# FLAT OUT

## The Story of 30 Squadron Royal Air Force

by John F. Hamlin

This book is dedicated to all those who served with
30 Squadron Royal Air Force

AN AIR-BRITAIN PUBLICATION

Copyright 2002 by John Hamlin

Published in the United Kingdom by:

Air-Britain (Historians) Ltd.,
12 Lonsdale Gardens,
Tunbridge Wells, Kent TN1 1PA

Sales Dept:
41 Penshurst Road, Leigh,
Tonbridge, Kent TN11 8HL

Correspondence to the Editor:

R. C. Sturtivant, 26 Monks Horton Way,
St. Albans, Herts. AL1 4HA
*and not to the Tunbridge Wells address.*

ISBN 0 85130 308 0

Printed by:

The Cromwell Press Ltd,
Aintree Avenue,
Whitehorse Business Park,
Trowbridge, Wiltshire,
BA14 0XB

Origination by Howard Marks, Hastings

Cover painting by Mark Postlethwaite
*Thunderbolt Mk.II KJ240 in action over Burma*

# FLAT OUT

No 30 Squadron, Royal Air Force
Royal Air Force Lyneham

# CONTENTS

# FOREWORD

## by Air Chief Marshal Sir John Cheshire KBE CB RAF

In 1984, Wg. Cdr. John Bell (then the CO of 30 Squadron) spotted an entry in the Royal Air Force News convening a meeting of former members of 30 Squadron. John, displaying that powerful combination of initiative and enthusiasm for which he has always been renowned, responded by saying that the crews currently serving on his Squadron would be delighted to gatecrash the meeting to greet their predecessors. Out of that first get-together in a London hotel was born the 30 Squadron Association, with Air Vice-Marshal David Dick as Chairman. As a young pilot, David had flown Thunderbolts with 30 Squadron in Burma.

Under the leadership of David Dick, the Association prospered. Reunions attractedformer Squadron members from the earliest days, and it soon became clear that, unless swift action was taken, the fascinating stories that they related would be lost. David was determined that this should not happen and, with great energy and determination, he set about compiling a record of the Squadron's remarkable history. Sadly, before the task was completed, David died, and it was left to his successors to see the history in print. I am in no doubt that David would have been the first to salute John Hamlin, John Bell and all those who have worked so hard to complete this task on his behalf.

Formed in 1915, when operational aviation was in its infancy, the Squadron's subsequent history has reflected the employment of airpower in many parts of the world. It spent its formative years in the Middle East before, in 1941, facing the Italian and German invasion of Greece. A year later its Hurricanes helped to turn back the Japanese fleet from Ceylon, keeping the seas free for vital fuel supplies to support the war in Europe. This was an action which Churchill rated as perhaps the most significant battle of the war. Later, the Squadron saw action in Burma, flying long-range missions against Japanese targets.

After VJ Day there was only a short respite before the Squadron was back in action, this time taking part in the Berlin Airlift. Then, in 1956, came Suez, and in 1982 the Argentinian invasion of the Falkland Islands. In 1991 the crews were committed to supporting the coalition force which evicted Saddam Hussein from Kuwait, and it was only a short time after the Gulf War that the troubles in the Balkans gave 30 Squadron another new operational challenge. But, if that was not enough, in between major operations the Squadron has been employed in a myriad of minor conflicts, in numerous humanitarian relief operations, and a miscellany of other activities, many of which have attracted critical acclaim in aviation circles.

I served on 30 Squadron for less than a year, in 1975, and much of that short tour was spent on detachment in Cyprus and the Middle East. However, I am very proud to add my name to the list of former Squadron members. Like its sister Hercules squadrons at Lyneham, 30 Squadron continues to uphold the traditions and reputation of its forebears. This book is a tribute to all of them, the crews of yesterday and today. *Ventre a Terre.*

# ABBREVIATIONS

| | |
|---|---|
| AA | Anti-aircraft |
| AAC | Army Air Corps |
| AACU | Anti Aircraft Cooperation Unit |
| AAR | Air-to-Air Refuelling |
| AC1 | Aircraftman First Class |
| AC2 | Aircraftman Second Class |
| ACM | Air Chief Marshal |
| ACSEA | Air Command South East Asia |
| ACW | Aircraftwoman |
| AEG | Allgemeine Elektrizitäts Gesellschaft |
| AFC | Air Force Cross |
| AFME | Air Forces Middle East |
| AHQ | Air Headquarters |
| Air Cdre. | Air Commodore |
| ALM | Air Loadmaster |
| AM | Air Marshal |
| 1/AM | Airman First Class |
| 2/AM | Airman Second Class |
| AMES | Air Ministry Experimental Station |
| ANZAC | Australia & New Zealand Army Corps |
| AOC | Air Officer Commanding |
| AOC-in-C | Air Officer Commanding-in-Chief |
| AQM | Air Quartermaster |
| ARCM | Associate of the Royal College of Music |
| ATDU | Air Transport Development Unit |
| AVM | Air Vice-Marshal |
| BABS | Beam Approach Beacon System |
| BAFO | British Air Forces of Occupation |
| BAFSEA | British Air Forces South East Asia |
| BAOR | British Army of the Rhine |
| BEA | British European Airways |
| BER | Beyond Economic Repair |
| Bf. | Bayerische Flugzeugbau |
| Brig. Gen. | Brigadier General |
| BSc | Bachelor of Science |
| Capt. | Captain |
| CAS | Chief of the Air Staff |
| Cat. | Category |
| CB | Companion of the Bath |
| CBE | Commander of the Order of the British Empire |
| C-in-C | Commander-in-Chief |
| CLE | Container Light Equipment |
| cm. | centimetres |
| CMG | Companion of the Order of St. Michael & St. George |
| CO | Commanding Officer |
| Co. | Company |
| Col. | Colonel |
| Cpl. | Corporal |
| CVO | Commander of the (Royal) Victorian Order |
| CWGC | Commonwealth War Graves Commission |
| DBF | Destroyed By Fire |
| DBR | Damaged Beyond Repair |
| DCM | Distinguished Conduct Medal |
| DFC | Distinguished Flying Cross |
| DFC* | DFC and Bar |
| DFS | Deutsches Forschungsinstitut für Segelflug (German Gliding Resarch Institute) |
| DGA | Director General of Aviation |
| DH | de Havilland |
| Do. | Dornier |
| DSC | Distinguished Service Cross |
| DSO | Distinguished Service Order |
| DSO* | DSO and Bar |
| DZ | Dropping Zone |
| ENSA | Entertainment National Service Association |
| F | Fahrenheit |
| FA | Fliegerabteilung |
| FAA | Fleet Air Arm |
| FIR | Flight Information Region |
| Flg. Off. | Flying Officer |

| | |
|---|---|
| Flt. Lt. | Flight Lieutenant |
| Flt. Sgt. | Flight Sergeant |
| FRCO | Fellow of the Royal College of Organists |
| FTS | Flying Training School |
| GCA | Ground Controlled Approach |
| GCB | Grand Cross of the Order of the Bath |
| GCI | Ground Controlled Interception |
| GCMG | Knight Grand Cross of the Order of St. Michael and St. George |
| GCVO | Knight Grand Cross of the (Royal) Victorian Order |
| GD | General Duties |
| Gen. | General |
| GI | Ground Instructional |
| GHQ | General Headquarters |
| GMT | Greenwich Mean Time |
| GOC | General Officer Commanding |
| GP | General Purpose |
| Gp. Capt. | Group Captain |
| He. | Heinkel |
| HF | High Frequency |
| HM | His/Her Majesty |
| HMS | His/Her Majesty's Ship |
| HMT | His Majesty's Troopship |
| HP | Handley Page |
| Hptmn. | Hauptman |
| HRH | His/Her Royal Highness |
| IAF | Indian Air Force |
| IEF | Indian Expeditionary Force |
| IFF | Identification: Friend or Foe |
| IFOR | Implementation Force |
| IFR | Instrument Flight Rules |
| ILS/PAR | Instrument Landing Sysytem / Precision Approach Radar |
| J/T | Junior Technician |
| Ju | Junkers |
| KBE | Knight Commander of the Order of the British Empire |
| KCB | Knight Commander of the Order of the Bath |
| KCMG | Knight Commander of the Order of St. Michael & St. George |
| KG | Knight of the Order of the Garter |
| KG | Kampfgeschwader |
| kg. | kilogram |
| kHz | kiloHerz |
| LAC | Leading Aircraftman |
| lb. | pound weight |
| LCT | Landing Craft (Tank) |
| LG | Landing Ground |
| Lt. | Lieutenant |
| Lt. Col. | Lieutenant Colonel |
| 2nd Lt. | Second Lieutenant |
| m. | metres |
| MA | Master of Arts |
| MAAG | Military Aircraft Assistance Group |
| Maj. | Major |
| MALM | Master Air Loadmaster |
| MAQM | Master Air Quartermaster |
| MBE | Member of the Order of the British Empire |
| MC | Military Cross |
| MEAF | Middle East Air Force |
| M.Eng. | Master Engineer |
| METS | Middle East Training School |
| MIMgt | Member of the Institute of Management |
| MM | Military Medal |
| MO | Medical Officer |
| MoD | Ministry of Defence |
| MP | Member of Parliament |
| M.Pil. | Master Pilot |
| MRAF | Marshal of the Royal Air Force |
| MRAeS | Member of the Royal Aeronautical Society |
| M.Sig. | Master Signaller |
| MU | Maintenance Unit |

| | |
|---|---|
| NAAFI | Navy, Army & Air Force Institute |
| NASA | National Aeronautics & Space Administration |
| NATO | North Atlantic Treaty Organisation |
| Nav. | Navigator |
| NCO | Non-Commissioned Officer |
| NFD | Northern Frontier District |
| OBE | Order of the British Empire |
| OC | Officer Commanding |
| OCU | Operational Conversion Unit |
| OTU | Operational Training Unit |
| PC | Privy Councillor |
| Plt. Off. | Pilot Officer |
| PMRAFNS | Princess Mary's Royal Air Force Nursing Service |
| PR | Photographic Reconnaissance |
| PSP | Pressed Steel Planking |
| PTS | Parachute Training School |
| PZL | Panstwowe Zaklady Lotnicze (Polish National Aviation Establishment) |
| QFI | Qualified Flying Instructor |
| QGH | Controlled let-down through cloud |
| RA | Royal Artillery |
| RAAF | Royal Australian Air Force |
| RAF | Royal Air Force |
| RAFA | Royal Air Forces Association |
| RASC | Royal Army Service Corps |
| RCAF | Royal Canadian Air Force |
| Regt. | Regiment |
| RFC | Royal Flying Corps |
| RIAF | Royal Indian Air Force |
| RN | Royal Navy |
| RNAS | Royal Naval Air Service/ Royal Naval Air Station |
| RNZAF | Royal New Zealand Air Force |
| RRAF | Royal Rhodesian Air Force |
| RSU | Repair & Salvage Unit |
| R/T | Radio Telephony |
| RTO | Railway Transport Officer |
| SAAF | South African Air Force |
| SAC | Senior Aircraftman |
| SAM | Surface to Air Missile |
| SAS | Special Air Service |
| SASO | Senior Air Staff Officer |
| SE | Servicing Echelon |
| Sgt. | Sergeant |
| SHAPE | Supreme Headquarters Allied Powers in Europe |
| SHQ | Station Headquarters |
| SM | Savoia Marchetti |
| SMO | Station Medical Officer |
| SNAFU | 'Situation Normal — All Fouled Up' |
| SNCO | Senior Non-Commissioned Officer |
| SOC | Struck Off Charge |
| Sqn. Ldr. | Squadron Leader |
| SS | Steamship |
| St. | Sturzkampfgeschwader (Stuka) |
| SWO | Station Warrant Officer |
| TAF | Tactical Air Force |
| TAP | Target Approach Point |
| TCASF | Transport Command Aircraft Servicing Flight |
| TCEU | Transport Command Examining Unit |
| Uffz. | Uffizier |
| UK | United Kingdom |
| UN | United Nations |
| USAAF | United States Army Air Force |
| USAF | United States Air Force |
| VC | Victoria Cross |
| VFR | Visual Flight Rules |
| VHF | Very High Frequency (radio) |
| VIP | Very Important Person |
| Wg. | Wing |
| W/T | Wireless Telegraphy (using Morse code) |
| Wt. Off. | Warrant Officer |

# INTRODUCTION

When I began work on this history of 30 Squadron at the request of the late Air Vice-Marshal David Dick, I was not yet aware of just how varied a life the squadron has had over its 86 years of almost uninterrupted service. I learned that from establishment as an ad hoc unit late in 1914 it grew to become what was at one time the RAF's total operational presence in Mesopotamia (now Iraq), where several men lost their lives and many more were taken prisoner by the Turks. Parts of a poignant diary kept by one of the 30 Squadron airmen at the time are included in my text. The squadron remained to police the country between the wars, using several types of aircraft over the years in order to deal with recalcitrant tribesmen. 30 Squadron then graduated to Blenheim twin-engined bombers before moving to Egypt when war was declared. These aircraft the squadron took to Greece to take part in the abortive defence of that country, but in the end had to evacuate to Crete, where severe losses of personnel were sustained.

On regrouping in Egypt, a change of role resulted in 30 Squadron flying Hurricane fighters in the Western Desert for a time before an emergency situation found pilots, ground crews and Hurricanes on an aircraft carrier bound for Ceylon (now Sri Lanka). There, the squadron took part in the air battle of Colombo and lost several pilots. However, remaining in Ceylon, 30 Squadron settled down to a defensive task, eventually moving to Burma and converting to fly the Thunderbolt, mainly in a ground-attack role. The war over, Tempests replaced the Thunderbolts, but in 1947 the squadron disbanded.

A completely new mission was given to 30 Squadron when it reformed in England after a few months, that of flying Dakotas on military transport services along routes in Europe and the Middle East. Before long, however, the squadron was called upon to take part in the Berlin Airlift, and this proved to be one of the squadron's finest achievements. Subsequently, the Dakotas were replaced by Valettas, which continued route-flying and also specialised in carrying Very Important Persons. A further change of role came about when the squadron converted to Beverley heavy-lift aircraft, which after a period in England were taken to Kenya and eventually to Bahrain. In both countries squadron crews became adept at using rough airstrips and in air-dropping supplies to the military and sometimes to civilians in urgent need of food.

When the Beverley became outdated and somewhat unreliable, 30 Squadron was wound down, but this time it was not disbanded, its number remaining current so that it could be reactivated with a minimum of effort. This duly took place at Fairford, when the C-130 Hercules became the squadron's equipment in 1968. After 33 years the same aircraft are still being flown, although some of them have been 'stretched' in the interim period. Just imagine the early 'sticks and string' aircraft flown in 1915 being in service after 33 years, in 1948! 30 Squadron, a constituent of the Lyneham Transport Wing, concentrates on long-distance routes which take the crews all over the world as demanded by military requirements. The new C-130J model of the Hercules is being taken on charge by the LTW and will be flown by pilots of 30 Squadron for the foreseeable future. Without doubt the crews will uphold the fine traditions of the squadron by being ready to go anywhere at short notice, carrying any load, just as their predecessors did.

Two translations are put forward for *Ventre a Terre*, the motto of 30 Squadron — the literal Belly to the Ground is one and Flat Out is the other. This latter is generally preferred, as it gives the justly deserved impression that the squadron works at full stretch.

# ACKNOWLEDGMENTS

My sincere thanks go to all those who helped in the compilation of this book, particularly to members of the Committee of the 30 Squadron Association, who gave positive support throughout. I must also offer my thanks to my primary contact on the present squadron, Flt. Lt. Pete 'Cockers' Cochrane, without whose help my task would have been much more difficult; to a recent Commanding Officer, Wg. Cdr. John Barrass, and his successor, Wg. Cdr. Pete Dixon; to Flt. Lt. Paul Hughes; and to Mr. John Smith, a prominent former member of the squadron. For providing a mass of information on the squadron's activities in Mesopotamia I am glad to acknowledge Mike O'Connor, who is without doubt a true expert on the subject.

The four pages of colour drawings were prepared by David Howley, while others who have contributed information and anecdotes include the following people, while those who provided photographs are mentioned in the captions. If I have inadvertently failed to mention any contributor I ask his or her forgiveness.

Mr. J. W. Adams
Sqn. Ldr. R. E. Chaney
Mr. D. R. Cherry
Mr. Tom R. Croxton
Mr. Tom Cullen
Mr. N. Douglass
Wg. Cdr. R. Evans RAF (Retd.)
Wg. Cdr. K. H. Godfrey
Sqn. Ldr. Hacke RAF (Retd.)
Mr. W. R. Harrison
Mr. Arthur J. Henderson
Wg. Cdr. J. A. Jarvis DFC AFC RAF (Retd.)
Mr. R. J. Lawrence
Mr. R. G. Ledieu
Wg. Cdr. R. A. Milward OBE DFC MRAeS RAF (Retd.)
Flt. Lt. P. W. Mobbs BEng

Geoffrey Negus, for considerable help with
    the Roll of Honour
Sqn. Ldr. R. Paul RAF (Retd.)
Wg. Cdr. T. D. Perry RAF (Retd.)
Sqn. Ldr. A. P. Presnail RAF (Retd.)
Mr. P. Skinner
Mr. R. J. Smith
Mr. J. N. Sowerby DFM
Sqn. Ldr. F. Stillwell
Mr. Ken Stone
Raymond Vann, who with Mike O'Connor read the draft of
    my chapters on the squadron's early days
Mr. R. R. Waughman
Mr. Dennis G. White
Mr. S. Wilmot

**John F. Hamlin, 2001**

*A Henri Farman of the RFC Egypt Detachment at Ismailia in November 1914*                    *[R. Vann and M. O'Connor collection].*

# Chapter 1: The Origins of 30 Squadron

As far back as 1911, Lord Kitchener, then the British Agent and Consul General in Egypt, had realised that if a war broke out there was a threat of a Turkish invasion of Egypt by forces crossing the Sinai desert towards the Suez Canal. He therefore ordered a survey of the area between Gaza and Beersheba and the borders of Egypt with the Turkish Empire, and the task was carried out by one Capt. Newcombe of the Royal Engineers. A member of the survey party was a young archaeologist named T. E. Lawrence, who in a letter to his mother wrote: "We are obviously meant as red herrings, to give an archeological cover to a political job." With the First World War already three months old, diplomatic relations between Turkey and Great Britain, France and Russia were broken off on 1st November 1914, and at once the decision was made to send a token force of Royal Flying Corps aircraft and personnel to the vulnerable Suez Canal area. Three days later Turkey declared war on the same three countries and on Serbia.

## The very beginning

On 4th November 1914 the SS *Beethoven* sailed out of Avonmouth docks with an RFC Detachment on board. In command was Capt. S. D. Massy (originally of the 29th Punjabi Regt.), and the others were Capt. H. L. Reilly, 2nd Lt. S. P. Cockerell and a number of other ranks. Aircraft on board comprised two Maurice Farman S.7 Longhorn aircraft which had been collected from the Aircraft Manufacturing Co. at Hendon the previous day, and a single S.11 Shorthorn. Road vehicles consisted of two Crossley light tenders and a Leyland repair lorry, and to accommodate the aircraft after arrival two canvas hangars were included. Enough fuel for aircraft and vehicles for six months was provided.

After thirteen days at sea the ship arrived at Alexandria, and Capt. Massy immediately travelled to Cairo to make arrangements for a base for the Detachment. Ismailia, close to the centre of the 100-mile long Canal, was selected, as it had good rail communications and was already the Headquarters of the Canal Defence Force. However, its drawback was that if reconnaissance flights over points east of Suez or Port Said were called for there would be a fifty-mile flight before the task could begin. For defence purposes, the Canal was divided into three sectors: Suez to the Bitter Lakes, Deversoir to El Firdan and from there to Port Said.

After another night on board *Beethoven*, the Detachment disembarked and began the job of off-loading. This was not as easy as had been anticipated, as everything had to be manhandled fifty yards from the ship to a waiting train, but eventually the train left Alexandria and the Detachment arrived at Camp Moascar, Ismailia, on 20th November. Over the next few days the equipment and stores were brought to the camp and a new double hangar, each section 60 ft. by 40 ft., was erected. In addition, three 'aircraft

*Capt. Seaton Dunham Massy, 29th Punjabi Regt, joined the RFC Egypt Detachment on 2nd November 1914 and became CO in April 1915. In November 1915 he went to Mesopotamia to command 30 Squadron after Maj. H. L. Reilly had been shot down*

*[R. Vann and M. O'Connor collection].*

sheds' which had seen service at Heliopolis were brought to Ismailia and re-erected. A forward landing ground complete with fuel supplies was quickly established at Qantara, on the east bank of the Suez Canal half way between Ismailia and Port Said, so that reconnaissance flights to the north-east would be easier to accomplish. To make flights in a southerly and south-easterly direction easier a similar landing ground was created at Suez on 2nd December.

Pilots and observers began to join the Detachment on 26th November, and next day erection of Shorthorn 369 was completed and it was flown by Lt. Cockerell, with Capt. Barlow as observer, on a reconnaissance over Bir-el-Gilban and Bir Abu Abuk. It was found that on a clear day Port Said and Suez were both visible from an altitude of 4000 feet over Ismailia.

The next aircraft to be erected was Longhorn 712, which took to the air on 6th December. Its sister aircraft, 713, was completed on 15th December, but that day 2nd Lt. Cockerell badly damaged the Shorthorn on landing at Suez, where a stretch of rough ground still existed. He also damaged himself, breaking an arm in the crash, and his observer, Capt. Royle, suffered severe bruising.

Politically, the situation in Egypt was stabilised on 16th December 1914, when Britain declared that Egypt was now a Protectorate. This move enabled military action deemed necessary by the military authorities to be carried out without reference to the Egyptian government.

More equipment in the shape of a BE.2a and two Longhorns, all without engines, arrived on 21st December in the charge of Lt. S. C. Parr and three civilian mechanics from the Indian Central Flying School. Two Renault engines also arrived, this time in the company of Capt. G. B. Rickards and two NCO pilots who had made the journey from England. At much the same time Capt. W. F. Stirling was transferred to the French Seaplane Flight at Port Said, which consisted of seven seaplanes operating from the *Aenne Rickmers*, a captured cargo vessel equipped as a 'mother ship'.

Flying during December was only possible after 08.00 due to early morning mists, and in the afternoons strong north-westerly winds and frequent sandstorms were experienced. Nevertheless, two more advanced landing grounds and fuel dumps were set up during the month, one at Mabeiuk and the other at Ras el Hagg. The ill-fated Shorthorn (369) took to the air again on 30th December after repairs.

### The Detachment in action

January 1915 was the month in which the RFC Detachment began to see the action which had been expected. The BE.2A had been erected, as had Henri Farman No.1, one of two such machines acquired by Capt. Massy from Heliopolis soon after the Detachment arrived. The Turkish forces had been reported as having aircraft, and a double Company of Indian infantry was drafted in to protect the airfield at Ismailia. Four 'look-out men' with binoculars, under the command of a British officer, maintained a watch, and one aircraft was kept ready to take off in the event of an alarm being given. These precautions were found to be justified when on 17th January Capt. Reilly, with Lt. D. R. Tweedie as observer, discovered 720 Turkish infantrymen and fifty cavalry at Bir el Abd and a hundred irregular cavalry at Bir Abu Raml, all advancing on Qantara. The aircraft was fired upon and hit, but no serious damage was inflicted. This event was significant in being the first in which aggressive action was encountered by the unit which later developed into 30 Squadron. Three days later, a thousand Turkish infantry and 200 cavalry were found at Bir el Abd by Tweedie and his pilot, Capt. Rickards, who promptly bombed them. Further reconnaissance flights were made on 25th January to a number of locations, including Bir el Abd. This time, Cpl. Power and Lt. Tweedie had to make a forced landing on the coast due to engine trouble, and only just managed to avoid a 300-strong Turkish cavalry patrol. On the same day 2000 troops were spotted two miles south of Bir el Mahadat, 3600 at Bir el Mabeiuk, and 1000 infantrymen and three hundred cavalry six miles from Qantara. Two days later a large body of troops making ready to move were seen and bombed at Moiya Harab, as were two thousand at Wadi Muksheib and three thousand at a point only fifteen miles north-east of Ismailia. The BE.2A was damaged on 28th January when it force-landed at Nefisha.

During the month weather conditions had been worse than in December 1914, and only twenty-five sorties had been flown by the three serviceable aircraft. It was now clear that a Turkish attack was imminent, and on 3rd February it materialised. The assault was directed against the central section of the Suez canal between El Firdan and Deversoir, and was quickly repulsed. The enemy forces, many of whose officers were German, were seen retreating towards Qatiya and some were concentrated in an old camp, which the Detachment soon bombed. On the first day of the attack the Detachment's aircraft spent five and a half hours in the air on reconnaissance, and on the second day the total increased to fourteen hours. This effort enabled the GOC of the Canal Defence Force to be kept informed of all enemy troop movements and strengths, and on 7th February Gen. Sir J. Maxwell asked the GOC to convey to Capt. Massy a message of thanks. "Will you please convey to Capt. Massy and the officers of the Royal Flying Corps, also the observers, my appreciation of the hard and good work they have done with inferior machines. I do not know what we should [sic] have done without them." Gen. Wilson, the GOC, added his

*A rare bird: a Henri Farman flown by the RAF Egypt Detachment. Its engine, nacelle, lower wings and undercarriage were Farman components, the upper wing was Farman modified with Short seaplane parts and the tail unit was of local design!* *[R. Vann and M. O' Connor collection].*

own plaudits a few days later, when he wrote: "I would like to express my high appreciation of the valuable work done by the pilots and observers of the French hydroplane squadron and the Detachment of the Royal Flying Corps in the numerous reconnaissances carried out by them previous to and during the advance of the enemy. They were constantly under shrapnel and rifle fire and carried out their difficult and dangerous duties with courage and resourcefulness."

With the possibility of night raids over enemy camps in mind, an electric 'searchlight' plant was installed at Ismailia in February 1915. Powered by two generators driven by belts from counter-shafts on the platform of the jacked-up repair lorry, the power provided was enough for two 20-inch projectors. Whether it ever went into action is not, however, recorded.

The second of the Henri Farman aircraft received from India in December 1914 was erected on 20th February and two days later repairs to the BE.2A which had force-landed at Nefisha on 28th January were completed. Another temporary advanced landing ground was established on 28th February, this one at El Rigum, for use by aircraft making reconnaissance flights over Bir el Themeda and Gebel el Maghara. In all, 41 sorties were flown in February, the average number of serviceable aircraft being four.

Twenty-six reconnaissance flights were made in March 1915, including one to El Murra which was the longest flight made by the Detachment. With an extra large fuel tank on board, Capt. Reilly and Captain Royle took off on the 176-mile journey, and on arrival over the target they saw over two hundred tents and three hundred troops, both of which they bombed. There was some retaliatory fire but the crew failed to locate the offending guns. On arrival at Ismailia, the two men found that they had been in the air for three hours twenty-eight minutes. In the middle of the month, however, bad weather and sand-storms prevented any flying at all for a week. The Bikanir Camel Corps, unaffected by such factors, busied themselves at Qatiya with the preparation of yet another landing ground for use by the Detachment.

Lt. Parr and the mechanics from India left on 30th March to join the Indian Expeditionary Force in Mesopotamia. Much more distressing to his friends was the death on 20th March of 2nd. Lt. S. P. Cockerell from acute smallpox. He was an original member of the RFC Detachment and was sorely missed.

## Spring at Ismailia

April 1915 brought much better weather to the Canal Zone, and fifty-nine reconnaissance sorties were flown. At the end of the month, the strength of the Detachment was four officers and 44 other ranks, and nine aircraft were in use when serviceable. These were the three Maurice Farmans brought out from England, two Henri Farmans collected from Heliopolis on arrival, two Maurice Farmans received from India in December (although these were sent to the Indian Expeditionary Force during April), a BE.2A received from India and a BE.2C (1757) which arrived from the UK during the month.

Having found and attacked the enemy at El Murra once, the Detachment made the most of the opportunity and tried again on 16th April. Five aircraft took off from Ismailia at 05.00 and landed on the new landing ground at Qatiya. Four of the aircraft were fitted with bomb frames carrying three bombs each. The plan was for these aircraft to attack an aircraft hangar, and three duly left on their mission, the fourth remaining at Qatiya with engine trouble. Not fitted for bombing, the fifth aircraft was to be used to search for any of the others which might have to force-land in the desert. The three crews which took part comprised Sgt. C. E. Foggin and Capt. O. M. Conran in Longhorn 712, Capt. Rickards and Lt. Tweedie in Longhorn 713 and Lt. Murray and Capt. Royle in the BE.2A. Seven of the nine bombs were dropped, the others failing to leave the bomb frame. The enemy camp appeared to the observers to be laid out in such a way that damage from air raids would be minimised, but all the crews were of the opinion that what had been reported as a hangar could not possibly have been one. During the mission one of the three aircraft developed serious engine trouble, but it managed to reach Qantara, where it landed with a broken connecting rod cylinder and the bottom half of the crankcase split. In all, 208 miles had been flown by each of the

***Above:*** *Maurice Farman 369 at Ismailia with the RFC Egypt Detachment. On 26th May 1915 it was wrecked when it crashed into the Suez Canal*
*[R. Vann and M. O'Connor collection].*
***Below:*** *A Henri Farman F.20 of the RFC Egypt Detachment, later 'C' Flight of 30 Squadron, in the autumn of 1915*
*[R. Vann and M. O'Connor collection].*

three raiders that day, which transpired to be the occasion of the last offensive sorties made by the Detachment.

Another enemy camp, thirteen miles east of the Suez Canal at Hawawish, had been located, and Brig. Gen. Watson, with a column of the Imperial Service Cavalry Brigade, a half battalion of the 27th Punjabi Regt. and a section of Egyptian Artillery, left Ismailia on 28th April with the intention of making a surprise incursion. Not to be outwitted, however, the Turks left the camp during the night, and, after making a small attack on Watson's column, retreated to a point not far from their former position, where aircraft of the RFC Detachment found them next morning.

In May an agent reported that a serious attempt to burn down the hangars at Ismailia was imminent, and consequently the buildings were surrounded by a barbed wire fence along which a number of electric lighting columns were erected. Guards were doubled in number and two men were detailed to sleep in each hangar to act as guards. Thirty-four reconnaissance sorties were flown that month, and one aircraft, Shorthorn 369, was lost when on 26th May it crashed into the Suez Canal. It was being piloted by Sgt. W. B. Power, with Capt. Conran as observer, when it struck the water at high speed and sank. Both men suffered bruises and Power had a broken rib, but they managed to swim ashore and soon recovered.

## The Detachment becomes 30 Squadron

Frequent spells of dense cloud hindered the work of the Detachment in June, and all flights had to be made between 04.00 and 09.00 to avoid the intense heat of the day. Similar conditions prevailed in July, but two new functions were added to the Detachment's task — signalling and photography. The first photographic reconnaissance flight was made on 19th July by Sgt. Foggin and Capt. Conran in Longhorn 712, and the first signalling flight was made four days later. The hugely important event of the month, however, was the arrival of a signal from the Deputy Director of Military Aeronautics dated 31st July, informing Maj. Massy that the Detachment had been retrospectively upgraded to become an element of 30 Squadron, with effect from 24th March 1915. Other units which would form the remainder of the new squadron were already in action in what was then referred to as Mesopotamia, the present-day Iraq.

Only fourteen missions were flown in August 1915, as the war with Turkey had by now diminished. However, a further Martinsyde Scout aircraft, 4250, arrived from Alexandria on 29 August for use by the squadron. September's activity was almost the same, the average number of aircraft available per day being

14

four. Maj. Massy said goodbye to the squadron in September and command was taken over by Capt. G. B. Rickards. October saw the arrival of two more BE.2c aircraft from the UK, enabling the squadron to have an average of five aircraft in an available state each day in November, when sixteen missions were flown.

The end of 30 Squadron's time in Egypt was now approaching, and on 26th November 'A' Flight of 14 Squadron arrived at Ismailia to take over the work. Five of 30 Squadron's observers and seven other ranks were then posted to 14 Squadron, which also took over all the aircraft. 14 Squadron was part of the 5th Wing of the RFC,

commanded by Lt. Col. Geoffrey Salmond, who with his adjutant, Capt. F. C. Shelmerdine, was on the quayside at Alexandria to welcome the new arrivals. These men would carry on the pioneering work started by the original RFC Detachment in the Canal Zone, and were to be involved in the further development of Ismailia airfield, which by the 1950s was an RAF Station of major importance.

Their task in Egypt over, the remaining personnel of 30 Squadron received orders on 9th December 1915 to proceed to Basra in Mesopotamia, where they arrived there on 27th December to become 'C' Flight of 30 Squadron.

*NCOs of the RFC Egypt Detachment (which became 'C' Flight of 30 Squadron) and probably some members of 14 Squadron, on a visit to the Pyramids. Second from the right, seated, is Sgt. E. J. Malkinson, who went with 'C' Flight to Mesopotamia and later trained as a pilot*
*[Mrs. Elliott, via R. Vann and M. O'Connor collection].*

*Maurice Farman S.7 Longhorn 712 after a bit of a prang at Ismailia. It had been shipped from England in November 1914 and was still in service in April 1915*      *[Sqn. Ldr. A. M. Verity via Wg. Cdr. R. Evans].*

# Chapter 2: In Mesopotamia 1915 to 1919

For several centuries, the country known today as Iraq had been under Turkish domination, but by the end of the 19th century this state of affairs began to change rapidly. From 1900, Germany had included Iraq in its eastward expansion plans. Archeological work had given the Germans a foothold in the country, and they had established schools and trading companies. A Consul had been appointed, with his office at Baghdad, and a Vice-Consul at Basra, where it was hoped that a German-dominated quarter of the town could be developed. Ships of the Hamburg–Amerika Line using the port there were subsidised to encourage the growth of German influence, and sailings became regular in 1906, bringing an influx of salesmen and agents and resulting in the ready availability of German products in Iraq. In the minds of politicians in Berlin, Iraq was destined to become part of the German empire.

In May 1901, Mr. W. K. D'Arcy, a wealthy Englishman, secured an oil concession from the Shah of Persia, and drilling began just inside Persia near Qasr-i-Shirin. Small quantities of oil were found there in 1904, although not enough to justify the construction of a pipeline. A much better strike was made in May 1908, prompting the establishment in 1909 of the Anglo–Persian Oil Co, and a site for a refinery was chosen on Abadan Island, on the Shatt-al-Arab south of Muhammara. In the spring of 1914 the British government acquired a controlling interest in the Anglo–Persian Oil Co., thus setting in motion a chain of events which lasts to this day. The outbreak of the First World War in August 1914, with Turkey on the side of Germany, swept away all the hopes that had been entertained in Iraq that at last the country was beginning a period of settled progress.

## Conflict develops

Apart from anxieties concerning the Suez Canal, the British authorities were very worried about the vulnerability of the Anglo–Persian oilfield and its associated pipeline, which was only thirty miles from Turkish-held territory. Even before the outbreak of war the Turks in Iraq had been outwardly hostile toward British interests, and British property had been commandeered. There was clear reason to believe that Turkey could quite easily take over the

oil wells, thus providing a source of petroleum for German use in Europe. In the longer term, a threat to India was predicted. In September 1914 a small force of Indian soldiers had arrived in Persia to combat any incursions into the oilfields, and to provide better security a Brigade of the 6th (Poona) Division's Indian troops was drafted in during October as Indian Expeditionary Force 'D'. After landing on the coast they advanced inland to capture Basra, where they set up a main headquarters and supply depot for any military activity which might take place in the region. War between Great Britain and Turkey was officially declared on 5th November 1914.

Early 1915 found the IEF firmly in control of both sides of the Shatt-al-Arab. This proved to be unacceptable to Turkish forces, of which 20,000 men made an attempt to recapture Basra in January, but they were repelled.

As part of the defence programme, airborne assistance was clearly required, and plans were set in motion. A memo dated 12th April 1915 sent by Brig. Gen. Holloway, Secretary to the Government of India, to the Chief of the General Staff, reads: 'The Govt. of India has sanctioned preliminary arrangements for a Flight of aeroplanes for service with IEF Force 'D' and for its concentration in Bombay prior to departure'. Initial personnel were then listed. Capt. P. W. L. Broke–Smith, the Deputy Assistant Director of Aviation, arrived at Basra from Bombay on 9th April 1915 and was taken onto the staff of the GOC Indian Expeditionary Force with orders to establish an airfield and Air Park near the city. After deciding what would be required, he returned to India to arrange supplies of material and equipment, which he brought back to Basra and set about constructing the airfield and maintenance facilities at Tanouma, on the west bank of the River Tigris, opposite the town. While he was away, Maj. Gen. C. V. Townshend arrived in Mesopotamia to take command of the 6th Division, which would see considerable action over the next three years, from Gen. Sir Arthur Barratt.

## The birth of a Flight

To command the somewhat anonymous new flying unit, Capt. H. L. Reilly of the Indian Flying School, formerly of the 82nd Punjabi Regt., was appointed, and arrived from the detachment in

*Capt. P. W. L. Broke-Smith of the Royal Engineers and RFC was appointed Deputy, then Assistant, Director of Aviation for the Indian Army in Mesopotamia in April 1915, established the Aircraft Park at Basra and the Australian Half-Flight and remained in overall control of the RFC until 1st August 1916* [R. Vann & M. O'Connor collection].

Egypt on 30th April. The engineering officer was a civilian, Mr. W. R. Wills, who was given a commission as 2nd. Lt. in the Indian Army Reserve of Officers.

Although the Royal Flying Corps was unable to send any pilots or observers, it did authorise the despatch of two Maurice Farman aircraft from Egypt. Flying personnel were therefore drawn from Australia and New Zealand. First to arrive were Capt. H. A. Petre of the Australian Flying Corps and Lt. W. W. A. Burn of the New Zealand Staff Corps, who reached Basra on 14th May with eleven other ranks who were British, five Indian mechanics and ten 'followers'. They brought with them one Longhorn and one Shorthorn aircraft which had reached Bombay from England, both without engines and in poor condition, and there were no bomb racks or machine guns. A week later, Capt. T. W. White and Lt. W. H. Treloar of the AFC arrived in the company of twenty NCOs and other ranks and the two Maurice Farman Longhorn aircraft (712 and 713) which had been sent, without engines, from Egypt. These men then became known as the Australian Half-Flight.

To avoid confusion with Turkish markings, a red crescent in a circle, it was decided that instead of the normal RFC roundel (a red dot inside a blue circle) the aircraft would be marked with a black stripe. Thus adorned, the Shorthorn took to the air with newly-promoted Maj. Reilly at the controls on 27th May 1915. During the thirty-five minute flight, the first in Mesopotamia, an altitude of 4800 feet was reached and it was found that the aircraft was flying at no less than 55 miles per hour!

## Into action

As yet without an identity of its own, the Flight went into action on 31st May. On the previous day an advanced landing ground had been established at Chirish, a mile and a half south of Qurna, from where the Flight was to cooperate with the army in a planned operation. During the battle which ensued, Maj. Reilly and Maj. Broke-Smith in the Longhorn and Capt. Petre and Lt. Burn in the Shorthorn flew over Turkish positions on the Tigris river as far as Sakrikiya, about ten miles from Qurna, and reported back on what they had seen. Next day, another advanced landing ground, at Bahrein, was set up to enable the Flight to keep up with the army, which was advancing in the direction of Amara, fifty miles away. The Turkish forces were pursued by the army, and the Flight reported on the enemy's movements and on areas of flooding adjacent to the river Tigris. Accompanying the Flight towards Amara were twenty men of the 120th Infantry. Amara was captured on 4th June and next day an advanced landing ground was set up there.

On 3rd June the Flight began to take on a more official status as a separate unit. Headquartered at Basra, it was officially staffed by four officers and was equipped with the two Maurice Farman aircraft and a stores tugboat (T3), which had a crew of twenty-three. At this time, the river was a vital line of communication, there being no roads or railways. There were thirteen British mechanics – where the Indian ones had gone is not recorded. That day, T3 set sail for Abu Rabah, from where Capt. Petre carried out reconnaissance flights to determine whether any enemy troops were in the area around Amara. As he saw none, it was safe for the Flight to carry on to reach that town on 6th June.

Growing more confident, Maj. Reilly and Lt. Burn made a long-distance reconnaissance to Kut-al-Amara, a trip of 123 miles, on 14th June so that enemy positions could be located. A refuelling point at Abu Gharbi, about sixty miles from Amara, was used, and a rough map of this uncharted area made at the time came in very useful at the time and in a later battle. Afterwards the Major flew back to Basra. With an operation against Nasiriyah imminent, a fuelling point was established on 20th June on the island of Abu Salabik in the Hammar Lake, forty-five miles from Basra. From there, Shorthorn MF.1 set off two days later to make a reconnaissance over Nasiriyah and Longhorn MF.2 to cover Hammar Lake. During one flight Maj. Reilly and Lt. Treloar had to make a forced landing in the desert south of the lake, but the aircraft and crew were saved when a magneto from the other Farman was taken to the 'mainland' by rowing-boat.

Two Caudron biplanes arrived at Basra on 14th July aboard SS *Tortilla* (pancake in Spanish!) and were quickly assembled and given the local numbers C.3 and C.4. Five days later they left to fly to Asani, but C.4 had to force-land on the way and wait for a replacement engine from Basra. Ground personnel were already on their way to Asani on the tugboat, which was towing a lighter. Flights over the Turkish positions at Nasiriyah began on 21st July, and it soon became possible for British artillery to be ranged onto enemy trenches. Gen. Sir John Nixon, the officer commanding the Indian Expeditionary Force, expressed his gratitude for the Flight's work in a despatch — "I have to place on record the excellence of the work performed by officers and men of the Royal Flying Corps, whose valuable reconnaissances materially assisted in clearing up the situation before the battle of 24th July." Nasiriyah was occupied on 25th July, and the army's next objective became Kut-al-Amara, where Turkish troops were concentrating.

In a letter sent to Lt. Col. E. J. M. Wood of the Army HQ in India on 19th July, Maj. Reilly described the conditions in

*Working in one of the three mobile workshops of the Australian Half-Flight at Basra Aircraft Park* [R. Vann & M. O'Connor collection].

*Above:* The camp of the Australian Half-Flight at Tanouma, Basra, in June 1915. The two lorries had been converted to workshops by Newport Railway Works in Australia and were the only mechanical transport in Mesopotamia at the time *[A. E. Shorland via R. Vann & M. O'Connor collection].*
*Below:* Maurice Farman Longhorn IFC2 of the Australian Half-Flight about to leave Basra for Kut-al-Amara, with Capt. T. W. White at the controls and Capt. W. R. Wills, the equipment officer, as passenger *[D. Phillips via R. Vann & M. O'Connor collection].*

Mesopotamia. "There is tremendous trouble due to heat. Engines are constantly failing as they are air cooled, and the air from 500 feet to 3000 feet is like a blast furnace. I like Caudrons — they are slightly faster than the Maurice Farmans and climb very much better. They are, however, very bad for observation purposes and I don't think one could drop bombs from them very accurately." In June and July the Shamal north-westerly wind blows almost constantly for about forty days, so that any flight between Basra and Baghdad would be into wind, and Farmans and Caudrons were unable to make any headway except at dangerously low levels. In spring and summer large tracts of land adjoining the Tigris and Euphrates rivers from Basra to Nasiriyah and Amara were flooded to a depth of up to three feet.

Sadly, there was a fatal consequence to the Flight's success. Both Caudrons had set out for Basra on 30th July, and C.3 arrived there after two forced landings. C.4, however, did not. As soon as it was reported overdue, Lt. Treloar and Sgt. Heath in Maurice Farman MF.1 took off to carry out a search, but were not able to find it or its crew, Lt. G. P. Merz and Lt. W. W. A. Burn. The missing aircraft was not found until 2nd August, when Maj. Reilly

and Capt. Petre located the crash site twenty-five miles west of Abu Salabik. Pilot and observer were both missing, and it was later established that they had been murdered by a group of Zobaah tribesmen after putting up a running fight. Cockpit instruments had been smashed and the frame damaged, but the remains of the Caudron were dismantled and brought to Basra on 8th August.

## 30 Squadron comes to life

Most significantly, the Flight received the news early in August that administration of flying units in Mesopotamia would be taken over from the Indian Army by the War Office in London and that the Flight would become part of 30 Squadron, Royal Flying Corps. Another Flight had been formed in Egypt and would be sent to Mesopotamia in November. All officers of the unit became members of the RFC with effect from 5th August 1915.

Engines for the two Longhorn aircraft which had reached Basra from Egypt some time previously arrived in August. The aircraft were then re-erected, but one proved so old that it was of no practical use and was therefore used as a source of spares. The

*Above: Caudron G.III IFC4 outside the only permanent hangars in Mesopotamia, at Basra Aircraft Park. This Caudron force-landed in enemy territory on 30th July 1915 and its crew, Lt. Merz and Lt. Burn, were killed by hostile Arabs    [A. E. Shorland via R. Vann & M. O'Connor collection].*
*Below: The remains of Caudron G.III IFC4, recovered after the incident on 30th July        [N. Clutterbuck via C. Schneidel and R. Vann collections].*

As the Flight was required for action in the forthcoming Tigris operation all personnel and equipment were collected at Basra by 4th August. At Basra, the SS *Braunfels* arrived on 24th August with four Martinsyde aircraft, the engines of which needed an immediate overhaul, and three road lorries. A second lighter was taken over and fitted out as a floating workshop, with photographic equipment and a darkroom. Meanwhile, Caudron C.3 and Farman MF.1 were sent on the platform lighter to Amara. There, from 25th to 31st August, their crews carried out practice in artillery observation and reporting by means of Verey lights, smoke balls and electric lamp signals.

On 6th September the Flight left Amara for Abu Gharbi with MF.1, C.3, MH.5 and MH.6 on the lighter, the two Martinsydes having arrived from Basra the previous day. While being unloaded, however, MF.1 was damaged and had to be returned to Basra. A reconnaissance of Sheikh Saad on 13th September confirmed that the area was clear of enemy forces and the town was occupied by the army next day. Soon after taking off during the army's entry into the town, Martinsyde MH.5 was wrecked, and to add to the troubles, Lt. Treloar and Capt. B. S. Atkins were captured on 16th September when their aircraft, Caudron C.3, was shot down by rifle fire. The Flight was now the possessor of just one service-able aircraft, Martinsyde MH.6, which Maj. Reilly flew on an evening reconnaissance and brought back detailed information on an enemy trench system. After this, the unit moved to Sannaiyat.

better aircraft had been equipped with floats to a Farman design, made in Bombay, while its engine was awaited, but this was not successful as the floats affected the aircraft's normal low flying speed. It was then reconverted to a landplane and was used from September until December 1915, at which point it was worn out.

*Martinsyde 4243 (MH.5), a Caudron G.III and a Maurice Farman Shorthorn of 30 Squadron at Basra, probably after BE.2cs had begun to arrive for the squadron*
*[R. Vann collection].*

*Maurice Farman Shorthorn IFC.1 and Caudron G.III IFC.3 being carried on RFC tug T.3 on the river Tigris* [R. Vann collection].

From East Africa, a seaplane Flight of the RNAS had arrived at Basra on 5th September under the command of Maj. R. Gordon RNAS, bringing four Short seaplanes, four officers and twenty-two NCOs and men. The intention was that the RNAS unit would work with 30 Squadron, and two of the seaplanes arrived at Sannaiyat with Farman MF.7 and Martinsyde Scout MH.8 on 23rd September. Soon afterwards the augmented Flight moved to Nukhailat.

During the first battle at Kut-al-Amara, the seaplanes were attached to the artillery for observation duties on 28th September, as they had the distinct advantage of carrying Stirling wireless sets. A lack of straight stretches of river facing into the prevailing strong wind made take-offs tricky, however. 30 Squadron's Lt. E. J. Fulton and Capt. F. C. C. Yeats-Brown in MF.7 and Maj. Reilly by himself in MH.6 flew reconnaissance sorties, watching and reporting enemy troop movements and maintaining communication between 6th Division Headquarters at Nukhailat and Gen. Delemain's column in the Suwada Marsh area. This force would otherwise have been out of touch, as telegraph facilities had broken down earlier in the day.

The Flight moved to Kut-al-Amara on 30 September when that town was taken, after which the retreat of the Turkish forces up the River Tigris past Aziziya as far as Ctesiphon, close to Baghdad, was monitored for several days. It soon became clear that the Turks had settled into previously prepared entrenchments at Ctesiphon, and a reconnaissance by Maj. Reilly on the evening of 5th October in Martinsyde MH.6 confirmed this. Next day MH.8 and MF.7 arrived at Aziziya, and MH.8 carried out the first sortie over Baghdad. Unfortunately, in the hands of Capt. Petre, it crashed on landing at base.

Another Maurice Farman, MF.2, arrived from Amara on 19th October, allowing more than the minimum number of sorties to be flown. Three aircraft of the Flight raided a hostile Arab village five miles south-west of Fraser's Post on 22nd October, dropping sixteen two-pound, two 20 lb and three 30 lb bombs, but it was eight days before the white flag of surrender was flown by the inhabitants. The remaining days of October were spent in finding enemy positions in the Ctesiphon area and maintaining contact with Army headquarters units.

During October 1915 two of the RNAS seaplanes were converted to landplanes at Kut-al-Amara. Meanwhile, at Basra the personnel of a complete Repair Section with two trucks and two equipment officers had arrived. Other newcomers were Capt. E. M.

Murray and Capt. S. C. Winfield–Smith, who brought the first two BE.2c aircraft, 4302 and 4350, (recorded at the time, flippantly or otherwise, as Betuccis). Eight men who were to form the nucleus of a second Flight of the squadron also arrived, followed by twenty-five more men who arrived from England on 5th November under the command of Maj. R. A. Bradley and Lt. L. A. Graves. Stores and two more BE.2c aircraft turned up at the same time.

Developed from the BE.2a, which had been the first British aircraft to reach France at the outbreak of the War, the BE.2c was built by the Royal Aircraft Factory and sub-contractors in large numbers. It featured a 90 horse-power RAF1a engine and was the first type to carry a machine-gun. Its maximum speed was 90 mph at sea level, and it could climb to 9000 feet and stay in the air for four hours. The BE.2c was destined to become the mainstay of 30 Squadron for some time and to prove itself as both a reconnaissance aircraft — its designed function — and a bomber. Unfortunately, the BE.2c's inherent stability proved to be a disadvantage when manoeuvrability in combat was called for.

## Restructuring the squadron

Now that these additional personnel had arrived, it became possible to restructure the existing unit in line with standard squadron protocol. Thus, on 7th November 1915, the personnel were organised into 'A' Flight, which was largely comprised of members of the original Flight; 'B' Flight, which consisted mainly of the newly-arrived men; and Headquarters, which comprised any remaining men, including MT drivers and a mule transport section. No. 4 Aircraft Park was also set up at this time.

'B' Flight left Basra on 9th November on board lighters towed by tug T3 on the River Tigris, bound for Aziziya in the charge of Capt. E . M. Murray, the Flight commander. Two aircraft were taken — BE.2cs BE.11 and BE.12 — and twenty-two NCOs and men made up the party. Four days later the tug grounded north of Kut, where the aircraft were taken ashore, erected and flown to Aziziya. The two RNAS converted seaplanes and Martinsyde MH.8 were already there, and flew with BE.2c BE.11 to Lajj on 20th November, but on landing there the BE.2c was wrecked. Two more 30 Squadron fliers, Capt. T. W. White DFC and Capt. F. C. C. Yeats–Brown DFC, had landed Longhorn MF.2 behind the lines north-west of Baghdad on 13th November so that an attempt could be made to cut telegraph wires, and they had also been taken by

*BE.2c 4302 of 30 Squadron was presented to the RFC by the Maharajah of Rewa and was named* Bandhava        *[R. Vann & M. O'Connor collection].*

*Martinsyde G.102 Elephant A1599*        *[J. M. Bruce / G. S. Leslie collection].*

*The waterfront at Basra late in 1915, showing RFC motor transport and a wingless Martinsyde Scout. These vehicles were mobile workshops and were almost the only motor vehicles in Mesopotamia at the time*        *[R. Vann collection].*

*Above:* Martinsyde S.1 4244 (MH.6) on an RFC barge at Basra, demonstrating that the RFC serial number and 'local' numbers were carried at the same time. This is the aircraft in which Maj. H. L. Reilly was shot down on 21st November 1915
[A. E. Shorland via R. Vann & M. O'Connor collection].

*Right:* In Turkish hands — Martinsyde S.1 4244 of 30 Squadron after being brought down by ground fire. Maj. Reilly, the squadron's CO, became a POW
[R. Vann & M. O'Connor collection].

*Below:* 30 Squadron mess, with officers taking breakfast at the beginning of the battle of Ctesiphon in November 1915. The aircraft is a Martinsyde Scout, and the tail of a Maurice Farman can be seen in the background. First and third from left are Capt. Petre and Capt. Murray, the two Flight commanders. They were the only two to escape from Kut-al-Amara on 7th December 1915 as the Turks closed in on the airfield.

*Above: Sqn. Cdr. Robert Gordon RNAS, who was the CO of the RNAS/RFC unit in Mesopotamia in late 1915, had been awarded the DSO for his work in East Africa* *[R. Vann & M. O'Connor collection].*

*Below: Ctesiphon Arch, the ruin of King Nebuchadnezzar's banqueting hall and the objective of British troops in November 1915.*

Turkish troops. However, by persuading them that he had TB, Capt. White induced his captors to take him to Constantinople, from where he eventually escaped. But far worse, the squadron CO, Maj. Reilly, was shot down by machine-gun fire behind Turkish lines, and the Major was taken prisoner. This event was to have far-reaching consequences.

In a narrative about the battle of Ctesiphon, Mehemit Emin, the former head of the Military Movements Section of the Turkish Army, wrote as follows: "An event which occurred that day [20th November 1915] had an effect out of proportion with reality. After midday an aeroplane flying at a height of 1000 metres [3280 feet] in a last attempt to examine our lines of defence and rear, was brought down and captured by means of machine-gun fire from the 51st Division. This little event was taken as a happy omen that the luck of the enemy was about to change. It caused a deeply-felt improvement in the general morale. The presence of the 51st Division, which turned the balance of success against the assailants in this battle, was ascertained in this fruitless reconnaissance and was shown on the airman's map. But the map containing this priceless information fell, not into the hands of the enemy commander waiting anxiously for it before making his last dispositions, but into those of the Osmanli commander ................Major Reilly's greatest gift to us was the sketch showing the course of the Tigris from the Diyala to Aziziya. This little sketch, probably of small account to the enemy, was an important map in the eyes of the Iraqi command. For at HQ and with the troops there was no such thing as a map."

When Maj. Reilly failed to return, Maj. Gordon took temporary command of 'B' Flight, and a further reconnaissance flight was made. Unfortunately, the observer failed to recognise enemy reinforcements, and so Maj. Gen. Townshend, the British commander, was unaware of the strength of the Turkish forces. The battle of Ctesiphon began on 22nd November, and an immediate loss was Lt. E. J. Fulton, who force-landed Martinsyde MH.8 in enemy territory and was taken prisoner. Only two other aircraft could be put into the air that day, a converted Short and Maurice Farman MF.7, but on 24th November another Short and a BE.2c joined in. During the battle the Flight spent its time on a variety of tasks: monitoring enemy troop movements and dispositions; watching for any possible flanking moves; watching the enemy's rear along both sides of the River Tigris for signs of reinforcement or withdrawal; keeping a watch on an enemy heavy gun battery which was commanding a stretch of river up which a British Naval flotilla could have approached with a view to taking part; and

*Ready for take-off is Martinsyde Scout 4250 of 30 Squadron, which, on 22nd November 1915, was shot down and its pilot, Capt. E. J. Fulton, was captured*
*[R. Vann & M. O'Connor collection].*

dropping 100lb bombs on enemy troops in the rear and on a bridge across the Diyala river. Quite enough to occupy the small number of serviceable aircraft of 'B' Flight!

Armed with Maj. Reilly's map of the Tigris below Ctesiphon, the strengthened Turkish forces were able to rout Maj. Gen. Townshend's 6th Indian Division, which began a retreat through Lajj and Aziziya to Kut-al-Amara, which was reached on 3rd November 1915. There, Maj. Gen. Townshend was ordered to halt and to hold the city against Turkish forces. This proved to be a fatal error of judgment.

After a short period without a CO, 30 Squadron was cheered by the arrival at Kut-al-Amara on 28th November 1915 of Maj. S.

D. Massy, who had commanded the original ad-hoc Flight which had left England for Egypt a year earlier. Under Maj. Massy were the two Flight commanders— Capt. H. A. Petre for 'A' Flight and Capt. E. M. Murray for 'B' Flight. Aircraft then in use with 'A' Flight were Shorthorn MF.1, Longhorn MF.7 and Martinsyde Scout MH.9, while 'B' Flight used three BE.2cs, 11,12A and 14. The four aircraft which had taken part in the battle of Ctesiphon returned to Kut on 28th November, but by 1st December no machines were available for reconnaissance sorties, all being under repair, while the seaplanes were on the way to Basra by barge to be refurbished.

*Short Seaplane 827 of Maj. R. Gordon's RNAS detachment being serviced at Basra in December 1915. Behind the Bessoneau hangar is the former Turkish hospital on the bank of the Shatt-al-Arab, which was put into use as the RNAS HQ*
*[R. Vann & M. O'Connor collection].*

*Short seaplane 822 being serviced at Basra in December 1915 after operating in support of the 6th Indian Division*

*[G. W. Sutcliffe via R. Vann & M. O'Connor collection].*

## The siege of Kut-al-Amara

On 6th December an order was issued by 6th Division HQ to the effect that as many aircraft as could be moved were to be sent from Kut-al-Amara to Abu Gharbi the following day. Accordingly, Shorthorn MF.1 and a BE.2c were flown out by the two Flight commanders, but remaining at Kut were two BE.2cs and a Martinsyde, all damaged. That day, 7th December 1915, the Turks effectively placed a siege upon the town of Kut which was to last nearly five months and cause great hardship to, among others, five officers of 30 Squadron and most of the other ranks of 'A' and 'B' Flights who were marooned there. A diary kept by 533 Cpl. W. H. M. Candy, who (as will be seen later) recorded the intense tribulations suffered by other ranks of 30 Squadron, provides us with an insight into life in the besieged town. "All drinking water being drawn out of the river, two of our men were detailed to look after three large pumps while the rest of us were making bombs and rifle grenades. We also made a trench mortar out of one of our old Gnome engine cylinders" is Cpl. Candy's note at the beginning of the siege. He goes on to say that on Christmas day he and his friends managed to buy a few 'extras'.

The 30 Squadron depot left Basra on 13th December aboard T3 and two barges for the three-day journey to Amara. Having dealt with this move, Maj. Massy flew back to Abu Gharbi in a Longhorn. During the remaining days of December a few reconnaissance sorties were flown in an attempt to discover and report on the dispositions and numbers of enemy troops surrounding Kut-al-Amara.

*Also carrying Indian Flying Corps serial number IFC.11, BE.2c 4500 was flown out of Kut-al-Amara on 7th December 1915 and took part in food-dropping missions during the siege of that town*

*[FAA Museum via R. Vann & M. O'Connor collection].*

Reinforcements in the shape of the personnel of the Flight which until recently had operated in the Suez Canal Zone arrived at Basra on 27th December under the command of Capt. G. B. Rickards. This Flight was then nominated as 'C' Flight of 30 Squadron.

For the first five days of January 1916 Shorthorn MF.1 was the only aircraft available to the squadron, while news came through of the first Turkish aircraft flying over Kut. A few days later a Turkish deserter told army officers that four such aircraft had arrived at Baghdad. On 4th January the battle to relieve Kut-al-Amara began when the 7th Division under Gen. Younghusband advanced from Abu Gharbi towards Sheikh Saad. 30 Squadron advanced with the army, and flew from Abu Gharbi, Musandag and Sheikh Saad before arriving at Orah on 16th January. There the squadron remained until the end of the month. Reconnaissance sorties were flown daily by the two available aircraft, a Shorthorn and a BE.2c, in spite of poor weather conditions. Aerial photography was gaining in importance, and on 24th January six photographs were taken of the enemy front line.

By 10th January 1916 the besieged RFC men had run short of materials with which to make bombs, so went out to try the mortars and to survey trenches. On 12th January Cpl. Candy wrote in his diary "We took over a gas engine to connect to a flour grinder which we had to put in order. While working on this engine I stopped a stray bullet in the thigh, which gave me a few days rest." A large quantity of wheat had been commandeered, and flour grinding machines were operating. As the stones were rough, the flour was rather coarse, but in Cpl. Candy's words "the bread was considered A1 in the circumstances. The bread [ration] has been cut down to 12 ounces, and as it is brown our appetites have proportionally increased. From the 20th to the 28th it has been raining practically all the time........It is very cold at night. Spent from the 22nd to the 1st of February on the sick list with a touch of malaria. On the 10th rations were cut down to 12 ounces of barley bread and 12 ounces of horse [meat], which is not bad after all."

Two Voisin biplanes and five Short 184 seaplanes arrived at Basra on 17th January 1916 for use by the Royal Naval Air Service, but as the RNAS was short of flying officers and the 30 Squadron had the personnel who had arrived from Egypt recently without aircraft, a composite Flight was formed with the two Voisins and two of the Short seaplanes, to cooperate with Tigris Corps. One of each type of aircraft joined 30 Squadron at Orah on

*Voisin 8506, which arrived in Mesopotamia on 8th February 1916 and was used extensively by the RNAS Detachment for dropping food into Kut-al-Amara during the siege, its usual pilot being Flt. Sub-Lt. W. H. Dunn*         *[A. E. Shorland via R. Vann & M. O'Connor collection].*

*Henri Farman 1540 soon after its arrival at Basra Aircraft Park on 8th February 1916. Flt. Sub-Lt. J. D. Hume RNAS carried out ten food drops to besieged Kut-al-Amara in this aircraft*         *[R. Vann & M. O'Connor collection].*

3rd February, allowing the Maurice Farmans and a nucleus of 'A' Flight to return to Basra to re-equip with BE.2cs which were on the way from Britain. This left a solitary BE.2c as the only RFC aircraft operational with 30 Squadron.

A force to relieve Kut, known as the Tigris Column, was created but was beset by great difficulties, not the least of which was bad weather which brought floods and hindered land transport. An initial attempt to break the siege late in January 1916 failed, as did a second attempt in March and a final effort in April. By that time, supplies in Kut were critically low, and a message from Maj. Gen. Townshend indicated that at least 5000 lbs. of food per day was the minimum quantity needed.

A much-depleted 30 Squadron was able in February to fly some reconnaissance and artillery observation sorties, and frequent flights were made to drop much-needed stores, medical supplies, spare parts for radios, and money into the beleaguered garrison at Kut-al-Amara. Although the presence of Turkish aircraft was known, none flew over British lines until 12th February. It was then arranged that the garrison at Kut-al-Amara would notify the Tigris Corps by wireless when an enemy aircraft was seen to take off from the Turkish airfield near Kut. Unfortunately, this ploy failed to be effective, as the enemy aircraft tended to reach British lines before

the message did. Kut was bombed by German aircraft flying from a forward landing ground at Shumran Bend on 13th February and again on th March, this raid causing casualties in a military hospital. A few of 30 Squadron's Voisins and BE.2cs were fitted with Lewis guns, and on 15th February one BE.2c was within fifty feet of an enemy aircraft, but the pilot of the enemy monoplane did not wish to fight and made for home.

Cpl. Candy records in his diary that 13th February was a nice clear day. "We had our first visit from a hostile aircraft. It dropped two bombs near a battery of artillery but did no damage. I discovered that they were two of our own bombs off the barge we lost on our retreat. They were both 20lbs. (Hales Patent). It [the enemy aircraft] paid us another visit just before sunset and dropped five bombs, doing no damage. The result of these visits was that we had to work till one the following morning getting stand ready for converting into anti-aircraft guns, after which Sgt. Taylor and myself took reliefs on the observation post from daylight to sunset. Next day nothing happened until sunset, when the German machine came over and dropped bombs.........We gave it a warm reception but it got away." By 20th February Candy suspected that three German aircraft in all were operating, and they and RFC aircraft were making their presence felt.

At about 16.00 hours on 5th March the Turks began to bombard Kut with heavy artillery from all directions, and before long three Moranes flew over and dropped 20lb. and 100lb. bombs. After returning to base, the enemy aircraft returned twice, each carrying two 100lb. bombs. A good deal of damage was done to houses in the town, killing six Arabs, wounding four and burying sixteen. One of the bombs fell in the courtyard of the Officers' Hospital but failed to explode, and two shells hit the mosque, killing two, wounding two and blowing several out of the door.

*Top: BE.2cs 4361, 4412 and 4459 being unloaded from an RFC barge on the Shatt-al-Arab waterway at Basra on 24th February 1916. They had been sent from Ascot Aircraft Park in England for use by 30 Squadron, then based at Orah*      *[R. Vann & M. O'Connor collection].*

*Above: BE.2c 4328, which crashed at Orah in February 1916* 
     *[R. Vann collection].*

*Below: Short Seaplane 822, which arrived at Basra on 5th September 1915 for use by the RNAS detachment which worked so closely with 30 Squadron during the siege of Kut-al-Amara. On 13th October 1915, 822 was converted to a landplane and was written off on 14th February 1916* 
     *[R. Vann & M. O'Connor collection].*

Reinforcements for the squadron began to arrive from Basra on 5th March, when a BE.2c arrived, followed two days later by a similar machine, and on 8th March 'A' Flight brought two more BE.2cs. Unfortunately, one of the RNAS Voisins, 1541, was shot down by machine-gun fire on 5th March while flying over Es Sinn, and the two 30 Squadron men aboard, Lt. R. H. Peck and his observer, Capt. W. G. Palmer, both lost their lives. A message notifying the squadron of their sad fate was dropped over Orah next day by the pilot of a Turkish aircraft.

On 6th March the GHQ Indian Expeditionary Force 'D' announced that Wg. Cdr. R. Gordon RNAS would act as Aircraft Commander of the Tigris Column and that 30 Squadron and the composite Flight would be attached to that column under his command. The RNAS section of the Flight was then split into two, one section to operate the Voisin landplanes and the other to fly the Short seaplanes. Meanwhile, 'B' Flight returned to Basra on 11th March to refit, and on 20th March a ship carrying thirteen long-awaited BE.2cs for the squadron docked at Basra. Three of these aircraft left for Amara by barge on 28th March and three seaplanes flew there.

Due to the lack of water for the relieving force, Gen. Aylmer was forced to fall back to a new position on 9th March, but next day Maj. Gen. Townshend sent a message to him asking how long it would be before Kut could be freed. Those inside the town, including a substantial number of members of 30 Squadron, were now faced with a rapidly-deteriorating future. Rain fell incessantly, accompanied by thunderstorms, adding to the feeling among the men that relief was becoming unlikely. On 18th March., Cpl. Candy wrote in his diary "We had another visit from 'Fritz' early in the morning, but no bombs were dropped. He returned in the evening and dropped a few bombs, only one of which did any damage. That one made up for all the rest because it dropped on the English hospital among the patients, killing three outright and wounding 28, three of whom died shortly afterwards................In a good many cases their nerve has gone." Shelling began again on 20th March, and more bombs were dropped next day. At dawn on 22nd March the Turks began a three-hour bombardment which caused considerable damage and some casualties. During the shelling, two Turkish aircraft dropped five bombs on the town, several hitting the mosque. Fifteen people lost their lives that day, and there was no respite during the following days.

From the middle of March, or perhaps a little earlier, 'wireless' was used by both RFC and RNAS aircraft to report back to the artillery. Seven field receiving stations, each with one wireless operator, were attached to gun batteries, and were under the general direction of the Wireless Officer, RNAS. Relays of aircraft working individually over each bank of the Tigris registered the fire of the

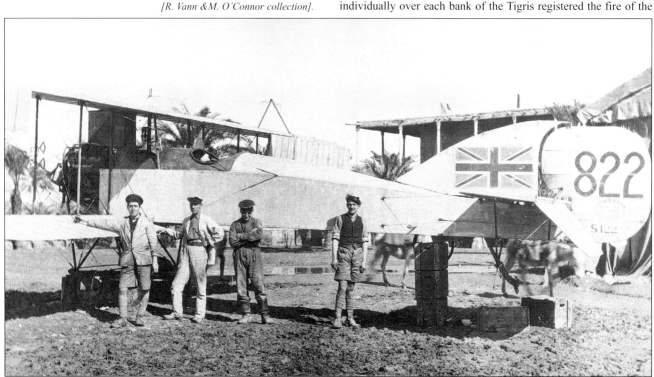

*RFC and RNAS aircraft at Orah during the siege of Kut-al-Amara*      *[C. C. H. Cole via R. Vann collection].*

gun batteries. One of the squadron's BE.2cs with such equipment flew up-river on 23rd March to direct a 5-inch gun battery, which then carried out some excellent shooting, achieving two direct hits on Turkish naval-type guns. Although Voisins, BE.2cs and Short seaplanes carried 'wireless' equipment, it was found that the one Maurice Farman aircraft still in service was best for this work. On one occasion its pilot registered twelve targets in 75 minutes. At times, an aircraft could work for two batteries simultaneously, a task which lasted until mid-April.

## The world's first food air-drop

By 1st April squadron HQ and 'A' Flight's four BE.2cs were located at Camp Wadi, where 'B' Flight joined them from Basra on 11th April, bringing three similar aircraft. The situation at Kut-al-Amara was now becoming very serious, and orders were issued that

*Voisin 8506 of the RNAS detachment flew several food-dropping missions at Kut-al-Amara before being struck off RFC charge on 11th October 1916*
*[C. C. Cole via R. Vann & M. O'Connor collection].*

*Ready for a recce! Two BE.2cs of 30 Squadron prepare for a mission. 4322 was presentation aircraft 'Gwalior' struck off Sqn charge 19th June 1916; second BE is 4352*      *[Blaker album via H. V. F. Winstone; R. Vann & M. O'Connor collection]*

*A close-up of BE.2c 4322 of 30 Squadron, with an unidentified crew. The handle and wire attachment by the rear cockpit was for releasing message bags*
*[Blaker album via H. V. Winstone and R. Vann & M. O'Connor collection].*

as much food as possible was to be dropped into the city, which was besieged by Turkish forces. Hastily-designed dropping gear replaced bomb frames on the aircraft, each of which could carry 150 lbs. (68 kg.) of food on each flight. After several methods of attaching and releasing the loads, a system invented by Capt.

*30 Squadron personnel on guard against enemy flying from Shumran Bend during the siege of . The gun mounting appears to be on a piece of telegraph pole* *[R. Vann & M. O'Connor collection].*

Murray was adopted, and all the available aircraft were hastily fitted. The gear consisted of a long bar attached to a bomb frame, from which the bomb guides and fittings had been removed. This bar was pivoted at one end, while the other end was essentially a quick-release mechanism operated by the pilot. Two bags were sown together and hung on each side of the bar, so that when the rod was released they slid off. In order to distribute the weight more evenly, the BE.2cs carried two 25lb. bags in this way, slung below the fuselage between the undercarriage struts, and a 50lb. bag on each wing close to the fuselage. These were attached by slip knots, so that the pilot pulled the bags over the trailing edge when he wished to release them. The aerodynamic effect of these unusual loads made the inherently stable BE.2c very difficult to fly, and it was considered at the time that only the most experienced pilots were suitable for the job. Much better suited to the task was the Voisin, which dropped by far the largest quantity of food into Kut. The distance flown from the landing ground at Orah was 23.5 miles.

Everyone on 30 Squadron was beginning to show the effects of short rations by 12th April, and fever and dysentery were common. According to Cpl. Candy's diary, an aircraft dropped emergency rations of dates and chocolate on 12th April, although the official start of the air-drop was three days later. The total weight of food dropped into Kut on 15th April 1916 was 3350 lbs., below the stated requirement but the most that could be handled by the aircraft. In view of this, it was suggested to Maj. Gen. Townshend that each man's daily ration should be reduced from six ounces to four ounces. Townshend's reply was that if that was so, a river-boat would have to try to run the blockade, and an attempt by the steamer *Julnar* was made to carry 270 tons of supplies. Unfortunately, she was captured by Turks who had laid a chain across the Tigris to foul her screw. The Candy diary for 15th April remarks "We don't seem any nearer relief than we did a month ago. Since the 12th nothing has been seen or heard down the river, but this afternoon a notice was issued saying that Gen. Gorringe had at dawn today taken a position on the right bank which enabled him to enfilade the Turkish position at Sannaiyat. Everyone is showing the effects of this ordeal, looking worried and worn out. I might note here that eight of the RFC are excused duty [as] they can hardly put one leg in front of the other."

All food drops were made from an altitude of between 5000 and 7000 feet, as the Turkish ground gunners did their best to shoot

*Short 827 seaplane 8046 at the RNAS base at Basra in March 1916, soon after arrival*    *[R. Vann & M. O'Connor collection].*

the aircraft down. Even so, it was not unusual for the aircraft to return with holes in the wings. The beleaguered garrison reported that the sacks used for food drops were received generally undamaged. Food dropped included flour, atta, sugar, salt, dal (lentils), gur and dates. In addition to food, large quantities of medical dressings and drugs, wireless parts, maps, mail and even a propeller for a launch, were dropped, as well as about 5000 lira in currency and 80,500 rupees in gold, silver and notes. Due mainly to sudden gusts of wind, a small amount of food was inadvertently dropped into Turkish-held territory or in the river. In 190 flying hours,140 sorties were flown, and combined with the RNAS element 19,000 lbs. (8.636 tonnes) of food was dropped, of which the recipients acknowledged 16,800 lbs. (7.636 tonnes). While on a food-dropping mission on 26th April, RNAS Short seaplane 8044 was shot down, with the deaths of the crew, Flt. Lt. C. B. Gasson RN and 2nd Lt. A. C. Thouless. On the same day, Lt. D. A. L. Davidson's BE.2c was attacked by an enemy aircraft and was riddled with bullets which shot away the aileron controls on one side and perforated the fuel tank. He suffered a wounded shoulder but managed to reach Orah. After that, escort aircraft flew on the Kut food-dropping operations.

Strangely, although perhaps understandable in view of poor long-distance communications, the RFC in London was not aware of the Kut food-dropping operation until a report appeared in the 'Times' newspaper quoting a Turkish statement about the loss of the RNAS aircraft!

In a memo sent to an unnamed Colonel by Maj. Massy on 12th April 1916 he lists all the pilots of 30 Squadron and comments on them. 'A' Flight consisted of Capt. H. A. Petre, Lt. R. E. Cuff ("an excellent pilot"), 2nd Lt. J. R. McCaudle ("a good BE.2c pilot") and 2nd Lt. Davidson ("a good BE.2c pilot"). In 'B' Flight were Capt. E. M. Murray ("suitable for squadron commander in a couple of months"), Lt. L. A. Graves ("sanctioned to be Flight commander"), Capt. I. D. Truman ("in his first two flights succeeded in smashing two BE.2cs! Clearly only half trained; should not have been sent here") and 2nd Lt. J. B. Walmsley ("quite a boy, without the most rudimentary knowledge of how to fly a BE.2c. Should not have been sent out here. I would like to exchange this officer for one a little older and better trained and he should go home for instruction"). 'C' Flight had only two pilots, Lt. H. P. S. Clogstoun ("not yet ready for Flight command. Pusher pilot being tried on Be.2c") and Capt. L. Wanless–O'Gowan ("pusher pilot but has been in Basra and Amara most of the time"). The Major went on to remark "When the other two pilots arrive we shall

have four pilots per Flight. This gives us no spare in case of casualties, sickness, etc. We are having fairly strenuous times and the hot weather and other unpleasantness are almost upon us. I am therefore most anxious for you to give if you can one spare pilot per Flight...........other wise we may very shortly be reduced to an almost unworkable minimum. I would point out that pilots sent out should be well trained on Betuccis [BE.2c]. We've had three crashes here in the last four days, two irrepairable, entirely due to half-trained pilots. Young Walmsley wrecked one in such a way that he is obviously untaught, and I'll have to send him back to the Maurice [Farman] Flight just when I'm very short of Betucci pilots. Ditto Truman, who has most completely accounted for two [aircraft]."

Maj. Massy's memo goes on in much the same vein, now complaining about the lack of transport and staff. "It has been a ceaseless howl for tugs, tugs, barges, barges. Five Maurices have arrived and I am now able to get C' Flight on its legs. I have asked for a photographic equipment officer.........demands on photography can only just be met, and they will, so far as I can see, increase. The same applies to wireless. At present the RNAS wireless equipment officer is helping me, but it is not altogether satisfactory as he has a great deal of work of his own to do."

As at 12th April 1916, 30 Squadron had six BE2cs 'in the field', another three on the way from Basra to Orah and four at Basra not yet erected, and five Shorthorns at Basra about to be assembled. More reinforcements arrived on 19th April, when a Shorthorn and a BE.2c flew in from Basra. Three more Farmans and another two BE.2cs turned up before the end of the month, by

*Short type 827 seaplane 822 of the RNAS detachment after conversion to a landplane. In conjunction with 30 Squadron, it was used to drop supplies during the siege of Kut-al-Amara in 1916*

*[A. E. Shorland via J. Clarke and R. Vann collection].*

*Above:* Lt. J. R. McCrindle of the 7th Gordon Highlanders and RFC, who served with 30 Squadron from 30th August 1915 to 27th June 1916. He is seated in BE.2c 4362, in which he carried out sixteen food-dropping sorties during the siege of Kut-al-Amara
[C. C. H. Cole via R. Vann & M. O'Connor collection].

*Left:* One of the five officers of 30 Squadron who became prisoners of war in Kut-al-Amara was Capt. Stephen Christopher Winfield-Smith, who had joined the squadron on 20th November 1915
[Mrs. Pugh via R. Vann & M. O'Connor collection].

*Below:* 30 Squadron BE.2cs at Orah before the final supply-dropping sortie to Kut-al-Amara on 29th April 1916 [C. C. H. Cole via R. Vann collection].

which time 'C' Flight was established at Camp Wadi with three Farmans. However, all three aircraft were wrecked in a storm on 4th May, so the Flight was forced to return to Basra to re-equip.

Easter Monday, 24th April 1916, brought a change in diet for the worn-out men of 30 Squadron in beleaguered Kut-al-Amara. The ration that day consisted of four ounces of white bread, half an ounce of cocoa, an ounce of sugar and some salt. A couple of days later, Cpl. Candy wrote in his diary "Yesterday we had the same ration as on the 25th except that we had three quarters of a pound of bully beef instead of horse. Early this morning we saw only about three and a half miles away one of our boats, which had tried in the night to break through with provisions, being captured."

Realising that British forces could hold Kut no longer even though 30 Squadron and the RNAS detachment were dropping supplies, Maj. Gen. Townshend went to meet the Turkish GOC on 27th April to discuss surrender terms. Next day a communique was issued stating that the RFC men would probably go on parole to India and that the Turks would allow the recently captured boatload of provisions to reach Kut. In his diary, Cpl. Candy echoed the thoughts of all when he wrote "Will the Turkish staff in Constantinople agree to this parole?"

It is of great significance that, aided by the RNAS detachment, 30 Squadron RFC carried out at Kut-al-Amara the world's first air-drop of food and supplies, and as will be seen, took part many years later in that other major humanitarian air supply operation, the Berlin airlift.

## The fall of Kut-al-Amara

Maj. Gen. Townshend surrendered Kut-al-Amara's garrison of 2750 British and 6500 Indian troops to Turkish forces at noon on 29th April 1916, and about forty-five members of 30 Squadron who had been trapped there during the Allied evacuation were taken prisoner — Capt. S. C. Winfield–Smith, Capt. T. R. Wells, Capt. R. D. de la C. Corbett, Capt. S. C. Mundey and 2nd Lt. C. H. Courthope-Munro and some thirty mechanics including NCOs. All guns, ammunition, wireless sets, aircraft spares and tools had been destroyed before the arrival of the Turks, who with Arabs set about systematically looting the town. Next day the 30 Squadron personnel were moved to a concentration camp about ten miles up-river and there they were given a little rice and some very hard biscuits, which were soon being referred to as 'paving stones'. Two ounces of potatoes, the first seen for a long time, were provided with half a pound of bully beef per man on 2nd May, but the food situation began to improve a little when supplies were sent by British forces down-river.

At mid-day on 5th May the men were ordered to pack their kits as lightly as possible and were issued with rations for three days — three biscuits, three ounces of jam and a few dates per day, the amount allowed by the Turks to allow a man to survive. The thoughtful Cpl. Candy wrote in his diary "What with the rations and the marching and taking into account our condition I wonder how many of us will be able to keep up with the column." These turned out to be prophetic words.

After the fall of Kut a letter was sent by the Chief of the General Staff at GHQ, Indian Expeditionary Force 'D' to the GOC Tigris Column, in which he expressed his thanks for the work carried out by all concerned with the campaign in the air. "The Army Commander desires you to convey to the combined air service — the RNAS and the RFC — his appreciation of their persistent and meritorious work during the last few weeks" the message read. It continued "They have been called upon for very arduous and trying efforts in keeping up the reconnaissance and observation services, at the same time as the transport of supplies to the beleaguered garrison of Kut. All this involved a very serious strain on all ranks, but every call for their services was at once responded to with readiness and resource."

Another of the violent storms which plagued the RFC in Mesopotamia made its presence felt on 2nd May 1916, when three Maurice Farmans, 5909, 7308 and 7346, were wrecked at Orah. Nine men tried to hold onto one aircraft, but it left the ground and landed atop the other two!

'A' and 'B' Flights moved from Camp Wadi to Sheikh Saad on 6 May. Two days later, during a reconnaissance flight east of Said

*Another pilot trapped at Kut-al-Amara was Capt. Thomas Ralph Wells of the 33rd Punjabi Regt. and RFC, who had joined 30 Squadron on 27th July 1915 [J. P. Wells via R. Vann & M. O'Connor collection].*

Hashim, the BE.2cs crewed by Capt. Murray and Capt. Glover was attacked by an enemy Fokker aircraft and was forced to land at Camp Wadi after bullets had penetrated the fuel tank and shot through three spars. Enemy aircraft were now believed to consist of a Fokker (Morane) fighter, two more Morane monoplanes and one or more Aviatik or Albatros biplanes. It was also believed that two of 30 Squadron's Martinsyde Scouts, a Caudron biplane and a Maurice Farman Longhorn which had fallen into enemy hands after force-landing were likely to be airworthy, but so far they had not used against British forces.

*Three Maurice Farman Shorthorns of 30 Squadron were wrecked by high winds and a dust storm while pegged out in the open on 2nd May 1916. Their serial numbers were 5909, 7308 and 7346*                          *[D. Phillips via R. Vann & M. O'Connor collection].*

## Forced to march

Those unfortunate members of 30 Squadron who had been trapped in Kut and taken prisoner were about to march north under escort. "Early this morning" recorded Cpl. Candy in his diary "we buried Cpl. Reid, the first of our English party to go. We left Eaves and Butler in hospital. At mid-day we left the camp and lined up for our march to Baghdad...........The road is awful, about as bad as marching across ploughed fields, [so] we only did about nine miles." He goes on to say "Every European will remember this day [7th May] as we had a forced march of 18 miles in the middle of the day because the natives who sold their rations to the Turkish guards then complained to the Turkish commandant that they did not have any rations. This march cost our column three Europeans and eighteen natives dead and about 300 to 500 sick." Next day the column rested, but all attempts to obtain food failed. "Three of our

party, Vincent, Hogg and Nicholls, have been sent to hospital" wrote Cpl. Candy, "so there is only a few of the batch left that came out on the SS Bamora." By 9th May he was forecasting a further deterioration in the condition of the column of captives, but in the morning each man was issued with six biscuits and a dozen dates, with no guarantee of how long this meagre allowance would have to last. On 11th May Cpl. Candy wrote "On account of so many sick we will not reach Azizeh until tomorrow. When we get there we are told by the Turkish officer [that] we will get some decent rations for a change. Every day gets much hotter. It is now about 100 degrees [F] in the shade and all the consolation we get is 'Wait till the really hot weather comes'."

The prisoners reached Azizieh on 12th May, only to find that no food was available. Further forced marches followed, but Baghdad seemed to be no closer. On 15th May, however, having marched past a very large arch which, unknown to Cpl. Candy, was

*A scene on the Tigris river at Camp Wadi on 5th May 1916. Maurice Farman aircraft 5909, 7308 and 7346, which had arrived in Mesopotamia in April for 30 Squadron's 'C' Flight, are loaded aboard an RFC barge and the RFC vessel T3 after being wrecked on 2nd May 1916*

*[R. Vann & M. O'Connor collection].*

almost certainly the Ctesiphon arch, each exhausted man was issued with half a pound of fresh mutton. Baghdad was reached on 17th May, and there the column camped at the railway station. Cpl. Candy had strained both legs in a gully and when most of the prisoners entrained for Turkey he was left behind, a meagre ration of bread, ghee and dates being provided. He wrote in his diary on 22nd May "I have heard that both men left at Shumran, Eaves and Keefe, have died, so our party is dwindling considerably. Late last night we had a terrible sandstorm, and as we have a job to get even drinking water we all look about as disreputable as possible. Later in the day we had a decent issue of lamb and we were able to get a few onions so we had a decent late dinner." Next day he heard that Hogg was in hospital in Baghdad and was unlikely to survive, and commented in his diary that it seemed very strange that Reid, Keefe, Hogg and Draper had been the fittest of the Kut detachment and yet were the first to succumb to their ordeal. On 26th May the Baghdad party left by train for Sammara, about 120 miles away, and then after a day's rest began another march northwards. Every day the bedraggled column was forced to march, although in Cpl. Candy's words, they were "absolutely done in."

Eventually, on 8th June, the exhausted men arrived at Mosul, where they found that more food was available. Cpl. Candy's diary entry for 9th June reports "Rations today are not bad at all and the SM [Sergeant Major] has paid each man four annas to get something for breakfast. We each got four eggs and three flat wheatcakes for the 4d. About an hour afterwards the Turks sent some boiled grain like rice and barley water and two one-pound loaves." On 20th June, however, the diary, which may be considered a unique historical document, contains a final unfinished and poignant entry, marking the death of Cpl. Candy — "Still with feet. Hope to resume marching tomorrow. Many men dying of starvation. Dinner 4 p.m. — two wheatcakes or chupatties. Tea — a small quantity of rice and..................." On that emotive note the diary ends. It came into the possession of another soldier who eventually passed it to a Mr. W. Haynes, who had served on 30 Squadron as Capt. Wells' mechanic, and was saved for posterity. Cpl. Candy lies buried in Baghdad (North Gate) War Cemetery in grave number XXI.B.24. He was one of 37 members of 30 Squadron known to have died in the hands of the Turks after the capture of Kut-al-Amara. Another thirteen men of the squadron are believed to have survived the ordeal.

Extremes of heat were beginning to take a toll of the 30 Squadron personnel who were still flying. Maj. Massy reported that "From eight pilots in April the squadron Flights in the field suddenly dwindled to two pilots and finally to one pilot each. All the others went to hospital more or less knocked up after the strain due to the feeding of Kut was over. The hot weather came on apace, and there were many admissions to hospital among the rank and file." 30 Squadron's camp at Sheikh Saad was pitched on the river bank between two hospitals, the downstream one being for cholera patients, from where many sad funerals took place at night. There was no fresh food, and half-rations were all that could be spared. Tinned 'bully-beef' turned to liquid, and while tinned fruit was issued in an attempt to counteract scurvy it had little effect. The only cool drink was the water in a 'chatti', a porous earthenware jar hung up on the tent-pole overnight, but during the day glasses became almost too hot to hold. Strangely, British personnel withstood the debilitating effects of the climate better than Indians. Lt. Col. J. E. Tennant DSO MC also had something to say about Sheikh Saad, in his book 'In the Clouds Above Baghdad'. "The sand flies at Sheikh Saad defied description" he wrote. "Mosquito nets were of no avail, the net specially designed against these pests entailing a mesh so small as to make ventilation impossible; the expedient of emptying the kerosene from one's butti [lamp] over bed and body gave relief for perhaps an hour till it had dried off, and the torture started again. In those days men sold their souls for kerosene." 30 Squadron men were in a way fortunate in using 'double-fly' tents, but even in them the temperature could reach well over 130°F during the day. Tennant's description of the beginning of a new day is graphic. "Horizons vanished, the sky became steel-coloured, another day had started to take its toll. About nine o'clock, with a few heralding puffs and 'sand-devils' the Shamal would be down, driving the sand five or six thousand feet high till nightfall; then the imagination would

stray to green fields of England or soft Highland rain."

Capt. E. M. Murray took over temporary command of 30 Squadron from Maj. Massy on 30th May 1916, pending the arrival from England of Maj. J. E. Tennant. On the following day a census of RFC aircraft in Mesopotamia (in other words, 30 Squadron) showed that thirteen BE.2cs and three Maurice Farman Shorthorns were serviceable, while four of each type were in a repairable condition — twenty-four aircraft all told. Personnel numbers, however, were augmented in June by the arrival of four pilots, one observer and seventy-seven other ranks. On the other hand, the RNAS element which had served so well during the siege of Kut-al-Amara departed for Egypt on 20th June, leaving two Voisins and spares for use by 30 Squadron.

Reference to Appendix VI of this book will provide information on all the 30 Squadron personnel who died following the capture of Kut-al-Amara. It should be noted also that a number of sick men, possibly including some of 30 Squadron, were shipped to Baghdad on the riverboat *Julnar* before marching across the desert. One of them, Flt. Sgt. P. W. Long, related his experiences in considerable detail in a book published in 1938.

## Operations after the Kut debacle

In June 1916 'A' and 'B' Flights maintained daily observation of the Turkish lines, flying down the river Shatt al Hai as far as Kut el Hai, where photographs were taken. 'C' Flight was still at Basra, but received orders to fly a reconnaissance over Safwan to report on the encampment of Ibn Rashid. To facilitate this operation, an advanced landing ground was established at Zobeir on 10th June, and the task was carried out by two Maurice Farman aircraft two days later. An enemy camp was also sighted at Jebel Sinam, and when more information on this site was required an advanced landing ground was created at Barjisiyah, about sixteen miles south of Basra.

The work of 30 Squadron in July 1916 consisted of daily reconnaissance flights over an area bounded by Sheikh Saad, Sannaiyat, Niadug, Kut-al-Amara, Shumran and Gussabs Fort. Intense heat curtailed operations, all of which had to be carried out in the early hours of each day. Flights along the Tigris river towards the Turkish airfield at Shumran were made by armed aircraft. A notable reconnaissance was made on 11th July to Mandali, a three-and-a-half hour flight over a distance of ninety-five miles each way, for which a spare fuel tank was fitted. On 12th July two aircraft of the squadron cooperated with troops on the ground to drive off an enemy raiding party six miles south of Sheikh Saad, afterwards bombing the village in which they had sheltered.

Two new BE.2cs arrived on board the T3 on 2nd July, accompanied by nineteen men and three officers. However, on 8th July BE.2c 4512 was wrecked when its engine failed. Seven more pilots arrived from Basra on 9th July, bringing the total number on the squadron to nineteen. This number was further increased by three when 'C' Flight, consisting of Lt. S. Haywood, 2nd Lt. J. B. Walmsley and 2nd Lt. A. Charig, arrived on 17th July. On that date 30 Squadron came under the administration of the Middle East Brigade, which was then being formed in Egypt, and on 31st July Maj. Tennant arrived at Basra from England and assumed command of the squadron. Thus far, 30 Squadron had not had a headquarters, each Flight operating almost as a separate unit, but now moves were made to regularise the situation. New equipment in the shape of BE.2c and Martinsyde aircraft replaced the early Farmans, Voisins and other types used up to this point, and a vigorous offensive was carried on against Turkish aircraft, which were set upon at every opportunity. Frequent raids were made on enemy airfields and daily reconnaissance flights were made. The squadron's field base was still at Sheikh Saad, while its depot was at Amara. 'C' Flight became attached to HQ of the 7th Division on 14th August, for which a move to Arab Village was made.

A reconnaissance report made by Lt. the Hon. H. B. Rodney after an early-morning flight on 7th August 1916 may be taken as representative of such flights. On this occasion the aircraft used was BE.2c 4414, and Capt. J. O. C. Orton was the observer. The report reads:

"*6.40 a.m., Bessouia:* fifty camels walking on mud flat west bank of Hai canal. Altogether about 300 camels grazing in this neighbourhood.

*RFC support vessels on the river Tigris at Sheikh Saad in July 1916. The yacht is the* Bahmashir, *and barges RFC.1 and RFC.3 contain 30 Squadron's workshop and photographic facilities*

*[R. Vann & M. O'Connor collection].*

*Lt. J. E. Tennant, Scot's Guards & RFC, photographed with 6 Squadron before his promotion to Major. He was C.O. of 30 Squadron from 7th August 1916 until 11th January 1917, then as a Lt. Col. commanded 31st Wing in Mesopotamia*

*[Via Barry Gray, R. Vann collection].*

*6.50 a.m., Dahra Reach:* four hangars on aerodrome (three white, one green); Shumran Reach: one steamer (appears to be painted white and seldom seen here).

*6.55 a.m., Nahrwan Ridge:* gun teams moving rapidly towards ridge from small camp on canal at 26.A6.4. Seen to halt at 25.B1.8 (our shelling of gun position behind ridge seen to be very accurate).

*7.15 a.m., Ataba camps:* unusual amount of transport and animals, much movement and tents being erected or struck (men seen around each tent).

*7.20 a.m., Suwada camp:* camp reported at 15.B5.4; has two large tents and ten long huts; two large white flags on mound to south; presumably hospital.

*7.25 a.m., Nakhailat position:* fresh water canal continued along line of communication trench and now reaches 16D.1.1. Still dry. Water only from Dahra to Ataba. Broad communication trench................now reaches the gun position SE of Suwada. Water is drawn from river bank.

*7.30 a.m., Sannaiyat position:* Appreciable amount of fresh digging in progress. Indications of work to reclaim former flooded portion of trenches. Old communication trench from 16B.10.7 to 16B.1.9 has been redug and widened. General defensive scheme appears to be the formation of a strong second line of defence from 16D.5.3 to 16B.6.3. The rapidly receding marsh has left the left bank very exposed. Photographs taken of this new continuation show how the work is being carried on to connect with the picquet trench at 16B.5.3."

One can imagine the delight with which the ground forces received such valuable and up-to-date information!

Many technical problems presented themselves to the hard-pressed ground crews and engineering officer in the very hot weather of Mesopotamia. Dust and sand did nothing to improve the performance of the aircraft engines, and lubricating oil thinned so much that it no longer lubricated. Engines then seized up, radiators boiled, and big-ends failed. Wing spars warped, fabric deteriorated and propellers delaminated. On the ground, buildings, including canvas hangars, became too hot to use after about 08.00, so the working day was very short. To make matters even worse, there was much illness among ground troops and RFC ground staff alike.

One of the potentially most useful devices invented during the war in Mesopotamia was a five-gun pack designed by Lt. C. J.

Chabot of 30 Squadron in August 1916 for ground-attack missions. This was the very first multi-gun armament carried by an aircraft, but official reaction to the idea was negative. Lt. Chabot then took the initiative, and scrounged four Lewis guns, all that could be found, and a quantity of steel tubing from a crashed Farman F.27 aircraft. He fitted the device between the undercarriage legs of a BE.2c and took off on a test flight. A long lever on the floor of the cockpit actuated wires to the triggers of all the guns. Extra weight and drag made the aircraft somewhat sluggish, but over the river Tigris Chabot fired several bursts without anything falling off the aircraft. Cheered by his apparent success, he made for base, where instead of a welcome he found an exceedingly irate CO. It seemed that the guns had been fired close to the spot where the cavalry watered their horses, which had been alarmed by the noise and had stampeded. Chabot was ordered to dismantle his device and return the guns to the armoury, and so they were never fired in combat. If they had been, who knows what benefits might have been felt?

Turkish pilots were now becoming more aggressive, and on 13th August one of their Fokkers attacked three BE.2cs over Kut-al-Amara, wounding Lt. Rodney in BE.2c 4141 before being driven to earth just behind enemy lines by machine-gun from from the aircraft flown by Lt. T. E. Lander in BE.2c 2690. The Fokker was then destroyed by artillery fire from Allied guns. The combat report submitted by the observer in 2690, 2nd. Lt. E. N. D. Barr, was typical of the period. It reads: " At 6 a.m., while on escort duty to a gun reconnaissance over Horseshoe Lake carrying one Lewis gun mounted to fire over [the] tail, we saw a hostile Morane coming from [the] direction of Sinn Banks, and dropped 2000 feet to attack him. We opened fire and continued manoeuvring for about fifteen minutes until two other BE.2cs joined in. After the appearance of these machines the Morane continued to attack us, but eventually went off in the direction of his aerodrome and was seen to land at 6.30 a.m." The report continues "About twenty minutes later a Fokker appeared, flying low over Horseshoe Lake, flying south. He climbed and attacked a machine which he followed over our lines; then he turned and manoeuvred rapidly into position facing us (time about 7.15 a.m.). He came straight for our machine, and we turned so that he crossed behind our tail, which gave the observer the opportunity to open fire on him. This was repeated several times and suddenly while firing the observer saw a part of the cowling (?) fall away. The Fokker at once dived steeply for the river with his engine apparently cut out, and landed just within his own lines on very rough ground between the river and Horseshoe Lake. He did not appear to be damaged by the landing. Damage done to our machine was as follows: one bullet through left bottom main plane rear spar; two through undercarriage strut; one through fuselage, grazing pilot's seat; one through rudder; two through elevators; one through right bottom main plane spar; one cutting outer planing wire on left wing."

The first night-time bombing raid was made during a full moon on 14/15th August, when BE.2cs piloted by Maj. Tennant, Capt. Hereward de Havilland and Capt. J. H. Herring dropped sixteen 20lb. and two 100lb. bombs on Shumran airfield. They all returned safely, although intense rifle fire had been encountered at the target. Capt. de Havilland's report states "Left the ground at 11.10. p.m. and keeping to the south and in sight of the river, approached Shumran at a height of 6000 feet. Started coming down when about three miles to the south of the pontoon bridge and arrived at the hangar on the aerodrome at a height of about 80 feet. Eight bombs bracketed about the hangar, damage uncertain. Some rifle shots were fired from the left bank of the river. Saw the flash of a bomb from the next machine on the pontoon bridge close to the right bank. Returned and landed at Sheikh Saad at 1.30 a.m." Capt. de Havilland was known as 'Mark 2', as he was the younger brother of the better-known Geoffrey. He is said to have feared neither God nor man, and on the rare occasions when he was not flying his vermillion-painted BE.2c named *Oo-Er* he was playing golf around whichever landing ground happened to be in use.

After information was received that three hundred hostile mounted men were encamped at Sahil, four aircraft of 30 Squadron took off on the morning of 26th August to raid their camp. Twelve 20lb. bombs were dropped from an altitude of 2000 to 3000 feet, but the first four bombs fell short, which brought people out from shelter. The next four bombs were dropped among the the shelters

*Lt. Charles Chabot's multi-gun experiment, using the four guns which comprised 30 Squadron's total armament in August 1916.*

*30 Squadron BE.2cs and Martinsyde Elephants atSheikh Saad airfield in August 1916          [de Havilland album via R. Vann collection].*

and into the crowd, doing considerable damage, and the last four bombs fell on shelters further away. The BE.2cs then descended and fired 850 rounds of machine-gun ammunition into groups of shelters, and although few people were seen to be hit the effect was reported as "............considerable, as bullets were seen to strike right in the middle of the shelters." Minor bombing raids were undertaken on numerous other targets during August, among general and photographic reconnaissance sorties.

Brig. Gen. (eventually Air Chief Marshal Sir Geoffrey) Salmond arrived on 29th August on a tour of inspection, accompanied by Maj. McEwan and Maj. Burchall (in command of Air Park Egypt), the three officers then making their way to Corps HQ to inform staff of the workings of the Middle East Brigade. They returned to Basra on 2nd September on the PS *Salimi* after completing a satisfactory tour. In Mesopotamia the RFC now formed part of the new Middle East Brigade, commanded by Brig. Gen. Salmond, and contact with HQ Middle East in Cairo, the Air Board in London and the Port Detachment in Bombay was direct, by means of 'cables'.

A similar pattern of operations occupied 30 Squadron in September 1916. Artillery cooperation was part of the daily routine, and on one occasion three enemy guns were destroyed by direct hits. Six more raids were made on Shumran airfield, on which eight 20lb., two 100lb. and four 112lb. bombs were dropped, generally with unrecorded results. One operation which was later documented took place at dawn on 23rd September, when Lt.

*Nicknamed* Oo-er *by 30 Squadron pilots, BE.2c 2702 was modified by covering the observer's cockpit and raising the sides of the pilot's cockpit [R. Vann & M. O'Connor collection].*

*Capt. Lawrence Hope King-Harman, Royal Horse Artillery and RFC, was an observer with 30 Squadron when, on 26th October 1916, he and his pilot, Lt. Sydney Harwood, were killed when Voisin 8523 crashed from a height of 1200 feet*

*[Col. A. L. King-Harman via R. Vann & M. O'Connor collection].*

*Maj. Tennant, the 30 Squadron CO, with Martinsyde Elephant 7493 at Arab Village in October 1916.*

*30 Squadron about to go on a reprisal raid on a Turkish camp, October 1916.*

Rodney flew BE.2c 4486 flew at under a hundred feet above the ground to drop two 20lb. bombs within thirty feet (nine metres) of a parked Albatros aircraft. 2nd Lt. J. S. Windsor followed ten minutes later, and descended into a hail of rifle bullets, dropped his bombs accurately and made off. For this exploit both pilots were awarded the MC, and the squadron was rewarded by a telegram from GHQ via the 3rd (Indian) Army Corps, which read "Please convey to the Royal Flying Corps [the] Army Commander's appreciation of the plucky work carried out this morning." Lt. Windsor was fortunate to escape with his life when the engine of BE.2c 4537 failed on 28th September and the aircraft was damaged in the subsequent crash. Before long, however, 4537 had been rebuilt, to fight on. Scheduled to boost 30 Squadron's equipment, six Martinsyde Scout aircraft arrived during September, but were not erected pending the receipt of a number of Maurice Farmans with Renault engines which were expected via Air Park Egypt.

Rapidly becoming more aware of the great usefulness of aircraft for reconnaissance and artillery ranging work, the GOC of the 15th Division remarked on 3rd October that "........an aeroplane would be of great assistance to me." The Army Commander approved of two aircraft being permanently attached, so on 15th October half of 'B' Flight, consisting of two pilots, two observers and nine other ranks, moved to Nasiriyah with two BE.2cs. As a stop-gap, Lt. Rodney flew from Basra to Nasiriyah on 6th October and two days later made a bombing raid on Shattra, on the Shatt al Hai. The other half of 'B' Flight moved to Arab Village on 7th October, followed two days later by squadron HQ and on 29th October by 'A' Flight. At the end of the month the squadron disposition was therefore —

    Squadron base at Basra
    Squadron depot at Amara
    Squadron HQ, 'A' Flight, half 'B' Flight and
        'C' Flight at Arab Village
    Half 'B' Flight at Nasiriyah

A draft of twenty-nine much-needed NCOs and men joined the squadron from Basra on 24th October. But there were two unfortunate casualties, caused not by enemy action but in an accident, the victims being Capt. L. H. King-Harman and Lt. S. Haywood. Their Voisin took off in the morning on an artillery observation mission and was climbing away when it suddenly spun into the ground.. A subsequent enquiry failed to decide what had caused the tragedy.

Seldom can the resources of the RFC have been put to a more unusual task than on 27th October 1916. Local Arabs had been stealing camels from Sheikh Saad camp, so two 30 Squadron aircraft were detailed to take action. The crews found twenty Arabs about twelve miles away and proceeded to machine-gun them until

*Martinsyde Elephant, BE.2c and two 'all-steel' F.27s of 30 Squadron at Arab Village in October 1916*

*[de Havilland album via R. Vann collection].*

*Seen here under tow by a light truck, Voisin 8523 was the aircraft in which Lt. S. Haywood and Lt. L. H. King-Harman lost their lives on 26th October 1916*
*[R. Vann & M. O'Connor collection].*

they disappeared into the foothills of the Pushti Kut, whereupon the cavalry arrived and began to drive the missing animals back to base.

During November the situation remained similar. Flying hours totalled 290, including five more raids on the enemy airfield at Shumran, which by now must have been somewhat the worse for wear! On one of these raids, Capt. de Havilland completely destroyed an Albatros by a direct hit with a 20lb. bomb. Eight aerial combats took place, none of them decisive, as the enemy pilots seemed to treat discretion as the better part of valour. Artillery ranging resulted in twenty-five hits on enemy gun positions and three direct hits on the guns. A Williamson Aero camera had arrived and was put to good use in taking 807 photographs, compared with 340 in October.

Military aviation in Mesopotamia was now becoming better and better established. At Amara an Advanced Aircraft Park was established on 2nd November 1916, consisting of two equipment officers, twelve other ranks and a 100ft barge fitted out to hold twelve months' supply of spares for 30 Squadron. Any spares issued from the barge would be replaced from the Aircraft Park at Basra.

At the end of November, 30 Squadron could call upon nineteen aircraft — thirteen BE2Cs, three Martinsyde Scouts and three Henri Farmans. These came into intensive use in mid-December 1916, when after a period of preparation Gen. Sir F. S. Maude launched a concentrated offensive on the river Tigris, with the recapture of Kut-al-Amara the immediate objective. 30 Squadron was ordered to carry out reconnaissances to check whether there were any hostile reinforcements within thirty miles of Kut in the direction of Bedrah, Aziziya or Afaq and to keep enemy aircraft away from Allied lines. Squadron crews were to make sure that army commanders were provided with up-to-the-minute information on enemy troop movements and to inform the artillery of III Corps on any progress made by enemy infantry and cavalry. In addition, cooperation with the artillery was required. A system of ground signals involving the use of white calico was devised to help the crews. 30 Squadron's CO then ordered 'A' Flight to have two Scouts available at one minute's readiness from 06.30 to dusk to prevent any enemy aircraft from reaching its base at Shumran. 'B' Flight was to carry out reconnaissance flights over a line from Arab Village to Jessan and Bughaila and twenty miles south from there to Gussabs Fort, and to search the desert within twenty miles of Kut-al-Amara. 'C' Flight was detailed to cooperate with the artillery of I and III Corps.

Part of GHQ moved forward to a new battle HQ at Sinn Banks on 13th December, and an advanced landing ground was set up immediately nearby. An officer was stationed there to receive reports from the observers of all aircraft as they landed, so that information could reach the Army Commander with the minimum delay. The opening operation was mounted next day, and consisted of a bombing raid on a bridge of boats spanning the Tigris at Shumran which formed the only way the Turks could bring troops across the river from the right bank to the left. One bomb struck the bridge but did not do any great damage. The British advance that day soon made it necessary for the bridge to be moved upstream,

*The grave of Capt. L. H. King-Harman*
*[R. Vann & M. O'Connor collection].*

*BE.2C 4194 off on a reconnaissance from Sheikh Saad in November 1916. Lt. 'Sally' Smallwood is in front and Lt. Charles Chabot in the rear. He gave 30 Squadron the honour of being the first RAF unit to equip its aircraft with multi-gun armament.*

30 Squadron personnel at Arab Village in November 1916. Rear row (left to right): 2nd Lt. M. L. Maguire; Lt. M. R. d'Arcy; Lt. H. St. Clair Smallwood; Capt. H. W. Hudson; Lt. G. Merton; Lt. W. A. Forsyth; Lt. J. A. Gibson; 2nd Lt. R. T. Colley; Lt. R. A. Rattray. Middle row (left to right): Lt. J. A. Ainscow; Lt. J. R. Burns; Capt. B. G. Nixon; 2nd Lt. L. H. Browning; unknown; 2nd Lt. H. C. Hopkinson; Lt. L. Beevor-Potts; Lt. C. Chabot; Capt. W. A. Hannay; Lt. E. R. Moxey; 2nd Lt. B. E. Berrington. Seated (left to right): Capt. L. Wanless-O'Gowan; Lt. J. R. McCrindle; Capt. J. H. Herring; Maj. J. E. Tennant; Lt. Col. N. D. MacEwan (Assistant Director of Aviation at GHQ); Capt. H. de Havilland; Capt. C. H. Elliott-Smith. On ground (left to right: Lt. R. M. MacFarlane; 2nd Lt. K. B. Lloyd; 2nd Lt. J. S. Windsor                    [Mrs. R. Nixon via R. Vann & M. O'Connor collection].

Posing in front of Henri Farman 'All Steel' 1572 at Nasiriyeh in November 1916 are (left to right): Lt. H. Richardson; 2nd Lt. F. M. Hawker; Capt. H. F. Gordon (OC 'B' Flight); Lt. E. A. Barr                    [G. T. Muir via R. Vann & M. O'Connor collection].

and Capt. J. H. Herring MC, of 30 Squadron, discovered this move in progress during the night of 15/16th December. He set about bombing the bridge at once, causing the tug to slip its load and pontoons to drift into the river bank. Twice Capt. Herring returned to Sinn Banks to re-arm, and continued bombing until he was satisfied that the bridge was effectively out of action. Next day the Turks had no contact between their forces, a situation which went a long way to demonstrating the effectiveness of air power in general and 30 Squadron in particular. For his exploits that night, the intrepid Capt. Herring was awarded the DSO. Further success was achieved on 20th December, when Lt. G. A. Merton and Lt. W. A. Forsyth in BE.2C 4423 fought off an Albatros over Shumran airfield, killing its observer and wounding the pilot, an NCO named Konrad, who crash-landed the aircraft. Some time later, the fuselage of the enemy aircraft was discovered in a workshop at Baghdad, the cockpit of the observer, Hptmn. Nimayer, the Kommandant of Aviation at Kut, drenched in blood. For this action, Lt. Merton was awarded the MC, and on 27th December Capt. J. R. McCrindle received the same decoration for his work in Mesopotamia.

Another notable bombing raid took place on 21st December with the town of Bughaila as the target for no less than seven BE.2cs and three Martinsyde Scouts, a major force by the standards of the time and place. In all, sixty-six bombs weighing up to 112lbs. each were dropped, causing a great deal of damage. The usual artillery cooperation and reconnaissance work occupied the last days of the year for 30 Squadron crews, one of the flights being made by Capt. de Havilland over Baghdad, where he saw no evidence of an expected build-up of Turkish troops.

Christmas Day 1916 in 'Mespot' was a cheerful time, probably more so than in England. A minimal amount of work was demanded, after which all concerned tucked into what must have been a feast by local standards. The officers' mess was bursting at the seams with merry men, many of them from army units in the vicinity who had wandered into the camp to exchange seasonal greetings. Singing, drinking and smoking went on far into the night, although in the afternoon a sports meeting had been held in an attempt to wear off the effects of the meal.

On 2nd January 1917 it was found that the Turks, no doubt a little upset by the constant raiding of their airfield at Shumran, had moved their operation to an alternative site five miles to the north-

*Lt. Skinner in a Martinsyde Elephant at Arab Village landing ground in December 1916. The long handle on the machine gun allows upward fire.*

west. Enemy aircraft were now becoming more active over the Mesopotamian front, and twelve combats took place, most of them on the enemy side of the lines. Two 30 Squadron aircraft were damaged in these confrontations, but there were no casualties.

## A change of command

Maj. J. E. Tennant, who had been CO of 30 Squadron since the end of the previous July, was promoted to the temporary rank of Lt. Col. on 11th January and left to take up a new appointment as the Officer Commanding the RFC in Mesopotamia. Into his position stepped Capt. Hereward de Havilland, who was promoted to Major, another temporary rank. These promotions formed part of a reorganisation of the RFC in Mesopotamia which became effective on 1st February 1917, when the post of Assistant Director of Aeronautics was abolished.

On the day of Maj. Tennant's promotion, a message from GHQ was dropped by 30 Squadron into Turkish entrenchments along the river near Kut-al-Amara inviting the Turks to surrender and promising proper treatment of captured troops.

Another landing ground was established on 13th January, this time at Atab to facilitate 30 Squadron's cooperation with III Corps

*An evocative picture for readers who are interested in road vehicles. Lt. J. A. Gibson was in charge of 30 Squadron's stores from 20th March 1916 to 15th November 1917. Four Leyland tenders shelter, while Lt. Gibson poses in a Crossley* [R. Vann & M. O'Connor collection].

at Shatt al Hai. Next day, while working with a cavalry regiment from Hai, Lt. Lander had the misfortune to suffer engine trouble and force-landed in enemy territory, wrecking the undercarriage of his aircraft in the process. The GOC of the Cavalry Division, made aware of the situation, ordered that the remains of the aircraft should be burnt after the engine and guns had been salvaged, and Lt. Lander and his observer were brought safely back to British lines.

Baghdad was the destination for 30 Squadron on 20th January, when three Martinsyde Scouts led by Maj. de Havilland dropped six 100lb bombs on the citadel. One bomb hit the citadel wall and two destroyed several houses, causing panic among the citizens, but two failed to explode and one was later reported as having "gone off very feebly." Six large steamers, three of them of the paddle variety, and nine barges were seen on the river below the bridge, but seemed to be out of use. As well as raiding the city the three observers made a comprehensive survey of Baghdad, Diyala and Ctesiphon, enabling good maps of the area to be drawn for future use by GHQ.

Violent rainstorms and a south-easterly gale on 21st January blew down two hangars, but the aircraft inside them were saved. Ten days later another storm left the landing ground at Arab Village partially flooded, and pilots found that taking off in the muddy conditions was very difficult.

Recently-arrived Lt. A. E. L. Skinner took off from Arab Village in BE.2c 4423 on 23rd January 1917 with Lt. L. Beevor-Potts as his observer, their task to register for artillery over the Dahra Bend region of the river Tigris. After two hours of this, they found that a Fokker was diving on their tail, and Lt. Beevor-Potts promptly fired at it. The ensuing dogfight lasted twenty minutes before the enemy aircraft made off, and the BE.2c was extensively damaged. Skinner therefore landed it at the Advanced HQ landing strip at Sinn and returned to Arab Village in the CO's aircraft, 2702.

'C' Flight moved to Sinn Abtar on 27th January as a detachment, a move made in fifteen wagon loads by the Australian Mule Transport section. Meanwhile, the half of 'B' Flight

*Left: Capt., later Maj., Hereward de Havilland, who joined 30 Squadron on 1st August 1916 and became CO on 11th January 1917, remaining in command until being posted to the UK on 21st April 1918*
*[R. Vann & M. O'Connor collection].*
*Below: An aerial view of the RFC Aircraft Park at Basra in 1917, by which time the original site had been surrounded by base hospitals and a camp for Turkish prisoners of war [R. Vann & M. O'Connor collection].*

continued to work with the 15th Division at Nasiriyah. Enemy aircraft were not much in evidence in February, when only two were seen, and only three combats took place. One was a Fokker which was shot down just behind Turkish lines on 1st February by Lt. J. R. Burns, who with his observer, Lt. Beevor–Potts, was cooperating with the artillery at the time. A document captured later indicated that the enemy pilot had been killed but his body was wedged in the wreckage of the Fokker and could not be extricated. A deserter had stated that the only Germans remaining on the front were aviators, and German records indicate that Gefr. T. Mileff was killed, or died, at Baghdad on 1st February.

Opportunities to obtain useful material locally were often taken by the squadron. Thus it was that when 2nd Lt. K. B. Lloyd, on patrol on 30th January 1917, spotted a large herd of cattle and sheep, he directed a group of cavalry towards them, resulting in the acquisition of 1000 animals and 60 tons of barley! What use was made of the haul has never been explained.

This was a period of exceptional success during which seventy targets were identified for the artillery, which then wiped out six active gun batteries, made two direct hits on a pontoon bridge at a range of 9800 yards (about 8.96 km.) and sank a barge. After one particularly accurate reconnaissance, the Chief of the General Staff sent a message to 30 Squadron: "I am directed by the Army Commander to express his appreciation of the excellent air reconnaissance carried out by Lt. G. Merton MC RAF [sic] on 8th February 1917 whereby the new system of Turkish entrenchments spanning the extremity of the Dahra loop was plotted with such accuracy that his trace was practically coincident with the trace of these works subsequently recorded by air photography." Two days later a further note of appreciation was received: "Army Commander's best congratulations to 104th Battery and Royal Flying Corps in their fine cooperation and the former's brilliant shooting."

Lt. Merton was the inventor of a simple but effective piece of apparatus known as the 'Mousetrap Plotter' after a mousetrap he had made from a kerosene tin. The plotter consisted of a sighting bar set at 45° to the horizontal and fixed to the lower wing. When flying at 5000 feet above the ground, any target sighted down the 45° bar would be 5000 feet from the position of the aircraft above the ground at the moment of sighting. This simple gadget proved very useful in the preparation of accurate maps, which were later used to good effect by the artillery.

Heavy rain and strong winds combined to flood the airfield at Nasiriyah in the middle of February, and the landing grounds at Arab Village and Sinn also became very soggy. The weather did not, however, prevent British forces from attacking and over-running the Dahra Bend trenches on 15th February, and 1995 troops were captured. Four of 30 Squadron's aircraft were kept busy throughout the day on army cooperation work, which by now the pilots and observers had made into a fine art for which the army expressed further gratitude. On 18th February another enemy aircraft fell to 30 Squadron's guns when Maj. de Havilland, on escort duty in a new Martinsyde G.100, attacked a Fokker, which attempted to make for its own airfield. Following the Fokker, de Havilland emptied a drum of Lewis ammunition into it, causing one wing to detach completely and the other one to fold back. Completely out of control, the enemy machine spiralled vertically down from 7000 feet to crash near its base. In German records there is mention of the death of Uffz. Ernst Jopp at Kut on this date.

## Turks in retreat

On 22nd and 23rd February a bridge was placed in position across the river Tigris near Shumran, and 30 Squadron undertook the task of preventing any Turkish aircraft from taking off and discovering the bridge, at least until it came into use. A standing patrol was therefore flown on 23rd February by the only two serviceable Scouts. One enemy aircraft managed to elude the Scouts late in the afternoon, but by then the bridge was in service and British troops were crossing. At the same time, an assault on Sannaiyat was launched, and the main work of the squadron in that area was to report on artillery fire and on the progress of British infantry. Lt. Lloyd made a reconnaissance of Sannaiyat on 24th February and after landing at Advanced HQ reported that the

*30 Squadron personnel at Sinn-Abtar in February 1917. Standing, left to right: 2nd Lt. R. T. Colley (pilot); Lt. A. E. Skinner (pilot); Lt. R. A. Heron (observer); Lt. G. Merton (pilot); Lt. E. W. Greswell (observer); Lt. L. S. Page (pilot); Lt. J. R. Burns. Seated, left to right: Lt. L. Beevor-Potts (pilot); Lt. R. M. MacFarlane (observer); Lt. A. R. Rattray (observer)*
*[G. T. Muir via R. Vann & M. O'Connor collection].*

enemy was in headlong retreat towards Baghdad. This was a great opportunity for an attack by 30 Squadron, and the crews made the most of it by bombing and machine-gunning the retreating troops. Notably, Maj. de Havilland scored twenty-two direct hits with bombs during the one day. In Order of the Day No.57, dated that very day, Capt. (temporary Major) de Havilland was awarded the DSO for conspicuous gallantry and skill. "He observed a Fokker attack a machine on photographic duty and immediately closed to attack", the citation reads. "The Fokker [pilot] dived for his aerodrome and was followed some way down by Maj. de Havilland, who blew one wing off. The Fokker then capsized and breaking up in the air crashed to earth. This is the second enemy machine he has destroyed. His services for the last eight months have been exceptional and he has done much damage to the enemy by bombing both by day and by night. His skill, dash and example are of the highest order." This fails to mention that the Major had to jettison twelve 20lb. bombs before being able to attack the Fokker.

Reconnaissance early on 25th February showed that the Turks were still in retreat, the main force having reached Bughaila. Lt. Col. Tennant, still taking an active part in the proceedings though no longer a member of 30 Squadron, machine-gunned a tug towing sections of a pontoon bridge up-river, and then Maj. de Havilland bombed it, which caused the tow-line to break and the pontoon sections to drift downstream.

By 25th February 30 Squadron, less half of 'B' Flight and 'C' Flight, was located at Arab Village, but a succession of moves then took place as the squadron kept pace with the advancing army. On 26th February Shumran, where Turkish aircraft had been based, was occupied, followed by Sheikh Saad on 2nd March, Aziziya the following day and on 5th March Zeur, where two Martinsydes crashed on landing in a high wind. There, 'C' Flight rejoined the squadron. In the advance, 30 Squadron had moved forward over 150 miles by land and had increased the river communications by 200 miles. During the advance, three tugs were used by the squadron, but due to the tortuous nature of the fast-flowing river Tigris it proved difficult to keep up with the moves forward made by the aircraft. However, two fast motorboats and three light tenders which carried two or three mechanics usually managed to reach the forward landing grounds at dusk in order to provide the necessary fuel. Landing grounds as close to the mobile GHQ as possible were chosen by survey from the air, but it was usually impossible to prepare the ground surface before the aircraft arrived. Nevertheless, no damage was suffered by any aircraft in landing on such rough strips. Pilots and observers flew with their day's rations in their pockets! No effort could be made to carry the portable hangars from place to place — there wasn't time. Constant air-to-ground communication with GHQ and the advancing troops and

*A sombre-looking group of RFC Wireless section personnel in 1917. Left to right: Cpl. Samuel Hall, who was awarded the DCM for his work at Ramadi on 11th July 1917, when he repaired his aerial three times under fire in order to maintain contact with supporting aircraft; Capt. P. L. Hunting; unknown airman; Cpl. Allen*  *[R. Vann & M. O'Connor collection].*

*Members of 30 Squadron at Aziziyah in March 1917: Potts, Burns, MacFarlane, Gordon and Brodie*
*[de Havilland album via R. Vann collection].*

## Baghdad falls

The army entered Baghdad at 05.45 on 11th March 1917, and the enemy, after looting or destroying everything possible, retreated to a position along a railway line fifteen miles north of the city, where troops were seen boarding trains. GHQ and the gunboats steamed in during the afternoon. A good deal of aviation material had been abandoned by the Turks, as well as an RFC barge which had been captured at Kut-al-Amara in April 1916. At this point it seemed doubtful that the enemy had more than one serviceable aircraft, although intelligence reports suggested that twelve were on the way, including some Halberstadts. The first pilot of 30 Squadron to land at Baghdad was Lt. Skinner in BE.2c 4585, with his batman, Pte. South, as passenger.

Availability of aircraft to 30 Squadron was also something of a problem by now. They were dilapidated, and as no hangars had been available for some time they had suffered continual exposure to the elements. Engines had not been properly overhauled or fabric repaired properly, but none of these shortcomings was the fault of the hard-pressed ground crews, who had neither the facilities nor the time to carry out their work 'by the book'. In addition, 30 Squadron's aircraft were spread over a wide area and were controlled by any staff officer of the formation for which they were working. To many of these officers, aircraft were a new toy, and they had little idea how to use them effectively.

Flying from Felujah on cooperation with the 7th Brigade on 19th March, Lt. Skinner and Capt. Brodie in BE.2c 4558 *Ginger* landed to give their report. Unable to restart the engine of the aircraft, Skinner jumped out to swing the propeller, with Brodie in the pilot's seat. The engine fired and *Ginger* moved forward with Skinner hanging onto the wing in an effort to stop it. Brodie, fearing for his life, jumped out, Skinner fell over, a wheel and the engine passing over him, and the aircraft nosed over! One of 30 Squadron's luckiest pilots lived to fight again.

After their retreat from Baghdad, the Turks divided into three separate forces. On the Tigris front north of Baghdad there were three Divisions which had seen service at Kut-al-Amara; on the Euphrates front there were two thousand troops; and on the Khaniqin front on the Diyala river the XIII Turkish Army Corps was found. These were very scattered positions, located about eighty miles from Baghdad to the west and north and 120 miles to the north-east, and to obtain accurate information on them the General Staff relied to a large extent on 30 Squadron's expertise. Long flights over unmapped territory thus became a regular feature of the squadron's work, but to ensure that as little time as possible was lost in transit, the Flights were repositioned. On 26th March 'B' Flight and a workshop barge were sent up the Diyala river to Baqubah, thirty-five miles north-east of Baghdad, to work under the direction of Gen. Keary's column against the Turks in the direction of Khaniqin, and three days later 'C' Flight was sent up the Tigris to work with III Corps at Kasirin. Headquarters and 'A' Flight stayed at Baghdad for work on the Euphrates front and to make long-distance reconnaissance flights if required by GHQ. The half-Flight at Nasiriyah was then brought back to Baghdad. As Baghdad is five hundred miles from Basra, the Advanced Park at Amara was moved to Sheikh Saad, a point about halfway between the two cities.

gunboats was maintained and all concerned were kept up to date with enemy dispositions and troop movements.

When it was discovered that the Turks were evacuating guns and stores from Baghdad to Samarrah by rail, Lt. J. S. Windsor and his observer, Capt. Cave–Brown, and 2nd Lt. R. K. Morris with Capt. Farley, were detailed on 7th March to destroy a vital railway bridge at Sumaikcheh, thirty-five miles north of Baghdad. After setting out in BE.2cs, the 30 Squadron crews landed within two hundred yards of the bridge, which was apparently undefended, but the observers, who were both members of the Royal Engineers, decided that the charges of dynamite they had brought with them were not capable of destroying the reinforced concrete structure. When a party of mounted Arabs of hostile demeanour appeared from a nearby village it became clear that a retreat was called for, but when they were airborne the two pilots took the opportunity of emptying their Lewis guns into the Arabs.

On 8th March the squadron moved to Bustan and next day 'C' Flight went on to Bawi to cooperate with I Corps. Another attempt to disrupt enemy rail transport arrangements was made on 9th March, when Maj. de Havilland scored a direct hit on a station near Khadimain, which is said to have blown the roof off the station building and to have destroyed a train. All that with a 65lb. bomb! An airfield at Baghdad was also raided, forty-seven bombs being dropped during that day. British troops were now approaching Baghdad, and on the night of 10/11th March the Turks evacuated their positions on the right banks of the Tigris and Diyala rivers. British forces then entered the city, and in the afternoon 'A' and 'B' Flights of 30 Squadron landed at the airfield they had so recently attacked. Next day they were joined by 'C' Flight from Bawi.

*Lt. Col. J. E. Tennant (second from left in front of Martinsyde Scout 7493) landed 24 miles east of Kasr-i-Shirin near the Pai Tak Pass on 2nd April 1917 to deliver messages to the Russian forces under Gen. Baratoff     [Mrs. R. Nixon via R. Vann & M. O'Connor collection].*

Russian forces were expected to arrive in Mesopotamia shortly, and on 22nd March Lt. Lander flew over Khaniqin and the area of Qasr-i-Shirin to try to find them, without success. Another attempt was made on 30th March by the CO, who flew for four and a half hours into Persia (today's Iran) but failed to see any Russians. It transpired later that they were held up at Miankul, about twenty-five miles east of Qasr-i-Shirin, where they were found on 2nd April by Lt. Col. Tennant, who was given an enthusiastic welcome when he landed his Martinsyde Scout nearby. Messages from GHQ to Gen. Baratoff were handed to the officer in command of the

**Right:** *A couple of days later, on 3rd April 1917, Lt. Page's BE.2C 4585 was in collision with a Halberstadt flown by Oblt. Schütz, damaging a wingtip, but both managed to return to their bases.*
**Below:** *The 30 Squadron Hupmobile car at Kuwar Reach. Lt. Skinner is standing behind. Others (l-r) were: Lt. Burns, Lt. Page, Lt. Brodie, Lt. Dennys and Lt. Colley.*

*'C' Flight camp at Kuwar Reach, the primitive conditions endured by the personnel being clear*        *[de Havilland album via R. Vann collection].*

Russian force. About fifty miles east of Baghdad, this area is very mountainous, with snow-capped ridges rising to 8000 feet.

Unusually, an award was made to an 'other rank' on 28th March 1917, when 1/AM 664 F. J. W. Adams received the Military Medal for his work as a wireless operator. Soon afterwards, 1/AM 4965 S. Hall was awarded the DCM for conspicuous gallantry. During operations at Ramadi, Hall's wireless station came under heavy gunfire, and the aerial was shot away three times. Each time he put it up again, and still under fire, he succeeded in contacting 'his' aircraft, enabling two enemy guns to be put out of action.

While flying a reconnaissance on 3rd April, Lt. L. M. S. Page and his observer, Lt. A. R. Rattray, their BE.2c was in combat with an enemy aircraft, and in jockeying for position the wingtips of the two machines touched. Recovering, the German pilot made off to the north, and Lt. Page managed to land the BE.2c safely at Kasirin. Subsequently, a German radio broadcast intercepted by the squadron reported "One of our Fokkers, piloted by Capt. Schütz, rammed a hostile machine in air combat and caused it to fall. Our machine brought back a wing torn off the enemy plane and landed safely in our lines." However, according to a report from Arab tribesmen, the Fokker crashed in the desert and was burnt out, a statement borne out when the remains were found by a patrol on 14th April. The Fokker was from Fliegerabteilung 2, based at Samarrah. Hauptmann Hans Schütz was said to be a fine airman and a sportsman; he would sometimes drop a note onto 30 Squadron's camp asking for copies of 'The Sketch' newspaper or the 'Bystander' magazine to be sent to him. Not content with that request, he said that the Germans were tired of the gramophone records they had captured at Kut and would appreciate some new ones, particularly 'Tipperary', in exchange for which he would drop fresh vegetables!

Fresh orders for 30 Squadron arrived from GHQ on 4th April 1917, when further offensive operations on both sides of the River Tigris were formulated. As a result, a Flight of 30 Squadron was to be allocated to each column. 'B' Flight was therefore withdrawn from Baqubah and moved to Fort Kermea to join Gen. Fane's column and 'C' Flight at Kasirin was instructed to move to Sindiyah (Kuwar Reach) to work with the column on the left bank under Gen. Marshall. Squadron HQ moved up the river to Fort Kermea on 7th April. Pilots flying reconnaissance sorties that day found that the Turks were digging trenches about twenty miles south-east of Samarrah and that there were new gun positions near the Adhaim river, while the XIII Turkish Army Corps was located at Qara Tepe, eighteen miles south of Kifri. Very high temperatures were now being reached, causing a number of engine problems and

forced landings. One occurred on 5th April, when the redoubtable Lt. Skinner, with 2/AM Griffen as gunner, took off in BE.2c 4348 to make a reconnaissance of the Duluie area. The aircraft refused to climb, so the observation to discover whether the Turks had bridged the Tigris was made from 2000 feet. On the return flight the engine failed altogether, and Skinner put 4348 down in the desert, where he and Griffen spent two days before being recovered. No sooner was he back in service than Skinner had to force-land BE.2c 4183 when fuel ran out. This landing was within shelling distance of the Turkish lines, but Skinner and Capt. Brodie managed to arrange for a Ford truck to tow the aircraft back to safety after dusk. Other forced landings followed, caused either by enemy action or by mechanical problems, not by any fault on Lt. Skinner's part.

30 Squadron's first Bristol Scout aircraft was collected from Basra by Maj. de Havilland, who left Baghdad on 4th April in a BE.2c at 07.00 and returned next day at 10.30 after a 750-mile round trip which kept him in the air for him eight hours fifteen minutes.

Bombing raids were carried out on 10th and 12th April on Samarrah, and direct hits on rolling stock in the railway station were claimed. Then the squadron suffered a sad loss when on 15th April Capt. C. O. Pickering and his observer, Lt. H. W. Craig, took off for a dawn reconnaissance flight in BE.2c 4500 but failed to return. Later it was discovered that they had been in combat with an enemy Halberstadt and had crashed, presumably with severe damage, and both officers had been killed. An impressive funeral service for the two men was conducted by Hauptmann Schütz at Samarrah on 17th April, attended by prominent German and Turkish officers, and their grave was marked by the propeller blade of their aircraft. Only two days earlier, Capt. Pickering had ferried the same BE.2c, which had seen service in the battle of Ctesiphon in November 1915, from Amara to Fort Kermea. In retaliation, 2nd. Lt. M. L. Maguire MC was able to destroy an enemy aircraft on 22nd April. Flying a brand-new Bristol Scout, he spotted a Halberstadt aircraft over Istabulat, and without further ado shot it to pieces, the two port wings falling off as the machine plummeted towards the ground from an altitude of 4000 feet. The enemy pilot was a German in Turkish uniform, possibly Sgt. Max Konrad of Türk FA2. Ironically, Lt. Maguire himself failed to return from a patrol in a Bristol Scout on 28th April, but was later found to be a prisoner of war. He had been shot down by the same Capt. Schütz who had fought with 30 Squadron four weeks earlier and who appears to have shot down Capt. Pickering. Sadly, as a result of his injuries, Lt. Maguire died in the Turkish hospital in Tikrit, but not before he had been awarded the MC for conspicuous gallantry. Schütz, after service in Palestine, was credited with ten victories, and survived until losing his life while flying from north Africa to Naples on 31st August 1941.

A particularly effective artillery barrage was carried out on 18th April, the subsequent report recording that "........at about 6 a.m. HMS Tarantula opened fire with 6-inch guns and HMS Waterfly with 4-inch gun. Observation difficult owing to clouds of dust hanging about Turkish position. Three aeroplanes cooperated with the RA from 5 a.m. to 10.30 a.m. and from 11.30 a.m. to 1 p.m., using 'smoke balls', very useful registration being carried out before bombardment at 12.30 p.m. Turkish prisoners report many wounded by our artillery fire." Another accomplishment for 30 Squadron!

'B' and 'C' Flights had moved to Barurah on 19th and 20th April, but were withdrawn from there on 4th May to Baghdad, where the opportunity was taken to give their aircraft a thorough overhaul. While this was being done, four BE.2cs and two Martinsyde Scouts led by Maj. de Havilland bombed camps and moving columns of Turkish troops at Bandi Adhaim, causing much panic and damage. During the raid, fourteen direct hits were made and the thirty-two bombs were all dropped accurately enough to be effective. Weather conditions were not conducive to easy operation, as ground mists often forced the squadron's aircraft to land without completing their tasks, while sandstorms delayed much-needed engine overhauls. A sandstorm blowing at 70 mph on 29th April caused an airborne Martinsyde to turn upside down, out of control, until the skilled pilot righted it.

## Samarrah captured

Samarrah station was captured on 23rd April, though the troops found that a great deal of destruction had taken place there. 30 Squadron continued to cooperate with the two army columns, the pilots landing close to the army commanders to hand over their

*Right:* 2nd. Lt. Matthew Laurence Maguire MC, of the 1st. Connaught Rangers and RFC 30 Squadron. He was shot down in combat on 28th April 1917 and died while a prisoner of war
[R. Vann & M. O'Connor collection].

*Below:* Hauptmann Schüz, a German pilot flying with the Turkish Air Service, was the leading fighter ace in Mesopotamia, credited with at least six victories. His Albatros D.3 carries Turkish markings
[A. Quoos via R. Vann & M. O'Connor collection].

*The graves of Capt. C. L. Pickering and his observer, 2nd. Lt. W. H. Craig, of 30 Squadron, who were killed in action on 15th April 1917 when flying BE.2c 4149. They were buried near Samarrah railway station in a site prepared by German and Turkish airmen* [R. Vann & M. O'Connor collection].

*30 Squadron Henri Farman 'all-steel' F.27 1573, which was returned to Egypt in May 1917* [R. Vann collection].

reports. Artillery ranging was becoming difficult, as the Turks were in a constant state of withdrawal. However, many reconnaissance sorties were flown, mainly in the early morning and evening, due to the intense heat. It was found that old-pattern radiators fitted to Martinsyde aircraft were of no use, as the water in them would boil away even if the aircraft was flown at dawn. Tropical radiators expected to arrive before the end of April would probably solve that problem, but difficulties caused by extreme heat in the cockpits remained a very severe strain on the crews. Such was the continual movement of the Flights that little or no hangarage was available, and to protect aircraft on the ground from the sun they were covered in Chuttai matting, made from palm leaves. It had already been found that BE-type hangars were useless in the field due to the frequent violent storms, apart from which they were not ventilated and the heat inside caused rapid deterioration of aircraft fabrics. One could often poke a finger through the fabric, and to carry out aerobatics in the aircraft would have been 'pushing one's luck'. Royal Aircraft Factory pattern hangars were much more practical and were awaited by 30 Squadron.

The tenuous link with Russian forces was maintained by 30 Squadron aircraft, one of which took off early in the morning of 4th May to make a reconnaissance over the Turkish 13th Army Corps in the Kifri area before reporting to Gen. Baratoff at Qasr-i-Shirin in Persia. Unfortunately, Lt. Windsor crashed the Martinsyde on landing there, and a Ford van with armoured escort had to be take mechanics and spares to the scene, about 110 miles from Baghdad. On the same day, Maj. de Havilland and three aircraft of 'B' Flight moved from Barurah to Baghdad, the personnel following by barge along the Tigris. 'C' Flight, meanwhile, sent its six BE.2cs and one Bristol Scout to Sindiyah.

Enemy aircraft still put in occasional appearance, and on 6th May Lt. Skinner in BE.2c 4191 and Lt. T. E. Lander MC in a Martinsyde encountered and tackled one, a Halberstadt. In the course of combat with Sgt. Maj. Pommerich, Lander was wounded and had to land behind enemy lines, where he was taken prisoner and hospitalised. It was many months before he could walk again, but he did survive, thanks partly to the kindness of a number of German aviators who provided small luxuries. Skinner, with little confidence in his engine, made for base with the reports of their reconnaissance. Turkish radio then reported that the Martinsyde had not been badly damaged and was fit for use against its former owners.

During May 1917 an extensive programme of aerial photography of hostile territory began so that proper maps could be made available. This task was expected to take three months, weather permitting. As there was now a lull in the activity on the ground and poor atmospheric conditions prevented much flying, the opportunity was taken to arrange regular courses of continuation training for pilots and observers. Subjects covered included artillery ranging, about which gunnery officers spoke, and practical tests on a variety of subjects, aided by printed information received from the Western Front. An elaborate model, made from mud, of the enemy position at Istabulat was made, complete with electric lights for simulating gun flashes, and was positioned in the RFC billet. An observer under training signalled from the roof and telephones were provided for the rest of the class on a gallery overlooking the model. On the last day of May the first BE.2e aircraft arrived for the squadron.

One of the infrequent combats with enemy aircraft took place on 13th May, when Capt. Merton was flying a Bristol Scout over Dali Abbas. His first action was a steep dive, the speed of which dislodged his toupee and affected his aim and fire! A second crew member in the enemy aircraft (which was variously reported as a late-model Albatros and a Roland) opened fire, hitting the Bristol's gun and exploding two cartridges. Unable to continue a fight, Capt. Merton returned to base. Those on the ground were reportedly puzzled by the appearance of an observer behind the pilot of what appeared to be a single-seat aircraft!

Wind and dust storms still combined to create poor visibility, which impeded operations by the squadron during the latter part of May 1917. A dust storm on 17th May ripped a hangar to shreds, but on the same airfield a Bessonneau canvas hangar stood up to the gale, only minor damage being caused. To make matters worse, the thermometer was rising day by day, and during the last week of May reached 107ºF at Baghdad.

The large photographic project continued in June, although frequent cases of jamming of the Williamson cameras hampered the proceedings somewhat. Pilots of BE.2cs were given training in flying 'scout' aircraft and there was some practice cooperation with the ground troops. One method of combat practice tried out at the time was for a pilot to make mock attacks on the shadow of another aircraft, but this was found to be impracticable, as the sun was too low during the hours when flying was possible. Shade temperatures were still rising, the temperature at Baghdad reaching 112ºF! No combats with enemy aircraft took place all month, although some were sighted on two fronts and over the Russian force. The Turks and their German allies seemed to be in the habit of sending one or two scout aircraft accompanied by a Halberstadt, all at very high altitude, and were known to have taken photographs of the Russian front over Kizil Robat, Khaniqin and Qasr-i-Shirin.

During the first few days of June, 30 Squadron pilots at Baghdad underwent night-flying training, taking off and landing by the light of flares. They became adept at navigation solely by the compass, a skill which would be required in operations to be mounted very shortly. Flying in much more stable conditions after darkness fell, Lt. Col. Tennant and Capt. Dent (GSO II Intelligence) reconnoitred the position of the 18th Turkish Corps during the night of 4/5th June. They were greeted by a barrage of AA fire when flying at 4000 feet, so descended to 1800 feet and machine-gunned the camp. To determine whether parachute flares would improve the lighting even more, they dropped some, but in the full light of the desert moon they made no difference. A similar mission was flown next night, each one lasting about five hours.

Administrative control of the RFC in Mesopotamia became the responsibility of the 31st Wing when it was formed on 15th June 1917 under the command of Lt. Col. Tennant.

More raids on enemy targets followed, and included a night attack on the Turkish steamer *Julna*, which was aground on the river Tigris ten miles north of Tikrit on 22nd June. Each dropping four 65lb. bombs from a Martinsyde Scout, Capt. L. J. Bayly and Lt. Skinner (in 'Tinsyde' 7461) succeeded in damaging the aft and one side of the ship severely and also scored a direct hit on a nearby

*Capt. 'Daddy' Merton, CO of 'B' Flight, in a Bristol Scout at Kuwar Reach in May 1917, just before he was seriously wounded in a dogfight with several Albatros fighters, three of which he shot down before he was downed himself. After being awarded the MC he returned to 30 Squadron in October 1917.*

dump. On 27th June six BE.2cs, in retaliation for enemy raids on Baqubah, Beled and Samarrah camps, raided an army camp south of Tikrit, making seven direct hits on the tents of the unfortunate infantry and dropping nine more bombs close by.

For logistic reasons, 'C' Flight moved to Khan Jadida, a point twenty miles downstream from Sindiya and an equal distance from Baghdad, on 23rd June, but was relieved by 'B' Flight five days later.

July opened with a raid on an Arab encampment about twenty-five miles east of Baqubah on 3rd July. One BE.2c and a Martinsyde Scout made this attack, carrying in all four 65lb. and eight 20lb. bombs. This time ten direct hits were claimed, and five drums of Lewis ammunition were fired into the Arabs, scattering them wide. Ramadi, which on 11th July was under attack by British troops, was the next target, and four BE.2cs of 30 Squadron played their part. One aircraft was used to bomb infantry, two flew on artillery ranging tasks and the fourth was used to provide up-to-date information on enemy dispositions. Three more aircraft would have taken part but were unable to gain height after take-off from Baghdad as the heat was so intense — 122ºF in the shade.

More activity than usual on the part of enemy aircraft was seen during July, but little combat took place. During the evening of 9th July the squadron heard that two 'hostiles' had left Ramadi that morning and that one had force-landed. Next morning a patrol took off to try to find it, but without success. Before long, two exhausted German aircrew surrendered to troops at Samarrah, reporting that their engine had seized up. The second Albatros had landed alongside, and after the crippled aircraft had been set alight an attempt to take off with all four men on the one aircraft had been made, two men in the fuselage and one on each wing! In addition, the Albatros carried three machine guns, all the personal kit of four men, four carbines, nearly 900 rounds of ammunition and a small Persian dog which acted as mascot. The German-built aircraft managed to stagger into the air and flew at 400 feet altitude for 23 minutes before the engine overheated and a precautionary landing was made. The men then decided to await the cool of the evening before trying again, but in the sparse shade of the Albatros and a very strong hot wind they soon became so parched that they began to drink very hot water from the radiator of the aircraft. At 18.30 they restarted the engine and began to taxy the Albatros towards the river Tigris, but before long the engine seized and they decided to burn the aircraft and to continue on foot. They marched for an hour or so before a Lieutenant and an NCO collapsed; the others, a Captain and an NCO, reached a British position at 05.30 next morning. One of them then accompanied a search party for two days, but the missing pair were never found. The German officer reported that 2nd. Lt. Maguire, brought down on 28th April, had been badly burnt and had died in a Turkish hospital two days later, but that Lt. Lander, who had been shot down on 6th May, was recovering from his wounds in hospital at Tikrit.

The Advanced Aircraft Park was relocated at Baghdad during July, and early in August it was decided that the best place for 30 Squadron would be Baqubah. Consequently, 'C' Flight arrived

48

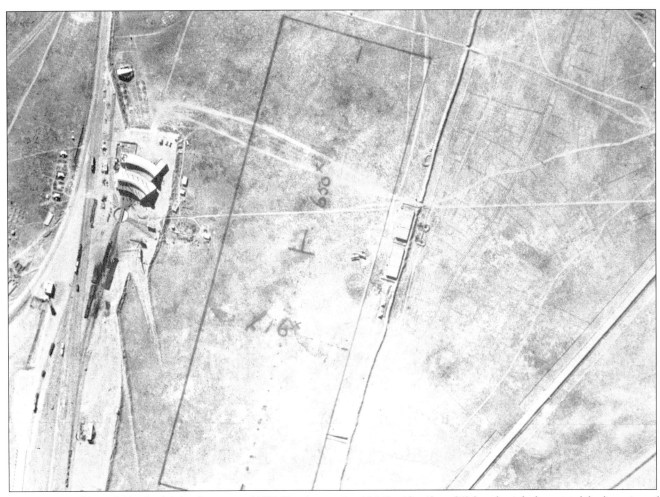

*A vertical view of the airfield at Baghdad in the autumn of 1917. The photographer, Maj. Everidge (then of 63 Squadron), had annotated the dimensions of the landing area, 650 yards by 216 yards. On the left is the new railway station and locomotive shed* [R. Vann & M. O'Connor collection].

there from Baghdad on 6th August and 'B' Flight three days later. It was also known at this time that another unit, 63 Squadron, was on the way to Mesopotamia to take part in the campaign against the Turks and would be based at Samarrah.

## Mission impossible

By now the weather conditions were almost intolerable. Intense heat had reached 122.8°F, a record even for this area, and resulting sickness was interfering with the squadron's work. Three of seven new pilots arriving at Basra had been admitted to hospital soon after their ship docked, and even Maj. de Havilland was not immune to heat stroke. Two of 30 Squadron's mechanics died, one officer and six mechanics were invalided the same week, and seven officers and thirty-two men of the squadron were in hospital. Of seven new pilots who arrived at Basra to replace the sick ones, three went straight to hospital and another was put ashore from the river-boat at Kut. Instead of building strength for an autumn campaign the squadron was deteriorating rapidly, and at one time had just one flying officer fit for duty, so Lt. Col. Tennant, the former CO and now in command of the Wing, stepped into the breach and flew for 30 Squadron for a few days. During this period, the only work carried out by the squadron consisted of early-morning practice artillery shoots.

August 1917 was a month of intense activity for those pilots and observers of 30 Squadron who were fit, and of course for those hard-working men on the ground who kept the aircraft in the air. A village on the trade route between Kerbela and Turkish-occupied Hit was bombed on 18th August, the five aircraft led by Capt. Bayly doing considerable damage to the place. Two days later two aircraft helped in the capture of Sharaban, and on 22nd August Fort Hamrin, seven miles north-east of Sharaban, was raided. Machine-guns were used to attack a concentration of troops behind a hill and direct hits on other troops were claimed. On 27th August a Turkish stronghold at Diwaniyeh on the river

Euphrates was bombed, this time using converted 4.5-inch howitzer shells fitted with forty-second time fuses. These were dropped from heights of 5, 20, 30 and 2000 feet, and although two failed to explode and nobody was injured by the two that did, the garrison surrendered to the Assistant Political Officer, fearing a similar raid in the future. There was one combat, when on 29th August a BE.2c and a BE.2e on reconnaissance over the Jebel Hamrin range were attacked by an Albatros. Lt. Page succeeded, however, in shooting away part of a wing strut of the enemy aircraft, which hurriedly made off.

For the first three weeks of September 1917, 30 Squadron crews concentrated on photography, although intense heat seriously delayed the programme. Martinsyde aircraft were particularly affected, and for days at a time were unable to take off. Even when conditions were a little cooler, pilots often returned to base worn out with the heavy strain of flying in temperatures which were still too high. Nevertheless, an area of 400 square miles was covered, and enemy positions were photographed in detail. Revised maps of the Tigris and Diyala river areas were then prepared and issued to the appropriate army commanders. On 12th September, while acting as escort to a reconnaissance aircraft, Lt. Page's BE.2c made a forced landing in hostile territory due to a cracked cylinder. He was saved by Lt. P. F. West and Lt. F. G. Dickinson, who landed their BE.2e close by, picked him up and took off just as mounted Arabs appeared!

At the Aircraft Park at Basra, some Spad aircraft had arrived for 30 Squadron, but air tests showed that their radiators easily overheated. Only by cutting away the cowling in front of the radiator and removing it from the sides was it possible to run an engine at all. Even then, specially cooled water had to be fed into the radiator before starting. After many attempts, Lt. Col. Tennant managed to reach Amara without the water boiling away, and after further delay he reached Baghdad on 15th September, a second example arriving two days later. Bristol Scouts were similarly affected, and were carried upstream on barges.

30 Squadron's work-load now eased a little, as 63 Squadron took over the responsibility for activity over the Tigris front, leaving 30 Squadron to cover the Euphrates and Diyala areas. Baqubah now being the squadron's base, HQ and 'A' Flight took up residence there on 13th September, but on 21st September 'B' Flight moved from Baghdad to Falluja and thence five days later to Mahdij to work with the 15th Division in a forthcoming operation against Ramadi. During these moves the only communication with the mobile flight was by means of light tenders on a desert track which was only just passable. The ten tenders carried stores and spares for two weeks, personnel and tents. A photographic sortie over Ramadi was made, and the assault by British troops took place on 29th September. This was completely successful, and the Turkish garrison surrendered next day. Thereafter, 'B' Flight was able to return to Falluja on 3rd October. Fortunately, a significant fall in temperature took place during this operation, and by 6th October was down to 100°F, described in the squadron diary as "........sub-arctic conditions." The general health of squadron personnel then began to improve.

Hostile activity in the air increased during October, and retaliation in the form of a raid on the enemy airfield of Fliegerabteilung 13 at Kifri took place on 16th October, when three Martinsydes flew from Baqubah carrying six 112lb. and twelve 20lb. bombs, which they dropped with reasonable accuracy. Dropping down to attack an enemy aircraft on the ground, Lt. Skinner's aircraft, 7494, was hit by machine-gun fire which pierced its fuel tank, causing a forced landing fifteen miles west of Kifri. There, Arabs and Turks opened fire with a machine-gun at 900 yards range. Lt. J. B. Welman landed alongside the stricken aircraft, and between them the 30 Squadron men set fire to it. To keep groups of hostile Arabs and Turks at bay, Lt. F. Nuttall circled above, letting loose his Lewis gun from time to time. Just in time, Lt. Welman took off with Lt. Skinner sitting on his lap! A safe landing was then made at Sharaban.

### New aircraft arrive

30 Squadron's first RE.8 aircraft (commonly known as the 'Arry Tate') arrived on 17th October, and next day Headquarters and 'C' Flight moved temporarily to Sharaban to cooperate with III Corps at Dali Abbas. Having provided artillery ranging services to the troops, both parts of the squadron returned to Baqubah a week later. Looking somewhat similar to the BE.2c but larger, the single-seat Royal Aircraft Factory RE.8 had been developed with the same task in mind — artillery spotting and reconnaissance. The power of its RAF 4a engine was much greater at 150 hp, and although not much faster it could climb to 13,500 feet. Its armament was fairly heavy and consisted of a forward-firing synchronised 7.7mm Vickers machine-gun and a Lewis gun mounted over the centre section of the upper wing. In addition, it could carry up to four 25lb. bombs. Like the BE.2c, it was inherently stable and could therefore become the target of enemy aircraft which could be thrown around the sky.

Sadly, 30 Squadron lost an officer on 22nd October when a BE.2e crashed near Sharaban airfield. It is believed that the engine of the aircraft, piloted by Lt. H. R. Gardner, failed on take-off, and

*Above: BE.2Cs and BE.2Es of 'B' Flight at Faluja in September 1917.*
*Below: 'A' and 'C' Flights' camp at Baquba in September 1917, a popular site opposite orange and date groves.*

*Above: Martinsyde Elephant 7494 at Basra Aircraft Park. On 16th October 1917, Lt. A. E. Skinner force-landed this aircraft 20 miles inside enemy territory after it had been hit by ground fire during a raid on Kifri airfield [R. Vann & M. O'Connor collection].*
*Below: The aftermath of a crash-landing of a Spad by Lt. Haight in October 1917. Soon after this photograph was taken, Haight force-landed behind Turkish lines and was taken prisoner.*

to avoid the HQ camp of III Corps Gardner tried to turn, causing the aircraft to dive into the ground. He was pulled clear with only slight burns, but Lt. A. N. Leeson DSO, the observer, could not be freed from the wreck.

On 24th October six aircraft of 30 Squadron took off to bomb a large party of Persian gendarmerie marching westwards towards Kifri. Unfortunately they could not be found, so the aircraft returned to base. A week later (by which time one would imagine the Persians were long gone!) another attempt was made, with even less luck, as one of the BE.2cs force-landed at Sharaban. The other five frustrated pilots again bombed Kifri airfield, the base of Fliegerabteilung 13, after which Lt. A. P. Adams had to force-land, his fuel tank having been holed. He set fire to his aircraft and was lifted away in a Martinsyde piloted by Lt. Nuttall, who treated a detachment of Turks to a burst from his machine-gun as the aircraft left the ground. Another Martinsyde was shot down, and its pilot, Lt. Welman, was captured. He spent three days in hospital at Kifri, after which he was sent in an open cart to Kirkuk. There he spent six months, during which he suffered from inadequate food, poor surgery and vermin. Eventually he managed to communicate with the squadron by persuading a German to drop a letter over British lines. Yet another machine force-landed with a punctured radiator ten miles from Qizil–Rabat, after which its pilot, Lt. C. Cox,

*Below: Two of 30 Squadron's Spad 7s on standby at Baqubah in October 1917 to intercept enemy aircraft over British lines. A8806, one of a batch of 100 built by Air Navigation Co., is in the foreground.*

*Lt. Hawkins (pilot) and Lt. Creery (observer) about to leave Qalat-al-Mufti on a reconnaissance in an RE.8 during the British advance up the Tigris in November 1917.*

*Lt. A. P. Adams in one of 30 Squadron's long-serving BE.2cs, at Baqubah in November 1917. Adams was killed in action near Khun, south Persia, on 6th September 1919.*

walked eighteen miles in six and a half hours to reach British lines. Not one of 30 Squadron's better days, although Lt. Nuttall was promoted to Captain and awarded the MC during week commencing 4th November.

The squadron's work during November 1917 consisted mainly of the ongoing photography programme, although this was hindered considerably by rain and a low cloudbase. A few reconnaissance sorties were flown, as were hostile patrols and a couple of bombing raids. The first of these was on 8th November, when enemy camps at Qara Tepe and Nahrin Kopri, in the Jebel Hamrin area, were attacked by three aircraft of 30 Squadron, a BE.2c, a BE.2e and an RE.8. From an altitude of 5000 to 6000 feet, these three aircraft dropped twenty-two bombs and two boxes of darts on the encampments, though what exactly the darts' function was is a matter for conjecture. Much alarm and despondency was caused among the inhabitants of the camps, which were raided again two days later by five aircraft. With a more friendly disposition, 'B' Flight of 30 Squadron made a 'flag-waving' visit to towns on the lower Euphrates river on 24th November "......for the benefit of Arabs of doubtful tendencies."

Enemy aircraft in the shape of Rumplers and Albatroses became much more provocative during the month, and were often pursued by 30 Squadron Spads. Gun trouble was a recurring

*Officers of 'C' Flight sunbathing outside their mess tent at Baqubah in December 1917. Left to right: Hawkins, Hancock, Herring, Creery, Williams.*

problem, but on 19th November the intrepid Lt. Cox engaged an enemy aircraft about six miles north of Baghdad. During the encounter, which ended when he had used all his ammunition, Lt. Cox's aircraft suffered damage to the main spars and aileron controls, though he reported that his opponent's machine must have sustained at least as much. Some time later, Capt. Nuttall was flying a Martinsyde over Sinniyah when he met an enemy machine, possibly the same one, which he followed to Dali Abbas. There, Lt. Morris appeared in his Spad and opened fire, but after sixty rounds his gun jammed. Several RE.8s were also in the air but none could catch its opponent.

Supported by two of 'B' Flight's aircraft, HQ and 'A' and 'C' Flights of 30 Squadron moved from Baqubah to Qala Mufti on 2nd December to cooperate with III Corps in operations against the Turkish forces in the direction of Qara Tepe. Surface transport, consisting of nine light tenders and two three-ton lorries, including one fitted as a workshop, had left two days earlier so that Lt. W. F. Creery could set up the camp. To avoid the possibility of enemy reconnaissance before the attack, two aircraft had bombed Kifri airfield again during the night of 30th November / 1st December, and although several of the bombs failed to explode it was believed that enemy aircraft on the ground had been damaged. The ground attack began on 3rd December, and within three days the enemy was in full retreat towards Kifri, and pursuit was discontinued. During the operation, 30 Squadron's main function was to make the usual reconnaissance flights, but some time was also spent, probably quite enjoyably, by pilots who fired machine-guns into the retreating troops. Three RE.8s and a BE.2c were allocated to each Division daily, while the Spads of 'A' Flight worked independently, but not much artillery cooperation was needed, as the Turkish retreat was so rapid. Not a single enemy aircraft entered the fray during the whole of the operation. On 5th December four enemy guns were made useless by one of 30 Squadron's crews, Lt. A. W. Hawkins and Lt. A. H. Lindop, who attacked the gun carriages from low level, scattering and killing many of the horses which pulled them. Next day Kifri airfield was seen to be deserted, and nearby coal mines were burning furiously. After a job well done, the 30 Squadron personnel all took their aircraft back to Baqubah on 8th December.

## Operations resume

By December the intense heat of the summer was a thing of the past, and in fact the health of the the squadron was suffering due to lack of warm clothing! However, more bombing of enemy airfields

*A minor landing accident to Spad S.7 A8806 at Sammarah on 19th December 1917. The pilot was Lt. W. L. Haight, a Canadian member of 30 Squadron*
*[R. Vann & M. O'Connor collection].*

*A somewhat damaged but interesting photograph of Bristol Scout A1768 at Baghdad in December 1917*
*[via G. S. Leslie and R. Vann & M. O'Connor collection].*

took place during the latter half of the month, the first being on Tuz Khurmatli airfield, which 30 Squadron visited on 19th December. During this mission, three enemy fighters took off, but one was forced down again, one circled ineffectively underneath the 30 Squadron aircraft, and the third followed the formation but did not attack. On 28th December 30 Squadron sent three RE.8s on a joint operation with eleven aircraft of 63 Squadron to raid Humr airfield. Over a ton of bombs was dropped by this large force, which left a hangar ablaze and, according to those who took part, destroyed four aircraft. Two hostile fighters (probably Halberstadts) were in the air during this raid; one of them made a hurried landing on the airfield amidst the falling bombs, while the other climbed and attacked from the rear. Its crew was given fire from three Lewis guns, causing the aircraft to dive steeply onto broken ground near the Tigris river, but which squadron shot it down is unclear.

A much more up-to-date aircraft in the shape of a DH.4 reached Baghdad for 30 Squadron on 23rd December 1917. Regarded by many as the best day bomber of the First World War, the Airco DH.4 was more powerful than anything 30 Squadron had flown before. Its engine was a 375 hp Rolls-Royce Eagle VIII inline which gave it a maximum speed of 143 mph and a service ceiling of 22,000 feet. Its armament was virtually the same as that of the RE.8, but the DH.4 could carry up to 460 lbs of bombs on racks under the fuselage and wings. This first example had been flown from Basra by Capt. F. Nuttall in four hours five minutes, the first time any aircraft had made that journey non-stop. Four more RE.8s and a Spad were also available for collection from Basra.

When three enemy aircraft were sighted on the airfield at Kifri on 30th December four RE.8s and the new DH.4 of 30 Squadron and four aircraft of 63 Squadron were sent to deal with them, but results this time were hard to define, although bombs were said to have fallen as close as 30 yards from the target.

### 1918 — make or break

No operations with ground troops took place during the first month of 1918, but bombing raids continued, as did the photographic campaign and the usual reconnaissance work. Twice, enemy aircraft ventured across British lines, and were dealt with by 30 Squadron. On 21st January an Albatros C.III force-landed near Falluja and the crew was captured, after they had managed to set their aircraft alight. More spectacularly, an enemy aircraft was shot down by Lt. Skinner and Lt. Morris, flying Spads, and landed near Qala Mufti, where the crew set their machine on fire before escaping.

With the object of escorting Col. Kennion, the HM Consul in Kermanshah (Persia), a wireless section and a group of surveyors, a ground party set out on 2nd January. This party was aided by an aircraft of 30 Squadron which took off next day to make a reconnaissance of the Qala Shirwin area to check for possible opposition. Finding none, the pilot dropped a message to the party on the ground, which made contact as planned. On the return journey, the column occupied Qasr-i-Shirin, where a landing ground was set out for use as a refuelling point for aircraft flying to or from Kermanshah.

While this was going on, three of 30 Squadron's RE.8s flew with nine aircraft of 63 Squadron to bomb the airfield at Humr on 3rd January, but as there was a great deal of cloud over the target

*Lt. R. K. Morris of 30 Squadron demonstrating the top-wing mounted Lewis gun fitted to the squadron's Spad S.7s*
*[R. Vann & M. O'Connor collection].*

*The top-wing Lewis gun mounting devised by Maj. de Havilland and Capt. Nuttall and fitted to Spad S.7 Scouts of 30 Squadron. This one is an aircraft of 'B' Flight at Fallujah in late 1917*    *[P. Liddle via R. Vann collection].*

*Rough-and-ready equipment for handling engine changes, with RE.8s of 30 Squadron in evidence*           *[S. Leslie via R. Vann collection].*

the results were inconclusive. Four Halberstadt fighters took off to deal with the RFC aircraft, and one attacked from above, but went into a steep dive, apparently hit. 30 Squadron remained very active during the second half of January, including an episode in which the crew of an RE.8, 2nd. Lt. W. Taylor and Lt. A. S. Mills, failed to return from a reconnaissance over Haditha, eighty miles along the Euphrates river from Ramadi, on 17th January. It was eventually heard that they had force-landed with engine trouble and after setting light to their aircraft had walked thirty miles before being captured by a Turkish patrol. It was conceded that 'B' Flight now had a competitor for mastery of the air in the Euphrates sector — an AEG based at Hit.

What was referred to as a 'demonstration' was carried out on 20th January by a Howitzer gun battery and seven aircraft of 30

Squadron. While the Howitzer bombarded Qala Shirwin the aircraft bombed and machine-gunned Kellar and Sheikh Saad Shakal, where forty bombs were dropped. A similar raid took place two days later, but by two aircraft only. On 21st January six bomb-laden aircraft of 30 Squadron, escorted by two Spads, joined six aircraft of 63 Squadron in a mass attack on the long-suffering inhabitants of Kifri airfield. Flying at 4000 feet, the pilots spotted eight enemy aircraft on the ground and proceeded to drop a large number of 20lb. bombs, not scoring any direct hits but probably damaging them. During this attack, DH.4 A7591, piloted by 2nd. Lt. W. S. Bean, was hit by AA fire, and he and his observer, Sgt. R. G. Castor, lost their lives when the aircraft exploded.

While visiting Falluja on 21st January, Lt. Col. Tennant heard that an enemy aircraft from Hit was approaching. He hurriedly took

*An evocative picture of 30 Squadron DH.4 A7621, which caught fire during a raid on Kifri on 21st January 1918 and force-landed in enemy territory. The crew, Capt. F. Nuttall and Lt. B. B. Sievier, reached British lines after walking 24 miles*         *[R. Vann & M. O'Connor collection].*

*Lt. Lancelot H. Browning and Lt. 'Col' Stokes, the squadron's political officer, leaving for Teheran in an RE.8 in January 1918.*

*A DH.4 returns from a raid on Kifri in January 1918.*

*Some of the forty Crossley tenders which maintained the supply link to 30 Squadron from a railhead sixty miles away during the advance up the Euphrates in January 1918.*

*Capt. P. Nuttall MC DFC (left) with Lt. R. K. Morris (pilot) and Lt. R. C. Williams (observer) at Baqubah on 31st January 1918 [R. Vann collection].*

*Remains of an AEG aircraft shot down by Lt. Skinner and Lt. Morris on 31st January 1918. The frame was of steel tubing and did not burn.*

off in his RE.8 (A3448) with Lt. Merton as observer, but missed the enemy aircraft, which had force-landed in the desert. After destroying their machine, the crew were sighted from the air and by the time A3448 landed at Falluja they had already been brought in by RFC personnel led by Flt. Sgt. Hammond. Capt. Merton, whose birthday it happened to be, shared his gifts of 'goodies' from home with his opponents, Lts. K. Halder and Kruse, who was a meteorologist.

Baghdad was raided by two enemy aircraft during the night of 24/25th January, when a hospital was damaged, though not severely. In retaliation, 30 Squadron raided Kifri airfield yet again next night, while 63 Squadron attacked Humr airfield. This raid on Kifri was made by one or two aircraft making five sorties each, the first at 20.30 on 25th January and the last at 06.35 on 26th January! Another DH.4 was lost that night, but this time the crew, Capt. Nuttall and Lt. R. B. Sievier, made a perfect landing in the desert, took out the Lewis gun and set fire to the aircraft (A7621) before beginning the trek back to base. Avoiding enemy patrols, the pair arrived at the British lines next morning after a twenty-four mile walk. The problem had been engine failure after damage by Turkish AA fire. "On the way home", reported Lt. Sievier, "the engine gave up the ghost and made noises as if everything had come loose. She caught fire, and a landing was made [on a road] three miles north-east of Qarah Tappah [Qara Tepe] town."

A flight to Kermanshah in Persia had taken place on 23rd January, when Lt. L. H. Browning and Lt. Hawkins had flown RE.8s to collect urgent despatches from Col. Kennion, the British Consul. They had made use of the recently-established landing ground at Qasr-i-Shirin for fuel. Now, at the end of January, one Col. Stokes of 'I' Branch had to be taken to Teheran quickly, and 30 Squadron was detailed to fly him there in an RE.8. The pilot was Lt. Browning, and Lt. Adams in another RE.8 acted as an escort and carried extra fuel and oil. Taking off on 25th January, the two aircraft set course for Qasr-i-Shirin, where they refuelled. Unfortunately, Lt. Browning crashed on take-off, and another aircraft had to be sent next day to replace the wrecked RE.8. On arrival at Kermanshah this aircraft

was refuelled from Lt. Adams' supply and completed the further 300 miles to Teheran on 28th January.

Spasmodic operations by 'Hun' pilots continued, and on 31st January one of them was reported to be bombing Mirjana. Lts. Morris and Skinner were about to take off in Spads to deal with him when an AEG appeared over the airfield at about 7500 feet. Lewis guns in dug-outs fired strongly at it, and when the Spads were airborne they closed with him and brought him down five miles from Suhaniya, where he set fire to his aircraft before escaping. When the enemy aircraft was located Lt. Morris landed nearby and found that it was built entirely from steel, including the wing spars. Its engine was undamaged and was salvaged.

Further bombing raids were carried out in early February, the first being on the settlement of Nehkidir, the base of Ali Shimal, who had been causing trouble locally. As the army on the ground intended to resume operations on the Euphrates river front shortly, a demonstration of strength was staged on 14th February. Ten aircraft of 30 Squadron played their part by flying over enemy lines and dropping bombs on any encampments they found. In conjunction with this operation, many photographic reconnaissance sorties were flown, none producing any sign on enemy troop movements or concentration. This allowed Uqbah to be captured without casualties on 21st February, and soon afterwards it was found that the enemy forces had evacuated their trench positions south of Hit. 'B' Flight moved from Falluja to Ramadi on 23rd February and was joined the same day by 'A' Flight from Baqubah and two of 'C' Flight's aircraft from the same place. In addition, a Flight of 63 Squadron arrived at Ramadi, and from these Flights a composite squadron under Maj. de Havilland was formed. This squadron then put its full effort into bombing and machine-gunning troops and aircraft at Hit, where one enemy aircraft was destroyed and others damaged, a gun team was wiped out and machine-guns obliterated, and lines of horses were stampeded. Lt. Skinner found himself in combat with an enemy aircraft near Hit, but lost sight of his quarry when his guns jammed. This campaign went on until 26th February, when the order was given to stop, the Turks having moved their airfield site back to Haditha, fifty miles away. 63 Squadron's Flight then returned to its base at Samarrah and the *ad-hoc* squadron was no more. On 25th February 30 Squadron's last BE.2c was struck off charge.

On the Diyala front, 'C' Flight was busy trying to locate the German Political Officer, von Drueffel, who was unwise enough to reveal himself by firing a machine-gun at the aircraft. This was too

*Spad S.7 A8812 of 30 Squadron carrying the top-mounted Lewis gun fitted in November 1917*    *[R. Vann collection].*

good an opportunity to miss, and on 26th February two RE.8s of 30 Squadron and two of 63 Squadron took off to bomb the position. One aircraft of each squadron found it and attacked, killing six signallers, but von Drueffel escaped.

30 Squadron moved its HQ on 1st March from Baqubah to Uqbah, where 'A' and 'B' Flights joined it a week later from Ramadi. 'C' Flight remained at Baqubah for the time being as a detached Flight. Unfortunately, the squadron suffered more losses on 4 March, when Capt. W. L. Haight and Lt. H. L. W. Hancock did not return from a reconnaissance flight over the road from Hit to Baghdadi. Searches were carried out at once, and the unfortunate officers' aircraft was found next morning, burnt out, north-east of Hit. It had been shot down by rifle fire, but according to a deserter the crew had survived to be made prisoners of war. On the same day, Lt. Morris, flying a Spad as escort to an RE.8, was attacked by an Albatros, but after a short combat the enemy aircraft broke away and disappeared into cloud.

### The capture of Hit

The town of Hit was evacuated by the enemy on 8th March and was soon in the hands of British troops. That evening retreating forces were machine-gunned and bombed by all available aircraft, bombs being dropped from low altitude, causing havoc among the enemy troops and motor and horse-drawn vehicles. This campaign continued next day, by which time the Turks had reached Sahiliya. During the night of 9/10th March the retreating columns arrived at Khan Baghdadi, twenty-two miles from Hit, but there was no respite, as on 10th and 12th March 30 Squadron sent RE.8s to raid the enemy encampments again. Hit now being in British hands, 'A' and 'B' Flights of 30 Squadron took up residence there on 11th March.

The residence of the elusive von Dreuffel was again raided on 11th March, when two aircraft dropped six bombs on it, and although no direct hits were claimed more of his native signallers were thought to have been killed. Oblique air-to-ground photographs of the house were taken on 21st March in an attempt to pin-point the German's actual headquarters.

On 25th March the intrepid Lt. Col. Tennant left base in a DH.4 with Maj. Hobart of the 8th Infantry Brigade to fly over the lines, but failed to arrive. Searches were flown to try to locate him, but without success, and it was then heard that he had been shot down over Turkish-held territory. Hopes of recovering him remained high, as the British advance was going in the right direction, and three days later he was released by armoured car crews about forty miles north-west of Anah after they had made a dash behind enemy lines. Tennant's capture did not go down well with senior RFC officers, and he was posted home on 17th April.

*Lt. Skinner on standby to intercept enemy aircraft in his Spad, Fifi, at Baqubah in February 1918. His favourite tactic was to fly beneath the enemy aircraft and rake it with gunfire from nose to tail.*

*BE.2c 4362 was used by 30 Squadron on food-dropping missions during the siege of Kut-al-Amara. Later, it was completely re-covered and doped khaki and was the last BE.2c on squadron charge, being struck off on 25th February 1918*    *[R. Vann collection].*

*30 Squadron personnel and RE.8 A4357 at Baqubah in February 1918. Left to right: Capt. G. M. Smith; Lt. A. P. Adams (pilot); 2nd. Lt. H. L. Hancock (observer); Lt. F. G. Dickinson (observer); Lt. W. F. Creery (observer, in the cockpit); Lt. A. W. Hawkins (at the controls)*
*[Mrs. D. J. Phillips via R. Vann & M. O'Connor collective].*

A conclusive operation which resulted in the destruction or capture of the whole Turkish army along the Euphrates front began on 26th March 1918. By that evening, cavalry and armoured vehicles had outflanked part of the enemy force which had been attacked by infantry in the morning. These troops were soon surrounded and forced to surrender. British cavalry continued apace, and occupied Anah on 28th March, while armoured cars pursued the enemy to a point 73 miles beyond the Aleppo road, taking many prisoners, including a number of Germans. Two Flights of 30 Squadron and two of 63 Squadron cooperated throughout 26th and 27th March by making constant reconnaissance flights and by bombing selected targets. This campaign of harassment continued next day, and direct hits were made on a river launch and on an ammunition dump, which exploded. No enemy aircraft were seen at any time. Meanwhile on the Diyala front 'C' Flight raided Kifri airfield, damaging one enemy aircraft.

A violent storm which raged for three nights at the beginning of April destroyed an RE.8 of 30 Squadron at Hit. Although held down by three screw pickets on each wing and two men were also doing their best to hold it, it was blown over and wrecked.

*Lt. Geoffrey Fielden of the 7th Hussars and RFC, a pilot with 30 Squadron from 29th August 1918, seen here while a member of 'C' Flight at Shiraz, south Persia, February and March 1918*
*[R. Vann and M. O'Connor collection].*

*An RE.8 and a Spad at Uqbah in March 1918.*

*Above:* An 'A' Flight picnic at Hit during the final stage of the advance along the Euphrates in March 1918, with Maj. de Havilland on the left.
*Below:* At Baqubah in April 1918: Capt. Nuttall, Lt. Morris and Lt. Williams.

Headquarters and 'A' Flight of 30 Squadron returned to Baqubah on 5th April, leaving 'B' Flight at Hit until 14th April, when it moved back to Ramadi. From there a half-Flight of three RE.8s went on 15th April to reinforce the squadron at Baqubah. No offensive operations were flown during the first three weeks of April, 30 Squadron being devoted to reconnaissance work, much involving photography. A change of command did take place, however, when Maj. H. de Havilland DSO left on 21st April to return to England. His place was taken by Maj. O. A. Westendarp.

*Above:* Maj. Oscar Alfred Westendarp of the Wiltshire Regt. and RFC was CO of 30 Squadron from 21st April 1918 to 11th May 1918, when he took command of 72 Squadron. He is said to have had a tendency to ride a motorcycle around the desert without the benefit of any clothing!
[R. Vann & M. O'Connor collection].
*Below:* The wreckage of RE.7 A4357, which struck two horses on landing at Hamadan, north Persia, on 10th April 1918. The pilot was Lt. A. W. Hawkins
[R. Vann & M. O'Connor collection].

*30 Squadron in April 1918. Back row: u/k, u/k, Smallwood, u/k, Merton, Forsyth, u/k, u/k, Rattray. Middle row: u/k, Burns, Nixon, Browning, u/k, Hopkinson, Potts, Hannay, Money, u/k. Seated: O'Gowan, McCrindle, Herring, Tennant (the CO of 31st Wing), McEwan, de Havilland, Elliott-Smith. Floor: McFarlane, Lloyd, Windsor. Apart from Maj. de Havilland, who was posted in May 1918, this picture shows the composition of the squadron in November 1918.*

Aircraft allocated to the squadron at that time were sixteen RE.8s (six of them unserviceable), one BE.2E, one unserviceable Spad and three Martinsydes, one of which was out of action. The amalgamation of the Royal Flying Corps and the Royal Naval Air Service on 1st April 1918 to form the Royal Air Force appears to have been of little interest to 30 Squadron and the other units in Mesopotamia, if indeed they were told about it!

This period of relative inactivity ended on 24th April, when military operations aimed at surrounding and destroying Turkish forces in the Tuz Khurmatli / Kifri area began. Four columns of troops were each allocated a number of aircraft to carry out reconnaissance and gunnery cooperation work. Column A was given six RE.8s of 30 Squadron 'A' Flight ; Column B1 was allotted three RE.8s of 'C' Flight; and Column C was given three RE.8s of 'B' Flight. The fourth column was allied to 63 Squadron, while for the duration of the operation 'C' Flight of 72 Squadron at Mirjana was placed under the orders of 30 Squadron. 30 Squadron crews took part with gusto, successfully dropping bombs on and machine-gunning retreating troops and carrying out many long-range reconnaissance flights to Kirkuk and elsewhere. An advanced landing ground was established at Umr Maidan on 27th April, and a succession of towns and villages were quickly captured. Also taken was Kifri airfield, the target so many times for 30 Squadron aircraft in recent months.

Meanwhile, on the border with Persia, troublesome tribes were known to be encamped north of the vital road from Qasr-i-Shirin to Kermanshah. It was considered necessary to take punitive action against them, and accordingly aircraft of 72 Squadron acting with a small ground element raided the site on 24th April. Next day, two aircraft of 30 Squadron led by two of 72 Squadron machine-gunned and bombed the settlement, dropping 25lb. bombs for a very low altitude and no doubt succeeding in putting considerable fear into the inhabitants. Another RE.8 was lost on 27th April when it landed near an army column to allow its crew, Lt. J. O. Allison and Lt. F. W. Atherton MC, to make a report. On touching down the aircraft lost a wheel and turned over, wrecking it completely. Its rear fuel tank was recovered to act as a replacement for another

aircraft, just before the wreck was captured by the Turks. However, next day it fell into British hands again and its engine was salvaged.

At the end of April orders from England were received by army GHQ to the effect that Kirkuk was to be captured. Ground forces were then reorganised into two columns, with an additional force to guard the lines of communication. As Kirkuk was about 130 miles from the nearest railway, 'C' Flight of 30 Squadron was put at the disposal of the columns of troops and its four RE.8s moved on 2nd May to Tuz Khurmatli, where it was joined by a Flight of 72 Squadron's Bristol monoplanes. That day, Capt. A. S. Edwards was flying on a sketch reconnaissance of the Tauq to Kirkuk road with Lt. Col. G. A. Beasley DSO as observer when their RE.8 was shot down. Intelligence reports indicated that the aircraft had force-landed behind Turkish lines after Capt. Edwards had been badly wounded by AA fire. Later reports showed that he had died of his injuries.

To facilitate the supply of stores to the Flight at Tuz from the squadron's base 110 miles away, an advanced dump was established at Chaman Kopri. Fuel and stores were then carried by tender from Baqubah to a half-way point, from where they were collected by similar vehicles from Tuz. Reconnaissance flights of Kirkuk and Altun Kopri kept enemy forces under constant observation, and camps around Arbil, sixty miles north of Kirkuk, were also watched closely. Taz Khurmatli was evacuated on 6th May and occupied by British troops on the same day. While they were doing so, Turkish forces were leaving Kirkuk, allowing British troops to enter the town unopposed on 7th May.

The first pilot of 30 Squadron to land there was Lt. F. S. Maxwell, who quickly discovered that not all the Turks had left and that several of them in a trench were firing at him! Luckily, he had not stopped his engine, so was able to take-off. In the air, Maxwell turned his aircraft so that his observer could retaliate, and the Turks fired no more. When he reached Kifri, Maxwell's colleagues were amazed that the aircraft could still fly, perforated as it was by countless bullet holes. Lt. Charles Brears, walking through Kirkuk a few days later with Lt. Maxwell, was taken aback by the number of starving children in the streets and even more alarmed when a group of Turkish soldiers surrendered to them!

*Changing an engine on RE.8 B7704 of 30 Squadron*        *[R. Vann & M. O'Connor collection].*

On 12th May five RE.8s and a Martinsyde Scout of 30 Squadron raided Turkish camps around Arbil, returning three days later to make another attack. On that occasion, the six 30 Squadron pilots divided to bomb and machine-gun Altun Kopri airfield, where they found nothing more than a bell tent and an empty hangar. They then decided to drop their bombs on more suitable targets and broke formation, but were set upon by six Albatros aircraft which had been concealed in a field six miles away. Enemy pilots succeeded in shooting down two of the 30 Squadron aircraft, including B5872, flown by Lt. Allison MC and Lt. Atherton MC, who were killed, but Lt. L. H. Browning MC and Lt. F. C. Kirk

managed to force an Albatros to land. Its pilot then made a run for safety, but Lt. Browning dropped a 20lb. bomb so close to the running airman that it completely eliminated him. Returning to base, Capt. Page was attacked by two Albatroses, one of which fatally wounded his gunner, 1/AM F. Suthurst. Five RE.8s again raided Altun Kopri airfield on 17 May, and subsequent reports from 'agents' indicated that these raids had been very effective.

Enemy aircraft raided Kirkuk on 18th May, and 30 Squadron took revenge two days later by making another attack on Altun Kopri airfield by four aircraft, accompanied by a Bristol monoplane of 72 Squadron. Severe damage was done to personnel and horses,

*Capt. Frank Nuttall, CO of 30 Squadron's 'A' Flight, about to takeoff with the Khan of Sultanabad in the observer's cockpit*
*[D. Phillips via R. Vann & M. O'Connor collection].*

*Lt. J. Chacksfield standing beside RE.8 B6585, which was fitted with a Davis gun. After a period with 72 Squadron, he served with 30 Squadron from 5th August 1918 to 13th February 1919*

*[R. Vann & M. O'Connor collection].*

and although AA fire was intense no aircraft were damaged. Two enemy aircraft were prevented from taking off by the 72 Squadron pilot, who liberally scattered machine-gun fire upon them.

Maj. Westendarp took command of 72 Squadron on 24th May, and was replaced as 30 Squadron CO by 37-year-old Maj. James Everidge, who after service in France had come to Mesopotamia as a Flight commander on 63 Squadron. Two days later 'C' Flight moved its three aircraft to Kifri, about fifty miles from a railhead from which all supplies were drawn. That month, about forty NCOs and airman who had served in Mesopotamia for the longest period of time left for a change of climate, leaving the squadron very short of experienced mechanics. Until the autumn only two NCO riggers were on the strength, with no NCO fitters at all. Great credit was given to these hardy individuals for keeping aircraft in the air under such adverse conditions. Not one of the squadron's aircraft was lost due to technical defects during the final months of the war.

British forces had begun to withdraw from Kirkuk on 11th May, leaving behind a mobile column which left on 24th May, so that by the end of the month the advanced positions in southern Kurdistan

were at Tuz Khurmatli and Kifri. There were no operations on the Euphrates front in May, although 30 Squadron continued to carry out reconnaissance flights. At the end of May, therefore, 30 Squadron was dispersed, its HQ, 'A' Flight and half of 'C' Flight being at Baqubah, 'B' Flight at Ramadi and 'C' Flight at Kifri.

From the beginning of June 1918 flying was reduced dramatically due to the extreme heat. Reconnaissance of Altun Kopri on 4th June provoked the Turks into putting five of their aircraft up, but there was no action. A flight over the Sulaimaniya area on 14th June revealed nothing of significance. Aircraft were still a source of magic and mystery to many of the native tribesmen, including those who had been a recent source of trouble. An attempt to intimidate such tribes in the area of Sermil on 26th June was made by four of 30 Squadron's aircraft which flew demonstration sorties over the region, and these had the desired effect, as the tribesmen then submitted to all the terms put forward by the Political Officers. This made punitive action unnecessary and showed the growing significance of aviation. The only other events of interest to 30 Squadron during June were trials of a Davis gun by Capt. Nuttall, who reported no significant difference to the aircraft's flying ability, and a trial carried out towards the end of the month with carrier pigeons which were thrown from aircraft at 5000 feet altitude to make their way back to base. Whether this method of communication was used in later action is not recorded, but certainly the new 'wireless' was now coming into use more and more. By the end of June communication had been established between Baqubah and Baghdad, and transmissions from Samarrah had been heard occasionally.

July 1918 began with the move of 'A' Flight from Baqubah to relieve 'C' Flight at Kifri. On 8th July two aircraft raided hostile Kurds who had been holding up a military patrol in the Kargamil Pass, but this was the only offensive operation during the month. Very little flying was done on the Euphrates front, although one RE.8 went to Rahaba to cooperate with the army against hostile Arabs only to find that the operation had been cancelled after negotiations.

Maj. Everidge flew to Baghdad about 20th July on his way to Qasr-i-Shirin to take Maj. Gen. Dunsterville, CO of forces in Persia, to his command. On his return journey, Maj. Everidge called at Kifri, where he inspected work in progress to provide four

*Capt. Percy Phillips of 30 Squadron in the cockpit of one of the unit's RE.8s at Baqubah in the summer of 1918 [D. Phillips via R. Vann & M. O'Connor collection].*

*The RFC landing ground at Kasvin in north Persia in August 1918, from where 'A' Flight of 30 Squadron operated*     *[R. Vann & M. O'Connor collection].*

hangars, engine workshops and stores. Two shelters of 'chattai' for scout aircraft had already been erected.

Two enemy aircraft ventured forth early in the morning of 3rd August and approached Kifri but were chased back to Kirkuk by three RE.8s of 30 Squadron, none of which could match the speed of the intruders, and two Bristol monoplanes of 72 Squadron. The pilots then took the opportunity of patrolling the Kirkuk region, but

did not see any enemy troops. Another demonstration of British strength was made on 8th August, when the Political Officer, Capt. Anderson, was flown by the CO in an RE.8 over villages where tribesmen were showing hostility to a sheikh who was friendly to Britain. Again, this ploy had the desired effect.

Sadly, 30 Squadron suffered a serious loss at Baqubah on the morning of 20th August 1918. While practising machine-gun

*Pleasurable pursuits – 30 Squadron's football team, 1918. Standing, left to right: Lt. F. W. Carryer; Lt. V. Soper; Capt. A. H. Mellowes; Lt. A. W. Hawkins; 2nd. Lt. E. D. Hughes; Lt. R. H. McIntosh; Capt. G. M. Smyth. Seated, left to right: 2nd. Lt. S. G. Bunster; Capt. A. P. Adams and dog 'Toddles'; Maj. J. Everidge; Lt. L. L. Leleu; Lt. C. H. Ridpath; Lt. A. E. Morgan*     *[Mrs. D. J. Phillips via R. Vann & M. O'Connor collection].*

techniques, the aircraft flown by Capt. L. M. S. Page stalled at an altitude of 600 feet and spun into the ground. He and his observer, Lt. L. Kirwan, the most recent addition to 30 Squadron, were killed instantly. Capt. Page was the senior Flight commander and had been with 'C' Flight of 30 Squadron since 1916, longer than any other officer.

During the evening of 21st August information was received from the 14th Division to the effect that an enemy attack on a post at Maidan was expected. Next morning, 30 Squadron put up an RE.8 with two escort aircraft to investigate, but apart from a few isolated parties of Turks no signs of life were seen. Subsequently, however, it was learned that the Maidan post had indeed been attacked before dawn by five hundred Kurds under Turkish command.

September produced a number of alterations to 30 Squadron's disposition. Firstly, on 17th September, three RE.8s of 'A' Flight

under Capt. Nuttall made a 200-mile non-stop flight over the mountains of eastern Mesopotamia from Kifri to Hamadan to bolster a detachment of 72 Squadron working in Persia. Two of the aircraft were then detached to Zinjan to cooperate with the North Persian Force. This Force was little more than a Brigade spread out over a large area of mountainous country and outnumbered by several Divisions of Turks who were advancing south on both sides of Lake Urumieh. With the 72 Squadron detachment, 30 Squadron's 'A' Flight carried out reconnaissance work and bombing raids. Supplies for the Flight had to be carried on the squadron's Crossley tenders over 400 miles of the mountainous Persian Road, which was often impassable. Wear and tear on the vehicles was severe, and Russian tyres costing twenty pounds each often had to be bought from local Persians. Working from Zinjan was found to be tricky, as the rarified air at high elevations meant that take-off speed of the RE.8s ('Arry Tates) could only be reached

*RE.8 B5877 of 30 Squadron's 'A' Flight after it had been overturned by Lt. A. L. Campbell at Kifri in September 1918*

*[R. Vann & M. O'Connor collection].*

*While engaged in co-operating with the 36th Infantry Brigade on 24th September 1918, 30 Squadron's CO, Maj. Everidge, crash-landed this RE.8, B3445, on Surmil advanced landing ground in Kurdistan*

*[R. Vann & M. O'Connor collection].*

after a run of 2550 feet (775 metres). Nevertheless, the crews carried out reconnaissance flights over roads in the mountains and dropped propaganda leaflets. On the day of 'A' Flight's departure from Kifri, 'B' Flight at Ramadi was relieved by half of a Flight of 63 Squadron and then joined the other half of 'A' Flight at Kifri.

## A new offensive

Orders for offensive operations against the Turkish 6th Army, which was covering approaches to Mosul on the River Tigris, were formulated on 5th October. The main part of the campaign was to be master-minded by Lt. Gen. Sir A. S. Cobbe VC, who commanded I Corps, and to protect the right flank of the Corps a small column of troops of III Corps under Brig. Gen. A. C. Lewin CB was detailed to advance toward Altun Kopri. 30 Squadron at Baqubah (less the half-Flight in Persia) and a Flight of 72 Squadron were attached to Brig. Gen. Lewin's column on the Diyala front. Before the main attack, 30 Squadron kept a constant vigil on roads and enemy troop dispositions. As early as 18th October, Lt. F. S. Maxwell and Lt. R. J. McNab had found small groups of enemy cavalrymen, which they machine-gunned "with good effect." Enemy camps at Taz Khurmatli were also dealt with, and before long the enemy was seen in retreat along the Kirkuk road. These troops were immediately attacked and messages giving news of the retreat were dropped on the advancing British troop columns. Next day Maj. Everidge and Capt. Adams in RE.8s bombed Kirkuk airfield, doing slight damage to an enemy aircraft and to tented accommodation. This raid was stated to have been in retaliation for an enemy raid the previous day on Ain Nukhaila, during which several casualties among British and Indian troops had been sustained.

The main assault in the campaign began on 23rd October, and Maj. Everidge and his observer, Lt. A. Bentley, carried out a reconnaissance of the area between Altun Kopri and Kirkuk. On their return flight, they took the opportunity of machine-gunning 250 troops holding a position south of Kirkuk with four guns, and caused severe casualties. Later Maj. Everidge took off again, leading two other aircraft to bomb and machine-gun camps in the area. The advance on Kirkuk continued next day, although some opposition was encountered by the ground troops at Taziyan, a

*Above: Brewing up tiffin at Kirkuk. 30 Squadron members enjoying a break on the former enemy airfield after its capture on 26th October 1918. Left to right: 2nd. Lt. E. M. Jenoure (pilot); Lt. R. Beresford; Capt. G. Cory Wright ('B' Flight CO); 2nd. Lt. S. P. Yeates (observer); 2nd. Lt. C. Brears; 2nd. Lt. A. Bentley (observer); 2nd. Lt. J. H. Southan (observer)*
*[R. Vann & M. O'Connor collection].*
*Below: 30 Squadron headquarters and 'C' Flight hangars at Baqubah, from where the squadron was supporting operations in Kurdistan in October 1918* *[R. Vann & M. O'Connor collection].*

village only two miles from Kirkuk. 30 Squadron's skill in artillery ranging therefore came into play again, and Lt. Adams and Capt. A. H. Mellows ranged a battery of the 66th Brigade onto a gun position south of the village. Attention then switched to another gun emplacement to the west of the village, and after eleven rounds had been pumped into it the gun was withdrawn and moved towards Kirkuk. Retreating enemy troops were constantly bombed and gunned, and information was supplied by the 30 Squadron crews to the appropriate column's headquarters. Two RE.8 crews turned their attention to Altun Kopri airfield, where they dropped six bombs and fired 400 rounds of ammunition on enemy aircraft and shelters.

So that patrols and reconnaissance flights could be carried out more expeditiously, an advanced landing ground at Brigade HQ six miles south of Kirkuk was established on 25th October. Lt. Maxwell of 30 Squadron, however, thought he would take the offensive even further into enemy territory and landed on the airfield at Kirkuk before the Turks vacated it. Intense gunfire convinced him and his observer, Lt. McNab, that this was not a good idea, and they took off again in haste, their aircraft considerably damaged!

While escorting a reconnaissance flight over the Kirkuk area on 25th October, an RE.8 of 72 Squadron had to force-land six miles from Altun Kopri. Lt. Adams landed his RE.8 alongside, helped to set the aircraft on fire and took off for Tuz Khurmatli with the downed pilot on board, badly damaging the undercarriage on boulders in the process. Other aircraft of 30 Squadron 'C' Flight circled above to ensure that a small group of enemy cavalry not far away did not interfere. This was the second time that Adams had performed a behind the lines rescue.

By 17.30 on 25th October the enemy had withdrawn from Taziyan and had begun to leave Kirkuk. By 03.00 next day that town was in British hands, and three aircraft of 30 Squadron flew into the airfield soon after daybreak. A supply of fuel, oil and other stores was soon set up. At 07.00 a reconnaissance of the area north of the town revealed that all enemy positions and gun emplacements had been abandoned. This knowledge allowed Gen. Lewin's column to move on, and his cavalry and armoured cars caught up with the retreating enemy troops ten miles from Altun Kopri. Further advance was hindered by a river which was impassable by the armoured vehicles, and to add to the problem difficulties in supply of stores made themselves felt. During the next few days Lewin's troops concentrated on containing the enemy forces, who were holding a bridgehead at Altun Kopri.

After a raid by 30 Squadron on the nearby airfield on 27th October, resistance to the British advance hardened considerably, but further raids followed, with considerable effect.

30 Squadron's new base at Kirkuk was over a hundred miles from the railhead at Table Mountain, and all supplies, including aircraft fuel, had to be transported by the ubiquitous tenders supplemented by mule-trains. This impediment limited the number of hours which could be flown by the squadron, but when the aircraft did take to the air they did so with good effect. Even those on reconnaissance duties carried bombs for use against 'targets of opportunity'.

Then, during the morning of 30th October, the commander of the Turks on the Tigris, Ismail Hakki Bey, surrendered his entire force. This momentous event led during the night to a retreat from the Altun Kopri area towards Mosul and to the unopposed occupation of that town next morning, the day on which an armistice was signed.

Meanwhile, in Persia, the detached half of 'A' Flight consisted mainly of reconnaissance flights, although bombs were carried and dropped on suitable targets. Three of the RE.8s were escorted by two Martinsydes of 72 Squadron on 11th October, when they made a reconnaissance of the Shibli Pass area, where the pilots spotted new trenches being dug. A ground attack was then made on this activity, supported by bombing of transport and troops on the Tabriz road between the Shibli Pass and Turcomanchi. Considerable damage was done, but one of 72 Squadron's aircraft was shot down, although it landed safely forty miles behind enemy lines. Seeing what happened, Lt. A. E. Morgan and 2nd Lt. J. Chacksfield of 30 Squadron landed their RE.8 nearby and collected the downed pilot. Unfortunately the RE.8 crashed on take-off, and the three officers had to take to the hills, watched over by other aircraft which kept hostile troops at bay. After many difficulties the three men managed to reach British lines a week later, after covering 120 miles of mountainous country. They had escaped from hostile Persians, but then had to survive on a diet of milk tablets and wild berries, but their arduous journey seemed to have done them no lasting harm.

Men of the Persia detachment were now living in billets alongside the officers' quarters, and their health had improved accordingly. Weather conditions in this mountainous terrain put a great deal of strain on the pilots, extremely bumpy conditions being normal. Many a pilot and observer returned from a flight minus the rations they had eaten before leaving!

*30 Squadron personnel at Baqubah in October 1918. Left to right: 2nd. Lt. A. Bentley (observer); Lt. A. W. Hawkins; 2nd. Lt. J. H. Southan (observer); 2nd. Lt. S. G. Bunster (wireless); Lt. C. H. Holland (observer); Lt. R. B. Herring (photographic)*      *[R. Vann & M. O'Connor collection].*

*RE.8 A4352 seen with 30 Squadron at Felujah, was one of a batch (A4334 to A4357), shipped to Mesopotamia for 63 Squadron as initial equipment. It was written off on 29th October 1918*                                           *[P. Liddle via R. Vann & M. O'Connor collection].*

*Two RE.8s of 30 Squadron in 1918. The nearer aircraft is B3449, which Lt. Morgan and Lt. Chacksfield landed in Persia in an attempt to rescue Lt. K. M. Pennington of 72 Squadron. The RE.8 with a white band around the fuselage is B5872*                 *[R. Vann & M. O'Connor collection].*

*Capt. Frank Nuttall, a New Zealander who was CO of 'A' Flight of 30 Squadron, standing beside a Martinsyde G.100 Elephant named Pan-K-Kos, which was used by the Flight when operating in Persia in October/November 1918*         *[R. Vann & M. O'Connor collection].*

*Capt. Frank Nuttall, CO of 'A' Flight of 30 Squadron, with an unidentified observer, about to take off from Zinjan airfield in Persia in November 1918*
*[D. Phillips via R. Vann & M. O'Connor collection].*

## Armistice in Europe

The war in Europe was now rapidly drawing to its close, although the forces in Mesopotamia may not have been aware of the fact. While the Armistice was being signed, 30 Squadron was in the process of leaving Kifri, HQ and 'C' Flight going to Baqubah and 'B' Flight to Baghdad. The 'A' Flight detachment in Persia moved from Zinjan to Kasvin on 13th November and took with them three Martinsydes which 72 Squadron had been using until returning to Baghdad. Maj. Everidge paid a visit to the detachment after a long journey from Kirkuk. He flew a new RE.8, and

returned to Kirkuk by road. Most of the flying carried out by 30 Squadron that month consisted of photographic reconnaissance for mapping purposes.

In December the squadron flew two VIPs on tours of inspection. Lt. Col. A. T. Wilson, the Civil Commissioner, was taken by Capt. Adams (who had just been awarded the DFC) on 1st December on a political tour of Sulaimaniya, Kirkuk, Mosul and Baghdad, and reported that use of the airfield at Sulaimaniya required caution. Mosul airfield, on the other hand, was excellent in all ways. A similar mission took place on 11th December, when Lt. Col.

*An RFC tender negotiating a sharp corner on the Takaguia Pass road in Persia. The aircraft remains being carried are those of BE.2c 5877, which had been force-landed by Lt. P Phillips of 30 Squadron*
*[D. Phillips via R. Vann & M. O'Connor collection].*

Wilson was flown by Capt. Morgan to Hilla, Nejef and Kebela. Inspection of landing grounds at Ahwaz, Amara and Basra was carried out by 30 Squadron, and a search for a suitable site in the Mandali area was also made. On 2nd and 3rd December the GOC RAF Middle East, Maj. Gen. Geoffrey Salmond DSO, visited most of the units in Mesopotamia, including of course 30 Squadron.

Lt. R. Beresford of 'A' Flight at Kasvin failed to return from a reconnaissance mission on 12th December after being seen over Hamadan. Other pilots of the Flight set out to look for him but after an exhaustive search he could not be found. Four days later he was discovered at Kherlileh, some forty miles from Hamadan, suffering from a fever, but made a good recovery at base. His RE.8 aircraft, A4356, was recovered on 22nd December and flown to Kasvin by Lt. P. Phillips.

## Operations against tribesmen continue

For 30 Squadron, hostilities were not yet over. With operations against the troublesome Qashqai and other tribes pending, Lt. S. Bull and Lt. C. Brears left Baqubah on 28th December to make arrangements for a move of 'C' Flight to Ahwaz and Bushire. The tribe had been active in the country bordering the road from Bushire to Kazarun and Shiraz and were considered to be similar in the way they carried out guerilla-like operations in the hills. The tribal chief, Saulat, had declared war on Britain and on the South Persian Rifles as far back as May 1918, largely due to the activities of German agents headed by a character named Wassmuss. As brigands, the Qasqai resented the proposal to build a railway through their territory and to fall under British-style law. As ground forces were usually ineffective, air power promised to

*Lt. P. Phillips (left) and the Civil Commissioner about to leave Kirkuk for Mosul. The aircraft is a presentation BE.2c*

*[D. Phillips via R. Vann & M. O'Connor collection].*

*On 12th December 1918, Lt. R. Beresford force-landed RE.8 A4356 forty miles from Hamadan, north Persia, after becoming ill during the flight. Ten days later, Lt. P. Phillips and Lt. A. L. Campbell flew A4357 to the scene of the landing so that Lt. Phillips could fly A4356 back to Kasvin. At the site, 5,000 or more feet above sea level, the ground and A4356 are covered in hoar frost*      *[R. Vann & M. O'Connor collection].*

*Another view of RE.8 A4356 after its forced landing on 12th December 1918*           *[R. Vann & M. O'Connor collection].*

*Unidentified 30 Squadron personnel in RE.8 B6585 with the result of a boar hunt. This RE.8 was fitted with a Davis gun in November 1918 and was also flown by 72 and 63 Squadrons*    *[R. Vann & M. O'Connor collection].*

play a major part in subduing them. 30 Squadron 'C' Flight personnel and transport left Baqubah on 1st January 1919 by rail and road for Baghdad, and continued from there by river boat to Bushire, where they arrived on 13th January. Two RE.8s left followed. Maj. Everidge and two other pilots flew RE.8s to Bushire from Baghdad on 14th January, arriving two days later. The country, which proved difficult for the RE.8s, had never been flown over before, and consisted of mountain ranges topping 11,000 feet, with few roads and no possible landing grounds. Operations began without delay when Capt. Adams and Lt. Hawkins bombed the rebel stronghold at Talleh on 10th January, dropping twelve 20lb. bombs on the village and a flock of sheep! Capt. Adams was active again on 27th January, when he led three other RE.8s to raid Robatak, a mission repeated next day by Maj. Everidge and four more aircraft. Inhabitants of the village ran to take cover in the nearby hills while the RE.8s dropped thirty-six bombs on their houses and on a camel caravan. It was then considered that the tribe had been adequately subdued.

At the end of January a landing ground was established at Bandar Dilam and another on the coast at Daiyar which could be supplied with fuel by sea. A further landing ground was built at Shiraz, where 30 Squadron's advance party was given a great welcome by the garrison, which had been under siege for several months. The landing ground there was 6000 feet above sea level and had to be carved out of the rocks. Work consisted of a few bombing raids and reconnaissance flights, but as all but one of the observers on the squadron had been posted, NCOs and airmen readily volunteered to take their places. The results of this campaign were completely successful, recalcitrant tribesmen surrendering after a few weeks when they realised that nowhere was safe from the attentions of the RAF. Without the help of 30 Squadron it was felt that the offensive would have taken much longer to draw to a successful conclusion.

Bad weather prevented much flying from Kasvin during the month, but mail from home was dropped there for the 30 Squadron detachment on 17th and 28th January. At Baghdad, 'B' Flight ferried several political officers around the country and carried despatches to isolated ground troops in January and February, with some photographic work in addition. Hostile Arabs were still creating difficulties here and there, prompting raids by 30 Squadron. On 31st January Capt. Nuttall in an RE.8 took as his observer Maj. Vincent Buxton from 31 Wing HQ, while Capt. Morgan took a member of 72 Squadron in a similar aircraft and Maj. O. T. Boyd, the CO of 31 Wing, flew a Bristol monoplane. These three aircraft carried out a raid on Arabs in the Samawah area, dropping sixteen 20lb. bombs which destroyed a number of houses and killed five Arabs and a number of cattle and sheep. Maj. Buxton was in the air again on 14th February, when he flew in an aircraft of 63 Squadron, accompanied by Capt. Morgan in an RE.8 of 30 Squadron, on a raid on hostile Arabs near Nasiriyah. This time the crews were met with heavy rifle fire from the ground, and the aircraft were badly damaged and Maj. Buxton suffered facial wounds.

The task of 'C' Flight at Bushire continued for a time, and effort was made to establish more landing grounds. On 29th January a site at Bandar Dilam was selected and fuel dump set up, but one already in use at Kazarun was found to be unsuitable after

the GOC had used it to make his official entry into the town, and was abandoned. However, a new site was chosen and two thousand labourers were set to work clearing rocks and filling up depressions. Capt. Adams flew to Shiraz, where a great deal of work had gone into cutting down trees, removing walls and levelling the ground. His aircraft was the first ever seen there, and when he left on 9th February everyone in the town turned out to watch.

On 18th February 1919 the 'A' Flight detachment at Kasvin was transferred to 63 Squadron, but the remainder of the squadron continued to do whatever was asked of it. After an aircraft carrying messages from the Consul General to the Governor of Kaki had been heavily fired upon from the village on 18th February, a reprisal raid was ordered for the following day. Flying a Martinsyde Scout, Capt. Adams led three RE.8s to the village, where they dropped thirty-six 20lb. bombs and fired over a thousand rounds of ammunition, causing a great deal of damage to buildings and cattle.

During the latter half of February 1919 Maj. Everidge made a demonstration flight over the Shustar/Dizful area at the request of Gen. Younghusband, following an attack made on the local Political Officer. Soon afterwards, Maj. Everidge returned from Shiraz to Baghdad via Bushire and Ahwaz in a total flying time of ten hours thirty-five minutes, a strong headwind slowing him down somewhat. Capt. Nuttall also had an interesting mission — he flew to Cairo in a DH.4, carrying Capt. Lapraik and the Civil Commissioner. Other news was that a draft of 39 men were about to be posted back to the UK and that DH.9 aircraft expected to re-equip the squadron had been held up at Damascus.

There was still some offensive action by 30 Squadron in clearing up vestiges of tribal resistance. Three RE.8s and a Martinsyde bombed the village of Kaki on 20th February in after leaflets had been dropped in an effort to persuade villagers to surrender. Their response was fire from a machine-gun. The pilots succeeded in causing severe damage to houses and cattle, but this was almost the last such mission by 30 Squadron. Rebel tribe leader Saulat was allowed to meet the Political Officer under terms of safe conduct on 3rd March and began to discuss surrender.

On 20th February 1919 Lt. E. H. P. Jolly of the Indian Cavalry embarked on HMS *Lawrence* to select sites for landing grounds along the Gulf coast., taking with him 2000 gallons of fuel and 200 gallons of oil to be deposited at chosen points. Having done so, he returned on 6th March, the ship now towing a raft carrying an aircraft which had force-landed at Daiyar with engine trouble. He left again four days later, and on his final return to Bushire on 30 March 1919 he was able to report that he had established a chain of landing grounds along the Gulf of Persia as far as Chahbar. It was now possible to fly an RE.8 from Mesopotamia to India, a huge step toward the early establishment of civilian air services throughout the Empire.

Never forgetting their comrades, a number of men of 30 Squadron left Baghdad by road on 5th March 1919 for Tuz

Kurmatli, where they erected a cross on the grave of 2/AM Suthurst, who had lost his life in action on 12th May 1918.

## The loss of Captain Adams

During the late afternoon of 6th March, Lt. Bull, Lt. Carryer and Capt. Adams were taking part in what turned out to be 30 Squadron's final offensive operation, a bombing raid on the village of Khun. While machine-gunning at low level, Capt. Adams' aircraft crashed into the ground and he died instantly. Lt. Bull, with AM Judge as observer, tried to land alongside, and actually touched down, but under heavy fire at close range they had to withdraw. Adams' body was brought brought back on 12th March to British lines at Chaghdaz, where it was found that he had been killed by a rifle bullet through the head. He was buried with full military honours next day, a firing party of 100 Sepoys from the Punjabi Regt. providing a last salute. His death was the last suffered by 30 Squadron in the 'wartime' Mesopotamian campaign. Capt. Adams had been an observer with 47 Squadron in Salonika and had served with 30 Squadron since August 1917.

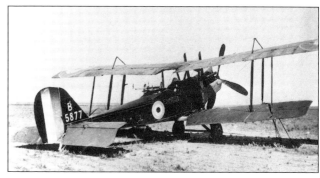

*RE.8 B5877 was flown by 30 Squadron in Mesopotamia until being SOC on 28th August 1919    [D. Phillips via R. Vann & M. O'Connor collection].*

Operations from Bushire were now almost completed, and following an order from Wing HQ on 1st April 1919 the squadron began to reduce to cadre status. Only two pilots and eleven other ranks remained, and Maj. Everidge left for Baghdad on 3rd April. The remaining aircraft soon followed, and a week later the cadre returned to Baghdad. Maj. Everidge was posted on 5th May, and it is not clear who took over from him to maintain the squadron's existence during the next few months. It is thought to have been Flt. Lt. F. Nuttall MC DFC AFC, who had joined 30 Squadron on 1st May 1917, had been in command of 'A' Flight since 1918 and was still listed as such. Certainly, Daily Routine Orders for 30 Squadron were posted to at least November 1919.

*The same aircraft seen after a forced landing in Persia*
*[D. Phillips via R. Vann & M. O'Connor collection].*

It is gratifying to know that in 1997 the Basra Memorial was resited, by order of Saddam Hussein, a man not known for his appreciation of Western sentiments. Originally built in Basra War Cemetery, the memorial was moved, with considerable effort, to a new site twenty miles (32 km.) along the road to Nasiriyah, in the centre of a major battlefield of the Gulf War. Consisting of a roofed colonnade of white Indian stone 262 feet (80 m.) long, the memorial has an obelisk 52 feet (16 m.) high as its central feature and the names of over forty thousand British, Indian and West African personnel who died in action in Mesopotamia between the autumn of 1914 and the end of August 1921 are recorded on slate panels fixed to the walls.

*Members of 'C' Flight at Shiraz, south Persia in March 1919. Left to right: Lt. F. S. Maxwell; Lt. A. W. Hawkins; 2nd. Lt. E. D. Hughes; Lt. F. W. Carryer; 2nd. Lt. E. N. Fletcher*                    *[R. Vann & M. O'Connor collection].*

TURKEY

SYRIA

LAKE
URMIA

⊙ Mosul

⊙ Kirkuk

⊙ Sulaimania

Zinjin 30 nm →

● TIKRIT

⊙ Tuz Khurmatli

Samarra ●

⊙ Kifri

⊙ Barura

Kasvin 90nm →

Hit ⊙

Qubba ⊙

Ramadi ⊙
Madhij ⊙
Fort ⊙
Kermea
⊙ Sindiya
Dhibban ⊙
Jadida ⊙
⊙ Qalat Mufti
⊙ Shahraban
⊙ Baquba
Falluja ⊙
Kasirin ⊙

Hamadan ⊙

● BAGHDAD

⊙ Hinaidi
⊙ Bawi

Ctesiphon ● ⊙ Bustan
⊙ Lajj
⊙ Zeur

PERSIA

⊙ Aziziya

R. Euphrates

⊙ Sheik Jaad

M E S O P O T A M I A

⊙ Arab Village
Shumran ⊙ ⊙ Camp Wadi
Kut-al-Imara ⊙ ⊙ Sheikh Saad
Sinn Abtar ⊙ Ora ⊙ Musandeg
⊙ Ali
Gharbi

⊙ Samawah

⊙ Nasiriyah

HAMAR
LAKE

R. Tigris

**30 SQUADRON AREA OF OPERATIONS IN MESOPOTAMIA**
**1915 - 1939**

30 Sqn aerodrome ⊙

SHAIBAH ● ⊙ Basrah
⊙ Zobeir
Barjisayah ⊙ ● ABADAN

Shatt-al-Arab

0 ————————— 100nm

*'B' Flight at Kasvin on re-establishment in 1920. In front of a DH.9A are (front row, left to right): Cpl. Simmonds, Flg. Off. H. G. W. Locke, Flg. Off. Bladon, Flg. Off. W. Bentley DFC, Flg. Off. Barrett, Flt. Sgt. Murton and Cpl. Blake. Others are unknown.*

# Chapter 3: A Troubled Iraq

Until October 1920 the administration of Iraq remained in the hands of the Commander-in-Chief of British forces, but was exercised through a Civil Commissioner, Lt. Col. A. T. Wilson. From 1919 Baghdad was the administrative capital of Iraq, and as new responsibilities were taken on, the Administration developed into something approaching the nature of a government. To control any elements of the population who might not appreciate the situation, the Police and the Iraq Levies worked from a common headquarters at Baghdad. Some of the railways built for military use during the war were refurbished and began to provide a very useful service to the population, and the port of Basra now came into its own as the main point of entry into the country.

However, the civil administration was essentially Christian in nature, and as might be expected, this did not please everyone in Iraq. Various tribes stuck to long-held religious beliefs, and unrest began to build, particularly when an influx of Iraqis began to return from exile. A number of trouble-makers were arrested and deported, and a general belief that the British would not maintain control over the country much longer prompted the dissemination of much propaganda material. Lt. Col. Wilson, horrified by an agreement between Britain and France signed in May 1916, proclaimed that nothing but firm British administration of whatever State might be created could prevent anarchy. From London, Wilson was authorised to conduct a referendum to determine whether the population wanted Iraq to be a single Arab state under British control; whether it should be ruled by an Arab; and if so who was the best candidate. The exercise was, however, indeterminate, as local tribes differed markedly in outlook. Britain's military presence in Iraq was diminishing rapidly, garrisons and outlying posts being abandoned and mobile forces being reduced in number. Those left behind were hard-pressed to maintain lines of communication and to guard stores and Turkish prisoners. In command of ground forces from March 1920 was Gen. Sir Aylmer Haldane, who tended to ignore warnings given by the Civil Commissioner that an outbreak of civil war was imminent.

Then came the news that at San Remo on 28th April 1920 a Mandate for Iraq had been offered to Great Britain by the other powers which had won the recent world war. This appeared to put an end to Iraqi aspirations of complete independence, but on 17th June the Civil Commissioner announced that an elected assembly would be convened and moves would be made towards the formation of an Arab state and almost-complete self-government. Nationalist feelings, had, however, already developed too far to accept this idea as anything more than words. By the late summer of 1920 the situation in Baghdad and central Iraq had worsened, and violence between opposing tribal factions, provoked by Turkish and Russian agents, was common.

**30 Squadron reborn**

Early in 1920, 30 Squadron still existed, in much-reduced form, with Flt. Lt. Frank Nuttall MC DFC AFC as its CO. The RE.8 aircraft which had performed well during the wartime period were being replaced by the more modern DH.9A. Designed to replace the earlier DH.9, the 9A had a larger wing area and was fitted with a 360 hp Rolls–Royce Eagle or a 400 hp LIberty engine, and had entered service in the UK in June 1918. 30 Squadron's HQ and 'C' Flight were at Baghdad West, while 'A' Flight was at Mosul and 'B' Flight at Kasvin in Persia. At Baghdad, quarters and messes were in separate buildings, and on the airfield, which adjoined the railway station, the hangars were Bessonneau canvas structures. Flg. Off. Bentley, who joined the squadron in the spring of that year, was posted to 'A' Flight at Mosul, to where he flew a brand-new DH.9A. This was not, he found, an easy aircraft to land on a small airfield, and wheel brakes were not provided, so if the pilot overshot on landing the undercarriage had a tendency to collapse. In command of 'A' Flight was Flt. Lt. Meredith Thomas, who eventually rose to the rank of Air Vice-Marshal. Flg. Off. Bentley remembers the life of 30 Squadron at Mosul: "At Mosul we occupied two Arab buildings, one a square built around a courtyard. This was the larger building alongside the airfield and was used as airmen's sleeping quarters and mess, workshops, stores and Flight office. The smaller building, a few hundred yards along the road and nearer the town, was used as the officers' mess and sleeping quarters. At that time each detached Flight had a ground W/T receiver and transmitter which occasionally worked, a W/T officer and one or two airmen. I believe W/T was not used in aircraft until early in 1921. Things were about as quiet and peaceful as they ever were, but even then we received quite frequent calls to go and search rivers for troublesome gentry reported to be sailing downstream on large rafts made of numerous inflated goatskins. There was seldom a week when we did not go and drop a few bombs on some village or other in the valleys of the Greater or Lesser Zab rivers in Kurdistan around Dohak or Zakho. Or else we might go after some Arab camp towards Tel Afar or Shergut, and sometimes out towards Erbil and Kirkuk. The bombs we used for this purpose were mostly the 20lb. Cooper."

Disorder which broke out in June 1920 among Iraqi tribesmen was caused by a number of factors — tribal unwillingness to be ruled, local ambitions among the sheikhs, reluctance to pay taxes, and other grievances. No serious disorder occurred in towns, but in the desert areas anarchy reigned for about three months. The Baghdad to Basra railway, an essential lifeline, was cut and remained closed for some time, and on many occasions the alternative form of transport between the two towns, military river steamers, were attacked from the banks of the river, and two were sunk. 'C' Flight of 30 Squadron was kept very busy in making attacks on hostile forces and dropping supplies to any British troops who became surrounded, a repeat of the squadron's pioneering activity at Kut-al-Amara four years earlier. "Most of the flying was done at low altitude, probably at 1000 feet above ground level" recalls Flg. Off. Bentley. "I think one surprising feature was the great success of hostile marksmen in bringing down aircraft with rifle fire. In that climate it only needed one bullet in the radiator or water cooling system to necessitate a forced landing. Quite a few aircraft of 30 Squadron were brought down in that way and several crews were captured. I remember in particular the case of Flg. Off. H. G. W. Lock and Flg. Off. G. A. Gowler..........who had a very unpleasant time. Among other things they were made to march long distances barefooted.......but were finally rescued and returned to Baghdad. Most of the fighting was to the south and around Baghdad. We of 'A' Flight were not quite so heavily pressed." On the morning of 4th June, however, the small town of Tel Afar, 35 miles west of Mosul, came under attack by a force of about six hundred tribesmen. They murdered the Political Officer and his assistants and the crew of an armoured car section which went to investigate but was ambushed in a narrow street. This was seen by the crew of a 30 Squadron aircraft, and led to a punitive column of troops being formed at Mosul. However, it was 9th June before they arrived at Tel Afar, which by then had been abandoned by the tribesmen. A few attempts were made to machine-gun the retreating horsemen, but with little effect. In his report, Flt. Lt. Thomas ventured to suggest that ".........had there been a reasonably strong air force in the country, such a situation would, with prompt action, have been nipped in the bud. The scene of operations being only 25 minutes flight from Mosul, fewer tribesmen would have escaped over open desert, where they offered excellent targets to aeroplanes. This and other cases of leniency had a serious effect on the general tribal situation in Iraq at this period. They proved our [Army's] inability to deal with disorder in its incipient stages, and were interpreted by the tribes as indicating weakness on the part of our Government. The prestige of our forces is lowered, and there is little doubt that these factors contributed largely to the rapid spread of the insurrection........."

The town of Rumaithah, on the river Euphrates, was besieged on 4th July 1920. Here the insurgents appeared to be under the command of former Turkish Army officers, as they were busy constructing a trench system north-west of the town. Aircraft of 30 Squadron observed a distress signal from the garrison to the effect that supplies were badly needed, but it was three days before a few boxes of ammunition could be dropped to the beleaguered troops. In addition to 'C' Flight of 30 Squadron, which was using RE.8s and DH.9As, 6 Squadron's Bristol Fighters were active in the area. A graphic description of a typical day's work came from Sqn. Ldr. Pirie of 6 Squadron but would apply equally to 30 Squadron. "Those days were very tiring. We would leave Baghdad at about 04.00 hours and fly to Dunn. There we would consult the Political Officer and the garrison commander and then proceed to Rumaithah. While one machine took messages off the Popham Panel in the Serai, the remainder of the Flight bombed and machine-gunned any gatherings seen nearby. After supplies had been dropped to the Panel messages, the Flight would proceed to Samawah, where the garrison was encamped on the aerodrome. Filling up our machines there was a laborious and unpleasant task, for we had to sit on the top planes of the [aircraft] and fill the tanks from five-gallon tins. The fierce hot wind from the north blew much of the petrol onto our clothes; these, consisting of a pair of shorts and a shirt, were no protection against the scorching and stinging pain of evaporating petrol. After a hasty lunch which we had brought with us, we used to load up with bombs and proceed to attack the tribes west of Samawah. This accomplished, we returned to Samawah, fixed on more bombs and started on the homeward journey." On the way to base, the opportunity was taken to drop 20lb. Cooper bombs on any hostile tribesmen who might be seen, and to check on the well-being of the garrison at Rumaithah, and often it was 20.00 before the aircraft finally landed at Baghdad. Flt. Lt. Thomas takes up the story by observing "By 12th July the garrison became short of food and other necessities, so a raid on the bazaar by the garrison was organised, with a covering force of nine aeroplanes from Baghdad. We warned the garrison of our plan by dropping operation orders on them the previous day. On 12th July five Bristol Fighters from 6 Squadron, reinforced by two old RE.8s and two DH.9As from 30 Squadron, set out in formation. One machine dropped two 112lb. bombs n the village. The remainder, one after the other, dropped four 20lb. bombs [each] on the houses round the serai, from about 300 feet. This caused a panic in the village, and the inhabitants rushed out into the countryside, where they were attacked with bombs and machine-gun fire. Meanwhile the garrison made a sortie and succeeded in collecting twenty sheep and twelve goats in addition to enough chickens and other food to feed them for three weeks." It was considered that if this action had not been taken the garrison would have been obliged to surrender through lack of food and would have been put to death. Before long, a relief force struggled through to free the garrison, which had held out for sixteen days, with considerable loss of life. The incident further confirmed the efficacy of air support in such situations, a lesson which was being learned in several parts of the Middle East.

On 14th July the situation around Mosul had become so precarious that the Army C-in-C and the High Commissioner proposed a withdrawal of forces from the entire area. They considered that pending the arrival of reinforcements from India the British forces in Iraq were not adequate, and only by withdrawing from the north and concentrating around Baghdad could the situation be controlled. But in the end a retreat was seen as too dangerous, so isolation had to be accepted.

Another opportunity for members of 30 Squadron to practice their supply-dropping skills came after the town of Kufah, on the river Euphrates, was captured on 21st July 1920. Food, ammunition, medical supplies and other essentials were dropped over a period of several weeks until the siege ended on 17th October, after 98 days of intense heat. In addition, the DH.9A crews maintained radio communication between the garrison and GHQ, passing messages of support and reporting on the daily situation.

Baghdad itself was prone to considerable unrest, causing concern about the security of Baghdad West airfield, the home of 30 Squadron. About the end of July 1920, sites were chosen for a series of earthworks, and work began without delay. Within two weeks, about forty brick blockhouses had been built around the city at half-mile intervals and were manned day and night. The technical area was surrounded with barbed wire, part of which had to be removed to allow an aircraft to gain access to or from the airfield. Several natives were caught near the hangars with matches and tins of petrol and occasionally rifle shots were fired at the airfield. This situation was remedied by issuing every able-bodied white man with a rifle.

Air Cdre. H. F. V. Battle OBE DFC, in his book 'Line', provides a vivid description of life at Baghdad West in 1920/21. Officers' quarters consisted of low single-storey huts built of sun-baked mud bricks, each hut having five or six single rooms with bathrooms at the back. A long verandah ran the whole length of each hut and had a flat roof for sleeping under in hot weather. Each unit at the Station had its own officers' and sergeants' messes, and in hot weather the practice was to dine under the stars. Unfortunately, the electric lighting around the tables attracted a wide variety of insects, ranging from locusts, sandflies, stag beetles, mosquitoes and moths to strange insects which were called Handley Pages and 'Arry Tates from their likeness to those aircraft! Living in close proximity to these and many other objectionable insects made everyone very careful. Precautions such as checking one's bed before climbing into it and shaking clothes and shoes before putting them on were followed closely. Food was very poor, and consisted mainly of 'bully beef', sometimes varied by 'hump' (Indian ox) which was tasteless. Potatoes were rare, and usually only available in dehydrated form. Onions were often the only fresh vegetable to be found. In hotels and clubs curries or a tough piece of chicken could be obtained, which varied the diet a little. For dessert the normal offer was tinned pineapple, which 30 Squadron officers once ate every day for two weeks! Beer was the standard liquid refreshment, but as the only British brew available had been 'doctored' to preserve it in the heat a Japanese beer which gave terrible hangovers was drunk.

The same officer asked for permission to design a marking for 30 Squadron. With the squadron's length of service in the Middle East in mind, all concerned felt that a palm tree would form the basis of an appropriate badge. "After making a stencil of the palm tree, which unfortunately looked more like a coconut tree than a date palm, I painted it in white on either side of the CO's machine" wrote Air Cdre. Battle. "As this emblem did not show up very well at a distance we had to paint a white stripe on either side of the tree. The stripes, measuring four inches across and a foot apart, were then carried round the top and under the fuselage. The result was duly approved by Wing HQ. When the time came for squadrons of the RAF to have their badges officially registered by the College of Heralds many of us were delighted to hear that 30 Squadron had been allowed to retain the palm tree, known by us all as 'The Shaving Brush'. The unit motto — Ventre a Terre — first proposed by Flt. Lt. H. G. W. Lock, was retained, to everyone's satisfaction."

Two members of 30 Squadron lost their lives on 18th September 1920, when RE.8 D4698 spun in from 300 feet when on approach to Kasvin. Frank Nuttall had taken off with LAC L. A. Dellow as his observer to raid Enzeli but due to bad visibility decided to return, a wrong decision, as Capt. Nuttall died instantly in the crash close to the airfield and LAC Dellow died later in hospital. Another pilot, Lt. Sidebottom, died on 17th November when he failed to return from a raid on the same target.

## Working 'in the field'

Small detachments of men and aircraft of 30 Squadron were frequently called upon to carry out tasks away from base, and Flt. Lt. Thomas described the way in which such detachments operated. "News comes through during the forenoon to the effect that trouble has arisen some 200 miles distant; possibly a Political Officer has been murdered" he wrote. "During the afternoon of the same day the aeroplanes arrive on the scene, complete with spares and other necessaries to last them from three to ten days. In all probability a bomb raid will be carried out that evening. Should any urgent spares become necessary, they will be transported by air from Baghdad. If an aeroplane becomes unserviceable and requires four or more days' work for repair, it will be flown back to Baghdad if possible, and immediately replaced. This system is a great help to detachments, which in most cases have to carry out operations with the few mechanics taken in the aeroplanes." He goes on to say that the work was strenuous, and pilots were called on to help the mechanics maintain the aircraft, to fuel them and to load them with bombs. Conversely, many of the mechanics acted as air gunners in addition to their normal work. "Aeroplanes are picketed in the open and are exposed to all weathers. They depreciate [sic] quickly under these conditions and require more man-hours to keep [them] serviceable than is the case with aeroplanes at home. It is surprising how much weather aeroplanes will stand if reasonable precautions are taken, such as keeping them head-to-wind, securing the control column and so preventing the ailerons and control cables being damaged, placing chocks behind the wheels and covering the engines and cockpits. In moderate weather a few well-trained pilots and mechanics who have learned to improvise can operate for considerable periods without hangars or the usual conveniences of organised aerodromes."

A source, not a member of 30 Squadron, recorded that the weather that summer was very trying. "At Baghdad the shade temperature was between 110°F and 118°F. Even at dawn it was quite a feat to fly through the hot belt (from 500 to 1500 feet) without losing too much water from the radiator. The new RAF authorities believed at first that it was impossible to fly after 0800 hours owing to the heat, and it was certainly difficult until the tropical radiator was improvised. GHQ, on the other hand, required flying at all times, although they did suggest an extra ration of ice to keep the radiators cool!" The hot belt referred to was a temperature inversion caused by the radiation surface cooling at night, creating a layer of cool air near the ground, which pushed up the hot air from the previous afternoon. Frequent sandstorms reaching an altitude of anything up to 8000 feet were another major problem. As it was impossible to see anything if caught in such a storm, the policy was to land ahead of an approaching storm, to allow time for the aircraft to be picketed down. Yet another problem for aircrews was thick haze which often developed into fog thick enough to prevent any flying. 'Dust Devils', caused by miniature whirlwinds passing over hot dusty ground, are columns of dust up to fifty feet high which career along until they collapse on hitting an obstruction, and are often the prelude to a dust storm.

During the 1920 insurrection, the entire burden of activity in the air was carried by two Flights of 30 Squadron and by 6 Squadron. Reinforcements were very slow in arriving, but the reason for this seems unclear. It may have been due to a lack of appreciation of the urgency by the British Government, although Sir Hugh Trenchard, then in the throes of a battle with the Army and the Navy over the future of the RAF, certainly realised the great importance of air power in Iraq and Winston Churchill, then Secretary of State for War and Air, had agreed that the number of squadrons in Iraq should be increased. More probably, the shortcomings were caused by a severe shortage of suitable aircraft in the post-war RAF and the very long time they took to reach Basra from the UK. Assembly of aircraft at Basra took time, and newly-arrived personnel, both fliers and mechanics, tended to suffer from the unaccustomed heat and humidity which was the norm there.

Early in October news was received of a Russian aircraft over Persia, and the detachment at Kasvin quickly asked for a DH.9A fitted with a front Vickers gun to be sent there, with an armourer to calibrate the Constantinescu interrupter gear. Aircraft H63 was prepared and Flg. Off. Battle was detailed to fly it, taking with him some mail and Flg. Off. Brewe from Wing HQ. After four very bumpy hours in the air Battle landed at Hamadan, a small rough landing ground at an altitude 6200 feet higher than Baghdad. Soon after their arrival a gale sprang up, and the DH.9A had to be put inside the sole Bessoneau hangar, where it remained for two days. Then a ninety-minute flight brought the aircraft to Kasvin, where the two men were able to spend a few days at leisure. Their return journey was as escort to another aircraft carrying Maj. Gen. Sir Edmund Ironside, recently appointed as GOC North Persia, but this plan fell through when the engine of H63 failed to start and the other aircraft went on ahead.

Winston Churchill, who succeeded Lord Milner as Secretary of State for the Colonies in November 1920, made a priority of

*The wreckage of Flg. Off. Ainscough's DH.9A being retrieved after his forced landing sixty miles south of Teheran on 11th January 1921.*

arranging a conference at which he hoped the peaceful futures of several Mandated Territories could be settled. He decided that a new Middle East Department of the Colonial Office should be created to control all these Territories. Another early decision was that Feisal should become King of Mesopotamia, which would then be renamed Iraq. After consultation with Sir Hugh Trenchard, Churchill put forward the idea of policing Iraq solely from the air. In a letter to the AOC-in-C Middle East, Sir Geoffrey Salmond, Trenchard wrote "Mr. Churchill is probably going out early in March to confer with the Palestinian and Mesopotamian authorities. The chief point will be the running of Palestine and Mesopotamia. He is very much in favour of the Air taking control, I believe. (Keep this to yourself). Broadly speaking, I am in favour of risking a good deal to Egypt and Palestine to equip Mesopotamia early. I am very keen on taking over Mesopotamia next cold weather, if not before." The Conference, held in Cairo, was very intensive, but in his report Lord Trenchard wrote "..........it is absolutely essential that the command of all forces in Mesopotamia is vested in an Air officer. Given the best will in the world, it cannot be possible for the instructions of a an Air Officer to be carried out through an intermediary military commander." He went on to describe the confusion and arguments which would be caused. And so air power in the region was encouraged to develop, as indicated in a memo written in May 1921 which stated "The role of the RAF has steadily increased from that of a subordinate auxiliary to predominance. The Mosul operations were conducted by the RAF entirely, to the entire elimination of an active military element."

## Flying in Persia

At Kasvin in Persia, where 'B' Flight of 30 Squadron still operated, weather conditions were very different. Sent there in November 1920 to take command of the Flight was Flt. Lt. Raymond Collishaw DSO* OBE DSC AFC, a Canadian fighter pilot with about sixty enemy aircraft to his credit in the recent War. In his book Collishaw recorded his arrival at Kasvin. "By this time the severe winter had set in, and this prevented either side from making any decisive moves. My detachment contented itself with desultory bombing and reconnaissance. In addition, we maintained

communication between our base and Baghdad. It was not unusual for one of our machines to take off from an aerodrome covered with several feet of snow, the temperature being below zero, and land at Baghdad to find the thermometer at 120°F. One of our problems was keeping the aerodrome free of snow, for we had no proper snow removal equipment. Once it became too deep we were unable to clear it from the area and had to pack it to enable our machines, which were fitted with normal wheeled undercarriages, to land. The British Army employed large numbers of pack camels for transport, and after the winter [*weather*] closed the mountain roads leading to Mesopotamia these camels were without employment. I realised that the large splayed feet of the camel, which enabled it to progress so rapidly through soft sand, were just as effective in loose snow. Therefore I had these camels deployed by their native attendants to plod up and down the snow-covered aerodrome packing the snow, and this worked very well."

Spare parts, particularly tyres, were in very short supply throughout 1920. Camelthorn undergrowth, which grew everywhere, caused continual punctures, and so all aircraft carried a spare wheel. In the autumn the supply of replacement aircraft dwindled away, and as a last resort a few RE.8s were brought out of storage, refurbished and issued to 'A' Flight. As they had been in Iraq for four years they did not last long, several of them being written off in perfectly good landings when the undercarriage collapsed due to deterioration of the wood in the oppressive climate. Others were scrapped when their engines refused to function properly. However, in December 1920, by which time the insurrection had been put down, the supply situation improved considerably, and by Christmas 30 Squadron was again completely equipped with DH.9As.

After serving with 'A' Flight at Mosul, Flg. Off. Bentley was transferred to Baghdad and then early in January 1921 to 'B' Flight at Kasvin. He remembered flying a DH.9A to Kasvin on 9th February in company with Flg. Off. G. C. Bladon in a similar aircraft. "After the first 45 minutes or so the route lies entirely over mountainous country, and we soon found ourselves over snow-covered ground." On arrival at Kasvin the two pilots found that a landing strip in the snow about fifty yards wide had been levelled

*30 Squadron at Baghdad in 1921, when the CO was Sqn. Ldr. Raymond Collishaw. The photograph was taken during a short period of co-location of the squadron's HQ and three Flights.*

by the camels employed by Flt. Lt. Collishaw. Bladon (in E821) landed first but swerved off the track into soft snow and turned over. Bentley was so intent on avoiding Bladon's aircraft that he over-compensated and swerved in the opposite direction, coming to a stop with nose in the snow and tail in the air. After a 'carpeting' from Collishaw, Bentley found that the Flight had been engaged in fighting off Russian aircraft which had flown over Persia from bases south of the Caspian Sea. Unknown to 30 Squadron, however, preparations were being made for the complete withdrawal of British forces from north-west Persia. During Flg. Off. Bentley's three weeks of service at Kasvin, the only flying done was an attempt to fly some mail to Baghdad on 18th February, with Gen. Ironside as passenger. The pilot was Flg. Off. G. Kidd, but the aircraft (H40) force-landed in the snow near Kermanshah, breaking the General's leg, and the hapless pilot and his passenger were only retrieved with great difficulty.

'A' Flight returned from Mosul to Baghdad on 15th February 1921. Two days later, four aircraft delivered wireless equipment to Hit, where one NCO and an operator erected it and put it into service the same evening, only ten hours after the order to deliver it was issued!

The hapless Gen. Ironside, flying as a passenger from Basra to Baghdad on 8th April, found himself in another unfortunate situation when the aircraft force-landed eighteen miles south-east of Samawah in a sandstorm. He was again injured, and an aircraft of 30 Squadron was sent with a medical officer to provide help.

As part of the general withdrawal, 'B' Flight of 30 Squadron left Kasvin on 24th April 1921 to return to Baghdad, and so all three Flights and HQ were, for the first time, based at one place. Flt. Lt. Raymond Collishaw was then promoted and given command of the squadron, which in the relatively peaceful conditions now being enjoyed, was to undertake a new task of great importance — surveying air routes for the future.

At that time, navigation was an almost unknown subject to most pilots. Blind-flying instruments did not exist, nor did the turn-and-bank indicator. Compasses were highly inaccurate, and it was claimed that a pilot was lucky to be able to steer within 30 degrees of his intended course. 30 Squadron crews had, of course, carried out a number of night operations without any dedicated instrumentation during the First World War, but generally by the light of the moon. Crews of flying-boat squadrons and others who flew over water were the only ones who learned navigation. A former CO of 6 Squadron recorded his thoughts about navigation in Iraq in the early 1920s. "Finding one's way in Iraq is difficult, to say the least" he wrote. "An airman can never hope for signposts, but usually he can hope for plenty of landmarks which he can

identify on an accurate map. Out here the landmarks are few and far between, and their positions as shown on the very bad maps may be miles out. Often maps show a mountain range as 6000 feet but when the unfortunate pilot gets there it is 6500 feet. The air is so thin that an aircraft won't go up as easily as at home. Rivers are our best friends in showing the way, but even they have ugly habits of altering their bends at short notice."

Wednesday 16th March 1921 was a historic day for the RAF in Mesopotamia, as that day a special demonstration flight was staged, with every available aircraft at Baghdad taking part. The recently-received RAF Ensign was flown for the first time, tied to the rudder of the DH.9A flown by Flg. Off. Battle. Unfortunately, when the ensign was streamed out it tore in half, right in front of the High Commissioner and the GOC-in-C! Nevertheless, it was a day to remember.

## Surveying an air route

With the development of aviation in mind, the authorities gave 30 Squadron the task of surveying and proving an air route between Cairo and Baghdad for use by commercial and military aircraft as part of the future Imperial route to India, Singapore and Australia. A rudimentary air mail service had already been opened between Europe, Cairo and South Africa, and the Far East now beckoned. To establish emergency landing grounds in the virtually uninhabited desert two survey parties were formed.

One ground party set out from Cairo, led by Dr. Ball, the Director of Desert Survey of the Egyptian Government, with Sqn. Ldr. W. L. Welsh and the DH.9As of 47 Squadron providing communications and supply functions. A similar group, equipped with Ford Model T trucks, left Baghdad, led by Maj. Holt of the Royal Engineers. 30 Squadron was given the job of providing support to this party, to which Flt. Lt. F. R. Wynne was attached as Air Liaison Officer. Both parties carried W/T sets, and the plan was for a meeting half way between Amman and Baghdad, which are 510 miles apart in a straight line. About 70 miles west of Baghdad was the former German airfield at Ramadi, and from there to Amman was uninhabited desert. It was decided that between Amman and Ramadi emergency landing grounds should be established at intervals of about 50 miles. To identify these sites, the original idea was to lay baked clay slabs about eighteen inches square which would be painted white. When it was realised, however, that a huge number of slabs would be needed and would have to be flown to each site a few at a time this idea was dropped. Then it was noticed that the tracks made by motor vehicles on the hard-baked sandy surface of the desert tended to remain for several months and were clearly visible from the air. Vehicles were therefore driven round the boundary of each landing ground to mark it thoroughly, and to add to the benefits of this system it was found that tracks marked between the sites could be followed easily.

About thirty miles west of Ramadi two outcrops of natural bitumen provided excellent landmarks. Further on, LG1 was established about fifty miles from Ramadi, and LG2 at mile 207 on a dry mud-flat giving a perfect landing surface two miles long in any direction. The position of LG3 was not recorded, but LG4 was about 200 miles from Ramadi.

30 Squadron's participation in the establishment of the air route was considerable. A detached Flight was at Ramadi between 5th and 18th May and again from 6th to 12th June 1921 to cooperate with the Desert Car Reconnaissance Convoy, and were used to carry surveyors to and from the sites of the projected landing grounds, as well as supplies for the road convoy.

Progress on the ground was slow, but aircraft from each end of the projected route flew missions to each newly-established landing ground to deliver water, food and fuel to the survey parties. It was usual for about five aircraft of 30 Squadron to set out from Baghdad in formation, one of them carrying a newly-provided and somewhat unreliable W/T set and operator. Eventually the two ground parties met as planned about half way between Ramadi and Amman. The first through flight was from Baghdad to Cairo and was under the command of Wg. Cdr. Peregrine Fellowes, a member of the staff in Egypt, who had been in charge of the entire project. On this momentous occasion he flew as passenger in a DH.9A piloted by Flg. Off. Battle. Three of 30 Squadron's DH.9As and two of 47 Squadron's aircraft which had arrived from Palestine took off from Baghdad just after dawn on 30th June 1921 with instructions that if one aircraft developed mechanical trouble and had to force-land in the desert another one was to follow it, mark its position and go for help. Fuel tanks were full, and in addition tins of extra fuel were fitted to the bomb racks. The operation decreed that the five DH.9As would fly to Ramadi, where their main tanks would be topped up from the cans, fly on to Amman to refuel, and then continue to Heliopolis airfield, near Cairo. The formation had not been airborne long when one of the 47 Squadron aircraft fell out with engine trouble and the other one duly followed it to offer assistance. 30 Squadron's aircraft flew on to Amman, where one overshot when landing on what was then a very poor airfield, leaving two to continue the operation after their crews had a meal and a couple of hours' rest. Soon after take-off from Amman, Flg. Off. Bentley noticed that his engine was misfiring intermittently, so he decided to make a precautionary landing. At the time he was near Jerusalem, and touched down in the desert near the village of Raffa. Safely on the ground, Bentley made use of the aircraft's tool kit and soon found a loose ignition lead, which he tightened before taking off. As darkness was now falling, he decided to land at the disused airfield at Qantara, where he and his passenger spent the night with an Army unit before flying on to Heliopolis next morning. The fifth aircraft, carrying Wg. Cdr. Fellowes, was the only one to reach Heliopolis without difficulty, in eleven hours flying time at an average speed of 79 mph. This operation had proved that mail could now be sent between Baghdad and Cairo in one day and could reach England in ten to fourteen days, as opposed to the five to eight weeks taken by sea via Basra and Bombay.

After a week in Cairo, the 30 Squadron aircraft flew back to Baghdad in company with DH.9As from another squadron. Subsequently, a regular fortnightly service in each direction was maintained by 30 and 8 Squadrons from Baghdad and 45 and another Squadron from Egypt. From time to time motor vehicles had to be sent into the desert to re-mark the tracks which the mail aircraft followed, and quite often engine failure caused an aircraft to be stranded along the route. Amazing feats of versatility were performed by the ever-willing mechanics. For example, they would dismantle a Liberty engine and pack all the parts so that they could be carried by a number of aircraft, which then flew them to the stranded aircraft. On site, a sheerlegs which had either been brought in by MT or flown in in parts was rigged, the replacement engine parts were assembled and an engine change carried out.

Flying time between Baghdad and Cairo was between nine and ten hours, so that in the summer the trip could be made in one day provided weather conditions were good. However, on 1st August 1921 Flt. Lt. Thomas did the trip in eight hours ten minutes! In the winter, a night-stop was made at Amman. There was keen competition to be rostered for the route, as two weeks was usually spent in Cairo before the return trip was made. One trip, though, was only as far as LG4, where Air Cdre. Brooke–Popham CB CMG DSO AFC had been deposited by a Vimy aircraft from Amman on 20th July. Two aircraft of 30 Squadron flew to collect him and bring him to Baghdad. Another 'rescue' was made by two aircraft of 30 Squadron in August, when 70 gallons of drinking water were flown to LG.1A for the benefit of the crew of a HP.O/400 aircraft which had force-landed there on its return journey from Baghdad to Cairo with radiator trouble.

A good deal of thought was given to the problem of supplying water to MT convoys moving along the route. Raymond Collishaw described an experiment which had such spectacular results that it had to be abandoned. "There happened to be some tyres and inner tubes at Baghdad for the massive wheels of the Handley Page bomber. The thought struck me that one of these inner tubes would hold a large amount of water and if encased in a tyre could be dropped from an aircraft with little likelihood of bursting" he wrote. "We decided to experiment, and a water-filled inner tube and tyre, weighing some 750lbs. in all, were attached to an aircraft. The idea was that when released a few feet above the ground it would hit in a horizontal position and skid to a halt. Sammy Kinkead brought his machine in low over the field in a line parallel with a row of hangars and released the load. The wretched tyre hit the ground as planned but as if possessed of some evil intelligence immediately bounced up into a rolling position and changed course for the hangar line. Those who saw the monster bounding towards them at close on a hundred miles an hour took violent evasive action, but nothing could save the hangar. Hitting the lean-to on the side of the hangar, [the tyre] went straight through the offices of several Flight commanders as if they were built of tissue paper and then continued into the interior, where it smashed an aircraft before coming to a halt. We continued to deliver water by less spectacular methods!"

The considerable amount of flying put in by 30 Squadron crews and aircraft brought about a major modification to the DH.9As. While serving with another squadron in south Russia, Sqn. Ldr. Collishaw had arranged for heavy cross-bracing wires to be fitted between the rear pair of undercarriage struts to provide greater strength. This 'mod' was now given to all 30 Squadron aircraft, and although the centre bomb rack could no longer be used to carry bombs it could still carry static loads. If bombing had to be carried out there were still the wing racks. There was some difference of opinion in higher echelons of the service about this procedure, but it went ahead with the proviso that the rear gun mountings had to be retained in order to ensure the 9A's readiness for immediate operations.

## A King for Iraq

From 1921, Iraqi affairs were handled by a new Middle Eastern department of the Colonial Office. Winston Churchill, the Colonial Secretary, convened a conference at Cairo on 12th March, with the task of selecting a ruler for Iraq and deciding on the desired level of British forces for the defence of the country after the withdrawal of British garrisons. For the position of Emir (King), there appeared to be no suitable candidate apart from Faisal, a Syrian leader who had been suggested by Lt. Col. Wilson in 1920. At first he turned down the offer, as he considered his elder brother Abdullah had a higher claim, but was persuaded to visit Mesopotamia to see the situation for himself. On 23rd August 1921 the Emir Feisal was crowned King at Baghdad, but the name of the country was not changed to Iraq until September 1922.

During the Cairo conference important decisions on defence were reached. British forces were to be reduced yet further, and the army was to hand over control to the Royal Air Force in 1922. The Iraqi Levies would come under the control of the British military, effectively the RAF, which would provide funding.

Life for RAF personnel in Iraq in the early 1920s is described by Flg. Off. Bentley. "In the early part of 1920 quite a number of the Army as well as British civilians had their wives with them in Iraq, but all were sent out of the country when the big revolt started that year" he observed. "The only remaining female society consisted of the service hospital nursing staffs. In the latter part of 1921 the ban was lifted, and wives began to return. In Baghdad there was a Sports Club with a golf course and tennis courts, whilst another social club, the Alwiyah, was opened, this lying out towards Hinaidi. At Mosul there was an Officers' Social Club. There was a fair amount of shooting to be had, including ducks, sandgrouse and geese. During 1920/21 30 Squadron had a good soccer team which won the cup for an inter-unit competition at Baghdad, though I do not remember whether the competition was confined to the RAF or if Army units also took part."

Bentley goes on to record that by the spring of 1922 many of the squadron's personnel had completed their two-year tours of duty and were being posted home in batches as replacements arrived. He had been acting as commander of 'B' Flight for about a year (without being promoted!) but on posting he handed over to Flt. Lt. S. M. Kinkead, who a few years later became well-known as a member of the British Schneider Trophy team. Eventually, however, he lost his life in a tragic accident. Flying Supermarine S.5 N221 over the Solent off Calshot on 12th March 1928, he felt unwell, and flew into the glassy calm sea, an accident attributed to the lack of a visible horizon. The body of this fine pilot is buried in the nearby Fawley cemetery.

A revealing insight into the conditions under which 30 Squadron ground crews lived is contained in a letter written in June 1922 by Fred Woolley to his family. Firstly he describes the bungalows in which the airmen lived. "These are built of bricks and have long sloping roofs so that there is a verandah 10 or 12 feet wide on both sides" he wrote. "The roof is made of reeds covered with a kind of rush matting and on the top is a thick coating of mud to keep the heat out. Inside they are like huts in Blighty but have fans to keep them cool. They also have two big fireplaces as it is very cold in winter." Fred went on to praise the food, writing "We get plenty of good grub at this time of year, but I don't know what it will be like later on. The following is a fair sample: breakfast — bacon with eggs, tomatoes or liver, tea and bread; tiffin [midday]: salmon and onions, jam,bread and tea; dinner: boiled or roast beef or mutton, onions, spuds, bread and tea. We seldom get any butter as it is tinned and is not much liked. We get any amount of onions and they are very nice." Next Fred describes the 'canteen', by which he presumably meant the NAAFI or an equivalent. "We have a good canteen, but prices are rather high. Tea is 2 annas (2d) a cup, beer is 1 rupee (1/4) a bottle and is either German or Japanese but is quite good. We can also get decent suppers such as eggs, fish, liver, chicken, mutton cutlets, chips and bread. The canteen is run by Indians who came over with the troops at some time or other. We can also get ice cream, chocolates and tinned fruits and practically anything [else] we want. English papers are supplied to the canteen for the benefit of the troops." If not exactly luxurious, the food and drink availabhle to the airmen seems to have been adequate. Outside duty hours, Fred complained, there was not much to keep him and his fellow airmen occupied. "We get pictures twice a week in a hangar" he reported. "There is also a concert party which gives a performance every two or three weeks and is quite good. We can also play cricket at night time or go swimming." Flies and mosquitos were an ever-present menace, and paraquat ointment was issued, to be rubbed on an airman's arms and legs before bedtime. One part of Fred's letter contains words and sentiments which are not 'politically correct' by today's standards but which are reproduced here nevertheless. "All the dirty work such as cleaning out latrines, cleaning the dining hall, washing dishes, etc is done by niggers. Indians do the guards during the day and our chaps do them at night. The Indians used to do all the guards but they are too windy at night. They shoot first and make enquiries after..........and the worst of it is they are just as likely to shoot a friend as an Arab." A description of the local Arab

*Accommodation for 30 Squadron under construction at Hinaidi in August 1922 in preparation for the move from Baghdad West, which took place in December.*

*The fin marking carried by DH.9A H3535.*

population which forms a later part of Fred's letter is so derogatory that reproduction here would be most unwise!

For 30 Squadron, 1922 was a very active year. In theory, the whole squadron was together at Baghdad West, but early in the year trouble flared up in Kurdistan, and a sizeable detachment was therefore sent to Kirkuk to be within striking distance of the scene. 30 Squadron took part in two substantial operations against a Kurdish rebel, Karim Fattah Beg, a supporter of Sheikh Mahmoud. His tribesmen killed two British officers, as a result of which they were harried by a small column of troops supported by aircraft. After he joined Turkish troops in Rowanduz in June, a concentrated bombing raid on that town was mounted by 30, 8 and 55 Squadrons. For the first time, long-delayed action bombs were used, with makeshift incendiaries which included some tins of petrol. In August the troops chasing Karim Fattah Beg, with support from these three squadrons, were brought to a halt by stronger forces and were obliged to retreat to Koi Sanjak after heavy losses. Many of the wounded were airlifted out by Vickers Vernon aircraft of 70 Squadron. When the Kurds moved towards the town of Sulaimaniya, where some seventy British and non-Kurdish civilians resided, the AOC made a reconnaissance himself and promptly ordered an immediate evacuation. With great efficiency, an airlift was arranged and was carried out in twelve hours on 4th September 1922 by DH.9As of 30 and 55 Squadrons, two Vernons of 70 Squadron and three Bristol Fighters of 6 Squadron. It is considered to be the first evacuation by air (other than of wounded soldiers) ever staged. Had it not been so successful, a massacre would have taken place, which would have had considerable repercussions throughout Iraq, encouraging Turkey to be even more troublesome.

## Trouble from Sheikh Mahmoud

When AVM Sir John Salmond became AOC-in-C Iraq on 1st October 1922 the RAF assumed responsibility for the security of the country, a unique situation in which the RAF was in total control of the army! In December, to forestall Turkish designs on Iraq, Sir John suggested a 'Forward Plan' for the defence of Kurdistan. In London the Plan was supported by Lord Trenchard if not by politicians, many of whom tended to be very nervous about the situation. During that month, Sqn. Ldr. Ernest H. Johnstone OBE took over as CO of 30 Squadron in place of Sqn. Ldr. Collishaw, and the squadron moved to Hinaidi.

Sir John Salmond's 'Forward Plan' was put into effect on 2nd February 1923 when the risk of losing the town of Mosul became clear. Prominent among dissident tribesmen was Sheikh Mahmoud, a Kurd who enjoyed great prestige among the inhabitants of areas

to the south of the Lesser Zab river. Although three years earlier Mahmoud had been sentenced to death for insurrection, he had survived, and it had been found politic to appoint him as Local Governor of the Sulaimaniya area. As soon as the Salmond plan was actioned, however, Mahmoud, who nurtured the ideal of an independent Kurdish state with himself at its head, reacted by sending a large force of Kurds and hill Arabs to occupy Kirkuk, where they looted the bazaar and frightened the population. The small garrison of British troops at Kirkuk would have been overwhelmed had not AVM Salmond staged the first major airlift of troops. Between 21st and 28th February 480 officers and men of the 14th Sikhs were airlifted to Kirkuk from a railhead at Kingerban, upon which Sheikh Mahmoud and his men took to the hills with all speed. Numerous flights from Erbil during the next few weeks enabled troops to recapture Sulaimaniya, while a force from Kirkuk reinforced the garrison at Mosul. Turkish forces

*Breakfast in the field, this one including eggs and sausages cooked over a Primus stove. DH.9A J7355 in the background sports the 30 Squadron palm tree motif.*

*Another breakfast picture, this one including several Kurds.*

*Kirkuk officers' mess and living quarters in February 1924.*

threatening Iraq were withdrawn, and for the time being the emergency seemed to be over.

But not for long! In July 1923 Sheikh Mahmoud turned up like the proverbial bad penny, proclaimed himself as King of Kurdistan and declared a Jihad (Holy War) against Great Britain. Renewed unrest in the south of Iraq encouraged him to stir up more trouble in Kurdistan, from a headquarters at Sulaimaniya, and warnings of the consequences of any action were given to him. Soon afterwards, forty-two DH.9A aircraft of 8, 30 and 55 Squadrons and Bristol Fighters of 6 Squadron dropped 28 tons of bombs on the town, causing a great deal of damage but no civilian casualties. The first 230lb. bombs were dropped on the Sheikh's house by Flt. Lt. Langford-Sainsbury of 30 Squadron and others.

Two columns of British-controlled troops code-named *Frontiercol* and *Koicol*, operating with strong air support based at Erbil, between Mosul and Kirkuk, succeeded in restoring order in north Kurdistan. The two RAF squadrons involved were 30 and 55, the DH.9As of which covered the advance of the ground troops by machine-gunning any enemy forces which appeared. The aircrews also helped to maintain communication between Air HQ and the two columns, while Vernon aircraft of 45 and 70 Squadrons dropped food and stores and airlifted two hundred sick troops to Baghdad.

**Unrest in the south**

30 Squadron was again active in November 1923, when the Iraqi government found it necessary to bring under control the large and recalcitrant Beni Huchaim confederation of tribes in the south of the country. The district in which the tribes lived was between Samawah and Rumaitha, and great difficulty had long been found in dealing with the residents, who tended to ignore government dictums. Even a fully-equipped infantry division of the Iraqi army had failed to deal with the situation effectively. Little up-to-date information on the tribes was available, as no government officials were prepared to venture into the area! Running nearby was the Baghdad to Basra railway line, which had been disrupted

previously and which was considered too important for further attacks to be made on it. Maps of the area were out of date, and two intelligence officers were sent to prepare new ones, which before issue were corrected by reconnaissance from the air. As a ground offensive was considered to be inappropriate, a major air campaign was decided upon, with support from a small number of armoured cars assigned to protect landing grounds and two important bridges. After a conference on 28th November to which many Sheikhs were invited but few attended, final plans were drawn up for an attack.

It was realised that the squadrons which would take part (1 Squadron with Snipes operating as dive-bombers and for low-level machine-gun attacks, 8, 30 and 84 Squadrons with DH.9As and a Flight of Vernons for night bombing) would have to operate from bases nearer the targets than usual. Three railway trains were therefore commandeered, two at Baghdad and one at Basra, each carrying a ground organisation, a W/T station and supplies of fuel, bombs and other necessities. These trains arrived at their destinations on 29th November and were ready for action next day. Offensive operations began at dawn and continued until noon on 1st December, during which time 25 tons of bombs were dropped with a high degree of accuracy, thanks to the recently-prepared maps. Results were almost immediate; by the afternoon of 1 December most of the Sheikhs had surrendered and others were on their way to give themselves up. A force of Iraq police accompanied by an RAF liaison officer was then able to begin a tour of the area. 30 Squadron returned to base on two days later, having taken part in an operation which had proved beyond doubt that in Iraq airborne action alone could effectively bring any dissident forces under control.

Life at RAF Hinaidi in 1923 was vividly described by Gp. Capt. Arthur Longmore (Later Air Chief Marshal Sir Arthur), who at the time was Gp. Capt. (Operations) on AVM Sir John Salmond's staff. "Office hours ran from 08.00 to 12.30 and from 18.30 to 20.30, when the day's reports from outstations would come in by wireless" he wrote. "Electric overhead fans in all offices and

*Above: DH.9A E961 over Kurdistan in 1924.*
*Below: The aircraft used by the AOC, AVM Higgins, with a 30 Squadron escort at Sulaimaniya a few days after the capture of the town on 29th July 1924. Three airman can be seen swinging the propeller of the centre aircraft.*

*The largest bomb-load carried by 30 Squadron in the Sulaimaniya campaign – 500 lbs.*

*Sqn. Ldr. J. Robb (eventually ACM Sir J. Robb KBE DSO DFC AFC) flying over the hills of Sulaimaniya on 27th May 1924.*

*Kirkuk serai after completion of the hangar in December 1924. Living quarters had been finished in August 1923 and the tennis court in the background earlier in 1924.*

*Sqn. Ldr. Robb in H3633 leading Flg. Off. Airey in H3632 and another pilot of 'B' Flight in J7124 during August 1924. Note the swastika emblem under the wing of H3632.*

*30 Squadron at Kirkuk in 1924 during operations against the elusive Sheikh Mahmoud. DH.9A H3633 is in the foreground.*

quarters were a welcome luxury, though it is surprising how healthy some of the personnel kept, living only in tents at the outstations." He goes on to record the many 'inconveniences' endured by Europeans "......such as sandflies, heat, dust, inoculations, restrictions resulting from indifferent water, the plague season [and] a cholera epidemic, [but] perhaps the most annoying was the 'Baghdad Boil'. It comes from the bite of a fly and may choose any exposed portion of one's anatomy. I got one on the point of my elbow and it remained for.......eight months before it finally faded." Additional problems recorded by Gp. Capt.

Longmore concerned flying activity at Hinaidi, where there was no radio and no air traffic control. "As there were four, and sometimes five, squadrons using the same aerodrome..........there was a certain congestion when taking off or coming in to land. This was not improved by clouds of dust thrown up by the running of engines or during take-off." An interesting description of Hinaidi follows. "This big air base about four miles outside Baghdad, at the junction of the Diyala river with the Tigris, was an air fortress, designed to survive isolation and investment (i.e. siege) for many months. In emergency it could accommodate.........at least six squadrons of

*DH.9A J7124 over Bazyan Ridge on 6th August 1924.*

*Kirkuk during the Sulaimaniya campaign. 30 Squadron is on the left, 8 Squadron on the right.*

aircraft besides the Air Depot and fine hospital already there. A bund, protected by barbed wire, surrounded the perimeter, on which armoured cars could patrol. It certainly would have withstood any attack by Arabs and could readily be reinforced by air from Basra or Palestine." This final comment relates to the air route from Baghdad to Cairo which had been established with the invaluable help of 30 Squadron.

In January 1924 Sqn. Ldr. Johnstone handed over the command of 30 Squadron to Sqn. Ldr. James M. Robb DFC, a recently promoted former Flight commander on 6 Squadron. He eventually retired as Air Chief Marshal Sir James Robb GCB KBE DSO DFC AFC, and on behalf of Her Majesty the Queen made the presentation of 30 Squadron's standard in 1954. On 4th January 'A' Flight returned to Hinaidi and 'B' Flight took its place at Kirkuk, Vernon aircraft of 45 Squadron being used to speed the changeover. February was used by 'B' Flight for low-level bombing practice on two days each week, and several flights were made to give air experience to W/T operators. On 14th March five aircraft carried out operations against Sheikh Mahmoud, who was thought to be hiding in one of four villages in the Halebja area, and similar sorties were flown on 16th and 27th March. On the first raid one aircraft was shot down when bombing the village of Kani Kawa, but the crew was picked up by another aircraft, probably with some difficulty. In all, 22 230lb, 28 112lb and 38 20lb bombs were dropped.

Religious disturbances in the bazaar at Kirkuk on 4th May were dealt with by a small force of British troops who were airlifted to the town by 45 and 70 Squadrons, and 30 Squadron's detachment made demonstration flights over the town. Two weeks later the remaining parts of the squadron left Hinaidi by train for Kingerban on their way to Kirkuk, all the aircraft flying to the new base next day. Leaflets were dropped on Sulaimaniya on 23rd May, and on 27/28th May no less than 101 sorties were flown. Several leaflet-dropping sorties were flown in June in an attempt to warn the local citizens not to harbour Mahmoud, and on 24th July Sulaimaniya was reoccupied. From September a serious Turkish incursion into

Kurdistan took place, and 30 Squadron was very much involved, dropping 26 tons of bombs in 34 raids during a 28-day period. Sqn. Ldr. Robb's usual aircraft was H3633, which suffered a cracked longeron and was replaced by E843 early in December.

A policy of destroying the elusive Sheikh's winter quarters and supply dumps began in December and was completed effectively. In spite of snowy conditions and very bad weather, aircraft of 30 Squadron bombed and destroyed four villages and damaged seven others. In 28 days and 230 flying hours, four 550lb, fifteen 230lb, 354 112lb and 36 20lb bombs were dropped. Two Flights remained at Kirkuk when the remainder of the squadron returned to Hinaidi in January 1925.

Not yet defeated, Sheikh Mahmoud made yet another attempt to gain power in Iraq in the spring of 1925, and another period of air operations began. In April, 30 Squadron, apart from a Base section, was again entirely at Kirkuk, where it was joined by 1, 6 and 55 Squadron detachments. The Sheikh's forces attacked a

*Sheikh Mahmoud (right), who was often referred to as the 'Director of Training' because he was the cause of so much action by the RAF.*

*Sheikh Mahmoud's home at Sulaimaniya under attack by aircraft of 30 Squadron. The large craters were caused by 500lb bombs.*

*30 Squadron aircraft at Kirkuk in 1926.*

*The armourers of 30 Squadron at Kirkuk in November 1926.*

small village near Sulaimaniya and were heavily defeated, prompting them to retreat into Persia in June. On the conclusion of this successful operation, Sqn. Ldr. Robb received a message from the C-in-C, AVM Sir John Higgins, reading "The fact that during the last fortnight your squadron has flown nearly 200 hours and has had an average of ten serviceable machines daily out of a total never exceeding eleven is, I consider, a very fine achievement, showing good and careful flying on the part of the pilots and hard and self-sacrificing work on the part of the mechanics. Please have the contents of this wire communicated to all ranks."

### Raiding Kurdistan

One of 30 Squadron's pilots, Flg. Off. C. G. M. Anderson, wrote a detailed account of a typical raid on a target in Kurdistan, affording an insight into the life of a pilot in Iraq in 1925. On the morning described, the first sound he hears is that of his native servant saying 'Sahib, sahib, five o-clock, sahib'. A mug of pale

yellow liquid, thick with condensed milk, had been deposited on the old bomb box which served as a chest of drawers and dressing table. The weather is cold, and the pilot is muffled to the eyebrows. Having drunk what passed as tea, he climbs out of bed, shakes his shoes to rid them of any reptiles or insects which may have settled down in them, and shaves. He has been detailed for the morning 'show' and knows that the CO will want to see all pilots in his office at 05.30. His fitter will be flying as gunner and bomb-aimer and the load will be four 112lb high explosive bombs and two 100lb cases of 'baby incendiaries'. He is not quite sure why he will be dropping bombs on a remote village of mud huts, but assumes it has something to do with persuading the inhabitants to stop aiding and abetting Sheikh Mahmoud. 30 Squadron, he knows, will continue this task until such time as Mahmoud surrenders or is captured or killed. Now fully dressed, he grabs his topee and hurries to the office block, hearing as he does so a 400 hp Liberty engine in a DH.9A being started.

The CO's briefing is short, and our pilot soon has the 'gen' he needs for a successful mission. He and his fellows hurry to the tarmac dispersal area, where one of them climbs into his aircraft, taxies out and takes off in a cloud of dust. His job is to fly ahead of the main force, dropping leaflets warning the inhabitants of the target village to evacuate at once and telling them why this punitive action is being taken. This is the only occasion when an aircraft is allowed to fly alone over enemy territory without W/T, as there is always the danger of a forced landing and capture by irate tribesmen who have never heard of the Hague Convention. Our pilot, however, is part of the main force, and when he is satisfied that his engine is running properly and all is well he waves away the chocks and lines up for take-off as No.3 in a formation of five. Airborne at 06.00, the formation forms up, and settles into a 75 mph cruise. At 800 to 2000 feet altitude it is already very hot, and radiators are liable to boil even with the shutters wide open unless engine revolutions can be reduced. This is tricky, as the air in this belt of heat is thin and therefore provides less lift. Apart from their bomb load, the DH.9As carry desert rations, five gallons of drinking water, ground strips, cockpit and wheel covers, a spare wheel, tools and 1500 rounds of ammunition, totalling a 200 lb overload. At 2500 feet, the formation reaches a cooler level, where engine revolutions can be reduced and the climb continued. Now the aircraft are over the foothills, with a range known as the Qara Dagh twenty miles ahead. To the left is the Brazian pass, near the foot of which is an emergency landing ground called Chemchemal, which is some comfort to the crews. Near the mountains flying conditions become bumpy, and the pilots find it difficult to maintain formation. For the gunners in particular this is very

*Flg. Off. Baggs of 'B' Flight had brought this badly damaged DH.9A back from a raid on Turkish irregulars in 1924. On landing at Mosul he lost control of the aircraft and, to prevent a ground-loop, he used 1 Squadron's mess tent as an arrestor gear!*

*Twelve aircraft can be seen in this photo of Kirkuk in July 1925, and, inset, another view of the Serai at Kirkuk.*

uncomfortable, but most of them have developed ways of overcoming airsickness.

Over the mountains at 5000 feet, the pilot loads his Vickers Mk.IV, which fires through the propeller by means of a Constantinescu synchronising gear, tests it and tells his gunner to test his Lewis gun. At 6000 feet, the leaflet-dropping aircraft spots the formation and joins it before a gradual descent to 4000 feet begins. Spotting the small cluster of flat-roofed huts which form the target 2000 feet below, the CO leads the formation towards them and drops a trial bomb to check whether he has judged wind-speed correctly. It falls short, but sights are adjusted before dropping in earnest begins. Each aircraft drops one bomb on each circuit; if the bomb falls on either side of the target, it is deemed to be the fault of the pilot, and if it falls short or long it is the gunner's fault! The pilot flies his aircraft into wind at a constant height and speed, looking over and down the starboard side of the fuselage, keeping the aircraft level and over the target. Standing up, the gunner works the gunsight, and at the right moment pulls a bomb-release toggle. He taps the pilot on the shoulder to indicate that the bomb has gone, and the aircraft immediately turns away to allow the next one to line up. When all the loads have been dropped, the crews indulge in machine-gunning for a few minutes before setting course for base, where each member of the formation tries to make a show of 'peeling off' before landing. With an airman on each wing-tip, the aircraft taxy in, and our pilot reports to the Flight Sergeant in charge of the ground crew that the aircraft was flying well. He also compliments our gunner on his good work. The CO

*One day in October 1926, LAC Hurst was Flg. Off. Denny's observer on a reconnaissance over Sulaimaniya when the engine of their DH.9A failed. Both men were taken prisoner by Sheikh Mahmoud's forces, and they wandered through the mountains with the tribesmen for several weeks. After they became very ill with jaundice the Sheikh sent them back to Kirkuk on horseback, where they recovered. Hurst is seen here in the Kurdish clothes he wore to combat the severe weather in the mountains.*

has gone to his office to send a signal to HQ while the other hungry pilots repair to the Mess. There, shouts of 'Boy! Bring me a large shandy gaff and tell the bearer to serve breakfast here — plenty eggs-i-bacon' and other demands can be heard.

Sheikh Mahmoud returned to stir up more trouble in the early summer of 1926, and in June 30 Squadron personnel once more found themselves all at Kirkuk. apart from a nucleus at Hinaidi. Mahmoud may have been aware that another Anglo-Iraq Treaty and an Anglo-Iraq-Turkey Treaty were in the course of preparation, with implications of the possible permanent control of Kurdistan by Iraqi

*J7352 was the reserve DH.9A of 'A' Flight at Kirkuk in March 1926.*

Arabs. These Treaties were signed in June and July respectively, confirming, among other matters, that Mosul was allocated to Iraq and that the border between Turkey and Iraq was to remain as it was. 30 Squadron was active against the Sheikh once more, and on of the DH.9As had to force-land behind his lines, where the crew, Flg. Off. F. M. Denny and LAC Hurst, were captured. After strong representations, however, they were released unharmed.

In command of 30 Squadron since 3rd June 1925 was Sqn. Ldr. F. H. Coleman DSO. By November 1926 ten of the squadron's twelve 'initial equipment' DH.9A aircraft were located with the forward detachment at Kirkuk, the other two remaining at the squadron's Hinaidi base. The aircraft and crews at Kirkuk were operating in cooperation with two columns of troops, code-named *Gocol* and *Bencol*, who were engaged in shepherding migratory tribes who were returning to Iraq for the winter. A third column, *Paicol*, left Sulaimaniya on 27th November to bring the right bank of the Diyala river under administrative control. All three columns returned to Sulaimaniya on 7th December, their task complete. During 1926 30 Squadron crews had spent 3767 hours in the air, and ground crews had ensured that aircraft serviceability in the difficult local conditions had averaged 87.2%.

Realising that 5th November was Guy Fawkes Day, the CO collected all the fireworks he could find and led a party to storm the fort at Kirkuk. One of two old Turkish cannon which stood outside the fort was captured by the 30 Squadron raiders, and the local armoured car company took the other one. Members of 30

*Flg. Off. Mizen's first landing at Kirkuk, on 1st May 1926, was something of a disaster!*

*Flt. Lt. Collins' aircraft, H3633, after colliding with another DH.9A over Sulaimaniya on 25th April 1927.*

*DH.9A E8580, flown by 30 Squadron between July 1927 and January 1928.*

Squadron hauled their booty back to the airfield before taking over the other cannon. Before long, they were set in concrete outside the officers' mess!

Six of the ten aircraft returned from Kirkuk to Hinaidi on 3rd January 1927, so that two Flights and Squadron HQ were there and just four were away from base at Kirkuk. However, on 11th April, with operations pending, a further reorganisation took place. From that date, a Base section, with stores, workshops and reserve aircraft, remained at Hinaidi, Squadron HQ and two Flights moved to Kirkuk and a detachment of four aircraft and crews went to Sulaimaniya. Operations comprising cooperation with army columns, bombing villages and chasing troublesome tribesmen, began on 22nd April and were completed on 7th May. The Sulaimaniya detachment joined their colleagues at Kirkuk on 26th June.

For their part in this short offensive, Sqn. Ldr. Coleman was awarded the DSO and Cpl. Beauchamp a well-deserved MM, while Flt. Lt. Harrison DFC, Sgt. Newman and Cpl. Reeves were mentioned in despatches. Cpl. Beauchamp was a wireless operator who had served with 30 Squadron from 1920 to 1923 and had been posted to the squadron again in 1926. During the 1927 operations he was in charge of a mobile W/T station at Halebja, in the heart of the mountains of Kurdistan, which was attached to an Iraq Army column chasing Sheikh Mahmoud. Such W/T stations were vital to the success of the troops on the ground and the aircraft cooperating with them. The W/T operators had to assemble, dismantle and move their equipment frequently, sometimes under fire. Cpl. Beauchamp eventually retired as a Squadron Leader.

### The 'wireless'

Communications between the various headquarters and the units under their control had always been a problem in Mesopotamia, but during the 1920s a sophisticated system of W/T (i.e. Morse transmission) was operating. Details of the organisation were provided by Wg. Cdr. James W. Gale, who joined 30 Squadron in 1927 as an LAC wireless and electrical mechanic, which included the trade of wireless operator. Between Air HQ at Hinaidi and Mosul and Kirkuk a continuous 24-hour intra-Command network operated on a frequency of about 1000 kHz (300 metres), and a liaison channel was open for an hour each day for contact with the French Air Force at Deir-es-Zor in Syria. When Kirkuk became an outstation in 1928 a supplementary link was introduced on 4.5 mHz (66.66 metres). RAF operational and administrative messages were passed to all Stations on the W/T system, which also handled traffic for Special Service (intelligence) officers and for Political Officers. 30 Squadron's signals section had the responsibility of manning Kirkuk W/T Station and its outstations and also provided operators and equipment to accompany mobile Army columns from time to time. When 6 Squadron left Iraq in October 1929, 30 Squadron took over its W/T work, becoming responsible for all communications north of Baghdad. Effectively, this consisted of Mosul, Diana, Barzan and Sulaimaniya.

At main W/T stations, a four-hour watch system was in force, day and night, which had the effect of isolating the personnel from the routine of squadron life, although if they were devious enough the operators also missed such events as AOC's parade! With regular time on their hands, they were able to enjoy hobbies, and many of them built their own radio sets, as they were all enthusiasts and

*'B' Flight at Kirkuk in 1927.*

wanted to make a contribution, however small, to the development of this new medium. Of particular interest was the potential use of high-frequency voice communication between aircraft and ground stations. For the time being, however, W/T was the only type of 'wireless'. Outstations were manned on a three-month detachment basis by two 'other ranks', who had to be self-supporting. They each received a subsistence allowance of three rupees per day, which at the time was equivalent to 4s. 6d. (22.5p.), which had to buy everything — fuel, food, hire of labour, water carrying and even sewage disposal! Accommodation was arranged by the squadron, and was often in buildings used by the local administration.

During the late summer of 1927 another Kurdish leader, Sheikh Ahmed of Barzan, began to cause trouble in northern Kurdistan, but was contained by 30 Squadron from Kirkuk and 6 Squadron and part of 55 Squadron from Mosul.

27th October 1927 was a red-letter day for 30 Squadron, as on that day the whole squadron was located on the same Station, the HQ, aircraft and crews having moved from Kirkuk to Hinaidi to join the base section. Sqn. Ldr. H. P. Lale DSO DFC took command of the squadron on 7th January 1928, after a year in which more hours had been flown than in 1926 (4158), but at 81.7% the serviceability record had suffered slightly. The early months of 1928 found a number of attachments to an army column known as *Akforce*, during which 30 Squadron aircraft were detached to

*Wapiti J9404 at rest, with two-wheeled trolley behind the rudder for use in manhandling the aircraft.*

*DH.9A J6961 at Sulaimaniya in 1927.*

90

Shaibah for operations against the Akwhan tribe in an area close to the border with Saudi Arabia. The Akwhans were noted for their aggressive incursions across the border into areas inhabited by southern Iraqi Arabs, who often fell victim to the ruthlessness of the invaders. Weather conditions were atrocious, gales, dust storms and very high temperatures adding to the normal difficulties. It was during one such detachment that on 2nd April one of the DH.9As crashed near Hillah, and the pilot, Plt. Off. J. W. Wood, and his gunner, LAC Waugh, both lost their lives.

1928 ended on a high note for 30 Squadron personnel, as the squadron had been awarded the Sassoon Bombing Cup for carrying out its bombing training more efficiently than any other unit in Middle East Command. More hours had been flown during the year than before (4766) and aircraft serviceability was recorded as 82.3%. On average, 13.7 pilots were available to the squadron each day.

Operations in the almost uninhabited desert west of Baghdad began early in 1929, with one Flight detached to Kerbela between 7th and 26th January. On 16th February one Flight left for Nukhaib for similar work, but did not engage in any offensive operations. Instead, the crews carried out many reconnaissance flights and photographic surveys before returning to base on 12th April. Meanwhile, another Flight had spent three days in March at Rutbah Wells assisting the civil authority to settle a tribal dispute.

### Goodbye to the 'Ninak'

On 19th April 1929, 30 Squadron took delivery of the first of the Wapiti Mk.IIA aircraft which were to re-equip the squadron. This was to be a slow process, and not without its problems. On 24th June two of the new Wapitis escorted three Potez aircraft of the French Air Force to Shaibah, but on the return flight to Hinaidi

*Wapitis at Hinaidi in June 1929.*

three days later one of them crashed near Luqait. On 29th June the three French aircraft were escorted to Deir es Zor in Syria.

First flown early in 1927, the Westland Wapiti incorporated as many DH.9 parts as possible and was of metal construction with fabric covering. The Mk.IIA was powered by a 550 hp Bristol Jupiter engine and carried a fixed Vickers gun forward and a Lewis gun in the gunner's cockpit. Wapitis cruised at 110 mph and had a maximum speed of 135 mph at 5000 feet. Service ceiling was 20,600 feet, and a range of 360 miles. Most of the improved performance probably came from an aerodynamically cleaner and deeper fuselage and a more efficient propeller. The Wapiti was provided with Frise ailerons, which gave much more effective lateral control. Handley Page slots fitted to the outer wings enabled control to be maintained at low airspeeds. It was thus an improvement on the trusty DH.9A, but hardly a major step forward over a period of ten years. The Wapiti did, however, carry W/T equipment, and the signals staff establishment was expanded to include wireless operator / air gunners. These men took great pride in their abilities and resourcefulness, and any failure to establish communication in the air was seen as almost a personal disgrace.

Many pilots were very fond of the DH.9A, which was colloquially known as the 'Ninak'. Gp. Capt. John Walker, who flew them with 30 Squadron, liked it immensely. "I had my 9A just as I wanted it" he said many years later. "I had a crate under one wing which took a case of beer. Then I had chargils, a canvas bag with a narrow neck with a string round it. You tied it on somewhere and the water used to evaporate slowly and cool everything. I used to have one at each side of my gun ring.......and it was slit down the neck so that it had a bottle of beer in each of them, one for my air gunner and one for me. In the .303 ammunition box you could get six bottles of beer if you put them in carefully and put ice all round them and shut them. An when you had been flying for seven hours and you got to the other end and it was still cold — beautiful!"

Although Hucks starters (a device by which the engine of an aircraft could be turned over by power from the engine of a Model T Ford) were provided at Mosul, they were seldom used, as the squadron pilots wanted to be sure that in the event of a forced landing in the desert the engine could be restarted by hand. So the procedure was for one airman to hold the propeller, another to hold his free wrist and the 'Chiefy' (Flt. Sgt.) to hold the central

*Wapiti J9407 of 30 Squadron in transit from Hinaidi to Mosul in September 1929.*

airman's other wrist. On the command 'one, two, three' the propeller was pulled, and with luck the engine burst into life.

Gp. Capt. Walker went on to describe flying the DH.9A. "The 9A took off at 50 and climbed at 55 to 60 and cruised at 70 to 75 mph. On a hot day I used to bring them in at about 90. The turbulence was so violent that if you didn't have your speed up...........I used to believe in coming in fast and getting the wheels on the ground and losing speed there. It worked very well. The 9A was very heavy on the ailerons. So if you were going that way and wanted to go that way it was much easier to pull the nose up, kick over the rudder and come back down!" Apparently the DH.9A tended to burn easily in a crash, as the battery was often flung out in the impact, causing sparks and an almost certain ignition of leaking fuel. If an aircraft turned over on crashing the wing centre section could collapse and trap the pilot.

He also recorded his thoughts about 30 Squadron's new aircraft. "The Wapiti was infinitely superior in performance, and many of the difficulties which we had with the DH.9A disappeared" he observed. "For instance, at Sulaimaniya you could take off any way you liked — uphill, downhill, it didn't matter. You could take off at (toward) the hills and get over them. The ailerons were not heavy like the 9A, despite having the 9A's wings." Another factor in the Wapiti's favour was that the deeper fuselage allowed more space for tools, bedding and personal possessions, all essential elements if an aircraft is to work for a squadron which at times must be highly mobile.

Two Flights of 30 Squadron had been equipped with Wapitis by 1 August 1929 and the third Flight by 15th September. Four of them, led by Wg. Cdr. J. A. G. de Courcy MC as senior RAF officer, made a flag-waving visit to Syria between 24th and 30th September,

*The result of a momentary lapse of concentration between Flg. Off. Hanton and Flg. Off. McCulloch on 3rd September 1930. Both had taken part in a leaflet drop on Sheikh Mahmoud's forces. Hanton pulled up into a wing-over but failed to see McCulloch above and behind him, and they collided. This is Hanton's aircraft. He died later in hospital and his crewman, LAC Cooper, died instantly.*

*The wreck of Flt. Lt. McCulloch's Wapiti near Aqra on 3rd September 1930 after colliding with Flg. Off. Hanton's aircraft. McCulloch escaped unhurt, but his gunner, LAC Kent, was seriously injured.*

*A lucky escape for Sqn. Ldr. Goddard, who went to search for the two aircraft which crashed on 3rd September 1930. In an attempt to land at the crash site, his undercarriage was smashed, so he flew to a nearby police post, where he crash-landed. Neither occupant was seriously hurt.*

*'A' Flight in a show of strength in support of the Iraqi army against Sheikh Mahmoud in November 1930. K1394 and the furthermost aircraft are carrying the 30 Squadron palm tree emblem on their fins.*

visiting Damascus, Aleppo, Rayak and Homs. While they were absent, 30 Squadron personnel had been making arrangements for a move to Mosul, to where an advance party travelled on 27th September. The move was completed on 25th October, and Sqn. Ldr. Lale assumed command of RAF Mosul as well as 30 Squadron.

RAF Mosul was intended to be fully defensible, and was surrounded by a barbed wire perimeter fence, apart from the water purification station and the ice plant, which were close to the right bank of the river Tigris. Ideally, all the necessities of life were available within the compound, enabling a siege of some duration to be withstood.

After settling down at Mosul, the squadron provided detachments to take part in Iraqi Army manoeuvres, one at Quaraghan from 13th November and another at Hinaidi from 23rd November, both of which returned to Mosul on 1st December. Apart from being available to lead any operations which might be required in the area of Mosul, 30 Squadron made many visits to Iraqi police posts to read messages which were put out on signal panels to indicate any problems, and to drop mail for the isolated personnel. Every pilot thus had the task of making himself familiar with the location of the posts, some of which were extremely isolated, and of usable landing grounds. 1929 turned out to be a busy year for 30 Squadron, during which 5492 hours were flown, with an excellent serviceability rate of 91.6%.

Sqn. Ldr. Lale was promoted to Wg. Cdr. on 1st January 1930 and left for the UK on 11th February. His position was taken by Sqn. Ldr. R. V. Goddard. Little seems to have disturbed a new-found even tenor of life on 30 Squadron that year, much of which was spent in shepherding other aircraft across the deserts of Iraq and being visited by VIPs. On 20th March HM the King of the Belgians arrived at Mosul in a Victoria aircraft of 70 Squadron piloted by Wg. Cdr. Maxwell MC DFC AFC, but left the same day. Four Potez aircraft of the 37iéme Regt. d'Aviation of the French Air Force flew in from Hinaidi on 1st April escorted by Wapitis of 55 Squadron. Two of them stayed for two days and the pilots of the other two decided that they liked Mosul and remained there until 5th April. On 3rd July the AOC arrived by air, escorted, as befitted

*Flg. Off. Nicholson of 'C' Flight on offensive patrol from Kirkuk in J9619 during the Flight's joint operations with a detached Flight of 55 Squadron in November 1930.*

*Wreckage of Flg. Off. Dustin's Wapiti, in which he was killed after trying to turn back when his engine failed on take-off.*

his rank, by Wapitis of 55 Squadron and next day made a reconnaissance flight over Karbchok Dagh, escorted by 30 Squadron, in connection with a border dispute which had flared up between Syria and Iraq. Meanwhile, the squadron had carried out extensive loading trials and other exercises with a possible move in mind, but this came to an end on 6th July.

## More trouble from the Sheikh

This period of relative tranquillity was not to last, however, as Sheikh Mahmoud and his followers came into the limelight yet again. In July 1927 the Sheikh had undertaken to go into exile with his family, but in September 1930 re-entered the country to proclaim himself yet again as the leader of an independent Kurdistan. He could understand that the Anglo-Iraq Treaty of June 1930 was a step toward complete independence for Iraq and knew that the strength of the RAF in Iraq had been reduced and that the Iraqi Army was now without British officers and was not yet battle-hardened. Furthermore, he was confident that the Kurdish tribes would support him completely. By mid-October it was clear that action would have to be taken against the Sheikh, and a force was assembled at Sulaimaniya. In view of the altered political conditions, the AOC gave control of the operation to Iraqi commanders, whose troops needed training without being embroiled in critical situations. Forthcoming operations seemed likely to be unsuitable for the well-established 'air control' methods, and the use of RAF squadrons was therefore restricted to reconnaissance, dropping of propaganda leaflets and to demonstrations.

At the end of October 1930 Mahmoud made a number of attacks on police posts but they were relieved by columns of troops working with strong support from 30 Squadron. From 27th October 'A' and 'C' Flights alternately were detached to Sulaimaniya, and on 1st November Sqn. Ldr. Goddard took command of a composite unit known as 'A' Squadron, comprising one Flight of 30 Squadron and one of 55 Squadron, which was based at Kirkuk. In addition there was a section of armoured cars from Hinaidi, but 'A' Squadron was disbanded on 26th November. After eight Wapitis of 30 Squadron had bombed rebels near Surdash on 30th November, intense activity and some offensive operations continued. When Sheikh Mahmoud was reported to be in the plain of Halebja on 4th January 1931, four aircraft of 'B' Flight carried out an unarmed demonstration flight, and discovered a gathering of horsemen at Kani Kawval. On landing at Sulaimaniya, the pilots asked for permission to take action against these tribesmen, but were refused. A second flight found a party of fifteen horsemen in much the same spot, and these proved to include Sheikh Mahmoud and his son. Next day three aircraft flew to the Halebja plain with orders to attack the hostile tribesmen, who suffered injuries before returning to their villages. Among them Mahmoud's son was alleged to be a casualty. Rebels succeeded in capturing a police post at Khurmal on 9th January, and took rifles and a large quantity of ammunition, a great boost to Mahmoud's arsenal as well as to his morale. Between 24th and 28th January reconnaissance flights were made in very poor weather. On 24th January Flg. Off. R. C. Warner and Sgt. Shaw located a wadi in which about fifty horsemen were taking cover, attacked and caused casualties. One of the squadron's Wapitis was itself a casualty on 30th January, when its engine failed in cloud over Tasluja, prompting the crew to abandon it by parachute, the first time this

*Sergeants' quarters at Sulaimaniya.*

had been done by 30 Squadron personnel.

To be closer to the scene of action, four aircraft of 'A' Flight moved to Halebja on 31st January, while two of 'B' Flight's Wapitis from Mosul made photographic sorties of mountain villages north-east of the plain. Next day four columns of Iraqi troops and police moved to that area, coordinated by messages dropped from aircraft of 'A' Flight. It was then found that the troublesome Sheikh had escaped into the mountains, and 'A' Flight returned to Sulaimaniya before moving back to Mosul on 3rd February.

At a social meeting in January 1931, W/T operator LAC James Gale realised that the Arab he was talking to was none other than the son of the elusive Sheikh Mahmoud. It soon came into the conversation that the Sheikh was in a village about ten miles away, not in Persia as was generally believed. On returning to their house LAC Gale and AC1 Clark went to bed for the sake of appearances, but later in the night they rose and made their way stealthily to the house of one Ismael Bilael, known as 'the interpreter'. He was an agent who gave information to the RAF Special Service officer at Sulaimaniya, and after checking the situation, he sent a message reporting the incident.

*30 Squadron pilots resting at the officers' mess at Mosul in 1931 during the final campaign against Sheikh Mahmoud.*

*Above: The road in Rowanduz Gorge, with an RAF vehicle*
*[J. Collins collection].*

However, after three months of operations, Sheikh Mahmoud had survived, and it was realised that the only way of dealing with him was by luring him into action. To do this, a mounted mobile force capable of living off the land was formed, to be ready for action by 25th March. Meanwhile, messengers from the Sheikh visited all Kurdish tribes to spread the notion that the British secretly favoured his cause, as the RAF had refrained from attacking villages. This ploy proved quite effective, as Sheikh Ahmed of Barzan asked the Air Intelligence Officer at Mosul whether the British wanted him to help Sheikh Mahmoud by rising against the Iraqi government!

In the extreme south of the area, a police post was attacked on 18th March and soon another post was under siege. For it to have fallen would have been a blow, and might have set the whole of southern Kurdistan in open revolt. On th March the Iraqi government asked for air action, which was handled by 55 Squadron. A Flight of 30 Squadron joined one of 55 Squadron at Kingerban on 2nd April and together supported the Iraqi Army in a sweep through the Qara Dagh valley, but the Sheikh escaped over the range at night, moving south-west with the aim of persuading the Jaf tribes to join his force. Before long he was located, and the decision was made to attack him on 5th April. An aircraft of 55 Squadron determined that he and his men were at Awa Barika, and four Wapitis from 30 Squadron and four from 55 Squadron then set about the task of bombing the village, dropping eight 112lb and nineteen 20lb bombs in all. At 15.30 the Special Force arrived after an eleven-hour trek, and attacked at 17.00, but were unable to hold the Sheikh, who made another miraculous escape, leaving behind a stock of weapons and ammunition and many casualties. Gales, dust-storms and heavy rain hampered the task, but on 9th April four aircraft succeeded in dropping four 12lb and sixteen 20lb bombs on a village, presumably a place where Mahmoud was thought to be hiding.

A plan of similar style was then put forward to deal a crushing blow to the Sheikh, but he had learned his lesson, and never moved by day or stayed anywhere long enough for the Special Column to reach him. Crossing into Persia on 23rd April, he immediately wrote to ask for terms of surrender, an event which took place on 13th May at Penjwin. There, he approached an RAF officer and remarked "You are the people who have broken my spirit."

*The village of Rowanduz seen from an altitude of 1500 ft. on 6th February 1932. On the left is the entrance to the famous gorge, mentioned above*
*[Wg. Cdr. N. W. Gale].*

Evidence indeed that air operations in a hostile environment could work. Other dissident tribal leaders quickly surrendered and sought the pardon of the King of Iraq, but not Sheikh Ahmed of Barzan, against whom action would have to be taken. 30 Squadron returned to Mosul on 14th April 1931, and a lull in activity followed.

A new CO for 30 Squadron and for the post of Station Commander at RAF Mosul, Sqn. Ldr. G. S. N. Johnstone, took over on 9th July 1931 when Sqn. Ldr. Goddard left to become CO of RAF Henlow. Preparations for a forthcoming campaign against Sheikh Ahmed continued, but in view of the severe winters experienced in the area concerned, the action was postponed until the spring of 1932. Meanwhile, 30 Squadron provided air cover for an Iraqi Army party which was looking for any Kurdish tribesmen not yet party to Sheikh Mahmoud's surrender.

On 5th October the AOC arrived at Mosul to carry out his annual inspection, and next day a ceremonial parade was held before he inspected 30 Squadron and the Station. On 7th October he watched flying exercises on the airfield and the local bombing range before leaving after lunch. At the end of November there was an outbreak of inter-tribal fighting, and 30 Squadron provided cover to units of the Levies who were withdrawing to their winter quarters at Diana. On 3rd December the squadron was ordered to search the Baradost area for signs of this fighting, but bad weather prevented flights for six days. Eventually the Iraqi Army unit from Billeh was found to be giving an ultimatum to tribesmen at Barzan but they were not cooperative. The troops were forced back, forty of them being lost in the process, and at midnight 30 Squadron was ordered to bomb Barzan and nearby settlements. Half an hour before bombing began, warning notices in Kurdish were dropped to encourage the inoffensive civilian population to leave their homes. In all, eighteen 112lb, 64 20lb and eight cases of incendiaries were dropped. During the bombing a wireless operator / air gunner, 506410 AC1 Gilroy, C. P. J. E., somehow fell out of the aircraft, but managed to use his lap-type parachute, and landed safely a mile or two south of the village. Fortunately, he had prior knowledge of the

*Filling a Wapiti with fuel from cans are ground-crew known as Paddy, Plonk, Tommy, Slim, anonymous and Milky*        *[J. Collins collection].*

*A typical 30 Squadron ground-crew: Leo, Coop and Ern. Note the palm tree motif on the fin of the Wapiti*        *[J. Collins collection].*

*A formation of Wapitis, with K1306 nearest*        *[J. Collins collection].*

area, having served as a wireless operator at Billeh camp with the Iraq Levies. When he arrived there on 11th December he contacted Military HQ at Mosul and was able to provide useful information on the condition of Billeh landing ground. This knowledge was particularly opportune, as a plan to evacuate wounded members of the Iraqi Army by air had been formulated. Gilroy was able to state that the ground was soft but serviceable, but as some doubt persisted that Victorias could land there safely OC 30 Squadron decided to test the conditions himself. For this, low-pressure 'doughnut' tyres were fitted to a Wapiti, and after landing the CO was able to confirm that Victorias could land with care.

By the end of December it was decided that although the situation in the Barzan area was static, a campaign against Sheikh Ahmed should be planned for the spring of 1932. Any military operations would be very tricky, and air support would be difficult to provide, as the terrain consisted of mountains rising to heights of 8000 feet, intersected by deep river gorges and valleys. Lower slopes of the mountains were covered with scrub, small trees and rocks, which would provide good cover for rebel forces, and villages were difficult to find. In later years it would become clear that this sort of environment is very appropriate for guerrilla warfare. For an aircraft in difficulties, there was nowhere to make a safe landing. The plan put forward was therefore for the advance party of an Iraqi Army column to occupy the Shirman district up to the river Kuchuk, establishing bases and a supply route, then in June to cross the Kuchuk to occupy villages and cut off Ahmed's escape route into Turkey, and finally for a second column to occupy Barzan.

The campaign began on 7th March 1932, when the leading column of the Iraqi Army marched through the Rowanduz Gorge, with 30 Squadron aircraft overhead to provide confirmation that the approaches to the gorge were free of rebels. On 12th March a Government ultimatum to Sheikh Ahmed was dropped on the police post at Billeh by 30 Squadron, for transmission to the Sheikh wherever he might be. That day, 'C' Flight moved to Diana to cooperate with the Iraqi Army and was put under the temporary command of Sqn. Ldr. M. B. Frew DSO MC AFC from AHQ. The Flight began daily reconnaissance sorties on 15th March, and on 19th March, after rebels mounted a strong attack at night , a dawn search was made, but the rebels had already dispersed. Two Flights of 30 Squadron and one of 55 Squadron bombed the village of Raizan on 2nd April, dropping 34 250lb and sixteen 112lb bombs, but although at least fourteen of the heavier bombs were seen to hit the target damage was only slight, due to the small proportion of explosive in the heavy case bombs. During the raid the engine of Sgt. Waylen's Wapiti cut out, and he and his gunner 'hit the silk', landing safely in friendly territory. The same target was bombed again next day, sixteen 250lb and eight 112lb bombs being dropped by aircraft from Mosul. Meanwhile the troops on the ground were becoming trapped in a narrow rocky defile and the column was being stretched and thus becoming much more vulnerable. A large force of Kurdish rebels realised this, and attacked, making for the supplies being carried by mules. Panicking, the mule drivers fled and a chaotic situation developed, only overcome by British officers in the column and by the intervention of two Wapitis of 30 Squadron. These made repeated attacks on the Kurds with bombs and machine-gun fire until darkness fell, at which time the enemy withdrew. Both aircraft had been hit by rifle fire, which had penetrated both fuel tanks of the one flown by Flt. Lt. Bradbury, and had wounded his gunner, AC1 Thomas, in the foot. With the other aircraft, flown by Sgt. H. V. Hudson, he then returned to Diana, from where the other three Wapitis, led by Sqn. Ldr. Frew, took off as replacements. Flt. Lt. Bradbury joined in again, this time with Sgt. Hudson as his air gunner. The three aircraft took up the attacks where they had left off, again coming under rifle fire as they flew low enough to do damage to the Kurds. When releasing his last bomb, Sgt. Hudson was hit in a lung, and subsequently died from his wound.

Sgt. Waylen, mentioned above, seems to have been the first NCO pilot attached to 30 Squadron, although the RAF Manual of

*DH.60M Metal Moth No. 1 of the Iraqi Air Force after its crash on a steep hillside. It had been engaged in exercises with 30 Squadron in April 1932.*

*A cartoon of 30 Squadron characters in the early 1930s, including Sqn. Ldr. Johnstone* [Wg. Cdr. N. W. Gale].

Manning Plans and Policy indicates that the introduction of airmen pilots began in 1921. King's regulations for the 1920s and 1930s certainly provided for airmen under instruction to volunteer for training as pilots.

The morale of the Iraqi Army had been severely damaged by this encounter, and all the column's supplies had been lost. The RAF came to the rescue by dropping food, tents and blankets, and under air cover escorted the column back to Zhazhok, where more food and blankets had been dropped, on 6th April. 30 Squadron was busily escorting another column from Aqra over the Piris Dagh and dropping warning notices prepared by the Ministry of the Interior on about twenty-four villages. On 8th April the first landing at Billeh since the previous December was made, using balloon tyres although the landing ground was almost suitable for normal use.

98

*An aerial view of Mosul airfield, with a Wapiti taxying towards the Watch Office. 'A' Flight's hangar is at right angles to those of the other two Flights*
*[Wg. Cdr. N. W. Gale].*

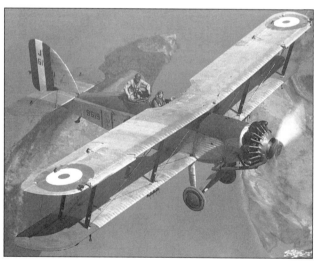

*A fine picture of Wapiti J9619 flying over a river scene on 28 April 1933. The pilot was Sgt. Noyes and the gunner LAC Bonny. Purists will note that the letter J has been omitted from the serial number on the fuselage*
*[B. Noyes].*

Three of the five DH.60M Metal Moths of the fledgling Iraqi Air Force's 1 Squadron arrived at Mosul on 17th April to operate with 30 Squadron. Next day one Flight worked from Billeh with two of the Moths, but unfortunately one of the latter crashed, killing both occupants. More proclamations were dropped by seven aircraft of 30 Squadron on 25th April and the opportunity was taken to complete a set of photographs of the 35 villages concerned. That day an 'air striking force' consisting of 55 Squadron and half of 70 Squadron arrived at Erbil, foretelling a new phase of the campaign against Sheikh Ahmed, but when one of 55 Squadron's Wapitis force-landed and was captured the plans were postponed. Trouble with the engines of 55 Squadron aircraft forced that unit's withdrawal from the force, and 30 Squadron stepped into the breach on 28th April. No less than 180 20lb bombs were dropped on two villages next day by 30 Squadron, and the Victorias of 70 Squadron added their weight to the offensive. Negotiations with Sheikh Ahmed continued through the period, ending on 24th May, when the Sheikh dismissed a government messenger with the warning that the bringers of any further messages would be shot!

55 Squadron returned to the fray on 25th May, and after both squadrons had flown over the villages to ensure that warnings by

*Two aircraft of l'Armée de l'Air. Potez 25 No. 1488 (right) and a Potez 29, visiting 30 Squadron at Mosul from Dera in Syria in 1933.*

*RAF Mosul seen from the air on 9th June 1933, with a Wapiti taking off. A few hundred yards behind the Station the river Tigris can be seen.*

*The ceremonial entrance to Mosul by 30 Squadron Air Firing team on their return from Hinaidi in 1933*                                                    *[B. Noyes].*

*A convoy of vehicles carrying 30 Squadron personnel and equipment to Ser Amadia on 7th August 1934 stopped in an almost-dry wadi.*

*Refuelling a Wapiti at Mosul in 1933* [B. Noyes].

*Dressed formally after their win, the members of the 30 Squadron team who won the Thomson Air Firing Cup in 1934 pose for the photographer. In the rear row were (left to right): LAC Bonny, LAC Rymer, LAC Gilbert, LAC Abbott. In front were (left to right): Wt. Off. Heffernan, Flg. Off. Grace, Flg. Off. Skelton, Sgt. Noyes, Sgt. Pebody* [B. Noyes].

*After the 1934 contest for the Thomson Air Firing Cup at Hinaidi. Just readable on the original print, the scoreboard shows that 30 Squadron gained 1374 points and 55 Squadron 1103 points, but 84 Squadron's total is not shown. The gentlemen in the picture are (left to right): LAC Rimer, Flg. Off. Skelton, Sgt. Noyes, LAC Gilbert, Flt. Lt. Prickman and Wt. Off. Heffernan*      *[B. Noyes].*

leaflet and loudspeaker carried by a Victoria had been heeded, a number of practice bombs were dropped, causing a great deal of noise but no damage, followed by a few 20lb bombs. By means of constant patrols and the use of delayed-action bombs, the striking force was able to impose a complete curfew on the core of Sheikh Ahmed's territory. Almost every day until 14th June offensive patrols were staged by 30 Squadron, directed by Gp. Capt. Breese at Erbil. Each day, four aircraft were usually provided for the one-hour patrols, loaded with 20lb bombs and machine guns. The pilots landed at Billeh for a briefing, and afterwards to make their reports on any activity they had seen and on the status of the villages in the area. After six days of this harassment, during which the Sheikh had been forced to move three times, and by 14th June he had arrived

near Zaita on the Turkish border and was trying to negotiate favourable conditions of surrender, having already sent his flocks and possessions across. When the Iraqi Army finally reached Zaita on 22nd June he crossed the frontier and gave himself up to the Turks, whereupon bombing ceased. The Barzan district was soon under the control of the Iraqi government, and at long last all rebellious tendencies appeared to have been overcome. Between March and June 1932, 30 Squadron had flown about 1400 hours operationally, had dropped 3131 20lb, 46 112lb and 52 250lb bombs and had fired 56613 rounds of ammunition. 'Air Control', in which 30 Squadron had played such a vital part, had proved to be the only practical way to bring the territory under administrative control. The avoidance of the total destruction which would have been the

*The first Hawker Hardy to arrive for 30 Squadron, in April 1935.*

*The fourth production Hardy, K4053, in 30 Squadron service.*

*'C' Flight of 30 Squadron on patrol after converting to the Hardy, August 1935.*

inevitable result of a protracted ground campaign meant that there was no lasting feeling of bitterness among the tribes. The RAF, and 30 Squadron in particular, were the architects of this policy.

## A different way of life

Soon after the Sheikh Ahmed campaign, a new CO took over from Sqn. Ldr. Johnstone. Commonly known as 'Tanks', the new man in charge was Sqn. Ldr. Paul Richard Tankeville James Michael Isidore Camille Chamberlayne AFC, a man with a strong personality as well as seven forenames! At Mosul, the HQ was in a fort-type building known to its occupants as Chappatti Castle, which was built around a square of grass, a rare commodity in Iraq. According to Mr. G. A. Rymer, who was the CO's confidential clerk, 'Tanks' did not like AHQ very much, and kept up a running battle with the AHQ staff on several matters. "One of the subjects"

*Hardy K3043 ready for take-off*

*[Gp. Capt. H. J. Walker].*

*30 Squadron's fencing team, winners of the RAF Iraq Novices Championship in 1935. Sqn. Ldr. Arthur Fiddament is seated in the centre of the group.*

recalled Mr. Rymer "was the vexed question of whether we should have one church parade a month or two, both parties knowing perfectly well that as we had no padre there were no such parades anyway. When the Tigris overflowed, someone told 'Tanks' that either the bombs or the pigs could be saved, but not both. His reply was typical — 'Save the pigs, b****r the bombs'."

Visitors in 1932 included the crews of two Flights of five Armstrong Whitworth Atlas aircraft from 4 FTS which arrived from Abu Sueir in Egypt on 30th August and the AOC on 17th October and 17th December. Between 6th and 16th November, however, the Station suffered an outbreak of diphtheria, but luckily there were no fatalities. On 21st January 1933 the Secretary of State for Air, the Marquess of Londonderry, paid a visit with the AOC and inspected 30 Squadron before leaving for Baghdad via

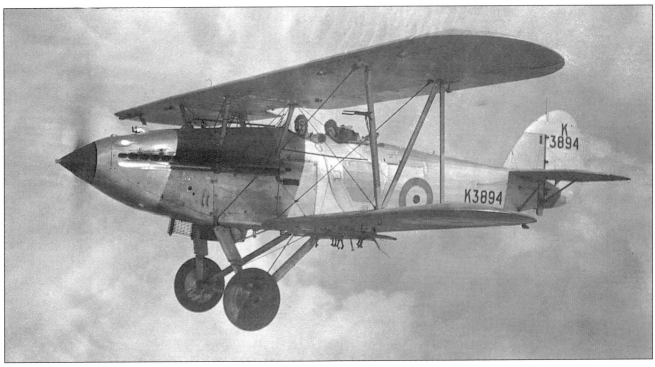

*A nice air-to-air picture of Hardy K3894.*

*A parade for the King's birthday: No. 3 Flight march past the CO*
*[J. Collins collection].*

Barzan and Diana two days later. Eight Potez aircraft of the French Air Force arrived on 8th March for an overnight stop, and on 24th March the delegate of the Syrian High Commission came to Mosul to discuss a new frontier with the Iraqi authorities. Yet another important visitor was the Under Secretary of State for the Colonies, who arrived on 25th April.

In July 1933 there was a certain amount of activity in connection with incursions of Assyrians into Syria, and 30 Squadron flew a number of reconnaissance missions over the area. On 31st August a number of Assyrian refugees were airlifted to Hinaidi in Victoria aircraft of 70 Squadron, and spasmodic reconnaissance flights continued into 1934. Festivities at Christmas 1934 followed the RAF tradition of officers serving dinner to the other ranks. Sqn. Ldr. Chamberlayne visited every decorated table to talk to the men under his command, accompanied by the Station Warrant Officer. 'Tanks', always a popular officer, was offered many drinks, and accepted them all, but unlike the SWO, who eventually slid beneath a table, he managed to stay on his feet!

On 26th March 1935 Sqn. Ldr. A. L. Fiddament DFC took over

from 'Tanks', and was given the task of restoring discipline, which according to some reports made him unpopular. His confidential clerk, inherited from his predecessor, has described him as quiet, firm, approachable and intellectual and very unlikely to be ruffled.

## Another change of equipment

The re-equipping of 30 Squadron with Hawker Hardy aircraft began on 30th April 1935, when 'A' Flight began conversion training to this relatively fast general-purpose biplane, which had been adapted from the Hart and Audax specifically for the use of 30 Squadron. Powered by a 530 hp Rolls-Royce Kestrel IB engine, or in later aircraft by a 581 hp Kestrel X, the Hardy had a maximum speed of 161 mph, a service ceiling of 17,000 feet and a three-hour endurance. A forward-firing fixed Vickers gun on the side of the nose and a Lewis gun on the rear cockpit mounting constituted the armament, and four 20lb bombs could be carried on wing racks, which could alternatively hold water containers. By 8th May 'C' Flight had taken delivery of Harts and on 14th August 'B' Flight followed suit. Compared with the Wapiti, elements of the Hardy's performance left something to be desired. RAF Iraq Command was not entirely happy with the new aircraft, complaining that it had a lack of carrying capacity, short endurance, and a high landing speed, a significant drawback when touching down at some of the small and high-altitude landing grounds used by 30 Squadron. Furthermore, take-off with a full load was tricky and there were overheating problems with the liquid-cooled engines. Low pressure 'balloon' tyres, considered an advantage in Iraq, were not provided. Although it had all these disadvantages, the Hardy was designed to deal with aircraft of the Iraqi Air Force in the event of hostilities. More importantly, it could out-perform the Italian Air Force in Abyssinia, allowing Sqn. Ldr. Fiddament to draw up battle plans in case the squadron was sent to help the Ethiopians in their fight against the Italian invaders.

By now, with only a routine policing role to perform, life for the men of 30 Squadron at Mosul had settled down. Gone were the days of 'roughing it' on desert landing strips or in the mountains,

*Mosul at Christmas 1935: a party at the '19th hole' in 'C' Flight's bungalow. The ladies were the wives of various consuls*          *[J. Collins collection].*

*'C' Flight of 30 Squadron during the Hardy period: (back row) Cpl. Arnold, Cpl. Cooper, Thomas, Gilbert, Renyard; (centre row) Sgt. Davidson, Cowan, Hughes, Baker, Lynch, Bonny, Middleton, Howlett, Milborn, Sgt. Pierson; (front row) Sgt. Alexander, Flg. Off. Tidd, Flt. Sgt. Lea, Flt. Lt. Scroggs, Plt. Off. Lynham, Plt. Off. Richmond, Sgt. Keates*       *[J. Collins collection].*

of moving on at frequent intervals and of eating and drinking what could be obtained. Gp. Capt. N. W. D. Marwood–Elton described the way of life by saying "In the mess there were six dinner nights every week. Every officer's batman, dressed for the part, stood behind his master to see that he was lacking nothing in culinary delights and also to see that his glass was kept full; this latter duty

was not always in the best interests of the officers! The following morning we rose at dawn for our first flights, and disciplinary action would be taken against anyone turning up with a hangover, which I knew to my cost!" The British Consul at Mosul from 1935 to 1937 was Sir Laurence Grafftey–Smith KCMG, who in his book 'Bright Levant' wrote: "The European civilian community was not

*The AOC inspecting 18 serviceable Hardys*       *[J. Collins collection].*

*30 Squadron cookhouse and dining hall at Mosul(?), which were well-appointed. Although the food was good, appetites in the summer were small due to the heat.*

*Two photographs above featuring William Ross-Jones, a wireless operator/ mechanic with 30 Squadron from 1933 to 1936 (and later a Sqn. Ldr.) posing on top of the squadron crest which he and Frank Griffin took a year to complete on a hillside two miles south of Mosul and near the 6 Squadron badge created earlier.*

large. It was to 30 Squadron RAF that we owed most of the excitements and pleasures of life in Mosul society. This squadron had been commanded by a redoubtable man, 'Tanks' Chamberlayne, whose overriding purpose had been to fit his men for war. Low-flying was encouraged, and every hazard accepted, if not imposed. Many of his officers had made the nightmare flight through the Rowanduz Gorge and back, and one initiation rite was the descent, first made by the CO, into a nauseous pit in the desert, where a myriad pigeons nested in a mass of guano centuries high. The squadron's bombing was the best in Iraq, and its esprit de corps was exceptional." Going on to discuss the local social affairs, Sir Laurence wrote: "These young men, denied any family life by

*Hardy K4053, carrying the 30 Squadron palm tree motif on the fin, flying over desolate Iraqi terrain.*

*Hardy K4056*                                                                                    *[J. Collins collection].*

service regulations, were something of a social problem. One expects a buzzing of bees around any available honeypot, but this was a hive of hornets. They worked hard to make life around Mosul enjoyable. They organised dances in the quarters where Gen. Bekir Sidqi was later assassinated, they organised picnics to the streams behind Nineveh or to the remarkable Partian ruins around Hatra. To drive to Hatra in the spring, when winter mud and summer dust lay hidden by a multi-coloured carpet of wild flowers, was a delight..........." Money was usually a problem among the young officers, as overseas allowances were not generous. Few of them were married, however, as the minimum age for marriage allowance was thirty. Gp. Capt. Neville Mason recalls one stormy meeting at which the Mess Secretary announced that the price of a gin was to raised from a penny-farthing (0.52p) to a penny-halfpenny (0.625p). This prompted shouts of anger from those present! However, they were assured that the new price would cover pink gin, gin and onion or gin and olive!

Conditions for NCOs were also considered quite good. Robert Burrows, who was on 30 Squadron from 1933 to 1936, recalls squadron dinners in the sergeants' mess. "We usually held three each year, one at Christmas, one in November and one in February, the latter two to welcome new drafts from the UK" he said. "The fish course never presented any problem, as there were plenty of fish in the Tigris, which flowed past Mosul, and the camp was only about half a mile from its banks. The armament warrant officer would issue a couple of the air gunners with a hand grenade apiece (for training purposes, you understand) and detail them to provide fresh fish for the dinner. The gunners would proceed to the river, collecting a couple of natives on the way.........and the grenades would be lobbed into the river. Downstream the natives would retrieve the stunned fish, which were anything up to five feet long." Christmas for the airmen was also as festive as they could make it, and decorated barrack rooms were often seen. It almost goes without saying that the airmen liked a drink or two when they could obtain it, and by today's standards it was extremely cheap. A pint of McEwan's ale was 7d (3p) and a bottle of Johnnie Walker Black Label was 8s 4d (42p). Spirits could not be bought in the NAAFI, but on special occasions was often spirited away from the officers' or sergeants' messes. For an airman, the pay structure at this time was determined by his Trade Group, the highest of which was Group 1. Within Group 1 the trades were Fitter Aero-engine, Carpenter–Rigger, Metal Rigger, Wireless Operator–Mechanic, Fitter Armourer and Electrical Mechanic. Weekly rates of pay were, for a corporal £2-16-0 (£2.80), for an LAC £1-18-6 (£1.92), for an

*One of the articulated coaches used by Nairn Transport Co. on their cross-desert route from Damascus to Baghdad.*

AC1 £1-8-0 (£1.40) and for an AC2 £1-1-0 (£1.05). His overseas allowance was one shilling (5p) per day, but this could be boosted by 1s 6d (7.5p) per day flying pay if he flew as an air gunner. Boredom could be endemic, but many sporting opportunities existed. Football, hockey, cricket and fencing were enjoyed, and there was a good, if rather small, swimming pool. An athletics day was held each year, everyone not on duty attending to take part or cheer on their friends. Those people with an interest in history were in their element, particularly those who flew over the country. One young pilot flying to Hinaidi to take part in the Command sports day was particularly fortunate to see the outlines of an ancient city near Baghdad which was normally covered in sand. Strong desert winds had blown much of the sand away, but on his return flight he was amazed to find that sand once again covered the city.

A training camp for use in the summer was established in the mountains at Ser Amadia, mainly for squadrons based in the south of Iraq to have a two-week break from the intensely hot weather. They flew to and from Mosul, and covered the remaining stage by motor transport and on the backs of mules. The training was light but enjoyable, and living in this wild mountainous area among Kurdish peasants who knew little of civilisation was quite an experience for those who took part. One officer who spent two weeks at Ser Amadia was Gp. Capt. Marwood–Elton, who took the opportunity of making a reconnaissance trek by mule. Accompanied by two Kurdish levies, he made for the northern border of Iraq where Kurdistan joined Turkey. When the party stopped for the first night outside a village to pitch camp, the entire population turned out to build them a 'kaprana house' of branches of trees interwoven with

*Hardys of 30 Squadron lined up for AOC's inspection in 1936, many of them carrying the palm tree emblem*      *[J. Collins collection].*

*MT vehicles of 30 Squadron awaiting inspection by the AOC*
*[J. Collins collection].*

rushes, the whole project taking half an hour! At dusk, the headman and a retinue of servants brought food, followed once more by all the inhabitants. "Everyone squatted down outside the 'kaprana', the headman dipped into a cauldron and brought out a sheep's eye, which he handed to me" recalled Gp. Capt. Marwood–Elton. "I only just managed to keep it down, and I hope my act of enjoyment passed muster! The meal went on into the night.......then the headman got up and we all exchanged courtesies and we were left in peace. I went behind the house and was sick..........then we opened a tin of bully beef to allow things to return to normal."

During the mid-1930s, it was discovered that members of 6 Squadron, which had been based at Mosul before 30 Squadron's arrival, had carved their squadron crest on a rock face. William Ross–Jones and Frank Griffin decided to do something similar, and began work on the 30 Squadron crest on the same hillside. It took about a year to complete, and the two men added their initials, W. J. and F. G., on the corners. One wonders whether these two

*The sight greeting newcomers arriving at Dhibban (Habbaniya) – the traditional 30 Squadron welcome!*

Some pilots had difficulty in coping with the higher landing speed of the Hardy and flared rather late, causing the aircraft to nose over. This shows an early arrival at Dhibban in 1936.

A 30 Squadron crew prepares to take-off from an up-country airstrip in May 1937. The Hardy's engine has already been started by one of the ground crew.

Hardy K4061 after a landing accident during intensive training for possible action against the Iraqi Air Force. The pilot was unhurt.

'Welcome to Dhibban'. One of the reception parties waits to greet new arrivals at this new RAF Station (later renamed Habbaniya).

110

*The sign which said it all – RAF Habbaniya-London 3287 miles!*

works of art have survived the trouble of recent years or if they have been destroyed.

## Life at Mosul

The same William Ross–Jones flew with 30 Squadron as a wireless operator, gunner, observer, photographer and bomb-aimer in addition to his engineering duties on the ground, and has described vividly some elements of his life at Mosul. "In Wapiti

and Hardy days all the squadron's wireless operators/air gunners, despite not being specifically employed as aircrew but very proudly wearing their 'flying bullet' emblem, were trained to do 'circuits and bumps', so that in case of emergencies they would be able to land and take off. We had a detachable joystick in the back cockpit, together with a parachute, Scarff ring, Lewis machine gun, four drums of ammunition, a wireless crate, trailing aerial, an Aldis lamp, and an HAD bombsight, not to mention a load of 20lb bombs on the wings. On special occasions, such as if we were on a long border patrol which could last four hours or more, [*we would carry*] a crate of beer (Allsop's and McEwan's were the brews out there in those days). There were two occasions on Wapitis when I had to take control. They were with a Flg. Off. X, who liked his beer, but I knew he was off course and refused to pass him another bottle. Having been refused, he unharnessed himself, 'upped it' out of the cockpit and threatened to 'walk the wing'. I suppose that, with enough struts and wires about to catch a shoal of fish, this was not desperately dangerous at a safe height and with a control column in the back cockpit, but with that gentleman it was certainly not inconceivable. It was certainly enough to petrify a young LAC WOp/AG in the back cockpit, but order was restored as soon as I could manage to grab another bottle without letting go of the control column, and wave it about. All in good fun perhaps, but admittedly a bit scary, even at 85 mph."

Most of the younger officers destined for service in Iraq travelled overland from Egypt, where they had been trained at 4 FTS at Abu Sueir on Avro 504N and AW Atlas aircraft. On being posted to Mosul, which was more than 750 miles away in a direct line, they travelled by train to Damascus, where they spent a night or more in a hotel before boarding a large desert bus owned by Nairn Transport. From Damascus there was no road, and in a sandstorm the marked track could be obliterated, the bus then diverting perhaps twenty miles off course. Nevertheless, the drivers always managed to find the half-way refuelling point at Rutbah Wells, where food and drink were available. For the next stage of the journey the bus took the new arrivals to Baghdad, where they caught a train to Baiji, about 100 miles south of Mosul. From there, RAF transport took them on the final stage of the thirty-hour journey.

*The 30 Squadron five-a-side officers' football team on Christmas Day 1937, with Sqn. Ldr. Stainforth wearing the back-to-front cap.*

*The staff of 30 Squadron orderly room at Habbaniya in October 1937. Although they are wearing KD uniforms, their jackets look less than comfortable!*

A major event in the calendar of any squadron was the annual inspection by the AOC. In 1936 this was scheduled for a Monday at the end of March, and by midday on the previous Saturday all was ready. The aircraft were all serviceable and had been polished, the hangars were spotlessly clean, billets had been cleaned until they shone, and the men's kit was immaculate. But during the Saturday afternoon a severe dust storm blew up and continued to rage with unremitting fury until 22.00 hours. At 18.00 Sqn. Ldr. Fiddament decided that he would not ask for the inspection to be postponed, and instructed his Flight commanders to arrange for several cases of beer to be taken to the billets so that the lads could drown their sorrows! At dawn next day all ranks reported to the

*New Blenheim Mk.Is arriving at Alexandria in crates in January 1938.*

*30 Squadron Amateur Dramatic Society's three-act play 'Almost a Honeymoon'. At the end of scene 1, AC Renyard, LAC Jarvis, LAC Bonny and AC Atkinson are on stage*
*[J. Collins collection].*

hangars, where a terrible sight met their eyes. The open-fronted hangars were full of sand! After digging some of the sand away, the Hardys were pushed out and cleaning-up operations began. Officers and NCO pilots were issued with overalls, with no badges of rank. A rigger standing on a high trestle was cleaning the upper wing of 'his' aircraft when a figure below began to clean the lower wing. In no uncertain terms, the rigger said "For Christ's sake use your loaf, you bloody idiot! Wait 'til I've finished up here before you start down there!" When the figure looked up to apologise, the rigger realised who it was — the CO, who later admitted that he deserved it!

Bob Burrows, who recounted this story, goes on to say "At about 12.30 the cooks arrived with 'char' and sandwiches and we had a twenty minute break. By about 17.00 hours all was ready again as far as the aircraft were concerned. We returned to the billets and found that the bearers had worked wonders in recleaning them. After dinner we only had our own kits to see to. At 08.00 on Monday morning, suitable attired in best shorts, tunics and Wolsey topees, we were on parade on the football pitch, complete with

*The outdoor cinema at Habbaniya, with benches at the front and more comfortable canvas chairs at the rear.*

rifles and bayonets. The AOC, [AVM W. G. S. Mitchell CB CBE DSO MC AFC], arrived, was duly saluted and inspected the parade, after which we marched past and were dismissed. We then changed into working kit and lined the aircraft up on the aerodrome for the AOC to inspect. In the sunlight twelve Hawker Hardys were a marvellous sight. The AOC ordered a squadron formation, and they took off in four groups of three aircraft and flew past [as a squadron]. The AOC congratulated the squadron on its turnout, both on parade and on the aerodrome, and in view of the hard work put in on the Sunday gave us the next day off. That evening we had a colossal party in the NAAFI."

Between 20th and 23rd April, one Flight of 30 Squadron acted as part of an enemy force in Command Exercise No.1, the establishment of an Advanced Air Station near Hinaidi. Also taking part were armoured cars and obliging tribesmen.

## First at a new Station

After a considerable length of time at Mosul, 30 Squadron was ordered to move to Dhibban, a brand new Station which had been designed from the outset as the permanent headquarters of the RAF in Iraq. Work on the Station had begun in 1934 under a clause in the Anglo-Iraq Treaty of 1932 which allowed a British base to be established west of the river Euphrates, although certain elements of the Iraqi military were anxious to see British forces leave Iraq completely. The squadron's advance party, consisting of 'C' Flight and a few personnel of other sections, left Mosul under the command of Flt. Lt. B. D. Nicholas on 19th October 1936 in three Valentias of 70 Squadron. A week later, 'B' Flight followed in the same way, and 'A' Flight flew south in four Valentias on 31st October. 30 Squadron's office at Mosul was closed on 2nd November, and the CO joined the squadron at Dhibban, where a few days later he became Station Commander. However, his presence at Dhibban was a short one, as he handed over his functions on 12th November to Sqn. Ldr. A. J. Rankin AFC and returned to the UK. No sooner had 30 Squadron arrived at its palatial new Station than an order was issued for training as a two-seat fighter squadron to be carried out.

On 12th April 1937 ten of 30 Squadron's Hardys flew to Heliopolis in Egypt to take part in an air display staged by RAF Middle East and the Egyptian Air Force. This satisfactorily completed, they returned to Dhibban, after a night-stop at Amman, on 21st April. At the end of July a further visit to Egypt was made, this time a training mission. Leaving Dhibban on 26th July, the four Hardys visited many RAF landing grounds for familiarisation purposes before returning to base on 31st July. A similar trip was made on 25th August, but this time to Palestine, where landing grounds used operationally against Arab terrorists were used.

On the day that this mission began, Sqn. Ldr. George H. Stainforth AFC took over as the CO of 30 Squadron. Six years earlier, he had become very well-known as the pilot who had secured the world air speed record of 407.56 mph in a Supermarine S.6b aircraft, and was regarded a a flying fanatic. Flt. Lt. U. Y. Shannon (later Gp. Capt. Shannon DFC) recalled that he used to take off and not return for many hours, which was most disconcerting for the staff of Flying Control. "Also, he had the idea of flying across the English Channel upside-down on his return to the UK" said Flt. Shannon "so he trained for this feat by hanging upside-down from a hook in the doorway of his quarters. He also spent a long time designing a new emblem for the squadron badge and was very particular how he placed the leaves of the date palm. The design was accepted by the College of Heralds as being authentic, but I think it

*30 Squadron's disciplinary Warrant Officer was Wt. Off. J. W. S. Carpenter, commonly known as 'Chips', who was not a man to be trifled with!*

*The fancy dress party to welcome the first incoming draft of the 1938/39 trooping season to 30 Squadron and to Habbaniya. These men were not really mad – they just went out of their way to give that impression!*

*This Blenheim, K7101, was written off when it swung on take-off from Habbaniya on 15th June 1938 and belly-landed.*

*This menu for the farewell dinner staged in 1938 for personnel of 30 Squadron who were to be posted elsewhere is remarkable in that it provides all their names. Prominent was Sqn. Ldr. Stainforth, the CO  [T. Morrow].*

*30 Squadron's Christmas festivities included all the food and drinks enjoyed back in 'Blighty'  [T. Morrow].*

has since been superceded. In passing, I understand...........that George declined promotion to the rank of Group Captain so that he could continue to fly." Sadly, Wg. Cdr. Stainforth was killed on operations in the Middle East in September 1942 at the age of 43. He was the oldest operational pilot in Middle East Command.

With a potentially dangerous situation developing in Palestine, arrangements were made in August 1937 for the complete

mobilisation of 30 Squadron. However, as existing squadrons were found to be capable of coping, reinforcement by 30 Squadron was not necessary, although the day-to-day state of affairs was watched closely. On 13th September four of the Hardys flew to Syria as a training exercise and to liaise with the French Air Force. Airfields at Damascus, Rayak, Aleppo, Ain Arous, Deir-es-Zor and Beirut were used before the Hardys returned to Dhibban on 19th September.

## A fundamental change

After flying Hardys for less than three years, 30 Squadron now began to re-equip with a much more modern twin-engined aircraft, the Bristol Blenheim Mk.I. Pilots and ground crews alike must have thought they were in a different Air Force! Powered by two

*A lorry convoy on its way to LG.5 in September 1938 during the Munich crisis.*

Bristol Mercury VIII engines of 840 hp, the Blenheim cruised at 200 mph, had a maximum speed of 260 mph and a range of 1125 miles. Its bomb-load was 1000 lbs, and armament comprised a fixed Browning gun firing forward and a Vickers 'K'-type in a dorsal turret. Its wing span was half as much again as that of the Hardy, and there was a crew of three.

30 Squadron had the honour of being the first overseas squadron to receive the Blenheim when on 13th January 1938 the first example arrived at Dhibban. After being shipped from the UK to Alexandria, the Blenheims were assembled at the Aircraft Depot at Aboukir, from where they were flown to Dhibban two or three at a time. Flt. Lt. Shannon had completed a conversion course at Wyton before leaving the UK, and he, the CO and Flg. Off. J. H. Slater flew the first three to be delivered. This trip was made in three hours at an altitude of 16,000 feet with no oxygen, as the CO was keen to set a record, but when they landed the three pilots wondered why they had headaches! About 38 flying days were taken up by the CO, the only instructor, in successfully converting all fifteen pilots on the squadron, and two others, to fly the Blenheim. Demonstration flights soon began, a notable one being the trip made by three of the Blenheims to the official opening of Basra airport (Margil) on 25th March 1938. While they were there, King Ghazi of Iraq inspected the aircraft and climbed into the cockpit of one.

During the conversion period, three Hardys visited all twenty-five useable landing grounds in northern Iraq, and one of the Blenheims also landed on some of them. Oblique photography and formation flying was still being practiced in the few remaining Hardys, but by 20th April dual instruction on the Blenheims had been completed. Good results were obtained in low-level bombing training in the Benheims, which were flown at 150 mph instead of 220 mph due to the distinct possibility of bird strikes, though what difference the reduced speed would have made to bird or aircraft is debatable!

*Blenheim K7096, now carrying code letters DP:A. This is the only photograph found so far of 30 Squadron's use of these code letters, which were issued in April 1939..*

*Members of the 30 Squadron gymnastics(?) team at Habbaniya in 1938*

*[D. J. Vellacott].*

*A Potez 25 of l'Armée de l'Air visiting 30 Squadron at Habbaniya.*

The name of 30 Squadron's airfield at Dhibban was altered on 1st May 1938 to become Habbaniya, a very familiar name for many years afterwards, meaning in Arabic 'of the oleander tree'.

Conversion to Blenheims meant that an additional crew member had to be found, and the CO asked for volunteers from among the ground crews to train locally as bomb-aimer/navigators. Keen to take up this offer was 'Lofty' Chaney, a Fitter II on 'A'

Flight, who had longer-term visions of becoming a pilot. He recalls that Sqn. Ldr. Stainforth did all he could to determine the capabilities of the Blenheim, and on hearing of the flight of a Westland Wallace at 30,000 feet over Mount Everest he decided to find out how high a Blenheim would fly. 'Lofty' was the navigator. "We had one oxygen bottle each" he said. "Off we went in KD and flying helmets (the temperature on the ground was about 100°F), and around 8000 feet we donned our 'Teddy Bears'. Can you imagine the front cockpit while we were doing this? The throttles were locked while the pilot was doing his trick and I was keeping the thing level. Then it was my turn............at around 10,000 feet and at about 0°C. We could still see Habbaniya through the haze directly below. We climbed in a five-minute square spiral and lost sight of the ground at 14,000 feet. At 15,000 feet we switched our oxygen on and used it sparingly and continued to climb, watching engine temperatures and the like. At 29,000 feet the temperature was minus 40°C and our breath caused ice to dribble onto our chests. The radio in the back contracted with the cold and the knobs wouldn't turn. We made more height very slowly and I estimated that we reached 31,000 feet. The aeroplane had reasonable control with the slipstream from the engines over the tail, but the ailerons were very, very light. Down we went in a gentle glide to thaw out slowly, still keeping our five-minute square orbit, with our oxygen full on. We saw the ground at about 10,000 feet, but Habbaniya was

*Although undated, this menu card must date from after the introduction of the Blenheim in 1938*      *[T. Morrow].*

*30 Squadron Blenheim K7177 of 'C' Flight in a rough shelter lent by the Iraqi Air Force at Mosul in 1939. The Blenheim was one of three which went to Mosul after local troublemakers had murdered the British Consul and destroyed the Consulate. On such detachments, a fitter and a rigger were usually taken.*

*The 30 Squadron rugby team*  [*J. Collins collection*].

nowhere to be seen. When I got it sorted out, we were 60 miles away. I have often wondered if we had unwittingly found a high-level jetstream. All that for £1-18-6 (£1.925) a week and flying pay of a shilling (5p) per day!" Air Cdre. H. J. Hickey CBE CEng MRAeS later wrote about the manning policy of the time. "I was an air observer with the rank of corporal, and the theory was that we worked 50% of the time on flying duties and 50% in our basic technical trade" he said. "The practical consequence was that, in the air, we were navigators and bomb-aimers and were required to be able to man the gun turret and the radio in emergency. In my case, on the ground I had to carry out all technical work on the engines and also sign for all first-line work on the airframe. In addition, as the CO's navigator, I had to do the work that in more

sensible years fell to the squadron navigation officer."

Sadly, it was not long before the first fatal accident occurred. While taking off from Habbaniya on 29th June, one engine of Blenheim K7102 failed, and the aircraft hit the ground violently and burst into flames. Both men on board, Plt. Off. C. A. Stephen and AC1 Davies, were killed instantly. Next day Sqn. Ldr. Stainforth, flying alone, tried to reproduce the effect of such a disastrous engine failure immediately after take-off, with the idea of either revealing the cause so that it could be avoided in future or developing a procedure for avoiding a repetition of the accident. Unfortunately, any conclusions he may have arrived at are not recorded.

The Munich crisis which so affected every part of western Europe reached as far as Iraq, and 30 Squadron was ordered to

*Blenheim K7097 at a wet Habbaniya in 1938*  [*D. J. Vellacott*].

prepared for immediate mobilisation. Squadron aircraft flew to Heliopolis on 29th September and a long convoy of motor vehicles left Habbaniya next day for LG5, where a stop was made to await further instructions. A recall was then issued, and the trek back to Habbaniya began, but the aircraft stayed at Heliopolis for twelve days to 'show the flag', as 30 Squadron was still the only Blenheim squadron in the Middle East.

With the distinct possibility of a major conflict still in the minds of politicians and military planners, 30 Squadron was instructed to carry the AOC Egypt and a number of staff officers on a tour of landing grounds in Egypt. Three Blenheims flew them to Mersa Matruh, El Dhaba, Amriya and Aboukir, from where the return flight to Heliopolis was made in 25 minutes at an average ground-speed of 245 mph. Soon afterwards, the whole squadron returned to Habbaniya, the

*Sqn. Ldr. Shannon surveys the wreck of Blenheim K7108 after an inexperienced pilot had landed the revolutionary aircraft at Habbaniya in March 1939.*

*'C' Flight at Habbaniya in April 1939. The picture shows the complete range of trades from armourers, electricians, wireless operators, instrument makers and tinsmiths to coppersmiths and carpenters. NCOs were all Group I tradesmen, while airmen were usually flight mechanics A or E, with some fitters II A or E, normally former apprentices.*

move being completed on 14th October apart from three aircraft which had force-landed and did not arrive for another six days.

Sqn. Ldr. U. Y. Shannon took over as CO from Sqn. Ldr. Stainforth on 3rd November 1938, and on 25th November led a Flight of four Blenheims on an inter-Command visit of some six weeks duration, probably the longest mission the squadron had ever flown, both in distance and in time. RAF Stations and landing grounds visited were Helwan and Aboukir (Egypt), Khartoum, Wadi Halfa and Port Sudan (Sudan), Malakal, Juba, where the crews slept in straw-covered mud huts, Kisumu (on the shore of Lake Victoria), Nairobi (Kenya) and Aden. At Khartoum and Aden the Blenheims made 'demonstration flights' before returning to Habbaniya on 5th January 1939. After the Blenheims had made a 300-mph low-level pass across Nairobi, the headline in the next morning's local newspaper was 'Flying Razor Blades Hit Nairobi'!

A second fatal accident since converting to Blenheims befell 30 Squadron on 10th December 1938, when K7097, on a flight to Ismailia, was reported missing. An extensive search was made for the aircraft and crew, but was abandoned after seven fruitless days. Then, on 20th December, a tribesman reported that he had chanced upon wreckage some forty miles west-south-west of Ramadi, and a party was sent out at once to investigate. It was soon established that the aircraft had flown into the side of a hill and that all six on board had been killed, but the cause of the accident was never determined, although weather conditions may have played a part. The pilot was Sgt. V. W. Garside, and also on board were AC1 F. O. Gamble, AC L. W. Cooper and AC R. W. Carpenter of 30 Squadron, Sqn. Ldr. P. Kinsey (the Command Signals Officer) and Capt. J. B. Harvey of the Argyll & Sutherland Highlanders but attached to the Iraq Levies. There were several very sad families that Christmas.

At Habbaniya, new arrivals from the UK were given a warm welcome as a matter of routine. Their voyage had usually taken about a month during which they were cooped up in a troopship as far as Basra and then had to suffer a long rail journey. One such 'sprog' was Freddie Greenhalgh, who recalls the reception. "What a motley crowd there was to meet us, like a carnival of broken and deranged figures with dire warnings and prophecies of madness; a 'black pageant' of inverted amusement which was obviously intended to make us feel that we should never have come, got up by inhabitants who welcomed any diversion from

their monotonous, heat-soaked lives. After being welcomed in a manner calculated to break our spirits we were taken to the canteen, where we enjoyed marvellous food and drink." As they were the centre of attention, new arrivals were always asked about events in 'Blighty'. Often, they would recognise old friends or acquaintances among the crowd, and for a time good cheer was much in evidence. "I was assigned to a bed in 'C' Flight billet" said Freddie Greenhalgh. "It was already made, and I just had to dump my stuff for the time being and be propelled — residents and new arrivals together — a few yards to the canteen shared by 30, 55 and 70 Squadrons. I cannot describe what it was like to be sitting in luxurious surroundings, being plied with drink and all talking at once, tired but marvelously relaxed. So many people to recognise, so many yarns to swap, and despite the warnings and prophecies earlier, so much to look forward to, with adventures and new horizons."

Johnny Vellacott's arrival six months earlier had been little different. "On reaching Dhibban, as it was still called then, the trucks dispersed to their various units and our truck stopped at 30 Squadron lines" he recalled in later years. "By this time we were tired and dusty and, at the command of a small man with a Warrant Officer's crown on his right wrist, we were very glad to get down out of the truck. The Warrant Officer was dressed in a smart khaki shirt and shorts well bleached by the sun, dark glasses and a large toupee. He barked at us 'Fall in in fours, facing the sun, with your kitbags'. He then called the roll. We were very grubby and weary

*Blenheim K7096 being refuelled and, below, refuelling a Blenheim from petrol cans.*

*A Blenheim of 'C' Flight about to leave Habbaniya for Ismailia as war looms.*

*Flt. Lt. Frank Marlow, who led the initial reconnaissance of western desert airfields in July 1939.*

*A rest period during the squadron's move to Ismailia.*

feel at home" said Johnny Vellacott. "After a shower and a change of uniform — long-sleeved shirt and slacks for evening wear — we were taken across to the squadron 'other ranks' mess hall for a special reception dinner. The food was wonderful, and there was plenty of it; so much better than the troopship. After the dinner we were asked 'Pray silence for a speech of welcome from the Sheikh of Aba Fluse'. This gentleman, in full Arab costume, spoke only in Arabic. At times there were grins and chuckles from the 'old sweats', and later it was explained that the Sheikh was in fact one of the lads, and the speech was not of welcome to us but told the tale of a certain airman's visit to a notorious part of Baghdad. In the evening there was a party in the combined squadrons' canteen, and much beer found its way down many a dry throat. Songs were sung and party pieces were done, including 'This Old Shirt of Mine' and a very good time was had by all. When the festivities came to a close we made our way back to our billet to our clean and comfortable beds, beds that were not on the move all the time!"

Habbaniya was a large Station with a twelve-mile perimeter, one side bordering the Euphrates river, which provided water for a large number of irrigation ditches. These watered lawns between the billets, trees and shrubs, and frogs breeding in the water fed happily on the insect life. There were three large hangars at Habbaniya, situated on the camp side of the airfield, which was a vast expanse of hard-baked clay known as mutti. The hangar at the far end from the main gate was 30 Squadron's, while the others were occupied by 55 and 70 Squadrons. About 6000 people lived on the Station, only a fifth of them British, the rest being a mixture of Arabs, Indians, Syrians, Assyrians, Kurds and Persians. Among them was a regiment of very smart Iraq Levies with British officers. Working with a company of RAF armoured cars, the Levies cooperated with the flying squadrons to protect the oil

from our long journey, and this sort of parade-ground stuff did not go down too well at the time! After he had made sure that the full draft was present, the WO ordered 'Leave your kitbags where they are. New draft, left turn, quick march'. As we marched away a hidden and strange-sounding band struck up 'Colonel Bogey' and came into sight from behind a nearby building. They were a motley collection of airmen in an assortment of very odd costumes, and they had trouble playing their instruments because they were laughing! Tired and dirty as we were, we realised that it was all very friendly and happy welcome for us and after they had marched us round the same building a couple of times we arrived back at our kitbags." It transpired that the Warrant Officer was really an LAC orderly room clerk! He told them which billet to go to, and the revellers picked up the new arrivals' kitbags and carried them to the billet, which was a bungalow-type building. "We found our beds already made and a bearer ready to do what he could to make us

*A night-stop in Transjordan for the 30 Squadron convoy.*

pipelines which ran from the Mosul oilfields to the Mediterranean Sea. Tom Donohue could recall the living conditions and domestic routine at Habbaniya. "There were at most a dozen white women on the camp" he said. "They were, with one notable exception, nurses at Iraq Command's main hospital. The exception was the beautiful blonde wife of 55 Squadron's CO. I think that any 'erk' who was at Habbaniya in those days will remember with pleasure seeing her ride her horse around the cantonment.........The sky was cloudless from mid-May to mid-September and the heat was excessive. From June to late August the daily maximum was never less than 105ºF, with up to 125ºF in the middle of that period. The minimum at night was 90ºF."

## Training for war

Preparation for hostilities continued in the spring of 1939. On 2nd May three Blenheims of 30 Squadron flew to Ismailia, where a dummy attack on the hangars was made from an altitude of 15,000 feet. Two of the aircraft returned to Habbaniya five days later, carrying out independent long-distance sorties with practice bombs on the North bombing range at 10,000 feet on their way. A new system of code letters to be applied to operational aircraft was instituted in April 1939, and 30 Squadron was allocated the letters DP. Squadron badges on aircraft were still permitted, as they could readily be obliterated in time of war.

In central Iraq, there is a short rainy season when even hailstones may fall. At times, Baghdad Airport was waterlogged, and for a few days airliners would be diverted to Habbaniya. One day on the extensive tarmac apron could be seen an Imperial Airways HP.42 aircraft on its way to India, a DC-2 of KLM on a journey to the Dutch East Indies, a Lufthansa Ju 52 inbound to Baghdad, and an Air France tri-motor Dewoitine *Arc-en-Ciel* bound for French Indo-China. Not far south of RAF Habbaniya was the lake of the same name, where flying-boats of Imperial Airways called weekly. It is interesting to note that mail from England took three days if sent on the KLM service, seven days by Imperial Airways and ten to twenty days overland.

An armourer on 30 Squadron, Ron Croxton, said that most of the squadron's time was taken up by bombing practice. "As armourers we spent many days filling smoke bombs, loading the aircraft and at times carrying out range duties or camera obscura operating" he reported. "Much of the training was needed because the introduction of the Blenheim necessitated an increase in aircrew. Although many aircraft were not initially fitted with rear turrets, wireless operators were needed as the radios were in the rear of the aircraft. Wireless operators were recruited and existing air gunners were trained to operate the radios. When turrets were eventually fitted, all had to be trained to operate the turrets and fire the VGO gun. Also needed were bomb-aimers. These were obtained from squadron volunteers — fitters, photographers, armourers etc." Ron also mentioned that 30 Squadron was known as a mobile squadron, and every so often there was, without warning, a practice 'pack-up'. All maintenance equipment, spares, food and personal kit was loaded onto the Chevrolet trucks, which then set off on a tour around the desert while the aircraft took off and flew cross-country for an hour or two. "Towards evening" Ron said, "everything, aeroplanes, lorries and all, arrived at camp with everybody clapped out, bad tempered and only fit to subside into the cookhouse and canteen, there to commiserate in swapping terrible experiences."

On 5th June 1939 one Blenheim flew to Rayak in Syria carrying the AOC's representative to the opening of Beirut civil airport. It returned to base after two days, and another aircraft then left for Amman, Heliopolis, Aboukir and Ismailia to demonstrate Blenheim armament at these RAF Stations. Another long-distance bombing exercise between Iraq and Egypt began on 19th June, when three Blenheims of 30 Squadron took off for Ismailia. Two runs with practice bombs were made in formation at 10,000 feet over the local range, and fighters made unsuccessful attacks on the 'intruders' between El Arish and Ismailia. After refuelling there, the Blenheims took off and further attempts by fighters from Helwan to intercept them were made. Next day, a flight around the Nile Delta was made, and on 26th June the three aircraft left for Habbaniya via Amman, where one had mechanical trouble which delayed its return to base until 3rd July.

*Seen at Dekheila, Blenheim L1166 of 30 Squadron is undergoing an engine run-up*     *[R. C. Sturtivant collection].*

A great deal of photographic work was also carried out, including high-level line overlaps and mosaics of the mountains of northern Iraq. High-altitude flying was practised constantly, and the bombing range was well used, often at the end of a long-range navigational exercise, and sometimes as far away as Egypt. On such a mission, three of the Blenheims left Habbaniya on 17th July 1939 to carry out practice bombing at Ismailia range and were subjected to a practice interception by Gladiators of 33 Squadron from Helwan. A dummy attack on Heliopolis was made by two of the Blenheims, and again an interception was made by 33 Squadron. Afterwards, a reconnaissance mission over the Western Desert landing grounds was flown by two aircraft, which visited Amriya, Ikingi Maryut, Burg el Arab, El Hamman, El Dabah, Fuka, Maaten Bagush and Qasaba before spending the night at Mersa Matruh. Next day, on the way back to Ismailia, landing grounds at Sidi Barrani, Sollum and Siwa were inspected. Unknown to the Blenheim crews of 30 Squadron, several of these names would in a couple of years become very well-known to aircrews and the British public alike. The three aircraft returned to Habbaniya on 20th July, carrying out more bombing practice on the way.

## Leaving Iraq

War now seemed inevitable, and on 19th August a Precautionary State under which the Middle East Reinforcement Scheme would be activated was brought into force. After some twenty-four years in Iraq (or Mesopotamia, to use its original title), 30 Squadron received the order on 23rd August 1939 to move to Egypt. Two days later, three Valentia aircraft of 70 Squadron left Habbaniya at 01.30 carrying key personnel and stores to the squadron's war Station, Ismailia. A ground convoy of 28 Ford and Chevrolet vehicles and a Morris ambulance, under the command of Plt. Off. Griffiths, left Habbaniya at 03.00, accompanied by Sqn. Ldrs. Barrett and Baker of 1 (Bomber) Wing. Finally, with Sqn. Ldr. Shannon as leader, twelve Blenheims took off at 03.15 and arrived at Ismailia in formation four hours later with no trouble except a slight shortage of fuel in some aircraft. On the ground convoy was Ron Croxton, who recalls that "........kitbags were laid along each side of the lorry. Bed mattresses (three biscuits) were

placed on top of the kitbags with one against the side of the lorry to form seats for the journey. We were escorted by armoured cars and travelled without incident to our first night stop at LG.6. Most night stops later were made at oil pumping stations. Breakdowns seemed to be limited to punctures on the armoured cars. We slept where we could, sometimes on the tops of the covered lorries, sometimes on the ground. We stayed two nights at RAF Amman to give us a rest and a chance to clean up. Through Palestine we were watched over by the Army personnel located on hilltops covering the road. When crossing the Sinai [desert] we were buzzed by aircraft from the squadron which had already arrived at Ismailia. We crossed the Suez Canal at Qantara and reached Ismailia after ten days." As the ground convoy had not arrived by 30th August, Plt. Off. Swann made a reconnaissance flight to find it, but failed to do so. It was not until next day that Flt. Lt. Darbyshire spotted the vehicles approaching El Kibri. The weary men finally arrived at Ismailia at 11.00 on 1st September.

A shortage of hangar space meant that only eight aircraft could be accommodated under cover, the others having to be picketed outside. For use as Squadron and Flight offices, a new temporary building was allocated, although it had to be modified before it was entirely suitable. Two more Blenheims were collected from Habbaniya on 28th August, and arrangements were made for the dispersal of the aircraft along the southern part of Ismailia airfield. Living conditions at Ismailia were very different from those at Habbaniya and quite a shock for the newly-arrived men of 30 Squadron. They found that the corrugated-steel barrack huts were bug-ridden, and everyone painted the iron beds with paraffin in attempt to dispose of the unwelcome visitors. However, the surrounding vegetation was lush, and the camp was close to a town with shops, bars, cafés, dance places and a railway to Cairo. So with some trepidation, the air and ground personnel of 30 Squadron settled down to await events.

After a conference on 1st September at which a practice bombing plan was formulated, it came as no surprise to anyone when an Operation Order for the first raid on commencement of hostilities was issued next day. On 3rd September 1939 Great Britain was at war with Germany, and 30 Squadron was ordered to stand by at two hours' notice.

*Passing through Jerusalem; the 30 Squadron convoy on its way to Ismailia*                                                                 *[W. Coventry].*

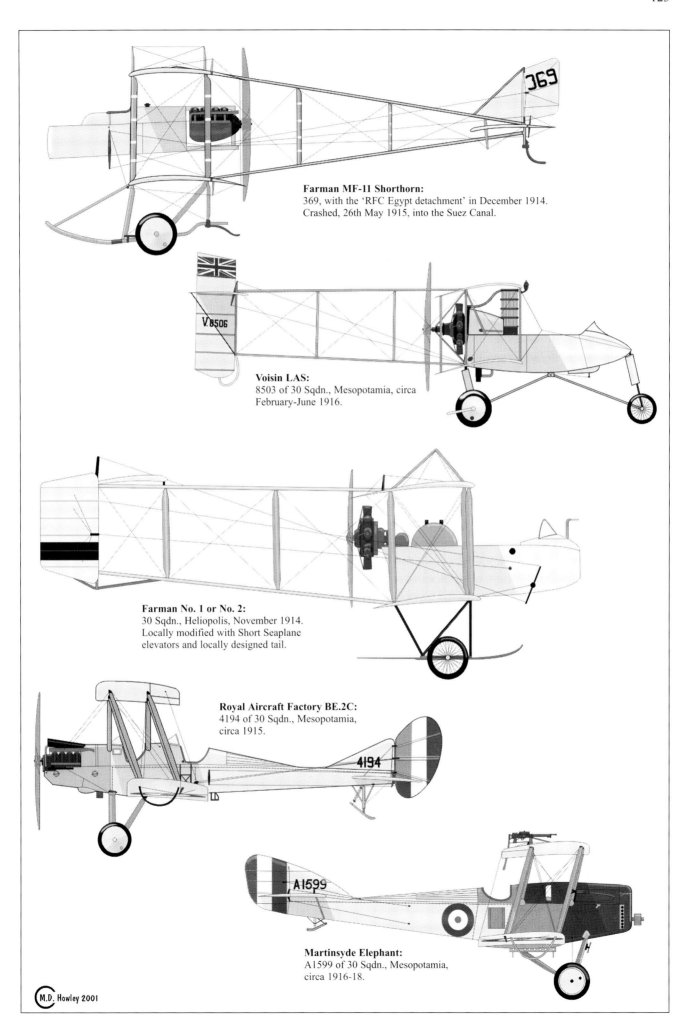

**Farman MF-11 Shorthorn:**
369, with the 'RFC Egypt detachment' in December 1914.
Crashed, 26th May 1915, into the Suez Canal.

**Voisin LAS:**
8503 of 30 Sqdn., Mesopotamia, circa
February-June 1916.

**Farman No. 1 or No. 2:**
30 Sqdn., Heliopolis, November 1914.
Locally modified with Short Seaplane
elevators and locally designed tail.

**Royal Aircraft Factory BE.2C:**
4194 of 30 Sqdn., Mesopotamia,
circa 1915.

**Martinsyde Elephant:**
A1599 of 30 Sqdn., Mesopotamia,
circa 1916-18.

M.D. Howley 2001

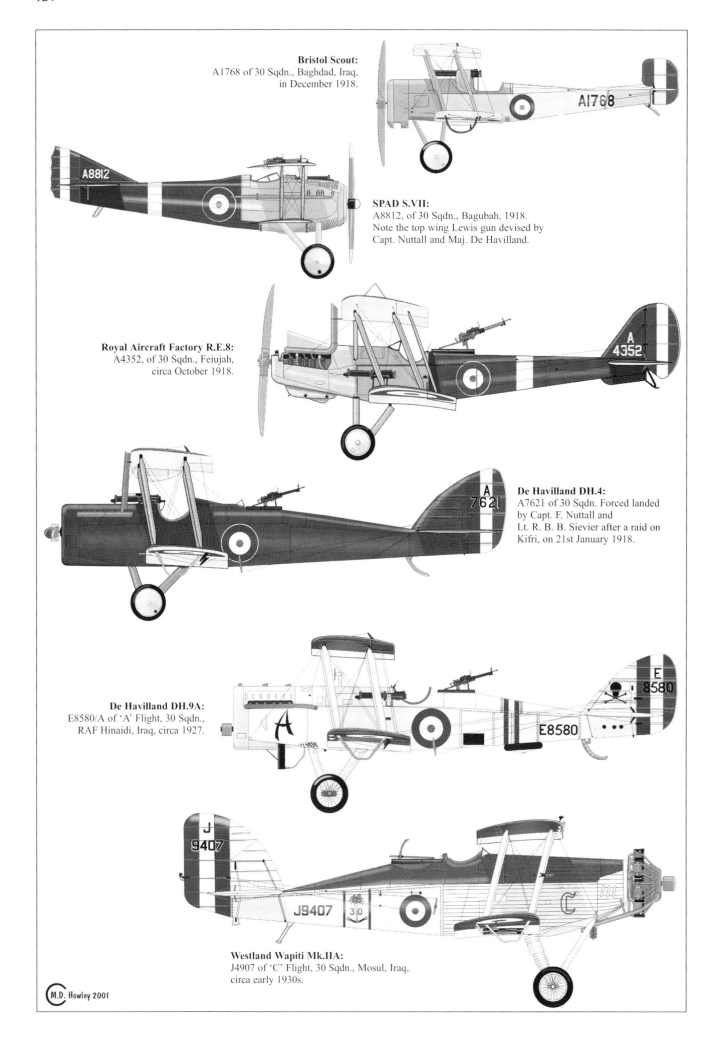

**Bristol Scout:**
A1768 of 30 Sqdn., Baghdad, Iraq,
in December 1918.

**SPAD S.VII:**
A8812, of 30 Sqdn., Bagubah, 1918.
Note the top wing Lewis gun devised by
Capt. Nuttall and Maj. De Havilland.

**Royal Aircraft Factory R.E.8:**
A4352, of 30 Sqdn., Feiujah,
circa October 1918.

**De Havilland DH.4:**
A7621 of 30 Sqdn. Forced landed
by Capt. F. Nuttall and
Lt. R. B. B. Sievier after a raid on
Kifri, on 21st January 1918.

**De Havilland DH.9A:**
E8580/A of 'A' Flight, 30 Sqdn.,
RAF Hinaidi, Iraq, circa 1927.

**Westland Wapiti Mk.IIA:**
J4907 of 'C' Flight, 30 Sqdn., Mosul, Iraq,
circa early 1930s.

M.D. Howley 2001

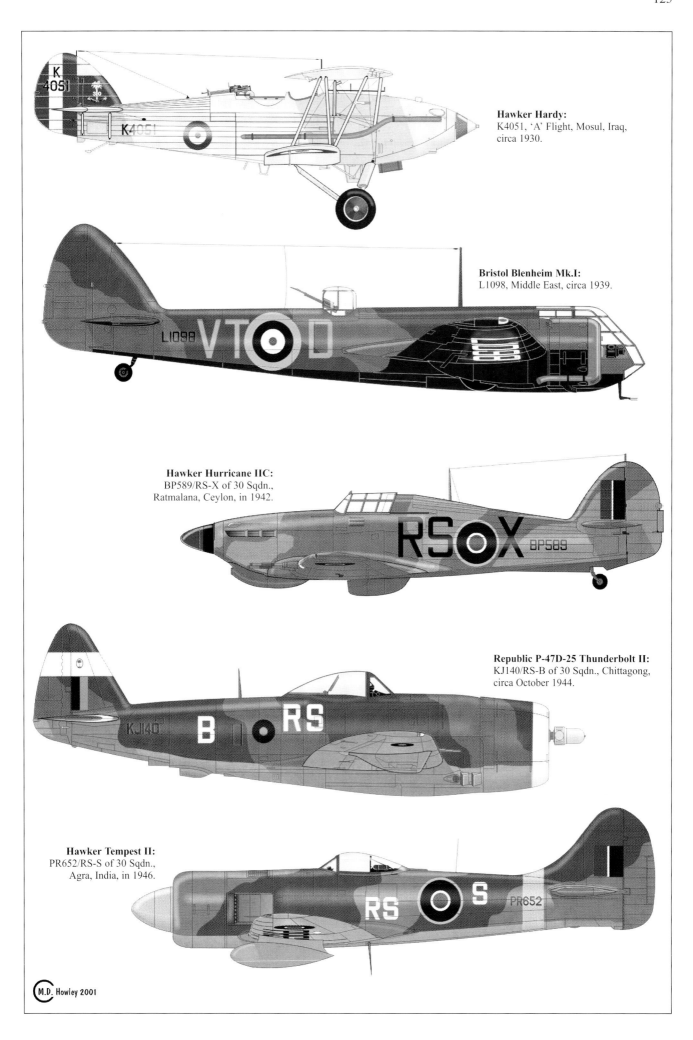

**Hawker Hardy:**
K4051, 'A' Flight, Mosul, Iraq, circa 1930.

**Bristol Blenheim Mk.I:**
L1098, Middle East, circa 1939.

**Hawker Hurricane IIC:**
BP589/RS-X of 30 Sqdn., Ratmalana, Ceylon, in 1942.

**Republic P-47D-25 Thunderbolt II:**
KJ140/RS-B of 30 Sqdn., Chittagong, circa October 1944.

**Hawker Tempest II:**
PR652/RS-S of 30 Sqdn., Agra, India, in 1946.

M.D. Howley 2001

126

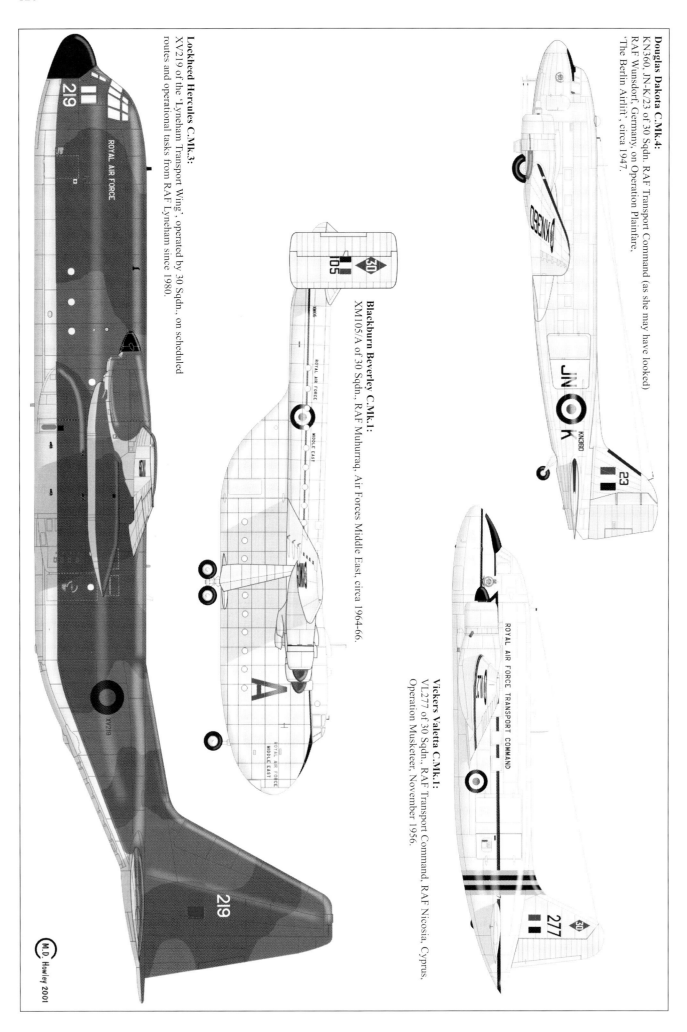

**Douglas Dakota C.Mk.4:**
KN360, JN-K/23 of 30 Sqdn., RAF Transport Command (as she may have looked)
RAF Wunsdorf, Germany, on Operation Plainfare,
'The Berlin Airlift', circa 1947.

**Vickers Valetta C.Mk.1:**
VL277 of 30 Sqdn., RAF Transport Command, RAF Nicosia, Cyprus,
Operation Musketeer, November 1956.

**Blackburn Beverley C.Mk.1:**
XM105/A of 30 Sqdn., RAF Muharraq, Air Forces Middle East, circa 1964-66.

**Lockheed Hercules C.Mk.3:**
XV219 of the 'Lyneham Transport Wing', operated by 30 Sqdn., on scheduled
routes and operational tasks from RAF Lyneham since 1980.

M.D. Howley 2001

*30 Squadron air and ground crews pose in front of a Blenheim, probably at Ismailia.*

# Chapter 4: Preparing for Action

As soon as war was declared, five officers and one sergeant were posted to 30 Squadron from 14 Squadron for training on Blenheims, bringing the number of pilots on the squadron to seventeen. The squadron's code letters (DP), allocated in April 1939, were now changed to VT. One of the aircraft was modified on 5th September to have dual controls, and the new arrivals began their conversion training at once. There were soon two cases of Blenheims being landed with undercarriage wholly or partly retracted, damaging the aircraft beyond repair by the squadron. By 19th September it was possible to carry out a simulated raid patrol in order to check fuel consumption. Six Blenheims were loaded with four 250 lb dummy bombs each and took off to fly the 688 miles from Ismailia over El Arish, El Dhaba, No.2 Suez Road live bombing range and back to Ismailia, where fuel remaining in the tanks was carefully measured and the information sent to HQ Middle East. Next day the first live bombing practice was carried out by six crews on the Ismailia range from an altitude of 15,000 feet, with satisfactory results. From that time, similar practice missions were flown each day.

Conditions at Ismailia were very different from those at Habbaniya, which was a much bigger Station. Freddie Greenhalgh provides an insight into the squadron's arrival in Egypt. "After the initial sorting out we found that the grey corrugated metal barrack-huts were bug-ridden, and there was a most unpleasant aroma of paraffin as everyone painted the iron beds with the stuff in order to do battle with the bug hordes. Some people were seen going over the bedsteads with a blowlamp or taper in an effort to burn out the enemy!" Nevertheless, Ismailia was not all bad, as Freddie goes on to relate. "Ismailia had a more pleasant feel about it than Habbaniya. The sand seemed yellower, and the vegetation more lush and greener. It took about ten days for the overlanders to make the trek, but when they did [arrive] there was great rejoicing as we were just about able to recognise figures sand-caked up to the eyes and barely able to see. There was only one remedy for that, what with 'Gyppo tummy' from bellies full of sand — a great revelling in showering and a glorious booze-up!"

Local tension gradually eased, and in mid-September it was possible to start granting 48-hour passes to squadron members. Although uniform was always worn, the practice of carrying side-arms was discontinued, except under special circumstances. Air Cdre. Raymond Collishaw DSO OBE DSC DFC, who had been CO of 30 Squadron in Mesopotamia from 1920 to 1922, paid a visit to Ismailia on 15th September and was no doubt pleased to meet the crews of the Blenheims and their supporting ground crews.

News of three new Blenheims on their way from the UK on board the SS *Queen Anne* was well received on 22nd September, as was the fact that the CO had passed Plt. Offs. Godfrey, Griffiths, Matthew and Barggren for training as operational pilots after five hours solo flying on Blenheims. Formation bombing practice now intensified, with up to nine Blenheims in three Flights of three taking part. On completion of the drop, R/T and visual signals between aircraft were practiced.

Between 26th and 30th October the squadron took part in a Command signals exercise which had been designed to evaluate the communication facilities throughout Middle East Command. The squadron's operations room was manned by every officer in turn, with Flt. Lt. F. A. Marlow in overall charge. At the end of the month a scheme of concentrated training for air observers was set up, and a marked improvement in results was quickly noted. During October the squadron's total flying time was 399 hours, the most time in the air since Blenheims had replaced Harts.

Long distance training entered the programme on 1st November 1939, when three aircraft left Ismailia at fifteen-minute intervals to carry out reconnaissance flights over the Western Desert. They landed at Dekheila, Amriya, El Dhaba, Maaten Bagush, Qasaba and Mersa Matruh before they returned to El Dhaba, where they refuelled in readiness for a night exercise. Rested and fed, the crews then made for the Ismailia bombing range, where they dropped practice bombs before returning to base. A different exercise was carried out during the same week, when the squadron practiced firing at drums floating in the sea, but as the drums were difficult to find this exercise was soon discontinued.

Sea markers were considered as an alternative but were found to be unavailable.

Every day, intensive reconnaissance flights and practice bombing missions at high and low altitudes were now being carried out. On 11th November one crew flew to Lydda in Palestine as an over-sea navigation exercise, and practice in the use of bombsights was a routine. Often, ships in the Gulf of Suez and the Suez Canal were the unwitting targets on these missions. Day and night formation flying, oblique photography, and Link trainer work also formed part of 30 Squadron's intensive preparations in November, and ground-based training for bomb-aimers was completed. However, towards the end of the month a number of failures of stern frames on the Blenheims occurred, reducing the overall serviceability somewhat.

Once 30 Squadron personnel had settled down at Ismailia, most of them enjoyed life, while remembering that there was a war on. Freddie Greenhalgh was one who had good times there. "There was an open-air cinema where one sat at tables on terraces, drinking 'John Collins' served by silent-footed 'wallahs' while watching the film. There was sailing and swimming in Lake Timseh and weekend visits to Cairo and the pyramids. We went in groups of three or four and met 'oppos' from the squadrons at Helwan and Heliopolis, mostly equipped with Gladiators, I think."

Another former member of 30 Squadron was Tom Donohue, who adds his memories of Ismailia, or 'Ish', as it was dubbed. "Ish as a camp was inferior to 'Habb', but its proximity to a town with shops, bars, cafés, dance places and a railway to Cairo made it a more desirable place to be" he remarks. "The town had been built by the French builders of the Suez Canal and was a very attractive place. In about a week [from arrival] the whole squadron was 'broke'. I had fellows borrowing pennies from me for cups of tea. Pay-day was fortnightly, then it all began again. Weekend passes began to be demanded again, much to the annoyance of our WO Discip., 'Chippy' Carpenter, who threw most of them out!" Warrant Officer J. W. S. Carpenter certainly had trouble in curbing the airmen's enthusiasm for the delights of Ismailia. When he began to receive a mass of applications for weekend passes for airmen wanting to go sailing or swimming in Lake Timseh he produced the highly dubious calculation that if 25% of each of the four Flights (including Maintenance Flight) were on leave the

*Flg. Off. R. G. le Dieu, 30 Squadron's adjutant in 1939/40.*

whole squadron would be absent!

Cooperation with searchlight batteries of the Egyptian Army was carried out for the first time on 4th December by five 30 Squadron crews who flew at various speeds and height over the Cairo district. By the end of the exercise the searchlight crews had become proficient in illuminating the Blenheims, so the exercise was regarded as highly valuable for both aircrews and 'defenders'. Evasive tactics which might be employed in future were the subject of a conference next day. A coastal air defence exercise was then planned, and on 9th December two road vehicles carrying a ground party left Ismailia on an overnight journey to El Dhaba. Seven Blenheims flew there on 12th December, each carrying four 250 lb high-explosive bombs and ancillary equipment, though why live armaments were taken is open to conjecture, as after refuelling the aircraft made dummy attacks on a warship and a floating dock in Alexandria harbour, the main railway station at Ismailia and the towns of Kubra, El Mahalla and Zifta. When possible, simulation of bombing using camera guns was carried out. Observer posts east of Port Said were then tested, and mock attacks on Cairo station were made, using 'tactical approach' methods.

More training in the form of direction-finding and homing practice was undertaken on 15th December, when two Blenheims and three crews journeyed to Lydda's civil airport, where presumably modern equipment had been installed. During the same week trainee bomb-aimers were given intensive instruction, and a good standard of efficiency was recorded. Link trainers were used by bomb aimers and air gunners, and some of the latter went to Heliopolis to attend a course on turret manipulation.

Christmas Day 1939 did not allow any let-up in the intensive training programme being undertaken by 30 Squadron, as on that day operational patrols of the Gulf of Suez began, the crews reporting all shipping seen in the area. Refuelling and rearming practice involved loading four 250 lb bombs, reloading front and rear guns and topping up fuel tanks, and this took between 23 and 50 minutes per aircraft.

A similar pattern of preparation for enemy attack and for offensive missions continued in January 1940. Simulated interception by fighter aircraft, including casualties among aircraft and crews, live bombing on Ismailia range and attacks on Amriya airfield were all included, and a good deal of benefit was obtained from the exercises. Patrols over the Gulf of Suez were now being undertaken every day, and every few days upper air temperature measurements were taken at altitudes up to 26,000 feet. Experiments in fuelling techniques were made on 31st January, involving the use of tins or drums of fuel and a hand-operated bowser or tins emptied by hand through a funnel. This latter method was judged to be the quickest, but further trials were considered necessary before a decision was made. In view of the mobility of both bomber and fighter squadrons which would be required in the near future, these trials can be considered as very forward-looking.

On 1st February six of 30 Squadron's Blenheims took part in army manoeuvres in the Wadi Natrun area by carrying out strategic reconnaissance flights. Next day the squadron cooperated with the Gladiators of 112 Squadron, based at Helwan, which carried out interceptions at heights of 15,000 to 20,000 feet. Simulated bombing of Helwan, with photographic evidence, showed an average error of 175 yards. At the same time, more crews went to Lydda for homing practice. Night cross-country exercises occupied many of the crews later in February, involving landings at Amriya and El Dhaba, and more dummy interceptions by Gladiators were made. A change of routine came on 19th February, when all crews attended an anti-submarine course, followed by coding and de-coding of signals in the Naval code.

Early in March three crews left Ismailia on a long-distance navigation flight, landing at Bahariya Oasis, Siwa South, Sidi Barrani and Mersa Matruh. From there the return flight was made at night in formation. For the rest of the month crews underwent continuation training in a number of tasks, all designed to bring them to peak efficiency. This continued through April, often involving the faithful fighter pilots of 112 Squadron, whose Gladiators were now being supplemented by Gauntlets.

As part of a Middle East liaison visit, Sqn. Ldr. J. Cox of the Refresher Squadron at Central Flying School, Upavon, paid a visit to 30 Squadron on 26th March 1940. The CO reported to him that no difficulty in the training of pilots had been experienced apart from a lack of aircraft fitted with dual controls and a slight overheating problem. The 'dual' Blenheim was placed at the disposal of Sqn. Ldr. Cox, who, for the benefit of the Flight commanders, demonstrated an engine failure immediately after take-off, followed by a circuit on one engine. He commented that the general flying ability of the five pilots who he checked for circuit efficiency was good, safe and methodical. All the squadron pilots then gathered in the crew room to listen to a 'pep talk', and all expressed their satisfaction with the Blenheim. Next day it was Sqn. Ldr. Shannon's turn to undergo the 'engine out' test, which he performed perfectly.

An air defence of Egypt exercise on 11th May 1940 involved nine of 30 Squadron's Blenheims, which carried out simulated bombing and tested the observer posts before landing at El Dhaba to refuel. After dark, the Blenheims returned to Ismailia, testing blackout conditions in the Nile Delta and cooperating with searchlight batteries on the way. On 31st May four aircraft flew to El Dhaba to carry out reconnaissance flights over the Western Desert under instructions from the Army Liaison Officer at Maaten Bagush. One such mission included an investigatory flight over the Libyan border, and a great deal of useful practice was obtained by the crews. Living conditions, however, were spartan, and the detachment personnel found themselves digging slit trenches in case there was an Italian raid. During the month three Beaufort aircraft of 22 Squadron, based at North Coates in Lincolnshire, were attached to 30 Squadron for training.

## Italy enters the war

All the training undergone by 30 Squadron crews was justified on 10th June 1940, when Mussolini brought Italy into the war on the Axis side. Next day, in accordance with an Operational Order issued by 202 Group, seven of the squadron's aircraft were loaded with 250lb GP bombs and took off at 06.30 in two Flights for El Dhaba. There, the Blenheims were refuelled, but a strategic reconnaissance of the Western Desert which had been planned was cancelled, and the aircraft returned to Ismailia, where their bombs were unloaded. Later in the morning, on the instructions of 252 Wing, two Blenheims were detached to Amriya and two to Helwan to shadow any enemy aircraft which might appear. At Ismailia, orders were received to send three Blenheims of 'C' Flight to 103 MU at Aboukir immediately so that four-gun conversion sets could be fitted, the first examples in the Middle East. This was achieved by removing the bomb doors and fitting two cradles into the bomb bay, replacing the bomb cradles. Each cradle mounted two .303 Browning guns and ammunition tanks. The whole bay was closed by a large tray secured to the underside of the bomb bay, the scheme effectively converting the aircraft into a fighter. These gunpacks were manufactured in England in the workshops of the Southern Railway.

On 12th June 1940, 30 Squadron, commanded by Sqn. Ldr. U. Y. Shannon, had fifteen Blenheim Mk.I aircraft on strength and was divided into three Flights, each with six or seven officer or NCO pilots. Flight commanders were Flt. Lt. A. C. Bocking DFC ('A' Flight); Flg. Off. I. C. Swann ('B' Flight); and Flt. Lt. F. A. Marlow ('C' Flight). Ground personnel comprised one Warrant Officer, six Flight Sergeants, nineteen Sergeants, 36 Corporals and 238 other ranks. By 15th June, nine Blenheims had been fitted with the four-gun pack, and three more had been allocated to 30 Squadron from other units. Only the six aircraft of 'A' Flight continued in the bomber role. Even with the benefit of a normal single forward-firing gun, the conversion gave an offensive power only a little over half that of a Hurricane. With its lack of speed and manoeuvrability, the Blenheim fighter was considered of little use as a bomber escort, but could be effective in the ground attack role, although it was very vulnerable to return fire, as there was no armour plating or self-sealing fuel tanks.

The aircraft detached to Amriya and Helwan were now replaced by fighter versions, just in time, as on 16th June a warning was received of three enemy aircraft approaching Helwan. However, as no contact was made, the warning may well have been a false alarm. Another alarm was sounded on 21st June, and one fighter Blenheim took off to patrol the area between Abu Sueir and Qantara, again without result. The remainder of the month passed uneventfully, allowing continuation training to proceed.

Two Blenheim fighters had been detached on 16th June to

operate from Qasaba, from where they carried out patrols over Italian territory south of Sollum and over Mersa Matruh. On 19th June they flew in company with six Gladiators over Sidi Barrani and Buq Buq. While the two 30 Squadron aircraft were patrolling over the sea the Gladiators had managed to shoot down no less than four Italian aircraft, but the Blenheims arrived on the scene too late to take part, to their crews' intense frustration! On 22nd June the detachment moved with 33 Squadron to a landing ground at Gerawla, from where patrols at an altitude of 18,000 feet at dawn, during the day and at last light were carried out, but no more enemy aircraft were seen. Gerawla was nothing more than a strip of desert between Sollum and Sidi Barrani from which camelthorn and scrub had been cleared. No flare-path was provided, so movements after dark were by the light of a red hurricane lamp at one end of the strip. Three days later the two Blenheims returned to Ismailia on being relieved by three of 'A' Flight's aircraft. A further Blenheim arrived early in July for conversion to fighter status.

On 1st July the AOC-in-C Middle East, AVM Sir A. M. Longmore KCB DSO, visited Ismailia to talk to pilots of 30 Squadron and the Pilots Reinforcement & Reserve Pool. Three days later the squadron was ordered to move to Ikingi Maryut, twenty miles south-west of Alexandria, where airfield construction had been in hand for several days. Frank Addington, a navigator, was in charge of four airmen who had the job of recruiting twenty or thirty Arabs to remove boulders and dig trenches. "My complete knowledge of Arabic" he wrote later "consisted of yalla (go), stenna (stop) shufti (look) and baksheesh (money). An English civilian came from Alexandria and did the pay parade for the Arabs, and severely criticised the fact that one of them was completely blind! Shannon came to pick me up and threatened a Court of Enquiry and flew me back to Ismailia. It was small comfort that he had forgotten to take the cover off the pitot head and was furious with himself". Packing began without delay. An advance party consisting of twelve vehicles and fifty-four personnel left Ismailia at 06.00 on 6th July and began pitching camp at Ikingi at 17.00. The main ground party of 28 vehicles carrying 191 men made the journey two days later, and the squadron's ten Ismailia-based aircraft flew in that morning. The squadron's photographic section, however, did not follow, and was disbanded. At Ikingi, most airmen had a camp bed of some sort, there was a good supply of water and beer was obtainable. Once a week, a bus was made available to take men to Alexandria, a welcome break for all concerned.

By 11th July one Flight of 30 Squadron, placed under 252 Wing as from that date, was at readiness, and next day the Helwan detachment arrived at Ikingi. Six aircraft were then put up for escort duty, landing at Maaten Bagush at the end of their mission. Airborne from there on 13th July, three Blenheims made contact with the fleet as ordered, and immediately spotted three hostile S.79 aircraft which were about to attack the ships, which included HMS *Royal Sovereign*, 160 miles north of Mersa Matruh. While one Blenheim shadowed the fleet in case of further attack, the other two engaged the enemy, one of which was seen to dive away trailing smoke from its starboard engine. The rear gunner in the enemy leader's aircraft was then put out of action. However, Blenheim K7181 was hit by enemy fire and crashed into the sea in flames. Its crew parachuted into the water, and one of the other crews went down to see whether

*Ablutions at Ikingi Maryut*        *[E. Wallis].*

a dingy could be dropped to them but could not locate them. Attempts were made to contact the fleet by radio, without success, so a return was made to Maaten Bagush, where the incident was reported. Further efforts to find the crew were abortive, and so Flg. Off. I. C. Swann, Sgt. C. F. Burt and Sgt. J. Young became 30 Squadron's first fatalities of the Second World War.

When the Amriya detachment arrived at Ikingi on 14th July the squadron was complete. Until 25th July, when bombs were dropped in Alexandria, there was no action, although AVM Sir Arthur Longmore, paid a visit to the squadron on 23rd July.

Eight aircraft went to Maaten Bagush on 27th July to work under the direction of 202 Group, and next day carried out operations along the Libyan border. On 28th July at 06.10 three of them took off to fly a reconnaissance at 6000 feet, but while flying in and out of cloud visual contact with K7178 was lost and it failed to return to base, with the loss of Flt. Sgt. Innes-Smith and Cpl. Stewart. At the same time, the crews of two 30 Squadron Blenheims escorting a similar aircraft of 113 Squadron on a reconnaissance flight sighted a Blenheim diving away with three enemy CR.32 fighters in pursuit, and this may well have been the missing K7178.

Severe dust storms inhibited flying during the first few days of August 1940, but afterwards local training was carried out, as well as some cooperation with the Gladiators of 80 Squadron, based at Amriya. Standing patrols recommenced on 9th August, mainly around Alexandria. On 15th August seven Blenheims flew to Maaten Bagush to attack flying boats and seaplanes moored in Menelaio Bay in the Gulf of Bomba (an appropriate name!) in conjunction with Fuka-based 55 Squadron, which flew similar aircraft. One aircraft returned to base, but the other six took off at 14.05 and took up position with eleven aircraft of 55 Squadron. After flying out to sea for about thirty miles at 17,000 feet, the formation turned towards the coast, and 55 Squadron went into line astern and descended. They dropped their bombs on the slipway and among the flying boats, and five minutes later 30 Squadron made a converging attack, all front guns firing until their ammunition was exhausted. One Cant Z506B seaplane was seen to tip onto its nose in the water, and it was believed that all the enemy aircraft must have been damaged by gunfire if not by 55 Squadron's bombs. A fuel dump caught fire, and the flames spread to an equipment store while burning fuel flowed down the slope to engulf two seaplanes. No enemy fighters were seen, and the only damage to a 30 Squadron aircraft comprised three bullet holes in a wing, probably from a rear gun in one of the moored flying boats. At 19.45 all six aircraft were back at Ikingi Maryut. When the area was captured by the British army, thirteen severely damaged flying boats were found.

Six aircraft of 30 Squadron were detached to Fuka on 17th August for fleet escort duty, as were aircraft of 33 and 80 Squadrons and the French Fighter Flight. Their task was to escort the fleet returning to Alexandria after carrying out raids on Bardia and Fort Capuzzio in Libya, but no enemy aircraft were encountered and the six Blenheims returned to base early next morning. For the rest of August, spasmodic patrols were flown without opposition.

Stormy weather again prevented much action in September, although a few patrols over Alexandria harbour were possible. When the weather cleared on 10th September, 202 Group ordered two aircraft to go to Maaten Bagush to carry out protective standing patrols over Mersa Matruh. Soon after the Blenheims had attained altitude, the crews saw a formation of six S.79 aircraft approaching from the north-east at 17,000 feet in two Flights of three. Gladiators and Hurricanes quickly appeared and shot down the leading aircraft of the second vic before dealing with one of the others, which went into a steep dive and crashed into the sea. While on patrol on 11th September, Plt. Off. S. N. Pearce received a message from his controller to the effect that an unidentified aircraft was approaching Alexandria. From an altitude of 17,000 feet, he climbed to 20,000 feet and spotted the intruder, an S.79 reconnaissance aircraft, flying in the opposite direction towards Aboukir. Following it, he drew to a range of 200 yards and opened fire, whereupon the enemy aircraft turned west and out to sea. A second burst of gunfire brought smoke from an engine, and after two more attacks the intruder lost height, circled and hit the water, although it was fifteen minutes before it sank. When four men were seen in the water, a dinghy was dropped from the Blenheim, which

then had to make for base as it was short of fuel.

Further patrols were flown on four subsequent days without any enemy aircraft being seen, but when on 15th September four S.79s dropped bombs east of Sidi Barrani they were chased by the two Blenheims of 30 Squadron, piloted by Flt. Lt. Marlow and Plt. Off. Jarvis. As the enemy aircraft were now diving from 10,000 feet to sea level, it took 25 minutes to catch them, but then the gunners were able to bring concentrated fire to bear. Pieces of fabric were seen to come off one enemy aircraft, which lost formation as if crippled, and later it was confirmed that it had not reached its base.

On 18th September a protective patrol was flown over HMS *Kent*, which was said to be lying disabled twenty miles from Bardia, but the vessel could not be located and when it was found to be under tow the mission was called off.

Three aircraft of 'A' Flight were detached on 1st October to operate from Haifa, to where kit and spares were sent in a Bombay aircraft. The Blenheims had not been there long before Plt. Off. T. M. C. Allison, returning from a patrol, overshot the runway, went round again, made a second approach with flaps up and over-ran, turning over in the process. The aircraft, K7106, was written off. Standing patrols were flown, and after one such mission Blenheim K7180 was caught in a downdraught just before touchdown and struck the built-up end of the runway. With its undercarriage wiped of, the Blenheim slid along on its belly and caught fire. After a time the French fire engine arrived but was found to be useless, and the aircraft was engulfed in flames and was destroyed. Luckily the crew were not injured. Flying with 30 Squadron from Haifa was a Potez 63 twin-engined fighter, presumably belonging to the French Air Force but possibly on loan to the RAF.

One Blenheim, crewed by Flt. Lt. Bocking, Sgt. Pease and Sgt. Vellacott, with LAC Spalding as the 'flying fitter' was detached to Nicosia in Cyprus in October. The airport there had been overflown a number of times by Cant 1007 aircraft of the Regia Aeronautica, probably carrying out photo-reconnaissance sorties. All the runways were therefore blocked by oil drums to prevent enemy landings but as there was no further activity the Blenheim returned to Haifa on 2nd November. At Ikingi Maryut, October was occupied by the usual standing patrols until the end of the month, when orders were received for a squadron move to Greece. The Haifa detachment therefore packed and returned to Ikingi Maryut on 3rd November.

One of the men who went to Haifa with the squadron was Mr. D. R. Cherry, who remembers that a British army infantry regiment was in charge of the camp. "There was no proper NAAFI, and we only got a few things dished out by an infantry sergeant," he said many years later. "We were on almost a starvation diet, and could not see why. There was a big fuss, and we had a meeting in the cookhouse with the 'Buffs' CO, and there was a proper row, I acted as spokesman but didn't get much support. A complaint was sent to the CO in Egypt, and later an investigation was made. It was found that the cookhouse staff were selling a lot of the rations in Haifa. Mr. Anthony Eden and some officials came to the camp and carried out a thorough investigation. Three days later the RAF took over the camp and things became more normal. We also had a proper NAAFI installed."

## The Greek campaign

At a meeting on 4th October 1940, Adolf Hitler agreed to the launch of an attack on Greece by Italy, largely because Greece was Great Britain's last remaining ally on the continent of Europe. He considered that such an attack would put Britain under increased pressure and should reduce its capability of continuing the war with Italy in Egypt.

Mussolini, the Italian Fascist dictator, invaded Greece on 28th October, following an ultimatum in which he demanded right of passage for Italian troops across the country. While aircraft of the Regia Aeronautica bombed Athens, ten divisions of Italian troops crossed the border from Albania through the Epirus mountains. The Greek defenders put up a strong resistance, and allowed the Italian troops to wear themselves out in frontal attacks until Greek reinforcements arrived.

Britain quickly determined to provide full support to Greece in resisting aggression, and an improvised force under AVM J. H. d'Albiac CB DSO was prepared. To avoid provoking Germany, no airfields further forward than those near Athens could at first be

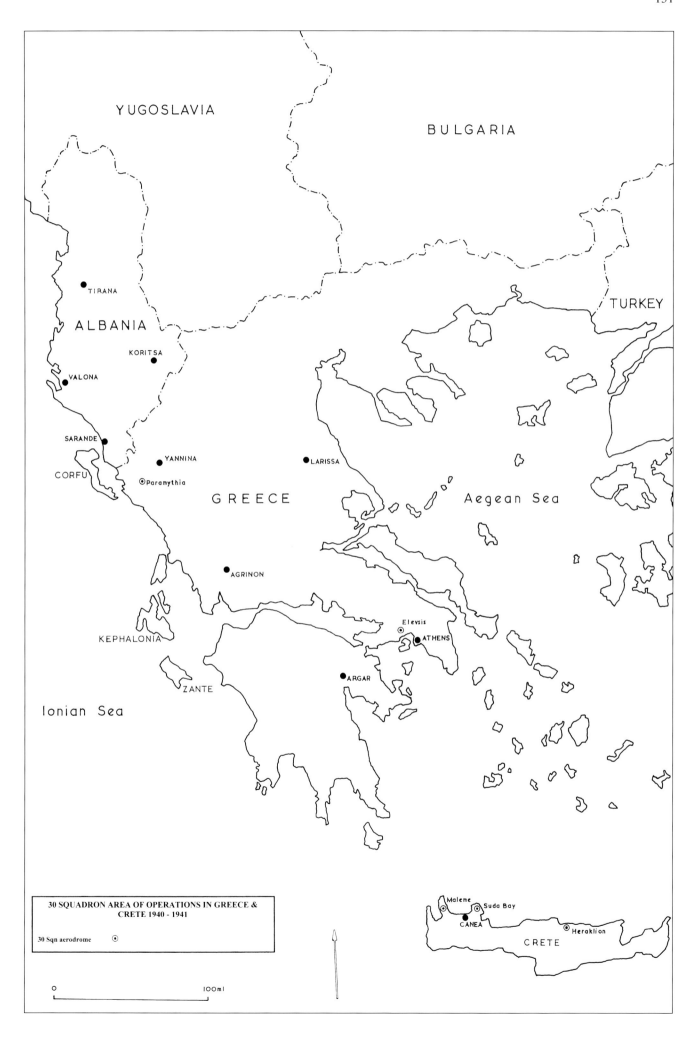

YUGOSLAVIA

BULGARIA

TURKEY

● TIRANA

ALBANIA

● KORITSA

● VALONA

● SARANDE

CORFU

● YANNINA

⊙ Paramythia

G R E E C E

● LARISSA

Aegean Sea

● AGRINON

KEPHALONIA

Elevsis ⊙

⊙ ● ATHENS

● ARGAR

ZANTE

Ionian Sea

**30 SQUADRON AREA OF OPERATIONS IN GREECE &
CRETE 1940 - 1941**

30 Sqn aerodrome          ⊙

0                    100 ml

Maleme
⊙      ⊙ Suda Bay
● CANEA
⊙ Heraklion
C R E T E

WHITE
STEWART
MORGAN
MILL.
RANDLE
FREW (kneeling)

*A group of 30 Squadron NCO aircrew at Ismailia in October 1940. Sgt. Stewart was the WOp/AG on Sgt. Childes' aircraft and was killed in the Koritza raid on 15th November 1940.*

used as bases for the RAF bombers. 30 Squadron was one of the units to be involved in this new campaign, and would be based at Eleusis, the uncompleted Athens airport, north-west of the city, to provide the air defence of Athens. After every item of stores and kit had been packed, Bombay aircraft of 216 Squadron air-lifted an advance party to Eleusis on 2nd November. At the same time, a small refuelling party moved to Iraklion in Crete to deal with aircraft which might land there. Next day eight of the squadron's Blenheims left Ikingi Maryut for the last time at 07.00 and made for Fuka, where they landed at 09.40 to refuel. Seven of them touched down at Eleusis at 13.10, the eighth having landed at Iraklion with slight engine trouble. After inspection, this Blenheim also arrived safely at Eleusis. Four Bombays were in the air by 06.30 carrying 24 men and 16,000 lbs of equipment, and after refuelling at Iraklion

they arrived at a rainy Eleusis at 14.00. The Bombays made their way back to Ikingi Maryut next day to uplift further loads of personnel and equipment, while one Flight of 30 Squadron was at readiness for operations and one Flight 'available'. It was not long before six Blenheims were in the air to intercept a Cant 501 aircraft, but they failed to find it. Better weather on 5th November allowed the squadron to make twelve patrols, although there were no interceptions, and four more Blenheims arrived from Ikingi via Fuka. The hard-working Bombays of 216 Squadron also arrived, bringing yet more men and equipment, including personnel of 'A' Flight who had been detached to Haifa. The squadron's main party, however, braved the rigours of the Mediterranean Sea by travelling aboard HMS *Orion* from Alexandria.

For the first three days, no cooking facilities were avalable at Eleusis, so the local people provided food, usually cold chicken and a bottle of beer. The mayor gave a speech of welcome, and arranged for personnel to visit the public baths in Athens. Eleusis, as remembered by Arthur 'Ginger' Henderson, was a draughty place but quite luxurious compared with 'digging-in' on detachment in Egypt. "The background of hills was quite beautiful" he says "and it was interesting to see the sun flashing on binoculars being used by interested watchers!" No doubt some of them at least had sinister motives. Former Cpl. R. J. Lawrence wrote many years later that "..........the scenery was quite spectacular, making it almost humourous to see airmen standing at the hangar doors gazing at the snow-capped mountains. Many 'old lags' had seen little but sand for years, so this was an invigorating sight for them."

At Eleusis, men of the Greek Air Force provided support of a general duties nature to the squadron. Unpaid and poorly clothed, they nevertheless welcomed the chance of helping the RAF men, who were considered to be Greece's potential saviours. For a time, Greek cooks fed the squadron, but when the war became more intense RAF cooks took over. In charge of the squadron's Inspection & Repair Flight was Sqn. Ldr. (then Flt. Sgt.) George Hartup, who remembered the feeding problems that were encountered. "As we were relying on the Greek Air Force for rationing, and food was not readily available at any rate, all we got for breakfast was a totally insufficient amount of black bread roll with some sort of jam!" he recalls. "We discovered a splendid mobile field kitchen which was not being used; this we

*Important members of 30 Squadron in Greece were the cooks, seen here with their mascot.*

*A formation of 30 Squadron Blenheims over Greece in November 1940.*

commandeered and appointed one of our junior fitters to service it and nurse it back to healthy production" he continues. "We also commandeered a mobile workshop lorry which was beautifully appointed with every tool a tradesman could wish for, including a lathe. We made good use of these vehicles, both of which were of German manufacture, and equipment."

Maintenance personnel soon became totally engrossed in keeping the overworked Blenheims in the air. For them, each 24-hour period consisted of work, eat and sleep. "Hardly had we received an aircraft for whatever reason than someone (the Flight commander, no doubt) would be asking 'How long will you have her for?' or 'Can we rely on having her for tomorrow's operation?'" says Sqn. Ldr. Hartup. Not far away there was a Stores Park, but it had little to offer in the way of spares for Blenheims. However, it was discovered that in an Athens workshop run by an Englishman the Blenheims used by the Greek Air Force were being repaired, so the stock of spare parts there was raided!

On 4th November Greek troops counter-attacked and pushed the enemy force back. This was extremely annoying to Hitler, who quickly realised that Germany might have to invade Greece, even though such a move would upset Yugoslavia, Turkey and Bulgaria, which had granted Germany the use of bases. Nevertheless, Hitler was determined to prevent the use of bases in Greece by Britain. In his eyes, the seizure of airfields in Greece from which the Luftwaffe might control the eastern Mediterranean seemed an excellent move.

Now fully prepared, 30 Squadron began offensive reconnaissance missions on 6th November, when three crews led by Sqn. Ldr. Shannon took off for Trikkala, where the aircraft would refuel. At Savaade two ships were seen and a salvo of three bombs was dropped but missed. The Blenheims then carried on to Valona in Albania, where about fifty Italian CR.42 and S.79 aircraft were spotted on the ground. Two salvos of 250lb bombs were dropped on this choice target from 2500 feet and 1000 feet, and one S.79 was hit. Personnel at the airfield were taken completely by surprise, and after the CO had fired on anything which moved the three Blenheims made off. One CR.42 took off in an attempt to effect retribution, and caught up after ten minutes, but after firing for twenty minutes without great success it broke off over Corfu. All three aircraft were riddled with holes, and unfortunately there was one casualty among the 30 Squadron crews. The air gunner in No.3 aircraft, Sgt. J. Mereifield, was killed, and his body was interred at the English Church in Athens next day.

Poor weather on 8th and 9th November prevented any offensive operations, but on 10th November three aircraft of 'A'

Flight raided and demolished a jetty at Konispol and damaged docks at Saranda, just missing a 7000-ton freighter. Blenheims of 'A' Flight were in action again next day, when three of them carried out a high-level raid on docks at Valona, and on 13th November, when the airfield at Argyokastron was the target. Located in the valley of the river Dhruno, the airfield was obscured by cloud at 5000 feet, so the Blenheims flew up the valley, bombed, and returned the same way. All bombs fell close to fighter aircraft at dispersals, and two of them took off to intercept, without making contact. There was a great deal of AA fire but no damage to the Blenheims was caused.

A raid by three aircraft on 70 Italian motor vehicles on the road between Pogradee and Koritsa on 14th November was deemed successful, and a large building thought to be a headquarters was also hit. Strongly-defended positions north-east of Koritsa were raided next day by three Blenheims, but this time five CR.42 and three Fiat G.50 fighters were in the air. Fighter escort was provided by seven Polish-built PZL-24 aircraft of the Greek Air Force, but all seven were shot down before the Blenheims' bomb-loads were released. Evasive action was needed, and unfortunately Blenheim L1120, piloted by Sgt. E. B.'Joey' Childs with Sgt. G. G. Stewart and LAC D. Stott as crew, was shot down in flames by an Italian fighter which made a single passing attack from forward and below as the Blenheim climbed away. It has since been discovered that the

*Flg. Off. Derek Walker and two 'Evzones' at Eleusis in November 1940. Their ceremonial costume, amusing to British eyes, belie the fearsome fighting qualities of these men.*

*Three airmen of 30 Squadron with a Greek serviceman during a day out in Athens.*

*Sgt. Maxie and ? Maudsley on Radio 'Taverna', a weekly show broadcast from Athens.* [E. W. Walker].

enemy aircraft was probably a Fiat CR-42 of 393 Squadriglia. The other two Blenheims, piloted by Flt. Lt. Bocking and Flg. Off. R. T. P. Davidson, set course for base.

After a night raid on Elbasan on 17th November, dawn to dusk standing patrols were maintained over a convoy of four cruisers and eight other vessels carrying anti-aircraft guns and the personnel of 80 and 211 Squadrons and their mobile equipment to Greece. At Eleusis, four Bofors light anti-aircraft guns were set up, and the squadron's motor vehicles were earmarked for use in defending the airfield. Standing patrols continued over the next few days, particularly on 20th November, when King George of Greece and Prince Paul paid a visit to 30 Squadron and other units at Eleusis.

The beginning of the squadron's route to the targets was always the same: west along the Gulf of Corinth to Patras and then north-west. After a time it was noticed that the Blenheims were being intercepted by enemy fighters on the way to the target, near it, and on the return journey. It was obvious that the enemy was receiving prior warning of the missions. Greek soldiers soon caught a man with a radio in an ancient temple just outside Eleusis and quietly dealt with him.

When not flying, crews sometimes made evening trips to Athens, where visits to night-clubs such as Zonar's, Maxim's and the Argentina were enjoyed. Most of the hostesses at these clubs were Hungarian girls fluent in German, some known to be employed by Greek security. Arguments with Germans posing as holiday makers at these places were not unknown, and sometimes came to blows! Another way in which personnel could relax was to listen to Athens Radio. Sqn. Ldr. R. A. Milward DFC, who took over from Sqn. Ldr. Shannon on 1st January 1941, remembers one of the programmes. "To keep the troops entertained during spells of bad weather, a weekly programme was arranged, which not only served [the forces] but became highly popular with the Greek public too, and made a direct contribution to the friendly relations which existed." The show became known as 'The Bafflers' and many RAF squadrons took part. 30 Squadron's contribution had the honour of being voted the best performance and was provided by Derek , one of the Flight commanders.

This happy state of affairs is also remembered by Mr. D. R. Cherry, who says that the men were allowed out quite frequently. "When we went to a Greek café or bar in uniform they all stood up and the band would play our National Anthem. We couldn't believe it at first. All our drinks and food were given to us and we couldn't pay for a thing. They took us to other cafés and really fêted us" he said. However, when the army arrived in Athens all the best places were put 'out of bounds' to other ranks!

"Operating in a country at war with Italy but with a strong and on the surface friendly relationship with the Germans was a strange experience" says Sqn. Ldr. Milward. "The Greek armed forces had largely been trained by Germans, many [of whom] remained in Athens. The German Legation was active, and there was an ever-present mass of German 'tourists' actively spreading rumours to damage relations between the British and Greek people. The Greeks, although welcoming the British help in their war against Italy, were most keen that their British friends' presence would do nothing to strain their relationship with Germany."

Three Blenheims of 'A' (Bomber) Flight set off at 03.45 on 21st November to raid the Tepleni area, but the crews found that the target was obscured by cloud. Bombs were dropped from one aircraft, but one returned to base with bombs aboard and the third became lost and belly-landed on a beach at Zagora, east of Volos, without injury to Flg. Off. Richardson or his crew. Operations for the remainder of November were affected by poor weather conditions, crews often bringing their aircraft back without having seen the target. However, the good news was that on 22nd November the Greeks defeated the Italian aggressors at Koritsa, the enemy HQ in Albania, where large quantities of stores and ammunition were left behind.

Another Blenheim of 30 Squadron was lost on 1st December 1940 when taking part in an abortive raid on Saranda by three aircraft. After suffering engine failure caused by carburettor icing, K7103 went into a spin. Sgt. Gallagher, the pilot, ordered his crew to bale out, but it was discovered that as the observer's parachute pack was out of reach they all stayed put. Still spinning, the Blenheim eventually broke into clear air at 7000 feet over a narrow valley, and Gallagher managed to stabilise the aircraft. A small field which turned out to be 14 miles north of Khalkis appeared, and Gallagher belly-landed the Blenheim, which before long had burnt out. All on board survived, and after a three-day trek returned, somewhat tired, to Eleusis. The same target was attacked again two days later, this time in good weather, and the three Blenheims dropped eleven bombs on Saranda harbour. The target was a troopship, but 30 Squadron's efforts failed to have any effect on it.

In Hitler's opinion, Mussolini should have succeeded in overcoming the Greek army, which was greatly outnumbered. A significant reason for the defeat was the dispersal of the Italian army between Libya and Ethiopia, rendering it less than fully effective, and another factor was that the Division which attacked Greece was weaker in many respects than the Greek army and the troops were not well motivated. Mussolini's motives for war with

Greece included a desire to bask in Hitler's successes, to establish bases from which British interests in the eastern Mediterranean could be attacked, and to reassert Italy's influence in Balkan states. With Greek forces in Albania, Hitler feared that German sources of strategic materials in Yugoslavia and Greece might be compromised and therefore ordered an invasion of the Balkans, Operation 'Marita'.

Further raids on Saranda were staged by 30 Squadron on 4th December, when a direct hit on a destroyer was scored, and on 6th December, although this mission had to be abandoned due to adverse weather. Conditions improved by 14.00 that day, and three fighter Blenheims of 'B' Flight took off to strafe enemy vehicles moving along a coastal road between Saranda and Valona. Two hours later one aircraft returned to Eleusis with engine trouble and the other two were reported as missing. Later both were found to have force-landed, one on the island of Corfu (Flg. Off. Blackmore's aircraft) and the other (Plt. Off. Crowther) 37 miles south-west of Agrimim.

In a briefing to war correspondents in December 1940, the AOC stated that flying conditions in Greece were more difficult than anywhere else in Europe. "The weather changes with great rapidity" he said "making accurate forecasts impossible, and the nature of the country does not always allow landings when pilots are unable to regain their bases. Ice formation is another difficulty; instruments freeze and airscrews get a covering of ice which makes it difficult to maintain sufficient altitude to clear the mountains. The temperature is never more than 28 degrees [F] and sometimes goes to minus 50 degrees." The two forced landings on 6th December served to confirm what the AOC had said about the difficulties often experienced.

Standing patrols continued, and on 10th December three fighter and two bomber Blenheims were flown in from Egypt as attrition replacements. No more offensive operations were possible until 18th December, when three bomber Blenheims of 'A' Flight took off to make an offensive reconnaissance of Valona harbour. They dropped bombs on the seaplane hangars there, but were soon engaged in a running battle with six CR.42s and three Macchi 200s. After the enemy aircraft had broken off the battle, the port engine of one Blenheim was seen to be on fire, and before long the aircraft ditched seven miles west of Saranda. One of the crew waved as the leader orbited the site, and a dingy was dropped and a distress message sent to base.

Even on Christmas Day there was little if any respite for the air or ground crews of 30 Squadron until 16.00, when they were stood down. Adverse weather had led to bad conditions on the airfield, and it was 28th December before the next mission could take place. This was a high altitude raid on Valona harbour in an attempt to dislocate disembarkation of troops, but the weather again prevented bombs being dropped. A similar raid was mounted next day, this time with more success. Bombs were dropped in the sea near the harbour, causing a number of small ships to disperse, and on MT vehicles and a warehouse, which was set on fire. However, the enemy decided not to take this without retaliating, and three CR.42s and a Fiat G.50 made an attack on the Blenheims. The aircraft flown by the leader, Flt. Lt. H. D. Card, was hit and was seen to crash into the sea, two of the crew taking to their parachutes. It is now known that this Blenheim was shot down by Sgt. Arrigo Zoli of 154 Gruppo. The other two aircraft returned to base, where one landed with its undercarriage retracted as a tyre had been burst in the attack.

Next day it was possible to retaliate. Six crews led by the CO were detailed to make a fighter patrol over the area between Previza and Levkas, and before long a Cant Z.506B twin-float seaplane heading out to sea was sighted. Sqn. Ldr. Shannon closed to within 25 yards and used all his guns to shoot it down into the sea. Flying as No.2, Flg. Off. Richardson closed in on another Cant Z.506B and also shot it down. Both 'kills' were later confirmed by the Greek Navy. In the course of the battle, Sgt. F. Goulding, the CO's gunner, was hit above the knee by an explosive bullet, and a landing was made at Agrinion to allow him to be taken to hospital. Unfortunately, serious loss of blood brought about the death of Sgt. Goulding, who was buried at Agrinion.

For the first two weeks of January 1941, 30 Squadron crews remained at readiness in weather which was sometimes bad enough to put Eleusis airfield out of action. The squadron was pleased to welcome the AOC-in-C when he paid a visit on 17th January to talk to the aircrews and ground personnel. Two days later came the first operation of the year, when two Blenheims of 'A' Flight on a three-hour anti-submarine patrol. At 13.00, an enemy aircraft, thought to be a He 111 carrying out a reconnaissance, was seen at about 1600 feet over Eleusis. No warning had been given, and the local AA did not open fire, but two fighter Blenheims of 'C' Flight took off to intercept. One of them followed the enemy aircraft for about a hundred miles but failed to catch it, and the opinion was that it had succeeded in making a good reconnaissance of both Eleusis and Menidi airfields and Piraeus harbour – not a good omen.

Early in the new year, the 30 Squadron 'immediate repair' ground-crews were moved out of Eleusis for sleeping and feeding, for security in the heavier air raids now taking place. Their new home was in Aspropiragus, a tiny white-walled village nestling in the foothills. It was soon discovered that the residents of one half of the village were strongly pro-British and those of the other half equally strongly pro-German, reflecting the stance of the Greek populace in general. At Aspropiragus the dividing line was the through road, so the RAF men were lodged on the 'correct' side! After settling down, Cpl. R. J. Lawrence, the squadron's supply corporal, established several outside contacts for cigarettes, beer, milk, bread, cocoa, cheese and other comestibles, an attempt being made to undercut the prices in the Eleusis NAAFI! Learning of the enterprise, men from Eleusis began to visit the village to partake of the service, but the manager of the NAAFI was not amused. A radio set was bought from profits made at Aspropiragus, and there was even a cash hand-out to regular customers when their pay was delayed by enemy action. This was not a loan but a gift, which surprised the recipients more than somewhat.

Things now began to 'hot up' in the Athens area. In view of the fact that an enemy aircraft had flown over the area, standing patrols were intensified, particularly over the Corinth Canal. In this, 30 Squadron was assisted by the Gladiators of 80 Squadron, which had been in Greece since 19th November 1940 and were now based at Iannina, with a detachment at Eleusis. On 20th January at 12.30 the alarm was sounded, and two Blenheim fighters and five Gladiators took off to intercept five enemy aircraft over Piraeus. At 13.15 five Cant. Z.1007 three-engined bombers of the Regia Aeronautica were sighted by a Blenheim crew, who opened fire, but it was a Gladiator pilot who succeeded in shooting one Cant down into the sea ten miles south of Athens. Four of the crew baled out and were taken prisoner.

After an abortive attempt by two Blenheims to intercept twelve enemy aircraft heading south from Salonika on 24th January, 30 Squadron mounted its next offensive operation next day. Three Blenheims of 'A' Flight were loaded with 40lb and 20lb bombs for a raid on a supply depot at Boultsar in Albania. While approaching the target at 15.05 and descending to below cloud level, the formation was intercepted by six Fiat G.50 fighters. No.3 aircraft was attacked three times and although the air gunner, Sgt. W. Ackroyd, was wounded each time he continued to return fire. In formation, the Blenheims proceeded to drop their bombs in the target area, causing many fires and explosions. All three aircraft returned to base badly holed. Sgt. Ackroyd was awarded an immediate DFM for the brave way in which he helped to fight off the enemy attack.

Apart from the Gladiators of 80 Squadron, other fighter squadrons were now arriving in Greece from Egypt to lend a hand. Nine Gladiators of 112 Squadron arrived at Eleusis on 23rd January from Amriya, and next day five Blenheims of 11 Squadron came from Helwan via Sidi Barrani. Neither squadron was destined to remain at Eleusis for long, however, as both moved to other Greek airfields within a few days, although 112 Squadron maintained a detached Flight at Eleusis for a time. This Flight and 30 Squadron were at high alert on 31st January on the occasion of the funeral of General Metaxas in Athens. In Athens that day was Arthur Henderson and his mate 'Frigger' Walker, who tried to keep a low profile but were pulled from the crowd and stood in front as the cortege passed. The first dignitary was the German ambassador, who, says Mr. Henderson "was the most arrogant, haughty slob we had ever seen. He looked us up and down and literally sneered. I reckon he knew what was coming in the near future."

*Seen at Eleusis in December 1940 or January 1941 were (left to right): 'Lofty' Lord; Flt. Lt. Card; unknown; unknown; 'Twiggy' Branch; Flg. Off. Carter; three unknown; Vellacott*         *[E. W. Walker].*

With better weather in the offing, formation flying practice was one of the exercises carried out by 30 Squadron early in February 1941. Greek islands which are now well-known holiday destinations, such as Zante and Cephalonia, were treated as navigation points on these trips, the Blenheim crews perhaps wondering what they were like. On 3rd February a nearly-completed all-weather runway at Eleusis was tested, and it was considered that the efficiency of the squadron would increase dramatically when the new surface came into use. There is no record of the construction of the runway, but it is safe to assume that it involved some form of tarmacadam or asphalt. Progress was also made in direction-finding techniques using both W/T and R/T, a number of Class 1 bearings being attained. These facilities would, it was felt, add to 30 Squadron's capabilities if and when the situation in Greece worsened.

Two of the Blenheim bombers of 'A' Flight were sent on 9th February to Paramythia, a landing ground in a deep valley close to the Albanian border, on overnight detachment. In ancient Greek 'the valley of fairy tales', Paramythia was within thirty minutes' flying time from targets which included the supply base at Valona. By taking off before dawn and arriving over the target at first light it was possible to avoid fighter interception. At Eleusis, meanwhile, standing patrols were maintained by the fighters of the other two Flights. Hostile aircraft were reported over the Athens area quite often, and there were small-scale bombing raids on nearby Piraeus docks. A further detachment to Paramythia left Eleusis on 12th February, this time with the specific task of working with 84 and 211 Squadrons on short-distance raids on Tepelene next day. When their crews arrived at Eleusis for refuelling, they were able to report a successful mission, having dropped their bombs accurately on gun emplacements and motor vehicles along the Buzi road. The Blenheims, augmented by a fourth aircraft, left for Paramythia for

*Sqn. Ldr. R. A. Milward, the CO of 30 Squadron, and Flt. Lt. Hogan at Eleusis in February 1941 [E. W. Walker].*

*Blenheim K7095, coded VT:G, at an unidentified location, possibly Paramythia. In the distance, a Wellington can be seen receiving attention.*

further missions, and on 14th February made two raids on the same area around Buzi, where gun posts and MT on local roads were attacked with great success in poor weather conditions. No enemy fighters intervened, and AA fire was minimal. After a similar raid in the afternoon of 15th February, the aircraft of 'A' Flight returned to Eleusis.

Members of the Paramythia detachment lived in tents, slept on the ground and ate bully beef and 'hard tack' prepared in a variety of ingenious ways. Some of the bully beef was dated 1917, and although well past its 'sell-by' date was in perfect condition. One night a storm developed, and before long small brooks and rivulets were coursing down the mountainsides. Many of the tents were blown over while the ground crews were bombing up the

Blenheims for the next raid. Later in the morning a fierce gale blew some of the tents right away from the site, but then the storm abated and the sun came out. The unfortunate tentless men walked with all their wet kit to the nearby village, where they werre accommodated overnight in the police station. There the chief of police produced bottles of the local brandy, ostensibly to ward off pneumonia!

Retired Sqn. Ldr. R. E. Chaney (formerly an LAC known as 'Lofty') claimed many years later that 30 Squadron may have been the first to fly Blenheims equipped with paddle-blade propellers! After a couple of years of use in sucked-up mud and 'mutti', the blades eroded significantly, especially at the tips. Combined with the evasive action of pilots returning from a sortie who flew low over the sea, with the likelihood of sea spray damaging the propellers, aerodynamic efficiency dropped alarmingly. On one occasion at Paramythia, 'Lofty' decided to deal with the problem by shortening the blades. After measuring each blade, he cut them off with a hacksaw and then ran the engines, which were "as smooth as a nut", and he flew back to Eleusis with a live lamb as freight, which equated to many drinks in an Athens night club.

Apart from the usual fighter patrols of Athens by 'B' and 'C' Flights, they carried out a search on 16th February for a Wellington thought to have ditched west of Corfu after a night raid on Brindisi. No trace of it was found, but one of the 30 Squadron Blenheims took the opportunity of chasing five Cant 1007 bombers almost to the coast of Italy, firing 600 rounds in the process. After breaking off the attack, the Blenheim was itself pursued by three Fiat G.50 fighters, which the pilot managed to evade by taking to the clouds.

More raids from Paramythia were arranged on 17th February, but this time the four aircraft of 'A' Flight were accompanied by four Blenheim fighters, which carried a number of ground crew personnel so that dependence on help from other squadrons could be reduced. Having deposited the men at Paramythia, the fighter Blenheims returned to Eleusis to take part in anti-aircraft cooperation exercises, which by now had become the routine on Mondays and Fridays. Meanwhile, the aircraft of 'A' Flight carried out raids on transport and troops on 18th February.

As the weather improved, so did offensive missions, which included raids on strategic targets such as Valona, Argyrovastron and Tepelene and support for troops in he front line. The 30 Squadron detachment often flew with 211 Squadron, which was also at Paramythia, usually occupying the box position behind and below the leading Flight. Flying in the treacherous air currents over mountains and up valleys, this was never a comfortable position. Tepelene was in the fork of three valleys and was approached up the southernmost one. As clouds often covered the mountains, this was like flying up a tunnel. Intense flak on the approach became even more severe as the Blemheims neared the target, and tracer shells appeared to be colour-coded depending on the location of the flak battery. One observer said that this was "just to help us find our way" while another remarked "if we do get hit we can get out and walk on the flak."

After several missions, Flg. Off. Derek Walker of 'A' Flight wrote the words of a song to the tune 'Clementine':

Took a Blenheim to Valona
Every morning just at nine;
Same old aircraft, same old aircrew,
Same old height and same old time.

'Do four runs down' said the CO
And make every one do well.
If you do you'll get a medal,
If you don't I'll give you hell.

Over Corfu weather clearing
And the sun begins to shine,
42s and G50s
All awaiting on the line.

On the way back same old fighters
And the gravy getting low.
How we wish we could see Eleusis
Through the snowstorm down below.

Oh Group Captain, our Group Captain,
Sitting coy at HQG,
How we wish that you could sample
'Musso' chucking muck at me!

How I wish I were at HQ
Drinking coffee by the score.
Then I wouldn't have to push off
To Valona any more.

To boost the fighter strength at Eleusis, seventeen Hurricanes of 33 Squadron arrived from Amriya via Crete on 19th February. 30 Squadron's Blenheim fighters were not called upon to carry out any

missions other than routine patrols, but the bomber crews and ground crews of 'A' Flight at Paramythia had been suffering in bad weather. Continuous heavy rain there had prevented any raids on 19th February, and the men had spent an uncomfortable day in their tents, one of which had taken off in gale-force winds. The four gunners and one observer who were in residence then had to spend the night in the nearby village, where they dried their clothing and equipment over a fire. Next day, however, the weather had improved a little, and a raid on troops on a section of road cut off by the previous day's rain was arranged. Bombing results were very disappointing, due, it was thought, to faulty airspeed indicators in all three aircraft, perhaps resulting from the rainy conditions. During the afternoon, the three Blenheims formed part of a force of eighteen aircraft escorted by six Hurricanes. The target was Berat in Albania, and 'A' Flight of 30 Squadron attacked a bridge south-west of the town, but the twelve 250lb bombs fell wide. Anti-aircraft fire was intense, and Fiat G.50 fighters were soon airborne, but the Hurricane pilots claimed afterwards that they had shot down eight of them with no loss of any RAF aircraft. 'A' Flight returned to Eleusis soon after midday on 21st February with four raids completed and the same number of bullet-holes in the Blenheims.

While leading a pair of Blenheim fighters on an offensive patrol over the west coast of Greece on 22nd February, Sqn. Ldr. Milward was warned of enemy aircraft near Zante. His No.2, Flg. Off. Davidson, spotted one and the pair gave chase. The aircraft turned out to be a Cant Z.506B floatplane, one of a number reported to be in the habit of shooting up villages and fishing boats. Attacking out of the sun, the Blenheims took the Italian crew by surprise, and after several rapid passes the rear gunner was put out of action. By this time, Sqn. Ldr. Milward's ammunition had all been used, so Flg. Off. Davidson made a further attack and forced the seaplane to make a heavy landing on the water with engines cut. Its crew waved white flags while Davidson orbited above, the Sqn. Ldr. having flown to Agrinion to report the seaplane's position. Although the Cant did not sink, it was believed to be too severely damaged to take off, and later reports stated that a Greek launch had been sent out to pick up the four surviving crew members, two having been killed in the battle. A reconnaissance flight next day revealed that the Cant was partially submerged, its floats in the air.

At much the same time, six enemy aircraft in box formation were sighted moving south-east towards Previza, from where heavy AA fire was being thrown up. Flg. Off. Walker dived down in a beam attack, and succeeded in shooting down one aircraft of the box into the sea south of Levkas. A second attack brought oil and smoke from the starboard engine of the enemy's No.5 aircraft, causing it to lose speed. At this point Flg. Off. Walker's guns jammed, so he broke off and made for Eleusis, but his No.2 made a series of rear quarter attacks, and another enemy aircraft broke away out of control and glided down to a crash-landing in the sea. No damage was sustained by any 30 Squadron aircraft in this morale-boosting encounter.

On 24th February the AOC-in-C and AOC paid a visit to 30 and 33 Squadrons at Eleusis and gave all aircrews a message, though what it contained is not recorded. Next day the spell of fine weather ended, and one of the Blenheims of 'C' Flight was blown from its picquets and was severely damaged when it came to rest in a ditch. However, these conditions cleared by the following morning, and Flg. Off. Davidson was able to fly the two high-ranking visitors to Paramythia on their tour of inspection. They returned on 27th February, when another three-day detachment of 'A' Flight to Paramythia for operations began.

'A' Flight opened their activities on 28th February by joining in an escorted raid on Codra, a village east of Tepelene, where a number of artillery positions existed. This mission was followed on 1st March by a raid in conjunction with 211 Squadron and an escort of Hurricanes, the target being a road under constuction near Buzi, and later the same day Berat was again targetted. Three enemy fighters were seen in front of the formation, but heading away from it! Joining the detachment that day was Sqn. Ldr. Milward, who arrived for operations in a Blenheim fighter.

A very different task befell 30 Squadron on 1st March 1941, when three Blenheims took off for Menidi, from where they were to carry urgently-needed medical supplies to Larissa, where an earthquake on 28th February had caused severe damage and injuries to the population. The Blenheims landed with some difficulty on the landing ground at Larissa, which had been damaged, and as the crews climbed out they could feel the ground under them shudder. The only reason why another three aircraft did not join in was that medical supplies were becoming scarce.

The defence of Athens from the air was now being shared between 30 Squadron's 'B' and 'C' Flights and the Hurricanes of 33 Squadron. Offensive patrols, however, were largely the province of 30 Squadron, and on 2nd March six of the Blenheims took off to carry out a patrol of the area between Kymi and Strati. Nothing untoward was seen, however, and this pattern persisted for several days. The 'A' Flight detachment returned from Paramythia on 3rd March, and that day RAF Greece declared 30 Squadron to be an all-fighter unit, 'A' Flight losing its bombing function. Conversion to the fighter role was completed on 9th March.

Another break from routine came about on 6th March, when two Blenheim fighters took off to escort a Sunderland flying-boat from Scaramanga towards Crete. On board were Mr. Anthony Eden, the Foreign Secretary, and several high-ranking War Office officials. For the next nine days nothing but routine flying was carried out, but on 15th March five Blenheim fighters led by Sqn. Ldr. Milward flew to Paramythia to take part in an attack on the enemy airfield at Valona early next morning.

Morale, which had always been high at Paramythia, seemed to climb to even greater heights once spring arrived. With the better weather, targets were easier to locate, and Paramythia valley began to bloom. It was even possible to see a family of bears sunning themselves at the entrance to a mountain cave.

At Paramythia the only motor transport was an old car, which was pressed into service to carry everything from bombs to food and fuel.The bomb dump was in the bed of a dry water-course, and there the aircrews fitted detonators to the 20lb and 40lb bombs, while the armourers concentrated on the 250-pounders. All crews bombed-up their own aircraft, regardless of rank.

At 03.30 on 16th March, the five Blenheims began to take off from Paramythia at ten-minute intervals, loaded with 20lb and 30lb fragmentation bombs. All bombs fell in the target area, but no crew could claim definite damage. Three AA batteries and a nest of pom-poms were silenced by accurate machine-gun fire from the Blenheims. In the harbour five ships were dispersed and a very large hospital ship was illuminated by the flames of explosions. One of the Blenheims was slightly damaged but there were no injuries to crew members.

Sometimes Swordfish biplanes of the Fleet Air Arm made an attack on Valona at the same time as 30 Squadron. After the 'Stringbag' had taken off and set course, the Blenheims would follow half an hour later. They would pass the Swordfish and give its crew an encouraging wave, and after bombing would pass it again on the return journey!

A permanent move of 'C' Flight to Araxos was now being considered, and on 22nd March Sqn. Ldr. Milward flew there to make preparatory arrangements. But before the move could take place more pressing matters came to the fore, and the move was postponed. When orders were received for five Blenheims to raid enemy airfields at Kalathos (Rhodes) and Scarpanto, from where attacks on shipping were being made, Sqn. Ldr. Milward took off at 09.30 for Iraklion on Crete to make arrangements for the operation to be mounted from there early the next morning in order to be over the target at sunrise. Later in the day the other five Blenheims flew to Iraklion.

Two of the 30th Squadron Blenheims took off from Iraklion at 04.10 on 25th March, led by Flg. Off. Davidson, bound for Scarpanto, but when they arrived over the target neither crew could see any aircraft on the airfield. The No.2 aircraft did not make an attack as an engine was giving trouble, and it returned to Iraklion. Flg. Off. Davidson dropped four bombs among buildings, causing considerable damage, and strafed other buildings and some 'tin' huts. Meanwhile, Sqn. Ldr. Milward had led the other two aircraft to the island of Rhodes, where 10/10 cloud meant that the airfield at Kalathos was not found before AA defences and fighters were warned of the Blenheims' approach. A diving attack was made, concentrating on a line of He 111 aircraft, five of which were hit and one destroyed. However, the leader was forced to drop his bombs into the sea, as a CR.42 fighter made an unexpected attack.

No.2 in the 30 Squadron formation claimed a successful strike on airfield buildings and a small factory, but No.3 failed to stay with the formation and the pilot found a target of his own, the island of Astipalaia, some 75 miles north-west of Rhodes. There he dive-bombed three merchant vessels, all bombs apparently hitting the mark. All 30 Squadron aircraft returned to base safely after what was regarded as a fairly effective mission.

Further operations from Paramythia were now being planned, and on 27th March six crews led by Flt. Lt. Horgan took off from Eleusis. Next morning at 05.35 they were on their way to a target in southern Italy, Lecce, where they arrived an hour later, gliding down from 10,000 feet to 1500 feet and then diving to machine-gun between eighty and a hundred enemy aircraft of several types lined up for inspection by a VIP at the anniversary parade of Regia Aeronautica! The enemy was taken completely by surprise. Two attacks lasting six to eight minutes were made, resulting in one aircraft being destroyed by fire and another having its undercarriage shot away, while about twenty other aircraft were riddled with bullets, putting them out of action for a few days at least. A little accurate AA fire was put up by the defenders, and the Blenheims suffered some minor damage, the one flown by Sgt. Ovens landing at Paramythia with a damaged oil cooler while the others returned to Eleusis.

A spell of fine weather was being enjoyed by all personnel when on 31st March 1941 the Foreign Secretary, Mr. Anthony Eden, paid a call on Eleusis in the company of the AOC, AVM d'Albiac. Mr. Eden chatted enthusiastically with members of the squadron before leaving for Athens.

The spell of fine weather continued during the early days of April 1941, and routine patrols were flown. Night flying and fighter tactics were practiced, and there was an occasional air raid alarm, though no enemy aircraft were seen. At 21.00 on 4th April an order was received instructing 30 Squadron to send a detached Flight of six Blenheims to Maleme in Crete on the following day for convoy protection purposes and to carry out offensive patrols. The six aircraft of 'C' Flight duly took off at 13.00 on 5th April, led by Flg. Off. Davidson, while a Bombay aircraft of 216 Squadron made two trips with the detachment's personnel and stores.

## Germany invades Greece

It was noted in the Squadron diary on 5th April 1941 that the situation in the Balkans had become so crucial that full-scale war was expected at any time. This remark was fully justified next day. After the German ambassador had handed a note to the Prime Minister of Greece, German troops crossed the border from Bulgaria and engaged in fierce fighting with the Greek and British armies. Two hours later, Germany sent twenty infantry divisions, seven armoured divisions and 1200 front-line aircraft into Yugoslavia from Austria. Opposition crumbled under this onslaught and Belgrade was sacked. Precautions for the defence of Athens were stepped up, and during the day three Blenheims each from 'A' and 'B' Flights joined six Hurricanes of 80 Squadron at readiness. Enemy reconnaissance aircraft were seen overhead, and one Cant 1007 was intercepted by 80 Squadron and shot down. At 22.30 high-flying bombers were heard over the Athens area, and ten minutes later bombs were dropped on the port of Piraeus, causing damage to a ship and buildings. Heavy AA fire drove the raiders off, and the all-clear was given at 01.30.

Flg. Off. R. G. Ledieu, who the previous November had arrived at Eleusis in advance of 30 Squadron to make arrangements for accommodation, was asked by the Greek Station Commander whether the RAF had any equipment for tracing radio transmissions. He seemed sure that one or two transmitters were operating nearby, acting as homing beacons for German aircraft to follow when raiding Athens or Eleusis. Furthermore, he said that he knew when to expect a raid because as dusk fell fires were lit on all the surrounding hilltops, almost like a flarepath to guide the raiding bombers. There were several other cases of blatant aid to the enemy. One involved a German-built Greek Air Force transport aircraft, probably a Ju 52, which had been assisting in the movement of detachments of RAF Gladiator squadrons. One day it failed to arrive on schedule, and urgent enquiries elicited that it had gone to Germany to collect spares! Its crew had been flying round all the RAF airfields and knew exactly where each unit was and what equipment it had!

Further enemy activity took place during the night of 9/10th April, and at 05.00 one Blenheim set off to put paid to a Ju 88 caught in a searchlight beam. A heavy burst of fire drove the enemy aircraft off, and an unconfirmed report from local inhabitants stated that it crashed near Scaramanga Bay. Later that day the two Flights of 30 Squadron were both required for operations consisting of strafing troops on the road between Monastir and Bitolj in southern Yugoslavia. The five available aircraft took off at 15.30 with Sqn. Ldr. Milward in the lead, and on arrival at the target made two dives on the troops at ground level, causing much mayhem and destroying three very large vehicles. Although there was heavy ground fire, the Luftwaffe failed to appear, and there was no damage to the Blenheims, which returned to base safely. Geoffrey Chapman flew with Flt. Lt. Horgan on that mission, and recalls the operation. "Soon after we had reached our operational height we spotted a formation of three aircraft approaching us head-on, or so it seemed. As they got closer we could see that they were Ju 88s, German bombers similar to Blenheims in size and performance. We watched them and they watched us and we passed each other at about 500 yards. Such was the discipline of both the RAF and the Luftwaffe, I imagine, requiring the appointed taks to be carried out regardless of any distractions!" He goes on to record the Blenheims' arrival over the target. "We found our German transport and flew in line astern to make a long run right down the road and back again. Trucks burst into flames and others overturned. Soldiers could be seen running for cover across fields. In attempting to play my part........I inadvertently fired a bullet through our own tailplane. This, I thought, is pure Plt. Off. Prune! Flt. Lt. Horgan said very little when I reported what I had done. On the ground Sqn. Ldr. Milward had a few terse words to say, for he feared the aircraft would be put out of action. Happily the ground crew found nothing of consequence had been damaged."

A similar mission was started next day, this time led by Flt. Lt. Horgan, but adverse weather caused abandonment of the operation. Late that evening, however, Sqn. Ldr. Milward took off to intercept an enemy aircraft reported to be laying mines in Piraeus harbour. It had been agreed that a Verey signal would be fired when engaging a target and the AA gunners would cease fire to allow the fighter to attack. "I quickly sighted a Ju 88 and closed for a stern attack, firing the special colour signal as I opened fire" recalls Sqn. Ldr. Milward. "As I broke away [my aircraft] received a direct hit, whether from the Ju 88 or from AA I was unable to tell. The cockpit filled instantly with thick smoke, and I instructed my gunner to bale out. I had no response from him and was unable to see in the smoke and flames, so baled out myself through the roof canopy, which I always left open during fighter sorties. When the parachute opened I was about 8000 feet over north Athens. There was still a large amount of activity in the air and I watched my aircraft spiralling down until it struck the ground. There was no [other] parachute. Just before landing I hauled on my shroud lines to avoid high tension cables and the next moment arrived with a loud sound of breaking glass in a greenhouse! Apart from cuts and bruises I was comparatively intact but very frightened." Greek soldiers soon arrived and took some time to be convinced of the CO's nationality, but the local mayor made a speech of eternal friendship and insisted that the mayoral car would be used to take the Sqn. Ldr. back to RAF Headquarters in the King George Hotel. "His driver was not so keen, as the heavy raid was still going on, but took me most of the way. On arrival at the hotel, I found that drinks were still being served in the basement bar! I was given a car back to Eleusis, where I was greeted as one back from the dead." The unfortunate gunner, who fell to earth with the stricken Blenheim, was Sgt. J. Crooks.

Offensive operations from Greece had now been increased, and 30 Squadron found itself sharing Eleusis airfield with Wellingtons of 38 Squadron, which raided Sofia on 13th April, and Swordfish of 815 Squadron Fleet Air Arm, which carried out a successful operation on Brindisi. However, the enemy began to retaliate, dropping a few bombs on the eastern end of Eleusis airfield at 03.30 on 15th April and parachute mines in nearby Scaramanga Bay. A further raid fifteen minutes later cause some superficial damage, but at 08.45 matters became serious. As soon as reports of about 25 Ju 88s approaching the Athens area were received, four Blenheim fighters of 30 Squadron and six Hurricanes took off to intercept. In the combat which followed, six Ju 88s were downed, four by Hurricanes and two by 30 Squadron crews, one of them most likely by Plt. Off. Allison, the youngest pilot on the squadron.

Enemy advances were now beginning to force the evacuation of airfields in the north of Greece, and on 16th April batches of men of 11 Squadron from Almyros, 33 Squadron from Larissa and 113 Squadron from Niamata arrived at Eleusis to be fed and accommodated for the night. Aircraft of many types flew in, including two S.79s and two Lockheed 14s from Paramythia with Yugoslav government officials on board, heading for Menidi.

By now it was becoming clear that British forces in Greece could not hold out, and that the country would have to be abandoned before long. In advance of such an evacuation, an order was received by 30 Squadron at 09.30 on 17th April 1941 detailing a move to Maleme in Crete to join 'C' Flight in carrying out escort patrols over convoys. Ground crews were told to return to their billets, prepare a minimum amount of kit and return to the flight-line. Loading of the aircraft then began, valuable spares, tools and stores being dealt with before as many men as possible embarked. At 13.30 the first heavily-laden aircraft took off, and ferrying continued until dusk. Meanwhile, a sea party was being organised for embarkation at the docks next morning. Movement of the remainder of the air party began at 07.00 on 18th April, and eight trips that day completed the move, although due to shortage of transport remnants of the squadron had to remain at Eleusis for several days.

The results of Cpl. Robert Lawrence's enterprise while he was lodged at Aspropiragus, totalling 33,000 drachmas (about £33), were deposited in the Ionian Bank in Athens, where the RAF itself banked. There it was hoped the money would be safe, but in fact all was lost in the German invasion. Lawrence had a lucky escape, not so much from the Germans, but from the family who owned the bakery in Aspropiragus and who were intent on marrying him to the fourteen-year-old granddaughter of the owner!

Cpl. Lawrence wrote a graphic description of his own evacuation from Eleusis to Maleme in a Blenheim piloted by his friend Jock Ratlidge. "Jock bade us all to jettison our rifles, tin helmets and all luggage, because he opted to carry the maximum number of men rather than equipment" he wrote. "In his aircraft there were eleven passengers. We could scarcely breathe, so absurdly tightly packed we were. I was pressed hard into the front cockpit, my back pressed into the curved shape of the Perspex nose panel, facing the pilot's knees, with other men squashed close to me so that breathing was slightly restricted and Jock had difficulty in operating the controls. Knowing every inch of Eleusis aerodrome as I did, I twisted my head round to watch for our hoped-for take-off. We all though little of our chances of reaching our destination, the island of Crete 450 miles away, and I watched Jock frantically trying to get the aircraft off the ground. As it dragged its weight toward the windsock I felt convinced we could not clear the hedge on the perimeter, which appeared all too swiftly. Miraculously, we just scraped over it with wheels up. We made no circuit of the airfield but were away at low level across the Aegean Sea, ever watchful for German fighters. Jock seemed the most unconcerned of us all, smiling and joking between spasms of tuneless Scottish humming. Somehow we made it. We lobbed down heavily on Maleme airstrip [after] approaching at almost sea level, despite German fighters dancing about above us hoping to destroy all evacuees on arrival. Jock bundled us out of his aircraft in great haste, keeping the engines running as we were in the middle of the small airfield. We ran for cover as he flew back to Eleusis for another load of men, and I certainly didn't envy him."

Stan Condra, an armourer, had a very different experience, as he relates. "I was in the main party to follow at a later date. We spent the interval clearing up and preparing to follow, but things took a turn for the worse, and one morning at dawn we were, together with our small arms, ammunition and supplies, boarding a train. We travelled for some time, and when the train halted we disembarked...... and spent the rest of the day and night on a hillside. There followed some days of walking. Several times we saw enemy aircraft, and I seem to recall some transport, which was welcome, and of crossing the Corinth Canal. During those days of travel we continued to carry our small arms, ammunition and supplies. We arrived at an evacuated airstrip (Argos) where we met other RAF personnel. Eventually, after a hair-raising journey by lorry over narrow roads and mountains we arrived at Kalamata, a port on the south-west of the peninsula. There we spent some days in, I believe, an old brewery. The day arrived when some personnel were air-lifted by Sunderlands flying very low. Those of us left then embarked one evening in a vessel of some sort, with only personal equipment carried. We spent the night on the top deck and arrived on a small island (Kithara) next day. We disembarked and spent some days on the beach area, as we were given to understand that we would be evacuate again by Naval vessels. During this time we had two Stuka attacks in which they strafed and bombed the ship we arrived in and another ship. Rations were getting fairly low, and we were given to understand that Greece had been occupied. After several evenings of waiting on the beach until dusk, some small Naval vessels did arrive, and to our relief we were evacuated and transferred to a cargo ship in Cretan waters, but were not landed in Crete. Eventually we arrived in Egypt after spending most of the time in the hold of that coal ship." These men rejoined 30 Squadron after the evacuation from Crete several weeks later.

### Crete: a disaster for 30 Squadron

30 Squadron officers found themselves in fairly comfortable accommodation at Maleme, where 815 Squadron Fleet Air Arm was in residence. As 30 Squadron had hosted 815 at Eleusis, it was felt that the FAA now had the opportunity of returning the compliment! Maleme was a dusty airstrip lying between the sea and the road from Khania to Kastelli. There were no hangars or workshops, and as no permanent living accommodation existed, ground personnel pitched tented encampments in the abundant groves of olive trees which almost covered the flat areas and hillsides toward the shore. A feature of the camp was that the occupants of each tent were encouraged to dig down one to two feet inside and then to build sandbagged walls to much the same height outside. The Flight office-cum-workshop was an EPIP (Egypt pattern/India pattern) tent erected very close to a slit trench which was to become very well used.

Operations began at 13.05 on 18th April, when Flg. Off. Smith took off to escort a convoy bound for Piraeus. He soon saw two S.79 aircraft in the vicinity of the convoy and attacked from the rear. Black smoke issued from the starboard engine of one aircraft and its undercarriage dropped. The second S.79 was also hit, and it was assumed that one of them did not return to base and one was severely damaged. On approach to Maleme, the Blenheim caught fire, but the observer, Plt. Off. Strong, quickly extinguished the flames, his prompt action preventing a complete write-off. Two days later the same pilot was on patrol 35 miles south-south-east of Gavdos when he spotted an S.79 at 6000 feet above a convoy. He made an attack, but quickly found that all four front guns jammed, leaving him unable to carry through the attack. On return to base, it was found that the ammunition was faulty.

More personnel continued to arrive for various squadrons expected to move to Crete, some of them travelling in Sunderland flying boats from Scaramanga Bay to Suda Bay and other in Bombays of 216 Squadron. During the last few days, Eleusis airfield had been heavily strafed by Bf 109s and Bf 110s and the entire MT and remaining equipment of the squadron had been burnt out. At noon on 22nd April orders were issued for Blenheims to return to Eleusis to evacuate any remaining personnel, although reports had been received that a 30 Squadron party had already left for Argos to await transport to Maleme. Crete was now also feeling the effects of the German onslaught, as Khania was strafed and shipping in Suda Bay was bombed.

An incident remembered by Wg. Cdr. J. A. Jarvis DFC AFC took place on 22nd April and almost made him and his navigator the perpetrators of regicide. That day they and six other crews flew to Eleusis to collect ground crew airmen of 33 and 80 Squadrons who had been stranded there. Each aircraft carried up to nine men."God knows where the C of G was!" remarked Wg. Cdr. Jarvis years later. "When we arrived over Eleusis there were three SM.79s in the circuit, so we started an attack. Bob Davidson suddenly shouted to hold fire, and I could see a bowler-hatted gentleman in the rear turret doffing his hat to us. It turned out that the aircraft were carrying King Peter of Yugoslavia and his court to safety. It was rumoured that the entire gold reserves of the country (nine tons) were packed in the aircraft, so it would have been an expensive splat." At 07.15 next day the Blenheims returned from Eleusis. To its credit, 30 Squadron had carried out a major task in ferrying over 300 personnel in difficult conditions.

Later that day, two Ju 88s were sighted over Suda Bay, and Flg. Off. Blakeway made a beam attack and managed to drive them down to sea level. No damage was reported and, perhaps due to 30 Squadron's intervention, there was no damage to shipping. Later in the day, 815 Squadron began to leave Maleme to return to its usual base in Egypt. Another 'kill' was recorded on 24th April, when Plt. Off. Basan shot a Ju 88 down into the sea while on convoy patrol.

Ships were now evacuating British forces and civilian evacuees from Greece, and on 25th April at 05.45 the CO led a formation of six Blenheims to meet a convoy south of Yora. Gunners on destroyers escorting the convoy seemed to be nervous, as they put up a barrage of fire on seeing the Blenheims approach. No enemy aircraft put in an appearance until 08.00, when Flg. Off. Smith sighted two Ju 88s ahead and below at 4000 feet. He intercepted, and saw one of the enemy aircraft trail black smoke and dive steeply into the water and the other one, also smoking, make a hasty departure. Escort patrols continued on 26th April, shared with Hurricanes and Gladiators of the RAF and Fulmars of the Fleet Air Arm. During the day many evacuees arrived from Greece and awaited the arrival of Bombay aircraft to take them to Egypt, and the remains of 815 Squadron FAA left. Maleme now became an RAF Station, with the CO of 30 Squadron in command. Every aircraft had to be picketed in the open around the perimeter of the airfield, where they were totally unprotected from the ravages of the Luftwaffe. Several wrecked aircraft lay around, the results of landing crashes or enemy action. Before long, the ground crews dug large square pits about ten feet deep with a slope into each one, so that a certain amount of cover from strafing could be found. In the pits, there was better shelter for men working on the aircraft, but moving Blenheims into and out was very hard work.

Daily life at Maleme is recalled by supply Corporal Robert Lawrence, who wrote "Life was pleasant, in blazing spring sunshine and amidst a veritable wilderness of scented wild flowers and blossom. Although locating urgently-needed spares to keep our aircraft airborne was a near impossible task, there was a noticeable air of false or temporary serenity and peace. It was easy to forget the insistent German air attacks and enjoy the immense respite from the hazardous Greek campaign and its devastating evacuation. Food was basic emergency rations and tedious in its repetition — tinned beans, bacon, sausages, potatoes, bread and jam. The trees were loaded with ripening olives...........and the fields were rich in grapes. I do not recall any sense of boredom.........nor can I recall anything of how we spent the evenings. Doubtless we gathered in groups, gossiping in the twilight, but later things deteriorated. I enjoyed fairly frequent excursions by truck.........scavenging for Blenheim spares. This strange pastime was justified because from time to time wrecked ships had beached and unloaded various aircraft spares, which were then swiftly dispersed into secret camouflaged areas under trees in the hills."

Another airman, Robert Smith, has recorded something of those strenuous days at Maleme. He never forgot his job of refuelling Blenheims after a convoy patrol. "Not for us the luxury of a petrol bowser" he said "but that infernal double-handled fuel pump, pumping straight from 40-gallon drums. I can still picture that pump to this day, bolted to a length of board that you stood on. I wonder how many gallons we actually pumped with that thing." In fact the fuel capacity of a Blenheim Mk.I was 276 gallons, or seven full drums.

German troops marched into Athens on 27th April 1941, and Allied troops began to withdraw from the mainland, under constant attack by Ju 87 Stuka dive-bombers. By this time, serviceability of the Blenheims of 30 Squadron was becoming an increasing problem, due to a lack of spare parts. On average, only six aircraft could be made available each day, out of thirteen on strength. Another one, K7177, was put out of action after a fighter escort mission on 27th April. Its pilot, Flt. Sgt. Innes-Smith, sighted a Do 17 flying at 5000 feet above a convoy, and while turning to attack he flew into the AA barrage put up by the ships. Although the Blenheim was badly damaged, he managed to reach Maleme, where he made a landing on a burst tyre. Next morning at 06.15, Flt. Lt. Walker flew a 'shufti kite' (a reconnaissance Blenheim) over the islands south of Argos to check on any Allied troops who might be awaiting evacuation, but he reported that "practically no-one" remained there. Neither did he see any sign of the destroyer HMS *Diewood*, which had been reported missing. During the day, while two Bombay aircraft left for Egypt with officers and men of RAF Headquarters, patrols were flown to protect shipping in Suda Bay. The last batch of evacuees from southern Greece arrived on 29th April in three destroyers which were guarded by three Blenheims of 30 Squadron until 203 Squadron, which had been posted from Aden to assist, took over. On their way to the comparative safety of Egypt that morning went 34 personnel of the squadron. Four air raid alerts were sounded that day when enemy aircraft appeared over Suda Bay and dropped some bombs without causing damage. More sinister was a report received at 18.00 that four troop-carrying aircraft had landed on the island of Melos, between Crete and mainland Greece, and on this news two Blenheims took off to reconnoitre and to carry out a strafing attack. However, no sign of any aircraft or troops was found.

It had been noted that photographic reconnaissance sorties were being flown over Crete, which was apparently being considered a potential base for future German and Italian operations. To fool the enemy into believing that the island was more strongly defended than it was, men of 30 Squadron and other units were ordered to construct wooden mock-ups of anti-aircraft guns around the Maleme airfield.

By the end of the evacuation of mainland Greece, several thousand Allied servicemen of many varieties had been moved to Crete. Many of them possessed little more than the clothes they wore, and food, equipment and other supplies were almost non-existent. As a fighting force, the war-weary troops and airmen were in a deplorable state, and morale was declining rapidly. Enemy air, land and sea power was known to be close at hand, and the chances of survival of the Allied force was considered to be poor. Added to the problem was a certain antipathy of ground troops to the RAF, which was commonly believed to have been ineffective during the Greek campaign. "Where was the ****** RAF when they were wanted?" jeered many soldiers. Of course, the unfortunate airmen on Crete could do nothing to rectify the shortage of aircraft and crews, but had to bear the brunt of hostility, particularly from Australian troops. "This stupid unjust bitterness deepened into active hostility in those first few weeks in Maleme" wrote Robert Lawrence. "Difficult as it is to believe, we of the RAF were savagely stoned by the Aussies. We had to mount guards on ourselves and move about stealthily, being wisely forbidden by our officers to retaliate. [The hostility] slowly faded out, but I suffered this stoning several times, especially when out in a lorry."

Sqn. Ldr. Hartup remarks that for the first time in his life he lost all sense of time and date while at Maleme. "We had to do amazing and unorthodox things to keep the old Blenheims flying" he says. "For instance we had an aircraft grounded with over-oiling, a known problem with the Mercury engine, and always recurring in the bottom cylinders. We knew that, tucked away at the far side of the aerodrome on the sea boundary was a Gladiator left behind by 80 Squadron. It was generally accepted that this aircraft was seriously unserviceable and unflyable. I knew that Gladiators and Blenheims both had Mercury engines, though I was not sure whether they were of different Marks. We had a 'recce' and satisfied ourselves that the cylinders were at least identical, so we 'borrowed' the two bottom cylinders for the Gladiator and fitted them to the Blenheim's engine. This worked, and without a word to anyone we ensured that one more tired-out Blenheim went home to roost at Aboukir."

Further air raids were made on shipping in Suda Bay on 30 April, again without great effect. A gradual evacuation of Crete was under way, and on 1st May a Bombay aircraft arrived at Maleme to take signals staff of 30 and 33 Squadrons to Egypt. Then the weather changed for the worse, a very strong westerly wind raising a great deal of dust. The break from flying did, however, allow time for some of the Blenheims to be made serviceable. Next day weather conditions improved, though 30

Squadron did not fly, leaving the patrols to 33 Squadron, pilots of which shot down three Ju 88s during a raid by fifteen aircraft on Suda Bay. A factor of this attack was that 33 Squadron pilots reported seeing four Blenheims Mk.I in RAF markings in use by the enemy. In hindsight, these may be identified as some of the batch of twelve ferried to Greece between October 1939 and February 1940 and subsequently captured in that country's fall.

Enemy bombing of shipping in Suda Bay was now a daily preoccupation, and the Hurricanes of 33 Squadron tackled them with vigour. Five of the raiders were shot down on 4th May, a day when 30 Squadron was restricted to a single reconnaissance sortie over Piraeus harbour. No shipping movements were seen there, and although aircraft were seen on the ground at Hassani airfield there seemed to be none at Eleusis or Menidi. A similar reconnaissance over Kithero was carried out on 5th May, again with little to report.

It soon became evident that Luftwaffe attacks had evolved into a regular schedule, raids being timed for 06.00, noon and 18.00 each day! To the chagrin of the RAF men on the island, the Bf 109s used for strafing were yellow-nosed training aircraft flown by student pilots since the defences of the island were so meagre. Other daylight raids were by Ju 87 Stuka dive-bombers, while at night Do 17s carried out their attacks.

Five of 30 Squadron's Blenheims, all unfit for operations, were flown from Maleme to 102 MU at Abu Sueir and 103 MU at Aboukir on 7th May, led by Flg. Off. Davidson. The squadron was thus seriously depleted in aircraft and personnel, but managed to put up single aircraft for reconnaissance sorties and to fly to Egypt to bring senior officers to Crete. There now seemed to be a lull before an inevitable storm. Little evidence of enemy activity was being seen apart from the daily raids on Suda Bay, until on 14th May, after fighter patrols had been operating from Iraklion, Crete was the target for three heavy bombing and strafing attacks by VIII Fliegerkorps. The culprits were Do 17Z and He 111 aircraft of KG.2 and II/KG.26, which made level runs at altitudes of 6000 to 13,000 feet over Iraklion, Suda Bay, Khania, Rethimnon, Kastelli and Maleme, while Ju 88s and Ju 87s of StG.2 attacked shipping, military camps depots and AA sites. Meanwhile, Bf 109Es and Bf 110Cs roamed around the island looking for targets of opportunity. Several enemy aircraft were destroyed by AA fire, but the attack was overwhelming. Any Gladiators or Hurricanes whose pilots tried to defend the area were promptly shot down by the roaming Bf 109s.

That night crews were ordered to fly all four remaining aircraft of 30 Squadron to Egypt at dawn next day. The enemy rose early, however, and dropped a stick of bombs on the airfield at 05.00, injuring three men and damaging a Blenheim. The other three took off for Amriya at 06.00, and half an hour later Maleme was strafed by about thirty Bf 109s, which succeeded in adding to the damage already sustained by the one remaining Blenheim and destroying a number of Hurricanes and Fleet Air Arm aircraft. Another assault was made at noon, this time ineffectual, and a third during the evening.

Matters were now coming to a head, and when the damaged Blenheim left Maleme for Egypt at dawn on 16th May 1941, piloted by Sqn. Ldr. Milward and carrying as many personnel and squadron records as possible, 30 Squadron then became non-operational. Just before leaving Maleme, the Sqn. Ldr. was asked by Cdr. Beale of the Fleet Air Arm to escort a Sea Gladiator which was suffering intermittent engine failure across to North Africa. This was agreed to very reluctantly, as it seemed an unnecessary risk to the pilot of the elderly biplane. About half an hour into the flight the Gladiator's engine failed and it ditched. An inflatable raft was dropped from the Blenheim, the location was marked and reported, but although a search was made the pilot was never found. "Another unnecessary waste of a life" remarked Sqn. Ldr. Milward.

Arthur Henderson says that after the last Blenheim had left the remaining ground crew personnel had one Bofors gun and a few hand weapons — he had a Smith & Wesson revolver with five rounds of ammunition. Fortunately there was plenty of food, but it was all tinned Machonachie's stew, which the men ate raw, fried, roast or grilled! He wonders whether the nearby river Tavronitis still contains rusty cans!

One of the Blenheims which had already gone to Egypt escorted two Hurricanes between Fuka and Iraklion before returning to Heliopolis and Flt. Lt. Davidson and three other pilots flew Hurricanes from Egypt to Maleme and Iraklion, escorted by a Maryland aircraft. These moves were, however, a last-ditch stand against a potentially overwhelming enemy.

During the early morning of 17th May Maleme was again heavily strafed, and the remaining ground personnel of 30 Squadron, led by Plt. Off. Crowther, took refuge on a hill overlooking the airfield. At about the same time, the Luftwaffe dropped leaflets, saying, in effect, 'Now, you British airmen, we're going to treat you to an air display on Monday 19th May at 14.00. Don't miss it: we promise it will be the finest display you have ever seen'. However, this display of enemy might did not happen after all, which was subsequently seen as a means of lulling the defenders of Maleme into a false sense of security.

By 19th May only three of the recently-delivered Hurricanes and three Gladiators were serviceable at Iraklion and one Hurricane at Maleme, and no replacements were available for the defence of Crete. Gp. Capt. Beamish, commanding the RAF on the island, therefore decided to evacuate, and this decision was sanctioned by HQ Middle East next day. One officer and fourteen airmen were evacuated from Suda Bay in a Sunderland flying-boat that day, with the four pilots who had brought Hurricanes to Crete a few days earlier. 'Lofty' Chaney was one of a group of men who made their way to Suda Bay, where they found HMS *York* laying on its side. A sailor told them that there was no transport to Egypt, so they began to make their disconsolate way back into the hills. But help then arrived in the shape of another Sunderland, which prompted a mass scramble back to the harbour. The pilot, asked how many men could be taken aboard, told Chaney and his mates "Get fifty men, no more, here at four o'clock in the morning." "I did, but they grew to eighty" says Mr. Chaney. "We got into a lighter, having thrown our guns and everything else into the sea to keep the weight down. The water was about half an inch from the gunwales, when a young Pilot Officer said to the pilot 'I say, sir, the water is nearly coming in'. 'Kindly step ashore' said the pilot, and we paddled with our hands to the Sunderland. All aboard, and we taxied or tried to take off for what seemed like about three miles before coming unstuck, and then flew at low altitude to Alexandria."

Crete was seen by Hitler and his planners as a serious obstacle to an attack on Egypt, while Winston Churchill stated that the island would be defended "to the last man." To achieve an invasion of Crete, Germany would have to gain control of the island's airfields and land troops by air and by sea. Feldmarschal Goering therefore allocated the complete VIII Fliegerkorps, under the command of Gen. Wolfgang von Richtofen, to Gen. Student for the proposed operation, named 'Merkur'. Aircraft at his disposal included 150 Ju 87 Stuka dive-bombers, three Gruppen of Do 17s, two of Ju 88s, a Gruppe of He 111s, three of Bf 109s and three of Bf 110s, plus forty aircraft for reconnaissance missions and, most significantly, 493 three-engined Ju 52 transport aircraft and eighty DFS.230 gliders. In all, 1223 Luftwaffe aircraft were ready to attack Crete. Defending Crete were 28,500 Allied troops, mainly ANZACs, and 6000 Greek soldiers, but not a single aircraft.

Between 07.00 and 07.30 on 20th May 1941, Luftwaffe fighters flew low over Maleme airfield, where the remnants of 30 Squadron personnel remained, and attacked with machine-gun fire. Twenty minutes later a heavy raid heralded the start of the landings. From airfields on the Greek mainland, including 30 Squadron's recent base at Eleusis, the Ju 52s towing gliders began to take off at 06.15, and at 08.00 they appeared over Maleme and the other airfields on the island and began disgorging paratroops, while the gliders, each containing eight heavily-armed troops, landed. Some of the gliders were riddled with Bren gun fire as they touched down, killing all on board; in the heat, the bodies soon discoloured, a fact which led to Germans to complain of atrocities and take revenge on local Cretans. It is thought that there were no survivors of the first wave of paratroops, who had been trapped by New Zealand soldiers and men of 30 Squadron as they tried to organise themselves. Nevertheless, several thousand enemy soldiers were quickly in possession of the airfield and its domestic site. Cpl. Croxton, a fitter/armourer, had joined 30 Squadron in Iraq in November 1938, and was one of the men stranded at Maleme. "On the morning of 20th May we had manned the trenches as usual, then had breakfast" he recalls. "We, the groundcrew of 'A' Flight, then went down to the airfield. Our task was to dig into the bank

*A hazy shot of the German invasion of Crete, with one Ju 52/3m falling earthward on fire.*

*Flt. Lt. 'Dave' Davidson, Flg. Off. Andy Smith and Flt. Lt. Derek Walker outside the makeshift mess at Malame.*

against the road and pile the earth up at the sides to make pens for Hurricanes we expected shortly. Not long after reaching the airfield the bombing started. We all managed to find trenches, where we stayed until the bombing finished. On emerging from the trenches we looked up and saw gliders and parachutes descending. A number of us had a quick discussion and decided our best course of action was to make our way back to camp using a direct route. We called all the others and as we were at the eastern end of the airfield this entailed crossing a road and making our way through vineyards. These we discovered were criss-crossed with barbed wire which we had to crawl under. Unknown to us, this was protecting a position held by a Company of the New Zealand 22nd Battalion. We called out to inform them who we were and were allowed to join them. There we stayed doing very little until about 5 p.m., when the New Zealand Lieutenant called for volunteers to supplement his depleted Company preparing to mount a counter-attack, supported by two light tanks. At the instigation of LAC Stewart, he, LAC Larter, another airman and myself volunteered. We were deployed twenty each side of the road along which the two tanks proceeded. We almost reached the other end of the airfield and our objective, the bridge over the river Tavronitis. Unfortunately the leading tank broke down and the guns on the other one jammed. Without their covering fire the counter-attack failed." The former Cpl. Croxton admits that much of the action is now a hazy memory, but remembers the whistle of bullets and a shout of "Hit the deck". Next came a call from a New Zealand corporal inviting the RAF men to join him in a trench, which they did with great speed.

Soon after diving into the trench, Cpl. Croxton and his new friends heard one of the tanks returning, and were told to crouch down and use the tank as cover while returning to base. He goes on to say "On return, I was asked to man a machine-gun position overlooking the airfield. During the night we were ordered to remove our shoes as we were to withdraw to the south-east. Before leaving I removed the breech-blocks from the heavy twin Browning guns, dismantled them and threw the parts away. At about dawn on 21st May we met a party from Hill 107. After a short stop we soon came under fire I remember the New Zealand officer giving two grenades to Cpl. Horner (a wireless fitter) and telling him to knock out the machine-gun post. Whether it was the look on Horner's face or another reason I don't know, but the order was withdrawn. At about this time about eight of us seemed to lose the main group and after a while we came to an RAF radio station on a hill. Here we were welcomed and I was allocated a Bren gun pit." Sadly, in the confusion LAC Stewart had been killed and LAC Larter wounded.

Flg. Off. T. H. Cullen, the 30 Squadron MO, had collected several wounded men together on Hill 107 and was attempting to return to the New Zealand lines with them. "We were over-run by a group of German paratroops, one of whom was a doctor" he recalls. "Later in the day we were moved back to the village at the western end of the Tavronitis bridge. The wounded were gathered together in buildings on the opposite side of the road from a German casualty clearing station. German medical staff were

helpful in supplying some instruments, dressings and chloroform. They thought their attack had failed and we would be released! This did not happen; a steady stream of wounded were brought in, including Sqn. Ldr. Howell, the CO of 33 Squadron, who was badly wounded in both legs."

Another airman who was taken prisoner was LAC D. R. Cherry, who had been wounded in the right ankle while retreating through woodland. "I reckon it was an explosive bullet" he remarked. "It made a terrific hole and a mess of my ankle. I laid there for a very long time, and an awful lot of fellows went by without offering to help me. Later a New Zealand corporal and one of our wireless operators, Cpl. Horner, stopped and picked me up. We struggled through streams and rough country until we got back to our lines. There a New Zealand orderly gave me a rough bandage and a tin of tomato soup, the best tin of soup I ever had. He kept rolling cigarettes for me; they helped a lot. I was taken on a bit further and lay with some other wounded for a very long time. Eventually they decided to take us to the field hospital. We went in a jeep with a Red Cross flag flying, right down in front of the German lines and were not fired upon." The wounded were then threatened with being shot, as German troops had been found with ears and other body parts cut off. However, when it was found that Cretans had done this a German officer came to apologise. After several days of painful delay, the captured RAF men were taken to Maleme airfield and from there flown in a Ju 52 to Kokinia hospital in Greece.

A report submitted later by Plt. Off. Crowther is worthy of reproduction in full. It details the events of 20th May 1941 in some detail, mentioning the names of several members of 30 Squadron who were directly involved:

"When the squadron was evacuated, I was left in charge of the rear party, consisting of five officers and 128 airmen. One officer and fourteen airmen were evacuated by flying boat a.m. 19th May. At 04.30 hours on 20th May the defence officers inspected all positions and satisfied themselves that everyone was on the alert. A second inspection was carried out at 06.00 hours.

At 07.00 hours on Tuesday 20th May 1941 the warning of approaching enemy aircraft was given and then 10 minutes later the alarm was sounded and within a few minutes very severe and prolonged bombing of the defence positions started, and a most intensive bombing attack was concentrated on the area of the camp site.

The Bofors crews, as the result of sustained bombing and machine-gunning attacks during the past seven days, were by this time almost completely unnerved and on this particular morning soon gave up firing. One Bofors gun was seen to go into action again but the shooting was rather inaccurate. While the camp was being bombed, enemy fighters made prolonged machine-gun attacks on the Bofors positions and inflicted heavy casualties. At the same time there was intensive ground strafing of troops over a wide area in the locality. These attacks lasted for two hours, with the result that the nerves of our men became ragged, and that intended reinforcements moving towards the aerodrome were unable to do so.

Meanwhile most of the personnel were taking cover in the slit trenches and other defensive positions. At approximately 09.30 hours we were warned of parachute troops landing in the vicinity of the river bed, the outskirts of the aerodrome and in the surrounding valleys. A fuller effect of the bombing was that the men kept their heads down and failed to notice the first parachutists dropping. This particularly applied to those which landed south-west of the aerodrome sheltered by hilly country. Gliders were already seen crashed in the river bed on the west side of the aerodrome and had apparently been dropped at the same time. There was no opposition to them except from the two RAF Lewis guns which kept firing throughout the landing. The remnants of RAF personnel and New Zealand infantry on the hillside were being subjected to persistent ground strafing from a very low height. The Germans were able to profit by the spare time allowed them to assemble trench mortars and field guns which later in the morning were instrumental in driving our men back. The RAF had been standing to since 04.30 hours, carrying out precautions

*How the 30 Squadron men survived. A tent in the woods at Malame.*

*Surviving the evacuation of Crete, a roadside meal.*

planned by the Station Commander, Commander Beale RN, and fire was opened on both parachute troops and gliders.

At this point our ambulance, under heavy fire, [with] driver 458485 LAC Betts [and] medical orderly 542821 LAC Darch, in response to an urgent call, was seen to travel across the exposed aerodrome towards the gun positions. Here they effected the rescue of wounded. LAC Darch, receiving two bullet wounds in the back, nevertheless carried on and brought the wounded back safely to the crash centre. This feature was the topic of squadron conversation for many days as being an outstanding act of bravery.

Meanwhile troop-carrying aircraft were landing along the beach at intervals of 100 yards. They appeared to land successfully in the most limited space, and the enemy did not seem to mind whether they could take off again or not. At least eight aircraft were seen crashed in this way. None of these aircraft did take off again to my knowledge.

At the beginning of the attack I reached the prearranged position [on a hill near the airfield] at the rear of the New Zealand troops and remained there during the morning. Those of our men not occupied in defending the lower slopes were withdrawn to this prearranged position to act as support troops. It was here that I gathered a handful of men and proceeded to the far side of the hill, where I heard parachute troops were obtaining a hold; the men in the deep dug-outs on that side had not been warned of the approach of parachute troops. After mopping up the parachute troops here I discovered that the enemy had obtained a foothold on the eastern side of the aerodrome, actually above the camp. I gathered 30 New Zealand troops who appeared to be without any leader and with my handful of RAF I made three counter-attacks and succeeded in retaking the summit. Throughout this period we were subjected to severe ground strafing by Me.109s the enemy's armament being very superior, namely trench mortars, hand grenades, tommy guns and small field guns. One particularly objectionable form of aggression was made by way of petrol bombs. These burst in the undergrowth and encircled us with a ring of flames.

At this time I was trying to obtain contact with the remainder of 30 Squadron personnel cut off at the bottom of the valley by the side of the camp, in order to withdraw them to more secure positions on the slopes overlooking the aerodrome. The time was now about 14.00 hours. The enemy drove our men who had been taken prisoner in front of them, using them as a protective screen. Any sign of faltering on their part was rewarded with a shot in the back. Our men were very reluctant to open fire and gradually gave ground. A small party of RAF led by 534164 Corporal Harrison succeeded in out-flanking them on one side, and I and a handful of New Zealand troops on the other were able to snipe at the Germans in the rear and succeeded thereby in releasing at least 14 prisoners.

Towards the close of the day we discovered that our communications with our forces in the rear had been cut and after an unsuccessful advance made by our two "I" tanks, we decided to withdraw under cover of darkness, in order to take up positions with the 23rd Battalion of the New Zealand Forces. During the next morning we were unsuccessful in locating them and had to withdraw from our cover under heavy aerial attack for another three miles where at last we made contact.

*Resting by the roadside.*

Throughout the day we held the left flank of a ridge and as evening approached took up new positions in a gully on a hill side. Here, Col. Allen, after consultation with the RAF officer, decided our men needed a rest. Unfortunately we were unable to contact the 5th Brigade; once more the enemy had cut it off. A message was prepared by Lt. Sutton RN to be taken to RAF Headquarters Canea, repeated to the Naval officer in charge at Suda Bay and volunteers were called for, to wit one officer and one airman to take this message. I, together with 522638 LAC Cooper, started off at 16.00 hours and reached 5th Brigade Headquarters in a village about half way between Canea and Maleme after a hazardous detour between sniping picquets. The rest of the Squadron followed the next day, about 30 strong. I proceeded to Headquarters RAF, arriving there 09.30 hours on 23rd May. LAC Cooper remained at Headquarters 5th Brigade. Here Group Captain Beamish had planned for the removal of 30 Squadron to a rest camp.

During the period of the rest camp, volunteers were called for to remove petrol from the dump behind Suda Bay to the quay side in broad daylight during dive bombing by Stukas. Again prominent were 534164 Corporal Harrison and 643789 LAC Campbell.

On 26th May we were moved at dusk towards Sphakia, where we lay hid in caves above the harbour. I reconnoitred the surrounding countryside and located what I considered would be an evacuation point.

On the evening of 29th May I was warned by Squadron Leader Kerr that an attempt might be made by the Navy to take off 30 Squadron personnel. In view of this I marched the men off under cover of darkness towards the beach, going through a stick of bombs and over hazardous country. I halted them on the hillside above the village and warned them [that] as there was no cover I would have to march them back into the hills if I considered the likelihood of the destroyers not turning up before midnight. The men remained in the charge of 563510 Sgt. Summers and I proceeded forward to make a solo reconnaissance. I discovered that nobody in the village had any knowledge of this impending withdrawal until I heard a Naval Commander asking for a working party to assist the wounded down to the beach and empty the picket boats of stores for those remaining. I promptly offered the services of 30 Squadron, which was gratefully accepted. The men worked wonders and in a very short period the stores were landed, and wounded, both walking and stretcher cases, were safely embarked. Our men were the last to leave the beach for the ships, and at 03.00 hours we set sail. During the early hours of the morning we were treated to our last dive bombing attack, which luckily proved abortive.

FOOTNOTE

Owing to the heavy casualties sustained by the squadron during the first day's fighting, I reorganised the airmen into three sections under the command of 513221 Cpl. Powell, 566195 Cpl. Pearce and 534164 Cpl. Harrison, using 563510 Sgt. Summers and 77863 Plt. Off. H. Black as my staff. A system of runners was used as a means of communication between sections; 592638 LAC Cooper was very prominent in this field. The high standard of morale shown by the squadron personnel was entirely due to the cheerful outlook maintained by the section commanders, who were always to be heard encouraging their men. Appreciation was voiced wherever we fought, both by the New Zealand and Australian troops, and [on] the last day [by] the Navy."

In this report, references to Luftwaffe aircraft landing on the beach are inaccurate — they landed, or crash-landed, on the airfield, which was of course close to the seashore.

Sheltering in a trench at Maleme camp were about nine members of 30 Squadron. One of them, 34-year-old LAC Ernest 'Mike' Walker, who had been confidential clerk to Sqn. Ldr. Milward, kept a diary of the events of the next few days and many years later wrote a book, 'The Price of Surrender', about their experiences in Crete and later as prisoners of war. Ernest had the most recent pages of the squadron's Form 540 (Operational Record Book) in his shirt pocket, given to him for safe keeping several days before the last Blenheim left. Although not much had been

*LAC E. W. Walker was one of the ground personnel of 30 Squadron*
*[E. W. Walker].*

written it would have been useful to the enemy, so he tore it up and buried the pieces. These men were not found for several hours, but when a hand grenade was thrown into their trench (and presumably failed to explode!) they gave themselves up. Apart from Walker, the inmates were Cpl. R. J. Lawrence, aged 24, a supplier; Cpl. A. W. 'Lofty' Bond, aged 26; Bill Austin, a 24-year-old stores accountant; AC1 Albert 'Dinger' Bell, aged about 22, a stores assistant; George Burwell, about 26, an aircraft hand; and Cpl. E. A. 'Darky' Dear, a cook. Others left behind included Flg. Off. Cullen and LAC Norman J. Darch, medical orderly.

By dawn on 21st May the whole district was in German hands. At about 14.00, the hill on which Cpl. Croxton and his mates had stopped came under attack by Ju 87 dive-bombers. The men then decided to make their way down the hill, and at the bottom they found a ditch in which they took cover from the circling enemy aircraft. Late in the afternoon, Ju 52s landed to off-load several hundred more troops and light armoured vehicles and guns. As dusk fell, Cpl. Croxton and his party, understandably confused, tried to decide what to do next. Six of them decided to head south and the other eight turned eastward toward Khania. That night they were given shelter in a village school and did manage to sleep for a time.

Opposition at this stage was limited, but on the morning of 22nd May two British guns four miles away succeeded in hitting the airfield to the extent that it was out of action for a few hours. The RAF evaders set off again, taking cover under trees whenever an aircraft was heard. Tom Croxton remembers picking a few oranges but cannot recall eating anything else. They reached Khania at about noon and found RAF HQ. That afternoon the town was heavily bombed, and the men spent a good deal of time under a table until in the evening, when the raids had finished, they were taken to a transit camp.

The prisoners were set to work clearing 50-gallon oil drums and the wrecks of aircraft from the airfield, filling craters, unloading Ju 52 aircraft and stretcher bearing. No food was available for three days, and to add to the men's troubles, there were spasmodic raids by Hurricanes from Egypt. After about three weeks of forced labour, the prisoners were taken to a transit camp near Khania and from there to Germany.

Tom Croxton and his group of men were much luckier. On 25th May they were loaded into lorries and taken to Sphakia, on the south coast of the island. "It was a nightmare trip over the mountains on roads with no lights and no moon" recalls Tom. "When nearing the coast we left the lorry, which was then pushed over a cliff, as there was nowhere to turn round. We rested where we could. Rations were short, and I was given two biscuits — hard tack — on the evening of 28th May and was told they were my rations for 29th May if the Navy did not arrive. I was hungry and ate them. Later that evening we were told that airmen from Maleme were to form a beach party for the evacuation. Once all the wounded were evacuated we could go too if there was room. At the cry of 'last boats', knowing all the wounded had gone, I left on HMS Kandahar. We only had one air attack on the journey to Egypt, and I remember what a wonderful sight it was, four destroyers at full speed on a glassy sea, zigzagging their way south. When we reached Egypt, we were re-kitted, but our personal possessions had all been lost in Crete."

Confirming this report, Mr. W. R. Harrison says "I remember standing up to my waist in water, passing packing cases over our heads to the shore, then assisting the wounded into small boats, and finally we were given permission to get into the boats ourselves and were taken to the destroyers, which set sail for Alexandria at about 3 a.m."

LAC Ken Stone, an instrument maker who had joined 30 Squadron at Eleusis, was one of those who made their own way towards safety. "We encountered a group of severely wounded men being nursed under the trees as best those who stayed with them could do" he says. "It was one of the saddest moments, for I knew some of them. We carried on up the hill in single file..........travelled all night and when dawn came took shelter under a wall. We had no idea where we were, but soon found that we were in the centre of fierce cross-fire. Any hope we had of joining up with our forces or of sleep we so badly needed was impossible." For the next seven days Ken and his colleagues travelled south, guided by Cretans. They did not eat until the third day, when they found a cheese maker in a hut high in the mountains. The shepherd's son led the

*The memorial to the many men of 30 Squadron who lost their lives in Crete with, below, a close-up of the panel listing their names.*

party to Souia, by which time they numbered abut 120. All the men were desperate for food, and an Australian killed a donkey which was cooked and shared out. At dusk an airman who had an Aldis lamp stood on the beach and signalled out to sea, and after a time everyone was overjoyed to see an answering signal, and waited expectantly. Unfortunately nothing happened, and the men decided to leave Souia and make for Sphakia. On the way they heard that evacuation was taking place there. "Passing through the Gorge of Samaria" recalls Ken Stone "some of us were able to get a little food from the monastery, although [the monks] had little themselves. Weary as we were, we kept going day and night to reach the evacuation beach. There, we were told to wait in a rocky clearing with hundreds of others and to appoint one [man] in charge of a group of fifty, all of whom must be of the same units. There were not a dozen RAF men, let alone fifty, so I made up a list of 'odd bods' and waited for the call which never came."

On the morning of 28th May, the Royal Navy was forced to abandon any hope of further evacuation from Sphakia, as heavy losses of shipping had already been suffered. Stuka dive-bombers were attacking everything that moved on the water, including some small boats containing men who had tried to leave under their own initiative. As the sun rose, a German officer with a loud-hailer ordered the men to lay out anything white to signify surrender to the Luftwaffe, and with assurances from the German that they would be well treated they did so. Ken Stone says that thousands of men stood in the clearing waving anything white they had, as wave after wave of aircraft flew over. "Down came the bombs, and the strafing carved visible paths through the mass of men caught in the open" he remembers. "How many died I don't know. I dived behind a rock with another [man] by my side. He was not fully protected by the rock and a hail of bullets took off his arm at the shoulder and he died by my side. Finally, they flew off, and the German officer apologised through his loud-hailer, explaining that due to the success of the hard-fought rearguard action he had lost touch with the Luftwaffe. He also told us of the Germans' amazement at our surrender, as plans were in hand for a German evacuation. A long and weary walk to a makeshift prison camp near Platanias began." Another report mentions that fraternisation between German troops and their captives was under way when the Luftwaffe appeared and shot up the beach area, killing some of their own countrymen as well as Allied servicemen.

Former Cpl. R. J. Lawrence, who was one of those captured in the fall of Crete and who after the war was a prosecution witness at

the War Crimes Trials at Nuremburg, discussed the campaign with a German officer who had taken part in the air drop on Maleme, Oberst Lt. Baron von der Heydte. During their conversation, the German asked "Why, at Maleme, did you surrender? At the moment when you did, we, the Germans, were at the point of capitulating!" This was hard to believe, but Mr. Lawrence remarked that the Germans' superior military might was very nearly equalled by the Allies' tenacity and bluff. "If only we'd known!" he said.

After the fall of Crete, Allied wounded were evacuated to Athens, the more serious in Ju 52 aircraft, and admitted to the prisoner of war hospital at Kokinia. This was staffed by a mixture of British, Australian and New Zealand medical officers, but Tom Cullen was the only RAF MO there.

As a result of the fighting, 30 Squadron lost one officer and 29 airmen, and two officers and 56 other ranks were taken prisoner. Only three of the graves in the Commonwealth War Cemetery at Suda Bay are those of 30 Squadron men, the remainder having no known burial places. At Suda Bay, only eighteen graves are marked 'Unknown Airman', so unfortunately the remains of the others could be anywhere.

148

In the late 1980s survivors from 33 and 30 Squadrons determined to try to have an appropriate Memorial built to record the names of those who lost their lives and to commemorate the event. No public funds were available, and building a memorial abroad presented formidable difficulties. After fund raising, the promoters were very fortunate to find invaluable help in Crete from a benefactor, Mr. Elef Tsiknakis, whose family had been brutally treated by the Germans and who had himself trained in England

*HRH The Duke of Kent and the late AVM David Dick during the dedication of the Maleme memorial on 25th May 1991.*

and later flown with the Greek Air Force. Without his great assistance the project would not have succeeded. The Memorial is situated on the lower slopes of 'Hill 107', facing north-east and overlooking the Tavronitis River and the old bridge around which much heavy fighting had taken place. It is in the form of an ellipse some eight metres (26 feet) across, with the names of fifty men engraved in granite tablets set into the rear wall, and identified with their Squadron. 30 Squadron Association hopes that it will remind Cretans and visiting Britons that men from other countries shared their own great sacrifices whilst defending Crete against tyranny. The Memorial was unveiled by HRH the Duke of Kent in a moving and most appropriate ceremony at 11 am on 25th May 1991, fifty years after the battle. He was accompanied by AVM A. D. Dick CB CBE AFC MA FRAeS RAF (Retired), the then Chairman of the 30 Squadron Association, who had done so much to foster the memorial project. Twenty-four veterans who fought in the battle whilst serving with the two squadrons were able to attend the ceremony, including the men who commanded the two squadrons in May 1941 and the two then current Commanding Officers. An ATC Cadet from 30(F) Squadron in Cardiff also attended.

The 50th Anniversary commemorated in Crete in May 1991 was very different from that commemorated in Britain in September 1990; it did not mark an historic British victory which saved the free world. Probably at least partly because of the prodigious effort required to achieve that victory in the Battle of Britain, the Commonwealth on its own did not have enough resources to defeat the German airborne invasion of Crete. But from the Battle of Crete came three consequences which affected the subsequent course of the war. Firstly, the delay of at least a month which this diversion entailed to Operation 'Barbarossa' (Hitler's invasion of Russia) may well have denied Hitler the ability to take Moscow before the onset of the Russian winter of 1941. Second, the severe loss of transport aircraft and air dropping capability had a very telling effect when they were so badly needed later in that campaign, especially at Stalingrad. And third, following the very heavy casualties inflicted on the elite German airborne forces, they were never used again operationally.

*Standards raised during the service of dedication*

*[B. Fraser].*

*Fitters, riggers and armourers of One Flight of 30 Squadron at Edku in mid-1941*  [*Sqn. Ldr. A. T. Roberts*].

# Chapter 5: A New Beginning

As soon as Sqn. Ldr. Milward reported to Headquarters Middle East he was sent for by Air Chief Marshal Tedder, who wanted an update of the position in Crete. When asked about re-equipment of 30 Squadron, the CO told Tedder that the pilots had a strong desire to fly Hurricanes rather than the Marylands proposed by higher authority. This was readily agreed, and new tropicalised Hurricanes began to arrive at Amriya on 5th June 1941. An intensive training programme began, helped by the fact that most of the pilots had flown Hurricanes unofficially in Crete to help the exhausted pilots of 33 Squadron. Within a week, operational flying began, with aircraft at readiness for the defence of Alexandria, but a move to Edku (otherwise known as LG.246) was soon ordered, and 30 Squadron personnel made the journey on 14/15th June by road. On arrival, they found that no communication between Edku and 252 Wing Operations Room had been installed, which meant that for the time being operations would have to be mounted from elsewhere.

30 Squadron Hurricanes began operating from Maryut on 16th June, four aircraft being held at readiness while carrying out practice interceptions. On 20th June R/T was installed in the Operations Room at Edku and two days later came into service, albeit not always effectively. During the next few days there were a number of 'alarms and excursions', but no interceptions took place. Reinforcing 30 Squadron, a Flight of 261 Squadron's Hurricanes was attached on 26th June. Enemy raiders appeared over Alexandria two days later, but 30 Squadron was not called on to go into action.

Sqn. Ldr. Milward was posted to the Far East at the end of June, but before leaving he met the fortunate few of the ground personnel of 30 Squadron who had managed to escape from Crete with the help of the Royal Navy. "They and their companions, lost or captured, fought with whatever weapons they could lay their hands on, and set standards of courage and devotion to duty second to none" wrote Wg. Cdr. Milward OBE DFC MRAeS RAF (Retd.) recently. In his place came Sqn. Ldr. F. A. Marlow, who took over the post on 28th June 1941.

July 1941 began with a pre-dawn intrusion by three enemy aircraft making for Aboukir at about 14,000 feet, but they were driven off by heavy AA fire. On 2nd July Wg. Cdr. Cross arrived to brief the pilots on dive-bombing, after which six of them took to the air to practice over the camp, to the consternation of some of its residents! Night flying practice was also carried out that evening, using Aboukir airfield, as Edku's eastern landing ground was not equipped with landing lights. More dive-bombing training followed on 3rd July, this time directed against ships in Alexandria harbour.

A squadron defence scheme was organised on 4th July, and protective revetments for the Hurricanes were built on the eastern landing ground at Edku. For the personnel, sandbagged protection was built instead of slit trenches, as the sand was surprisingly wet.

## A night fighter role

Night flying was given priority over the next few days, usually carried out from the western landing ground at Edku. The 261 Squadron detachment left for Abu Sueir on 9th July, depleting 30 Squadron's strength, but to make up for the deficiency six Yugoslavian officers and seven other ranks were posted in. To help them gain local knowledge of R/T procedures, they paid a visit to 252 Wing Operations Room. On 11th July 252 Wing ordered that 30 Squadron was to operate as a night fighter unit as from 22.00 that evening, and from that point only practice flying was carried out during daylight hours. During one such

*Hurricanes of 30 Squadron 'B' Flight at Edku. No squadron code was being carried at this time, only individual aircraft letters.*

**Above:** *30 Squadron Hurricanes in a neat line at Edku*       *[G. Titmas].*
**Right:** *30 Squadron personnel in their living accommodation at Edku. There seems to be an appreciable number of empty beer bottles awaiting removal! The names are (left to right) Anderson, Edwards and Pierce*          *[E. Wallis].*

*Hurricane T9531 of 30 Squadron, probably at Edku.*

*A water bowser delivering its load to thirsty airmen at Edku. As water was in very short supply, many airmen had their hair cut short to minimise washing* [N. Lancaster].

*A group of 30 Squadron airmen pose in front of their tent at Edku* [N. Lancaster].

*Hurricane Z4186 at Edku [N. Lancaster].*

sortie, Plt. Off. H. K. Cartwright force-landed on mud flats ten miles west of Rosetta, not injuring himself badly but severely damaging the aircraft. Another Hurricane was written off when on 23rd July one of the Yugoslavians, Plt. Off. Cranjanski, crashed near Edku following engine trouble. Later the same day, while carrying out night flying cooperation with searchlights and

Wellington bombers, Sgt. L. A. Ovens crashed on landing, destroying Hurricane Z6988 but again luckily suffering no injury. To make up for the deficiency in aircraft numbers, four new Hurricanes arrived on 25th July, with an elderly Hart biplane for use as the squadron 'hack', and seven more Hurricanes followed by the end of the month. To conform to regulations, all the

***Above:*** *A Hurricane line-up at Edku* [N. Lancaster].

***Right:*** *Armourers in a tent at Edku reading books and papers* [N. Lancaster].

152

*Inside a semi-dugout tent at Edku, N. Lancaster studied for his pilot's course* *[N. Lancaster].*

*A group of satisfied armourers* *[N. Lancaster].*

*More Hurricanes of 30 Squadron at Edku* *[N. Lancaster].*

*A nice sunset picture of 30 Squadron pilots at Edku (left to right: Flt. Lt. Davidson, Flg. Off. Jarvis, Sgt. Owens, Sgt. Marrack, Flg. Off. Basam and Sqn. Ldr. Marlow.*

*Two, six! Airmen using their backs to lift a Hurricane out of a hole*       *[N. Lancaster].*

Hurricanes went to Aboukir on 29th July to be painted black for night-flying.

At last, on 1st August, 30 Squadron was able to intercept an enemy aircraft. At 21.30 three Hurricanes were airborne to follow up a report of an intrusion, and when approaching the AA fire being directed at the raiders Flt. Lt. R. T. P. Davidson spotted one about 500 feet below him on a conflicting course. He put in a two-second burst of fire, but then had to break away as he was dangerously close to the AA fire, and lost sight of the intruder. After a number of false alarms on succeeding nights, 30 Squadron's next chance to tangle with the enemy came on 7th August, when seven aircraft were in the air nine minutes after being scrambled.

Thirty minutes later two cries of 'Tally Ho!' were heard over the R/T, indicating that enemy aircraft were being engaged. In each case the pilot let off violent and effective bursts of gunfire, but Sgt. Marrack had to break off the engagement when he was too close to the AA fire. Flt. Sgt. G. W. Ratlidge, however, made a three-quarter stern attack on an enemy aircraft and followed it towards the sea. When last seen it was continuing to descend, and a later report from 252 Wing confirms that an eye witness saw it go into the water. Next day a German broadcast admitted that four of their aircraft had not returned to base, and it was known that searches for survivors were being made fifty miles out to sea. A similar raid was made next night, but his time no interception was possible.

*30 Squadron Hurricane 'E' at Edku*       *[G. E. Titmas].*

*Away into the desert! A truck-load of 30 Squadron personnel about to leave*
[N. Lancaster].

**Above left:** *Wt. Off. 'Jock' Ratlidge in the Western Desert.*
**Above right:** *The bearded Flt. Lt. R. T. P. Davidson seen at LG.121 in January 1942. He had received the very unusual permission to grow a beard two months earlier*                [D. A. McDonald].

**Above left:** *Flt. Lt. Cartwright.*
**Above right:** *In command of 30 Squadron at LG.05 was Sqn. Ldr. Marlow.*

The Yugoslavian pilots, now deemed to be proficient in R/T procedures, were put on daytime standby on 15th August, and over the next few days carried out practice scrambles and interceptions. To improve the efficiency of interceptions, a new vectoring station with the call-sign 'Lofty' came into use on 26th August, and although using unsophisticated equipment it soon proved an asset. Meanwhile, scramble times were steadily improving, and on 30 August one of 30 Squadron's aircraft was in the air 48 seconds after the command, an all-Egypt record.

Then a tragedy took the life of a pilot who 'pushed his luck' a little too far. At 09.10 on 31st August 1941 three Hurricanes piloted by Yugoslavians took off to carry out a practice formation exercise. About an hour later, 252 Wing reported that they were shooting up Alexandria harbour, contrary to all the flying regulations which had been explained to the Yugoslavians many times. All three Hurricanes then approached Edku from the west at 150 feet above ground level in vic formation, climbed to 550 feet and split up. One pilot, however, found himself in difficulties, and his aircraft went over onto its back. He tried to extricate himself by using right and left rudder, but with insufficient height he could not pull out and the Hurricane (Z7004) hit the ground, bursting into flames. The fire was beyond the capacity of the antiquated fire-fighting vehicles, and the pilot had clearly been killed instantly. Sqn. Ldr. Marlow immediately grounded all the Yugoslavians, which meant that other pilots had to take over the 'readiness' function even though they had been on standby all night. Nothing more is known of the remaining Yugoslavians.

That evening, a panic call was received from control and within twelve minutes nine Hurricanes and a cooperative Beaufighter were in the air. Light bursts were fired at enemy aircraft without apparent effect, but before midnight it was confirmed that a large number of incendiary bombs had been dropped on the area of Aboukir.

September was occupied with routine scramble practice, the occasional raider and on 11th September a formation flypast by twelve Hurricanes over the Alexandria area. As the squadron diarist recorded, "It was really a sight to please the eye of even the less informed Plt. Off. Prune", a reference to a cartoon character of the time. The only mishap of the month occurred when Plt. Off. R. C. Graves, returning from an interception at dawn on 15th September, experienced engine trouble and crashed into Lake Edku, luckily not damaging himself but writing off his aircraft, W9132. October followed much the same pattern, until on 13th October a preliminary warning of a squadron move into the Western Desert was received. The CO flew in that direction on 17th October to try to elicit more information, followed on 21st October by Flg. Off. Smith, who had the misfortune to force-land at

*A pair of 30 Squadron Hurricanes await refuelling.*

LG.104. During his absence, eighteen Hurricanes arrived at Edku from 94 Squadron, to be taken over by 30 Squadron for use in desert conditions.

## Life in the Western Desert

Details of 30 Squadron's new task having been arranged, an advance party left Edku at 07.00 on 24th October and arrived at LG.102 (located at 31°36'00"N 27°33'30"E) fifteen and a half hours later. The eighteen Hurricanes flew in next day, and the main ground party also made the journey. The next two days were spent in arranging the accommodation and drawing stores, and in the evening 'hospitality' visits were made to other squadrons in the area. There was also a unique reunion of four former members of 30 Squadron now attached to other units — Wg. Cdr. A. C. Bocking DFC (who as a Flt. Lt. had been in charge of 'A' Flight in Egypt and Greece), Sqn. Ldr. Horgan (a veteran of the Greece campaign as a Flt. Lt.), Sqn. Ldr. Walker (another Greece veteran as both Flg. Off. and Flt. Lt.) and Sgt. Stammers.

Administrative alterations had placed 30 and 33 Squadrons and a Fleet Air Arm fighter squadron under the control of 264 Wing, which was formed at Sidi Haneish on 24th October 1941, only to be renumbered 269 Wing six days later!

Having settled down at LG.102, the squadron took up its night-flying task again. It was not long, however, before LG.102 was considered unsuitable for night operations, there being too many obstructions there. One wonders why the squadron had been sent there if that was the case. Whatever the reason, the decision was taken on 1st November to use LG.07 (Mersah Matruh West, otherwise known as LG.Z), a detachment of ground crew personnel making the journey both ways each night. From there on 3rd November two scrambles took place, but no interceptions were made. Ground mist began to cover the landing ground, and Flt. Lt. Allison had to force-land. Flg. Off. Jarvis landed at LG.104 (Qotafiya II), but there was no news of Sgt. Davies until next day, when he returned to base after force-landing fifteen miles from LG.07. On 5th November Sgt. C. W. Anderson became lost while on the way to LG.07 and could not be contacted by W/T, but next morning it was found that he also had crash-landed, without injury. A request was then made to Wing HQ that the use of LG.07 be discontinued, and this was quickly agreed.

Sgt. Ovens, a gentleman whose name would reoccur in the annals of 30 Squadron, was flying Z4710 on dawn patrol on 13th November when he sighted a Ju 88 very close to him at about 5500 feet and moving in the same direction. His approach was not seen, and he was able to make stern-quarter attacks from port and starboard, causing the enemy pilot to turn to port to give his gunner an opportunity to open fire. However, he was promptly silenced, and after Ovens had fired a few more bursts a bright orange glow appeared in the port engine of the Ju 88. By that time Sgt. Ovens had used all his ammunition, so had to return to base not knowing whether the enemy bomber had survived.

A captured Bf 110 twin-engined fighter was demonstrated to 30 Squadron pilots by Wg. Cdr. Barnes on 14th November, after which dummy attacks were made on it by pilots of 'B' Flight, which they considered "..........excellent practice for things to come." Then came another move, this time to LG.05, near Sidi Barrani (located at 31°32'30"N 26°01'00"E and otherwise known as LG.X), to where the squadron travelled on 16 November. As soon as everyone had arrived, work began on setting up a sub-sector operations room so that the task allocated to the squadron by Wing HQ, protection of shipping and of LG.75 and LG.76, could be carried out effectively. All 'scrambles' would now be controlled by the squadron itself, and fighter controllers, operations clerks, telephone operators and others all had to be co-opted from within the squadron.

Life at LG.05 has been described by 'Canada Mac' McDonald, who wrote "LG.05 was a large flat area surrounded by PACs,

*The captured Bf 110 which was demonstrated to 30 Squadron crews in the Western Desert. There are no clues as to its former identity.*

individual rockets spaced about 40 feet apart and wired to a sandbagged sentry-post. If enemy aircraft started to strafe the airfield, the sentry would fire the rockets, which would go up several hundred feet, trailing chains. A parachute then deployed to suspend the chains for several minutes, entangling any enemy aircraft which tried to fly through them." Whether this somewhat Heath Robinson-like contraption was ever used in anger is not recorded. 'Mac' goes on to say "We were housed in tents, usually in a dug-out two to three feet down surrounded by sandbags. The squadron operations room was in a dug-out where there was a telephone and a radio transmitter and receiver. I expected the desert to be hot and dry, but found LG.05 to be cool and wet, as it was quite close to the Mediterranean Sea. There was only one tent for eating, and you had to take your own plate, mug and 'irons'. After eating, you washed your utensils in a pan of water just outside the tent. After having up to 200 plates swished through it, the water was usually pretty grungy. Fortunately, we had a five-gallon drum of water sitting on top of a Primus burner in each tent, which helped in our cleaning-up. There were usually four officers in each tent, and the first to wake would light the burner. In a few minutes the tent would be reasonably warm and we would have warm water for our ablutions."

Early interceptions made by 30 Squadron from LG05 were all of friendly aircraft such as Marylands, Martlets and Blenheims, but on 29th November at 17.50 six aircraft carrying out a dusk patrol were ordered to proceed to LG.75 to investigate a possible intruder. Twenty minutes later Plt. Off. (ex Flt. Sgt.) Ratlidge in Z4230 sighted an enemy aircraft not more than a hundred yards away and thirty feet above him. He immediately turned to attack, opening fire from the stern quarter. The enemy pilot tried evasive tactics by turning steeply to port, but Plt. Off. Ratlidge, now slightly above the enemy aircraft, fired a long burst, causing a stream of fuel vapour to pour from the starboard wing, which burst into a dull red glow of fire. At that moment another enemy aircraft appeared and fired at the Hurricane from its rear turret, but a violent explosion on the ground then occurred. Later it was confirmed that a Ju 88 had crashed in flames and the crew had been taken prisoner. For 30 Squadron, victory was in the air!

Convoy patrols were usually somewhat boring for the pilots, but occasionally there was some action. On 17th December Flt. Lt. Davidson and Sgt. Ovens, who were nearing the end of a convoy patrol, were given vectors by a destroyer onto a He 111, which they saw a mile ahead heading out to sea at about fifty feet above the water. Catching up with it, the two Hurricane pilots opened fire from both stern quarters at 300 yards, closing to 100 yards. The enemy gunners returned fire with what appeared to be a cannon or large-bore machine-gun using explosive bullets. After making several attacks, Davidson and Ovens had used all their ammunitions and had to break off, feeling bitter that the enemy aircraft had not dived into the sea after having expended so much

*Flt. Lt. L. Bush, the squadron intelligence officer, with 'Rommel', his dachsund mascot.*

ammunition on it. Their only compensation was that the He 111 was seen to be losing speed and seemed to be in difficulties.

Former Plt. Off. P. M. Hamilton, who arrived to join 30 Squadron on the last day of 1941, also remembers the somewhat basic conditions at LG05. "Our diet consisted mainly of bully beef, soya links, raw onions, biscuits and jam, and of course tea," he says. "However, everyone seemed reasonably healthy and the weather in January was quite pleasant, apart from the odd sandstorm. Some evenings we played bridge. My usual partner was Sgt. Marrack, one of two veteran sergeant pilots on the squadron (the other one was Tony Ovens), and I think he had flown Hinds on the North-West Frontier." Mr. Hamilton goes on to say that he flew regularly, his usual No.1 being Flg. Off. Atwell. "He was the most laid-back character I ever met and often flew in red carpet-slippers! He liked to land in formation, and taught me a system of hand signals for lowering flaps, wheels, etc. The Hurricanes Mk.I were pretty 'clapped out'. When sixty miles out over the sea one was very conscious of the engine note. Several times one or other of us had to return to base with engine trouble. We were controlled by 'Twiggy' Branch from his dug-out. Our aircraft were equipped with old TR.9 radio sets which we tuned in to signals from base. Once or twice we were vectored after 'bandits', but without success."

Convoy patrols were dispensed with on 21st December, when six of 30 Squadron's Hurricanes took off to escort the AOC-in-C's aircraft to Mersa Matruh, from where, after handing over the VIP they flew to LG.102 to enjoy some hospitality and a well-deserved lunch. Next day it was back to the routine, and even on Christmas Day standing patrols were flown. As it happened, there was a some action that day when Flt. Lt. Davidson noticed transport activity in Halfaya Pass. Knowing that opposition was unlikely, he made an attack, putting two MT vehicles out of action.

Boxing Day of 1941 proved to be a day of activity for the pilots of 30 Squadron, four of whom ('A' Flight) took off at dawn to patrol the Sollum area and to intercept Ju 52/3m transport aircraft which were thought likely to drop supplies to the defending troops. While 'stooging around', these four pilots noticed some enemy movement, and when relieved by 'B' Flight carried out a diving attack from 6000 feet to just above sand-level on machine-gun posts and vehicles. Leading the assault was Plt. Off. Ratlidge, who later confirmed that the guns had been silenced and three gunners had been seen to drop to the ground. Led by Flt. Lt. Davidson, members of 'B' Flight, after finishing their patrol, attacked two enemy vehicles moving along the road parallel with the coast at the foot of Halfaya Pass, stopping both of them. Later in the day, nine aircraft took off on a dusk ground-strafing mission in the Sollum area, where they put a number of gun posts out of action and machine-gunned slit trenches and fortifications, scattering their inhabitants. Visibility in a heavy dust haze was very limited, but many successes were believed to have resulted from this enervating mission.

'Canada Mac' remembers a Colonel in command of British troops visiting the squadron to ask for the Sollum area to be strafed so that when enemy AA guns were fired at the Hurricanes Allied gunners on the ground could plot their location and shell them. The Colonel also remarked that at night enemy aircraft would fly over Allied lines and fire a Verey pistol. German troops would then light flares as a guide to Luftwaffe aircraft dropping supplies to them. "Bob Davidson devised a plan," said 'Canada Mac'. "He would fly over Sollum at night, fire off a Verey pistol and when the flares on the ground were lit he would go down and strafe them. He would then fly back over the area and release a parachute flare and the next Hurricanes would go down and strafe in its light." This operation took place on 28th December, when Sgt. Paxton took the first of eleven aircraft into the air in hazy conditions at 17.30. During the course of the strafing, AA guns, dispersed MT vehicles and a heavily fortified defence line and dugouts were attacked. Opposition was put up by AA fire, machine-gun fire and even rifles. Unfortunately, Hurricane Z4709, flown by Plt. Off. Theobald, failed to return after the operation, and he was not found in a subsequent search. It was known that he had been active over the target, and it was thought that he might have fallen foul of enemy aircraft which paid a retaliatory visit to LG.05 at 19.15 that evening, dropping a stick of bombs two miles south of the airfield and others at Sidi Barrani.

For 30 Squadron at LG.05, 1942 began with three convoy patrols of two Hurricanes each, but deteriorating weather brought an end to flying at 14.45. Next day the Luftwaffe put in an appearance when a solitary Ju 88 dropped four bombs on the south-east corner of the airfield, but during the afternoon eight aircraft were at readiness for any help which might have been required by a convoy. As it happened, no assistance was needed, and night patrols off Bardia were cancelled. Heavy rain on 3rd January put the airfield out of action.

## More gains and losses

Then came a day of sadness for the squadron, for on 4th January during a convoy patrol Plt. Off. F. A. Scott broke away from the loose formation and disappeared, without any obvious reason. His opposite number, Plt. Off. A. D. Wagner, was unable to say in which direction he had gone, and needed help himself when he returned to base, as weather conditions had worsened. Verey pistols were fired to guide him in, and more were fired in the hope that Plt. Off. Scott would appear, but when his fuel must have run out hope was abandoned. Information on the missing aircraft was given to army units in the area, but to no avail. Further attempts to find Plt. Off. Scott and his Hurricane were made next day, and a Walrus amphibian joined in, but without result, so he had to be posted as missing. Eventually Scott's body was recovered by the Navy and he was given a proper burial at sea.

Two other pilots, returning to base after a patrol, had a unique experience. Acting on information provided by South African troops, the squadron operations room vectored the two aircraft onto a small craft becalmed four miles north of Barrani Point. On being sighted, six men aboard the twenty-foot long vessel waved to the

Hurricane pilots, and subsequently the craft was captured and about thirty Germans taken prisoner. It was found that they had attempted to escape from Bardia after heavy shelling by Allied forces, but engine failure and adverse tidal conditions had brought them to a halt. Routine convoy patrols then continued, and on 6th January one Hurricane crashed on landing, luckily without serious injury to the pilot. Another one suffered engine failure on take-off on 8th January, the pilot sustaining a beautiful black eye but nothing worse.

Poor visibility conspired to limit 30 Squadron's operations over the next few days, but at noon on 11th January there was some excitement when Flg. Off. Jarvis, on solitary patrol, spotted a submarine near the convoy he was shepherding. From out of the sun he dived on the vessel from 3000 feet, raking it with machine-gun fire from stern to bows. The submarine crash-dived, and although Jarvis informed the escorting destroyer of its position so that further action could be taken, no results were seen. Altogether, 30 Squadron pilots sighted twenty-five submarines in two weeks of convoy patrols.

Another loss to the squadron was experienced on 12th January, when two aircraft were on dawn patrol over the Sollum – Halfaya area. Spotting some Ju 52/3m transport aircraft, the two pilots made an attack. Plt. Off. Cartwright noticed two bursts of fire from his colleague, Plt. Off. Ratlidge, the first a three-second burst of tracer delivered downwards over the sea. A second burst, a minute later, was seen two miles east of Sollum Point at low altitude. This fire was long, and an orange flame appeared which burnt for about five seconds before dying out. Flying out to sea, Cartwright identified some exhaust flames as those of a Ju 52/3m and made a head-on attack, only breaking away at the last moment but unfortunately not seeing the result. Meanwhile, Ratlidge had disappeared without trace, and searches throughout the day failed to find him or his aircraft.

More of the Luftwaffe's 'Tante Ju' aircraft were seen next day by Flt. Lt. Davidson, who made several attempts to shoot one down, machine-gunning enemy ground positions at the same time. On 14th January Sgt. Ovens, out on patrol early in the morning, strafed enemy motor vehicles at Halfaya Pass. All three vehicles were brought to a rapid standstill. Meanwhile Sgt. Ovens' 'oppo', Sgt. T. G. Paxton, had spotted a submarine and three motor launches near Bardia, which he reported to Wing. A Swordfish torpedo-carrying aircraft was soon on its way to the scene.

Sgt. Paxton was in the news again on 17th January when operating from Ber el Gabi. While on patrol at an altitude of 4000 feet, he saw bombs being dropped near the convoy, and after being warned over the R/T he spotted two Ju 88s above him. After climbing to 10,000 feet, Paxton chased the enemy aircraft from out of the sun, causing one of the Ju 88s to show signs of becoming uncontrollable. When he attacked again, he had the satisfaction of seeing an explosion between the port engine and the fuselage of the enemy aircraft, followed by the total disintegration of the engine. Although dense cloud prevented his seeing the Ju 88's fate, Paxton's kill was confirmed by HMS *Carlisle*. Vastly cheered by his success, he engaged the second Ju 88 by firing a burst from 600 yards, but it was able to escape into cloud. While on similar duty later in the day, Sgt. Marrack sighted a submarine on the surface about twenty miles from an Allied convoy. Although the submarine began to dive, he opened fire at the conning tower, but failed to inflict any visual damage. These exploits were the highlight of 30 Squadron's day.

One of the two pilots who answered a panic call on 18th January, Sgt. J. P. Morris, crashed his Hurricane at LG.75 while on his way back to base, but until 22nd January there was little activity. That day was spent in preparing for a move to LG.121, a new landing ground at 31º32'00"N 26º11'30" E, a move which would reunite the squadron, part of which had been at LG.05 and part at LG.102. The move from LG.102 was made on 23rd January

*Above left: Seen at LG.121 in the Western Desert in January 1942 is Plt. Off. Wagner* [D. A. McDonald].
*Above right: Probably photographed in the chill of early morning at LG.121 was Flg. Off. Cartwright* [D. A. McDonald]

*Sgt. Ratlidge (right).*

in good time, although five of the vehicles had broken springs! By late afternoon, all the domestic tents and some of the working tents had been pitched, with the willing help of Indian troops in the area. The party from LG.05 arrived next day and were soon busy putting up their tented accommodation. A general air of pleasure at meeting old friends developed at mealtimes, and everyone settled down very quickly. Before long, it became clear that the site of the camp, on the main road from Sidi Barrani to Mersa Matruh, would be used by passing convoys as a staging post. Even during the first few days, the cookhouse served an average of forty extra meals per day!

Flying from LG.121 began on 25th January with four aircraft on convoy patrol and a number of air tests. However, conditions were about to change in a big way. After convoy patrols in the morning of 26th January a rising wind developed into a gale, and by lunch-time the camp, which had been ready for the CO to inspect, had assumed the appearance of a wasteland. Despite ingenious methods used by the occupiers of the tents to keep them intact, at least half the camp was flattened. Even the staff of the orderly room, who struggled to keep their impeccable filing system in order, lost the battle, their 'bumph' soon spreading from their tent to the beach! This was much to the dismay of the staff, who spent the remaining hours of daylight collecting the elusive paperwork. Throughout the night the gale continued unabated. Some untoward event must have taken place elsewhere as well, as during that day all MT vehicles were sent 'poste haste' to Mersa Matruh to be loaded with petrol to be taken to Gambut.

Relaying of roads within the camp with earth-filled petrol tins began next day, but a dust storm did nothing to improve matters. On 28th January a convoy of forty vehicles on their way to Gambut arrived from Helwan in the evening. With no rations, each driver was issued with supplies for four days, given tea and breakfast next morning and sent on his way.

LG.121 proved to be something of a Mecca for visiting aircraft. Sixteen Hurricanes refuelled there on 1st February, and next day the arrival of a number of Hurricanes, Blenheims, Fulmars,

Albacores and various transport aircraft gave the airfield something of a feeling of peacetime routine flying. Little of importance took place until 10th February, when Sqn. Ldr. G. F. Chater DFC, a South African who had fought in the Battle of Britain, took over as CO in place of Sqn. Ldr. Marlow, who expressed his appreciation of the work done by the squadron while under his command.

Next day, in answer to a 'scramble' call Flt. Lt. Davidson took off at 09.30, and while flying at 8000 feet saw a Ju 88 4000 feet above him and 2000 yards ahead. Unable to close with the enemy aircraft, he opened fire, which prompted its pilot to turn ninety degrees and to jettison two large bombs. Davidson took advantage of this movement and fired the rest of his ammunition, causing parts of the port wing to detach, but with no more ammunition he was obliged to end the attack and did not see any further result of his action. The intrepid Sgt. Paxton, however, airborne on 12th February for a 'panic' call, did have the satisfaction of shooting down a He 111 off Mersa Matruh. Further excellent results for 30 Squadron pilots came on 15th February, when S.79 aircraft of Regia Aeronautica were intercepted while attempting to attack a convoy with torpedoes. Sergeants Marrack, Bate and Lawrence each 'bagged' one; one crashed into the sea in flames and a large piece of wing of another was shot away. No damage apart from a few explosive bullets in one fuselage and a damaged tail wheel were suffered by the Hurricanes.

### Goodbye to the desert

Then came the amazing news that 30 Squadron was to move again, not within the Middle East but to Singapore to take part in the fight against the Japanese. This move was unlike any move yet made by the squadron, because it involved a long sea voyage for men and aircraft on board an aircraft carrier. Packing began on 16 February, maintenance personnel in particular working very hard to ensure that all the Hurricanes were airworthy. An advance party left for Heliopolis next morning, and early on 18th February the main body of the squadron was ready to follow. By 20.00 on 19th February the whole squadron was there, and time was spent in issuing blue uniforms, arranging for surplus personnel to be posted, arranging promotions to meet the new establishment and issuing three weeks' advance pay. The Hurricanes were flown to 108 MU, as they were no longer required by 30 Squadron. Not wanting to miss their last chance, many members of the squadron visited Cairo's many bars, an evening remembered by 'Canada Mac'. "As we went about Cairo, Bob Davidson's beard caused quite a stir. Nobody had seen an RAF officer with a beard before, and several people tugged at it to see if it was real! We also noticed that when we went into a bar as a group, being somewhat boisterous, we caused a bit of a commotion. In some places some of those present put on a monocle to look us over with a certain air of disdain. Next day, Bob had his beard shaved off, and all of us went out to buy [plain glass] monocles. After that, when anyone put up a monocle to look us over, we as a group would do the same and stare back. We became known as the Monocle Squadron."

After travelling by train overnight, personnel of the squadron arrived at Port Tewfik at 06.00 on 22nd February and embarked on the *Princess Kathleen*, a former Canadian Pacific ferry which before the war had plied between Vancouver and Victoria, which sailed at 11.00 for Port Sudan, where it docked at 09.00 on 24th February. In view of the possibility of a long-range Luftwaffe bomber attack on the area, it was arranged that Kittyhawk fighters based at Port Sudan should be brought to readiness, and six of the 30 Squadron pilots each made one familiarisation flight to qualify on the type. However, this precaution turned out to be unnecessary.

Two hundred of 30 Squadron boarded the aircraft carrier HMS *Indomitable*, which sailed at 16.00 on 25th February, seventy of the squadron's personnel having returned aboard *Princess Kathleen* to Port Tewfik to join the rear party. By this time, however, Singapore had fallen to the Japanese, and so the destination of the *Indomitable* was changed to Ceylon.

*The aircraft carrier HMS* Indomitable, *in which 30 and 261 Squadrons travelled from the Canal Zone to Ceylon in February 1942.*

*30 Squadron's first accommodation on arriving in Ceylon was at The Blind School.*

# Chapter 6: Ceylon, 1942 to 1944

On board HMS *Indomitable*, the personnel knew only that they were bound for the Far East. In fact, the original intention had been to send 30 and 261 Squadrons to Java to help stem the seemingly unstoppable Japanese advance southwards towards Australia, but Admiral Sir Geoffrey Layton, the recently appointed C-in-C Far East, countermanded this order on his own initiative when he came to the conclusion that Hurricanes could contribute very little in Java and were much more urgently needed in Ceylon. So he ordered the *Indomitable* to divert, and it made its way toward the island.

During the ten days or so of the voyage, all personnel of 30 and 261 Squadrons worked night and day to assemble new Mk.IIb Hurricanes, so that by the evening of 6th March 1942 no less than seventy had been completed. Next day, twenty pilots of 30 Squadron were called on to do something not one of them had done before (and would not do again): fly their aircraft off the deck of the carrier. They were briefed by the Fleet Air Arm CO, who told them to apply the aircraft's brakes and rev up the engine and when the deck officer gave the signal brakes were to be released and full power applied. All made good take-offs, but one aircraft, piloted by Sgt. Whittaker, developed a glycol leak, and he decided to return, a doubly risky thing to do. With *Indomitable* steaming into wind at top speed and crash barriers raised, Whittaker made one dummy approach and then touched down, bringing the Hurricane to a stop some fifteen yards from the barrier, without benefit of an arrestor hook! Fleet Air Arm pilots were 'highly chuffed' to see that this could be done with a Hurricane Mk.IIb, and made Whittaker an honorary deck landing instructor, with an ornate scroll to prove it! Another six pilots took off later in the day to make the short flight to Ratmalana airfield, which was to be 30 Squadron's base. The carrier then continued on its way around the island to Trincomalee, where it docked on 7th March. Apart from a rear party of seven men, the 30 Squadron personnel then boarded a train for Colombo, where they arrived at 09.00 next morning, and Ratmalana was reached four hours later.

## A proper airfield at last

Situated seven miles south of Colombo and almost on the palm-fringed coast, Ratmalana (in Singhalese 'the red flower

*After flying off HMS* Indomitable *off the coast of Ceylon on 6th March 1942, Sgt. Fred Whittaker's Hurricane developed a glycol leak and he decided to return to the carrier, and made a successful landing. This photograph was taken from the bridge of the carrier just after the landing, with Sqn. Ldr. Chater in front of the aircraft with a naval officer*

*[D. A. McDonald].*

160

*A long shot of the airfield at Ratmalana, with Hurricanes airborne and on the ground.*

place') was Colombo's civil airport. There was a paved runway, but as it was rather short, work on an extension began without delay. A villa named 'Kandawala' was requisitioned as SHQ, and living quarters for the ground crews were quickly built among the surrounding coconut plantations, which provided both shade and camouflage. Although they had concrete floors, most of these buildings were made of 'kadjan', plaited fronds of coconut palm, which allowed cool sea breezes to blow through.

On that first morning in Ceylon, three of the senior pilots flew over Colombo in formation, after which one landed on the grass in front of the Galle Face Hotel and took off again, just to prove that it would be possible to make a landing ground there on which to disperse aircraft if the need arose. Partly in recognition of their hard work on board the aircraft carrier and partly as the squadron's stores had not arrived, the ground crews were given a day off for rest and relaxation. Lack of transport meant that the stores did not turn up until 11th March, allowing work to begin on readying the Hurricanes for whatever action might occur.

30 Squadron took over the 'readiness' and 'available' functions from 131 Squadron on 15th March and began operations with a dawn patrol. At 13.45 the aircraft at readiness were scrambled and the remaining pilots taxied their Hurricanes to the end of the runway, where they remained until at 17.00 the alarm was declared as false. Another false alarm was acted upon next day,

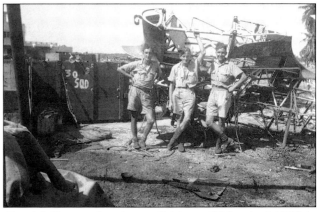

**Above left:** *The somewhat vulgar unofficial crest of 30 Squadron's 'A' Flight.*
**Above:** *Cpls. Walker, Brown and Butcher and the remains of a wrecked aircraft.*
**Left:** *In the sergeant's mess at Ratmalana.*

*Left: One of the stalwarts of 30 Squadron was LAC 'Syd' Sharr, an MT driver*
[D. A. McDonald].
*Above: Plt. Off. Jimmy Whalen at Ratmalana in March 1942*
[D. A. McDonald].

*Flt. Lt. Bolton, the squadron adjutant, at Ratmalana in March 1942. Apart from the 30 Squadron Hurricane Mk.I in the background (carrying code RS) there is an Albacore of the Fleet Air Arm* [D. A. McDonald].

when 'bogeys' were reported over Colombo at 12,000 feet. On 17th March six Hurricanes took part in dive bombing and ground strafing exercises with the 99th Indian Infantry Brigade, but apart from that there was no activity.

The squadron's rear party and seventy men who had been left at Port Sudan arrived at Colombo on board HMT *Talma* on 18th March, bringing the squadron together once more when they appeared at Ratmalana at 17.00 that day.

## Preparing to defend Ceylon

A major exercise was staged on 21st March, when nineteen Hurricanes of 30 Squadron made dummy interceptions of Blenheims which were returning to Colombo. To make conditions as authentic as possible, no indication of the position or height of the Blenheims was given in advance, so sections of 30 Squadron patrolled at several altitudes from 500 to 5000 feet. A section flying west of Colombo harbour spotted the Blenheims, and spectacular dog-fights then took place, albeit without any guns being fired. It

*A group of 30 Squadron pilots pose on and around a Hurricane. On the left is an army liaison officer. None of the men seems to be wearing 'wings' on his KD uniform.*

*An important member of 30 Squadron was Cpl. Cooper, the barman and mess steward*          *[D. A. McDonald].*

was assumed at the time that none of the Blenheims would have survived! Two days later an exercise to give the 30 Squadron pilots practice in dive-bombing ships at sea was staged, attacks being carried out in cooperation with HMS *Royal Sovereign* and its escort. Due to rapid evasive action by the battleship only near misses on the port bow could be claimed. The Hurricane pilots also worked with four Blenheims practising torpedo attacks. Later in the day a practice scramble was carried out by twenty Hurricanes which patrolled various areas in a search for four Blenheims making for Colombo as a dummy target. Only two Hurricanes succeeded in the interception, and then only after the mock raid had taken place. However, before returning to base the other Hurricane pilots managed some good practice in attacking the bombers, the gunners of which were given many opportunities off fighting off the fighters.

Over the next few days routine patrols formed the only activity for 30 Squadron pilots, but the ground crews excelled themselves by working hard to provide twenty-four serviceable aircraft — the complete establishment. By the end of March the squadron was well established in Ceylon, old and new personnel working well together, ready for any operations which might be called for. They needed to be!

A ground radar station, 524 AMES (Air Ministry Experimental Station), was set up on Mount Lavina and began operating on 1st April. There were many unconfirmed reports of Japanese naval forces near the island, and a false report of paratroops being dropped at Kandy prompted a thorough aerial search, but nothing untoward was found. Another misleading report was investigated on 2nd April, this time when a warning was sounded at China Bay, but again there was no substance in the report. Pilots not involved in this carried out practice dog-fighting or stood by to await the call to action. Dawn patrols were flown on 3rd April, and sadly, while flying some eight miles off the coast Flt. Sgt. G. E. Lawrence, leading a section of three aircraft, was seen to dive into the sea. Both the other pilots circled the scene, and after ten minutes an empty 'Mae West' lifejacket popped up and a small amount of wreckage was seen. On hearing about the loss, Sqn. Ldr. Chater took off to investigate, but in the strong light of the setting sun he was unable to see even oil patches on the water. A destroyer also searched, but without success, and the unfortunate pilot had to be posted as missing.

### Red Alert!

By now a Japanese attack on Ceylon by air was considered inevitable. The crew of a long-range Catalina flying-boat had

spotted a small speck on the horizon almost 350 miles south-south-east of the island and had gone to investigate. As they approached, they found that what they had seen was just the vanguard of a large armada of battleships, destroyers, aircraft carriers and attendant vessels, which initially the Catalina's captain, Sqn. Ldr. L. Birchall, believed to be the Royal Navy's Eastern fleet. He therefore had no qualms about flying low and close to the ships, and for some minutes his aircraft was joined by fighters. Their pilots waved in a friendly way, but when the red disc markings on the fighters were seen it became only too obvious that these were not aircraft of the Fleet Air Arm! They were in fact Mitsubishi A6M Reisen fighters, known to the Allies as 'Zeros', from the carrier *Hiryu*, and it is now known that by coincidence a Japanese flying boat had been expected to arrive to help with navigation. Even though the Catalina was in the most serious danger, a signal informing base of the situation had to be sent, and the wireless operator began to transmit as Sqn. Ldr. Birchall beat a hasty retreat northwards. The flying-boat, with a maximum speed of 180 mph, was no match for the Zeros, which could fly at twice that speed, and six of them pounced. The vital message was transmitted, and the wireless operator began to repeat it in accordance with regulations, which demanded three transmissions. Firing 20mm cannon shells into the Catalina, the Zero pilots succeeded in bringing it down, but the message had been received in Colombo in time for action to be taken. A second Catalina was sent to shadow the enemy fleet, but after one ominous message about a Japanese destroyer sailing northwards nothing was heard, and the flying boat was presumed to have been shot down.

Several significant facts about the Japanese fleet were unknown to the Allies at that time, or perhaps had been disregarded. One was the sheer striking power of the force and another was that the Zero fighter had sufficient endurance to enable it to escort naval bombers for a considerable distance. A Zero was quite capable of flying 200 miles to engage in combat for up to twenty minutes before returning to its carrier. It is now known that Commander Mitsuo Fuchida of the *Akagi*, who had led the attack on Pearl Harbour which precipitated the United States into the war, had 125 aircraft at his disposal, consisting of 36 Type 99 Val dive-bombers, 53 Type 97 Kate attack bombers and 36 Zero fighters.

An inter-service dance was held in Colombo on the evening of Saturday 4th April, but during the proceedings all personnel were ordered to return to their units immediately. On arrival at Ratmalana, the 30 Squadron pilots were told that a Japanese force including aircraft carriers had been sighted and that the squadron was to be brought to a state of readiness before first light next morning in anticipation of an attack.

### Ceylon is attacked

On that fateful Easter Sunday, 5th April 1942, the Japanese aircraft took off when 200 miles south of Ceylon and made for the south-west coast. On reaching land they expected opposition, and as they planned to continue well offshore, the Zeros dropped their auxiliary fuel tanks at about that time. Six Fulmar aircraft of the Fleet Air Arm, returning from a patrol, sighted the approaching force, but it did not occur to the crews that they were hostile. As their main targets the Japanese had selected warships in the harbour, the railway at Ratmalana and oil depots east of Colombo.

At dawn, the pilots of 30 Squadron were ready for action, while ground crews worked to ensure that as many Hurricanes as possible were serviceable, and defence posts were manned. In conditions of 8/10 to 10/10 cloud with a base of 2000 feet, frequent heavy showers and gusting winds, a patrol was flown, but when nothing had happened by 07.30 small numbers of men were allowed to go for breakfast. About twenty minutes later a huge formation of enemy aircraft was sighted approaching Ratmalana from the south at about 8000 feet. Pilots of 'A' and 'B' Flights who were standing by rushed to their aircraft and took off, but although it was obvious that the formation was hostile none of the ground defences opened fire. The enemy aircraft did not attack immediately, but instead continued to fly north over the airfield, by which time Hurricanes of 30 and 258 Squadrons were beginning to engage them in combat. One enemy aircraft was seen to burst into flames and crash near the railway workshops. Five Val dive-bombers circled, formed line astern and dived from the east. As their first bomb was released, Bofors guns on the ground opened up. Four Hurricanes not yet airborne took off while bombs exploded around the control tower, but continuous fire from the Bofors guns seemed to discourage enemy aircraft from 'jumping' the Hurricanes as they lifted off. Just one Hurricane did not take part, as it was damaged by blast from an exploding bomb. Several of the pilots had no aircraft to fly and therefore made the most of the chance to fire Thompson machine guns at any enemy aircraft coming within range.

Former Sgt. G. G. Bate, then a pilot on 30 Squadron, remembers standing by his aircraft while some of his colleagues went to breakfast, as did his No.1, Flt. Lt. 'Dave' Davidson. "As it was starting to drizzle, my 'erk' and I climbed onto the wing of my aircraft to close the cockpit. As we were doing so we heard the sound of aircraft, and looking up through the broken cloud we saw formations of aircraft passing over, heading in the direction of Colombo. My airman said 'Look at the Spits. They must be reinforcements!' I looked and said 'Those are Japs.' I jumped into my aircraft and along with Flt. Lt. Davidson started up and headed for the end of the strip for take-off. At the same time the lorry carrying the other pilots headed back to the aircraft. We were caught on the ground with no warning. Dave and I started our take-off as the first bombs hit the field, and we became the first airborne. Still no Verey light!" This comment refers to the firing of a Verey pistol from the control tower to signal a scramble, and rumour has it that in his haste the airman responsible fired it inside the building! Mr. Bate goes on to describe the battle by remarking that as soon as the two Hurricanes were in the air the pilots lost visual contact. "When I broke out on top I was jumped, and headed back into cloud. It seemed to me that every time I came out of cloud the Jap aircraft were waiting. It was impossible to gain any height to get above them. I decided to head out to sea and climb back into the area. I was fortunate to gain some height and came back to attack a number of single-engined aircraft flying in a V formation. I.........shot down two aircraft on the starboard side of the formation. From then on it was a real hornets' nest. I cannot remember seeing any of our aircraft during this time. Everyone had their private go. Because we were caught on the ground any squadron tactics we had were not available to us." With two enemy aircraft to his credit, Sgt. Bate returned to base. "When I arrived back at the field" he says, "I did not make a circuit, but flew straight over the trees and onto the ground, maybe even downwind. The ground crews had the bowser out in the open, so I taxied straight up to it. The armourers hit the wings, the refuelling crews began refuelling, all out in the open. As this was going on the Japs again strafed the airfield. I jumped off the wing, heading for a ditch not far away; one of the armourers threw me his rifle and suggested in no uncertain terms that I shoot at the b*****s! As I looked out from the ditch, [I saw that] not one airman had left his job; all were carrying on refuelling and rearming as if everything was normal. To me the 'erks' were the real heroes of the raid, and to my knowledge have never received any official recognition. If it means anything, I do so now." Many will echo these sentiments.

Another pilot who took part in the defence of Ratmalana that day was Plt. Off. P. M. Hamilton, who at 07.30 was standing outside the officers' mess waiting for the remaining pilots to finish breakfast. "Suddenly we heard the sound of many aircraft," he recalls. "We looked up and there, in open sky between great banks of cloud, were two vics of nine aircraft passing over at about 3000 feet in the most perfect formation. Suddenly someone shouted 'Japs'! Then followed a mad rush to get into the 'gharri' and a high-speed dash to dispersal. No instructions were given; it was clear what we had to do and that was to get airborne as quickly as possible. As I taxied towards the runway I noticed the CO's aircraft still parked outside the Flying Club building. Half way to the runway a 'Val' passed above my head at about 500 feet. I watched,

*Flt. Lt. T. P. 'Dave' Davidson, the officer in command of 'B' Flight of 30 Squadron at the time of the Japanese raid on Colombo. He was unusual in shooting down aircraft of three air forces – German, Italian and Japanese.*

fascinated, as a bomb slowly toppled from the rack towards me, but by the time it landed I was out of harm's way. Once airborne I looked around; there was not a single aircraft to be seen. I headed for the harbour, and was flying at about 1000 feet round a large black cloud when a 'Val' suddenly appeared. I wrenched round in a steep turn and got on its tail very close behind it. I fired a long burst as we both plunged into cloud. Eventually I came out of cloud at about 700 feet above the harbour [but] there was no sign of the 'Val'." Hamilton then set course south and climbed to gain an advantage. As he approached Ratmalana he spotted a vic of three aircraft several miles away at about 8000 feet and gave chase. Climbing all the time, he laboured to catch up with the Japanese aircraft, but did not want to overtax his Hurricane because he suspected that he might need as much endurance as available. "After what seemed like an age I began to close on them" he says. "I would have liked to get above and ahead of them in order to deliver a proper quarter attack, but I felt that I could not spare the time. I decided to attack from below so that their tails would hinder their rear gunners. As I got within range I put my finger on the button, but at that instant the 'Vals' began to jink about madly. I got a bead on the left-hand aircraft. Tracer was now coming back from all three in that typical lazy undulating manner. I dived under them again and came up for another go. I pressed the button but was shocked to discover that I had no ammunition left. There was no point in hanging around, so I turned for home. As I did so I looked back and was gratified to see that the left-hand aircraft had left formation, lost height and was emitting grey smoke."

Twenty-one Hurricanes took part in the proceedings that fateful day. Low cloud enabled them to secure cover soon after take-off, so few ground personnel were able to see the combats except when an aircraft emerged from cloud being chased by another one, the rattle of twelve machine guns being easily distinguished from the sound of cannon fire from the Zeros. The CO could not take part, because when he arrived at the airfield in his car, 'Chick' Evans, the engineering officer, told him that his aircraft was unserviceable after a bomb had exploded close to it and it had to be inspected to ensure that no damage had been caused. After half an hour the attack was over and the Hurricanes began to return to Ratmalana, where ground crews rapidly refuelled and rearmed them, but apart from a few combats which could be seen some miles away to the south-west the raid there was no more action. At 09.00 a check revealed that eight Hurricanes were missing and several more had been badly damaged. As telephone lines were out of action the CO flew to Colombo Racecourse airstrip to find out whether any 30

*One of the five pilots of 30 Squadron who lost their lives in or just after the Easter Sunday 1942 raid on Colombo was Plt. Off. Don Geffene from California. He is seen here on a motorcycle at Ratmalana soon after the squadron arrived from the Middle East*                    *[D. A. McDonald].*

Squadron pilots had landed there, but found only one. However, Flg. Off. D. A. 'Canada Mac' McDonald had crash-landed his badly shot-up aircraft on the grass at the Galle Face Hotel (which had been evaluated as an emergency landing ground earlier) without injury. An RAF officer drove him to the Galle Face Hotel, where he was given a glass of an amber liquid which looked very much like Scotch whiskey but turned out to be cold tea, as the bar was closed! During the afternoon it was heard that Plt. Off. Cartwright was safe in hospital at Colombo after surviving a crash when flying too low in an attempt to escape from a Zero, and in the

evening Flg. Off. Allison was reported to be in hospital with a bullet wound to his neck. He had been carried there in a bullock cart from a paddy field where he had crashed. That dreadful day's final event was the arrival of an officer of the Ceylon Light Infantry, who brought the body of Sgt. C. J. Browne. This officer had watched the combat between Browne and a Japanese aircraft in which Browne had shot down his opponent but had then been attacked himself, his Hurricane diving into a paddy field in flames, killing him on impact.

## Aftermath

At the end of the day 30 Squadron had no more than seven serviceable aircraft, and only those because the ground crews worked so hard. It was claimed that eleven enemy aircraft had been shot down, seven more were 'probables' and five had been damaged, a total of 23 which almost certainly failed to reach their carrier. This was for a loss of one pilot known to have been killed, four missing and two injured, and eight aircraft written off. Eventually it became known that Flt Sgt. Paxton, who three months earlier had shot down two Luftwaffe aircraft over the Western Desert, had been badly burnt in combat with a Zero. Plt. Off. G. E. Caswell and Plt. Off. D. Geffene, an American, had also been shot down and killed, while Flt. Sgt. L. A.. Ovens' Hurricane (BM910) was not discovered for two days, lying near the Kandy road. All the surviving pilots learned that day how substantially built the Hurricane was. Among the ground crews, the only casualty during the raid was one airman who was hit on the head by a coconut when the tree under which he sheltered was shaken by a bomb blast!

Shortly after the raid a Flight of Fulmar aircraft of the Fleet Air Arm landed at Ratmalana and the leader said to Sqn. Ldr. Chater "Nothing to report, sir, we didn't see any enemy aircraft." The CO pointed at a bomb crater and said "What do you think caused that — mice?"

Why the Japanese aerial armada had not been spotted as soon as it reached landfall has never been explained satisfactorily,

*Clearing wreckage of Japanese aircraft at Ratmalana after the Easter Sunday 1942 raid.*

neither has the fact that Fighter Operations staff at Colombo were not aware of the attack until after 30 Squadron was in combat. It has been claimed that the radar was unmanned due to a watch changeover and that the attack was not expected to take place until later in the day when the Japanese fleet would be closer to the island. More plausibly, it seems that the radar was closed down every Sunday at 07.00 for maintenance, and no order was issued to

**Above:** *In command of 'A' Flight at Ratmalana was Flt. Lt. John 'Attie' Attwell*       *[D. A. McDonald].*
**Right:** *The grave of Flt. Sgt. T. G. Paxton at Colombo (Kanatte) General Cemetery*       *[D. A. McDonald].*

*Taking a well-deserved rest in the officers' mess at an unrecorded location, probably Colombo Racecourse. A 'rogues gallery' graces the area above the bar.*

*A 30 Squadron Hurricane at Ratmalana, with Sgt. 'Bowser' Norton below the propeller.*

cancel this routine. But the radar had only been operational for four days! Whatever the reason, the attack was only marginally successful, the most significant effect being that it lowered the morale of the local people dramatically. This attack on Colombo and a later raid on Trincomalee (on the other side of Ceylon) cost the Japanese some seventy aircraft and crews. The fleet had to return to Japan to refit, and thus only two of the five aircraft carriers were available to take part in the Japanese attack on Port Moresby in New Guinea a month later. Their participation there might well have made all the difference to the outcome of that battle and perhaps of the war.

The fortitude of Sqn. Ldr. Birchall and his Catalina crew in providing their warning of the attack on Ceylon on 5th April 1942 had an interesting sequel. He and his surviving crew had been captured and had spent the remainder of the war as prisoners of the Japanese, who tortured, starved and beat them. However, Sqn. Ldr. Birchall survived this ordeal and returned to Canada to take up his career. In July 1967 the Prime Minister of Canada, Mr. Lester Pearson, revealed that at a dinner held by Lord Halifax at the British Embassy in Washington just after the end of the Second World War the conversation had turned to the critical moments of the struggle which had eventually led to the Allied victory. When asked what he felt had been the most dangerous and distressing moment in the war, Winston Churchill gave a surprising reply. In his opinion the most dangerous moment, and the one which gave him most cause for alarm was when he received the news that the

*Sqn. Ldr. A. W. 'Alf' Bayne, CO of 30 Squadron and seen here at Dambulla [D. A. McDonald].*

Japanese fleet was making for Ceylon. The capture of Ceylon, he said, and the subsequent control of the Indian Ocean, combined with a possible German conquest of Egypt, would have "closed the ring", and the future would have been bleak. When told that Sqn. Ldr. Birchall had survived, Churchill was delighted.

Flt. Lt. Grossmark, the MO, and several other officers began the task of checking crashed aircraft next day, 6th April. One of them was believed to be that of Plt. Off. Caswell. The MO also visited the mortuary in an attempt to identify several bodies but was not able to do so. Funerals occupied many of the officers and airmen, as apart from the laying to rest of Sgt. Browne in Kanatte Cemetery in Colombo Sqn. Ldr. Chater, Flt. Lt. Bolton and Plt. Off. F. L. Bush represented 30 Squadron at the burial of four pilots of 258 Squadron.

That day the CO heard from his opposite number on 258 Squadron, based at Colombo Racecourse, that Flt. Sgt. Paxton was in the City General Hospital suffering from second degree burns. He was visited by the CO and the Intelligence Officer, who learnt that he had definitely shot down two enemy aircraft, one of which was attacking Flg. Off. McDonald's Hurricane. He also confirmed having seen the aircraft which McDonald was dealing with crash into the sea. When other enemy aircraft succeeded in hitting Paxton's Hurricane it began to burn, and Paxton reported that ".......although it was getting hot in the cockpit and the throttle became too hot to hold" he carried on firing at an aircraft ahead before he had to bale out at 1600 feet. He fell in a tree, from where he was rescued by local inhabitants who took him to hospital. His condition was not considered to be serious, and when the MO paid a visit to make sure he was being looked after Paxton was asleep.

Flg. Off. Cartwright considered himself lucky to be alive, as only by taking violent evasive action was he able to escape the attentions of the Zeros. On crashing, his aircraft hit a tree and was completely wrecked. He could not make any claims, as he had not been able to engage the enemy before he was set upon. Flg. Off. Allison was in no condition to provide any details of his experience other than he had fired on two enemy aircraft before they had shot him down. 30 Squadron's final score was claimed to be fourteen aircraft shot down, six probably so and five damaged.

Sadly, the after-effects of the Japanese attack persisted, as Flt. Sgt. Paxton succumbed to secondary shock which caused his death on 7th April. The body of Flt. Sgt. Ovens was recovered from a small reservoir but after immersion for two days was not immediately identified, while the body of Plt. Off. Geffene was found in the wreck of his Hurricane.

*An unidentified Hurricane carrying the 30 Squadron RS code sits in the sun at Ratmalana*         *[R. C. Sturtivant collection].*

*30 Squadron's bungalow, used for rest and recuperation purposes*         *[Bill Binch].*

## Routine patrols

Over the next few days the squadron concentrated on dawn patrols and repairs to damaged but still airworthy aircraft. Four replacement Hurricanes arrived on 13th April, which was a help, but one aircraft was lost in an accident on 20th April. Five aircraft had taken off to practice formation-flying, and all went well until Flt. Sgt. J. B. Lisle in BG916 appeared to turn into the slipstream of another aircraft. This caused his Hurricane to turn over and enter a dive from which Lisle was unable to recover. His aircraft crashed into a lake, bursting into flames as it hit shallow water about ten yards from the shore. The cockpit and engine were buried deep in the mud, but later in the day Sgt. Lisle's body was recovered and was buried at Kanatte Cemetery without delay. So ended one of those tragic incidents which were all too common at the time.

For the remainder of April a state of readiness was maintained, sometimes in heavy rain and with occasional reports of approaching bomber formations which all turned out to be false alarms. On 2nd May the CO decided to arrange some exercise for both Flights, the objective being 258 Squadron's base at Colombo Racecourse. Six Hurricanes from each Flight took off at 11.15 and made a low level attack on the target without opposition, much to the surprise of 30 Squadron pilots. Still anticipating reprisals, an increased level of readiness was maintained at Ratmalana, but 258 Squadron failed to appear!

By 7th May the runway at Ratmalana was in bad condition, causing undue wear to the wheels of Hurricane undercarriages. Flying was therefore suspended while the runway was repaired, any movements taking place on the grass area while the work was done. The possibility of bomb racks being fitted to the Hurricanes was the subject of a talk given on 11th May by one Gp. Capt. McDonald, and several aircraft awaiting inspection in Maintenance Flight were duly fitted with the racks, which one assumes were brought to Ratmalana by the Gp. Capt.

An accident with only minor consequences, and no injury to the pilot, occurred on 14th May, when Plt. Off. J. H. Whalen took off to test his guns. At about fifteen feet off the ground, his engine failed, so as his undercarriage was not yet retracted Whalen, with great presence of mind, landed the Hurricane on rough ground on the other side of the road from the airfield. In doing so, the starboard wing hit a bullock cart, and the Hurricane came to a halt after its undercarriage had been ripped off, the lower part of the engine had buried itself in the soft ground and the propeller blades had been smashed. As soon as he had seen the MO, Whalen was airborne in another aircraft!

## A new Commanding Officer

During this continuing period of readiness, two of 30 Squadron's officers received promotion. Flt. Lt. R. T. P. Davidson became a temporary Sqn. Ldr. and was posted to command 261 Squadron at China Bay, while Sqn. Ldr. Chater was given the

*Squadron engineering officer at Ratmalana was Plt. Off. 'Chick' Evans [D. A. McDonald].*

*Sgt. Corps was known as 'Trunkie' [D. A. McDonald].*

*Canadian pilots on 30 Squadron in Ceylon (left to right): Sgt. C. I. Nutbrown; Plt. Off. D. A. McDonald; Sgt. Jack Hurley; Plt. Off. Jimmy Whalen; Sgt. Grant Bishop; Sgt. G. Murray; Sgt. G. G. Bate.*

*Sgt. 'Slim' Mills with his flying kit after a mission.*

temporary rank of Wg. Cdr. He handed over command of 30 Squadron on 29th May to Sqn. Ldr. A. W. A. Bayne DFC, who spent most of the day inspecting his new squadron's accommodation and the Flights. Next day he spoke to all the pilots to explain a 'Balbo' exercise which would take place that afternoon. Every pilot was to take his place in the formation as quickly as possible, and afterwards was to touch down without delay. Twelve aircraft took part in the exercise, which lasted twenty-five minutes and involved a flight over Colombo. In view of the order which had just arrived from 222 Group stipulating the maximum engine hours of all operational aircraft in Ceylon this may have been the last unrestricted exercise of its type. From that point, very little individual flying by pilots at readiness was sanctioned, and all exercises were to be of short duration and in formation. A significant exercise was flown on 20th May, however, principally to test the radar defences of the island without notifying the radar controllers. It involved three aircraft of 'A' Flight, which took off and flew on a south-south-east course over the island for about forty miles at low altitude before turning west out to sea, climbing to 6000 feet and returning to base. No IFF was switched on, and the flight was not picked up on radar. On a visit to Ratmalana that day, the AOC, AVM J. H. d'Albiac CB DSO, was told about this, and must have been less than impressed.

June began with two sessions of night flying, followed by a period of cooperation with the Fleet Air Arm. On 5th June twelve of 30 Squadron's Hurricanes were placed on stand-by to escort a force of Swordfish aircraft taking part in a mock attack on Naval forces approaching Colombo. After being given the order to scramble they attempted to join the Swordfish but it was decided that the fleet was too close to Colombo and the exercise was abandoned. It was eventually carried out a week later. Next day the Fleet Air Arm carried out a practice attack on RAF airfields defending Colombo, including Ratmalana, and it appears that once

*Flt. Lt. Dick Graves was 'B' Flight commander between August 1942 and April 1943, when he became CO of 261 Squadron. He is seen here outside the pilots' dispersal hut at Dambulla*  [D. A. McDonald].

*Above left: Terry Cutting joined 30 Squadron as a sergeant pilot and was later commissioned*  [D. A. McDonald].
*Above right: Bob Davies, an Australian on 30 Squadron [D. A. McDonald].*

*Above left: Flg. Off. 'Smokey' Harris, an American member of the squadron from Oklahoma, who lost his life when his Hurricane crashed on 15th June 1943*  [D. A. McDonald].
*Above right: Flt. Lt. D. K. 'Aussie Mac' McDonald at Dambulla*  [D. A. McDonald].

*Above left: The unfortunate Sgt. Jimmy Morris, who was killed in the crash of a Tiger Moth at Colombo Racecourse on 21st September 1942*  [D. A. McDonald].
*Above right: Plt. Off. D. K. McDonald.*

again the radar system did not warn 30 Squadron early enough for the Hurricanes to take to the air in defence. A similar exercise was staged on 18th June, and this time six Hurricanes were scrambled. Unfortunately the weather was too bad for an interception to be made, so 30 Squadron went home. On 23rd June twelve of the Hurricanes escorted six Swordfish in a dummy attack on naval vessels leaving Colombo, but although 30 Squadron found the target the Swordfish crews decided not to press home their attack.

In Ceylon at that time, visits by dignitaries were few and far between, so when HRH the Duke of Gloucester came to Ratmalana on 27th June 1942 there was some excitement. All twenty-one serviceable Hurricanes of 30 Squadron were lined up, with the pilot and ground crew standing in front of each one. Headquarters and Maintenance Flight formed the head of the parade, and when the Duke arrived he was escorted on his inspection by the AOC, Sqn. Ldr. Bayne and Wg. Cdr. H. L. P. Lester, the Station Commander. The Duke then left to carry out a similar function at Colombo Racecourse, while two sections of 30 Squadron provided defensive cover. Next day the Duke's fleet of aircraft (a DC–3, two Hudsons and a Lodestar) was escorted by twelve Hurricanes of 30 Squadron for the first hundred miles of its flight northwards.

At the end of June, authorisation was given by AHQ India for 30 Squadron to have three Flights instead of two, but this alteration was considered quite impracticable, unnecessary and a waste of manpower. Presumably no increase in the number of aircraft or personnel was allowed. It is a credit to the squadron that all twenty-two Hurricanes were available for business at that time.

July 1942 was another month of practice flying for 30 Squadron, with the occasional noteworthy event to add spice to the proceedings. After practising a battle climb procedure on 7th July Sgt. R. Greyvensteyn force-landed in a paddy field near the airfield, but escaped injury, although the Hurricane was written off as far as the squadron was concerned. Two days later the same sergeant had an argument with a bullock cart while riding his motor-cycle on the Galle Road, and ended in hospital!

An advanced landing strip at Dambulla was now being considered for use by the squadron, and to check its suitability the CO and several other officers and SNCOs went there by road on 13th July. New aircraft were now becoming available, and on 19th July six pilots went to India to collect Hurricanes Mk.IIc for the squadron. However, it was 7th August before the first three arrived at Ratmalana.

More cooperation with Naval forces took place on 28th July, and on this occasion the pilots made mock dive-bombing attacks on

aircraft carriers approaching Colombo. Sadly, Sgt. P. B. Kember lost his life when he misjudged his dive and hit the side of a carrier, his Hurricane crashing into the water.

Exercises planned for the early part of August 1942 involved a detachment of 30 Squadron using an advanced landing ground at Kalmetiya, where an SNCO and twenty airmen set up camp. Six pilots flew there on 3rd August and immediately began to take part in practice interceptions of aircraft making mock attacks on the Naval fleet. Control of the 30 Squadron aircraft by R/T from the ships was found to be completely successful. One Hurricane developed engine trouble on the way home, but landed without incident. All six returned to Ratmalana next day, while another six made a trial flight to Dambulla.

## New aircraft, new base

Familiarisation with the new Mk.IIc aircraft began on 10th August and included firing of the cannons, which at first suffered many stoppages. Eight Hurricanes Mk.IIb and one Mk.I left for Katakurunda on 15th August to be handed over to 273 Squadron, followed by another eight five days later, but little flying was

*Six of 30 Squadron's Hurricane Mk.IIcs in formation near Madras. The squadron code, RS, was not in use at the time, only individual aircraft letters being carried.*

carried out otherwise as a squadron move to Dambulla was afoot. An advance party comprising one officer, five SNCOs and 49 airmen left Ratmalana on 25th August and a servicing party of about the same size followed four days later. On 31st August the main party of three officers, twelve SNCOs and 177 airmen took leave of Ratmalana and after a six-hour journey arrived at Dambulla, the pilots of twelve new Hurricanes timing their forty-five minute flight so as to land at exactly the same time. Three more turned up next day.

Dambulla airfield was situated alongside the main road between Kandy and Trincomalee and was surrounded by hills up to 1000 feet high. The landing strip was about 3000 feet long and was subject to a continuous cross-wind of up to 25 mph — not an ideal site for an airfield, one might think! Its surface was clay, which although not affected by light rain, was considered a likely hazard in heavy rain. Other than local flying and a few communications trips, there was no activity for a time, but on 12th September Air Cdre. Peake, the Director of Welfare at Air Ministry, paid a visit to judge the general feelings of the personnel. What the outcome was is not recorded! By mid-September the squadron was more active, carrying out practice in battle formation, homing by R/T, and dog-fights as well as maintaining a state of readiness. For night-time readiness, aircraft had to be flown to Minneriya, as Dambulla was not suitable for use after dark.

At this time the squadron had the use of a Tiger Moth aircraft for communications purposes and no doubt for use of a more recreational nature. On 21st September Sgt. Hamilton flew it to Colombo Racecourse to take an airman who needed treatment at the dental centre. With Sgt. J. P. Morris as passenger, the Tiger took

*Above left: 30 Squadron's armaments officer at Dambulla was Wt. Off. 'Tubby' Whymark* [D. A. McDonald].
*Below right: Jeff Newell, seen at Dambulla, converted to Thunderbolts with 30 Squadron, but lost his life in a crash on 14th August 1944* [D. A. McDonald].

off for the return flight but had gained no more than a hundred feet of height when it spun into a tree, killing Sgt. Morris and badly bruising Sgt. Hamilton.

Routine patrols and reconnaissance flights combined with exercises in dog-fighting and 'Balbos' occupied 30 Squadron during the latter half of September, as did an army exercise code-named *Wilfred* in which the squadron took part. The object of this was to test communications, and after repositioning at Colombo Racecourse no take-offs were required.

On 2nd October Flg. Off. D. K. McDonald flew to Manin to carry out shoot spotting, after which he allowed Dambulla Operations to give him homing bearings by R/T from a distance of 100 miles, an experiment which was completely successful. From 6 October the CO was laid low by an attack of fever which kept him in his tent for most of the time, but when AVM d'Albiac paid a visit on 14th October with Gp. Capt. Meek, Wg. Cdr. Louis and Capt. Vyne he escorted them on a comprehensive tour of inspection of the Station, fever or no fever. In Maintenance Flight, the AOC spent some time in inspecting tools made by LAC Govan, an armourer, for use when servicing cannons. AVM d'Albiac also saw a Browning gun taken from an aircraft and adapted for mobile ground defence by squadron armourers. These initiatives seem to have pleased him, as he expressed great approval, and did again when he saw the cup given by members of the squadron for the Inter-Flight Football Competition. Next day both the CO and Flg. Off. McDonald went on leave to a tea plantation in the hills near Kandy to recover from their attacks of fever.

As a result of rapidly-increasing United States intervention in the Pacific area, the threat of Japanese attacks on Ceylon had now almost disappeared. Japan's long-desired expansion of its empire had to be postponed so that action could be taken against the American forces, which left the opportunity for Allied forces in India and Ceylon to be reinforced and brought up to a more effective level of performance. So for 30 Squadron and all the other units the constant practice in tactics and on exercises continued, but states of readiness were still maintained. For reasons which remain obscure, one Wg. Cdr. Leather of AHQ India visited the squadron on 24th October to give a lecture on tactics used in the Western Desert, a far cry from the requirements of Ceylon and India and a subject on which several members of 30 Squadron could have lectured!

To improve the condition of the airfield, work began on 27th October on laying Sommerfeld track on the landing strip at Dambulla. It had taken two weeks for the MT section to carry this material from Matale railway station, which indicates that the task was a major one. All the work of laying the mesh was carried out with only three aircraft being grounded, and these could have taken off within thirty minutes in an emergency. Meanwhile, the remainder of the squadron had gone to Minneriya to take part in an Army cooperation exercise, Exercise *Cod*, during which AVM d'Albiac visited the pilots again. Unfortunately, Sqn. Ldr. Bayne succumbed to fever again, and the MO sent him back to Dambulla forthwith. In his place he designated Flt. Lt. Cartwright to oversee the remainder of the exercise, which ended on the last day of the month. Thirteen Hurricanes then returned to Dambulla, where the final 400 yards of Sommerfeld track was being laid on the landing strip. It was 10th November before the job was finished and thirteen Hurricanes were able to make use of it for the first time. By this time the CO had recovered enough to show six officers and twelve NCOs of the Queen's Own Regt. the Hurricanes and to give a lecture.

## A detachment in India

For 30 Squadron, Exercise *Minx* was the significant event in December 1942. On 6th December at 17.50 an advance party of 45 ground personnel under the command of Flg. Off. F. L. Bush left Dambulla for Kekirawa to board a train. The wireless tender had gone to Colombo the previous day to be shipped to Madras, but as loading it from a lighter proved impossible it returned to Dambulla with its crew of three airmen. Equipment on the vehicle was then crated and loaded onto the train, which left Kekirawa in pouring rain at 19.40. Meanwhile the Hurricanes were air-tested, and took off at 09.57 on 9th December for St. Thomas Mount, near Madras, where they landed at 16.30, presumably having refuelled on the way. On arrival, the pilots found that recent heavy rain made taxying to dispersals impossible, so the aircraft were parked near the end of the runway ready for an immediate take-off. The ground party arrived at Madras station at 07.40 and were quickly taken to the airfield.

Throughout the morning of 10th December preparations were made for operating the twelve aircraft independently. Refuelling facilities had to be arranged and R/T had to be working, but by noon everything was ready. No demands were made on the squadron that day, so the pilots contented themselves with local flights and sector reconnaissance, during which the CO had to make an emergency landing at Arkonam with engine trouble. Calling up Sgt. Davies, he told him to land there too so that they

*Three of 30 Squadron's ground crew making the most of a chance for a bit of boating on a home-made raft.*

*30 Squadron transport on the way from Ratmalan to Dambulla.*

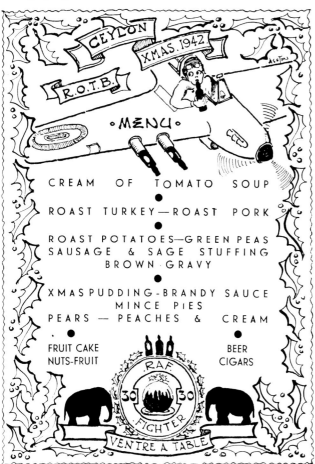

*The menu from the Christmas dinner enjoyed by 30 Squadron in 1942.*

*Sqn. Ldr. Peacock-Edwards, 30 Squadron's CO from February 1943 to May 1944.*

*A roadside rest for 30 Squadron's 'erks' on the journey to Dambulla.*

*Plt. Off. Hamilton on the wing of his Hurricane at Dambulla.*

could exchange aircraft, and the engineer officer, Plt. Off. Pringle, then went to deal with the problem and to collect Sgt. Davies.

30 Squadron pilots were brought to readiness at dawn on 11th December and were ordered to sit in their cockpits and maintain radio contact. At 13.15 four sections were scrambled to intercept intruders, which turned out to be four Vengeance aircraft, all of which were held in 30 Squadron sights at least once. It has to be admitted, however, that these aircraft were 'sitting ducks'! On landing, the Hurricane pilots were told that as the Vengeances should have been seventy miles out to sea no claims would be allowed! Later in the day the CO flew to investigate a possible satellite landing ground at Vellore, but brought back the information that there was a large soft patch in the middle of the landing area.

Next day the pilots went on readiness before dawn, only to be told by guards at the gate of the Station that they were all captured! There was no flying on 13th December, and in the late afternoon orders were received for 30 Squadron to leave St. Thomas Mount for Arkonam. Twenty NCOs and airmen left by train at once under the command of Flg. Off. Bush and arrived at the new base at 21.15. Eleven Hurricanes flew in on 14th December, and the remainder of the ground personnel arrived. Seven sorties consisting of troop-strafing and reconnaissance were made next day, concluding the exercise and enabling some of the squadron personnel and all the aircraft to return to St. Thomas Mount.

To give all the pilots further experience in cross-country flying, the CO decided to send them back to Dambulla at ten-minute intervals on 16th December. Weather reports indicated fair conditions, but then deteriorated, and several pilots found Trichinopoly with difficulty. The weather then cleared, and they took off for Dambulla, but more heavy rain then made things difficult. Fortunately Dambulla remained fairly clear, and the CO landed there at 12.34, followed by two others, but the other eight Hurricanes landed at Ratmalana before going on to Dambulla at the end of a hazardous trip.

The ground party left St. Thomas Mount on 17th December and was ready to board a train at Madras when the officer in command was told by the RTO that seating could be provided for only forty men and that the luggage van could not carry the two tons of equipment. Although arrangements for this journey had been made two days in advance, the party had to return to St. Thomas Mount to await developments. Next day, the equipment was loaded into railway wagons and the party boarded the train at Madras, leaving behind Plt. Off. Pringle and three airmen to fit a new engine to an aircraft stranded at Arkonam. At noon on 20th December the ground party arrived at Kekirawa station, from where three lorries carried them to Dambulla, completing 30

Squadron's somewhat minimal participation in Exercise *Minx*.

Christmas 1942 was celebrated in the traditional RAF manner when all officers and SNCOs waited on the airmen at dinner. A general consensus of opinion was that the meal was the best most of the men had experienced since joining the service! Practice in several aerial skills continued, particularly air-to-sea cannon firing at Puttlam or China Bay, and at times elements of the squadron were brought to readiness. for an hour or two at Dambulla or Ratmalana. Opportunities for newly-arrived pilots to practice 'circuits and bumps' were provided at Sigeriya. Practice interceptions and drogue towing also occupied the pilots during January 1943.

The entire ground personnel of 'A' Flight plus three pilots journeyed to Colombo by road on 29th January and were followed by eight aircraft next day. Sadly, LAC S. Smith, an aircraft hand (General Duties), died in the 57th Indian General Hospital at Kandy on 30th January from multiple burns after a stove used for cooking in the officers' mess exploded.

## Another move and a new CO

On 9th February a new CO arrived to take over from Sqn. Ldr. Bayne. The new man was Sqn. Ldr. S. R. Peacock-Edwards DFC, who was posted from 273 Squadron at Ratmalana. He was one of those who flew a Hurricane off HMS *Indomitable*, after which he had joined 258 Squadron. On 5th April 1942 he had claimed two Japanese fighters before his own Hurricane was shot down, colliding with a tree and losing its wings. Soon after his arrival, the squadron began to prepare to leave Dambulla and move to Colombo Racecourse, to where an advance party of two NCOs and 37 other ranks under Flg. Off. M. R. Ridley journeyed on 13th February. That day, the squadron lost Flg. Off. B. Le B. Smith, who was killed when flying as a passenger in a Beaufort aircraft which crashed at Colombo. The new CO formally took over the squadron on 15th February, and Sqn. Ldr. Bayne left on posting to 136 Squadron, a Hurricane squadron then based at Chittagong. The main party of the squadron with Flt. Lt. H. E. Andrews in charge of eleven SNCOs and 103 airmen left by road for Colombo that day. At Colombo each Flight was billeted in a large house, which made

*Plt. Off. Fred Whittaker, who as an NCO pilot had landed on HMS* Indomitable *when a glycol leak developed.*

*Hurricanes of 30 Squadron dispersed among the trees at Dambulla.*

*Flt. Lt. D. A. 'Canada Mac' McDonald, the OC of 'B' Flight at Dambulla in 1943* [D. A. McDonald].

a considerable contrast to the tents used at Dambulla and elsewhere. Such unheard-of luxuries as flush toilets, hot and cold running water and airy rooms were now available.

Routine tasks continued, enlivened on 21st February by a flypast by twelve aircraft to celebrate Red Army Day! Apart from a visit on 16th March from the deputy AOC-in-C, Air Marshal J. E. A. Baldwin CB CBE DSO and the AOC, AVM A. Lees DSO AFC, little occurred to disturb the routine that month. One ceremony that did take place was arranged to award his third Good Conduct Badge to Wt. Off. E. L. Whymark, the armaments officer, with a retrospective date of 27th May 1941. At the same time, three sergeants, eight corporals and seventeen airmen were awarded their first Good Conduct Badge. Among them were the first airmen to enlist at the outbreak of war.

On the 25th anniversary of the formation of the RAF, 1st April 1943, twelve aircraft carried out a flypast. Other Hurricanes were airborne that day, two making a mock attack on Colombo harbour, two intercepting a Hudson aircraft and two flying locally. For the rest of the month it was a case of 'the mixture as before', the few aircraft intercepted turning out to be friendly Hudsons, Liberators, Swordfish or Catalinas. The same situation persisted in May, June and July, but at the end of that month a move back to Dambulla was ordered.

Radar surveillance had improved since that disastrous day in April 1942, but was still not fully effective. One moonlit night in July 1943 two Hurricanes were scrambled to intercept a 'bogey', but an attempted radar vector failed to bring the Hurricanes even close to the intruder, which was identified by ground crews at the Racecourse as a Japanese flying boat. A similar aircraft which flew over in August fell victim to a Beaufighter equipped with AI radar.

**Back to Dambulla**

Four SNCOs and fifty-eight airmen under the command of Plt. Off. Whittaker made the move to Dambulla on 31st July as the advance party and the main party followed on 3rd August, as did the Hurricanes. By now, to the relief of the personnel, Kadjan huts had been erected to house them rather than the tents of earlier days. It was found that an outgoing squadron had left the domestic area in a very bad state and a good deal of time had to be spent in clearing up. To help in this work, Group HQ was asked to sanction the use of native labour, at least until the squadron's rear party arrived on 7th August. Within a few days the situation had been rectified, the camp in general was looking much tidier and the

*AC1 J. Henderson died on active service and is buried at Colombo* [D. A. McDonald].

everyday routine was being run smoothly. To maintain the health of the squadron, a squad of Ceylon Pioneers with an RAF corporal in charge was carrying out measures to combat malaria. A great asset was a bungalow at Darawella which was taken over by the squadron for the use of airmen, who went there in weekly batches for rest and recuperation.

By October 1943 a Harvard two-seat training aircraft was available for the squadron's use, and on 13th October it was used to carry out a search for a missing aircraft, although its main functions were as an instrument flying trainer and as a communications 'hack'.

**Leaving Ceylon**

30 Squadron's days in Ceylon were now coming to an end, and on 12th January 1944 an advance party consisting of a SNCO and sixteen airmen left for Dohazari in India on their way to Feni, an airfield in Bengal. A trial of Hurricanes carrying jettisonable long-range fuel tanks was put into force, and aircraft to be left behind were flown to Ratmalana. A farewell party was held in the officers' mess on 18th January with several senior officers present. Three days later the CO led fifteen pilots on the first stage of the long flight to Feni. After refuelling at St. Thomas Mount, they flew on to Vizagapatam, on the east coast of India, for a night-stop. Meanwhile the main party was moving baggage and equipment to the railway station at Kekirawa and loading it all into closed wagons. On 22nd January the aircraft flew on to Alipore, where twelve refuelled before making the final stage of the journey and the other four, held up by minor technical trouble, followed next day. 30 Squadron's main party, made up of eight officers, twenty-four SNCOs and 161 other ranks left Dambulla for the last time on 23rd January, and their train arrived at Talaimannar at about 23.00 hours. Baggage was then unloaded by 'coolies' and hoisted aboard the ferry steamer, but clumsiness caused many of the lighter containers to be damaged. It was 06.00 next day before the job was finished, and an hour and a half later the ship sailed for India.

*During conversion from Thunderbolts to Tempests at Agra in July 1946, these 30 Squadron pilots posed in front of one of their new mounts. (Rear) unknown; Flt. Sgt. Rex Taylor; Wt. Off. Les French; Wt. Off. Ken Gardener; Wt. Off. Roy Skinner; Flt Sgt. Ken Kenyon; Wt. Off. Jack Coombs; Flt. Sgt. John Paterson; Flt. Sgt. Bert Tatlow; Wt. Off. Les Banks; Wt. Off. Ray Dark. (Centre) Flt. Sgt. John Webb; Wt. Off. Derek Hewetson; Plt. Off. Frank Watson; Flg. Off. Willie Birkett; Wt. Off. Keith Twynam; Wt. Off. George Simpson; Flg. Off. Doug Allan; Flt. Sgt. Ken Steel. (Front) unknown; Flg. Off. Frank Skinner; Flt. Lt. Williams; Sqn. Ldr. Tim Meyer; Flt. Lt. Les Meehan; Flg. Off. Phil Archer; unknown.*

# Chapter 7: India and Burma, 1944 to 1946

The steamer carrying the main party of 30 Squadron from Ceylon left the dockside at Talaimannar at 07.30 on 24th January 1944 and arrived two hours later at Dhanuskodi, where instructions were given that all personnel were to be marched to a transit camp, apart from a small number of men who would supervise the transfer of baggage to another train. A meal was gratefully received, and facilities were available for a good wash before the personnel boarded the train for Trichinopoly, where a change of rail gauge meant yet another spell of moving baggage from one train to another. A meal served at the station helped to sustain the personnel. Travelling on via Arkonam and Nellore, progress was slow, with frequent stops, but the airmen remained cheerful, which was just as well, as it was 30th January before they arrived at Docks Junction, Calcutta. There the officers were accommodated in the Grand Hotel and the airmen in a nearby transit camp. Next morning was spent in moving baggage to the SS *Islami*, a vessel of about 6000 tons, at the docks. All personnel, however, boarded the SS *Ethiopia* on 1st February.

While the *Ethiopia* was at sea on its way to Chittagong, the Hurricanes already at Feni were flown in groups to Agartala and Singarbil to be re-camouflaged. At 09.00 on 4th February the *Ethiopia* and the *Islami* docked and the laborious task of off-loading baggage and personnel onto lighters began. Baggage was then loaded aboard railway wagons while the men were carried by road to 47 Army Rest Camp nearby. Next morning a state of 'snafu' arose when the train allocated to carry the squadron was cancelled,

and the situation was repeated on 6th February after everyone had boarded the train. To solve the problem the CO borrowed motor vehicles from 224 Group's MT section and sent squadron drivers to fetch transport from Feni. This arrived next day, and with the addition of three more borrowed vehicles it was possible to carry most of the personnel and their kit to Fazilpur, the squadron's ultimate destination. According to Wg. Cdr. Ken Godfrey, during this final stage, over seventy miles of the roughest road imaginable, the trucks were never able to exceed ten miles per hour.

## Operations begin

After their long and frustrating journey from Ceylon, the personnel of 30 Squadron were gratified to find that the accommodation at Fazilpur, in 'basha' huts for two men, was clean and in good condition. Recent rain had put the grass airstrip, which had been bulldozed through paddy fields, out of action. The next few days were spent in retrieving the baggage which had been sent on from Chittagong by train, the bad state of the roads making this task a difficult one.

On 12th February fifteen Hurricanes were flown from Feni to Fazilpur, where the landing strip was now usable. That same day, the pilots took off at 15.00 to escort five Dakotas which were dropping supplies to the army in the Kaladan valley, and another two followed half an hour later. Most of them landed at Feni after the operation as only one small fuel bowser was yet available at Fazilpur and there was no fire engine.

Practice scrambles and GCI interceptions occupied everyone for the next few days, until on 16th February another escort mission came the squadron's way, and eighteen sorties were flown to escort Dakotas and C–46s dropping supplies to beleaguered Allied troops. This task soon became 30 Squadron's routine, and continued for some time, interspersed with convoy patrols to cover the arrival of shipping in the Kodnaphut River. A description of a typical escort mission has been provided by D. A. 'Canada Mac' McDonald. "We were only given a vague idea as to where the drop was to take place, but were given specific instructions as to where and when to rendezvous with the Dakotas. We would escort one to eight Dakotas at a time. I usually led a Flight of six aircraft. My number two and I would fly at about 1100 – 1500 feet from the Dakotas; another two Hurricanes would fly about 2000 – 3000 feet above us and the top two would be about 2000 – 3000 feet above them. I had a great deal of admiration for the Dakota crews. On most of their drops, they had to fly low over Japanese positions. On one occasion, a squadron of Vengeance dive bombers were off to one side, bombing Jap positions, and an artillery spotting plane was flying on the other side. Artillery shells were exploding on the ground and the Dakotas were serenely dropping their supplies. We went to several different locations, sometimes deep in the mountains. Our flying clothing changed considerably. In Ceylon we had flown in shorts and a shirt, with a Mae West, of course. In Bengal we wore overalls with long legs and long sleeves. We carried a long knife, a revolver, a money belt, maps, compass, first aid kit, fishing line, matches and a 'gooley chit'. This was piece of cloth printed in several languages which assured any local native who found us that he would receive a suitable reward for helping us to get back to Bengal." So equipped, the pilots were ready to go, and 'Canada Mac' continues his memoirs. "One extremely hot day we took off, met the Dakotas and proceeded some way north into the mountains. All at once, we came to a plateau. It was delightfully cool and all the foliage looked lush and green. I thought it was Shangri La. Actually, I think it was Imphal. The Dakotas made their drop there. On all of these sorties, we never saw a Japanese aircraft. It was surprising that they didn't try to stop the dropping of supplies." Had the Japanese succeeded in curtailing this supply lifeline, the outcome of the campaign, and indeed of the whole war, might well have been very different.

A small village compound close to the airfield caught fire on 2nd March, and a large number of drums of 100 octane fuel had to be moved to safety, but luckily there was no wind. Huts occupied by villagers were reduced to piles of ashes, however.

Escort missions for supply-dropping Dakotas continued, and in addition 'Rhubarb' operations were flown. Night-flying practice took place at Feni, as no facilities were available at Fazilpur, and a Harvard was flown in from Chittagong for a short period, probably to polish the pilots' instrument flying abilities. On 7th March two Hurricanes took off to help search for a Wellington bomber which was believed to have crashed in the Lushia hills, but no trace of it was found. That night, four Hurricanes carried out individual night sorties from Feni to attack enemy river traffic and communications targets. Two of the pilots fired at river craft without observing any results, and had to land at Chittagong when thick mist developed at Feni.

A daytime attack on a storage area at Zibingyi by 'B' Flight on 12th March proved less than successful, as every Hurricane taking part suffered gun stoppages. The problem reoccurred on 15th March, when six aircraft flew to attack shipping on the Kaladan and Mayu rivers, only one pilot being able to use his guns. Strangely, it was six days before the 3rd Tactical Air Force armament officer, Wg. Cdr. Buchanan, arrived at Fazilpur to try to remedy the situation. The Commander of the 3rd TAF, Air Marshal Sir John Baldwin, KBE CB DSO, had meanwhile visited the squadron and chatted to pilots at dispersal.

Before Fazilpur landing strip became unserviceable on 26th March after heavy rain, 'A' Flight pilots were scrambled to intercept 'bandits' flying from the south, but no contact was made. When the rain started, the Hurricanes made for Feni. The airstrip dried out by 29th March, and escort missions were resumed.

During the month, 295 operational sorties were flown by 30 Squadron, many under adverse conditions.

At Fazilpur, administration continued to suffer from lack of facilities. No furniture had arrived, only small quantities of equipment had been acquired and a recently-obtained electric power trailer proved to be unserviceable. A lack of medical equipment resulted in the MO having to carry out a blood transfusion on the floor. Food was below average in quality and quantity, and while bully beef and canned fish were fairly plentiful, milk and sugar were in very short supply. Nevertheless, the squadron lived up to its reputation in sport, with football being played almost every evening on a pitch at the north end of the airstrip.

Poor weather early in April hampered escort operations somewhat. A few night-time 'rhubarbs' were flown from Feni, but targets were few and no claims were made. Conditions improved on 4th April, allowing thirty escort sorties to be flown, and Daily Routine Orders that day announced the award of the Africa Star to 83 airmen and the 1939-43 Star to six officers and nine airmen. Then came news of a move, as Fazilpur was needed by the United States Army Air Force.

## The move to Comilla

On 6th April an advance party left by road for Comilla, 30 Squadron's next base. Next day, heavy showers in the morning put Fazilpur airstrip out of action, but after conditions improved eleven USAAF C–47 aircraft of the 35th Troop Carrier Squadron, 64th Troop Carrier Group, touched down without any prior warning. Five days earlier, this squadron had been ordered to make the lengthy move to India from Comiso in Sicily and the crews had expected to find Fazilpur empty, although their arrival was scheduled for 11th April. In the best traditions of the RAF and 30 Squadron, help was given to the new arrivals at once, and all spare accommodation was handed over. This proved to be a shrewd ploy, as on 9th April the Americans provided three C–47s to carry some of the 30 Squadron personnel to Comilla, two days ahead of schedule. Twelve of the Hurricanes made the move to Comilla that day while the remainder of the airmen and their kit travelled by road.

On arrival at Comilla, the pilots found that as the paved runway was under repair the fair-weather landing strip alongside had to be used. Escort missions covering supply-dropping Dakotas, most of them belonging to 62 Squadron, continued from Comilla, as did night 'rhubarb' sorties, some flown from Chittagong. By now the weather had improved dramatically, and the maximum sun temperature had risen to 120 degrees Fahrenheit. Domestic conditions at Comilla were certainly better than at Fazilpur, the messes and canteen even having electric light! Ken Godfrey, who had suffered from attacks of dysentery and dengue fever, wrote in his diary "........our food supplies have been very poor and we are existing on a diet of dehydrated mutton, dehydrated potatoes and tinned soya links."

By 1st May the paved runway was in use, and the number of escort operations was increased. Indecisive 'rhubarbs' were flown at night, and two VIP escort missions were also started, but bad weather on their routes caused them to be aborted. On 4th May a new CO, Sqn. Ldr. T. A. Stevens, a friendly Scotsman, arrived from 146 Squadron to take over from Sqn. Ldr. Peacock–Edwards, who left for the UK at once.

Ken Godfrey's diary continued "I have now done 80 hours operational flying. Since arriving at Comilla we have been on 'readiness' from dawn till dusk. The trips have been taking as much as three and three-quarter hours from here. One day we were unexpectedly scrambled early in the morning after an all-night drinking session in the mess. Miraculously, twelve inebriated pilots got off the ground and landed back without mishap. Most of us had to be helped up into the cockpit. I have had several narrow shaves. My long-range tanks packed up on one trip and I landed back with only a few drops of petrol in the reserve tank. On another trip I became disorientated while flying [in] formation in thick cloud and broke out of the cloud upside-down at 3000 feet. Vera Lynn visited Comilla last week (mid-May) and we all went into the village to hear her sing."

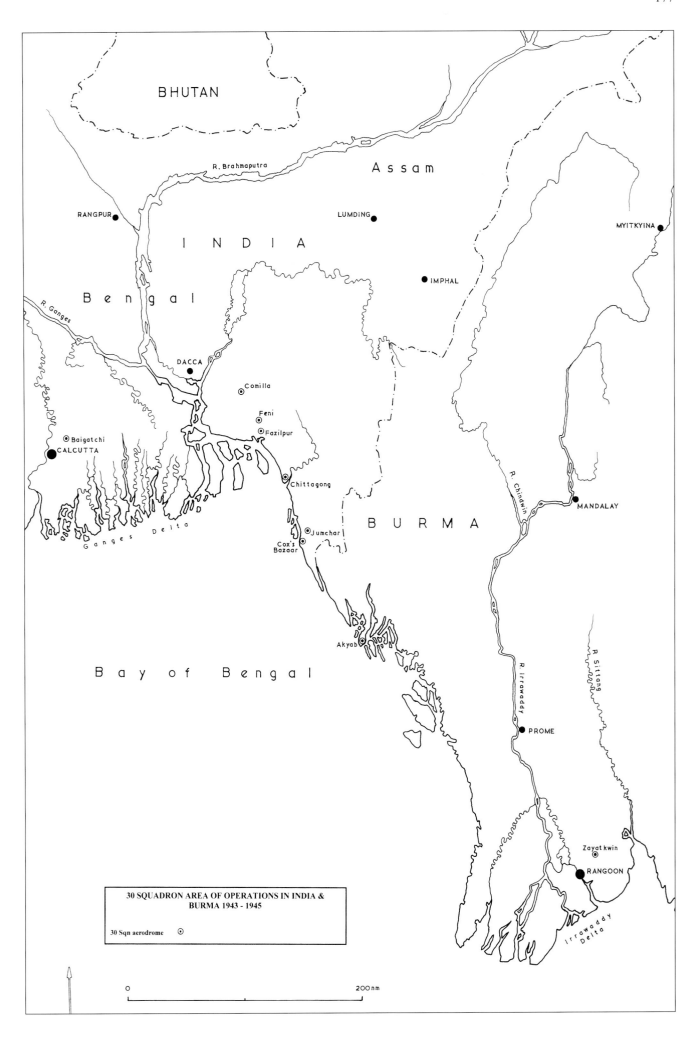

BHUTAN

R. Brahmaputra

Assam

RANGPUR

LUMDING

MYITKYINA

I N D I A

B e n g a l

IMPHAL

R. Ganges

DACCA

Comilla

Feni

Fazilpur

Baigatchi
CALCUTTA

Chittagong

B U R M A

R. Chindwin

MANDALAY

Jumchar

Cox's
Bazaar

Ganges Delta

Akyab

B a y   o f   B e n g a l

R. Irrawaddy

R. Sittang

PROME

Zayatkwin

RANGOON

Irrawaddy
Delta

30 SQUADRON AREA OF OPERATIONS IN INDIA &
BURMA 1943 - 1945

30 Sqn aerodrome ⊙

0                                    200 nm

One of the VIP sorties on 4th May involved Wt. Off. Geoff Newell and another pilot who were given the job of flying to Chandina and thence to Imphal as escort to Gen. Slim's Lodestar aircraft. On landing at Chandina Geoff went in search of the VIPs, leaving his colleague sitting in his aircraft. Minutes later he returned 'ventre a terre', shouting that they were at the wrong airfield, boarded his aircraft and took off like a rocket. His partner managed to stay with him until almost to the end of the runway, when his engine cut, as he had forgotten to switch on the fuel! After taking off downwind, he caught up with Geoff Newell and they carried out their task as ordered. On returning to Comilla, however, they felt that they had aged by ten years!

Flt. Lt. H. F. Whidborne has provided a detailed account of a typical night 'rhubarb' operation, "As we also experienced in daylight, possible targets were scarce. I think it was generally thought that as so little by way of supplies transport was ever seen beyond the bomb line by day, the Japs must have been moving some or much of it under cover of darkness, probably using boats and barges etc. on the waterways. These could be readily spotted out in the water by moonlight. We were briefed to search for and attack any likely target in order to cause damage, harassment and disruption to possible supply movement. I do not remember being tipped off for any particularly likely spots or targets – we had no aerial photographs at that time. We just decided which rivers to patrol in discussion during briefing with the Intelligence Officer, Flight Commander and perhaps other pilots who were flying that night. The safety factor regarding flying time overlaps (over the target area, between different pilots) was of course always discussed, agreed and understood. I remember flying along to one side of fairly wide rivers, particularly hoping to see possible targets on the far side. I think that only once did I sight a target sufficiently far enough ahead to go straight in. Otherwise it usually entailed making a 270º turn outwards in order to come into a firing dive across the water. This manoeuvre inevitably entailed losing sight of the target during the turn and then having difficulty in picking it up again visually from a different angle against the background of dense vegetation on the banks. Any river craft which were about seemed to have been very well alerted to keep near the bank and to go into the shadows at the first alarm. I also found that, particularly in the firing position when using the reflector sight, it was very difficult to judge height and distance from the target in moonlight. After experiencing this I remember initially low flying over the water to zero my altimeter and then using this to help me to judge the pull-out using quick glances at the altimeter during manoeuvres and the dive attack. The 20mm canons on our Hurricane IIcs were effective at longer range than .303s would have been. I think the sides of wide rivers were not usually very steep. There were always tall rushes, mangrove and palm trees around. As you know, air to ground firing always entails a critical last-second pull-out and one was always conscious of potential disaster if one left it too late. As mentioned, judging height and distance was difficult in moonlight."

Adding to this account, former Plt. Off. P. M. Hamilton has said that there was no black-out of base airfields. A goose-neck flarepath which was left burning for a considerable time in case of an emergency landing showed up clearly from a long distance but there were no other regular lights. Mr. Hamilton also provides information on operating the Hurricane. "The jettisonable long-range tanks held 45 gallons each – enough for two hours at cruising power. They were not gauged. Fuel was fed by positive air pressure delivered to the tanks, directly to the engine fuel pump. If a airlock materialised the idea was to switch smartly over to the gravity tank. Aileron trim was quite satisfactory. Hurricanes were trimmed (laterally) by doping a few inches of flex on the upper side of the appropriate aileron until you got it right. We had VHF [radio], but no control was exercised – we were too low. We were on our own. We were not given specific times or areas. Long gaps between take-offs were sufficient to keep us apart." The Hurricane's only navigation instruments were a P4 compass, the standard flight instruments and the pilot's watch; not even homings by R/T were available. At night, detailed reading of a 1:1,000,000 map, much of

which was printed in red, presented a problem by the light of the dimmable red cockpit lighting.

An analysis of operations carried out by 30 Squadron Hurricane pilots over the Arakan front between February and May 1944 reveals that 829 sorties (89% of the 931 total) were escorts to supply-dropping aircraft, 44 (4.75%) were 'rhubarbs', 24 (2.5%) were VIP escorts, 18 (2%) were convoy patrols and escorts, ten (1%) were interception scrambles and six were searches for missing aircraft. It should be stressed that the dropping of supplies to ground troops was absolutely vital to the outcome of the Burma campaign, and 30 Squadron's participation in escorting the Dakotas and C-46s equally important. The official historian, when dealing with this subject, has said that "It is fantastic to think that what was in fact the world's first major experiment in basing a complete campaign on transport aircraft should in fact have been staged in what was also the world's worst flying country." It is doubtful, however, whether the intrepid pilots of 30 Squadron realised that fact at the time, or even whether officers higher up the ladder did.

Yet another squadron move was announced on 23rd May, this time to Yelahanka, where conversion to Thunderbolt aircraft was to take place. Next day the Harvard, followed by sixteen Hurricanes, took off for Vizagapatam, with a refuelling stop at Baigachi, while ground personnel spent the day loading baggage onto a special train. On 25th May the aircraft left Vizagapatam for St. Thomas Mount, where they were refuelled while the pilots ate lunch, and eventually arrived at Yelahanka at 15.30 hours. During the night the baggage train left Comilla, and at 07.00 on 27th May the main party of personnel left for Laksham, where a wait of fourteen hours on the station platform had to be endured as their train had been subjected to a series of delays. It arrived at 22.30, with 134 and 258 Squadrons already aboard, which placed 30 Squadron at a major disadvantage. At 03.30 next morning, however, the train arrived at Chandpi and squadron personnel began to board the riverboat *Prince of Wales*, a paddle steamer of 1916 vintage. Food was provided at 07.00 and the steamer set off two hours later up the river Padma. The voyage took over ten hours, and owing to a hold-up at the landing stage at Goalundo nobody was able to disembark until 23.30. A troop train awaited the exhausted men, but there was an acute shortage of water and there was no fuel for the kitchen car.

After a five-hour delay on 29th May while the train was being watered, Howrah Junction, Calcutta, was reached at about midnight. Only one meal had been served during the day. In the evening of 30th May, the train reached Bhadrak, where it was learned that rations were running short, and the officer in charge of the train had to telegraph ahead for further supplies. These were taken on board next day, and the kitchen car staff then began to provide three meals a day. Slow progress continued, and on 3rd June the train reached Madras in the morning and Arkonam about noon. There, the other two squadrons disembarked, and 30 Squadron personnel changed trains for the final stage of this lengthy journey. At 08.00 on 4th June, the train arrived at Bangalore Cantonment station, from where the men were transported in road vehicles to RAF Yelahanka, twelve miles away.

On arrival at Yelahanka, Flt. Lt. 'Canada Mac' McDonald was reminded by Flt. Sgt. Godwin, the SNCO in charge of 'B' Flight ground crew, that Mac had said that a party would be organised for the men on return to civilisation. This seemed a good time and place for such an event. "All the pilots donated money, a reservation was made at a local restaurant and a keg of beer was obtained" says 'Canada Mac'. "The owner of the restaurant took one look at the keg of beer and told us that he didn't want it opened on his premises. No problem! We ate dinner, loaded the beer and all personnel on a truck and drove to 'B' Flight dispersal tent. Everyone had his own mug, a big bonfire was lit, the beer started flowing and all the Air Force songs were sung that night. It was a great party."

Weather conditions at Yelahanka contrasted greatly with those in Bengal, as the airfield was at an elevation of over 3000 feet, which led to a cooler and more pleasant environment. As soon as the baggage train arrived on 5th June, all hands began unloading it. Next day was of course marked thousands of miles away by the

*After Hurricanes and before Thunderbolts. Seen at Yelahanka were: (rear) Wt. Off. Mills; Flg. Off. Kidd; Flt. Lt. Holmgren; Flt. Lt. Boyer; Flt. Lt. Fulford; Plt. Off. Hamilton; Wt. Off. Pyman; (front) Don Blair; Plt. Off. Newell; Wt. Off. Knodler; Flg. Off. Wright; Flt. Lt. Whidborne. Not all these pilots survived.*

invasion of France, a factor which gave an added impetus to everything the squadron personnel did. Radio bulletins giving the latest available news were listened to with great interest.

It was soon discovered that three other Hurricane squadrons were already at Yelahanka for conversion to Thunderbolts, so as it was likely to be the middle of July before 30 Squadron pilots could begin their training course a programme of continuation flying in the Hurricanes was formulated. An opportunity to allow leave for both pilots and ground crews was also taken, and a party of 24 airmen duly left for 8 Hill Depot at Wellington, in the Nilgiri Hills. After giving the pilots a brief description of the conversion course they awaited, Sqn. Ldr. Stevens left on 12th June for Delhi, where he was to take a Junior Staff Officers course lasting three weeks. Flying was carried out when weather conditions allowed, and consisted of formation practice, dog fighting, aerobatics, camera gun exercises and sector reconnaissance.

As at 30th June 1944, the strength of the squadron totalled 320, consisting of 13 officer (including nine pilots), 44 SNCOs (including 19 pilots), 180 corporals and British other ranks, 28 Indian other ranks, and 55 'enrolled followers'.

### Enter the Thunderbolt

First considered by the Air Ministry in 1941 for use by the RAF as an alternative to the Kittyhawk, the Republic Thunderbolt, known as the P–47 in USAAF service, was a powerful single-seat fighter. However, when the USAAF found certain shortcomings in the P–47B the Air Ministry lost interest, despite good reports from RAF pilots who had flown it. A partial redesign, the P–47C, incorporated a strengthened tail unit, an engine mounting which allowed rapid detachment and shackles to allow an external fuel tank. Air HQ India, aware of the ground support capabilities of its Hurricane squadrons, proposed that some squadrons be re-equipped with the P–47D, which was effectively the P–47C with

minor modifications. On 8th November 1943 the Air Ministry informed AHQ India that the Thunderbolt was a high-altitude fighter and was not designed for ground attack missions. This was a strange comment, because the P–47 had already begun to make successful ground attack sorties in Europe.

In January 1944 the RAF Delegation in the United States had ordered 420 P–47D aircraft, to be delivered at the rate of sixty per month with the intention of equipping an initial eight squadrons and a Conversion Unit in India. This order was closely followed by an order for a further 180 aircraft to cover attrition. The first aircraft, a Thunderbolt Mk.I, was delivered to 301 MU at Drigh Road in February 1944, and like the next 241 aircraft was fitted with a Curtiss Electric propeller. On the remainder of the first 420 Thunderbolts Hamilton Standard Hydramatic paddle-blade propellers were standard. Commencing with serial number HD182, the Thunderbolt Mk.II was fitted with a bubble cockpit canopy in place of the framed sliding version, but tended to be unstable laterally and to oscillate when being pulled out of a dive. This feature was to have tragic consequences for more than one 30 Squadron pilot.

Although the 40 ft. 9 in. wing span of the Thunderbolt was only nine inches greater than that of the Hurricane Mk.IIc, it was much longer at 36 ft. 2 in. Most significantly, the Pratt & Whitney Double Wasp engine of the Thunderbolt turned out 2300 hp compared with the 1280 hp of the Hurricane's Rolls Royce Merlin XX, giving a vastly different performance. Where the Hurricane Mk.IIc could fly at a maximum of 339 mph the Thunderbolt could attain 427 mph and had an operational range of up to double that of the Hurricane. The under-wing bomb load carried by the Thunderbolt, 2000 pounds, was also double that of the Hurricane. All in all, the new aircraft was a formidable machine, and one which it was hoped would play a major part in beating the Japanese enemy.

180

*A group of 30 Squadron pilots at Yelahanka during their conversion to the Thunderbolt.*

## 30 Squadron converts

Three years of flying Hurricanes came to an end on 6th July, and next day they were taxied away from the dispersal area and replaced by seventeen Thunderbolts which had arrived during the previous week. 30 Squadron pilots then began to learn about their powerful new mount by attending lectures about its airframe and engine and practising cockpit procedures. Wt. Off. Milne, the SNCO in charge of the armament section, lectured on the 0.5-inch Browning machine guns fitted to the Thunderbolt and gave a demonstration of stripping them down. The CO talked about the conversion syllabus and told all concerned that longer working hours would be necessary in order to meet the extensive programme.

Everyone was out and about early in good weather on 15th July, when the CO led a number of pilots into the air in Thunderbolts for the first time. Altogether, twenty-six pilots made their first flights without incident. More flights took place over the next few days and included some aerobatics and section formations. Pilots' comments on their new mounts were, almost without exception, favourable. They flew as a complete squadron

for the first time on 26th July, but next day it was learnt that a pilot of 1670 Conversion Unit had crashed a Thunderbolt, as a result of which they were all grounded pending an enquiry. The aircraft had been on fire in the air before the fatal crash. Until this incident occurred, 30 Squadron pilots had flown 228 sorties, so were already well advanced, and any interruption to the conversion programme would be a problem.

On of the first 30 Squadron pilots to fly the Thunderbolt was Flt. Lt. D. A. McDonald, who remembers the day well. "It was delightful to fly. A big, spacious cockpit and controls that handled very well. A water injection button on the throttle was intruiging. I always thought that water and gasoline didn't mix, but to my surprise and according to instructions, when the button was pressed there was a very appreciable boost in power. I also found out that you had to help the Thunderbolt get airborne. With the Hurricane, you would be airborne at 100 mph airspeed with little or no back pressure on the stick. On my first take-off in the Thunderbolt, I was surprised to see the airspeed indicator at 150 mph. I pulled back a little more and was airborne."

A great deal of sporting activity was undertaken by squadron personnel, football and hockey being played against teams from within the Station and from other units. In spite of the better climatic conditions at Yelahanka, there was a high incidence of stomach trouble among the men, many of whom had to be admitted to the military hospital. Food at Yelahanka was regarded by most as being poor in quality, and this may have been the root cause of the problem.

By 2nd August the cause of the fire in the Thunderbolt which crashed had been found to be a faulty fuel feed pipe, and some of them were therefore sent away for modification. While they were unable to fly, the pilots attended a series of lectures and film shows on combined operations and recognition of Japanese aircraft. Flying was resumed on 14th August after a frustrating interruption lasting seventeen days, and consisted of flight formations and climbs to 35,000 feet, but no sooner had these exercise begun than two 30 squadron pilots lost their lives. After taking off at 14.00, Wt. Off. Geoff Newell failed to return from a height climb, and before long it was learned that he had crashed about five miles from Deyannalli. Two and a half hours later Wt. Off. K. J. Knodler

*The 'office' of a Thunderbolt Mk.II.*

RAAF left on a similar exercise but crashed about forty miles west of Bangalore. Next day, height climbs were banned until further notice. Both pilots were buried at Cosseer Cemetery in Bangalore, with full military honours. The loss of two senior NCOs on the same day was keenly felt by their compatriots. At a Court of Enquiry convened to investigate these deaths it was concluded that one, and possibly both, pilots had been unable to pull out of a compressibility dive. Wt. Off. Knodler had been carrying out aerobatics at 20,000 feet. According to Flt. Lt. D. A. McDonald, "........we think he had a problem with oxygen supply, causing him to pass out temporarily. It's possible that he came to and was in a dive, and in trying to pull out wound the elevator control full back. We surmised that when the aircraft hit denser air the controls took over and pulled the aircraft up so sharply that it pulled the wings off. The fuselage was found in one field and the wings in another." Ken Godfrey also referred to these tragedies in his diary. "Other squadrons converting onto T-bolts [sic] have also had a lot of fatal prangs. As most of them occurred from high altitude, we had assumed that they were due to failure of the oxygen systems. But we have just discovered that they have been due to compressibility, a phenomenon which occurs when the aircraft nears the speed of sound in a dive, resulting in the loss of control and the aircraft breaking up. Until now, no-one knew anything about compressibility, and we have only just received word of it from England. Now we have to adhere rigidly to speed limitations while diving. The T-bolt, being so heavy and powerful, can soon reach compressibility in a dive." How right he was. A sudden reduction in engine power caused a nose-down trim change, which steepened the dive and increased the speed still further. Pilots who went too far beyond the aircraft's compressibility threshold found that they regained control at too low an altitude to pull out of the dive.

Practice bombing began on 18th August at a range a few miles north of Yelahanka, and continued over the next few days, intermingled with low flying practice and camera gun exercises. Restrictions on height climbs were relaxed, but additional precautions were laid down.

Early in September orders were received that the squadron, its conversion programme complete, was to move to Chittagong after a three-week period at Arkonam. An advance party under the command of Flg. Off. F. J. Kibble left Yelahanka by road early on 11th September and completed the 200-mile journey after eight and a half hours. The main party loaded kit and equipment into 'gharries' next day and made the move on 13th September, the

*The CO takes the salute at the funeral of Wt. Off. Geoff Newell, who lost his life on 14th August 1944.*

*The firing party at the funeral of Wt. Off. Knodler, who died in a Thunderbolt which went into a high-speed dive on 14th August 1944.*

sixteen Thunderbolts and the Harvard flying in during the morning.

Having spent a day in organising quarters and offices, squadron personnel paraded outside HQ on 15th September, and the CO gave a short address in commemoration of the Battle of Britain, which had culminated four years previously. Two days later the local padre held a service of commemoration, but although it had been promulgated in Daily Routine Orders only two officers and two

*A minor inspection in progress on a Thunderbolt Mk.I at Arkonam before 30 Squadron moved to the Arakan front in mid-September 1944.*

*The officers' mess at Arkonam was basic but functional.*

*A height climb in Thunderbolt KL308 [RS:C]. Note the white spot on a dark stripe across the fin.*

airmen attended! Practice flying continued, and now included army cooperation exercises, cross-country flying and dive bombing practice. Conditions at Arkonam, which is at sea level, were unpleasantly hot after the cooler weather at Yelahanka.

Their short stay at Arkonam over, the squadron pilots flew the seventeen Thunderbolts and one Harvard to Vizagapatam on 2nd October 1944, the first stage of the move to Chittagong. At the same time the advance party of ground personnel left by train. Baigachi was reached by the air party next day, apart from Wt. Off. D. A. Smith, whose aircraft suffered plug trouble, forcing him to make a hasty landing. The air party arrived at Chittagong on 5th October, and next day the main party left Arkonam by train. While they were in transit, the pilots spent 7th October in trying to acquire accommodation and furniture for the squadron. For the first time, the airmen of the squadron were allowed to organise their own canteen, which was successfully established by the end of October, but sporting facilities were almost non-existent, the nearest football pitch being in the town some six miles away.

## Back to business!

To set the scene, it is as well to provide details of the structure of air forces in the Burmese theatre of operations at the time 30 Squadron joined the campaign. Operations were divided into three fronts, with three major tactical air formations responsible to Eastern Air Command. 224 Group, commanded by Air Cdre. the Earl of Bandon DSO, a well-respected former Blenheim pilot and a highly effective staff officer, was responsible for the Arakan front. The central front, covering an area between Imphal and the Chindwin, came under 221 Group, commanded by AVM Stanley Vincent CB DFC AFC, and in the north-eastern area the US 10th Air Force held sway, under the command of Brig. Gen. John F. Egan. These three formations operated as part of 3rd Tactical Air Force under Air Marshal W. A. Coryton CB MVO DFC until it was disbanded in December 1944, after which they worked directly under Eastern Air Command.

30 Squadron pilots began operations on Thunderbolts on 16th October 1944, when in company with 135 Squadron they flew 'rhubarbs' in support of XV Corps and West African troops advancing south to clear enemy forces from the Arakan coast. However, the operation was impeded by low cloud and the last of the monsoon rains over the mountains east and south of the Imphal valley. Next morning four Thunderbolts carried out individual attacks on about eighty bashas concealed in the jungle, but without definite results. On 20th October six aircraft made an offensive reconnaissance of the Pi-Chaung, Kaladan and Lemro rivers, but apart from a two-masted boat and some bashas targets were not in evidence. According to Mr. W. V. Evans, however, two pilots, of whom he was one, made an attack (contravening their orders) on

*30 Squadron's 1st XI: (rear) Burgess, Kenyon, Lowe, Birkett, Kibble, Wilson (umpire); (front) Sumner, Archer, Simpson, Jenkins, Calder, Rolfe.*

Japanese troops in tunnels in riverside cliffs at Paletwa. He claims that large numbers of Japanese were killed, enabling British troops to occupy the town without a single casualty later in the day. Further offensive sorties were flown over the next few days, and during one of them the description 'low flying' was taken literally by Flt. Lt. E. Holmgren, whose aircraft (HD267) hit a treetop when he set upon a 20-foot boat moored under trees just north of Rathedaung. He was fortunate to return safely to base. For the first time, machine-gun fire was encountered on 24th October during a successful attack on a Japanese camp at Yezogyaung, where several bashas were set on fire.

In his diary, Ken Godfrey wrote "We are getting plenty of action now. Bombing and strafing jobs and long range jobs to Rangoon. The first one I did left me a wreck for three days afterwards. We have to fly with dinghy, Mae West, parachute, jungle suit, water bottle, revolver, jungle knife and many other articles strapped to our person. Remaining constantly alert in a very hot, cramped and confined cockpit for five to six hours is a very big strain on one."

Several Mk.II Thunderbolts arrived for the squadron in the last week of October 1944, and it was learnt that this Mark would re-equip the squadron and that long-range fuel tanks would be fitted. Long sorties were seen to be a forthcoming feature of 30 Squadron's life, and on 26th October Capt. Seeley of the 459th Fighter Squadron, USAAF, (which was also based at Chittagong) visited to talk to the pilots about his operational experiences in Burma, flying P–38 aircraft over long distances. Next day, seven aircraft fitted with Lockheed 137-gallon tanks took off to evaluate fuel consumption, after which the CO spoke gave advice to pilots on taking off with long-range tanks and on the subject of tactics. It was found that although the runway at Chittagong was 6000 feet long there was little to spare on take-off. This problem came to a head on 31st October, when six Thunderbolts carrying long-range tanks were detailed for formation flying. The fourth aircraft, piloted by Sgt. V. A. Waters, failed to climb away and crashed about 200 yards from the runway, bursting into flames on impact and killing the unfortunate pilot. Orders were then given that no Thunderbolt was to take off from Chittagong carrying full long-range tanks. The

funeral of Sgt. Waters was held on 1st November at Chittagong New Cemetery, attended by a representative party from the squadron.

Fourteen Thunderbolts and the Harvard flew to Cox's Bazaar on 2nd November, while C–47s carried the ground crews, in anticipation of an operation to be carried out in conjunction with 135 Squadron and the USAAF 1st Air Command Group, which was based at Asansol. In the afternoon pilots were briefed by Sqn. Ldr. Corfe, the senior Intelligence Officer of 167 Wing, Wg. Cdr. Parker from 224 Group Operations, and Air Cdre. the Earl of Bandon. As Air Marshal Coryton, the Commander of 3rd TAF, was also present, the following day's operation promised to be a particularly important one, code-named Operation *Eruption*. This was a two-day mission in which forty-nine new B–29 Superfortresses and twenty-eight B–24s were used to mount a devastating attack on targets in the Rangoon area. As part of *Eruption*, twelve of 30 Squadron's aircraft took off at 07.30 on 3rd November in fine weather for a sweep over Mingaladon airfield, Rangoon, in partnership with 135 Squadron. One of the Thunderbolts suffered complete oxygen failure and another a serious oil leak and had to return, but the others pressed on. On the approach to the Irrawaddy river, Wt. Off. Webster noticed that the Thunderbolt flown by Wt. Off. H. C. Edwards was on fire and called him on the R/T to suggest that he bale out. There was no response, and it seemed that Edwards had decided on a forced landing at a point north-east of Pathwe. His

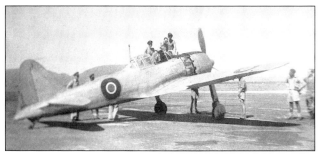

*Interested men of 30 Squadron inspecting a captured Zero fighter.*

*At disperal at an unrecorded location, with 30 Squadron Thunderbolts and a Mosquito in the background.*

aircraft hit the waterlogged ground and overturned, smashing a wing, and although the fire had gone out it seemed unlikely that Wt. Off. Edwards could have survived. After orbiting the area to check for any sign of life, Wt. Off. Webster returned to base with the news. Meanwhile, six aircraft arrived over the target at 20,000 feet, jettisoned their long-range tanks and circled for ten minutes to provide top cover for 135 Squadron pilots who had begun their attack. Heavy but inaccurate AA fire was being thrown up, and 30 Squadron then went into an attack. Two or three Oscars were seen but did not approach. One pass over the airfield at very low level was made, and although no Japanese aircraft were in evidence attacks were made on hangars of various sizes, gun positions and bashas. Apart from the heavy AA, a great deal of light AA and machine-gun fire was experienced. Wt. Off. Wright, arriving late, saw three aircraft which in the heat of the moment looked like Thunderbolts, but on nearing them he realised that they were Oscars in green, brown and yellow camouflage and carrying the Japanese red disc marking. After firing at one, he found another one on his tail, so beat a hasty retreat into cloud. The Japanese fighter known to the Allies under the code-name Oscar was the Nakajima Ki–43 Hayabusa (Peregrine Falcon), an important component of the enemy air forces, although not common in Burma.

A second, but very different, operation was flown from Cox's Bazaar next day. At 09.00 twelve Thunderbolts of 30 Squadron took off and set course for Cheduba Island, where they and other aircraft were to join Liberator heavy bombers and escort them to their target, the Insein railway workshops at Rangoon. However, the Thunderbolts arrived at the meeting point too early and after making a wide sweep out to sea came back too late! Only the leading four aircraft of 30 Squadron (Red Section) and P–38s of the USAAF 459th Fighter Squadron found the Liberators and successfully escorted them, while the remainder of the squadron returned to Cox's Bazaar. As the Liberators turned away from the target after dropping their bombs, two enemy aircraft identified as Tojos appeared at 12,000 feet and made an attack on the trailing bombers. Red leader, Flt. Lt. Whidborne in HD289, managed to shoot one Tojo down in flames, a victory confirmed later by P–38 pilots. The Nakajima Ki–44 Shoki (Demon), code-named Tojo, was similar to the Oscar, and is thought to have been fairly unusual in this theatre of war, being largely restricted to the defence of Japan, so what the 30 Squadron pilots were dealing with may in fact have been Oscars. Earlier, at least six enemy fighters had been seen in the target area, but although they made individual attacks on the Allied force there seemed to be no coordinated effort on their part. After returning safely to Cox's Bazaar, the 30 Squadron aircraft and personnel returned to Chittagong.

During the next few days no operations involved 30 Squadron, but on 8th November four pilots were detailed to escort a Dakota carrying ACM Sir Richard Peirse, the Allied Air C-in-C in India, from Barisal to Cox's Bazaar and then to Chiringa and Chittagong. In fact Sir Richard was flying in a Mitchell, and there was some degree of confusion before the four Thunderbolts were told to proceed to Cox's Bazaar. Making a farewell tour on relinquishing his post, Sir Richard visited squadron dispersal and spoke to airmen and pilots. Next day he was escorted to Agartala without incident.

30 Squadron flew fourteen sorties as escort to C–47s dropping supplies for forward troops on 9th November, while two pilots were sent to continue a search for a crashed Beaufighter. This they spotted on the southernmost of the Donmanick Islands, on a beach and surrounded by local inhabitants. More escort and patrol sorties for C–47s were flown on 10th and 11th November, after which a day was spent in preparing for a forthcoming long distance

*Twelve Thunderbolt Mk.IIs of 30 Squadron carrying out a fighter sweep over Burma.*

*Thunderbolt Mk.II HD298 [RS:U] at Chittagong in November 1944. 30 Squadron's badge is carried on the white identification band applied to all Thunderbolts in the region.*

operation. It had been decided that it would now be safe to take off from Chittagong carrying long-range tanks and using about half flaps. The mission, flown on 13th November, comprised a fighter sweep by twelve aircraft of 30 Squadron and twelve of 135 Squadron over the mouth of the Sittang river in support of Liberators bombing bridges in the area. Weather conditions were cloudy and no enemy aircraft were seen.

Before the next operation, 30 Squadron received a visit from Air. Cdre. the Maharaja of Baroda, who spent a short time talking to the pilots on 16th November. Next day, twelve Thunderbolts carried out a fighter sweep over airfields around Rangoon. Setting course from Chittagong at 09.30, they made a gradual climb to 23,000 feet in battle formation, with 135 Squadron slightly above them. On approaching the target area they descended to 19,000 feet. Pabst airfield was reached at 11.55, but no enemy aircraft were seen there or at Zayatkwin or Hmabwi. Between there and Mingaladon, however, things were very different, and twelve or more Japanese fighters were seen to be adopting defensive orbiting patterns at

*Thunderbolt Mk.II KL308 [RS:C] in the hands of Wt. Off. Keith Twynam over the east coast of India near Vizagapatam.*

*30 Squadron Thunderbolt KL881 taxying at Vizagapatam.*

8000 to 10,000 feet. It was observed that most were camouflaged but highly polished, with large red disc roundels well toward the wingtips, but one aircraft was in silver finish. Dropping their fuel tanks, Red Section of 30 Squadron dived to attack. An engagement lasting about ten minutes allowed the pilots to make individual attacks, but no claims could be made. Blue Section followed about a thousand yards behind and made a concentrated attack on three enemy aircraft at 8000 feet, but Blue 3 had to pull out owing to an oily windscreen. The others had difficulty in closing the range, as the Japanese pilots were in the habit of making extreme manoeuvres at the last moment. Again, Blue Section could not claim any success. White Section made its attack on three aircraft at 10,000 feet, but in every case the enemy pilots managed to avoid a confrontation. 30 Squadron aircraft were over the combat area for about twenty minutes, and left it at about 8000 feet, apart from some which had dived to lower levels to evade the enemy. Use had been made of superior altitude to dive upon the enemy, strike, zoom up and away and return for another attempt, but it was found that the Sections could not be held together, and pilots had to operate individually after the initial attacks. Enemy fighters, on the other hand, flew in line astern in a wide defensive circle, the leader apparently acting as a decoy. If one of the RAF pilots persisted in pursuing an enemy aircraft he soon found another one on his tail. During this operation, three 30 Squadron pilots experienced 'hang-ups' with their long-range tanks, two were troubled by oily windscreens, and two had persistent engine trouble and were lucky to survive. Three diverted to Hatharazi and five to Cox's Bazaar, while four managed to reach Chittagong, where unfortunately two of the Thunderbolts, HD294 and HD298, collided on landing. As a result, Wt. Off. I. G. Hardy RAAF died of his injuries, and was buried with military honours at Chittagong New Cemetery next day.

Twelve Thunderbolts of 30 Squadron provided low cover for twenty-two Liberators of 355 and 356 Squadrons, both based at Salbani, on 19th November, while they bombed railway yards at Mokpalin, with 135 Squadron as top cover. Red 4 soon aborted with fuel trouble, but the remainder found the Liberators and climbed above them, so that Red Section was at 11,000 feet, Blue Section at 13,000 feet and White Section at 14,000 feet. At about ten miles from the target, White Section was 'jumped' twice by Oscars approaching from the north. On the first attack White Section jettisoned tanks and broke away to 12,000 feet to avoid the four enemy aircraft, which were reported later to have a silver finish apart from red upper wing surfaces. The Thunderbolts were attacked again by three Oscars and so dived to about 6000 feet. Blue leader made a pass at an Oscar, but failed to damage it. Seven of 30 Squadron's aircraft continued to escort the bombers to the target, where there was heavy but inaccurate AA fire, and part of

the way back before returning to base or to Hatharazi, where one aircraft overshot the runway.

Avoidable accidents during recent months were the subject of a talk given by the CO to the pilots on 20th November, and the squadron engineering officer spoke about operational failures. Next day the Wing armament officer talked to pilots about bombs, as the squadron was expected to switch to short-range bombing missions in the near future. Soon, practice bombing using 100-pounders began on the Kathkali range. However, on 23rd November twelve Thunderbolts took off to provide low-level cover to eighteen B–24s of the USAAF 7th Bombardment Group, based at Pandeveswar, a mission which included 135 Squadron as medium cover and the USAAF 459th Fighter Group at high level. The target was Bridge No.71 on the Pegu to Moulmein railway line, and there was no opposition, but this was 30 Squadron's longest trip yet, the Thunderbolts being in the air for six hours and five minutes.

## 7030 Servicing Echelon

A radical alteration to the squadron's structure was ordered on 29th November, when HQ ACSEA Administration Instruction No. 298 (Org.) was put into effect. Under this order, almost all the ground personnel were posted to a new unit, 7030 Servicing Echelon. It was understood that the Servicing Echelon scheme had been adopted successfully in England for mobile squadrons and it was hoped that it would increase efficiency in SEAC. In charge of 7030 SE as engineer officer was Plt. Off. Ivan de la Plain, who over the next few months would prove to be a credit to his unit and to 30 Squadron. The establishment of 30 Squadron now allowed for eighteen officers (fifteen pilots, an adjutant, a medical officer and an intelligence officer) and twenty-one NCOs (fifteen SNCO pilots, a signals Wt. Off., a corporal clerk GD, a corporal electrician and three SNCO fitters).

Two pilots carried out a special experimental incendiary bomb exercise on 1st December 1944, a trial of armament which later in the war was used frequently. They each carried a long-range fuel tank filled with what was described as an inflammable substance and dropped them on a target on a beach near Cox's Bazaar, where they caught fire very effectively on impact. Such was the squadron's first experience of Napalm. Other pilots continued to practice dropping 100lb. bombs on the Kathkali range and flying GCI exercises.

However, another squadron move was on the cards, and on 2nd December a farewell dinner party was held by 30 and 135 Squadron officers at the Chittagong Club. Shades of the 1930s! Guests were Gp. Capt. J. B. Lynch, recently the Station Commander at Chittagong, Sqn. Ldr. J. D. Morison of 89 Squadron and Maj. Leuring, the CO of the 459th Fighter Squadron, USAAF. Before the move to Jumchar, though, there was work to be done,

*30 Squadron Thunderbolts taxying at Vizagapatam.*

and on 4th December six Thunderbolts made the squadron's first bombing raid, an attack on a supply dump at Kindaung. Eight 500lb. GP bombs were seen to burst in the target area, and this was followed up by a strafing attack. Next day, six pilots took part in Exercise *Earthquake*, which was a mock attack on a hill feature about six miles north-east of Imphal by Liberators, Mitchells, Hurricanes and Thunderbolts. Their efforts were controlled by a VCP and were followed by a ground-based attack by armoured vehicles. 30 Squadron's final missions from Chittagong consisted of a raid by eight aircraft on a suspected supply dump at Htizwe on the morning of 6th December and a mission to bomb a bridge at Awrama in the afternoon. Although during the morning mission assessment of the results was difficult, fourteen 500lb. bombs were seen to fall in the target area. The afternoon raid was marred by misidentification of the target, which was found only after another site had been attacked.

The move of 30 Squadron and 7030 SE to Jumchar began on 7th December 1944 with the departure of the advance party by road under the command of Flg. Off. M. J. Kidd. There were two main parties, the first of which boarded a river steamer at Chittagong at 07.30 on 8th December and arrived at Cox's Bazaar at 15.00 to join road transport for the final seven-mile stage to Jumchar. The second main party followed a day later and the aircraft on 10th December. Baggage and kit turned up at Cox's Bazaar on 11th December, but then had to be transferred to landing barges and rafts and taken up the river Baghkhali and off-loaded at jetties near the airfield. A great deal of time and effort went into procuring furniture for domestic and office use.

It was soon found that the open spaces of the camp at Jumchar provided a welcome contrast to the somewhat confined surroundings at Chittagong. Billets were the usual basha huts, situated along the slopes of small hills, providing good natural light, and fitted with built-in beds of bamboo. Another advantage was that there were few mosquitoes, so few cases of malaria were reported, other than relapses. Nevertheless, not everybody was happy with the new surroundings. In his diary, Ken Godfrey wrote on 10th December "We have moved to Jumchar; right in the wilds and complete with roaming tigers, deadly snakes and other nasty things associated with the wilds of Burma. About twenty of us are living in a long bamboo hut [with] dirt floor and bamboo poles for a bed which was too hard

*Thunderbolt Mk.II KJ131 [RS:Y] about to take off from Jumchar carrying two 500 lb. bombs for a 'cabrank' sortie for the 14th Army.*

for me. I have since constructed a bed from bamboo and sprung with electric light cable. Also erected a shower which works quite well. The mess is very crude and the food is lousy."

At Jumchar the 6000-foot runway consisted of rolled 'paddy'. 30 Squadron, now under the control of 904 Wing, used it for its first operation on 13th December, when twelve Thunderbolts took off, with twelve from 135 Squadron, to escort twelve Liberators of 99 Squadron. Their targets were Bridges 41 and 71 on the Pegu to Moulmein railway, and top cover was provided by P–47s of the 5th and 6th Fighter Squadrons of the USAAF 1st Air Command Group, based at Asansol. Over the target a few Oscar fighters were seen, but no significant engagements took place. Patrols and escorts for supply-dropping C–47s over the Mayu and Kaladan fronts were flown over the next few days, largely uneventfully, as well as some VIP escort flights. Among the personages looked after were the Viceroy of India, Field Marshal Sir Archibald Wavell, and the Allied Air Commander, Air Marshal Sir Guy Garrod, who flew from Comilla over Japanese-held territory to Imphal and back. One of the two pilots who flew the escort Thunderbolts was 'Taff' Evans, who on arrival at Imphal was asked "Do you always land like that?" "Like what?" he replied. "Well, the first Thunderbolt stalled at exactly four inches above the runway and the second landed in exactly the same way." "Oh yes" replied Taff, "We

*Part of 30 Squadron's dispersal at Jumchar, with the CO's aircraft visible under the awning.*

188

*Engineering staff of 30 Squadron at Jumchar.*

*Flg. Off. Ivan de la Plain was 30 Squadron's engineer officer and then the CO of 7030 Servicing Echelon.*

*A somewhat ramshackle-looking ambulance of American make forms the backdrop to this picture of 30 Squadron personnel listening to their wind-up gramophone during a rest break.*

roll above the starboard wing and another one above the port side, followed by a giant barrel roll around the amazed VIPs. Later, the squadron received a letter from Lord Louis Mountbatten in thanks for the escort that day.

Bombing missions began in earnest on 16th December, when twelve aircraft raided a suspected enemy HQ east of Buthidaung. Ten aircraft reached the target, and a subsequent message from the army congratulated the squadron on its success. One Thunderbolt which did not take part was KJ187, which swerved off the runway during take-off and overturned. Its engine was thrown from its housing, the tail broke off, the undercarriage was torn away and the aircraft caught fire. Some minutes later, the fire crew, with Cpl. Harvey in charge, arrived and extinguished the flames. Earth was dug away from underneath the cockpit, and the pilot, Wt. Off. E. M. 'Curly' Lacasse, was pulled out, still conscious but burned and gashed on the head. He was rushed to hospital and eventually recovered from his ordeal.

Next day, twelve aircraft bombed supply dumps east of Thaungdara, and on 18th December the same number went to the southern end of the Nataguna valley on a similar mission. An enemy staging post at Ponnagyun was the target on 19th December and another one east of the Mayu river next day. On 21st December the squadron was fully occupied in escorting Dakotas on supply-

always fly like that. Is there any other way to land?" "Does the whole squadron land like that?" was the next question, to which 'Taff' replied "Oh no, they're much better than us, that's why we were sent on this escort job. The squadron's much too busy fighting...." A few minutes later, 'Taff' overheard one NCO say to another "Did you see those two Thunderbolt pilots? They look like a couple of rough b*****s. I wouldn't like to meet them on a dark night!" An altogether incorrect assessment, one feels sure! During the return flight, 'Taff' decided to enliven the VIPs' journey by carrying out some aerobatics. After tucking the Thunderbolt's starboard wing a foot behind the port wing of the VIP aircraft he slid underneath and did the same trick on the other side. This told him the exact airspeed of the VIP aircraft, so he then carried out a dropping missions in forward areas, and more attacks on Japanese gun positions followed. Even on Christmas Day there was little respite, but the 30 Squadron officers did carry out their time-honoured privilege by waiting on airmen of 7030 SE at dinner, which was said to have been excellent in both quality and quantity. Seasonal food and drink had been brought back from Calcutta by Ken Godfrey, who flew the Harvard there for the purpose. "I had so much stuff in the Harvard it was a wonder it flew" he says.

For the remainder of the month the offensive missions continued, largely in close support of the 25th Indian Division advancing down the Mayu range and the 81st West African Division in the Kaladan valley. It was when returning to Jumchar in Thunderbolt KJ132 on 30th December that the CO, Sqn. Ldr. Stevens, experienced engine failure in the circuit, not a pleasant thing to happen to anyone. Luckily, he was able to force-land in a paddy field and suffered only a few bruises, but the aircraft was written off.

During the month 205 operational sorties had been flown, involving 349 flying hours. It was already becoming apparent that the Servicing Echelon system was a success, and the monthly serviceability average was fourteen aircraft, the best recorded since re-equipment with Thunderbolts. If airframe spares had been more readily obtainable the average would have been even higher. A stated policy of re-equipping 30 Squadron with Mk.II aircraft with Curtiss Electric propellers had not been fully activated, and only seven such aircraft were yet on strength. The change of role to bombing had meant that a maximum effort had been required from the armourers, who had performed very well in view of the fact that they had only three bomb trolleys and no tractor for shifting 500lb. bombs. To add to the armourers' troubles, bombs were delivered at short notice and needed extensive modifications which should have been carried out elsewhere. 'Taff' Evans has recorded his admiration for the men on the ground. "Led by Flg. Off. Ivan de la Plain, they were the greatest" he says. "They worked day and night to keep us in the air and they succeeded. We had sixteen aircraft and were the only squadron to put sixteen in the air in combat at the same time. There was no token of recognition for them (the ground

crews); we would never have been the effective fighting machine we were if it were not for the untiring and conscientious work done by our ground crews. Bless 'em all!"

The final year of the Second World War began for 30 Squadron on 2nd January 1945, when bombing and strafing of Japanese troop concentrations was the order of the day. An elaborate operation for an assault on Akyab Island in which the squadron was to have taken part was cancelled at the last minute because the island had been captured without opposition. After frequent raids since 1942, the island was now derelict, but was needed by the Allies as a base from where Dakotas could begin shorter flights to their dropping zones. In addition, it was seen as a potential base for fighters such as those of 30 Squadron.

Strafing missions continued until 6th January, when very heavy overnight rain made the runway unusable and brought about a stoppage of all road traffic on the camp. Many of the bashas were

*A mystery! 30 Squadron seems to have taken over these premises from 88 Squadron, but the latter did not leave the UK until after the Second World War!*

*Readying a 30 Squadron Thunderbolt for action.*

*Sqn. Ldr. Stevens has just shut down the engine of Thunderbolt Mk.II KJ146 [RS:I] after a long-range sortie.*

found to have leaked, due to high winds lifting the roofing thatch, much to the discomfort of the occupants. More rain fell next night, and although the weather improved dramatically on 8th January it was a further two days before any use could be made of the runway. On 11th January it was found possible to send four Thunderbolts on patrol over Dakotas dropping supplies in the Kaladan valley and for nine aircraft to go to Cox's Bazaar to be bombed up for a mission next day.

Flying from there, twelve of 30 Squadron's aircraft took off on 12th January to attack enemy positions on the Myebon peninsula, where Combined Operations forces had landed from the sea. Next day, the Thunderbolts raided Japanese positions near Kangaw, and later four aircraft went to look for enemy river craft reported near Myebon, but without success. Afterwards, all the Thunderbolts returned to Jumchar, where the runway was now in service. Twelve seems to have been the usual number of aircraft put up by 30 Squadron at this time; that number bombed and strafed Japanese positions on the Myebon peninsula on 14th January, attacked enemy positions on a hill feature north-east of Teinnyo on 15th January, flew as medium-altitude cover to Liberators bombing Zayatkwin airfield, near Rangoon, on 16th January and raided hill positions north of Kantha on 18th January. It was noted that forward air controllers were becoming more numerous, and it was now possible to contact them by R/T before bombing commenced.

To hone the pilots' gunnery skills, a detachment from 23 Armament Practice Camp arrived from Dhubalia on 18th January, bringing three Harvards and two Vengeances. That day was also marked by the arrival in a B–25 of Col. C. M. Kellogg, a Chemical Warfare Officer of the USAAF, who gave a short talk and then showed a film on the use of Napalm bombs improvised from 165-gallon jettisonable tanks.

Defensive patrols were flown over the anchorages and recently-established landing beaches at Myebon on 18th January, and five pilots flew to Akyab, where they met two Dakotas which they escorted to Kalemyo, one of them said to be carrying Admiral Lord Louis Mountbatten. After a twelve-aircraft raid on Japanese positions near Kantha on 19th January, Flight commanders were briefed for a major combined operation, an assault on Ramree

Island to take place on 21st January. 30 Squadron aircraft, each carrying two 500lb. bombs and a 90-gallon belly tank, made two patrols over the beachhead, during the second of which the pilots were allocated a target by the forward air controller. This tactic enabled ground troops to capture a prominent hill position. Awaiting the pilots when they returned to Jumchar were two visitors from Eastern Air Command, Gen. Shulgen of the USAAF and Gp. Capt. Spotswood DSO DFC, who were anxious to obtain first-hand information on the mission.

Similar missions were flown over the next few days, earning compliments from a forward air controller on the pilots' bombing accuracy. After the mission on 24th January, Gp. Capt. J. L. Airey DFC, who had served with 30 Squadron in Iraq (then Mesopotamia) in 1926 and was now the CO of 1670 Conversion Unit at Yelahanka, was welcomed by the pilots, to whom he spent time chatting at dispersal. With him was another prominent person, Gp. Capt. H. I. Edwards VC DSO DFC of Bomber Command.

The squadron then spent three days on gunnery training with the 23 APC detachment before operations were resumed on 28th January, when accurate bombing was carried out by twelve aircraft on the road east of Kangaw and later a gun position in the same area. After a similar attack on 29th January, the Thunderbolts landed at Cox's Bazaar, where they were fitted with two tanks containing Napalm, which they proceeded to drop on enemy positions near Kangaw. This attack was repeated next day and on 31st January, and the army was able to make a significant advance. By the end of the month, 30 Squadron had disposed of its Mk.I Thunderbolts in favour of Mk.IIs, with which a serviceability averaging 88% was attained. This figure, however, was only attained by the transfer of components from other aircraft awaiting repair and by the prompt delivery of replacement aircraft in generally good condition. January was the busiest month for 30 Squadron since its arrival in SEAC, and the CO paid tribute to the men of 7030 SE, who entered wholeheartedly into their task and often worked into the small hours of the morning to ensure that the aircraft were in top condition for the next day's mission.

February 1945 began with an attack by twelve Thunderbolts on

*A motley selection of 30 Squadron personnel at an unrecorded location. Back row, left to right: LAC Mannion (intelligence clerk); Flt. Sgt. Frank Sumner; Flt. Lt. H. F. Whidborne; Flt. Lt. Dunlop; Plt. Off. D. Calder; Wt. Off. Knowles; Sgt. Allan; Sgt. Coombes; Flt. Sgt. Cook; Flt. Sgt. Keith Twynam. Front row, left to right: Sgt. Simpson; Flt. Sgt. Ledbury; mascot 'George'; Flg. Off. MacKenzie; unknown.*

Japanese hill positions at Kangaw, but results could not be determined owing to the thick jungle which covered it. Later in the day a 'rhubarb' over Magwe airfield, Magwe satellite landing strip and Maida Vale was carried out, but there was little sign of activity and no enemy aircraft were sighted. A compound at Kolan said to contain a Japanese HQ was raided next day after the target had been indicated by Thunderbolts of 134 Squadron, based at Ratnap, and damage was inflicted on the bashas. On 3rd February twelve pilots flew over to Cox's Bazaar so that Napalm tanks could be fitted to their aircraft, but as no operation was detailed they left the Thunderbolts and went back to Jumchar by road. Returning next day, they took off to attack Japanese defensive positions on Ramree Island, and returned to base after a successful raid, although small arms fire had damaged three aircraft. A road bridge near Thangyo was the target on 5th February, but although near misses were scored the bridge survived. Over the next three days similar missions were flown, but then the weather began to deteriorate, with a change in wind direction from north-east to south-west and a build-up of low cloud. Heavy rain fell on 9th February, making the Jumchar runway unserviceable, but twelve aircraft waiting at Cox's Bazaar took off when the weather improved in the afternoon to drop Napalm bombs on that bridge at Thangyo, scoring at least one direct hit.

B–24 heavy bombers of the USAAF making for stores dumps north of Victoria Lake, Rangoon, were escorted by 30 Squadron Thunderbolts on 11th February. This was one of three waves of bombers which made successful attacks, and although AA fire was heavy no enemy fighters were seen. Flying was still taking place from Cox's Bazaar, as at Jumchar improvised pumps were in use in an effort to drain water off the runway. The efforts of the 'coolies', who removed 10,000 gallons of water, were rather wasted, as more rain fell on 14th February. Pilots waiting at Cox's Bazaar were frustrated, as 6/10 cloud at 2000 to 3000 feet prevented any operational flying. However, when the wind veered to the north-east matters began to improve, and two operations were flown on 15th February, both by the usual twelve aircraft. The first comprised a Napalm attack on Sakanmaw and a strafe on Kywegu

and the second was a raid with delayed action bombs on a river bridge, when direct hits were scored. By 16th February good progress had been made in de-watering the Jumchar runway, but for the next few days all operations had to be staged from Cox's Bazaar. Missions included defensive patrols over an area where 53

**Dear friend,**

I am an Allied fighter, I did not come here to do any harm to you who are my friends, I only want to do harm to the Japanese and chase them away from your country as quickly as possible. If you will lead me to the nearest Allied Military Post, my Government will give you a good reward.

*A 'gooly chit' printed in English and Burmese as issued to aircrews during the Burma campaign.*

Indian Brigade had just made a fresh landing, raiding bridges and villages and strafing Japanese troop concentrations.

Jumchar airfield became operational again on 21st February and aircraft began to return after operations. Over the next two days, Japanese concentrations including positions east of new Allied landings in the Ru-Ywa area, were attacked. Then, on 24th February, twelve aircraft flew to Cox's Bazaar to be fitted with Napalm tanks for two operations later that day. On landing, Thunderbolt KJ128, piloted by Sgt. B. A. Rattenbury, whose first operation this would have been, suffered a burst tyre, swung off the runway and overturned on sandy soil. The aircraft was wrecked, and unfortunately Sgt. Rattenbury was found to be dead. While twelve aircraft were attacking two targets in the Dalet Chaung area next day, the sergeant's body was buried in the cemetery on nearby Kurushkaul Island.

On the last day of the month, escort was again provided for B–24s of the USAAF's 7th Bombardment Group, based at Pandaveswar, which were raiding Mingaladon airfield near Rangoon. Flying with 30 Squadron were 135 Squadron and P–47s of the 1st Air Commando Group. Enemy aircraft were conspicuous by their absence, although Mingaladon was the most important

Japanese airfield in Burma. Over the target R/T silence should have been observed, but to the disgust of 30 Squadron pilots the B–24 crews monopolised the airwaves to such an extent that it would have proved impossible to warn them of the approach of enemy aircraft.

During February, 30 Squadron dropped 192,000 pounds of GP bombs and 11,748 gallons of Napalm in 326 operational sorties over 756 flying hours. Aircraft serviceability was, at 93.1%, the highest average achieved by the squadron so far in the war, but the spares position improved only marginally. Components were always sourced locally rather than through official channels if possible, in order to minimise delay.

After a period of dropping Napalm, 30 squadron reverted to the use of 500lb. GP bombs on 5th March 1945, when twelve aircraft made very successful attacks on enemy positions south-east of Ru-Ywa under the direction of a forward air controller. Most operations were still being mounted from Cox's Bazaar due to inclement weather, but on 6th March a return to Jumchar was made, which pleased all concerned, as a great strain had been put on the MT section and maintenance was inconvenient.

A squadron record was set on 9th March, when sixteen aircraft, the complete establishment, took off to escort B–24s of the 7th

*Flt. Lt. Kidd, the 'A' Flight commander, landing at Jumchar in Thunderbolt Mk.II KJ248 [RS:B] after a long-range escort sortie for Liberators bombing Rangoon. The round trip would have involved up to six hours in the air and at least 30 minutes more in the cockpit.*

*Thunderbolt Mk.II KJ223 [RS:A] seems dwarfed by a 137-gallon drop tank.*

Bombardment Group which were attacking storage dumps at Rangoon. As the squadron records state "This was a most inspiring day for the new engineer officer and CO of 7030 Servicing Echelon to arrive — Plt. Off. G. R. Calder, ex UK."

Allied forces made a new landing on 13th March, at Letpan, and 30 Squadron sent sixteen Thunderbolts to carry out 'cabrank' patrols over the area, a mission known as Operation *Turret*. Two days later a railway bridge at Thawatti was bombed, using 11-second delay fuses, and direct hits were scored. This target was visited again on 20th March, after which weather conditions prompted another temporary move to Cox's Bazaar. Progress made by XV Corps was now beginning to leave 30 Squadron behind, and after 14th March the squadron's operations in direct support of the army came to an end. Pin-point targets all over southern Burma and from the west coast to the border of Siam (now Thailand) continued to be bombed, however, road and rail bridges, stations, riverside settlements, stores dumps, living quarters and military headquarters sites far behind the front line feeling the effect of the squadron's efforts. To carry out a prominent operation on 29th March, consisting of a raid on Japanese troops and dumps at Ngedaung, it was necessary to fly a 720-mile round trip, but after 3 hours 45 minutes in the air every pilot reported having at least 100 gallons of fuel remaining on return to base. For these operations, every Thunderbolt was fitted with a 90-gallon jettisonable fuel tank under the belly and carried two 500lb. bombs with either instantaneous or delayed action fuses. A record number of operational hours were flown in March, 809, in 268 sorties during which 201,000 lbs of GP bombs and 9147 gallons of Napalm were dropped on enemy targets. Aircraft serviceability remained constant at 93.1%.

Personnel reporting sick at Jumchar began to increase in number in March, a result, it was believed, partly of the rise in temperature and humidity and partly that the many recent new arrivals from the UK had not yet had time to establish immunity to mild alimentary infections. It was noted that the ages of the new personnel were the extremes, some being under 21 and some over 35, and the younger ones seemed to stand up to the climate better. A plague of flies did nothing to help the health of all concerned, and vigorous spraying of DDT had to begin. Furthermore, all personnel were inoculated with anti-cholera vaccine.

On 28th March, Flg. Off. A. D. Dick and Sgt. L. F. French, were the pilots on 30 Squadron's only supply-dropping mission in Thunderbolts. Each aircraft was fitted with three long-range fuel tanks from which the ground crews stripped out the baffle plates and fitted doors to the sides. These containers were used to drop 'goodies' to ground troops at Lebon. Why the squadron did this rather than the usual Dakotas has never been explained. Since the Thunderbolts were carrying containers, no extra fuel was available, so the two-hour ten-minute round trip had to be flown without any navigation problems.

Dive-bombing techniques used in close support operations were well rehearsed, and accurate results were usually obtained. Twelve aircraft carrying 500lb bombs took off, joined up in fours, line astern, and as soon as the leader set course re-formed in three sections of four, Red, White and Blue, in finger formation. An easy climb at 170 mph (indicated) took them to 10,000 feet. Bombing was carried out from a deep echelon, with Blue and White leaders line astern to Red leader, aircraft being spaced at about 150 yards, each one at the same altitude as the one in front and just outside its slipstream, with the exception of Blue and White leaders. Targets were identified on one-inch or 1:25,000 scale maps, sometimes with the help of photographs, and pilots were also briefed by the squadron's army liaison officer. Forward air controllers equipped with VHF radios had been set up in forward areas, and at times the army was able to provide smoke indicators. An interval of one second between the time each aircraft 'peeled off' to bomb was normal; a 120 degree turn was found to be most satisfactory, eliminating the need to make an aileron turn back onto the target during the dive. The angle of dive was between 60 and 80 degrees, bombs were released at 4000 feet, and at the bottom of the dive

*Flt. Lt. Harry Whidborne DFC, one of 30 Squadron's stalwarts.*

indicated air speeds often reached 500 mph! Engine rpm was set at 2500 before the dive began.

### The beach disaster

Operations such as these continued in early April 1945, although the weather was by no means good, several missions being flown from Cox's Bazaar. On 13th April, however, orders were received that a move by ship to Akyab Main airfield scheduled for about 20th April was to be brought forward to 15th April and was now to be made by road. Little did anyone know what trouble that change of plan would cause! Tremendous activity took place on 14th April, and by evening most of the squadron kit had been loaded onto vehicles provided by 57 MT Company, although more trucks were awaited from Chittagong. On 15th April all personnel were up and about at 05.00 and two hours later eighty-three vehicles carrying the main parties of 30 and 135 Squadrons with 7030 and 7135 Servicing Echelons left Jumchar at the beginning of their long journey south. The Thunderbolts and

*Servicing the Pratt & Whitney Double Wasp engine of a Thunderbolt at Jumchar.*

pilots were to remain at Cox's Bazaar until Akyab Main airfield had been made ready for aircraft and a small rear party was left behind to clear up remaining baggage. In spite of rough roads and and heavy loads Razabil was reached at noon and a stop made for 'tiffin'. Progress during the afternoon was slower, due to the bad state of bridges along the road, and it was dark before the convoy arrived at Indin airstrip, where a hot meal was provided. That night everybody slept in the open air, in, under or alongside the vehicles. Next day the party was under way just after dawn to begin a stage of the journey which involved driving fifteen miles along a sandy shore at low tide. It was soon found that the sand was wet and soft in places, and as several MT drivers were inexperienced it was not surprising that some thirty vehicles became bogged down. About fifteen of them were extricated by a four-wheel-drive wrecker before the fast-incoming tide could reach them, another seven were pulled out after being submerged, but the rest had to be surrendered to the water. Most of the kit on the trucks was saved in the nick of time and moved to a drier part of the beach. Personnel, however, were stranded all along the beach to Donbaik, where the road to

*Sgt. French talking to a member of the ground crew of Thunderbolt KJ128 [RS:X] after returning from a long-range escort mission.*

Foul Point could be accessed. Only eighteen vehicles were able to reach Foul Point in time to be ferried to Akyab Island in a LCT efficiently loaded by a Combined Operations officer.

One airman who remembers this catastrophic trip is Mr. A. Brown, who says "When the squadron was stranded during the trek to Akyab we ran completely out of drinking water. [There was] plenty of food among the stores but staff began to suffer [from] thirst. The adage 'Water, water, everywhere but not a drop to drink' was very true as the waves came crashing on the beach. The army transport drivers drained their radiators, strained the water and boiled it for use. They then refilled their radiators with sea water. One member on the trek was so thirsty that he opened a tin of fruit to drink the juice. This unfortunately caused his mouth and tongue to thicken terribly. Eventually contact was made with a local native who agreed to show us where there was a water hole. A party of half a dozen, including 'Doc' Jones, set off into the jungle laden with containers. The water hole lay in a clearing surrounded by bales of rotting Japanese rice and other stores. All that could be seen was a thick layer of brilliant green scum. After looking at it for some time, 'Jonah', as he was called, knelt down to scoop the cover away and dipped a can into the water underneath. He looked at it and barely took a sip, said 'Fill them up, we'll boil it and should survive'. We survived!" The main cause of this catastrophe was a lack of knowledge of the condition of the beach between Indin and Onbaik, which monsoon tides had softened. It was also noted that the CO of 57 MT Company, Sqn. Ldr. Potter, had no experience of the route.

Next day more vehicles reached Foul Point, which then became a staging post. Food and water supplies still presented a problem until American 'K' rations were made available. Thirty trucks were ferried to Akyab Island that day, and a further fourteen on 18th April. Men arriving at Akyab Main were directed to a temporary domestic site, as the permanent site for the squadrons had not been prepared. This area was decided upon next day, and work began at once on clearing and burning scrub and jungle. Only two bashas were being built, and tents had not yet arrived. In warm and humid conditions, officers and airmen were soon busy digging latrines,

*Thunderbolts of 30 Squadron at an airfield close to the Arakan front. Note the squadron palm badge on the fin of KJ140 [RS:B]; HD265 [RS:G] behind; and in the background B-29 42-6255, an aircraft which must have seemed enormous to the 30 Squadron personnel.*

building cookhouses and cooking ranges, laying concrete floors and indeed doing everything else which was required. The site contained several large bomb craters and a number of crashed aircraft and was very rough. Tents arrived on 21st April and work began on erecting them at once. With the arrival of the MT vehicles, it was possible to move baggage from the temporary site to the permanent one on 22nd April. Work continued over the next couple of days, and included another basha which was to be the airmen's dining hall. Writing his comments on the month's activities, the CO remarked "............ it should be stated that the camp site for the squadron at Akyab had been barely started, and it was to the credit of our personnel that so much hard work was done in such a short time so that the squadron might become operational at the earliest possible moment." The area where tents were pitched was on a slope, with a Japanese burial area at the bottom. Every tent had a drainage ditch around it, which at night was inhabited by bullfrogs. As Mr. A. Brown recalls "We had no radios, just frogs!" It was soon found that the damp ground did not make for comfortable nights and that snakes found the warmth under the ground sheets attractive. Within a few days all the tents had been floored with PSP (perforated steel planking used for runways), but when a gun pit lined with the same material was struck by lightning and its Indian crew killed every piece of PSP was hurriedly removed!

Akyab Main airfield came into use at noon on 24th April 1945, and shortly afterwards the Spitfires of 67 Squadron flew in, followed by the Thunderbolts of 30 and 135 Squadrons and a detachment of 27 Squadron's Beaufighters. One runway was 6000 feet long, surfaced with a hessian/bitumen material and the other one, which was parallel, was covered with what was described as 'metal stripping', probably PSP. Now under the control of 903 Wing, 30 Squadron began local flying on 26th April, but most attention was given to the domestic site, where tents had to be fortified against the forthcoming monsoon. Between May and October, no less than 250 inches of rain could be expected!

Six aircraft were brought to a state of readiness for a close support operation on 28th April, but were not called upon. The Allied armies were now sweeping towards Rangoon, and Operation *Dracula*, the capture of the port of Rangoon, was the subject of a talk given by Gp. Capt. D. C. Yorke, the CO of 903 Wing, to the pilots of 30 Squadron. A sweep over Mingaladon airfield was then planned, but with the rapid advance of the ground troops this was cancelled and an attack on the Letpadan West railway bridge and a nearby road bridge was carried out instead.

30 Squadron's good standard of serviceability was maintained in April, but due to the protracted move from Jumchar to Akyab Main the number of sorties flown, 120, was much less than the previous month. An epidemic of main fuel cell defects had been apparent and had caused four aircraft to undergo repairs. 7030 SE had lost a considerable amount of equipment during the move, and by the end of the month it had not been replaced, giving cause for worry about servicing in the immediate future.

Operation *Dracula* began in earnest on 1st May 1945, when forty Dakotas took off from Akyab Main soon after dawn carrying paratroops to be dropped on Elephant Point, at the mouth of the Rangoon River. 30 Squadron stood by to take off at 06.30, but as there was now 10/10 cloud almost 'on the deck' and heavy rain had caused the runways to be waterlogged it was impossible to take off. Conditions improved in the afternoon just enough to allow twelve aircraft to attack specified targets in the Rangoon area. The terrible weather continued next day – D-Day in Burma – and although six Thunderbolts took off to provide 'cabrank' patrols around Rangoon only two were able to bomb a prearranged target. A seaborne landing that day by the 26th Indian Division was almost unopposed. Later in the day six more aircraft of 30 Squadron patrolled as before and attacked targets specified by Naval personnel on board the HQ ship. Japanese forces evacuated Rangoon on 3rd May and Allied troops were able to continue their rapid progress, and 30 Squadron found that its services were not required for several days. Some squadron pilots flying over

*The CO's bath-time! With a mug of 'char' and a paper, this was the height of luxury.*

Rangoon saw a curt message on the roof of the prison: JAPS GONE – EXTRACT DIGIT, and no time was lost in releasing the prisoners of war inside. On 5th May Flg. Off. C. W. Weir in the squadron Harvard carried an RAF pilot who had just been released from Rangoon prison to Barrackpore for interrogation at HQ Eastern Air Command. He had been shot down while flying a Mohawk over Burma two and a half years earlier.

30 Squadron's next participation in the campaign was on 8th May, when two aircraft made contact with two Dakotas off the west coast of Burma and escorted them to Rangoon. During the afternoon eleven aircraft took off to attack enemy troop positions just west of the Sittang river, but only eight pilots found and attacked the target. This day was of course VE-Day in Europe, but celebrations at Akyab Main were confined to the firing of AA guns by local units. Nevertheless, when AVM the Earl of Bandon DSO visited the squadron next day he was in very good spirits, and spoke to the pilots about future prospects with great confidence.

Apart from escorting a Sunderland flying boat carrying a VIP from Akyab to Rangoon and back, 30 Squadron was engaged in the usual attacks on Japanese troops over the next few days, often with Wg. Cdr. M. G. Riggall from 903 Wing leading. During this period, it was learned with pleasure that Wt. Off. H. C. Edwards, who had crash-landed on 3rd November 1944, had survived with a broken leg and had just been freed from Rangoon prison. While six Thunderbolts were on supply-dropping escort on 13th May a Hurricane with a very light-coloured under-surface and markings that could not be identified repeatedly flew from the east, up-sun, toward them. The 30 Squadron Thunderbolts were at 9000 feet and the Hurricane two or three thousand feet higher, and while its pilot did not actually make any dummy attacks the Thunderbolt pilots found its activity most disconcerting. One wonders whether it was an aircraft which had been captured intact by the Japanese.

Yet another move for the mobile 30 Squadron was demanded on 15th May, when a period of rest and training at Chakulia was

*Not exactly the Ritz, but it served its purpose. The airmen's mess at one of 30 Squadron's locations.*

196

ordered. Three days later the weather, which had been appalling, cleared to allow seventeen Thunderbolts and the Harvard to fly to their new base, while a Dakota carried a small ground party with enough equipment to service the aircraft for a short time. Another Dakota took more personnel next day while the main party were packing all the remaining kit. As will be seen, it was some time before the squadron's main party was able to leave Akyab Main, a case of bureaucratic confusion having arisen.

30 Squadron was now non-operational. The Thunderbolt had proved to be ideal for close-support operations in this theatre of war, with long range and good fire power. Opposition from Japanese fighters had rapidly diminished, and to this must be attributed the fact that the squadron had shot down only one enemy aircraft and damaged another, both in the first month of operations. Not one pilot had been killed on operations. Sqn. Ldr. Stevens wrote in the squadron records "It was very gratifying to find the squadron taking part in the successful assault on Rangoon, thus ending the season with the campaign in Burma virtually over." Soon after this, he was posted, and the squadron found itself without a leader for the time being.

During the time that 30 Squadron had been flying the Thunderbolt the pilots had flown 1485 sorties, 70% of them (1038) offensive missions. Army support missions had accounted for 207 sorties (14%) and long-range fighter escorts and sweeps 148 sorties (10%). Escorts to supply-dropping aircraft had fallen to a mere 49 sorties (3%), while VIP escorts totalled 33 sorties (2%) and other tasks made up the other 1% of the total.

At Chakulia, disaster struck almost at once. On 23rd May a severe gale gusting to more than 100 mph caused much havoc, and although picketed down, three Thunderbolts and the Harvard were damaged beyond repair. Two nights later another gale caused more damage to aircraft, including one which was completely destroyed. Domestic buildings were also badly damaged and had to be repaired without delay. High temperatures did nothing to help matters, causing many cases of severe prickly heat.

## Back to India

Flt. Lt. H. F. Whidborne, who was in command of the squadron pending the appointment of a new CO, flew to Akyab Main on 3rd June to find out whether any movement order had been received by the main party, but learned that the matter was still in the hands of HQ RAF Burma. There was still no news on 7th June, when he returned to Chakulia. When he made another attempt to sort the matter out on 9th June, however, he was told that the squadron was to move yet again, this time to Vizagapatam, and the main party had at last been given a movement order. Consequently, most of the heavy technical equipment was taken to the Arakan jetty at Akyab on 10th June and loaded into landing craft for transfer to the HMT *Santoy*. All MT vehicles loaded with equipment were put aboard *Santoy* on 12th June. There seems to have been no hurry to effect the move, however, as it was 20th June before the remaining pilots at Akyab Main were flown in a Dakota, not to Chakulia as they expected but to Vizagapatam, where they carried out the function of an advance party. Meanwhile, Flt. Lt. Whidborne had been posted to 22 Armament Practice Camp and on 21st June had to present himself at Amarda Road to explain why he had not reported for duty at that unit. As he complained, he was the only Flight commander on 30 Squadron and was thus put in the unenviable position of acting as CO. On 22nd June it was learned that the main party at Akyab was at last about to begin the move, and next day, in torrential rain, baggage was taken to Arakan jetty and transferred to HMT *Pulaski*, a 6000-ton ship built on the Clyde in 1896. Rain was still falling heavily when the main party embarked on *Pulaski* on 24th June, and within a couple of days most of the men were suffering from the heavy seas being encountered. Even the Indian stokers were affected, and stopped work. A call for volunteers was then made, and a number of airmen stepped forward, presumably ones who were not laid low with sea-sickness. Had they not done so, the ship would have had to return to Akyab, but their hard work enabled the voyage to Madras to be completed. *Pulaski* docked there on 30th June after what should have been a two-day voyage,

*At Vigazapatam in July 1945: (rear) Flg. Off. Kent; Wt. Off. Hewetson; Flg. Off. Birkett; Wt. Off. Coombs; Flt. Sgt. Moore; Flt. Lt. Kibble; Flt. Sgt. Webb; (front) Flt. Sgt. Taylor; unknown; unknown; Flt. Sgt. Kenyon; Flt. Sgt. Paterson; Flg. Off. Sumner.*

*The funeral of Flg. Off. Fred Kent, who lost his life at Vigazapatam on 12th August 1945.*

and the slow process of unloading baggage and kit into barges began, inevitably leading to a loss of some items. The disembarkation is remembered vividly by Mr. A. Brown, who recalls that "On arrival at Madras we found that the ship could not enter harbour, and we watched in horror as small tugboats came out to us, each towing several small rafts about 15 feet square. We scrambled onto these, holding onto each other until we were standing in five or six inches of water. What a climax, and what a way to land back in India." Feeling like a group of refugees, the 30 Squadron men were greeted at the landing steps by a number of white women who treated them to bars of scented soap, tea, sweets and cakes. "Things were looking up" says Mr. Brown. Personnel, thankful to be on dry land, were taken to Patchiapolis College, about five miles outside Madras, a disused school with marble floors, toilets and showers, and reasonably good food. Most of the airmen had over a year's pay in credit, so for the first few days in Madras they gorged themselves on steak and chips, apple pie and ice cream.

While the men were disembarking, Flg. Off. E. A. McKenzie RAAF was taking off to fly from Chakulia to Vizagapatam to make arrangements for the arrival of the remaining Thunderbolts, but on the way was taken ill in the cockpit and had to make a belly-landing in a paddy field at Kallikota, near Cuttack. Luckily, he suffered nothing worse than a broken leg and cuts, but his aircraft (KJ193) was destroyed.

The task of transferring baggage from ship to railway wagons was finished on 2nd July, and next day the main party boarded a train at Rayapuram station, Madras. This train was said to have been the best military train that 30 Squadron personnel had used for a very long time. It was 23.00 on 4th July before the main party arrived at Vizagapatam and were promptly taken to the domestic site at Kottapalem, about four miles from the airfield. This site was found to be pleasant and well-equipped apart from a lack of electric lighting! The next few days were spent in organising the various sections of the squadron and making sure that the domestic arrangements were up to scratch. Battledress green uniform was issued to all personnel, and a major effort was made to ensure that everyone had a short leave period. On return, time was spent on a short course of weapons training in anticipation of Japanese

infiltration, and inoculations against TB and cholera were provided.

After a talk by the local air traffic control officer on 8th July, fourteen pilots took to the air next day to carry out a sector reconnaissance, following which cross-country exercises and section formation flights were made, though the cloud-base hampered the proceedings to some extent. By 14th July, however, no fuel was available, as there was no bulk fuel installation on the airfield. A limited supply of fuel arrived next day, and a training syllabus consisting of 21 hours 15 minutes on Thunderbolts and two hours of instrument flying in the Harvard commenced. However, as four aircraft had been written off in the storms at Chakulia and another two or three had been damaged or were unserviceable, the programme soon proved to be difficult to carry out. Furthermore, many personnel were reaching the end of their tours of duty and were being posted, while Dominion pilots were being withdrawn from SEAC, reducing the pilot strength of the squadron by about half. Nevertheless, 217 flights were made during July.

A number of new pilots now arrived on the squadron, largely from 8 Refresher Flying Unit at Yelahanka, but some were woefully inexperienced. Six who arrived on 20th July had flown only Spitfires, and even Flt. Lt. B. Jutsum, who arrived on 17th July to become a Flight commander, had only three hours on Thunderbolts to his credit. Nevertheless, eight pilots, led by Flt. Lt. Whidborne. flew to Santa Cruz, Bombay, on 18th July to cooperate with the army and navy in Exercise 'Attic'.

At Vizagapatam, catering in the airmen's mess seems to have been something special. Mr. Brian Rowlands remembers that the corporal cook, Jim Reed, was a bluff Mancunian who in civilian life had been a sheet metal worker. "Rumour had it" says Brian "that Jim was in the habit of somehow securing rations for 1001 rather than for the 101 on squadron strength. There was never any shortage of things to eat and at breakfast time one could cook one's own meal. It seems that the Royal Indian Army Service Corps, from whom rations were drawn, either never realised what our numbers actually were or failed to recognise the significance of the additional 0."

Flg. Off. A. D. Dick, an officer who in later years was to make

*Thunderbolt Mk.II KL306 at Vizagapatam in November 1945.*

a distinguished career in the RAF and who was the President of the 30 Squadron Association from 1985 until his death in 1999 was promoted to Flt. Lt. on 19th July. He was soon in action to help a fellow pilot in trouble. With Flt. Lt. Jutsum, he took off on 24th July to practice section formation flying. Jutsum, however, hit a twelve-foot high bund at the end of the runway, shearing off the port undercarriage leg and damaging the other leg and a flap. A belly-landing was considered, but after a discussion over the R/T it was decided that it would be safer to bale out. The Thunderbolt was therefore flown along the coast and Flt. Lt.. Jutsum 'hit the silk' about eight miles from the airfield. Flt. Lt. Dick orbited until his colleague had come to earth safely and then returned to base and set out with a truck to collect him. He was found at Appikonda, where he was being cared for the the chief of the village. Suffering from a severe cut on the head, Flt. Lt. Jutsum was taken to hospital. His Thunderbolt was no more, having exploded on impact not far from the beach.

Four of the pilots who had been detached to Santa Cruz returned on 25th July, but it was learned that the other four, Flt. Lt. H. F. Whidborne, Flg. Off. R. B. Barlow RNZAF, Flg. Off. C. W.Weir RNZAF and Plt. Off. J. M. Ledbury, had been in trouble with the civilian police there and would be delayed. In fact they became involved in legal proceedings and did not return to the squadron until 12th September, after being acquitted by a court martial. Their aircraft, which were urgently needed at Vizagapatam, were collected on 27th July by spare pilots flown to Santa Cruz in Harvards.

Flt. Lt. Dick, who many years later became a test pilot, flew what was described as a new type of Thunderbolt Mk.II to Bobbili on 27th July to carry out take-offs with long-range fuel tanks fitted. This aircraft was fitted with a dorsal fin extension to counteract a

tendency for lateral instability and which was claimed to make it fully aerobatic. In all probability, the aircraft flown by Flt. Lt. Dick was from the batch numbered KL318 to KL347, which had been modified on the production line, as the RAF did not make this modification to any Thunderbolts at MUs or 'in the field'.

After nine weeks without a Commanding Officer, Sqn. Ldr. T. H. Meyer arrived on 29th July 1945 to take up the post. He had been serving in SEAC for three and a half years, latterly as CO of 615 Squadron.

## The end at last

Another shortage of fuel restricted training during the early days of August, but everyone was greatly enthused when on 10th August the first indications of a Japanese surrender were heard. Sadly, on 12th August, Plt. Off. F. G. Kent became 30 Squadron's final casualty of the Second World War. After taking off normally to carry out practice bombing on the Balacheveru range, his Thunderbolt (KJ222) was seen to crash about two miles south-west of the airfield and catch fire. He was killed instantly, and as a mark of respect further flying that day was abandoned. His funeral took place that afternoon with full military honours. Three days later Japan's unconditional surrender was announced. It had been anticipated that 30 Squadron would soon be employed in driving the Japanese from South-East Asia, and it came as something of an anti-climax to know that this would not now be necessary. Although considerable relief and pleasure was expressed by everyone, an entry into Malaya and the East Indies would have been very satisfying.

After two days of celebrations, during which a special dinner was provided for the airmen, with officers and SNCOs acting as waiters, and a large party was thrown, the training syllabus was recommenced. Eight pilots carried out cross-country flights of about 1000 miles, the first leg mainly over water with air-sea rescue launches in attendance, and air to ground firing was another feature. Then came news of a squadron move, and on 23rd August training came to a halt. By 27th August almost all the equipment had been packed by 7030 SE pending further instructions, but as a shortage of replacement Thunderbolts persisted, two were taken from 139 Repair & Salvage Unit for the SE personnel to repair themselves, which, of course, led to a certain amount of unpacking.

## A move to the Dutch East Indies

It was 11th September before instructions were received for the squadron to leave for Baigachi at once on the first stage of a journey to the Dutch East Indies. Briefing for this long move was given by Wg. Cdr. Watson (Wg. Cdr. Flying), and a mobile briefing section sent to Vizagapatam for the purpose. Fourteen Thunderbolts took off at 08.00 next day and the Harvard a little later, while the pilots' kit were flown in an Expediter. Two remaining aircraft were flown to Baigachi on 13th September, leaving the way clear to pack most of the equipment used by 7030 SE. Time was found, however, for ground personnel to attend a colour-hoisting parade and a church parade in commemoration of the Battle of Britain five years earlier and to play football and cricket matches and to enjoy an ENSA show. It was also decided that limited leave at 48 hours notice might be given to some of the airmen.

This period just after the end of the Second World War must have been very unsettling for service personnel, particularly those who had been serving overseas for a long time and who just wished to go home and resume their civilian careers. At Vizagapatam, a Ministry of Labour official gave a talk to everyone on the subject of resettlement and rehabilitation, and there were many grumbles about the slow rate of demobilisation. The length of time it was taking for mail from home to reach India was also a source of complaint, but a large batch of letters arrived on 28th September, some of it having been in transit for twenty days. But orders had to be obeyed, and the planned move had to go ahead.

On 24th September, sixteen Thunderbolts of 30 Squadron left Baigachi for Zayatkwin, an airfield about twenty miles north-east

*This photograph, marked 'Some of the boys', shows unidentified 30 Squadron ground crew members enjoying themselves on a beach, perhaps near Vizagapatam.*

*Dispersals at Vizagapatam, with Thunderbolt Mk.II coded RS:J in the foreground.*

*The wreck of Thunderbolt KL287 at Bhopal on 23rd March 1946.*

*Awaiting the squadron 'pancake'.*

*Flt. Lt. Jones, Flt. Sgt. Wilson, Sqn. Ldr. Newbery and Wt. Off. Auton in a jeep.*

of Rangoon, where the pilots found that the hessian/bitumen runway surface was in bad condition. Food was also inadequate, as personnel already there were on half rations. The ground party, still at Vizagapatam, knew nothing of the movements of the squadron aircraft and no information had been received about their own movement by sea. Then the pilots at Zayatkwin learned that they had to return to Baigachi, as the whole move had been a mistake and they should not have left Vizagapatam! The acronym SNAFU must have been in the forefront of their minds! So on 30th September back to Baigachi they flew. While the ground party had been awaiting the order to move, they had indulged in an extensive sports programme, with football, cricket, hockey and swimming being available to all.

Sixteen Thunderbolts and the Harvard arrived at Vizagapatam from Baigachi on 1st October at the end of a wasted journey to Rangoon and back. On arrival, the pilots found that no plans for the future of 30 Squadron were known, and they were to continue routine training. On 8th October, however, notification was received from HQ ACSEA that the squadron's establishment was to be reduced to 25 pilots, and so three SNCOs were posted at once, six officers and a Wt. Off. following three days later. Heavy rain began to fall on 18th October, and a gale-force winds blew the roof off the officers' mess, the sergeants' mess and some of the billets at Kottapalam, and tarpaulins had to be used to cover the damaged areas temporarily. The north-east monsoon had arrived! Flying was impossible until 24th October, when a programme of air-to-sea firing began. Over the next few days 30 Squadron pilots also carried out air tests on Thunderbolts serviced by 139 RSU and ferried some of them to 308 MU at Allahabad via Kailakunda.

Members of 30 Squadron were gratified when on 23rd October news was received from the Air Ministry that Flt. Lt. H. F. Whidborne, formerly 'B' Flight commander and the officer who had filled the breach during the period when no Commanding

Officer had been available, had been awarded the DFC. It was felt that the award was not only a tribute to his courage and skill but a recognition of the part played by everyone on 30 Squadron and 7030 Servicing Echelon in the campaign in Burma.

Although official records are hazy on this point, the original aborted move to the Dutch East Indies must have been reinstated, as at the end of November plans were put in hand to take the squadron to Padang in Sumatra. December 1945 began with a farewell party in the officers' mess on 3rd December, after which sixteen Thunderbolts and the Harvard took off for Baigachi on the 500-mile first leg of the journey. From there they would fly to

*An inspection line-up, with Wt. Off. Auton in the cockpit of Tempest PR760 [RS:N].*

Rangoon (about 700 miles), on to Port Swettenham (1100 miles) and finally the 500 mile leg to Padang. All the pilots could carry in their Thunderbolts was their sleeping bag and small kit, which was not likely to be adequate for such a journey into the unknown. Referring to this factor, the CO wrote in the squadron records at the time "Such lack of arrangements for personal comfort is always a good way to lower the morale of pilots, especially when transport aircraft were flying all over the place."

Eighteen airmen and some squadron equipment sailed on a LCT on 5th December and arrived at Padang two days later, but once again a 30 Squadron deployment turned out to be an error. On 8th December Wg. Cdr. Adams of 225 Group visited Vizagapatam to investigate the situation, as it seemed that the move to Sumatra had been cancelled for the second time. Meanwhile the pilots at Baigachi pressed on with continuation training, including GCI interceptions of Mosquitoes of 176 Squadron, and ground crews still at Vizagapatam organised a hugely successful dance, presumably enjoying the company of WAAFs. The personnel who

*Posed in front of a Tempest are: (rear) Johnny Autors; Rex Taylor; Les French; Ken Gardener; Roy Skinner; Ken Kenyon; Jack Coombs; Johnny Paterson; Bert Tatlow; Les Banks; Ray Dark; (centre) Johnny Webb; Dicky Hewetson; Frank Watson; Wally Birkett; Keith Tynam; George Simpson; Doug Allan; Ken Steele; (front) Ted Slinger; Frank Sumner; Willie Williams; the CO; Less Meehan; Phil Archer; Jeff Sorrel [L. F. French].*

had left for Sumatra never rejoined the squadron and are thought to have gone to Japan as part of the occupying force.

By 19th December the condition of the aircraft at Baigachi was deteriorating due to lack of maintenance personnel, although the few men available were working very hard under the eagle eye of Sgt. McIntosh. Next day, a strong rumour that 30 Squadron was to be disbanded began circulating, and that personnel of 7030 SE would soon be sent to Calcutta for embarkation or posting to other units. No official order to this effect had been received, however, by Christmas Day, when a dinner of turkey, Christmas pudding, mince pies and almost unlimited beer was enjoyed by all those remaining at Vizagapatam. Disbandment was confirmed on 27th December, and four days later the first party of 7030 SE personnel left for 35 Personnel Transit Centre at Calcutta.

On 5th January 1946 the final group of 7030 SE personnel arrived at Calcutta, where they found severe problems in accommodation. Almost the only task available to occupy the airmen were guard duties, the attractions of which, if any, soon palled. Their stay at Calcutta was understood to be indefinite, but on 11th January the good news that 30 Squadron was not to be disbanded after all was given by Wg. Cdr. Gardner, who made a special flight from BAFSEA HQ to deliver the message. The squadron was to relinquish its faithful Thunderbolt aircraft and convert to Tempests Mk.IIs, and this involved the Servicing Echelon returning to Baigachi. Morale immediately improved enormously, and the men at Calcutta made themselves ready to move at a few hours' notice. However, before beginning work on Tempests, eight airmen were earmarked for posting to Drigh Road airfield at Karachi to familiarise themselves with the new aircraft. At Baigachi, several pilots took the opportunity of flying Thunderbolts for the last time before they were put up for disposal.

By 25th January the airmen detailed to go to Drigh Road had still not been told to begin the journey, and Calcutta was out of bounds due to recent rioting among the population. Next day, news of a move to Bhopal arrived, cancelling any previous orders, and on 29th January the exodus began. The personnel of 7030 SE arrived at Bhopal on 6th February, and disposal of Thunderbolts took place between 19th and 22nd February, when they were ferried to Kancharpara by locally-based pilots.

*Newly-delivered Tempest PR686, already carrying 30 Squadron's RS code but no individual aircraft letter, at Bhopal*            *[L. F. French].*

*Lord Tedder on a visit to Agra in 1946.*

*An impressive line-up of 30 Squadron Tempests at Agra.*

*Pilots of 30 Squadron making their way to their Tempests; the nearest two aircraft are PR653 and PR660.*

*PR605, a Tempest of 30 Squadron, being refuelled.*

## Tempests arrive

The first three Tempests arrived at Bhopal on 4th March and were inspected by everyone on the squadron, with the unanimous comment "Wizard!" Sqn. Ldr. Murphy DFC, representing the Hawker Aircraft Co., gave a talk on the new aircraft next day, and on 6 March Sqn. Ldr. Meyer, Flt. Lt. Williams, Flt. Lt. Meehan and Flg. Off. Sumner all made their first flights without incident, expressing themselves very happy with the type. After a public holiday on 7th March eight more pilots took to the air in Tempests, and a confidence-inspiring demonstration of low-level aerobatics was given by Sqn. Ldr. Murphy. Already, a shortage of Tempest spares had developed, so a number of Thunderbolts were borrowed from 3 Fighter Support Training Unit. To confirm this problem and to discuss its consequences, the AOC Base Air Forces, South East Asia, Air Marshal Sir Roderick Carr KBE CB DFC AFC, visited 30 Squadron (and others in a similar situation) on 16th March.

After flying one of the borrowed Thunderbolts to Calcutta on 17th March, Sqn. Ldr. Meyer was marooned there with technical difficulties, and on 22nd March Flg. Off. Sumner took off in Thunderbolt KL343 from Bhopal with spare parts for him. Unfortunately he was almost blinded by hydraulic fluid which sprayed into the cockpit, and crash-landed in a paddy field near Pableau, a hundred miles north of Calcutta, luckily without injury. Next day another Thunderbolt was written off when Flt. Sgt. Tatlow experienced engine trouble in KL287 while in the circuit

and had to crash-land it near the runway to avoid hitting the nursing sisters' mess. Again there was no serious injury to the pilot. By the end of March, only five Tempests had arrived, and it had been possible to fly only 100 hours on the new type. It was felt that Tempests were a distinct improvement on Thunderbolts, and all personnel were proud to be flying them or working on them. Problems were caused, though, by the recent reduction of the overseas tour to three years and by the number of men being demobilised. Off duty, football proved to be the only sport in which most airmen were interested, and at this 30 Squadron excelled, coming out top against ten teams from various units at Bhopal. A visit from ENSA to the Station cinema on 6th April to perform 'Stars in Battledress' was well received.

By 13th April the Tempest spares situation had worsened to the extent that the aircraft had to be grounded, and the compiler of the Squadron diary remarked "Perhaps it will now be realised how really grim the spares situation has become." A week later a Dakota delivered some spares, and flying resumed. Then came the loss of Tempest PR686, the first one delivered to the squadron, when on 23rd April Flt. Sgt. Simpson crashed on landing and cartwheeled, luckily without hurting himself. It was suggested that his crash might have been the result of a lack of oxygen, and the Tempests were therefore grounded again until new supplies arrived on 28th April.

Fifteen Tempests were on 30 Squadron strength by the end of April 1946, the complete establishment. Flying had consisted of fuel consumption tests, low-level navigation, aerobatics, formation flying, mock rocket attacks, tracking exercises and bad-weather flying, but it had not yet proved possible to take full advantage of the new aircraft. The squadron's Harvard aircraft was still in use for instrument flying practice and 'shopping' trips to Agra, Delhi, Nagpur and Cawnpore. During the month 30 Squadron and 7030 Servicing Echelon lost thirty of their older members who were repatriated for release from the service, and postings of pilots were beginning to cause a problem. It was considered that if new pilots did not arrive by mid-June there would be more aircraft than men to fly them! Ground crew airmen were being relinquished at an alarming rate, the essential trades being especially badly affected. To clarify the release situation and to explain the plans for a post-war RAF, a visit was made by Air Chief Marshal Sir John Slessor GCB DSO MC, the Air Member for Personnel, on 15th April.

*'Plumbers' arming the CO's aircraft [RS:D] with rockets at Agra.*

The spares shortage was not improved by the brake failure of new Tempest PR661, which was being delivered on 3rd May by Flg. Off. Haddow. This incident prompted another grounding to allow pneumatic systems to be checked, but eleven aircraft were back in the air on 8th May, when the pilots made their first attempts at rocket firing, with very good results. Four days later Sqn. Ldr. Meyer, Flg. Off. Sumner and Wt. Off Dark flew to Santa Cruz to take part in an exercise which involved firing rockets at pontoons off the coast near Bombay. Support for this detachment was provided by Wt. Off. Auton and seventeen ground crew airmen who flew to Santa Cruz in two Dakotas.

While the three Tempests were at Santa Cruz, a number of trips were made in the Harvard to deliver spares. More significantly, orders were received at Bhopal on 13th May for the squadron to move to Agra by 1st June, and the first advance party left on 20th May, under the command of Plt. Off. Watson. Two days later the first three Tempests were flown to their new base, while at Bhopal packing of equipment reached fever-pitch. The three pilots at Santa Cruz returned to Bhopal on 25th May after two weeks of rapidly-increasing efficiency. After a slow start due to unfamiliarity with the gyro sighting instrument, the CO and Flg. Off. Sumner in particular had become very proficient, seldom missing the pontoon

*'Chota' Brown standing on the wing of Tempest PR734 at Kohat*
*[A. Brown].*

*Loading rockets onto a 30 Squadron Tempest for operations in Waziristan*
*[A. Brown].*

*Ken Gold refuelling a Tempest at Kohat*                                                                                                                                         *[A. Brown].*

*Maintenance on a 30 Squadron Tempest at Kohat. Note the rocket rails*                                                            *[A. Brown].*

Sqn. Ldr. Meyer, Flt. Lt. Sumner, Flt. Sgt. Wright and a ground crew at Kohat [A. Brown].

30 Squadron armament section staff at Kohat          [A. Brown].

Tempests of 20 and 30 Squadrons lined up at Agra on 7th October 1946 for inspection by the AOC of 3 (India) Group, Air Cdre. Perry-Keene.

Tempest PR751, known as the 'Christmas Tree', being serviced at Agra. Working on it were Cpl. Sinclair, Sgt. Hewitt, Sgt. Badley (in overalls), an unknown LAC, and Cpl. Cookson (under the wheel well).

*30 Squadron pilots at Agra on 10th October 1946, being briefed for a search for a missing aircraft.*

target towards the end of the exercise. The ground crew personnel returned to Bhopal in a Halifax aircraft, which must have been very much less comfortable than a Dakota!

On 27th May the main move took place when ten Tempests flew to Agra in formation, followed by the Harvard. A rail party under Flg. Off. Wallace and a road party under Flt. Lt. Wootton left at the same time, and the rail group arrived at Agra next day in extremely hot weather. Unloading of the railway trucks began at once, and on 30th May the squadron orderly room was set up, so that by the stipulated date the entire squadron was at Agra, ready for business. Members of the squadron were pleasantly surprised by the accommodation at Agra, and though repairs to most of the airmen's billets were needed they were carried out without delay. Morale remained high, although replacements for repatriated personnel were still not forthcoming, and the squadron's efficiency was becoming ever more difficult to maintain. Indoor sports such as badminton and table tennis were enjoyed, and a swimming pool on the Station was used intensively, but other outdoor activities

were impractical in the extreme heat.

A party was held in the officers' and sergeants' messes to celebrate 30 Squadron's arrival at Agra, and the other resident unit, 20 Squadron, joined in. Five pilots left by train for Karachi on 3rd June to bring back new Tempests for 20 Squadron, which was just converting from Spitfires. The AOC of 4 (India) Group, Air Cdre. Perry-Keene OBE, visited Agra to welcome 30 Squadron and complimented the pilots on their successful conversion to Tempests, particularly in view of the shortage of spares and personnel.

A highlight for members of 30 Squadron during June was the visit by about seventy of them to the Taj Mahal on the 9th. Whether or not this trip was successful is not recorded, but as the monsoon season was in full swing it seems doubtful. Nevertheless, on 14th June several pilots visited the famous monument to see it by moonlight. A typical day brought 10/10 cumulus and stratocumulus cloud, heavy rain and strong gusts of wind. Much of the squadron's working time that month was spent in helping 20 Squadron's conversion programme, either by ferrying Tempests or by providing instruction on the ground. Essential spares arrived by air and road on 16th June, and oxygen charging equipment was fetched from Bhopal two days later, allowing 30 Squadron to begin flying its own Tempests again on 19th June.

A two-day cricket match between the squadron airmen and the SNCOs and officers began on 21st June, the first such contest since the squadron was at Vizagapatam. The score on the first day was 108 for the SNCOs and officers, but next day the airmen put in a good effort with 117 runs for four wickets, winning the match. The weather was very hot and oppressive, with prickly heat, an acutely uncomfortable disease, affecting most of the personnel, so it is to their credit that the cricket was played at all.

Repatriation and demobilisation was still affecting the squadron severely, and it was recorded that if new personnel were not forthcoming soon almost everyone would have left! Serious efforts were being made to fill the vacancies in pilots and ground staff, but when Gp. Capt. Cliff from Air HQ India visited the squadron on 1st July he told the pilots not to be downhearted at the

*The wreck of Tempest PR583 [RS:C] being studied after it collided with PR672 in formation near Agra on 10th October 1946.*

*A variety of aircraft attended the 'At Home' day at Agra on 8th August 1947. Visible are a late-Mark Spitfire, a Harvard Mk.IIb which appears to be KF115, an earlier Spitfire, an Oxford, a Tiger Moth, an Auster, three Tempests and a Dakota, all aircraft to gladden the heart of an enthusiast today.*

lack of flying, stating that the situation in the RAF in Europe was almost as bad! He also spoke of trouble brewing in the North West Frontier and said that four of 30 Squadron's Tempests might be firing live rockets in that area within a week.

In the meantime cricket became a major preoccupation in the squadron, and it was possible to form two teams, which played almost every day, either against each other or teams from other sections or units, among them 20 Squadron, which was well and truly thrashed! This activity continued while a spell of good weather lasted. Continuing depletion of personnel did not help matters, either on the cricket field or at work, however. By the end of July only ten pilots remained on the squadron, and of these four were due to leave in August. On 24th July a Mr. Finney from the

Ministry of Labour spoke to everyone about conditions in the UK and prospects for newly-released servicemen to take advantage of Government schemes and grants designed to help them back into civilian life.

In the first days of August a number of pilots ferried Tempests for 152 Squadron, which was based at Risalpur and was converting from Spitfires. Two redundant SNCO pilots joined the squadron on 2nd August and were warmly welcomed, although conversion onto the Tempest was expected to be difficult as neither man had flown for over a year. A third such pilot arrived next day and a fourth on 5th August.

The anticipated detachment to the North West Frontier began on 4th August 1946, when six Tempests flew to Kohat,

*A 30 Squadron Tempest about to depart on a mission*

[A. Brown].

*Tempest PR841 [RS:A] apparently withdrawn from service* [A. Brown].

accompanied by fourteen ground personnel. From Kohat, they carried out live rocket attacks on tribal villages, each pilot flying an average of three sorties in the four weeks of the detachment. They used the Mk.IID gyro gunsight and found little difficulty in hitting the targets. Damage caused by the 60lb rocket with a high explosive warhead seemed to be greater than that inflicted by 250lb or 500 lb bombs. Afterwards, it was felt that the detachment had been very successful from the point of view of flying and of servicing and that the experience gained should be an advantage in similar circumstances. One wonders whether those involved realised that 30 Squadron had carried out very similar missions in Iraq about fifteen years earlier!

Just before the detachment left, fire broke out in the officers' lines, completely destroying two tents and a quantity of personal kit. Two days later, while he was away, Sqn. Ldr. Meyer was posted to Ambala, and his replacement, Sqn. Ldr. R. A. Newbery DFC*, arrived at Agra on 6th August. That night, the officers held their first dining-in night in the mess, which was said to be quite an experience for the younger officers, who had never been involved in mess ceremony before. The new CO flew a Tempest for the first time on 8th August and was duly impressed with its performance.

Sqn. Ldr. Meyer returned from Kohat on 10th August, and three days later Sqn. Ldr. Newbery and Flg. Off. Sumner flew to Kohat to replace him. The personnel situation, which had been improved by the arrival of the four SNCOs earlier in the month, now deteriorated again, and Flt. Lt. Wootton travelled to Bombay on 27th August to attempt to persuade someone in authority that immediate action was needed. At times, the pilots carried out practical work on their aircraft, including tyre changing and cleaning and testing sparking plugs, as well as daily inspections under the supervision of the NCOs in charge of the Flights. For most of the month the weather was typically monsoon, with heavy rain and dense cloud. At times the temperature fell dramatically, but it was always very humid and uncomfortable until the last few days of the month, which were brilliantly sunny and cloudless.

The Kohat detachment returned to Agra on 3rd September, ground crews making the journey in a Dakota. Conversion training of the newly-arrived pilots continued, and the 'old hands' were amazed to see how well they coped, considering that the Tempest was the first British aircraft they had flown and that they were out

of flying practice. Early in September the squadron was warned of a move to Peshawar, but when this was cancelled an air of great disappointment prevailed. Everyone had been looking forward to the move and had worked hard to ensure that the Tempests were up to standard. A party to mark the move had already been organised, and rather than waste an opportunity it went ahead and was greatly enjoyed.

In order to give the pilots practice in bombing, it was decided that an Indian Army firing range at Babina, about 135 miles south-east of Agra, could be used if found suitable. To check this, a small party left by train on 24th September and returned next day with a favourable report.

The personnel situation had improved somewhat but remained fluid. More airmen had arrived to work with 7030 Servicing Echelon, which although still not up to full strength was better manned than for several months. Both flying and ground personnel were judged to be at 85% of the establishment numbers. Improved autumn weather also helped in many ways, and a lot of sport was played, which may have helped maintain the general health of the squadron.

On 10th October an unfortunate accident, luckily not fatal, occurred when Flt. Sgt. Whyte's aircraft, flying as No.2 in a formation of three, collided with the Tempest flown by the leader, Wt. Off. Hewitson. Finding his aircraft (PR672) out of control, with an aileron missing, Wt. Off. Hewitson bailed out at an altitude of 8000 feet. Its propeller damaged, the other Tempest (PR583) was vibrating excessively, and Flt. Sgt. Whyte was obliged to put it down in a paddy field without the benefit of an undercarriage. Neither pilot was hurt in this incident. The month of October was very much a routine period, with instrument flying, low level cross-country trips, aerobatics, formations and sector reconnaissance flights filling the pilots' time. During some of the formation flights, quarter attacks were made by single aircraft, but as no camera guns were fitted to the Tempests it was not possible to make any assessments.

This, however, was 30 Squadron's swan song, for on 1st December 1946, without fuss, all personnel were posted and the squadron was reduced to a 'Number Plate' basis. Surviving records, which for units based in SEAC tend to leave a lot to be desired, do not indicate any further activity, but it is believed that official disbandment took place by the stroke of a pen in April 1947.

*Dakota Mk.IV KN512 of 30 Squadron, still in camouflage finish, with the squadron emblem on the nose. In the background is a similar aircraft in natural metal finish*      *[via author].*

# Chapter 8: A Transport Role

For the first time in its long existence, 30 Squadron was located in the United Kingdom when it reformed on 1st November 1947 at Abingdon from a nucleus provided by 238 Squadron. The squadron's new role was to be in transport, vastly different from flying powerful fighters in Burma or medium bombers in Greece. In command (officially from 24th November) was Sqn. Ldr. R. C. Wood, whose first task was to organise an efficient unit from a collection of assorted aircrews and ground crews, many of whom were due for release from the service and were therefore somewhat lacking in enthusiasm. Dakotas C.4 were already in use on scheduled passenger, mail and freight services to Germany, principally Berlin, Bückeburg and Utersen.

The embryo 30 Squadron's time at Abingdon was short, as a move was made on 24th November to Oakington in Cambridgeshire, which was to be its base for three years, although, as will be seen, many of the aircrews did not see much of it for long periods. When Sqn. Ldr. Wood left, his place was filled by Sqn. Ldr. A. McC. Johnstone OBE DFC, a forthright Scot, who took over command of the squadron on 18th January 1948. Apart from the nucleus from 238 Squadron, many of the crews were inexperienced in the European transport role. Sqn. Ldr. Johnstone and Flt. Lt. J. F. Manning, the Flight Commander Training, strove to work up the squadron. Their task was done well; by June 1948 all crews carried Transport Command categories and, where relevant, instrument ratings.

In February two more routes were added, to Berlin and Warsaw (CBW) and to the Canal Zone (UFD), which staged through Istres to Castel Benito for a night-stop before going on to Fayid via El Adem. Of particular significance was the occasion when five of the squadron's aircraft took ground crews of a Lincoln squadron from

Wyton to Shallufa in the Canal Zone in support of their three-month *Sunray* detachment before flying back to Waddington with the ground crews of a returning squadron.

30 Squadron's first detachment from the comforts of Oakington was to Schleswigland, an airfield on the Baltic coast of Germany which had been a Luftwaffe night-fighter base during the recent war and was now being used by the RAF as a practice camp for airborne forces. On 29th April 1948 eight Dakotas were sent there, together with 27 Squadron (also from Oakington) in support of the 16th Independent Parachute Brigade, which was taking part in a major exercise. Sqn. Ldr. Johnstone, who was in the habit of keeping his personnel well informed of all that was happening, as long as it was not secret, asked the senior customs officer at Oakington how much foodstuffs each man would be permitted to take and was told that five pounds would be allowed, with not more than two pounds of any one item. At the time coffee was highly prized in Germany, and the CO was told that it could be one of the

*Outside the CO's office at Oakington (right) where this Nissen hut (left) served as 30 Squadron ground crews' bolt-hole.*

*The 30 Squadron detachment at Schleswigland in May 1948, with Sqn. Ldr. Johnstone in the centre of the front row. The letters BC on the nose of the Dakota are part of the aircraft's radio call-sign*
*[Sqn. Ldr. Stillwell].*

items to be carried. Johnstone immediately gave everyone the news and when the aircraft took off each man carried the permitted two pounds of coffee. After landing at Schleswigland, however, the pilots received a message ordering all crews to remain in their aircraft. Before long, trucks arrived carrying RAF police, who shifted toolkits and personal kits from the Dakotas onto the trucks. 30 Squadron personnel were then ordered to climb on board the trucks, which were driven to an airfield building and unloaded. Each man was told to pick up his kit and under the scrutiny of a commissioned policeman a group of SNCO and corporal 'snowdrops' moved aircrews to one side of the building and groundcrews to the other side before beginning a detailed search of everything and everyone. In doing so, a corporal gave Sqn. Ldr. Johnstone a push, intentionally or otherwise, whereupon the CO demanded to know what was going on. The police officer said that he had been told to confiscate all food carried on the flight, but although Johnstone explained that he had permission from customs in England to do so he was adamant. The CO then demanded to see someone in higher authority, and when it became clear that everyone of Wg. Cdr. rank was away he asked the name of the Station Commander and was told it was Gp. Capt. Biggar. When told that he was not allowed to leave the building, Sqn. Ldr. Johnstone demanded, and was given, the use of a telephone, on which he proceeded to tell Gp. Capt. Biggar just what he thought of his Station. Not to be outdone by another Scotsman, Gp. Capt.

Biggar told Johnstone that he was not in the UK now and that BAFO regulations were paramount. So all the CO could do was to watch the confiscation of his men's property take place, unable to tell them to resist, as that would be mutiny. When the police tried to take his own two pounds of coffee, however, he said "No, you can arrest me if you wish, but I will NOT give this stuff up." The 'snowdrops' let him keep it, and the confiscated food was released when the squadron returned to Oakington. When the groundcrews had settled into their billets, Sqn. Ldr. Johnstone went round to ask them how they felt about the incident, and naturally enough found that they were most unhappy. He did what he could to placate them, and then went to the officers' mess for a drink. There he found every officer of the squadron ".....moaning like so-and-sos." Then in walked Gp. Capt. Biggar. He was a little taller than Johnstone, and was in a bad mood, but he offered to see the groundcrews' accommodation, and Johnstone went with him. Afterwards, the two officers had a fierce argument, which made the CO even less impressed by Gp. Capt. 'Wally' Biggar.

Part of the task carried out by 30 Squadron at Oakington and Schleswigland involved towing Horsa troop-carrying gliders. Sqn. Ldr. Frank Stillwell remembers an incident when an officer of the Glider Pilot Regt. was being teased by some of 30 Squadron's aircrews when there was a delay in inspecting glider tow-ropes before a flight. He replied "It's all right for you. You can run up an aircraft. I can't run up a rope". Back came the reply "The flippin' Indians do!"

During the detachment the island of Sylt officially became a British Leave Centre, and the opportunity was taken to fly a load of squadron members there. As some of the staff of the Control Commission had arrived by train there was no shortage of feminine company. A number of couples took advantage of the warm evening to retire to the beach to carry on their new-found friendships in a more peaceful atmosphere away from the bars.

30 Squadron did not return to Oakington until 25th June. Men of the squadron had enjoyed their time in Germany, and some had found new friends among the frauleins who spent time basking in the sun on Sylt. Sylt was, however, five hours from Schleswigland by road, so navigation exercises were indulged in by 30 Squadron, ground and air crews making the 25-minute flight to Sylt when the weather was suitable. But all good things come to an end. While taxying to his dispersal at Oakington on arrival from Schleswigland, Sqn. Ldr. Johnstone was instructed by the air traffic

*A Horsa glider about to be towed off by 30 Squadron at Oakington in April 1948*
*[Sqn. Ldr. F. Stillwell].*

controller to report to the Station Commander as soon as he had cleared customs. As he had taken the opportunity of leading the seven Dakotas in two circuits of Sylt on the way home he thought he was in for a dressing-down, but instead he was told that the squadron was to return to Germany. "How soon can you go back?" he was asked. As all the squadron stores and kit were still on board the Dakotas, the CO replied "We can go back now, if you like." "No need for that" said the Station Commander. "You can have two days here, but don't unpack anything." Little did the crews realise the scale of the task in which they would become involved.

## The Berlin Airlift

By mid-June 1948, relations between Russia and the Western powers had deteriorated to the point where military supplies were being prevented from travelling across the Russian Zone to the Allied zones of Berlin by surface transport. On 19th June BAFO began to plan an airlift to ensure that urgent supplies would not be held up, and two days later the Russians stopped barge traffic between West Berlin and the Western Zone and cut electricity supplies to parts of the western sectors, where electricity generation was very limited as the one modern power station had been destroyed. Rail services between West Berlin and the west came to a complete halt on 24th June, leaving the Allied sectors of the city, into which 12,000 tons of fuel, food and industrial and consumer goods had flowed daily, completely devoid of normal supplies. It had already been made clear that the interests of British troops and their dependents in Berlin would be safeguarded by air, and this scheme was put into action on 26th June as Operation *Knicker*, which involved delivering sixty tons per day using sixteen Dakotas of 53 and 77 Squadrons, based at Waterbeach. At this stage there was no plan to support the civilians of West Berlin.

It was 29th June before five Dakotas of 30 Squadron, piloted by Sqn. Ldr. Johnstone, Flt. Lt. Harper, Flt. Lt. Haines, Flt. Lt. Ward and Pilot 2 Pullen, flew to RAF Wunstorf with their ground crews to take part in what would become the Berlin Airlift and was already known as Operation *Carter Paterson*. On arrival, it took an hour to find a parking space for the five aircraft, as Wunstorf was already crowded. The CO was then able to go, with his crew (Flt. Lt. Hunter, the squadron navigation leader, and Flt. Lt. Goggin, the

signals leader) to the control tower, where they found overworked personnel who told them that somewhere around was an operations room. Before reporting there, though, they were advised to find accommodation. There was none in the officers' mess, but eventually they found space on the top storey of one of the former Luftwaffe barrack blocks, where beds and a jury-rigged lighting system had been installed and a large number of men were already in residence. It soon became clear that aircraft and ground crews were to be pooled for this operation, only the aircrews of the nine units involved (18, 27, 30, 46, 53, 62, 77, 238 Squadrons and 240 OCU) retaining their identities.

Next day, Sqn. Ldr. Johnstone and his crew flew three trial sorties to Berlin (Gatow) in Dakota KN512, and the CO attended a conference of squadron commanders, where he was not too pleased to meet Gp. Capt. Biggar from Schleswigland again. The SASO had explained that essential supplies were to be moved into West Berlin by air, and that the USAF had already begun a similar operation code-named *Vittles* from Wiesbaden and Frankfurt (Rhein Main). An advance operations room was to be set up at Wunstorf under joint RAF, Army and civilian command, and Gp. Capt. Biggar, now the RAF Commander, would be answerable to BAFO headquarters. A Brigadier would oversee the Rear Air Supply Organisation to handle loading of freight at Wunstorf and the Forward Air Supply Organisation to unload it at Gatow. Wunstorf had been chosen as the rear airfield because it was situated close to the central air corridor into Berlin, even though as a fighter airfield it lacked equipment for handling transport aircraft.

On its first day of duty on the airlift, now renamed Operation *Plainfare*, 30 Squadron flew nineteen sorties to Gatow, the first one by the CO in Dakota KN238. Among other loads flown that day was 6500 lbs (2.95 tonnes) of flour. Rear and forward freight handling systems were still being developed to meet the rapid growth in demand, which was estimated to total 5000 tons per day.

There had not been time before the start of the airlift for crews to be put through the intensive training which they needed. A number of pilots did not hold full instrument ratings, which limited their activity, and those pilots who were fully qualified had to fly more hours to make up the shortfall. Transport Command regulations were strict; for pilots with a Green rating a visibility of

*Paratroops boarding Dakota KN442 at the Transport Support Practice Camp at Schleswigland in June 1948. This Dakota is still in service as G-AMPX with Air Atlantique, based at Coventry*

*[Sqn. Ldr. F. Stillwell].*

*They're off! Paratroops leaping from Dakota KN512 over north Germany in June 1948* [Sqn. Ldr. F. Stillwell].

100 yards was necessary before being allowed to take off, and those with a White rating needed better conditions. Pilots holding Green ratings could land, with navigational aids in use, with a cloud base not lower than 200 feet above ground level and a visibility of not less than 800 yards. Sqn. Ldr. Johnstone, who held a Green rating, was surprised to find that the CO of one of the other squadrons had no rating at all and had only flown to Berlin twice compared with Johnstone's twenty-five times.

In the early days of the airlift Flt. Lt. Don Skeen found his Dakota taking an unduly long time to come unstuck on take-off from Wunstorf, and to be distinctly soggy when airborne. On landing at Gatow it was discovered that his Dakota had been erroneously loaded with the cargo intended for a York!

A Dakota crew consisted of pilot, navigator and signaller; the flying was tiring, demanding a high and sustained level of accuracy and concentration. Aircraft of one type flying in the same direction flew at the same assigned altitude and at a set airspeed, with a horizontal separation equivalent to three minutes flying time. A vertical distance of only 500 feet separated them from a similar stream of aircraft of a different type, flying at a different airspeed. Only if in danger were pilots permitted to descend to the emergency level, 3000 feet. Navigation aids consisted of GEE, Eureka and radio beacons. In VFR conditions aircraft landed at three-minute intervals at all three airfields throughout the twenty-four hours, but when IFR conditions prevailed this interval was increased to five minutes. The value of the new Ground Controlled Approach (GCA) equipment was really proved during the airlift, as a missed approach meant an immediate overshoot and a return to base with the load on board. At the RAF base airfields the only instrument approach other than at Wunstorf, where there was GCA, was Rebecca/BABS.

Norman Douglass, who flew as a signaller with 30 Squadron on the airlift, recalls the pressure at the start, and an incident which took place when the initial pressure was lifted after a period of two weeks of flying without a break. A night out in Hanover was arranged, and the NCOs went to a Senior NCOs' Club which had a lake around it. Most of the members of the Club were from the Civil Control Commission in Germany, and were rather stuffy, not taking kindly to uniformed aircrew interlopers. Norman says that after a heated discussion the civilians ended up "........with a cooler in their lake" and the NCOs of 30 Squadron had to cool off in the 'Red Hat Hotel', where it took most of the night to convince the Military Police that they had to fly at 05.30. They arrived at Wunstorf just in time! Norman also remembers another incident which occurred about eight or ten days after the start of the airlift. "I was flying with Flt. Lt. Haines when we had engine trouble shortly after take-off. As we could not maintain height the Captain ordered us to start to jettison our cargo of hay. We had a RASC Private as loader and as it was more trouble keeping him in the aircraft than getting the hay out Flt. Lt. Haines flew the aircraft back to Wunstorf and landed on one engine."

It was not long before it became clear that the RAF's contribution to the airlift could not be maintained from Wunstorf alone, particularly after the introduction of four-engined York aircraft. It was therefore decided that the Dakotas would move to Fassberg, a former Luftwaffe experimental site about forty miles to the north. Gp. Capt. Biggar was given the task of reopening the airfield, which contained a concrete runway and several large hangars to which railway lines ran. The miracle of opening Fassberg was completed in seven days, during which a parking area measuring about 1500 feet by 2400 feet was laid. Eight squadrons of Dakotas, of which 30 Squadron was one, moved into Fassberg and on 19th July began a task which had hitherto been considered impossible — transporting coal to Berlin by air. However, it was soon decided that USAF C-54s should be brought into Fassberg to

*Dakotas lined up at Wunstorf in July 1948* [Sqn. Ldr. F. Stillwell].

take advantage of the shorter distance to Berlin compared with that from Wiesbaden or Frankfurt. The Dakota squadrons would therefore move to Lübeck.

Very soon, a convoy of USAF trucks carrying equipment deemed necessary to sustain life, such as huge refrigerators, arrived, quickly followed by a large number of frauleins carrying babies in arms. Within a few hours, the aircrew mess had become a joint RAF/USAF operation, with long rows of trestle tables attended by local waitresses. The serving counter was also a joint venture, with USAF food to the right and RAF food to the left, a large coffee dispenser to the right and a tea urn to the left! It was not long before RAF men were queuing for coffee and USAF men for tea!

### Down to business

At Lübeck, enormous efforts went into making the airfield and its support services fit for the forthcoming operations. Perforated steel planking was removed from a disused runway and the material was relaid to form 118,000 sq. metres of aircraft standing area, in addition to which 25,000 sq. metres of hardcore was laid. Tarmac 63,000 sq. metres in area was put down and new lighting was provided on the airfield and in the proposed loading area. The capacity of the existing railway siding was doubled, and buildings for use as dining rooms and living accommodation for aircrews and ground personnel were rapidly erected. For storage purposes, three small hangars were taken over by the Rear Air Supply Organisation. On the airfield, a new VHF 'homer' was installed, and at Tremsbüttel a navigation beacon was set up. To accommodate the influx of extra personnel, RAF St. Hubertus, a mile from the airfield, was taken over, but even then arrangements were made for a hotel near Lübeck railway station to house some men.

### A fatal flight

The first Dakotas moved into Lübeck on 5th September 1948, and the first sorties were flown on 13th September. All went well until the night of 17th November, when 30 Squadron was the only Dakota squadron to fly from Lübeck, as almost enough Yorks and USAF C-54s were available to carry out the night's task. The weather was poor, and after carrying out its task Dakota KP223, piloted by Pilot 1 E. F. Trezona, crashed in the Russian Zone while making an instrument approach to Lübeck airfield, which was situated only just inside the British Zone. The fate of KP223 and its crew is recorded in some detail in the log of 46 Group Advanced Operational HQ, as follows, verbatim but with this author's comments:

21.43 Lübeck reports Dak 223 called on finals and [has] not been heard since; flash of flame sighted off runway; they fear an accident.

21.49 Lübeck Daks being diverted to Wunstorf and confirm crash of Dak 223 half mile off end of runway.

22.35 Chat with Lübeck re crashed aircraft; duty Sqn. Ldr. says aircraft cannot be found in or anywhere near position reported. Suspect it may be in Russian Zone.

22.39 Asked ACCBE to report possibility of 223 crashing in Russian Zone to Berlin Air Safety Centre.

23.00 Lübeck report crew of Dak 223: P.1 Trezona (captain), Flt. Lt. Wilkins (navigator), S.3 Lynch (signaller). [This was incorrect: his name was Lough]

23.07 Captain, Cat. C, holds no instrument rating. Air Traffic Control states weather at time was visibility 1000 yards, cloudbase 900 feet. [Then the log says that visibility was 500 yards!].

23.21 Lübeck re P.1 Trezona — say as far as they can ascertain he has never been instrument rated. Still no further details except that MO has contacted Russian guards, who confirm they saw what appeared to be an aircraft crash in flames in their Zone.

23.55 ACCBE report Dak 223 crashed at Schönberg in Russian Zone, 5/6 miles due east of Lübeck. Pilot killed, two crew in hospital.

00.40 (next day) Spoke with AOC re crashed Dak; he requests I contact BAFO duty staff officer, who should liaise with Air Cdre. Waite in seeking permission to enter Russian Zone.

01.08 Gatow reports Air Cdre. Waite contacted but he states little can be done until the usual formalities are completed.

Trezona was a very competent pilot, although he held no instrument rating. Sqn. Ldr. Johnstone had sanctioned his flight that night even though Transport Command regulations might be broken. As a safeguard, Trezona's aircraft went off in the middle of the nine which flew that night, with rated pilots in front and behind. Take-offs from Lübeck outbound were at the standard five-minute intervals, the weather at that time being reasonable. By the time the squadron returned, however, the cloud base was lower, although visibility from the top of the control tower was about 1000 yards. Lübeck was not equipped with GCA, so BABS (Beam Approach Beacon System), on which Trezona approached the airfield over the Russian Zone, and on finals at five miles they would be at 1500 feet altitude, lined up with the runway. Sqn. Ldr. Johnstone, in the control tower as duty operations officer, heard Trezona call "King Peter 223, turning finals, six miles." And that was his last transmission. Pilot 2 Pullen, at the controls of the following aircraft, called when he was three and a half miles from the threshold

*A Dakota at Gatow between sorties.*

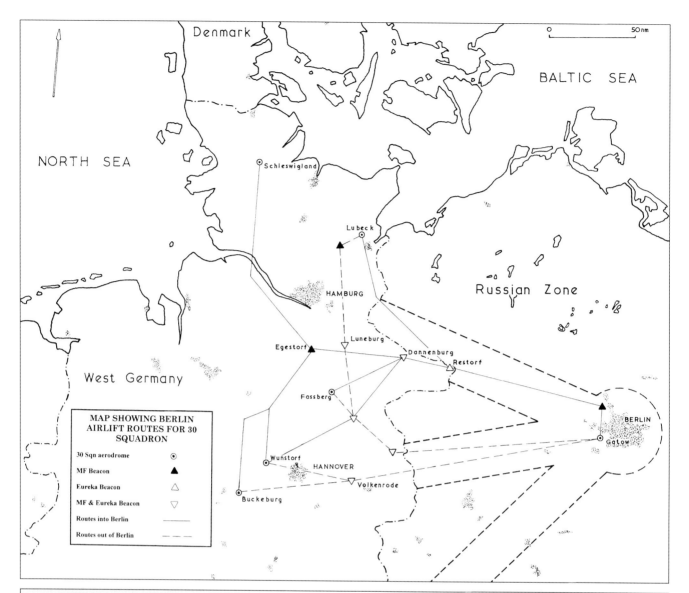

MAP SHOWING BERLIN
AIRLIFT ROUTES FOR 30
SQUADRON

| 30 Sqn aerodrome | ⊙ |
| MF Beacon | ▲ |
| Eureka Beacon | △ |
| MF & Eureka Beacon | ▽ |
| Routes into Berlin | ——— |
| Routes out of Berlin | – – – |

*Pre-jump inspection of paratroopers about to fly in Dakota KN507 at Schleswigland in June 1948*

*[Sqn. Ldr. F. Stillwell].*

"Jesus, the whole place is lit up! There's a ruddy great fire here." It was then obvious that KP223 had come down. After making vain attempts to enter the Russian Zone, Sqn. Ldr. Johnstone was given permission to overfly the area to discover what had happened. His Dakota laden with volunteers, he flew a mosaic search extending eight miles from Lübeck into the Russian Zone, but was unable to locate the crash site. Later, it became clear that Russian reports of the crash were more accurate. Apart from the two members of 30 Squadron who died in the crash, Sgt. Dowling, a soldier of Air Movements section at Gatow, also lost his life. Flt. Lt. J. G. Wilkins was taken to hospital at Schönberg in the Russian Sector.

With the intensity of the 'Cold War' at the time, the humanity shown by the Russian authorities was quite uncharacteristic and received considerable publicity in the British press. Flt. Lt. Levy, the SMO at Lübeck, was allowed to visit Flt. Lt. Wilkins freely and to go back and forth with medical supplies. In addition, ACW Jeanne Burns, a nursing orderly, comforted John Wilkins throughout his stay. For the first two days, Russian surgeons operated on him, gave blood transfusions and consulted with Flt. Lt. Levy. As John Wilkins' condition showed signs of worsening, the Russian authorities offered to allow his wife to visit him. so she was flown from Northolt to Lübeck and taken direct to the hospital to be at his bedside. Sadly, however, he died on 25th November and with the three other casualties was buried in the British Military Cemetery in Hamburg.

As the airlift grew, Gatow airfield in Berlin became inadequate, and a site at Tegel, in the French sector, was selected for a completely new terminal. US Army Engineers began the construction on 5th September with the intention of making the airfield operational on 1st January 1949. They took rubble from bombed buildings for hardcore and railway track ballast for use in concrete, while dismantled construction equipment was flown into Templehof. Much of the construction work was done by Berliners of both sexes, up to 17,000 of whom worked round the clock in three shifts. Only ten weeks after construction began, Flt. Lt. Manning, with the CO as co-pilot, became the first pilot to land there, on 18th November 1948! Flying Dakota KN446, which carried a load of tractor tyres, cooking oil and condensed milk, plus a number of staff officers from 46 Group, he touched down safely on the 5400-foot runway. Soon afterwards, he made a night landing at Tegel, accompanied by P.2 Pullen, with a cargo of coal. A hazard to operating at Tegel was an 800-foot radio mast which belonged to the Russians but stood within half a mile of the runway. Repeated requests to remove or shorten it bore no fruit, so in the end French engineers blew it up!

According to former Nav.1 J. N. Sowerby, an imposing mansion which was the residence of the Russian Supreme Commander was close to the approach to Gatow, as was a Russian airfield. "On one occasion" says Mr. Sowerby "we noticed the pilot ahead of us making an approach to the Russian airfield and he was about five miles on finals when we managed to get him on R/T. They would have welcomed his load of pig carcasses, no doubt. ....... A few weeks after the airlift started the Russian Commander was reported to have moved to East Berlin — he couldn't put up with the noise."

As the Airlift settled down into a routine, the Dakota squadrons adopted an 18-day cycle of 14 days operations followed by four days rest in the UK. Other Stations had different routines, and it was thought desirable to standardise the pattern. Accordingly a conference was called at which 'The Brass' proposed a 28-day cycle. Andrew Johnstone was quick to point out that there was also a 28-day human biological cycle, which meant that for some chaps the UK rest time would not be a happy one. The proposal was hastily dropped.

The 50,000th sortie made into Gatow by the RAF was flown on Christmas Day 1948, when Flg. Off. J. G. Beddoes of 30 Squadron (later AVM J. G. Beddoes CB) arrived with a load of coal, whereupon he was made an honorary member of the Berlin Schörnsteinföfer (Chimney Sweeps') Club! Later in the day the Club donated a load of cigarette lighters, all engraved with the Schörnsteinföfer logo, to Flt. Lt. Manning for distribution among the aircrews as a token of gratitude. By now, it was considered that the blockade of Berlin had been overcome, but there was still a great deal of flying to be done.

Sqn. Ldr. Ray Paul has provided some details of his Christmas of 1948. "At Christmas Eve I was detailed to fly from our base at Lübeck to Hamburg to provide a back-up service to Berlin for the British European Airways schedule which had gone unserviceable. The rest of the squadron stood down because of persistent fog over the North German Plain, which restricted the airlift to the 'Heavy Boys' from Wunstorf. I returned to Lübeck in the evening to find most of the squadron sipping soft drinks in the bar in view of an impending 04.00 take-off on Christmas Day. I was plied with questions regarding the weather and reported the unanimous opinions of the 'Met' men at both Berlin and Hamburg that there was no chance of flying next day. Soft drinks rapidly changed to something more festive whilst I and my crew repaired to bed after a hard day's work. Well, as you can guess, the 'Met' men got it wrong and the fog cleared in the night. So early calls were given at 02.00 hour, and a sick and sorry lot of 30 Squadron crews took off at 04.00 on Christmas morning for two lifts to Berlin. One crew was reasonably bright-eyed and bushy-tailed and I was not the most popular chap on the Squadron that day."

Continuing bad weather grounded many crews in Berlin on New Year's Eve, and at first the consumption of alcohol was forbidden, in case a sudden improvement made flying possible. At midnight, everyone was stood down until 09.00 on 1st January, and Sqn. Ldr. Johnstone, who happened to be the senior officer present, allowed the bar to be opened. However, he knew that orders could be changed, and not only refrained from drinking but also forbade his crew to drink. This was a wise move, as at 02.00 the weather improved and all crews were ordered back to their billets. Johnstone then checked on every pilot and navigator to determine whether they were fit to fly. Some were sound asleep and were left alone, as were signallers. Although Transport Command decreed that every flight must include a signaller, his job was merely to transmit one W/T message on the outbound sector and one on the inbound, and on this occasion this service was dispensed with. So the airlift was maintained that night, although later Sqn. Ldr. Johnstone, who had just received an OBE in the New Year's Honours List, was interviewed by higher authority about this episode.

*South African AirForce officers on attachment to 30 Squadron in 1948. Lt. Haskins in the doorway, Lt. Norman-Smith and Lt. Attie Bosch on the ground. The Dakota belongs to 240 OCU*     *[Sqn. Ldr. Hacke].*

*A Christmas party at Lübeck* *[Sqn. Ldr. Hacke]*.

Keeping the Berlin airlift going in all weathers by day and night was a major task for air traffic controllers, who had little modern equipment to help them. At Gatow, GCA was in use for final approaches, and it was found that USAF CPS-5 radar located at Templehof could be used to position aircraft onto the Gatow

*Mr. Arthur Henderson, the Secretary of State for Air, talking to South African crews on the Berlin airlift* *[Sqn. Ldr. Hacke]*.

*The temporary Officers' Mess at RAF Lübeck* *[Sqn. Ldr. Hacke]*.

approach path. Without that facility, life would have been far more difficult for all RAF aircrews. Unfortunately, GCA suffered from weather clutter during rain or snow, ironically when the aid was most in demand. At Lübeck, BABS was used for instrument approaches. Four VHF and one HF R/T frequencies were available, as was a VHF direction-finding service, which was used by air traffic controllers for QGH let-downs. Call-signs used on VHF R/T usually consisted of the aircraft type and the digits of its serial number, for example 'Dakota 916' for KN916, while for W/T transmissions the parent unit's callsign plus individual aircraft letter was used, for example 'MODBV'.

Aircrew fatigue was a common problem and was aggravated by the unreliability and lack of servicing of autopilots, which were considered to be unnecessary because of the short duration of airlift sorties. At the best of times, the autopilots fitted to the Dakota needed constant monitoring and resetting, as the gyros precessed badly and caused the aircraft to wander off heading. One 30 Squadron crew flying back to Lübeck one night with autopilot engaged fell asleep. Some time later one crew member woke up and was horrified to find the aircraft flying back towards Berlin against all the outbound traffic, the heading gyro having precessed through 180 degrees.

From Lübeck, every sortie was flown as required under a Master Flight Plan, compliance with which was the responsibility of the navigators, particularly those in the lead aircraft of each 'wave'. When up-to-date weather conditions were known, an elapsed time was determined for the sector between Lübeck and the Frohnau beacon, about ten miles north of Gatow. A three-minute interval between aircraft was set, accurate navigation being required to maintain separation, and a precise climb to a route altitude of 5500 feet and a cruising speed of 125 knots was normal. When about twenty nautical miles from Frohnau beacon, the signaller made contact with Gatow approach on VHF R/T and then, if necessary, changed frequency to contact Gatow GCA director.

After landing at Gatow, the aircraft were expertly marshalled into position, the marshaller sometimes signalling to the captain to cut his engines even before coming to a halt. The cargo doors were opened within seconds and a truck was backed up so that unloading could begin. By the time the crew had left the flight-deck, German labourers had often unloaded half the cargo, particularly if it was

*An airman uses an Aldis lamp to control the flow of Dakotas at Lübeck in 1948*                    *[Sqn. Ldr. Hacke].*

*A mess party at Lübeck in 1948, with a few RAAF personnel involved. The CO of 30 Squadron, Sqn. Ldr. Johnstone, is the gentleman with the moustache and visible 'wings' in the centre of the group*                    *[Sqn. Ldr. Hacke].*

*Checking aircraft serviceability on the flight line at Lübeck. The officer in the foreground is Flt. Lt. (now Wg. Cdr. retired)* [D. J. Harper].

*Refuelling a 30 Squadron Dakota at Lübeck in 1948* [Sqn. Ldr. Hacke].

coal! Turn-round time was twenty minutes, just enough for 'char and a wad' and for any calls of nature. On the return flight evacuees were often carried as passengers. About fifty miles from Gatow the signaller of the leading aircraft transmitted up-to-date weather actuals to Lübeck for use by subsequent flights, a facility known as 'Carmet'. After flying over Lüneburg, the Dakotas made for the beacon at Tremsbüttel, about fifteen miles south-west of Lübeck, from where a straight-in approach to runway 08 was favoured, as a landing in the opposite direction involved flying over the Russian Zone.

30 Squadron crews, ever ready to concoct a song to fit the occasion, did just that during the Berlin airlift. First heard in the officers' mess at Lübeck, the words of one song were sung to the tune of 'Lili Marlene':

*Flying down the corridor*
*In an ancient Dak,*
*Thirty inches on the clock;*
*I wish that we were back,*
*Back in the mess all safe and sound,*
*With both our feet upon the ground;*
*We're pressing on regardless*
*For the skipper's OBE!*

Another ditty used the tune 'Balling The Jack':

*First you do your safety belt*
*Right up tight,*
*You look out to the left*
*And you look out to the right.*
*Line up on the runway*
*In the sodium light*
*Then with throttles wide you heave it off,*
*With all your might.*
*Flying back to Lübeck,*
*Night shift nearly done,*
*Your boost is 32 and your revs are 21.*
*You've got the crew asleep*
*But you're bang on track.*
*Now that's what I call*
*Floggin' the Dak.*

The thirty inches referred to was the barometric pressure in inches of mercury, as used in American-built aircraft, while the 21 refers to 2100 rpm.

Other personnel who maintained 30 Squadron's intense efforts were the dedicated members of the ground crews. Working around the clock, they ensured that Dakotas were available to meet the requirements of the airlift planning staff, and in fact contributed more than was asked of them. When the airlift operation was analysed some time later it was decided that in any similar future operation greater emphasis would be placed on ensuring that mobile canteens and messes close to hand would be provided, so that delays could be minimised and morale maintained.

One day in January 1949 Sqn. Ldr. Johnstone and his crew collected twenty-five children to be taken from Berlin to Lübeck, the eldest a girl of sixteen who spoke some English. Obviously scared of flying, she asked what would happen if the aircraft crashed. "My dear, this is a most exclusive aeroplane" replied the CO. "It never crashes. Also, this is the most experienced aircrew in the Royal Air Force", which seemed to satisfy her. On 9th March the 50,000th passenger, a small girl, was flown out of Gatow to

Lübeck, where she was welcomed by Gp. Capt. Hall with a bunch of flowers and some Lübeck marzipan.

Sqn. Ldr. Paul remembers one example of lack of cooperation during the airlift. "At one Station we had a particularly obnoxious Station Accountant Officer whose leisurely peace-time routine he found rudely interrupted by large numbers of airlift personnel on detachment from the UK. Since we were on detachment and not on posted strength, the only way we could obtain money was by drawing cash from said accountant on a Transport Command Pay Book. He insisted that this could only be done on Tuesdays and Thursdays between 14.00 and 15.00 hours - very difficult for crews operating 24 hours a day seven days a week. At that time we had aircraft returning to the UK practically every morning for servicing, and this individual approached Andrew Johnstone to ask for a lift home on one of these flights. Johnny was delighted to tell him that he could go only on a Tuesday or Thursday between 14.00 and 15.00 hours!"

Attempts by the Russian authorities to intimidate the airlift crews were numerous. Flying training schools and firing ranges had been established below and close to the air corridors, and cases of Yak fighters flying close to the RAF and USAF aircraft were frequent. On airfields near Berlin, the Russians brought together large numbers of aircraft, which they then flew along the corridors, often against the flow of Dakotas, Yorks, C-54s and others. Never, though, did the Russian and East German pilots succeed in preventing an airlift mission reaching its destination.

One day, Sqn. Ldr. Johnstone, never one to worry too much about the strict letter of regulations, found himself without a signaller in his crew. As Johnstone could not find a spare 'bod' he decided to fly without one, hoping that the statutory calls from one Dakota would not be missed among the mass of messages being passed. He took off from Lübeck and was looking forward to an easy landing at Gatow when the port engine of the Dakota failed. After trying to restart it without success he had to decide whether to carry on to Berlin with a valuable load or to return to base. As the Dakota was losing height and speed and was becoming a

liability to other aircraft in the corridor, he considered going down to 3000 feet, the designated emergency altitude, and carrying on. That, however, would involve flying a replacement engine to Berlin, a waste of freight space. So he made a 180° turn and set off for base. Without a signaller he could not report his difficulties, as his R/T had insufficient range, but after a while he was able to talk to the pilot of another Dakota, who passed the message on via a USAF C-54, which had enough altitude to talk to the controller at Lübeck. Johnstone then thought about throwing out some of the cargo so that the Dakota could maintain altitude, but as the cargo consisted of two huge rolls of newsprint which when unleashed could cause havoc in the fuselage this idea was quickly rejected. He then opened up the good engine to maximum power, ignoring the oil-pressure and temperature gauges. "We've got to keep going" he told his navigator "whether the gauges show we're haywire or not. If we keep on this course where do we hit the British Zone?" On his map, the navigator pointed out a lake which straddled the border. "If we can't make Lübeck, we'll plonk it down on the British side of the lake" said Johnstone. Then they waited, wondering whether the one good engine would survive the hammering it was being given and whether there would be enough fuel to allow them to reach Lübeck, ninety miles away. By the time the border was reached fuel from the last tank was being used, and the Dakota had descended to 1200 feet. From that point there was still twenty miles to be covered when the overstressed engine spluttered and stopped. Reacting automatically, Johnstone turned the fuel cock through the starboard wing tanks, with no success, then to the port tanks, for which the gauges read 'empty', whereupon the engine burst into life. On the R/T, he told Lübeck tower that he had to make a proper landing there rather than crash-landing, because of the hazardous load he was carrying. That decision made, he entered his final approach over the Russian Zone, exactly as Pilot 1 Trezona had done, and told his navigator that he did not want the undercarriage to be lowered until the Dakota had crossed the runway threshold. "If you can get it down

*The Secretary of State for Air, Arthur Henderson, talking to German children about to be flown out of Berlin to West Germany*          *[Sqn. Ldr. Hacke].*

in time after that, good" he said. "If not, we'll land on our belly. We'll have no flaps, either, because I daren't do anything that might cut our speed and make us stall. We have to keep the speed up. Then as long as we land clear and don't come to a sudden stop, we won't get the newsprint down the backs of our necks. When I shout 'When', slam the undercarriage down." Just as the Dakota was floating down, he shouted, and as the undercarriage indicator lights showed three greens the wheels touched the runway. After recovering from the ordeal, the CO watched airmen drain the fuel tanks, which contained exactly four gallons! It transpired later that an ancillary drive in the port engine had sheared and only half its cylinders were operating. Had it not been shut down in time it might well have fallen out of the wing. This incident culminated in the award of a 'Green Endorsement' which was placed in Sqn. Ldr. Johnstone's log book in July 1949 to reflect his "..........great calmness and exceptional airmanship."

*An influential group at RAF Lübeck in July 1949. Left to right – Sqn. Ldr. A. McC. Johnstone (CO of 30 Squadron); Air Cdre. Mercer (AOC 46 Group and Deputy Commander of the Berlin Airlift); Wg. Cdr. Ford-Kelsey CBE AFC BA (Wg. Cdr. Flying, RAF Lübeck); the CO of the RAAF detachment; the CO of the SAAF detachment; Sqn. Ldr. Kirwen (CO of 18 Squadron)*
*[Sqn. Ldr. Hacke].*

*At Bückeburg in May 1949: Flg. Off. F. Stillwell, Sig.1 Barlow and Flt. Lt. J. Manning*
*[Sqn. Ldr. F. Stillwell].*

The flying programme for 30 Squadron covering the period between 1st and 7th April 1949 shows 22 sorties:

| | 'A' Flight | 'B' Flight |
|---|---|---|
| 1st April | 20.45 | 22.45 |
| 2nd April | 01.51, 16.45 and 21.51 | 03.51, 18.45 and 23.51 |
| 3rd April | 12.45 and 17.51 | 14.45 and 19.51 |
| 4th April | Stand-down | Stand-down |
| 5th April | 08.45 and 13.51 | 10.45 and 15.5.1 |
| 6th April | 04.45 and 09.51 | 06.45 and 11.51 |
| 7th April | 20.45 | 22.45 |

The Berlin airlift was brought to a successful conclusion by a statement issued in London, Paris, Washington and Moscow on 5th May 1949, in which the Russians promised to lift the blockade of the city provided trade restrictions imposed by the Allied powers were removed. However, it was considered prudent to stockpile supplies just in case the Russians failed to comply with the agreement, so for a time the airlift continued. 30 Squadron continued, and indeed increased its effort.

Unfortunately for 30 Squadron, the privilege of taking the final Dakota sortie from Lübeck was given to a 10 Squadron crew. At 18.30 on 23rd September 1949 Dakota C.4 KN652 of 10 Squadron took off from Lübeck for Gatow on the last Dakota flight of the airlift. Piloted by P.1 Brown, with Nav. 2 Pearce and Sig. 1 Batson, the aircraft carried two passengers – Gp. Capt. A. J. 'Wally' Biggar and Wg. Cdr. Foord-Kelsey, the OC Flying. Waiting to meet the Dakota was the Father of the Royal Air Force, MRAF Viscount Trenchard GCB GCVO DSO, the AOC-in-C, Air Marshal T. M. Williams CB OBE MC DFC, and the AOC of 46 Group, Air Cdre. J. W. Mercer CB. Gp. Capt. Biggar presented an illuminated scroll to Gp. Capt. B. C. Yarde CBE, Gatow's Station Commander. The last sack to be offloaded from the Dakota carried the inscription:

*Positively the last load from Lübeck*
*73705 tons*
*Psalm 21, Verse 11*

The wording of that cryptic message is 'For they intended evil against thee; they imagined a mischievous device, which they are not able to perform'. As if in confirmation of this sentiment, on the previous day at 16.03 thirty-eight Russian fighter aircraft had flown over Gatow from north to south, followed by another twelve nine minutes later. On its return flight, KN652 carried the last German passengers to be taken to the British Zone of Germany by *Plainfare* aircraft.

The following statistics show just how much effort the air and ground crews of 30 Squadron contributed to the Berlin Airlift:

| Month | Freight carried (lbs.) | Mail carried (lbs.) | Passengers carried | Operational hours flown |
|---|---|---|---|---|
| **1948** | | | | |
| June | 143,123 | nil | 95 | 105:50 |
| July | 1,470,817 | 64,906 | 3386 | 670:25 |
| August | 3,324,023 | 540 | 1093 | 956:50 |
| September | 1,348,074 | 7266 | 2226 | 506:50 |
| October | 980,067 | 38,942 | 3560 | 536:15 |
| November | 1,156,978 | 5696 | 835 | 419:40 |
| December | 1,796,633 | 7960 | 491 | 596:25 |
| | | | | |
| **1949** | | | | |
| January | 1,105,882 | 19,917 | 1015 | 410:45 |
| February | 655,503 | 47,210 | 2882 | 398:30 |
| March | 1,214,671 | 30,950 | 757 | 429:55 |
| April | 1,294,183 | 12,000 | 819 | 195:05 |
| May | 1,866,832 | nil | 1632 | 603:25 |
| June | 5370 | 1742 | 105 | 20.00 |
| July | 1,101,556 | 3799 | 998 | 450:50 |
| August | 1,551,306 | 19,707 | 3696 | 747:20 |
| September | 537,240 | 15,982 | 1546 | 297:35 |
| | | | | |
| **TOTALS** | 19,552,257 | 276,617 | 23,746 | 7345:50 |
| | (8728 + tons) | (123 tons) | | |

## Back to routine

Not until October 1949 did 30 Squadron crews return to Oakington. They then began intensive preparations for a new series of scheduled services to the Middle East and Gibraltar via Istres in the south of France. In addition, special flights were carried out on demand, and in October included a trip piloted by Flt. Lt. Hacke from Northolt to Copenhagen (Kastrup) with the fifteen members of an RAF boxing team and one by four Dakotas to take the Central Band of the RAF to Valkenburg in Holland. A more mundane task was carried out by P.2 Burry, who flew freight from Honington to Dishforth and back. Another interesting function for 30 Squadron was carrying personnel of bomber squadrons to Shallufa in the Canal Zone in connection with Operation *Sunray*, usually with a night stop at Luqa in Malta. This type of work was carried on until the spring of 1950, by which time routes to Germany and Poland, usually via Manston or Northolt, were once more being operated. Routes flown were given flight letters, as follows:

| | |
|---|---|
| UB | Bückeburg |
| UBB | Bückeburg and Berlin |
| UBD | Northolt–Bückeburg–Northolt–Oakington (twice weekly) |
| UFD | Istres–Luqa–El Adem–Fayid and return |
| UIG | Gibraltar |
| UME | Middle East |
| UU | Casualty evacuation from BAFO carrying nursing sisters of PMRAFNS and orderlies for training purposes: *Schedule A:* Oakington–Manston–Fühlsbuttel– Bückeburg– Lyneham–Oakington *Schedule B:* as Schedule A but omitting Bückeburg *Schedule C:* as Schedule A but omitting Fühlsbuttel |
| UWD | Oakington–Northolt–Bückeburg–Berlin (Gatow)–Warsaw and return same route |

The UWD service was considered the most interesting, with the overnight stop in Berlin always looked forward to by the crews. One of the pilots involved was Flt. Lt. R. R. Waughman, who recalls that he and his colleagues had never seen anything like the 'topless' bars in the Kurfurstendamm clubs before. In one bar he was told to have just one drink. "Having eyed the females and had our one drink we left. Later we were told that there hadn't been one woman in the place!" he said years later. "Air Traffic Control in the Russian sector was just as devious" he continued. "I felt that they were out to be as obstructive as possible. The allocated corridor from Berlin to Warsaw was three miles wide. I cannot remember anyone straying outside the limits, although we were accused of doing so. Our allocated height on one trip was 40,000 feet! We went at 4000 feet and argued later. On landing at Okecie (Warsaw airport) an armed guard in a car escorted you to a parking space. Your identification (Form 1250) was taken away as you left the aircraft, to be returned as you re-entered it for departure. These military guards were allowed into the passenger compartment but the flight deck was taboo. After parking, passengers and crew were escorted to a reception room. Passengers were mainly Embassy staff and families and the King's Messenger with his diplomatic bag. After customs and immigration clearance the crew were allowed into the airport restaurant, which was like a run-down transport café. We usually had a fried egg sandwich and a soft drink before being escorted back to the aircraft for departure. A very young soldier, under instruction, met us on one occasion, took our identification and promptly handed it back. Later, he arrived, rather sheepishly, in the restaurant with an armed escort to demand our identification. We never saw him again. I imagine he ended up with snow on his boots. The [Polish] officials were dour, officious and most unhelpful. Once they made an eight-year-old girl passenger handle her own luggage through customs. We were prevented forcibly from giving any help".

Retired Sqn. Ldr. Paul Presnail also recalls the weekly flight to Warsaw, which involved positioning the Dakota at Northolt on a Monday, flying to Berlin via Bückeburg next day, on to Warsaw and back to Berlin on the Wednesday and finally returning to base via Bückeburg and Northolt on the Thursday. During the latter part of 1950, a certain amount of consternation was caused when the Communists demanded to be notified, some weeks in advance of each flight, the names of the crew, the serial number of the aircraft and its radio call-sign. In the end, the problem was overcome by repainting every Dakota C.4 on the squadron with the same serial number, KN222! An aircraft not on the UWD schedule showed its correct serial number painted on canvas strips stuck over the fictitious one! "This strategy worked well" says Paul, "although I wondered what the Communists thought on the day we turned up in KN222 in camouflage paint instead of the usual polished livery. The only other hiccup was when a much-delayed aircraft returning to base encountered an outgoing aircraft at Northolt using the same call-sign." Sgt. Pete Bougourd, then an airfield controller at Oakington, remembers the same confusion happening there.

To present the 1949 Transport Command Accident Prevention Trophy to RAF Oakington, Air Chief Marshal Sir John C. Slessor GCB DSO MC, the Chief of the Air Staff, visited the Station on 10th February 1950, accompanied by Sir Frederick Handley Page and the AOC-in-C Transport Command, Air Marshal Sir Brian Baker KBE CB DSO MC AFC. In the presence of officers from Command and Group and all the transport Stations, Sir John remarked that it would have been quite reasonable to expect an increase in accidents during the Berlin Airlift, but this had not happened. Unfortunately, 30 Squadron had been one to suffer.

Sqn. Ldr. Johnstone left in March 1950 and was replaced by Sqn. Ldr. A. Reece DSO DFC AFC, who had previously been in charge of 46 Squadron. Officers of the squadron bought a squadron crest on a plaque which in June 1950 they presented to the officers' mess at Gatow in recognition of the hospitality extended to them while on scheduled services.

In October 1950 two crews were detached to North Luffenham to carry out conversion training on the then new Valetta aircraft with 240 Operational Conversion Unit. After the medium-range element of 24 Squadron was absorbed into 30 Squadron on 15th November 1950 a move to Abingdon was ordered, and so 30 Squadron left Oakington between 24th and 28th November. The first two Valettas for 30 Squadron, VW949 and VW855, arrived at Abingdon in December, and by the end of the month the full establishment of eight aircraft had been taken on charge.

*The Airlift Memorial in Berlin at the time of the 50th anniversary celebration.*

222

More adventures in Warsaw are recalled Flt. Lt. Waughman, who on one flight in December 1950 was the captain, with Flt. Lt. Jackson as wireless operator, Flt. Lt. Robinson the navigator and Cpl. Cunliffe the AQM. "I arrived at Warsaw" says Mr. Waughman "and on entering the reception room I found that the handles had been removed from the inside of the doors. After two hours the passengers were released [but] we were detained for nearly twelve hours without being able to contact anyone. We passed the time looking for 'bugs', thinking there were microphones behind the pictures on the wall. We also endeavoured to memorise as many of the serial numbers of foreign aircraft as we could. We were released in the small hours of the morning and beat a very hasty retreat to Berlin, although we were not supposed to night-fly over occupied territory. A Foreign Office

official met me at Hendon and quizzed me about the trip. We never did find out the reason for our detention".

Thus the huge contribution paid by 30 Squadron Dakotas to the Berlin Airlift and to military air transport in Europe and the Middle East drew to a close. The scene was now set for a more modern aircraft carrying heavier loads over longer distances in greater comfort — the Vickers Valetta — although during the month route flying by the faithful Dakotas continued.

**In remembrance**

To mark the fortieth anniversary of the final Dakota sortie of the Berlin airlift, a Hercules of 30 Squadron flew to Gatow on 22nd September 1989 carrying Wg. Cdr. Andrew McC. Johnstone OBE

*30 Squadron in July 1950.*

*Dakota C.4 KN419 was diverted to Wunstorf on 2nd July 1950 while on the UWD service, due to work in progress on the runway at Bückeburg. In the background is Dakota G-AGIZ of British European Airways and the Wunstorf control tower.*

The crew of KN383 about to depart from Northolt on the UWD service on 23rd July 1950 (left to right) – Flt. Lt. Fuller (captain), Flt. Lt. Raymond (signaller), Cpl. Duff (AQM), Nav. 1 Aitken and Nav. 1 Revers.

Loading Dakota KN383 on 23rd July 1950.

AFC, the CO of 30 Squadron at the time of the airlift, and his wife and fifteen other Airlift veterans. This flight, captained outbound by Wg. Cdr. D. M. Guest, was considerably less fraught with danger than those of 1949! Routed from Lyneham around London to join the airways system over Clacton, the Hercules (call-sign Ascot 4951) flew east over Amsterdam and Osnabruck before joining the Bückeburg–Berlin corridor. Carrying its own internal navigation aids, the Hercules could be navigated accurately without recourse to external help, although the entire flight was routinely monitored by radar. On arriving at Gatow, the party was taken to the terminal building and then to a hangar in which stood a Dakota carrying Royal Australian Air Force markings, ready to serve as a backdrop to the forthcoming ceremony. The party was welcomed by Senator Wagner of the Berlin Legislature, to whom AVM David Dick presented a symbolic piece of coal, which now sits in a display case in the foyer of Berlin's main power station. In addition, commemorative presentations were made by Wg. Cdr. Guest to RAF Gatow on behalf of 30 Squadron and to Senator Wagner. It was then the turn of Wg. Cdr. Johnstone to talk to the Senator, recalling some of his personal experiences on the Berlin airlift. These formalities completed, the small group then paid visits to the Airlift Memorial, on which are inscribed the names of the 30 Squadron personnel who lost their lives in the crash at Lübeck, to the Brandenburg Gate and the Berlin Wall and enjoyed

lunch at the Reichstag before beginning the return flight to Lyneham.

Among some of those who served on the Berlin Airlift there is a lingering resentment that they are not entitled to any form of decoration for having done so. As the airlift was deemed to have been flown to aid the civilian population of Berlin rather than the military garrison and no offensive action was involved, no decoration was permitted under British law. However, the Prime Minister did authorise the issue of ten AFCs and ten AFMs in recognition of the efforts made by aircrews of Transport Command. Of these, 30 Squadron members were awarded three:

> Flt. Lt. J. F. Manning the AFC,
>     Birthday Honours List, June 1949
>
> Sqn. Ldr. A. McC. Johnstone the AFC,
>     Birthday Honours List, 1950
>
> Nav.1 J. N. Sowerby the AFM,
>     Birthday Honours List, 1950

In addition, Sqn. Ldr. Johnstone was honoured with the award of the OBE in the New Year's Honours List, 1949.

**Above:** Sqn. Ldr. A. Reece DSO DFC AFC in his office at Oakington.
**Above right:** Dakota KN628 of 30 Squadron at Oakington in 1950
[Flt. Lt. A. Thomas].
**Right:** Nicely polished Dakota C.4 KN360 [JN:K] of 30 Squadron in post-Airlift days
[R. C. Sturtivant collection].

*Sqn. Ldr. Reece and the aircrews of 30 Squadron pose in front of a Dakota at Oakington in 1950.*

*At the 40th anniversary celebration in Berlin on 23rd September 1989 (left to right) – Herr Wagner; Sqn. Ldr. Johnstone, the CO in 1948/49; Wg. Cdr. Guest, the then CO of 30 Squadron; and the Station Commander at RAF Gatow.*

*Just about the whole of 30 Squadron's personnel seem to be in this picture, taken at Dishforth on an unrecorded date.*

# Chapter 9: Short Range Transport, 1951 to 1957

Now based at Abingdon, 30 Squadron settled down to flying the new Valetta aircraft, the military version of the Viking civil airliner which had first flown in June 1945. Adapted to the requirements of the RAF under Specification C.9/46, the Valetta was powered by two 2000 horse-power Bristol Hercules 230 engines and had a range of 1460 miles at its 211 mph cruising speed. This compared with the Dakota recently flown by 30 Squadron, which had a range of 1600 miles at about the same speed but could carry only 7800 pounds of freight as opposed to the Valetta's 11500 pounds. In size, the Valetta had a smaller wing span and was approximately the same length as the Dakota.

During January 1951 Valettas began to replace Dakotas on 30 Squadron's scheduled services. However, Dakota KN628 was retained for the use of Field Marshal Viscount Montgomery and was usually flown by a crew captained by Flt. Lt. J. Haughton, at least until January 1952. February was a month of intense training for the 30 Squadron crews, who flew 354 hours on conversion exercises as opposed to 155 on operations. Nights away from base were frequent, even on tasks within the United Kingdom, an example being a trip from Northolt to Cosford, Turnhouse and Leuchars which began on 23rd February and ended two days later. During March the last Dakota (apart from the one used by 'Monty') was withdrawn, and several extra freight schedules were flown to enable crews to build up their route hours and become qualified to carry passengers.

A problem suffered by the Valetta for the whole of its life was jamming of the aileron controls. One of the first to experience this fault was Russ Hooper, captain of Valetta VX484 on a UFV service returning from Fayid on 11th January 1951. After take-off from Benina he realised that the ailerons were locked and assumed that the locking pins had failed to withdraw. An attempt at flexing the wings in zero G-force had no effect, but on landing back at Benina aileron control returned, and he learned later that the problem was caused by the high temperatures of the Middle East. In fact the phenomenon was more widespread, and caused an emergency landing at Berlin (Templehof), which ruined the tight schedules on the route. A technical team was flown to Berlin and eventually discovered a greasing problem, which was generally solved by increasing the size of the grease pocket.

Typical of the use to which Dakota KN628 was put was a flight which began on 2nd March, when Flt. Lt. Haughton flew Field Marshal Montgomery to El Adem in Libya and on to Farouk Field in Egypt. After a respite for crew and passengers, the Dakota flew to El Adem and Castel Benito on 6th March and two days later made the journey to Istres and on to Villacoublay near Paris. The final leg of the tour was from there to Odiham to allow the Field Marshal to disembark, and thence to Abingdon. Other VIPs flown by 30 Squadron that month included Field Marshal Sir William Slim, the Chief of the Air Staff, MRAF Sir John Slessor GCB DSO MC, the Secretary of State for Air, Rt. Hon. Arthur Henderson, Rt. Hon. Anthony Eden MP, MRAF Sir John Salmond GCB CMG CVO DSO, and the Minister of Defence, Rt. Hon. E. Shinwell MP.

Special flights carried out by the squadron are noted meticulously in the Operational Record book, but the purpose of each flight is seldom mentioned. It is impossible without a great deal of further research to know, for instance, why 'Monty' was flown from Blackbushe to Exeter and on to Paris on 15th May. Again, we may never know the reason why on 18th May three Valettas began special flights carrying freight and passengers from Abingdon to Exeter, Martlesham Heath, Llandow, Acklington and Honiley, a task which took three days to complete. In June an interesting five-day trip was made to carry AVM McDonald from Northolt to Villacoublay, Maison Blanche (Algeria), Marrakesh (Morocco), Meknes, Gibraltar, Bordeaux and back to Abingdon. An increasing number of missions were now being flown to carry

*30 Squadron Valetta VW190 at Dishforth early in 1951*

*[Sqn. Ldr. A. Thomas].*

*Valetta VW863 displaying the 30 Squadron diamond marking and the 'last three' of the serial number on the fin*          *[R. C. Sturtivant collection].*

personnel of Fighter Command on detachment, some within the UK and some to Germany. In addition, Bomber Command ground crews were being flown to Shallufa in the Canal Zone to take part in the annual *Sunray* exercises.

Gatow airfield in Berlin was replaced in July 1951 by Templehof as the terminal of the scheduled services. Now in use by the USAF, Templehof had been the civil airport for Berlin in prewar days and had then seen service as a Luftwaffe airfield.

## Swedish Rhapsody

In August 1951 three of 30 Squadron's Valettas acted as support for a squadron of Vampires from North Weald which were to make a goodwill tour of Sweden, led by Don Kingaby. Within minutes of arriving at the first point on the tour, Angelholm, the 30 Squadron crews were all stark naked in the sauna! Flg. Off. Paul Presnail found himself being beaten with hazel twigs by the C-in-C of the Swedish Air Force, by no means a normal experience. At dinner that evening, the C-in-C told how eager he was to learn from the RAF pilots about operating the Vampire, with which the Swedish Air Force was also equipped. Unfortunately, the RAF pilots had more than a fair share of unserviceability problems, particularly involving engine starting, and were much embarrassed. At Barkaby airfield, just outside Stockholm, the Swedes challenged the RAF to a scramble race, their aircraft from massive underground hangars and ours from the hardstanding at the end of the runway. The outcome was only too predictable, the Swedes putting most of their Vampires into the air before the first RAF aircraft, several of which failed to start.

Socially, 30 Squadron was well to the fore, and many good friendships were made. At that time several Commonwealth officers were serving on the squadron, one of whom, Flg. Off. Jimmy Fitzsimons, was a signaller who proudly wore his RCAF Radio Observer's brevet on his RAF uniform, much to the annoyance of one Gp. Capt. Beisiegel, a Station Commander who had told Fitzsimons not long earlier to remove it. At a cocktail party in the British Embassy in Stockholm, Jimmy was mortified to hear a familiar voice booming "I thought I told you to change that Brevet." The fact that the Gp. Capt. had been posted to Sweden had been forgotten.

Apart from the Swedish expedition, a large number of tasks for Fighter Command and VIP flights were carried out during August 1951, one of the passengers being the Prime Minister, the Rt. Hon. Clement R. Attlee, who was ferried from Turnhouse to Northolt. A new CO, Sqn. Ldr. R. S. Kerby, took over on 15th August.

30 Squadron suffered its first Valetta mishap on 5th February 1952, when VW827, flown by Wg. Cdr. Kane, the new Wg. Cdr. Flying, crashed into houses at Iffley near Abingdon when carrying out a single-engined overshoot, the cause remaining a mystery. Flt. Lt. Waughman had just air-tested this aircraft, as the engine had

been reported as not unfeathering quickly although within limits, after which the inexperienced Wg. Cdr. had decided to investigate. Some injuries were sustained, but no fatalities.

Activity in Fighter Command remained high, several squadrons being transported hither and thither in the Valettas. Among the tasks were trips between Horsham St. Faith and Wymeswold and between Acklington and North Weald .Some of the fighter squadrons were those of the RAuxAF (Royal Auxiliary Air Force) on their way to and from summer camps. Freight carried included a Ghost engine for a Vampire fighter, complete with a servicing crew, flown to Istres near Marseilles on 17th March.

An ever-popular schedule was the UFV service to Fayid and back, particularly if the weather was good. Former Flt. Lt. Waughman remembers night-stopping at Istres, near Marseilles, where a bar was run by Mrs. Robinson, the French wife of an Englishman. "In return for various favours we were asked to take her a giant whisky bottle, the sort used for marketing in the UK" he says. "We had no end of fun getting that through customs." He went on to recall that flying over the north African desert and along the coast could be spectacular. "We tried to fly as low as possible. Old tank tracks, tanks and crashed aircraft, relics of the north African campaign, could still be seen. At Fayid we were not allowed to go into the native villages alone – there had been a stabbing or two. Transit crews were housed in tented accommodation. You were advised to sleep with your kit as pillows or by your side [but] even so they could be, and were, pilfered. In the village you could get a greatcoat turned or a pair of shoes made, more or less overnight. We made a trip to Ismailia one rest day – the road went parallel with the Sweetwater Canal. The things that floated in the canal turned the strongest constitution. Outside the French Club we noticed potted palm trees in tubs. These reminded us of our emblem. To our undying shame we 'acquired' one when darkness fell. This was brought back to Abingdon, where it stood outside our offices. I wonder how long it lasted."

VIP flights continued, and in April 1952 those carried included MRAF Sir John Slessor, ACM Sir Ralph Cochrane, ACM Sir Hugh Pugh Lloyd, Field Marshal Lord Alexander of Tunis, Air Marshal Curtis, the CAS of the RCAF, the Secretaries of State for War and Air, and Gen. Yamut. Among the Stations and other sites visited by Air Marshal Curtis were Avro at Woodford, Langar, North Luffenham (both RCAF Stations), Hucknall, Prestwick and Moreton Valence, the Gloster Aircraft Co. airfield.

## What a welcome!

Then came another change of address for 30 Squadron, which moved on 2nd May 1952 to Benson, a Bomber Command airfield where parent unit facilities were provided. The move was completed quickly without interruption to scheduled services, but a few days later the whole squadron assembled so that the Station

Commander could make a speech. He stood on a box and said "You are a Transport Command squadron on a Bomber Command Station. I will feed you, pay you and clothe you. Other than that I want nothing to do with you. And keep away from the Queen's Flight next door". With that he left, and members of the squadron looked at each other and said "What a greeting", or words to that effect. Next day the Station Equipment Officer arrived to find out how much fuel, lubricants and de-icing fluid was required. He did not believe how much de-icing fluid the Valettas used, and it was only a couple of weeks before the Station ran out of stock. Transport then had to be sent to Abingdon to acquire some, and ground crews soon learnt to look after the squadron and forget about the Station.

Soon after the move, Flt. Lt. Williams and his crew flew the body of the late Dutch Ambassador from Northolt to Schipol, an unusual task carried out with great efficiency. During May, a series of mysterious flights between Boscombe Down and Stornoway began. Mr. 'Buck' Taylor, then Sgt. Taylor, has an explanation for them. "One day a number of civilians walked through the hangar accompanied by some officers from [Transport] Command" he says. "We were told to supply them with an aircraft with a trolley accumulator plugged in and not to interfere. A couple of hours later they disappeared. A few weeks later a lorry arrived with a large cage in sections. Its walls were of two-inch wire mesh. It was assembled in the rear of the aircraft, aft of the main spar on the starboard side. It had a normal entrance door with a lock on it. Nobody could think of any reason for it, nor were we told anything. Then we were allotted VW190 [as] an extra aircraft to carry the cage. Every week, it would leave us at about six in the morning, fly to Boscombe Down, pick up a professor and fly him to Stornoway, together with his packages. There he left the island by Royal Navy pinnace and was taken to a ship anchored off shore. Very hush-hush. Many years later we were told that the professor was working on germ warfare, his packages contained guinea-pigs and the cage in the aircraft was used to prevent any animals escaping."

In July one of the Valettas, captained by Flt. Lt. Lawson, carried the Secretary of State for Air, Lord de l'Isle and Dudley VC, the Minister of Defence, Maj. Gen. McKonnell USAF and Gen. Griswold USAF on a tour which included the US Strategic Air Command bases at Mildenhall, Lakenheath, Bentwaters and Sculthorpe and thence to Farnborough and West Malling.

30 Squadron took part in the relief operation after the Lynmouth (north Devon) disaster on 16th August 1952, when nine inches of rain had fallen, causing disastrous floods and landslides. Some personnel went to Zurich in Switzerland, from where sandbags were flown to Manston, to where other personnel were detached. Another gang of men were sent to Lynmouth to dry out some of the houses with the squadron's heaters.

## A disaster for 30 Squadron

Tragedy struck at 01.14 on 29th August 1952 when Valetta VX559, carrying out continuation training at night, crashed three minutes after take-off from Benson and exploded. The three members of the crew, Flt. Sgt. N. Cross (pilot), Sgt. W. E. Garnes

(navigator) and Flt. Sgt. T. F. W. Lomas (signaller), were killed instantly in the crash, the cause of which was not determined.

During August Sqn. Ldr. Kerby relinquished command of 30 Squadron on posting to Transport Command Examining Unit, and until the arrival of Sqn. Ldr. D. A. Peacock DFC on 1st September, Flt. Lt. S. R. Dixon was in charge. In September one of those more interesting tasks was carried out, involving Flt. Lt. Williams and his crew carrying Admiral Sir Patrick Brind from Fornebu to Fearn and Turnhouse on 5th September and taking him back next day. They then began a short period of attachment to the Admiral's HQ, during which they flew sorties to Bodø, Aalborg, Karup, Kastrup, Schleswigland, Hamburg and Kristiansand. By 14th September this crew was back in business at Benson, ready to take the Rt. Hon. Anthony Eden to Strasbourg, Belgrade, Zagreb, Vienna, Klagenfurt and Bückeburg. Such was the life of a 30 Squadron Valetta crew!

Another trip halfway round the world began on 2nd November, when Flg. Off. d'Oliveira and his crew positioned at Northolt in VX576 to collect the RAF Director General of Organisation, AVM Sharpe. Their first staging post was Istres, from where they flew, over a period of twenty-one days, to Malta (Luqa), El Adem, Nicosia, Habbaniya (where 30 Squadron had spent time before the Second World War), Maffraq, Fayid, Port Sudan, Aden (Khormaksar), Hargeisa, Nairobi (Eastleigh), Entebbe, Khartoum, Fayid, Benina, Tripoli (Idris), Maison Blanche, Gibraltar and Madrid before landing back at Northolt. On the same day Flt. Sgt. Hyland and Flt. Sgt. Willbie took a party from the Central Fighter Establishment at West Raynham to Istres, Luqa, Nicosia, Habbaniya, Fayid, Kabrit, Deversoir, Khartoum, Salalah, Mauripur, Sharjah and El Adem, returning to base on 24th November.

While these intrepid airmen were away on business, the squadron's establishment of aircraft was reduced from ten Valettas C.1, three Valettas C.2 (the VIP aircraft) and two Dakotas C.4 to six, two and two respectively. At least one of the C.2 aircraft, WJ504, had been fitted with fifteen seats for high-ranking officers and other Very Important Persons, and for an increased range it carried 116lbs of extra fuel in saddle tanks in the engine nacelles, as used in the Viking airliner.

*After use by 30 Squadron for VIP transportation, Valetta C.2 VX576 saw service with 233 Squadron and the Metropolitan Communications Squadron*       *[R. C. Sturtivant collection]*

*The prefabricated aluminium huts used by 30 Squadron groundcrews at Benson.*

*30 Squadron aircrew posing in front of a highly-polished Valetta carrying the squadron badge.*

*Valetta VX494 parked on a brick-paved dispersal, probably on an airfield in Germany.*

On 25th November 1952 another serious accident occurred when Valetta VW203, flown by Flt. Sgt. 'Jock' Campbell to demonstrate the versatility of the aircraft to eight senior Commonwealth army officers, collided in mid-air with Venom FB.1 WE258 of the Aircraft & Armament Experimental Establishment near Boscombe Down, the Venom's base. On board, forward of the main spar, was a jeep, and the army officers sat behind the spar. Hardly had the Valetta taken off when the Venom flew across the airfield at low level and struck its tail. The Venom pilot bailed out, but his parachute failed to open in time, with the inevitable consequence. The Valetta belly-landed heavily a mile and a half from the airfield, and the jeep, though chained, broke away, came forward through the bulkhead, severed one of the legs of the Air Quartermaster, who was sitting in the signaller's position, and broke the hip of the navigator. First to reach the crashed Valetta was a helicopter pilot who happened to be flying nearby. He flew the injured crew one by one to Boscombe Down, from where ambulances took them to hospital. No passengers were injured, proving once again the effectiveness of rearward-facing seats in saving lives. Blame for this mishap was placed upon the unfortunate pilot of the Venom.

December was a quiet month, with fog preventing several flights. However, on 29th December Flt. Lt. Setterfield and his crew took the RAF Rugby Football team to Bordeaux and Mont de Marsant and brought them back two days later. Another unusually quiet month followed, adverse weather affecting the squadron's operations, although a full training programme was carried out.

In February 1953, 30 Squadron's most important task was an uplift of sandbags in four aircraft from Zurich to Manston and Waterbeach in connection with the floods which were inundating east coast areas at the time. For this project, known as Operation *King Canute*, all leave for squadron personnel was cancelled, and some were sent to Manston and Zurich to handle the aircraft. At Manston, the same attitude found earlier at Benson was found – if you're Transport Command we don't want you! One officer in particular was most unhelpful, but a cooperative Warrant Officer suggested that his feelings should be ignored and went on to help the 30 Squadron men do the work they were sent to do. In addition, some of the squadron's ground crews went to the affected area to help dry out flooded houses with the aid of heater trolleys. Similar floods were being experienced in Holland, and 30 Squadron helped by carrying rubber dinghies from Burtonwood and other supplies from Lyneham to Valkenburg.

The annual Fighter Command uplift season was opened by two Valettas which carried ground crews from Tangmere to Wahn on 13th March and brought them back ten days later. Next came a similar mission between North Weald and Acklington on 29th March, and VIP flights continued. In April a large part of 30 Squadron's work consisted of fighter squadron uplifts, and while they were being carried out the squadron moved in three stages to a new home at Dishforth in Yorkshire. Transport Command had decreed that apart from a couple of 'Queen Mary' low-loaders no help would be provided, so squadron personnel carried out the task themselves between 12th and 17th April.

July 1953 was the month in which the Royal Review of the RAF was held at Odiham, an event never matched in size or quality before or since. To take part in the training programme for the Review, two crews, one of them captained by Flt. Lt. d'Oliveira, flew to Colerne on 26th May, and in June one of the VIP Valettas was sent to Odiham to act as a static exhibit. No doubt a good deal of 'bull' was applied to the already polished Valetta! VIP flights carried out in July included a three-day round trip by ACM Sir Basil Embry, the C-in-C Allied Forces (Air) Central Europe, who was making a tour of airfields involved in Exercise *Coronet*, and a visit by ACM Sir William Dickson, the Chief of the Air Staff, Lord Trenchard, AVM Sir Harry Broadhurst and ACM Sir J. Whitworth-Jones, who boarded two Valettas at Northolt and flew to Cranwell to attend a passing-out parade. A third aircraft carried representatives of the press.

Most of 30 Squadron's effort in August 1953 involved fighter squadron uplifts and special flights required in connection with exercises taking place in Germany. The routine scheduled flights and flights between Boscombe Down and Stornoway, now referred to as Operation *Hesperus*, also continued. An unusual task was air-sea rescue duty in connection with Operation *Momentum* under which one aircraft stood by at Acklington, but was not called out. Another task was to fly the Imperial Defence College course on a protracted tour taking in Paris, Wahn, Bückeburg, Hamburg, Copenhagen, Oslo, Lohausen and Brussels before returning to Northolt, three Valettas being involved. Deviating slightly from this route, some senior officers of the College were collected at Klagenfurt on 8 September, and between Vienna and Klagenfurt the Valetta was intercepted by MiG fighters, presumably belonging to the air force of East Germany. Resolutely maintaining height and course, Flt. Lt. Lofting reached safer territory without any shots being fired at his aircraft. Sighs of relief could be heard when the party reached Northolt!

One of the VIP missions involved flying a certain member of the Cabinet to Germany. On boarding the Valetta at Northolt, this rather corpulent gentleman slowly eased himself into a seat, and the AQM went to help him fasten his seat-belt. The ends of the belt failed to meet! The Minister looked up and with a smile on his face said "Ee, lad, tha'll have to get a bit bigger booger than that". On another VIP flight a party of government officials and their secretaries were being taken to Germany when over France 'George', the automatic pilot, suddenly and without warning took over. The Valetta went into a dive and all the passengers became airborne above their seats. The head of one official went through the netting of the luggage rack and when the pilot took control again he remained suspended by his neck until the AQM cut him loose! It seems that Valettas C.1 had been cleared for autopilot use but not the VIP C.2 version, from which the autopilot fuses were soon hastily removed.

In October several missions were flown for Coastal Command in connection with Exercise *Mariner*. A typical task involved three of the Valettas, captained by Flt. Lt. Claxton, Flt. Sgt. Hyland and Flt. Sgt. Whiteight, which flew from St. Eval to Lisbon and Bordeaux and then to Lyneham, to Lisbon again and back to Lyneham and finally to Aldergrove, taking four days in all. Another aircraft, with Flt. Lt. d'Oliveira in command, took a naval servicing party from Lee-on-Solent to Keflavik in Iceland in connection with the same exercise, and Admiralty freight was flown to RNAS Hal Far in Malta. On 25th October another mammoth trip began, when the C-in-C Transport Command, Air Marshal Guest, began a comprehensive tour of the RAF in the Middle East. Flying from Lyneham in a Valetta of 30 Squadron with Flt. Lt. Topley at the controls, the party visited Istres, Tripoli (Idris), Fayid, Habbaniya, Bahrain, Sharjah, Masirah, Aden (Khormaksar), Hargeisa, Nairobi (Eastleigh), Juba, Khartoum, Fayid again, El Adem and Luqa before returning via Istres on 15th November. During the trip the Valetta suffered a number of technical problems but completed its task without undue delay. Another airlift for Coastal Command began on 23rd November, when four Valettas, one of them captained by Sqn. Ldr. Peacock, positioned at Lyneham and flew to Luqa in Malta via Istres to pick up Royal Navy personnel and equipment. Next day they returned but were diverted to their own base, Dishforth, instead of landing at nearby Topcliffe.

A feature of 30 Squadron's work during December 1953 was a twelve-day airborne support course at Abingdon, which was completed by three crews in poor weather conditions. It was intended that three crews would undertake this course each month until April 1954. The adverse weather included several days in which Dishforth was fogbound, hampering the training commitment, although two aircraft did leave on New Year's Eve for Nairobi for the annual Bomber Command *Sunray* airlift.

After taking off from Lyneham on 20th January 1954 on a flight to Istres, Valetta VL282 of 30 Squadron reached an altitude of about 200 feet when it suddenly dived to the ground two miles south-south-west of the airfield. Only one of the occupants, the navigator, Plt. Off. A. Robinson, was unlucky enough to lose his life, and the other four crew members survived. The pilot, Flt. Lt. R. Topley, was seriously injured, while the signaller, Sgt. Goodwin, the screen signaller Flt. Lt. Sheen and the AQM, Sgt. Hiscock suffered minor injuries. The eight passengers, including two children, escaped. One woman passenger said afterwards "We owe our lives to the fact that we were seated facing the tail. When I looked forward the whole of the nose of the plane was missing." A Court of Enquiry was established at once, and soon found that elevator control had been lost soon after take-off. As a consequence, at 09.30 that day all Valettas were grounded for three days for inspection. Several aircraft were then flown to Edzell in Scotland for modification, a factor which had an effect on continuation training for the rest of the month and into February. Nevertheless, occasional Fighter Command uplifts were flown, the one which began on 26th February consisting of a flight to Leuchars, West Raynham, Odiham, Hooton Park, Tangmere and Honiley before returning to base two days later.

## Life on the squadron

LAC A. Franklin was a National Service member of a 30 Squadron ground crew, and remembers life on the squadron at that time. "As a working squad it was one weekend off, one on" he says. "According to work load, if you gave up a weekend leave you could fly to Sylt as engine mechanic and stay while your aircraft flew back and forth to [Northern] Ireland ferrying air crews for gunnery practice. Nylons in Sylt were 1/6 per pair and Scotch was 10/- a bottle. But it could go wrong if your plane broke down in Ireland and you were in Germany. Mine never came back for a week and I was the engine mechanic for that plane. No court martial, just 'Chiefy' saying 'It's about time you did some bloody work. Get on with it'."

30 Squadron had many a brave man, according to Mr. Franklin, "..........but none braver than the one who stole the Station Warrant Officer's bike from outside a pub at Dishforth, a crime that could have put him in front of a firing squad or sent him tyre-checking at the North Pole! It did not take long for the police to arrive at 30 Squadron block, in fact they were downstairs when the bike left from a top-floor window, but that was the undoing of all. Our wireless got tangled up with the bike, and out that went too. Bakelite wirelesses do not bounce well! The outcome was 2/6 each for a new wireless, the culprit 5/- for being drunk!"

With the arrival of better weather in March came an increase in the demand for special flights. These included two flights to Gibraltar on 29th March to bring survivors of the SS *Empire Windrush* to Blackbushe, three to Nairobi for Operation *Sunray* and one to 30 Squadron's prewar base at Habbaniya in Iraq to carry sandbags for use in floods which were threatening Baghdad. Scheduled route flying continued, of course. In May the squadron flew 533 hours, the most achieved for several months. Several Fighter Command uplifts were included, and one of the special flights was a short tour of France carrying wartime agents to a reunion with French resistance leaders from 28th to 30th May. May's high number of flying hours were small in comparison with the number flown in June, which totalled 702, added to which were rehearsals for the forthcoming presentation of the squadron's standard. Special flights that month included two to France on the occasion of the tenth anniversary of the D-Day landings and several tasks for Fighter Command.

## Presentation of the Standard

On 1st July 1954 at Dishforth 30 Squadron was honoured by the presentation of Her Majesty the Queen's Standard by Air Chief

*On parade to receive the 30 Squadron standard at Dishforth on 1st July 1954. The standard was presented by ACM Sir James M. Robb GCB KBE DSO DFC AFC, who had been the Commanding Officer of 30 Squadron in Mesopotamia in 1924/25. Apart from the five Valettas parked around the parade, another three can be seen on the perimeter track, and four Devons, a Hastings, an Anson, a Chipmunk and a Dominie are also in the picture.*

*Some of the veterans of 30 Squadron and others who flew to Dishforth on 1st July 1954 to take part in the ceremony of Presentation of the Standard to 30 Squadron (left to right): Maj. H. Petre DSO MC; Sir Thomas White KBE DCF (Australian High Commissioner); ACM Sir James Robb GCB KBE DSO DFC AFC; Gp. Capt. H. St.C. Smallwood OBE; Gp. Capt. Piper (Station Commander); Gwynne Hughes (adjutant in 1918); Wg. Cdr. J. Everidge (CO in 1918); Sqn. Ldr. Whitaker (CO); Lt. Col. S. Barnes (observer in 1918); R. K. Morris MC; R. C. Williams MC; Brig. S. Windsor MC; A. E. L. Skinner MC [Wg. Cdr. R. Evans].*

*Air Chief Marshal Sir James Robb carrying out an inspection at Dishforth on the occasion of the presentation of the 30 Squadron standard. The white webbing belts and rifle slings were clearly highly 'bulled' and boots laboriously polished, facts which Sir James no doubt realised. Where are these men, some very young at the time, now, one may wonder [Wg. Cdr. R. Evans].*

Marshal Sir James Robb GCB KBE DSO DFC AFC, who had been the squadron's Commanding Officer in 1924 and 1925 in Mesopotamia and had recently retired. The Rev. Canon A. S. Giles CBE MA QHC, Chaplain-in-Chief to the RAF, conducted the ceremony of consecration, supported by other chaplains, after which the Standard Bearer, Flg. Off. M. J. Rosenorn-Lanng, advanced to Sir James Robb, who formally presented the Standard to 30 Squadron and addressed the parade. The Standard Warrant Officer was Master Signaller F. W. Walker AFC, and its escort was provided by Flt. Sgts. F. R. H. Seal and R. C. T. Dorsett. A march-past followed, with music provided by No.1 Regional Band under the Director of Music, Flg. Off. H. E. Wheeler Mus. Bac. FRCO ARCM.

Fighter Command requirements later in July included carrying personnel of RAuxAF squadrons to summer camps in Germany and Malta and within the UK, while routine services continued. Towards the end of August the Imperial Defence College annual tour began with flights to Paris, Fassberg and Bückeburg, and a special flight to Klagenfurt was arranged to bring home the Foreign Secretary, the Rt. Hon. Mr. Anthony Eden, for talks on the troubles in Cyprus. This task was not without its problems, as the first aircraft, VX576, was struck by lightning and had to land at Frankfurt, where it was replaced by WJ504.

September 1954 was a much easier month, as the uplifts of RAuxAF squadrons had finished, which allowed three Valettas to take part in Battle of Britain air displays at Castle Bromwich, Hendon and West Malling. An unusual task was carried out by two aircraft, piloted by Flt. Sgt. Phillips and Flt. Sgt. Whiteight, which carried salvage equipment from Llandow to Guernsey for the recovery of a Sunderland flying-boat from Pembroke Dock which had sunk in St. Peter Port harbour after striking hidden rocks. Although efforts were made to lift the wreck it was eventually scrapped on site. In October, apart from maintaining all its training commitments and route services, 30 Squadron sent two Valettas carrying VIPs to Alexandria for the El Alamein memorial service and another one with BBC and press correspondents. During October, Sqn. Ldr. P. L. Whitaker DFC took over command of 30 Squadron from Sqn. Ldr. Peacock.

## Behind the Iron Curtain

The weekly UWV service to Warsaw was flown by five nominated crews during any four-month period, and provided transport to and from the Polish capital for members of the staff of the British Mission there, couriers and British subjects. Diplomatic mail escorted by Queen's Messengers and a variety of small freight ranging from car spares to Christmas food were also carried as required. Departures from Northolt were at 11.00 each Tuesday, the 30 Squadron Valetta having positioned there on the Monday afternoon, allowing the crew a chance to visit the fleshpots of London. The first touch-down was at Bückeburg, after which a course was set along the central corridor through the Russian Zone of Germany to Berlin (Templehof), a flight of about an hour with powerful beacons at each end to aid navigation. The UWV schedule was by no means hurried, as a night stop was made at Templehof in the airport hotel, which was in the terminal building. Next morning the take-off was set for 07.15 GMT, although the Polish border had to be crossed at Frankfurt-am-Oder at 07.30 to satisfy the Polish bureaucrats. From there, a six-mile wide corridor led to Warsaw, 250 nautical miles distant, with few navigational aids to help the pilot keep on course. Altitudes were set by the Polish authorities and often bore no relation to prevailing weather conditions. On touching down on the 6600-foot runway at Warsaw (Ocekie) the Valetta was escorted by security police in a jeep to a terminal building, which crews were not allowed to leave. All paperwork carried by the crew was scrutinised intently, including their Form 1250 identity cards, just in case an unapproved person might have the temerity to enter Poland! Take-off for the return flight was at 11.00 GMT on the same route, and although crews enjoyed going through the Iron Curtain they enjoyed returning to England even more! Sometimes a Russian navigator was on board to make sure that the aircraft stayed on course.

Special flights carrying VIPs were provided regularly by 30 Squadron, using the Valettas C.2 allocated for the purpose. One such trip on which LAC Franklin flew was to the Paris Air Show,

with Sir John Harding, the Governor of Cyprus, on board. It was a terrible day, with heavy rain pouring down. "My last sight of Paris was when we were taxiing away with the plane's steps stuck in the doorway and an officer covered in gold braid and tassels [was] laying on the tarmac after a vain attempt to help! For an encore the skipper said he would feather both props and fly by on the wipers! On the following Monday we went to Lisbon to inspect the Portuguese Air Force. What luxury, an American de Soto car and all flags flying, all for an LAC. On arriving home, the AQM was congratulated on the in-flight dinner. The VIPs said that the chicken could have been warmer but the soup was excellent. When we opened the tins just solid lumps lay in the bottom but with plenty of boiling water and a good bashing the result was, as the man said, excellent! We ran an aircraft behind the Iron Curtain to Warsaw regularly. Other routine jobs involved picking up casualties from Germany and dropping parachutists at Abingdon. There I saw Alan Ladd filming *The Red Beret*."

January 1955 began quietly, the only special flight of importance being the start of a protracted tour of Middle East airfields and staging posts by Air Chief Marshal Sir William Dickson, with Flt. Sgt. Whiteight in command. Bad weather prevailed in February, but in the middle of the month Flt. Lt. d'Oliveira made three consecutive special flights on the same route: Northolt–Wattisham–Heathrow–Northolt–Boscombe Down–Heathrow–Northolt–West Malling–Brussels–Scampton–Dishforth. These flights were for the benefit of the Australian Minister of Air and twelve Members of Parliament. The same captain was in charge of a Valetta which on 19th February carried the Secretary of State for Air from Manchester to Dishforth, Northolt, Brussels, Lydd (Ferryfield), and back to Northolt before returning to base next day.

A successful proving flight between Germany and Cyprus was carried out by Flt. Lt. Claxton on 28th March with the intention of increasing freight loads and shortening journey times. From Wildenrath, the Valetta flew to Treviso, Naples and Athens before landing at Nicosia, unloading, and returning via El Adem, Luqa and Istres on 2nd April. Another flight, on 20th March, was organised to bring home from Salzburg and Linz a number of soldiers who had been badly burnt in a fire during an exercise. The first of the summer season's squadron uplifts, began on 20th April with two trips between Honington and Wunstorf, and the final UXV schedule was completed on 30th April. Several flights for members of the Canadian National Defence College occupied the squadron during the month, but time was found to carry the RAF Rugby team to Barcelona and Biarritz.

Members of the Fighter Weapons School were customers of 30 Squadron on a long tour of the Middle East which started at Leconfield on 9th May 1955. After clearing customs at Lyneham, the Valetta, captained by Flg. Off. Daykin, flew to Luqa, Istres, back to Luqa, El Adem, Nicosia, Abu Sueir, Wadi Halfa, Khartoum, Aden, Khartoum again, Wadi Halfa again, Fayid, Amman, Habbaniya, Shaibah, back to Habbaniya, Nicosia, El Adem, Luqa, Istres and Lyneham before returning to Leconfield a month later. Quite a jolly by anybody's standards! On 31st May

*In 1953, Valettas of 30 Squadron took part in Operation 'Stage Coach', the transport of mail during a railway strike. This cartoon sums the task up nicely! [A. Dilke-Wing].*

*Valetta C.1 VL277 was used extensively by 30 Squadron, but in 1958 was relegated to use as ground instructional airframe 7476N*   *[P. Davis collection].*

three aircraft positioned at Northolt and one at Filton to take part in Operation *Stage Coach*, an emergency mail service which was to operate during a national railway strike. This operation formed a major part of 30 Squadron's activity until 17th June, and about 1,090,000 lbs. of mail were carried to major towns and cities in the UK in 500 hours flying time. Meanwhile, all other flights except the scheduled services were cancelled. Most weekends in July were occupied with Fighter Command airlifts within the UK, from Horsham St. Faith to Glasgow and from Aberdeen (Dyce) to Pembrey for example.

In August two Valettas were used in support of a team of Hunter aircraft from the Day Fighter Leaders School, West Raynham, which left on a tour of mid-southern Europe and the Middle East as far as Iraq. One of the other more interesting tasks was to fly the Secretary of State for Air from West Malling to Prestwick, Benbecula and Stornoway and back to Northolt on 29th August. Even more interesting to the author of this book is the fact that on 27th August he flew in VL277, one of three 30 Squadron Valettas which uplifted personnel of 604 Squadron RAuxAF from North Weald to Wunstorf for their summer camp. September was also a busy month for the squadron, mainly in bringing hung-over RAuxAF airmen back from Germany.

A new scheduled service from Northolt to Berlin (Gatow) via Wildenrath, known as UBV, began on 4th October 1955, and during that month special flights included the movement of Territorial Army personnel from Blackbushe to Guernsey, soldiers from Wiesbaden to Blackbushe and casualty evacuation from Gibraltar. VIP flights continued, using the faithful Valettas VX576 and WJ504.

Very bad weather in January 1956 hampered the squadron, only two VIP flights being possible. However, Flt. Lt. Bunn captained VL277 to Lagos in support of aircraft of the Queen's Flight which were on a month-long Royal tour of West Africa. The spring of 1956 became much more lively, and in May 30 Squadron had the honour of flying the Rt. Hon. Sir Winston Churchill and Lady Churchill to Germany, with Sqn. Ldr. Whitaker in command of the aircraft. On 7th May Flt. Lt. Langley carried the Secretary of State for Air in WJ504 to Warton to inspect the new English Electric P.1 fighter, which eventually developed into the Lightning.

In August there were signs of unusual activity and a programme of training for paratroop and supply-dropping at Abingdon began, continuing in September. A number of CLEs (Containers Light Equipment) were dropped at Watchfield and several sorties were flown to drop troops at Frensham Ponds, near Farnham in Surrey. A roller conveyor fitted to the floor of the Valetta and curved towards the rear door allowed panniers to be pushed out by hand as soon as a green light was seen. CLEs were fitted to the belly of the aircraft and were released by the navigator using Second World War type bomb release gear. As it was rarely used, most of the bomb release gear proved to be faulty. When power was switched on, all six CLEs could fall off, short of the DZ, instead of at intervals, or none of them disengaged, or they could drop late, among the

paratroops. The pilot had a jettison handle for emergencies, so a technique of only switching on the apparatus when crossing the DZ boundary was developed, when the release button was hit and the jettison handle was pulled in quick succession!

Among the pilots on 'B' Flight of 30 Squadron, which flew the VIP aircraft, was Flg. Off. (later Wg. Cdr.) Trevor Perry, who recalls the preparations being made to deal with possible conflict in the Middle East. "On 20th August we started to fly formation cross-countries for an hour, then an hour and a half, with timing to a simulated drop" he says. "I was crewed with the CO as formation leader, flying on 21st and 29th August by day and at night on 30th August. On 2nd September I returned to flying with the VIP Flight. We took Lt. Gen. Stockwell (who was to lead any operation) from Gutersloh to Algiers for talks with the French, then to Idris and Luqa before returning to Bovingdon. The Valetta's extra fuel tanks allowed us to fly direct from Gutersloh to Algiers in seven hours 25 minutes. That was the longest flight that I did in a Valetta. On the way back from Bovingdon to Dishforth, at about 2000 feet, the aircraft suddenly pitched nose down. The quartermaster, who was down the back cleaning and stacking crockery, hit the roof, together with the plates! About two months earlier, a Valetta did the same in the London Control Zone, with a mixed Parliamentary party on board. As a result, the Valetta C.2 had to carry two qualified pilots, one strapped in and able to disconnect the autopilot. For VIP flights, it was difficult to find another available pilot with A or B VIP category. In this case we had borrowed an examiner from the TCEU and he disconnected the autopilot p.d.q!" In an attempt to deal with this problem, in January 1957 Sperry (the makers of the autopilot) configured an aircraft for trials. It was then discovered that the autopilot servos to the elevators produced three times the power required.

One of the VIPs carried by 30 Squadron on 5th September was Air Chief Marshal Zhigarev, whose Soviet Air Force delegation was flown by Flt. Lt. D. A. Lawrenson from Northolt to Honington, Manby, Cranwell and Little Rissington. After dropping more paratroops in mid-September, Trevor Perry returned to VIP duty and on 26th and 27th September went to Paris as back-up to the Queen's Flight aircraft carrying Sir Anthony Eden for talks with his French opposite number. While waiting at Le Bourget until Sir Anthony and his staff arrived, the 30 Squadron crew witnessed a panic when a BEA Elizabethan arrived carrying a VIP who was said to be injured. It transpired that the VIP was Liberace, the pianist, who had been stung by a bee!

It was during September 1956 that the first personnel, two navigators, were posted to Abingdon for conversion to the Beverley aircraft with which 30 Squadron was scheduled to re-equip. Sqn. Ldr. P. G. Coulson DFC MBE also arrived, to take over from Sqn. Ldr. Whitaker as CO of 30 Squadron. In October four special flights to Vienna carried food and medical supplies, and several VIP flights were made, one of them classified as 'Secret', possibly in connection with the troubles developing between Israel and Egypt.

## The Suez campaign

In July 1956, the President of Egypt, Col. Nasser, decided to nationalise the Suez Canal Company, in which Great Britain and France owned a large proportion of the shares. The two countries immediately protested and threatened military action, Britain being particularly concerned, as three quarters of the nation's oil supplies were shipped through the canal. Prime Minister at the time was Sir Anthony Eden, whose government declared a State of Emergency, calling up reservists, while Transport Command scheduled services were suspended and Bomber Command squadrons were placed on standby. Israel decided to take action against Egypt, which had provoked Israel in a number of ways since the State was created. On 30th October Britain and France, fearing that any war between Egypt and Israel might damage the canal, issued an ultimatum to both countries, ordering them to withdraw to positions ten miles from the canal and to allow British and French troops to occupy Port Said, Ismailia and Suez in accordance with a treaty drawn up two years earlier. While Israel concurred at once, Egypt blatantly ignored the order. RAF and Armée de l'Air aircraft then attacked Egyptian airfields, while Israeli forces routed the Egyptian army in Sinai and advanced toward the Suez Canal. At this point, the United nations Security Council requested a cease-fire, to which Israel agreed, but Col. Nasser's response was to sink ships in the canal to block it as a waterway.

On 31st October ten aircraft and crews left Dishforth for Nicosia in Cyprus to become part of an Air Transport Task Force, together with two MEAF-based Valetta squadrons, 70 Squadron's Hastings from Akrotiri and detachments of 99 and 511 Squadrons, also with Hastings aircraft. For Operation *Musketeer*, all these aircraft were hurriedly painted with black and yellow stripes on wings and fuselages, similar to the markings on aircraft which took part in the D-Day landings. This armada began to take off from Cyprus airfields at dawn on 5th November, led by a Valetta captained by Sqn. Ldr. Delaney of 114 Squadron. Each Valetta carried twenty paratroops, while the Hastings carried heavy equipment. The DZ was at Gamil airfield, Port Said, which was situated on a strip of land about half a mile wide with the sea on the north and marshes of Lake Manzala on the south. Fighter support

was provided by aircraft of the Fleet Air Arm, which put a stop to any retaliation by Egyptian ground gunners, but when the FAA departed a nasty barrage of fire was put up. Nevertheless, all the troops were dropped on the DZ with few injuries. Next day Valettas began to land on the recently-cleared airfield to deliver reinforcements, and continued to do so until 17th December. By the time they returned to Dishforth, 30 Squadron crews had flown 167 sorties between Nicosia and Gamil.

A first-hand account of the short-lived Suez campaign is provided by Trevor Perry, who as a VIP pilot was not included in the original list of personnel of the detachment. However, when on 30th October the C-in-C Transport Command decided that a maximum effort would be staged and only one VIP crew would remain at Dishforth, he was included. "The new CO was not yet fully qualified, but was to fly with the OC 'A' Flight, Flt. Lt. Macleod, and I joined them as formation leader" he recalls. "Departure was set for 01.15 on 31st October. I had to rush around collecting maps, revolver (a .38 Smith & Wesson), parachute and anti-flak garments. The parachutes would be of limited use, and we used the anti-flak garments to cover the cockpit floor. We took our ground crews with us. 01.15 is not a good time to start work! Work really began two hours before, and included flight planning, filing the plan and checking the aircraft. We had to stage through Lyneham for customs and fuel and Istres for refuelling, before arriving at Luqa at 13.30. The rest of the detachment followed, with about thirty minutes between each aircraft. Our task at Luqa was to keep the transit bar open until the next crew arrived. Take-off from Luqa was at 03.00, with a refuelling stop at El Adem, to arrive at Nicosia at 10.30." Once on the ground, commissioned crews were taken by bus to the Dome Hotel in Kyrenia, with armed escorts due to the activities of EOKA terrorists, but NCO air and ground crews remained at RAF Nicosia, which was extremely crowded. "From our arrival on 1st November to 4th November it was R & R in comparative luxury, except for the odd crew needed to fly air tests" says Trevor Perry. "On 4th November we were warned for the operation, to leave the hotel at about 20.00 by escorted convoy. We arrived at the aircraft at 22.00 to find that stripes had been painted on wings and fuselage. Our paratroops had been there since 17.00, fitting 'chutes. We went to a main briefing, then to specialist

*Roughly-applied black and yellow stripes on this 30 Squadron Valetta indicate its use in the Suez Campaign of 1956. This photo was taken on 7th November at El Gamil, with (left to right) Commandant Labachine, commanding the French air element, 'Dinger' Bell, Flt. Lt. Bob Andrews (navigator) and Flt. Sgt. Lewis (signaller)*                                                    *[Bell].*

briefings. The Escape & Evasion briefing was confusing about where to go if shot down on and and if [shot down] at sea where to be picked up by submarine. There was no submarine! Take-off was for 05.00 on 5th November, to drop at about 07.00, in daylight, after the ground attack [aircraft] had suppressed the ground forces. There was to be radio silence. The Cyprus Valettas would drop first, followed by the UK Valettas and then the Hastings. After take-off we went into a long climbing orbit to form up and gain height to cross the mountains. I went up and down into the astrodome giving a running commentary on the formation assembly. We departed without our No.3 (Flt. Lt. Andrews), thinking that that was quite good. After coasting out, the navigation timing became my main concern as we descended to transit [level] at 2000 feet. Another check in the dawn light showed that somehow No.3 was with us on station. We were to coast in about fifteen miles west of Port Said at a little headland and then turn east for the drop. As we approached the coast, we descended to about 1000 feet and caught sight of the lead formation and the ground attack fighters. We slotted in behind the lead and descended towards the approach point. The paratroops had been going through their checks for some time. We normally dropped at 800 feet, but I think we were to drop at 500 feet. Port Said (Gamil) airfield was the drop zone, with the first part for the heavy stores containers (our CLEs and the Hastings very large containers), followed by a sterile area and then the paratroop dropping area."

So far, so good. "As we approached the drop" says Trevor, "there was evidence of ground attack damage and the control tower seemed to be on fire. Streams of men in white galabias were leaving the airfield towards the beach. Short of the DZ were stores containers from early releases from the lead formation. After our drop it was hard to port and full power and low. As we crossed the coast there were splashes in the water from tanks on the beach which were optimistically firing [at us]. Over to the east we could see the French Noratlases heading back to Cyprus after their drop. Only one aircraft was damaged. Flt. Lt. Bell (he may have been from the OCU) did not complete his drop and went round again. His aircraft got a bullet hole on the second run, after the Hastings had dropped. There were very few awards; I believe Pete Coulson was awarded the OBE for planning, while Dinger Bell and our signaller were Mentioned in Despatches. We were back at Nicosia by 09.00 for debriefing and wind-down, then went back to Kyrenia."

Another officer, a QFI with 242 OCU who had been loaned to take part in the Suez operation, recalls the magificent work of the ground crews. "In spite to the conditions they worked all hours and never once failed to produce the aircraft on time, including a 100% on the day of the operation. On their own initiative they organised a spare aircraft, with engines running, positioned to the side of the queue of squadron aircraft waiting to take off, together with a tractor plus towing arm, and fitters to change over the CLE containers. Pilots had been briefed that should any last-minute unserviceabilities arise, to flash their landing lights and they would be pulled out of line, replaced and reloaded within minutes. They [the ground crews] maintained this sort of enthusiasm without respite throughout the detachment."

After that resupply was the task for 30 Squadron and the others. Trevor Perry believes that his aircraft was the first to land at Gamil, on 7th November, when a sailor who had fallen from a ladder had to be airlifted. This landing was made after dark, at 18.00, and the Valetta was on the ground for just twenty minutes. For 30 Squadron crews there was no more flying until 16th November, giving them the opportunity for a spell of what is officially referred to as Rest & Relaxation but which in this case turned out to be a test of stamina! A typical day consisted of a morning trip to the NAAFI in Kyrenia to stock up with beer, followed by visits to the Harbour Club and the hotel bar and a good deal of lazing around. Officers and NCOs from the Parachute Regiment, who had been recovered from Suez, came to Kyrenia for an evening party, and it was learnt that one paratrooper had been hit by small arms fire during his descent and had to release his personal kit container. On landing, he found that his rifle was bent, so he used it as a club until being rearmed! Resupply sorties to Gamil then began, and were flown on 16th, 19th, 22nd, 24th and 26th November. On the last of these, Trevor Perry's aircraft was carrying a young reporter, Robin Day, but had to return to Nicosia with an engine fault. "Robin Day looked most uncomfortable" says Trevor "and when we took off again an hour later he was not with us!"

Normal services were resumed in January 1957, when nine scheduled services UGV and UWV and eight special flights, all but one with an overseas element, were flown. By now the only VIP Valetta C.2 in service with 30 Squadron was VX576, which in February was used only twice, piloted by Flt. Lt. D. A. Lawrenson on both occasions. In March VX576 was flown by Flt. Lt. G. Garforth DFC between Northolt and Odiham and from Northolt to Chivenor, both times with Lt. Gen. Rubio, the C-in-C of the Spanish Air Guard, on board. It appears that a detachment was maintained at Northolt for VIP flights at this time, Dishforth being somewhat distant from where the passengers wanted to fly.

## The Valetta is phased out

The Valetta's days were now numbered, and conversion to the four-engined Blackburn Beverley heavy freight aircraft was about to begin. On 8th April 1957 six pilots of 30 Squadron travelled to Bristol Aeroplane Co. at Filton, presumably to inspect the Bristol Centaurus engines which powered the Beverley. At the same time, six signallers were sent to Abingdon for a conversion course, and six navigators began converting on 27th April. While the strength of the squadron was thus diminished, only four scheduled flights were made, all in VL277, and two VIP flights carrying the CAS, Air Chief Marshal Sir Dermot Boyle, both using VX576.

By the end of May the first phase of the conversion programme had been completed. A large number of personnel had enjoyed a visit to the Blackburn Aircraft factory at Brough in Yorkshire to see the Beverleys under construction, each man being given a handsome propelling pencil as a souvenir. Another visit, which proved very popular with most of the squadron, was to John Smith's Brewery at Tadcaster! No route flying took place in May, but was recommenced in June.

On 3rd June the CO, Sqn. Ldr. P. G. Coulson AFC, and six other pilots, went to Bristol to begin conversion to the Beverley. While he was absent, the CO was awarded the OBE in recognition of distinguished services in the Near East between October and December 1956, and at the same time Flg. Off. A. S. Douglas was Mentioned In Despatches and Flt. Sgt. H. F. Krombach and Sgt. R. W. Hewett received the C-in-C's Commendation. All these awards were Gazetted on 13th June 1957.

Progress towards conversion to the Beverley was slowing in July due to a lack of aircraft for the second phase of the course, a situation aggravated in August by the effects of an uprising in Oman which prompted the loan of the newly-arrived Beverleys to other units. The faithful Valettas were still in use on an occasional scheduled service and VIP flights, usually with Flt. Lt. Lawrenson at the controls. By the end of October all crews had completed their Beverley conversion course, allowing Transport Support exercises to begin in November.

In January 1958 30 Squadron's VIP Flight was disbanded, and the final scheduled service, UGB006, was flown on 19th January by Flt. Lt. G. Garforth. Thus ended the squadron's busy and highly effective period of flying the Valetta, but the newly-qualified crews had much to look forward to in flying their new aircraft.

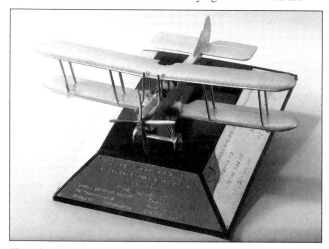

*This silver model of a BE.2c aircraft was presented to 30 Squadron at Dishforth by members of the squadron who had served in the First World War [Wg. Cdr. R. Evans].*

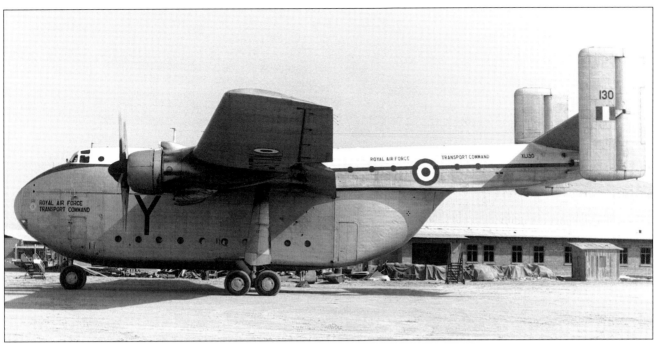

*Beverley XL130 [Y] at an unrecorded location*                    *[R. C. Sturtivant collection].*

# Chapter 10: The Beverley era

A very different aircraft from any type yet flown by 30 Squadron, the Blackburn Beverley was a somewhat unusual-looking high-wing machine with a fixed undercarriage. Originally designed by General Aircraft as the GA.60 Universal Transport, the Beverley was at the time the largest aircraft to enter service with the RAF and the first to be designed specifically to drop heavy army equipment through removable rear loading doors. Its unique features included a payload of 94 troops or 70 paratroops or 45,000lbs. of freight, which could be carried over a radius of action of 230 miles, although the Beverley's maximum range was 1300 miles. Powered by four Bristol Centaurus 173 engines, it cruised at 173 mph but could attain 238 mph and had a service ceiling of 16,000 feet. In size it boasted a wing span of 162 feet, a length of 99 feet five inches and a height of 38 feet nine inches. A crew of four kept the Beverley in the air.

Still under the command of Sqn. Ldr. P. G. Coulson AFC MBE, 30 Squadron crews had converted from the Valetta over a period of time after the first three aircraft arrived at Dishforth in April 1957. All crews had completed the conversion course by October and then began tactical exercises with the new aircraft. By now they were no longer involved in VIP flights, and only occasionally flew scheduled services. On 15th November the first crew to take the Beverley overseas left for Aden (Khormaksar) for a short detachment, other crews following later. Sadly, while on detachment Beverley XH118 crashed on landing at Beihan on 27th February 1958 after both engines on one side had failed at altitude. This mishap resulted in the death of the signaller, Sgt. W. Rose, and minor injuries to Flg. Off. A. Douglas, Flt. Lt. J. Lister, Sgt. S. Justin and Sgt. J. Whittaker. Passengers on board escaped unhurt, but the aircraft was written off.

During the second half of April 1958, 30 Squadron was engaged on Operation *Quickstep II*, which entailed transporting troops from Nairobi (Eastleigh) to Khormaksar, a task in which all available aircraft and crews took part. This operation continued into May, with the ultimate objective, it was believed, of evacuating British personnel and families from Lebanon, where political tension was strong at the time. However, in addition to *Quickstep II* time was found for Exercise *Sunspot*, a routine airlift of Bomber Command personnel. *Quickstep II* came to a climax in the middle of June, when an initial 1000 troops, and then a further 6000, had to be flown from the UK to Cyprus, the Beverley crews 'slipping' at Luqa in Malta. In view of this major commitment, the squadron's periodic detachment to Abingdon for training with the army came to a premature end on 12th June.

## More trouble in the Middle East

Restlessness in the Middle East continued, and in July a military coup in Iraq and increased tension in Jordan resulted in all 30 Squadron crews being detached to Cyprus. From there several uplifts of troops were made to Amman, the capital of Jordan. The situation had improved by August, although a token transport force was maintained at Nicosia, crews spending an average of six weeks there and no doubt making the most of the opportunity. In September the tensions had eased to the point when all detached crews were brought back to Dishforth and the squadron settled down to flying routine schedules.

However, no sooner had the crews become accustomed to the routine when they were again mobilised. On 22nd October 1958 four crews and three Beverleys were sent to Nicosia, with eight Beverley crews from Abingdon, to help 70 Squadron's Hastings aircraft evacuate troops and equipment of 16 Independent Parachute Regt. from Amman. After a period of planning and replanning and discussion with the nations concerned, agreement was reached and UN observers were posted at Amman and Nicosia. In order to check routes and timings, Flt. Lt. W. MacLeod and his crew flew a 'pathfinder' aircraft on the day before the start of the operation. The schedules were very precise, and the timing, route and altitudes imposed called for careful navigation. Aircraft serviceability was very good, and the operation was completed ahead of schedule without incident. The Beverley performed extremely well and proved that given a chance to carry out its designated tasks it was an outstanding aircraft. Although crews had to climb out of bed at 02.00 each day their morale remained high, and when they returned to Dishforth on 31st October they had the feeling, for once, of a job well done. A final task was to carry two Arab horses which had been presented to Her Majesty the Queen by King Hussein of Jordan, to Abingdon, where the Beverley's arrival was televised.

In November 1958 Sqn. Ldr. Coulson left to take up an appointment involving guided weapons and was replaced as CO by Sqn. Ldr. E. J. Churchill AFC. The outgoing CO was remembered for his good example and inspiration, which created a happy and willing spirit among the personnel. Sqn. Ldr. Churchill, although not a newcomer to Transport Command, came to 30 Squadron from an administrative position at 7 School of Recruit Training at Bridgnorth. On arrival at Dishforth he was immediately thrust into a heavy trooping commitment, with little time to acclimatise himself. One officer who left in November was Flt. Lt. Rayson, one

*Yes, it's still there! Visual inspection of Beverley XL152, which spent its whole working life with 30 Squadron.*

of the squadron's all-time best athletes and keenest men, who took up a highly desirable posting with the Royal Canadian Air Force.

At Khormaksar, meanwhile, Flt. Lt. K. Smale and his crew enjoyed a protracted detachment, with plenty of time in the air. An airlift of soldiers from Aden to Nairobi occupied them for some time, and they also visited two desert airstrips within the Sultanate of Oman, at Azeiba, near Muscat, and Firq, in the Nizwa area.

December's weather was poor, and the routine Transport Support detachment to Abingdon was curtailed, although in the second week a number of heavy drops were made and paratrooping sorties flown. At Khormaksar the detached crew was now that of Flt. Lt. Andrusikiewicz, and on 4 December a tragedy occurred there when Flg. Off. D. A. P. Mayoux fell from the open rear doors of a Beverley while carrying out a pre-flight inspection. He was taken to Steamer Point hospital, where he died a few hours later.

January 1959 proved to be the most settled month for a considerable time, allowing crews to meet new personnel, some of whom had appeared on the squadron just before being sent off to take part in the recent operations. Three Beverleys were provided to take part in Exercise *White Christmas*, a large-scale support exercise from Abingdon which involved dropping paratroops in the Stanford Battle Area near Thetford. In February fog hampered the squadron's activities somewhat and there was little improvement in March. Two aircraft, though, were sent to Cyprus to assist in bringing helicopters and Pioneer aircraft back to the UK, while Flt.

*The swimming pool at RAF Eastleigh.*

Lt. Macleod flew XH124 to the French paratrooping school at Pau in the Pyrenees for a static demonstration.

Close cooperation with the army continued, and on 8th May one aircraft carried 56 troops to Blackbushe after a local exercise. Although squadron records reveal nothing, it is possible that the airstrip known as Starve Acre, in the military exercise area of Hawley Common and only two miles from Blackbushe airfield, was used. At the end of May two Beverleys were used for support duties and 572 paratroops jumped out of them. June was a Transport Support month at Abingdon, during which 22 heavy platforms and 1926 troops were dropped, but one aircraft was withdrawn from this task to carry out a shuttle service between Luqa and Tripoli (Idris). The month's highlight, however, was the success of Flt. Lt. Garforth and Flg. Off. Douglas and their crews in winning the Lord Trophy for the first time. Flying as navigators during the contest were Master Nav. Gunn and Flt. Lt. Pierson.

In July 1959 the monthly eighteen-day route task to Singapore (Changi) was cancelled, much to the disappointment of the crews. It was not until 16th September, when five aircraft were detached to Vaernes in Norway for Exercise *Bare Frost*, a major NATO exercise which lasted until 2nd October, that anything more than routine flying was carried out. Then came news of a move to sunnier surroundings in Kenya for 30 Squadron. The move was to take place during the first two weeks of November, prior to which many members of the squadron were posted to Beverley squadrons at Abingdon and replaced by others from Abingdon or from 242 OCU. A change of command also took place, the new CO being Sqn. Ldr. T. C. Waugh DFC. Before the move, a number of special flights were made to north Africa to uplift fighter squadrons under Exercise *Sambar*.

## Life in Kenya

Between 2nd and 12th November 1959, 30 Squadron successfully moved to its new base at Eastleigh, Nairobi. Due to the untimely death of Flg. Off. D. G. K. Longman, a navigator, who took his own life a few days before the move, the illness of an engineer and the non-arrival of three people who were travelling with their wives, the squadron was not at full strength. Little flying was done until 24th November, when the squadron took part in Exercise *Summer Flight III*, an air mobility and ground loading training exercise for 24 Infantry Brigade Group.

Having settled down at Eastleigh, the squadron found that aircraft unserviceability was proving a problem. However, three special flights to Aden were made in order to provide crews with experience of operating the Beverley from desert airstrips in the Aden Protectorate, and another special flight was to Entebbe in Uganda. In January 1960 a Beverley was sent each week to Aden or Bahrain. One of them was detained at Sharjah on 5th January to fly 95 tons of equipment and supplies to an army camp at Ibri in Oman, a task which was carried out in eight trips over five days. In command of this aircraft was Flt. Lt. G. J. Calvert DFC, who then took the Beverley to Aden before returning to Eastleigh on 12th January.

The sixth Beverley for the squadron arrived at Eastleigh on 5th February after being delayed at El Adem with engine trouble. Flights to Aden and Bahrain continued on a routine basis, but at the end of the month news of a damaging cyclone in Mauritius was received, and three crews then stood by in case it became necessary to fly supplies to the island. On 3rd March Flg. Off. F. G. Welch and crew took off from Nairobi Airport for Mauritius as Spec.06, but next day suffered an engine failure and landed at Ivato in Madagascar. Another Beverley was then earmarked to fulfil the commitment or to fly out a repair team as Spec.07, and was eventually flown to Mauritius by Flt. Lt. Calvert's crew. On 5th March Spec.06 became serviceable and left Ivato for Mauritius, returning to Eastleigh next day. March had not been a good month for the squadron, as the murram runway at Eastleigh was out of service for several days and various technical snags had cropped up.

Exercise *Firebird I* was held on 11th April 1960, and involved the movement of a large number of troops and equipment from Nairobi to Embakasi, its success prompting a letter of appreciation from East Africa Command. Earlier in the month, Flt. Lt. A. P. Brown had, for reasons unknown, been marooned on the side of a mountain at Arusha. As he had a Sarah unit, it was hoped that a Pembroke aircraft could be homed to his position, but the

*Beverleys of 30 Squadron at Dishforth about to leave for Eastleigh*     [*Norman Wood via Paddy Porter*].

*The technical area at RAF Eastleigh, Nairobi, with the control tower, signals square and three hangars prominent, but no aircraft visible except a Venom between the hangars.*

Pembroke crew had no success, unlike a herd of buffalo which found him easily, much to his discomfort!

May 1960 was the most successful since the squadron moved to Kenya. Two of the Beverleys and crews were placed on twelve-hour standby on 2nd May, with the remainder of the squadron on 48 hours notice, in case trouble anticipated in Somalia when that country gained independence flared up. Luckily nothing untoward occurred and the squadron stood down on 13th May. While this operation, which had been named *Tomahawk*, was awaited, Flt. Lt. G. D. Dorricot flew an aircraft carrying the band of the King's Regiment to Bulawayo on 10th May so that they could play at the

opening of the Kariba Dam by Her Majesty the Queen Mother. Another Beverley went to Aden on 13th May with Flt. Lt. Moran at the controls, carrying the advance party of 24 Brigade to preposition for Exercise *Egress*, the major military exercise in East Africa, which began on 18th May. Staged in two phases, *Egress* involved moving large numbers of men and equipment from Nairobi to Aden and back again. Originally, it was planned that Britannia aircraft would carry the men while Beverleys took the equipment, but during the outbound phase the Britannias soon became unserviceable and Beverleys had to carry troops, which involved several extra sorties by 30 Squadron. In consequence,

*The officers' mess at RAF Eastleigh.*

ground and air crews had to work very long hours, but on completion of the exercise it was felt that an excess of work made a pleasant change. May ended with a dramatic engine fire in a Beverley flown by Flt. Lt. W. Howell, who was about to force-land in the bush when the fire went out, allowing him to land safely at Embakasi.

During June a hundred troops of the Parachute Regt. were flown from Nairobi to Cyprus and each man jumped three times from a Beverley onto a DZ 5000 feet above sea level, with, as the squadron diarist wrote, ". . . only the normal number of injuries." A herd of buffalo which wandered onto the touch-down area did not cause any great problems. Beverleys were often flown to airstrips in the desert of Arabia and in the bush of East Africa, and time was spent by 30 Squadron crews in making themselves familiar with such out-of-the-way places. On 18th June Flt. Lt. Howell spent three days in charge of a Beverley when checking airstrips in Uganda, and some photographs of angry elephants were taken to prove it! Towards the end of the month Flt. Lt. Calvert flew to Abingdon to take part in the Lord Trophy on 30th May, but this time 30 Squadron only came second to 84 Squadron.

For some time a small group of bandits had been causing mayhem in north-eastern Uganda and had killed a number of native people. In the second week of June they ambushed a police patrol and killed a European Inspector. This prompted a request from the Uganda Police for RAF help, and three Beverleys of 30 squadron were sent to Jinja, on the north shore of Lake Victoria. A Company of King's African Rifles and two Land Rovers were flown to Moroto, a grass airstrip near the scene of the outrage. What happened then is not recorded, but one can assume that order was restored.

*Worried-looking ground crewmen studying a copy of 'The Yorkshire Post' in which news of a one-day rail strike in the UK is headlined.*

July 1960 was another active month for 30 Squadron, which was brought to a state of readiness during the second half of the month. Before that, Flg. Off. D. G. M. Wright had flown a Beverley to Thornhill in what was then Southern Rhodesia on 3rd July to carry freight and some of the aircrew of 8 Squadron, which was detached from Aden to Thornhill and was flying Hunters. Four days later Flg. Off. Welch flew a Beverley to Nicosia to take part in Exercise *Desert Hawk*. The venue for this exercise, originally Libya, had been altered at the last minute as the army had failed to obtain permission from the Libyan government. Two Land Rovers were dropped from the Beverley, but the parachute of one failed to open and the vehicle crashed and burnt out, while the other one fell upside down and was badly damaged. The Beverley returned via Akrotiri, where an engine for a Canberra was uplifted and flown to El Adem. On the way back to Eastleigh an oil leak on one engine developed and the captain diverted to Entebbe airport, where the civilian authorities were most helpful and even provided a three-course meal at 03.00 hours.

The Belgian Congo became independent on 30th June 1960, prompting severe rioting among Africans and an exodus of Europeans. Beverleys of 30 Squadron helped evacuate refugees from Entebbe and Stanleyville to Nairobi in four sorties, two from each place. However, one aircraft returned empty, as a deadline for take-off from Stanleyville passed before the refugees arrived at the airport.

Little of significance occurred during August, and in September schedules were reduced and hours flown fell short of normal. One interesting trip was carried out by Flt. Lt. A. T. Scorey and his crew, who flew to Wajir in the Northern Territories with a load of fuel for a Pembroke aircraft which was staging through from Aden to Nairobi. An initial attempt to land was baulked by a giraffe on the runway, and when a second attempt was made two giraffes were seen. Flt. Lt. Scorey decided to ignore them, and they left the airstrip in a hurry when reverse thrust was selected! The Trucial States were the destination for Flt. Lt. Calvert, who flew repair equipment to Buraimi, a small desert airstrip south of Sharjah, where a Pembroke had force-landed. During the second of the two sorties a strong sandstorm blew up. On 12th September a Beverley was flown to Nakuru so that army personnel could practice loading and off-loading of Land Rovers and trailers. Other vehicles carried by the Beverleys included a Tasker trailer which had to go to Karachi on 16th September.

Morale at this time was both high and low – high because the squadron was visited on 23rd September by Admiral of the Fleet the Rt. Hon. Earl Mountbatten of Burma KG PC GCB GCSI GCIE GCVO DSO, Chief of the Defence Staff, who inspected three crews and their aircraft, and low because a letter was received from Air Ministry via British Forces Aden Protectorate stating that it was not official policy to short-tour co-pilots on overseas tours for Captains' courses in the UK.

30 Squadron's operational commitment increased in October 1960, when the scheduled service to Bahrain via Aden was reintroduced, resulting in two or three Beverleys being on the route at any time. On 1st October Flt. Lt. D. R. V. Molloy was flying Beverley XH119 between Aden and Nairobi when an engine failed, and he therefore diverted to Hargeisha. There the crew stayed overnight, much to the delight of the Somali Scouts who provided hospitality. A servicing party was quickly flown to Hargeisha and the faulty engine was serviceable within two and a half hours of their arrival. More checks on rough up-country airstrips took place in October, when Sqn. Ldr. Waugh flew to Entebbe before visiting strips at Gulu, Soroti and Murchison Falls, where two large bull elephants decided to block the airstrip until the Beverley was at 300 feet above the ground on finals, when they lumbered off.

In November the aircraft of 84 Squadron all went unserviceable, placing a great load on the shoulders of 30 Squadron personnel, who had to take over some tasks. These included the ferrying of an engine to Mauripur for a Shackleton aircraft and airbags to Entebbe to lift a Boeing 707 of South African Airways which had crash-landed there. These extra tasks completed, 30 Squadron sent three Beverleys to Sharjah via Khormaksar and Salalah on 5th December to take part in Exercise *Warden*, carrying ground crews of 30 and 208 Squadrons. During the exercise 30 Squadron flew seven sorties from Bahrain to Sharjah. This was followed by Exercise *Firebird II*, which involved five uplifts from Nakuru to Eastleigh. More pleasurable, perhaps, was Operation *Father Christmas*, which took place on 23rd December and involved dropping 6743 lbs. of seasonal food and drink by parachute to a detachment of the King's African Rifles at Wajir. The operation went so smoothly that not a single egg was broken. Just after Christmas Operation *Catechism* took place, with the object of positioning troops at Jinja in Uganda in anticipation of disturbances after an election, when Buganda stated that it would secede from Uganda.

Further exercises took place in January 1961, one of them named *Placard* being something of a washout. Bahrain and Sharjah were to be used by the squadron, but when more rain fell in that area in two days than in a normal five-year period the exercise did not proceed as planned. However, a new airfield at Das Island was opened up to Beverleys and a spare engine for a marooned Pembroke aircraft was flown in. In February a number of flights were made to rough airstrips in the Aden Protectorate, under the guidance of 84 Squadron, so that 30 Squadron crews could practice the techniques involved.

## Not enough water . . .

During March 1961, Kenya suffered the worst drought since 1933, and 30 Squadron was tasked to fly maize, dried milk and biltong (sun-dried meat) to the remoter areas for the native population. The first sortie was made by Flt. Lt. Dorricott and his crew, who at Oropoi free-dropped food in specially-made sacks from a height of fifty feet before landing at Todenyang to pick up further supplies. Referred to as Exercise *Oliver*, the six such trips made by 23rd March provided a great deal of sustenance to the local people and as a result the RAF received well-deserved publicity in the East African newspapers and on radio. Meanwhile, trooping flights and military supply drops in and around Kenya continued as required by local army commanders, and transportation was provided to and from Nicosia for the ground crews of 208 Squadron for Exercise *Sweet Orange*.

Disturbance among the population of Zanzibar early in June 1961 gave 30 Squadron the task of carrying troops of the King's African Rifles to the island. Seven crews were involved, three of them landing at Pemba, the Beverleys being the largest aircraft to have touched down there. More serious trouble was brewing in the Persian Gulf, where Iraq was claiming sovereignty over Kuwait. On 29 June the whole squadron was placed on standby for possible intervention, and four Beverleys set off for Bahrain via Khormaksar. From 1st to 26th July 1961 the whole squadron operated from Bahrain, flying large quantities of men, equipment and supplies into the new, unfinished, airport at Kuwait. No approach or landing aids were available, and for most of the first two weeks sandstorms reduced visibility to 800 yards or less. The only incident during the operation, named Exercise *Vantage*, was

*A view from the astrodome of a 30 Squadron Beverley at Eastleigh in August 1961. Note the Hunters in the background   [Brian Webb via Paddy Porter].*

when Flt. Lt. R. J. Holloway's aircraft suffered an engine failure, but a successful landing at Bahrain followed. Although two crews had returned to Eastleigh, the detachment to Bahrain continued in August, and thirteen sorties were flown to Kuwait. Continuation training was also carried out at Bahrain.

September and October 1961 followed much the same pattern, flying being largely between Bahrain and Kuwait and a few positioning flights. On 25th October, however, a new regular service was initiated, from Eastleigh to Masirah and Sharjah, with a night-stop before returning by the same route. On the last day of October the squadron said goodbye to Sqn. Ldr. T. C. Waugh, who left the RAF to become a Second Officer on the Dakotas of East African Airways. He was replaced by Sqn. Ldr. C. R. Evans, although he and his family did not arrive until 20th December. He remembers the occasion well. "As I got off the aircraft I was met by an old friend, Wg. Cdr. Don Taylor, the Wg. Cdr. Flying at Eastleigh, who told me that I had to fly to Bahrain in a couple of days' time to take over the Beverley detachment there. With friends like that, who wants enemies? My wife was not best pleased, as I had no time to find her a car before I left for Bahrain. My detachment [there], the first of many such detachments, lasted four weeks, and I was away from Kenya for Christmas and New Year." However, while in Bahrain 'Dicky' Evans became aware of some of the problems being experienced by squadron personnel on detachment.

## . . . and too much

Early in November severe flooding in Kenya created a further demand for 30 Squadron's services, which began on 16th November and continued unabated until the end of the month. Rainfall was far in excess of the usual amount, and roads and railways were soon out of action. As the rain had made Eastleigh runway unsuitable for Beverleys, all relief operations were carried out from Nairobi Airport, where an operations room was set up, with a radio link to Eastleigh and to the civilian flood operations centre in the city. Wishing to see a supply drop, the Governor of Kenya, Sir Patrick Renison KMG, flew in Flg. Off. D. G. Wright's Beverley and, entering into the spirit of the occasion, helped dispatchers of 16 Company RASC in the arduous job of pushing the sacks of maize out of the aircraft. Also taking part in the relief work were four Beverleys and four Sycamore helicopters specially flown out from England. In all, 30 Squadron dropped 591 tons of food that month.

Many of the tasks tackled by 30 Squadron in December 1961 were also from Nairobi Airport, as Eastleigh's runway was still out of use. Among the work carried out before Christmas was the transport of personnel of 208 Squadron to Bahrain via Khormaksar, and a few flood relief sorties were flown. These continued in January 1962, and included some aid to areas of Tanganyika which were now also feeling the effects of considerable rains. Prominent in this task was Flg. Off. Wright and his crew, the ground crew who took part and the air dispatchers of the RASC, all of whom worked very hard while on detachment at Dar-es-Salaam with Beverley XH122. In return they were entertained in a grand manner by the Government of newly independent Tanganyika.

*Beverleys of 30 Squadron at Eastleigh in October 1961, with a wingless Hastings in the background* [Wg. Cdr. R. Evans].

Exercise *Foamex II* began on 5th January with a reconnaissance of Yas Island by Sqn. Ldr. Evans. Lying just off the coast of Qatar, Yas Island was to be used for a combined landing exercise by sea and air, with Bahrain-based 2nd Bn. of the Parachute Regt. taking part.

The oldest African employee at Eastleigh, Mayo Amotha, who had worked for the RAF for fifteen years, was taken aloft by 30

*A Beverley of 30 Squadron loaded and ready to carry out yet another supply-dropping mission over Tanganyika during flood relief operations. The officer is Wg. Cdr. Evans, and on the right is the Prime Minister of Tanganyika.*

Squadron on 12th January in the Beverley which dropped the 5,000,000th pound of food to malnourished citizens. At Eastleigh on 21st January a VIP visitor was HRH the Duke of Gloucester, who watched 30 and 21 Squadrons make demonstration supply drops while Hunters of 208 Squadron gave a display. The whole process was repeated at Gil Gil next day.

On 15th January the CO left Bahrain in XM107 bound for Kenya, and very quickly experienced the unreliability of the Centaurus 173 engines fitted to the Beverley. "I had an engine failure on the way into Salalah and after a three-engine landing had to wait there for an engine change," he recalls. "We arrived back at Eastleigh on 19th January. The Centaurus 173 engine was notoriously unreliable in the Middle East, particularly on aircraft based at Aden. The parking area at Khormaksar was adjacent to a stone-crushing plant that produced clouds of coarse dust, which didn't contribute much to the lubrication of the engines. Records will show that the engines of Aden-based Beverleys had a much shorter life than those of others. The trouble was eventually traced to the cylinder holding-down bolts, which were too weak. When they stretched, an engine fire could result. It used to be said that every time you got airborne the chances were that you would land on three engines, hence the Beverley's reputation as the best three-engined transport aircraft in the Royal Air Force! The 173 engines were eventually modified with stronger bolts and called the 175."

The first heavy drop to be made in the Middle East for a considerable time was to be made on 25th January by Flt. Lt. Dorricott and his crew. Manama, a small airstrip about forty miles east of Sharjah, was selected as the DZ, and the Beverley flew there from Bahrain carrying a Land Rover and a half-ton trailer on a pallet. Having disembarked, the DZ party checked the load and the Beverley began its take-off run, but as it lifted off the load fell out onto the airstrip! The aircraft immediately landed, picked up the DZ party and returned to Bahrain to face the inevitable leg-pulling by other members of 30 Squadron and by rival 53 squadron. Five days later the remains of the disastrous drop were collected and flown back to Bahrain.

Flood relief in Tanganyika continued on a small scale in February, Flg. Off. Wright and his men still flying from Dar-es-Salaam. On 1st February, during a supply drop at Zombe, HE the Governor General of Tanganyika, Sir Richard Turnbull GCMG,

*The presentation of the 'East African Standard' award for supply-dropping missions.*

and the Tanganyikan Minister of Commerce, Mr. George Kahama MP, were on board the aircraft. This was Flg. Off. Wright's final sortie, and next day XH122 was able to return to Eastleigh after a job well done. When Pioneer aircraft of 21 Squadron and Beavers and Alouettes of the Army Air Corps operating in the bush against hostile tribesmen needed supplies, Flt. Lt. Howell and his crew carried fuel in 44-gallon drums to Lodwar. On the way back to Eastleigh he made roller landings at Isiolo and Nanyuki to check the condition of the airstrips.

When Sqn. Ldr. Evans returned from Bahrain he set about finding out what problems were being experienced by the 70 aircrew and 100 ground crew. At least a third of the personnel were detached to Bahrain at any one time, and this was found to be the cause of many personal and administrative difficulties. It was also true that being at Eastleigh was a most unhappy time for many of the wives of 30 Squadron personnel, although it was a delightful Station, with azaleas, bougainvillea, roses and many more exotic plants growing in great profusion. 'Dicky' Evans himself spent more than fourteen months of a two-year posting away on detachments. There was also a significant security problem in 1962/63, caused by Uhuru, the granting of freedom to Kenya. Whenever married personnel were on detachment arrangements had to be made to provide security guards outside their houses.

On 7th February Flt. Lt. Dorricott and his crew were detailed to take members of the 5th King's African Rifles to Wajir and others from there to Nanyuki. Landing at Wajir, the Beverley bogged down, but with the aid of the soldiers it was extricated. The crew was then told that they should have landed on a wartime airstrip twenty miles away called N'degis Nest which had just been cleared after seventeen years of disuse. So there the Beverley went, lifting fifty troops to Nanyuki before returning to base. A similar task was flown next day by the same crew.

March 1962 was a fairly quiet month for Bahrain-based 30 Squadron crews, the main tasks being transportation of troops,

among them members of the Gordon Highlanders, the Royal Horse Artillery and the Parachute Regiment. Supply sorties for the forces at Lodwar continued, and on 8th March a parachute drop was made at Juweiza, a desert airstrip near Sharjah, followed the same night by two drops at nearby Falaj al Ali. During the month further famine relief sorties were flown from Dar-es-Salaam, 196 tons of food being dropped in 30 hours flying time. This mission is remembered by 'Dicky' Evans, who took part in it. "On 22nd March 1962 I took XL152 to Dar-es-Salaam to set up British-supplied flood relief for Tanganyika, as it was then known. My crew comprised M.Plt. James (co-pilot), Flt. Lt. Macgregor (navigator), Sgt. Brooks (signaller), and Flt. Sgt. Mangnall (engineer), together with sixteen members of 16 Co. RASC (Air Despatch). While we were taking part in this flood relief the crew

*This hardly seems the place for an aircraft, particularly one the size of the Beverley! The aircraft was XB124 [G] and the location is believed to be Lodwar* [Wg. Cdr. R. Evans].

*A tight fit, but it worked! Loading Alouette AH.2 helicopter XR382 of the Army Air Corps into a Beverley of 30 Squadron at Eastleigh on 13th June 1962.*

and I set up what was claimed to be a world record when we dropped 200 tons of pocho and maize in seven days. We started by free-dropping 22,000 pounds of pocho and maize from a height of fifty feet, doing two sorties a day to Mtanza, Utete and Zombe, but very quickly increased to three sorties a day, dropping 30,000 pounds each time. This was quite hard work, particularly for the Air Despatchers. Some of the DZs were extremely short and usually surrounded by trees, and on one occasion it was claimed by one of our ground crew that the aircraft returned with palm fronds stuck in the wheels, which were of course always 'down and welded'."

The period of relative quietness continued in April, and at the end of that month all aircraft and personnel were withdrawn from Bahrain, where they had been on standby in case of action by Iraq against Kuwait. The last 30 Squadron crew to return to Eastleigh was that of Flt. Lt. Brown, who flew XH119 from Bahrain via Sharjah and Khormaksar to arrive at Eastleigh on 29th April. However, two aircraft and three groundcrew remained at Bahrain to be ferried home a few days later. One casualty of the Kuwait crisis was Beverley XL131, which was damaged by a bomb placed aboard by sympathisers of General Kassem. The aircraft had to be ferried back to Abingdon for extensive repairs, and did not return to Eastleigh until 9th July.

Now all together at Eastleigh, 30 Squadron personnel began the task of aircraft servicing and rectification necessary after the harsh conditions found at Bahrain. Subsequently, it became possible to reinvigorate the training commitment, as more aircraft and crews were arriving from the UK, and it was hoped that it would soon be possible to achieve fully the squadron's allocated task. On 9th May two crews began to practice dropping one-ton containers on the airfield, the first time that crews, aircraft and a supply of parachutes had all been available together! Two hundred flying hours were allocated to the squadron for April, the minimum period needed for the Eastleigh to Khormaksar scheduled service, transport support, and continuation training. All the plans were subject to no sudden operations being imposed on the squadron. These objectives were not helped by the unserviceability of the runway at Eastleigh due to heavy rain, which caused the loss of several flying hours each morning while crews waited for the runway to dry after early

morning downpours. A three-day army/RAF exercise named *Hartley Wintney* (did the planner come from Hampshire?) was affected but came to a satisfactory end after 30 Squadron crews had dropped containers for troops operating in hilly country. A different type of task came the squadron's way on 17th May, when the CO, who was checking out a co-pilot, was diverted to look for a missing C-130 Hercules of the USAF which had been reported missing while on approach to Nairobi Airport. After a short search, the smoking wreckage of the aircraft was spotted at the southern end of the Ngong Hills. Rescue was initiated by the RAF Eastleigh Land Rescue Team, but it was found that all thirteen on board the C-130 had been killed. The aircraft had been flying from Evreux in France to Nairobi via Entebbe in connection with Operation *Mercury*, the US programme of manned space probes.

As a result of an accident to a Beverley of 242 OCU in the UK, an intensive investigation into the condition of all Centaurus 173 engines was carried out in June 1962 and many engines had to be changed. This delayed the squadron's training programme, and before it could be reinstated a comprehensive exercise in the Northern Frontier District of Kenya involving the RAF, the army and the Kenya Police Air Wing kept the squadron busy until the end of the month. The exercise did, however, provide useful experience to the crews, particularly newcomers.

Later in the month the CO flew XH122 to Mombasa on the first leg of a proving flight to the Central Africa Federation, Basutoland, Swaziland and Bechuanaland to inspect airfields and airstrips which might be suitable for Beverleys. Departure from Nairobi was on 28th June for Mombasa and thence to Salisbury, Southern Rhodesia, but an hour after take-off the starboard hydraulics system failed and the Beverley diverted to Dar-es-Salaam. After repairs the Beverley was airborne at 18.10 for Salisbury and a night stop. Next day the destination was Francistown and then Bulawayo. On 30th June airfields visited were Serowe, Mahalapye, Gaberone and Matsapa, where the aircraft was featured in an air display on 1st July. The crew had two days rest at Livingstone and were able to visit the Victoria Falls. Completed on 6th July, this mission caused much favourable comment in the local press in all the areas visited. During the month, Sqn. Ldr. Evans also flew to Dar-es-Salaam, where his crew uplifted starter and oxygen trolleys to be returned to Eastleigh. This equipment had been placed at Dar-es-Salaam for use by the RAF's V-bomber force in an emergency, but now that Tanganyika was independent the situation had changed.

All crews of 30 Squadron took part in Exercise *Air Wings* from 22nd to 28th June 1962, the object of which was to test the control of aircraft operating in the Northern Provinces and the efficiency of signals communications. First, 21 Squadron was moved from Eastleigh to Isiolo, from where the Twin Pioneers operated until being transferred to N'degis Nest airstrip. Troops of the 5th KAR were then flown in and exchanged for others, and finally 21 Squadron and its equipment were flown back to Eastleigh. Other units taking part included 8 Ind. Recce. Flight of the Army Air Corps, operating Beaver aircraft and Alouette helicopters, and the Kenya Police, flying Cessnas.

A series of extensive training flights began in July 1962, entailing two Beverleys leaving Eastleigh at intervals and landing at different remote airstrips in Kenya. They then met at a prearranged point, carried out practice supply drops and flew to either Entebbe or Kisumu in close formation or in station-keeping positions. After instrument let-downs and landings and flight planning, they flew to Nairobi Airport on airways to carry out night approaches before returning to Eastleigh. Crews generally agreed that this task was very interesting and rewarding. Another exercise that month involved the General Service Unit of the Kenya Police, 173 members of which were flown to Nanyuki with their equipment in three sorties by 30 Squadron. Later in the day four one-ton containers were dropped to them before the men returned to base.

One of the more interesting projects carried out by 30 Squadron at this time is described by 'Dicky' Evans. "On 23rd August 1962 Flt. Lt. Don Selway in Beverley XH124 and myself in XL152 took off for some formation practice over Mount Kenya and Kilimanjaro. My crew was Flg. Off. David Crys-Williams (later an AVM), Flt. Lt. Bill Ewens (navigator), Sgt. O'Mahoney (signaller), Flt. Sgt. Smith (engineer) and Sgt. Berkeley (AQM). In the unpressurised Beverley all crew members had to be on oxygen above 10,000 feet. This was not a normal training exercise and so we had to make special arrangements to ensure that we all had plenty of oxygen, as most of the trip would be above 10,000 feet. We left Eastleigh and climber to the north, heading for Mount Kenya, which is just over 17,000 feet high. After taking some photographs of this magnificent mountain we turned south and continued climbing towards Kilimanjaro (in Tanganyika in those days), which at 19,340 feet is the highest mountain in Africa. It was quite a struggle to get the Beverleys above Kilimanjaro, but nevertheless we made it and got some superb photographs of this wonderful mountain, which had taken me five days to climb back in 1953."

Apart from carrying out routine training exercises and scheduled flights, 30 Squadron prepared in August to take up its new commitment of providing two aircraft, three aircrews and fifteen servicing personnel as part of a standby Beverley force at Bahrain for Operation *Tantrum*. One of the first to leave Eastleigh on this month-long detachment was the CO, Sqn. Ldr. Evans. At Eastleigh, a shortage of aircraft and crews developed, and continuation training began to suffer. Check flights to remote airstrips were made when possible, and on 17th September an Alouette helicopter of the AAC was flown in Beverley XB263 from Eastleigh to Kasese to replace a similar machine which had crashed. From 30th September to 9th October the crews at Bahrain were heavily involved in Exercise *Duffel II*, which covered the movement of 6th Parachute Brigade from Bahrain to Juweiza. On 4th October, 30 Squadron's task was to air-land more troops at Juweiza, but when contact was made with the ground party the captains were told that in view of thick fog they should divert to Sharjah. From the air the fog appeared to be very thin and the outline of the strip could be seen, so the decision was made to land anyway, which the pilots did at the first attempt. Waiting generals and observers standing in ground-level fog were taken completely by surprise, but the Beverley cockpits were above it, and at least two other Beverleys were able to land because their crews could see the tail fins of aircraft on the ground sticking up through the fog. During the exercise, an airborne assault was carried out on the airstrip at Manama, followed by several resupply drops. At the end of the exercise, all troops and equipment were uplifted to Bahrain by the 30 Squadron aircraft.

Uganda became independent in 1962, and 30 Squadron was tasked with supporting 208 Squadron and its Hunter fighters, which took part in the celebrations. As part of this programme, two of the Beverleys flew to Entebbe on 5th October, and four days later another aircraft went to Tororo, Jinja, Arua, Tororo again and back to Eastleigh. On 11th October the places visited were Murchison Falls, Arua and Gulu.

Another unusual task was flown on 9th November, when Sqn. Ldr. Evans and his crew in the faithful XB263 went from Nairobi to Aldabra, a small island in the Seychelles group about 800 nautical miles east of Dar-es-Salaam, where they dropped supplies to an RAF party surveying the site as a possible airfield to replace others in India, Pakistan, Ceylon and Gan which were no longer available as staging posts. The idea had been mooted by Air Cdre. McDonald, who asked Sqn. Ldr. Evans whether he could do it. "Yes, of course I can" was the reply. With the help of Station workshops, a huge metal fishing hook about six feet long with three large barbs on it was made. This was attached to about a hundred feet of nylon rope which was then wound onto a giant reel borrowed from the electrical section, and the reel was then mounted above the parachute exit in the boom of the Beverley. On the island, the RAF men were asked to cut down two ten-foot poles, across which was strung a length of rope. After trials at Eastleigh some modifications were made, but when deemed satisfactory off they went to deliver the mail. They then snatched mail from the beach before returning to Eastleigh after a total sortie time of eleven hours thirty-five minutes. On the return flight the captain franked the sixty or so letters with the 30 Squadron stamp. As it happened, the survey team found that Aldabra was honeycombed with subterranean chasms, so the project was abandoned.

Meanwhile, possible operations on the border between Aden Protectorate and South Yemen had meant the diversion to Khormaksar of Beverley XH119, which had been on its way to Eastleigh after extensive servicing in the UK. However, the standby ended a few days later and XH119 returned to Eastleigh on 14th November.

More unusual work for 30 Squadron is recalled by Flt. Lt. Al Aked, who was the captain of Beverley XB263 on 6th November 1962. At the time, Jomo Kenyatta was still under detention at Lodwar in the Northern Frontier District, a very hot area many miles from civilisation. With the coming independence of Kenya in mind, it was decided that he and his colleagues should be moved closer to Nairobi, and that the local airstrip should be improved. Suitable graders were in the hands of the British Army, and one was made available. "I took 263 to Nakuru, where the grader was stored," says Al Aked. "On a lovely sunny morning the army driver drove the 26,000lb. vehicle up the ramp without blinking. It was a

*A piece of earth-moving equipment being loaded into a 30 Squadron Beverley.*

*Sqn. Ldr. R. Evans when CO of 30 Squadron in East Africa*
*[Wg. Cdr. R. Evans].*

very tight fit, but seemed to present no trouble to the army. As soon as we had secured the load we were airborne for Eastleigh, where there was a better runway for all-up weight considerations. On arrival at Lodwar the grader was unloaded with equal skill and was used immediately to smooth the soft airstrip and lengthen it. Although by then we were much lighter, there was a large drag on the wheels, particularly the nose-wheels, which made the take-off run unpredictable. I believe we caused quite a bow-wave on our take-off run!"

1962 drew to a close with claims by 30 Squadron of two altitude records for supply-dropping by Beverley aircraft. The Mountain Club of Kenya had asked whether it would be possible to drop two prefabricated huts on Mount Kenya for use by climbers.

After a reconnaissance of the area and a couple of practices at 15,000 feet to judge how the Beverley would behave it was decided that the task was feasible. The first sortie place on 15th December, when Sqn. Ldr. Evans and crew in XB263 dropped sand and cement for the foundations of the huts high in the Naru More valley at Klarwill's Camp, at an altitude of 13,500 feet. The weather was satisfactory on the approach but then violent turbulence was encountered, and to add to the difficulty No.3 engine failed with a loud bang. With only part of the load dropped, the mission had to be abandoned and a return to base made. The crew, consisting of co-pilot Flt. Lt. Allen, navigator Flt. Lt. K. Schuck, engineers M.Eng. Marr and Sgt. Gifford and the AQM, Sgt. Robinson, all carried out a dangerous task under very difficult conditions. Sections of one hut were parachuted onto the site on 20th December and another hut was dropped at Kami Tarm, at 14,700 feet. Later, an emergency arose when a mountain-climber was taken ill with suspected pneumonia, and the CO then took Beverley XH124 to drop emergency oxygen equipment at Klarwill's Camp and to coordinate a rescue by helicopter and Twin Pioneer.

From 5th December the runway at Bahrain was back in full operation, after being under repair for some time. Apart from weekly flights to Kuwait and Masirah, 30 Squadron crews now took part in Exercise *Desert Nimble*, involving the resupply of paratroops at Jebel Ali, and Exercise *Relax*, the retrieval of paratroops from Juweiza and Jebel Ali. Later in the month, heavy rain at both places forced the use of Sharjah as the recovery airfield.

The detachment at Bahrain was still in position in January 1963, and was involved in several minor exercises. During that month the remainder of the squadron took part in two exercises involving the movement of troops and equipment. On 21st January the CO had the task of flying a party of future District Commissioners, a BBC 'Panorama' team, and an ITV news team around new farming projects in the Northern Frontier District of Kenya, at the request of the Kenya Institute of Administration. This flight was routed from Eastleigh to Lodwar and Kitale before returning. Having completed this task, the CO left for Bahrain for another period of detachment.

Exercises flown in February included *Ibrex II* in Bahrain and *Seabird* and *Sharp Panga* at Eastleigh. *Seabird* involved ferrying 799 troops and over 54 tons of supplies from Mombasa to Zanzibar,

*Spectacular scenery for the crew of XL152 [A] – the crater of Mount Kenya*　　　　　　　　　　　　　　　*[Wg. Cdr. R. Evans].*

*Refuelling a Beverley at Eastleigh during Exercise* Sharp Panga *in February 1963* [J. Robinson].

while *Sharp Panga* was the largest exercise held in East Africa. Taking part was a detachment of Canberras of 73 Squadron from Akrotiri, with Twin Pioneers of 21 Squadron, Beavers and Alouettes of the AAC and of course the Beverleys of 30 Squadron, supported by two from 84 Squadron. The role of the Beverleys was to maintain a line of supply between Eastleigh and Isiolo, the base camp airstrip, to where Sqn. Ldr. Evans was detached as Air Transport Operations Controller. All squadron personnel other than those in Bahrain took part in this exercise, and the ground crews paid a particularly efficient part in keeping the Beverleys in top condition. In all, 959 troops and 282 tons of freight were carried during *Sharp Panga*, which ended on 4th March.

When the Ruler of Kuwait was recognised as such by the Military Government of Iraq on 17th March 1963, tension in the area relaxed a little, and the size of 30 Squadron's detachment was reduced to two crews, two aircraft and nineteen ground personnel. Publicity was given to the squadron when the CO took a Beverley to Wilson Airport, Nairobi, where he took part in a set piece to demonstrate the Beverley's capabilities. Another Beverley was in the static display and proved to be the most popular exhibit. Further publicity stemmed from a 'casevac' flown by Flg. Off. B. W. West on 10th March. A Lascar seaman who had been taken ill on an oil tanker, the *Caltex Wellington*, had been transshipped to the RAF Masirah rescue craft and was then flown from Masirah to Bahrain for hospitalisation. Flg. Off. West was only in Masirah because he had just delivered a load of 5 tons 16cwt. of gelignite from Kuwait!

Extensions to the squadron offices at Eastleigh began in April 1963, using a load of timber which had been airlifted from Tanganyika. Heavy rain hindered the work and also held up resurfacing of the runway. The Bahrain contingent carried on with supply tasks and checked a number of desert airstrips, including one at Abu Dhabi, which was then a small village but is now a major city with an international airport. While taxiing for take-off there on 25th April, Beverley XH119 became bogged down in soft sand. A large number of local Arabs surrounded it to offer advice to the captain, Flt. Lt. Selway, and his crew, but all but two beat a hasty retreat when asked to help dig the aircraft out! Eventually some more helpful bodies were recruited, and in temperatures of 110° in the shade made half-hearted attempts to free the Beverley. With the help of the Beach Survey Team who were to be the passengers, it was freed, and was taxied onto some PSP, which prevented it sinking back into the sand. What happened then is not recorded, but the surveyors were flown out in another aircraft next

*The reception committee on 30 Squadron's arrival at Mandira (Kenya) during Exercise* Sharp Panga [J. Robinson].

day and XH119 lived to fly again until the end of 1967.

After using Nairobi Airport since 15th March 1963, 30 Squadron moved back to Eastleigh on 12th June. On the previous day, the squadron had been placed on standby for Operation *Alfred*, a possible detachment to Swaziland, where a general strike was threatening the country's economy. At the time, the CO was in the Central African Federation, conducting a check of usable airstrips in Swaziland, Bechuanaland and Basutoland. He then deployed to RRAF New Sarum at Salisbury, Southern Rhodesia, from where he flew tear gas to Matsapa. While Air Cdre. J. C. McDonald, the AOC RAF East Africa, was discussing the situation with the Political Resident of Swaziland, Sqn. Ldr. Evans was requested to 'show the flag' by making as much noise as possible over trouble spots. This he did by 'beating up' Havelock, Mbabane, Manzizi and Piggs Peak, and found the natives friendly. Next day (12th June) he flew 37 Bechuanaland tribal policemen from Gabarone to Swaziland. The first four Beverleys of 30 Squadron apart from that of the CO arrived at New Sarum on 13th June and began operations next day by flying troops of the Gordon Highlanders to Matsapa, the nearest usable airfield to Mbabane, the country's capital city. Sqn. Ldr. Evans became RAF Detachment Commander at New Sarum for the duration of the operation, after which one aircraft returned to Eastleigh of 23rd June and another two days later. The other two Beverleys continued to carry out resupply flights until leaving on

6th July. During the operation, 422 troops, 242 passengers and over 110 tons of freight were moved by 30 Squadron aircraft.

A possible tragedy which was averted more by luck than judgment is recalled by 'Dicky' Evans. "On 29th June 1963 I was involved in another bit of excitement," he says. "Beverley XB262 had been badly damaged when the captain made a heavy landing in the undershoot area at Matsapa. After being thrown back into the air it came down on its nose wheels to register a 9G landing! I happened to see the aircraft about half an hour later and it really did

*Beverley XL131 making a drop at Isiolo while its starboard outer engine was feathered*                              *[J. Robinson].*

look quite sick. The boom had whipped and the top halves of the clamshell doors were badly damaged. After about a week the aircraft seemed to shake itself and lose some of its hang-dog look, so after my ground engineer, 'Chiefy' Davis, had given it the once-over we decided to fly it back to Salisbury and Eastleigh. The flight to Salisbury was uneventful, and next day I asked John Lancaster to take it to Eastleigh. That ferry was also uneventful. However, when I returned to Eastleigh on 6th July, the Wg. Cdr. Tech., George Young, asked me to look at XB262. He showed me a gigantic crack in the tailplane main spar, which he said could have fallen off at any time during the two flights from Matsapa, with disastrous results. This shattered me when I thought that I could have been responsible for the deaths of John Lancaster and his crew, not to mention my crew and myself!"

Another operation, *Installment*, kept 30 Squadron personnel on their toes in August 1963. A preparatory phase which provided valuable training for new captains involved the resupply of troops of the King's African Rifles deployed at forward airstrips at Isiolo, Wajir, Garissa and Mandera. At Bahrain, the detachment took part in a larger than average exercise, *AWEX 10*, in September, which involved landings on the desert airstrip at Sohar, on the coast of the Trucial States (now the United Arab Emirates). By the end of the exercise the strip was so badly cut up that a Provost of the Sultan of Oman's Air Force pitched forward on landing in a rut; the pilot was last seen trying to straighten a bent propeller with a hammer!

Airstrip familiarisation flights were continued in October, and touch-downs were made on several strips not often used by Beverleys, including Voi, Ferguson's Gulf and McKinnon Road in Kenya and Kasese, Jinja and Murchison Falls in Uganda. Towards the end of November Operation *Bootleg* required the deployment of three aircraft to New Sarum, from where they assisted in the changeover of troops who had been positioned around the capital of Swaziland.

On 1st December 1963 the name of the RAF airfield at Bahrain was changed to Muharraq, reflecting the name of the island on which it was located. Unfortunately, Muharraq means in Arabic 'the place of the dead', which personnel there did not consider a very appropriate name for an RAF Station!

After a period of very active service as CO of 30 Squadron, Sqn. Ldr. Evans handed over command on 20th December 1963 to Sqn. Ldr. R. A. W. Harrison, who arrived from 242 OCU at Thorney Island. That month was also notable for the coming to independence of Zanzibar on 10th December and Kenya two days

*Somewhat bemused ground crews watch local musicians perform. The Beverley, XH124, saw two periods of service with 30 Squadron before being displayed at the RAF Museum, where eventually it was, regrettably, scrapped.*

later. 30 Squadron had the honour of supporting 208 Squadron, whose Hunters made a flypast after refuelling at Dar-es-Salaam. As the RRAF was to be split when Northern Rhodesia gained independence, a 30 Squadron aircraft flew to Ndola with a supply of oil for the Northern Rhodesia Air Wing, and from there continued to New Sarum to take ground equipment to Livingstone. In all, four sorties were made before the aircraft returned to Eastleigh on 23rd December.

At Eastleigh in January 1964, 30 Squadron was greatly involved in uplifting troops and supplies to quell mutinies by the armies of Tanganyika, Uganda and Kenya. In addition, the African population of Zanzibar threatened to overthrow their Asian masters, which presented a problem to British citizens living there. From 20th January a total of 16 hours 35 minutes were flown in carrying troops to Mombasa, where they boarded HMS *Owen* and HMS *Rhyl*, which then stood by off the coast of Zanzibar in case armed intervention was called for or if British families had to be withdrawn from the island. In the end no such support was necessary, and the troops returned to base at Nairobi. Meanwhile trouble loomed in Tanganyika, where President Nyerere had disappeared from Dar-es-Salaam. It was rumoured that he was on board a boat in the Indian Ocean, but in his absence his army revolted because of low pay and the use of expatriate white officers instead of their own men. British troops and marines flown in from the UK were flown to Tabora and Dar-es-Salaam, where they disarmed the army and policed the area to put down any further trouble. 30 Squadron then began a series of resupply drops to all areas until a railhead could be established. On one such flight two Beverleys were held at Dar-es-Salaam so that an armed landing could be made at Machinwea, an army camp on the border of Tanganyika and Mozambique, where the third uprising took place. The Commander of the Tanganyikan Army contacted the mutineers there and told them that a landing would be made by helicopters from HMS *Centaur* at 13.30 on the playing field. What really happened was that two Beverleys of 30 Squadron led by Sqn. Ldr. Harrison flew in at low level to drop paratroops, who soon overpowered and disarmed the mutineers. Subsequently, the ringleaders were taken to Dar-es-Salaam. Troops of the Uganda Rifles who were rioting at Jinja were dealt with by means of a night armed landing by 30 Squadron Beverleys flown by Flt. Lt. D. S. Selway and Flt. Lt. M. H. Letton, who landed at Entebbe Airport on 23rd January. The revolt of the Kenyan Army at Lanet occupied 30 Squadron for just over one hour of flying time, so it could not have been too serious!

Apart from these tasks, 30 Squadron crews spent time in dropping supplies to elements of the Kenyan Army at Moyale, Mandera, Wajir, El Wak and Garissa in the Northern Frontier District, where unseasonal amounts of rain had cut the roads. This operation, known as *Late Gesture*, involved 130 hours 20 minutes of airborne time. Several trips were also made to Taveta, on the southern border between Kenya and Tanganyika, carrying an army team which was to establish a fresh water supply from Lake Chala, a volcanic lake feared by the local population as a place of evil spirits. But, as the squadron diarist remarked: ". . . none of these were encountered by 30 Squadron." At Muharraq, Flt. Lt. R. Humphrey and his crew were kept busy on 10th and 11th January by an exercise at Azeiba Two airstrip on the Oman Peninsula, where they joined detachments of other squadrons in dropping paratroops and Land Rovers. Due to high winds and seas, naval landing craft which were standing by to take men and equipment back to Bahrain Island were unable to do so, so time was occupied in returning most of the troops by air on 14th January.

February's work by 30 Squadron was confined to resupply flights to Dar-es-Salaam and Tabora and a few more trips under Operation *Late Gesture*. While on an air test, Beverley XH123 was struck by a marabu stork, which collided at the point where the captain's windscreen joined the nose coaming. Serious damage was caused, and the manufacturers had to be called in to carry out repairs. Unfortunately, nobody could be found to repair the stork! Probably the most significant event that month, certainly the one which caused the most celebration, was the marriage of Sqn. Ldr. R. A. W. Harrison to Miss Paola Bianchini on 29th February.

Resupply missions to outposts of the Kenyan Army and Police in the Northern Frontier District continued in March 1964

*Attending to a problem with the Beverley's tailplane was not a job for anyone who suffered from vertigo!*

before the onset of the rainy season. Equipment was flown from Khormaksar to Wajir airstrip, where the runway was to be resurfaced by the Ministry of Public Buildings & Works as it often became unusable due to the soft topsoil. One piece of equipment was a power shovel which was 11 ft. 3 in. (3.43 metres) high, fifteen inches (38 cm.) higher than a Beverley's hold. Eventually, the front wheels of the aircraft were lifted onto a ramp and the rear tyres were let down, enabling the ten-ton shovel to be fitted in the best position for transportation. As a complete change from flying the heavy Beverley, Flt. Lt. R. G. Statham and Flg. Off. M. G. Gale were detached to the Kenya Police Air Wing, with which they flew single-engined Cessna 180 aircraft on sorties in the Northern Frontier District. Another large load, a Britannia loading platform, was carried by a 30 Squadron aircraft to Dar-es-Salaam on 26th March in addition to a complete mobile air movements section, to assist in the changeover of Marines and Nigerian troops.

April 1964 was notable for the lack of serviceable aircraft, several having restrictions placed on the number of hours they could fly before refurbishment became necessary. Nevertheless, all planned tasks were completed. One unplanned mission was flown to assist 21 Squadron, which was engaged in dropping flares at night at timed intervals to alarm the Shifta gangs which were creating mayhem in the NFD. As the pilots of the 21 Squadron Twin Pioneers found it difficult to fly without navigation aids, a Beverley was sent to the Garissa area to act as an aerial beacon.

Following considerable comment in the local newspapers on the subject of formation flying over Nairobi, several members of the press were invited to fly to Marsabit and Moyale on a resupply flight. On landing at Moyale the Beverley sank into the soft ground up to its axles. In the next Sunday paper appeared the headline "What happens to a 50-ton Beverley when it lands on a soft runway." This was considered good publicity for the squadron, of which the crews may have felt that their work was not recognised as valuable.

A shortage of aircraft continued in May 1964, but both aircraft detached to Muharraq were replaced with ones having longer hours available. Operations in the NFD continued, and on 8th May Exercise *Slumber* was carried out, involving flying 448 troops of the Scots Guards and 23 tons of freight to Lanet from Eastleigh. Operations continued in this vein in June, with the added excitement for the crews at Muharraq of searching for two Hunters of 208 Squadron which had crashed while practising low-level rocket attacks near Jebel Dhanna. One pilot was found when his Sarah beacon was heard transmitting from an Arab dhow which had picked him up from the sea, but the few remains of the other pilot's body were found on a sand-bar by Flt. Lt. G. H. Smyth and Flt. Lt. D. J. Fewell, who had been taken there in an oil company launch. On a happier note, Flt. Sgt. J. N. Payen, the NCO in charge of ground servicing, was awarded the BEM on 13th June and Sgt. B. H. Smith, an air engineer, received a Queen's Commendation for Valuable Services in the Air.

Another country to become independent was Nyasaland, which on 1st July 1964 became Malawi. Flt. Lt. Letton and his crew flew Beverley XH124 to take part in the proceedings, taking a band to Blantyre, Zombe, Salima and Lilongwe. In addition, fly-pasts were made at Monkey Bat, Dedza and Mzuzu. The Beverley was marked with the Pegasus symbol of Malawi Airways and Flt. Lt. Letton was ceremoniously presented with a white topee which he wore to all the functions before returning to Eastleigh on 9th July.

Changes were now in the air at Eastleigh. Over a period of several weeks, the Beverley Servicing Flight moved to Khormaksar, aided by the aircraft of 30 Squadron, and in August a rumoured move of the squadron to Muharraq was confirmed, to commence on 1st September 1964. This was the result of an independence treaty for Kenya which specified that all British troops would leave Kenya by 12th December. Provisional arrangements were made for two crews to fly to Muharraq that day to relieve 84 Squadron of its commitment, and two more crews would move in the middle of the month, as soon as 84 Squadron could provide a detachment at Eastleigh. The remainder of the squadron would follow in October, by which time accommodation for families could be provided. Meanwhile, normal flights to the NFD as part of Operation *Late Gesture* continued in support of the Kenyan Army's action against Shifta raiders who had a habit of coming over the border from Somalia to cause damage to local villages and their inhabitants. Other missions outside the squadron's routine that month included the journey made by Beverley XL152, which left Eastleigh on 2nd August in the hands of Flt. Lt. Statham and his crew. At Khormaksar a Whirlwind helicopter was loaded aboard for delivery to Wroughton for major attention. From there the Beverley staged through Khartoum, El Adem, Luqa and Abingdon, and after unloading at Wroughton it flew on to Dishforth to be refurbished. Another unusual task was carried out on the night of 23rd August, when Flt. Lt. Humphrey and his crew flew Beverley XM105 to Entebbe to collect 32 Greek men, women and children who had escaped from the Congo. They were quickly flown to Nairobi Airport to connect with an onward civilian flight. Called out at one hour's notice, the 30 Squadron crew had been in the air in fifty minutes. As none of the refugees could speak English, an interpreter was carried, and afterwards the mission was praised by the Greek Consul in Nairobi.

## On the move again

30 Squadron duly began the move to Muharraq, led by Sqn. Ldr. Harrison, who brought Beverley XH119 in via Khormaksar and Masirah on 2nd September 1964. Flt. Lt. B. Clinch and his crew made the trip on 5th September in XM105 via Khormaksar, where a full day was spent to allow service wives to see how their husbands were looked after in Aden. This enabled 84 Squadron to withdraw from the Bahrain detachment. A third crew, captained by Flg. Off. C. W. Ellis, arrived on 17th September in XH123, which left three crews with Beverley XH124 at Eastleigh to assist with 84 Squadron's detachment there.

During the second week of September the annual Lord Trophy was contested at El Adem. Assembled for the competition were Beverleys, Hastings and Argosies from all parts of the RAF world. The competition consisted of a night-time low-level cross-country flight over the sea, followed by a landing and harness pack drop after three hours' flying. A 'spoof' DZ was illuminated for a short time at the expected target approach point (TAP) of each aircraft, confusing many crews. Unfortunately, the 30 Squadron crew, headed by Flt. Lt. A. A. Clark, was unable to drop on time as they missed the TAP, which showed that Doppler-equipped aircraft had an advantage over aircraft relying solely on conventional astro-navigation.

At Muharraq, Exercise *Sandstone* was under way at Al Khatt, an airstrip north-east of Sharjah. There, several drops were made by day and night, and a recovery phase allowed an uplift of men of the 3rd Parachute Battalion. Two scheduled services were now being flown. AFME.8 was a weekly schedule from Muharraq to Masirah via Sharjah and Azeiba Two, returning the following day, but every other week extended to Firq to rotate the Omex patrol of the Sultan of Muscat's Armed Forces; and AFME .10, a weekly ration flight to Sharjah and back. In addition, two resupply flights were made each month to Kuwait. On 21st September two

Beverleys were recalled from the AFME.8 service and were sent to Sharjah to carry armoured Ferret scout cars and troops to Salalah, where dissident tribesmen were attacking installations in a campaign against the Sultan of Muscat & Oman. After three sorties the Beverleys returned to their routine tasks.

As planned, 30 Squadron completed its move from Eastleigh on 14th October 1964, when the three crews and one aircraft arrived at Muharraq. Apart from AOC's inspections, this was the first time since August 1962 that the complete squadron had been in one place. On the previous day, the Ruler of Bahrain and its Dependencies, His Highness Sheikh Isa bin Sulman al Khalifa KCMG, made an official visit to RAF Muharraq, accompanied by the Heir Apparent, Sheikh Hamed bin Sulman al Khalifa, and his brother, Sheikh Mohammed bin Sulman al Khalifa, the Chief of Police and President of the Council of Education and Training. After a parade at which the 30 Squadron standard was paraded, the Ruler toured the Station, commencing with 30 Squadron's premises, where paratroops in full kit demonstrated exit procedures by jumping from a Beverley onto matting on the ground below. Another Beverley contained two Land Rovers and trailers, and on the Ruler's approach the doors were opened, ramps lowered and vehicles driven out to show how quickly this could be done.

Always ready for an interesting exercise, 30 Squadron crews took part in *November Handicap* in November 1964. This was a combined services exercise in which Beverleys and Argosies took part, using a dropping zone at Sohar. This site had the advantage of proximity to a beach suitable for use by tank-landing craft Some elements of the 'enemy' force were dropped and air landed on 11th November, and the assault began next night. Four Beverleys led by Sqn. Ldr. Harrison flew over Sharjah and descended to dropping altitude over the sea. At a point about thirty miles from the coast a formation of Argosies of 105 Squadron from Khormaksar was seen, the Beverleys fell in behind them and the whole fleet proceeded to the TAP, which was HMS *Meon*. From there to the DZ was a distance of thirteen miles or so, but the formation leader became confused and missed the DZ. An orbit then had to be made, and a successful drop was made on the second attempt. Three Beverleys of 30 Squadron made a combined paratroop and heavy equipment drop over the DZ, and the whole exercise was repeated after a rapid turn-round at Muharraq. Six recovery flights were made on 15th and 16th November to bring back men and vehicles, but heavy equipment was recovered by sea.

After diplomatic clearances for flights over Sudan were withdrawn in December 1964, new routes had to be devised for aircraft flying to and from the UK. 30 Squadron crews now had the chance of night-stopping in Cairo, where earlier members of the squadron had spent many a happy hour.

As an indication of the amount of work carried out by 30 Squadron, the following record of activity in December 1964 is of interest. There were nine complete crews, plus an extra captain, at the time.

| | |
|---|---|
| Total hours flown: | 281:55 |
| Operational hours flown: | 226:40 |
| Training hours flown: | 55:15 |
| Air miles flown: | 30,710 |
| Passenger miles flown: | 307,852 |
| Troops carried: | 258 |
| Passengers carried: | 1,053 |
| Freight carried: | 212 tons |
| Paratroops dropped: | 132 |
| Freight dropped: | 25.25 tons |
| Mail carried: | 6,253 lbs. |
| Casualties evacuated: | 5 |

1965 began with little to disturb the routine, but with an assault exercise in February to add a little spice to life. In March a double crew flew to Socotra, where 34 troops of the 3rd Parachute Battalion had been carrying out a map survey of the island. Paratroops were dropped at Yas Island and Al Khatt, and a search was carried out for two members of the Saudi Arabian Air Force who were reported to have ditched 75 miles north-east of Muharraq. At the end of March Sqn. Ldr. Harrison left on posting to HQ Technical Training Command at Brampton, and was replaced by Sqn. Ldr. R. P. J. King, who had previously been Flight Commander Operations with 47 Squadron at Abingdon. On of his first actions was to fly a team of naval divers to Masirah on 25th April so that offshore pipes used to transfer aviation fuel from tankers could be repaired.

For 30 Squadron crews, the highlight of May 1965 was Exercise *Jay Trump*, which involved a formation of Beverleys with Argosies of 105 Squadron dropping heavy equipment and troops at Al Khatt and afterwards landing to recover them. While *Jay Trump* was under way, a team from the Transport Command Examining Unit watched the proceedings and subsequently placed emphasis on Transport Support in their categorisation.

Due to an increase in the activities of dissidents in the Salalah area, 30 Squadron flew troops of the Sultan of Muscat's army there from Firq on 16th June. Three days later Flt. Lt. Clinch and his crew carried twenty-three political prisoners from Salalah to Azeiba for questioning. Detachments to Khormaksar allowed crews to gain experience of operating into rough airstrips in the Radfan area, under the guidance of 84 Squadron.

On 14th July, 30 Squadron had the honour of a visit by the Inspector General of the Royal Air Force, Air Marshal Sir Augustus Walker KCB CBE DSO DFC AFC MA. As 1965 would be the fiftieth anniversary of the formation of the squadron, preparations were put in hand for celebrations, and Flg. Off. Jackson, who had suffered the indignity of an arm broken while playing football, was nominated as the officer in charge. By October he was organising guest lists and coordinating various sections of the Station which were to be concerned with the planned tattoo and reception. 30 Squadron celebrated its fiftieth anniversary on 20th November 1965 at Muharraq, but unfortunately the reviewing officer, ACM Sir James Robb, was taken ill at the last minute. The salute at the parade was therefore taken by the Political Resident in Bahrain, HE Sir William Luce. In the evening the tattoo included demonstrations by the Station Defence Flight, police dogs of the Provost Flight and the band of the 1st Battalion of the Parachute Regiment. Four Hunters of 208 Squadron led by Wg. Cdr. D. J. Rhodes gave a flypast. Afterwards the Station entertained the guests at a cocktail party in a hangar, after which members of the squadron repaired to their appropriate messes to continue the festivities.

In the air, meanwhile, the first of a series of route training flights to Eastleigh was flown by a double crew. The introduction of this route was welcomed by squadron members, as it gave them the opportunity of re-establishing contact with old friends in the Nairobi area.

Exercise *Meadow Court* occupied several crews at the end of November, and involved dropping troops at Hafira DZ and flying resupply sorties consisting of fuel for tanks and water for the men. When this exercise ended on 1st December, disturbances on Das Island caused aircraft and crews to be placed on standby at Sharjah so that troops of the Trucial Oman Scouts could be ferried there if required. Trouble in Rhodesia and Zambia also affected the squadron, which took over some of the RMS schedules, which were flown three times weekly through Salalah and Masirah.

January and February 1966 were uneventful, but in the middle of March when there were disturbances around Salalah paratroops and troops of the Sultan of Muscat's Army were flown in to reinforce the garrison. At the end of the month the squadron cooperated with a film unit recording heavy equipment drops from Beverleys and paratrooping from Argosies. Scheduled routes AFME.8 and AFME.10 were still being flown by the squadron. Life was not without incidents for the 30 Squadron crews, two of which left Muharraq on 12th April on a training sortie to Eastleigh. Shortly after leaving Khormaksar, where the Beverleys had refuelled, fuel was discovered leaking into the freight bay of one aircraft, which was loaded with explosives. A hurried return was made, and the aircraft remained on the ground for four days before being flown back to Muharraq with its inboard No.1 fuel tank isolated, as no reason for the leak could be found.

The recently-completed airstrip on Yas Island was visited for the first time by a Beverley on 18th April, when Flt. Lt. P. F. Walker touched down to collect a number of construction personnel to be ferried to Muharraq. Another airstrip to be 'christened' by a

*30 Squadron Beverley XL152 [A] on a desert strip in the Radfan in 1965*
*[Sqn. Ldr. A. Thomas].*

Beverley of 30 Squadron was Bait al Falaj, which was used for the first time on 30th May after being extended. On that occasion the aircraft, piloted by Flg. Off. Ellis, was on scheduled service AFME.10. The approach to the strip proved somewhat difficult, with a tortuous narrow valley at each end. It was considered that experience of the site would reduce its apparent hazards, and it was hoped that Bait al Falaj would become a regular port of call, perhaps taking over from nearby Azeiba. Before long the schedule did indeed include Bait al Falaj.

In June 1966 Exercise *Junex*, involving an attack on Yas Island, was held, and 30 Squadron took part in the assault, resupply and recovery phases. In the extreme heat and humidity there were many casualties among the troops, and 30 Squadron flew a number of casevac missions to the island to repatriate them to hospital.

An unusual award was made in June 1966 to SAC M. W. Bailey, an air radio mechanic, who received a Commendation from the AOC Middle East. Another visit to Muharraq by Air Marshal Sir Augustus Walker took place on 16th July, and he made sure to spend time with 30 Squadron.

*The heights one had to reach to service the engines of a Beverley, this one at Muharraq on 5th May, 1966.*

*A view of RAF Muharraq in May 1966, showing SSQ in the foreground, administrative buildings behind and the frame of 30 Squadron's new hangar in the background* *[S. Wilmot].*

While engaged in a search and rescue exercise on 1st July, the CO was diverted to take part in a real search. A Trident aircraft of Kuwait Airways had been reported as missing, but before the Beverley arrived n the Kuwait area it had been found, four miles from the airport on the extended centre line of the runway. Another search was called for on 10th August, when a Hunter T.7 of the Kuwait Air Force disappeared while on a training flight. 30 Squadron crews flew about 43 hours in an attempt to locate this aircraft or its crew, but to no avail. In the search, some 'Sarah' equipment was used after being removed from an RAF launch and installed in a Beverley, replacing the usual 'Sarbe' equipment.

Two major incidents in August 1966 brought 30 Squadron crews into action. On the morning of 6th August Sheikh Shakbut, the Ruler of the Abu Dhabi sheikhdom, was deposed and replaced by his brother, Sheikh Zaid, leading members of his family stating that he was totally unable to govern properly or to use the country's increasing oil revenues for the benefit of his people. Under Operation *Hazland* two Beverleys, captained by Sqn. Ldr. King and Flt. Lt. J. Blount, lifted troops of the Trucial Oman Scouts into Abu Dhabi, while two other Beverleys, captained by Flg. Off. D. Jenkins

*The morning of 1st September 1966 found Beverley XB266 at Bait al Falaj, Muscat*         *[S. Wilmot].*

and Flt. Lt. S. K. Mulligan, held off at Tarif and Sharjah in case they were needed. Sheikh Shakbut was then flown to Bahrain.

Published in August 1966 was a squadron newsletter, although whether a second issue ever saw the light of day is doubtful. An item from the newsletter refers to a new building for the squadron and provides an insight into the airmen's domestic arrangements. "We should be moving into our new quarters in the large hangar about October. The accommodation will be luxurious in comparison to our present building and there will be toilet facilities and showers so that people can try to wash off the 100u and general gunge and go to their meals feeling reasonably civilised. There won't be any reason then for people to have to carry their clean clothes back to the billets before washing and hanging out their working garments. Too many people have dropped their wallets and similar valuables doing just this. It has accounted for more money and more F.1250s lost than you would believe possible. The fine for a lost 1250 remains for the moment £5 for the first one and you-name-it for the second loss. So whatever else you lose don't lose your 1250, as the security implications of one of these getting into the wrong hands is frightening." The Form 1250 referred to was the RAF Identity Card, the loss of which has always been a serious matter.

The same newsletter reported that at the end of August most of the squadron seemed to have taken up residence at Masirah, where the climate was delightful and the fishing superb. Turtles could be seen coming ashore to lay their eggs, which predators of various sorts then promptly devoured! Leave at Masirah could be arranged, the CO there being willing to accommodate squadron members for a few days of rest and relaxation.

The first of several ferry flights to Hong Kong (Kai Tak) began on 16th September 1966, when Flg. Off. C. J. Dyson took off from Muharraq in XH122, bound for Masirah, Bombay, Calcutta, Butterworth and Saigon. Arrival at Kai Tak was on 20th September, and the Beverley was left in the hands of the MU there for major refurbishment. The crew brought an 84 Squadron aircraft, XH121, back from Kai Tak to Khormaksar along much the same route. It is interesting to note that in November 1966 the total number of Beverleys allocated to 30 Squadron was only five, and

*XB266 starting up at Muharraq in October 1966. The start-up crew consisted of Ch. Tech. 'Chick' Ellis, shown on the left, J/T 'Fred' Abbott with the fire bottle trolley, Sgt. 'Batty Jim' Batten standing under the entrance door, and SAC Phil Kelly standing forward of the nosewheels*         *[S. Wilmot].*

*Beverley XL122 at Phuket in Thailand on 22nd January 1967 when on the way back to Muharraq from Hong Kong after major servicing. An interested crowd is inspecting the aircraft, which was an unusually large visitor to this airport* [S. Wilmot].

this included the Command spare aircraft. Serviceability was beginning to present real problems, as engine failures, oil leaks and other troubles were becoming almost everyday occurrences. On more than one occasion crews had to spend a lonely night in the hold of their aircraft at a desert airstrip after 'gremlins' had been up to mischief! Personnel numbers remained much the same at nine complete aircrews.

At the beginning of December 1966, 30 Squadron was engaged in Exercise AWEX 17, and was obliged to borrow one aircraft from 84 Squadron. The DZ for this exercise was at Kalba, an airstrip on the east coast of the Trucial States peninsula. Flg. Off. Dyson positioned the base party there on 2nd December, and next 35 personnel and equipment were air-landed there. Two pairs of aircraft, led by the CO with Air Cdre. Topham as passenger, dropped 225 troops on 5th December, and next day the resupply phase began when two one-ton containers were dropped. Then a series of technical troubles started. Flt. Lt. Walker had to abort his take-off from Kalba on 7th December as his Beverley refused to gain speed, and on his second attempt an engine failed when the PCU drive sheared, forcing him to divert to Sharjah. Next night Flt. Lt. J. K. Drew and his crew spent a cold night at Manama due to engine trouble, but were entertained by the Trucial Oman Scouts. The recovery phase of the exercise involved five sorties over two days, during which 250 troops, their Land Rovers and other equipment were uplifted. Another example of hospitality occurred on 23rd December, when Flt. Lt. Jenkins was forced to land at Sharjah with an engine feathered. He and his crew were then offered a flight back to Muharraq in a C-54 of the USAF which was in fact scheduled to go to Dhahran but which its captain kindly offered to divert so that his RAF passengers could spend Christmas at home.

In January 1967 Beverley XH122 was ferried back from Hong Kong by Flt. Lt. Jenkins and his crew after refurbishment. This trip, which began on 19th January, was not without excitement. The first leg of the journey tested the range of the Beverley, and the only solution was to fly over South Vietnam, not the best place to be at the time! But apart from a radio malfunction all went well. The aircraft spent two days at Seletar before making the short flight to RAAF Butterworth for another night stop. On the Butterworth to Calcutta leg, a precautionary landing had to be made at Phuket in Thailand when it was thought that a dinghy hatch was lifting. This was put right, but at Calcutta J/T Steve Wilmot, an airframe mechanic on board, noticed that the captain's windscreen was cracked, although fortunately the problem did not become dangerous. Then, at the top of the climb out of Bombay an engine failed when the PCU control became detached. After a return to Bombay for rectification the trip was resumed, and the aircraft landed at Muharraq on 24th January, the crew tired and hungry as they had been wary of rations given to them in Bombay and had not eaten them.

## An uncertain future

By now, rumours of a change of aircraft were circulating, and there was much speculation about the future of 30 Squadron. Positive information was soon received, to the effect that the Beverleys were to fly to the UK in September and that the squadron, reduced to seven crews, would re-equip with Argosies previously used by 105 Squadron. Families would return to the UK in August, but no information was available on the future of the ground crews. Meanwhile, scheduled services AFME.8, AFME.9 (to Kuwait) and newly-instituted AFME.7 (to Khormaksar) continued.

Beverley XH120, being ferried to Kai Tak by the CO, became unserviceable at Bangkok in January and was not airworthy until 7th February, when its journey continued via Seletar with Flg. Off. Bond as captain, allowing the CO to return to Muharraq.

In March the squadron spent time in Operation *Snaffle*. In company with two of 84 Squadron's aircraft, two from 30 Squadron positioned at Khormaksar and then flew to Riyan on 7th March. Next morning troops of the Hadramaut Bedouin Legion and their Land Rovers were loaded at Al Ghaydah and flown to Hadibo on Socotra Island, where the object was to round up rebels who had been terrorising the island. This was completed in six hours and the rebels were flown back to Al Ghaydah with their captors.

Scheduled services were becoming plagued by technical difficulties, some of them potentially dangerous. On one occasion Flt. Lt. Drew was forced to divert from AFME.8 to land at Dubai when a dinghy hatch came adrift and part of the dinghy streamed across the wing. On 16th March Flg. Off. T. J. Michaels was practising asymmetric landings after ILS approaches when another engine failed. He restarted the feathered engine and made a good landing and was later awarded a Flight Safety commendation by the CO. Very unusual weather conditions were met by AFME.8 crews in late March at Masirah, where the first rain to fall for six years completely swamped the island, washing away the sand runway and creating large lakes. Later, Salalah, Riyan and Khormaksar were similarly affected.

April 1967 proved to be an active month, with two flights carrying airstrip development equipment from Sharjah to Dibba, Rostak and Bait al Falaj given prominence. One crew flew to Nairobi on 19th May to take part in flood relief operations, but in general the number of flights made was beginning to diminish, with only six complete crews available. At the end of May squadron personnel were told that the first three Beverleys to be ferried to the UK would leave Muharraq on 3rd September, and the other three would follow on 15th September. The future of 30 Squadron was still, however, under discussion, the earlier plan to re-equip with Argosies not having been confirmed.

On 8th June, however, the squadron was brought to a state of immediate readiness to evacuate British civilians in Jordan, where security was threatened by the conflict between Arabs and Israelis.

By recalling all aircraft on scheduled services and the loan of one aircraft by 84 Squadron, the 30 Squadron groundcrews produced six serviceable Beverleys, but in fact they were not called upon and the squadron was stood down four days later, when the airlift had been completed by aircraft from Mediterranean airfields.

The last Beverley to be refurbished in Hong Kong, XH120, was collected by Flt. Lt. Walker and his crew on 15th June, but unserviceability resulted in a 24-hour delay at Calcutta and dysentery contracted by a member of the crew meant two days being spent in Bombay. Finally, the aircraft reached Muharraq on 25th June. The monthly AFME.7 schedule to Kuwait was cancelled when relations between Britain and Kuwait deteriorated due to the Arab/Israeli war, and there were no plans to reinstate the service. One aircraft was detached to Salalah from 14th June to ferry fuel to Riyan for helicopters operating against terrorists, as a strike by fuel company employees at Aden was having an adverse effect.

Several more airfield development sorties were flown in July 1967, mainly involving delivering bulldozers and graders to airstrips used by Twin Pioneer aircraft. In some cases the strip was lengthened while the Beverley was on the ground so that it could take off! In addition, flights were still being made to ascertain the suitability of new airstrips for use by Beverleys, although the aircraft was about to be withdrawn! By the end of the month a roster of crews to fly the aircraft back to the UK had been prepared, although the exact route had not been finalised. All crew members had received their postings, some to join Hercules squadrons, some to communications squadrons and others as captains at the Central Flying School.

One of the squadron's main tasks in August 1967 was the uplift of equipment and stores from Khormaksar to Muharraq and Sharjah. At maximum take-off weight, the Beverleys were able to carry 6 tons 14 cwt. of freight. Later they routed through Salalah in order to refuel there rather than at Khormaksar. Sqn. Ldr. King flew the final AFME.8 schedule to Sharjah, Bait al Falaj and Masirah on 31st August, the crew bidding farewell to their many friends on the route. The CO gave Masirah and Bait a flypast.

Several social events marked 30 Squadron's departure from Muharraq. On 14th August, just before the first families were due to leave, there was a squadron party in their honour. The squadron officers were 'dined out' in the mess on 24th August, and a final briefing and presentation of tankards was arranged for 3rd September. In the words of the squadron diarist, Flg. Off. B. C. Dickens, "It will be hard to ever truly replace the Beverley's role in the Gulf, and by the army it will be sorely missed. Over the past three years at Muharraq, the squadron has supplied the route Stations in the Gulf, supported 1 and 2 Parachute Battalions and maintained a search and rescue standby for the Bahrain FIR." He went on to remark that very few of the aircrew would be sorry to leave, as some whose tours had been extended had been at Muharraq for three summers. "Our groundcrews, most of whom are not returning to the UK, have worked many long hours in trying conditions to maintain

and lately to surpass the squadron's tasked hours. They too will be glad to be moving on to a less fickle old lady."

A comparison with activity in December 1964 is appropriate here:

| | |
|---|---|
| Total hours flown: | 274:25 |
| Operational hours flown: | 263:30 |
| Training hours flown: | 10:55 |
| Air miles flown: | 37,190 |
| Passenger miles flown: | 269,200 |
| Troops carried: | nil |
| Passengers carried: | 1,039 |
| Freight carried: | 269 tons |
| Paratroops dropped: | nil |
| Freight dropped: | nil |
| Mail carried: | 2,967 lbs. |
| Casualties evacuated: | 15 |

At midnight on 6th/7th September 1967, 30 Squadron ceased to function as an operating unit, but was not disbanded and continued to exist on a 'number-plate' basis. The squadron standard had been taken to the RAF College at Cranwell on 26th August for safe keeping and subsequent return to a newly-activated 30 Squadron, planned for September 1968 at RAF Fairford.

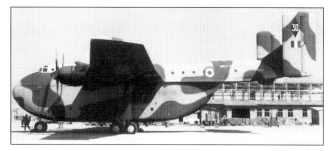

*Beverley XH122 at Muharraq in 1967*          [Flt. Lt. A. Thomas].

*One of a number of Beverleys parked forelornly at 27 MU, Shawbury, in 1967 was XM105 [A] of 30 Squadron, still wearing Royal Air Force Middle East markings*          [R. C. Sturtivant collection].

*After withdrawal from service, Beverley C.1 XL148 [U] is seen at 27 MU, Shawbury, in 1967*          [R. C. Sturtivant collection].

*Students of the Kenya Institute of Administration surround the Beverley of 30 Squadron in which they were flown on a tour of Kenya's intensive cultivation areas. Apart from the 30 Squadron crest displayed prominently on the nose, the call-sign of the aircraft, MOBEA, is marked in full, an unusual feature*
*[Wg. Cdr. R. Evans].*

*The Operations Room at Isiolo during Exercise* Sharp Panga                    *[Wg. Cdr. R. Evans].*

*XH122 during 30 Squadron's tour of High Commissioner's Territories in June 1962. A small piece of the fuselage of this aircraft is, at the time of writing, exhibited in the Norfolk & Suffolk Aviation Museum at Flixton*
*[Wg. Cdr. R. Evans].*

*Seen here at Dar-es-Salaam airport in March 1962, XL152 [A] is being refuelled while taking part in flood relief operations*   [*Wg. Cdr. R. Evans*].

*Local residents admire the cavernous hold of Beverley XH122 during the June 1962 tour of High Commissioner's Territories*   [*Wg. Cdr. R. Evans*].

*Beverley XB263 at Isiolo during Exercise* Sharp Panga *in February 1963, with a Twin Pioneer and a Beaver in the background*     [*Wg. Cdr. R. Evans*].

*A line-up of Beverleys of 30 and 84 Squadrons being readied for a para-drop at Muharraq in 1962*     [*Wg. Cdr. R. Evans*].

*A Beverley on the Isiolo airstrip*     [*Wg. Cdr. R. Evans*].

*Beverley XB263 [K] performing the mail drop and pick-up at Aldabra on 9th November 1962*                                *[J. Hartup].*

*Surveyors at Aldabra Island await the pioneering mail drop by the 30 Squadron Beverley*                      *[J. Hartup].*

*The view from the 'office'. Taking on fuel from a VC10.*

# Chapter 11: Life with 'Fat Albert'

30 Squadron, dormant for nine months, was brought back to active life on 10th June 1968, when the first personnel were posted to RAF Fairford in Gloucestershire. Their new aircraft was to be the Lockheed Hercules C.1 (C-130K in USAF parlance), and in command was Wg. Cdr. K. J. Parfit, a navigator whose rank reflected the high status being given to squadrons flying the Hercules. For the first two weeks, time was spent on internal administration and acquisition of equipment.

The Hercules was a very different aircraft from the Beverley, which had been flown so intensively during the squadron's previous incarnation. Powered by four Allison T56-A-7A turboprop engines of 4050 ehp, the Hercules C.1 can cruise at up to 375 mph, has a maximum loaded range of 2450 miles and a maximum fuel range of 4770 miles. Empty, it weighs 72,367 lbs., and its normal take-off weight is 155,000 lbs. With a flight crew of five,'Fat Albert', as the aircraft is fondly known by its crews, can carry 92 fully-equipped troops or 64 paratroops, and by virtue of its low-pressure tyres it can use unmade airstrips. In all, the new aircraft had much greater potential than the Beverley. In size, however, it is somewhat smaller than the Beverley, as its wingspan is 132ft. 5in., length 97ft. 9in., height 38ft. 3in. and wing area 1745 square feet.

Continuation training began on 25th June and the first route trip left on 7th July for Changi, Singapore. A week later there was a considerable influx of newcomers, who joined an operational if somewhat basic squadron. Acceptance checks were carried out on newly-arrived aircraft, and a sixteen-hour three-shift day was instituted, with the hope that rectification time could be boosted to 3000 hours per month. Aircraft engineering was centralised and aircraft were assigned to RAF Fairford and were allocated to 30 and 47 Squadrons as required for a flight.

Since 1968, 30 Squadron's main task has consisted of long-distance flying to anywhere in the world, often at short notice, carrying personnel, equipment and supplies, either for operational purposes or on exercises. A great deal of the early flying was carried out in support of fighter and bomber squadrons. An ongoing task which began in 1969 is the redeployment of troops on detachment to Northern Ireland, known as Operation *Banner* or *Banner 2*. In the early days a secondary task was Transport Support, which consisted of low-level air drops of paratroops and

their equipment, but, as will be seen, this was withdrawn later. Another regular and enjoyable task over the years has been the provision of support for the Red Arrows aerobatic team in the UK and overseas.

As one of the first interesting extra-mural activities, the CO and five members of the squadron travelled to Shawbury (by car!) on 17th July to present three medals to former Flt. Sgt. Clews, who was a member of 30 Squadron from 1915 to 1919. In 1921 he had applied for his medals and had been told that they would be forwarded. The 50th anniversary of the formation of the RAF found him still waiting for them, so he contacted a RAF Recruiting Office, and at his request his medals were at last presented to him by his old Squadron.

By August 1968, 30 Squadron was working a full programme, with seven Changi slip flights and seven other route trips. Poor serviceability played havoc with the timings, however. A further intake of captains and co-pilots, navigators, engineers and AQMs, thirty-two in all, arrived on 19th August, by which time the squadron offices began to feel a little crowded. The first squadron party was held that month, and the CO hoped that similar functions would encourage wives and girl-friends to become friends, as the living quarters were so widely spread that loneliness while husbands were away could be a problem. Another 'thrash', the Autumn Ball, was held by the Station on 20th September and was judged a splendid success. One route trip to Germany provided beer for a German Beer Cellar, a trip to France brought back champagne, and another to Scotland meant that seafood was available!

Most significantly, the 30 Squadron standard was brought to Fairford from its resting place at Cranwell on 26th September 1968. Squadron badges soon adorned almost all flying suits, and squadron ties were to be available. The standard was on show at a guest night on 5th October, to the delight of all concerned.

On the flight line, however, poor serviceability still dogged the squadron, and bad weather did not help matters, with fog, low cloud and drizzle conspiring to inhibit the training programme. Personnel were cheered in November, however, when 30 Squadron came fifth in the contest for a trophy presented by the 14th Air Despatch Regt. for the best squadron drop. Seven squadrons competed at El Adem — 30 and 47 from Fairford, 24 and 36 from Lyneham, 114 and 267 (Argosies) from Benson and 46 (Andovers) from Abingdon. Each squadron sent three crews on the ten-day detachment, and the competition consisted of two drops, one by day and and one by night. Umpires carried on board awarded points or penalties for everything from the quality of briefing to a dropping error. Winner that year was 46 Squadron with 4619 points out of 6000, while 30 Squadron collected 3894. Congratulations were given afterwards to the ground crew who provided an excellent serviceability rate.

The beginning of 1969, and the usual bad weather, meant that flying was restricted to routine training, but social events flourished. Exercises and competition for the Lord Trophy, in which unfortunately 30 Squadron came last, occupied February. The reason for such a poor showing was an unserviceable aircraft, but it was considered that the three crews who went to El Adem for the competition had nevertheless gained valuable experience.

## A tragedy for 30 Squadron

Then disaster struck. Flying a training sortie on 24th March 1969, Hercules XV180 had just completed a practice three-engined 'touch and go' at Fairford when the other engine on the same side failed. The aircraft struck the ground just north of the overshoot area of runway 28 and burst into flames. There were no survivors. Flying the aircraft was the squadron's training officer, Flt. Lt. John Coutts; the two co-pilots were Flg. Off. Robin Plumtree, the deputy squadron adjutant, and Flg. Off. Alan Walsingham, and the navigator was Flg. Off. Ian Moir. Flg. Off. Peter Medhurst was the engineer and deputy engineer leader; and AQM was Flt. Sgt. Bryan McGing, who was in charge of weight and balance data. All but Ian Moir were buried at All Hallows cemetery, South Cerney, on 28th March with military honours, and Ian was buried in Scotland next day.

But life had to go on. A more exciting selection of trips was flown in March, and included three to Nairobi and a detachment to Bermuda and Antigua to deal with unrest in Anguilla, where rebels decided to declare unilateral independence from the St. Kitts, Nevis & Anguillan Federation. Great Britain quickly decided to impose direct rule, and Operation *Sheepskin* began. All four Lyneham-based squadrons were involved, 30 Squadron making history when Flt. Lt. M. Letton dropped the first two vehicles from an RAF Hercules operationally, a Land Rover and a trailer. Flt. Lt. R. Humphrey was the captain of the first aircraft ever to land on Anguilla. In April '*Westabout*' trips were also becoming more frequent, and Exercise *Bitter Breath* in Canada was also on the programme. Another exercise, *Flush*, involved seven trips to Iceland, all of which were delayed. These tasks meant that many of the crews were away for long periods.

Exercise *Montalvo* took six crews and four Hercules in May 1969 to El Adem, where they took part in stream assaults. A NATO exercise, *Olympic Express*, was held at Thessaloniki in Greece, to where passengers and freight were flown. On the return flight, the empty Hercules managed to reach an unusually high cruise altitude of 33,000 feet.

On 1st June 1969 the two squadrons based at Lyneham took over the Changi slip tasks, leaving 30 Squadron to concentrate on exercises and training flights. These proved interesting, covering Greece, Denmark, Germany, the United States, Canada, the Middle East and Far East, Greenland and South America. In England, the squadron carried out two stream assault parachute drops at Imber DZ on Salisbury Plain on 24th June, the first operation of its type in the UK since equipping with the Hercules. Another unusual task was participation in the Open Day held at Fairford on 7th June, when four crews flew by in formation and Sqn. Ldr. Henley gave a convincing demonstration of the tactical capability of the Hercules.

Variety continued to be the spice of life, one of the more out-of-the-ordinary tasks in July being a practice call-out for crews on Strike Command standby. Three crews were involved in the initial phase, providing dispersal and logistic support for Vulcan bombers and their crews. In August the squadron reverted to general route flying, and that month there were eleven return flights to Changi and several 'pond-jumpers' to military airfields and civil airports in the USA. Of enormous significance, 30 Squadron first became tasked to ferry troops and equipment to Belfast, a task which continues to this day. Three crews were on standby each day to carry out these missions, but this was later reduced to one crew.

Use of the simulator at Lyneham began in August 1969, and consisted of an hour's briefing, three hours in the simulator carrying out various exercises, and an hour's de-briefing. September's work included Exercise *Unity 69* on Salisbury Plain, a joint Service demonstration of Britain's fighting capabilities in which 30 and 47 Squadron crews took part.

During the first half of October, 30 Squadron participated in Exercise *Ranular*, a Strike Command exercise which used Marham for the airlift of No.1 Air Control Centre (based at Wattisham) and 25 (SAM) Squadron (based at North Coates) to Akrotiri in Cyprus. Communications played an important part in the proceedings, and operational cells were established at Marham and Fairford with HF SSB radio capable of air/ground and ground/ground operation. Most crews were from 30 Squadron, with sixty Hercules sorties flown. Crews were given only an hour or hour-and-a-half turn-round time at Akrotiri. On three days when fog obscured all UK airfields, diversions had to be made to Luqa in Malta, but otherwise the exercise went as planned. Fairford provided a detachment commander, operations staff, groundcrews, servicing equipment and spares.

On 17th October, Flt. Lt. Jack Huntington completed 10,000 hours of flying in the RAF. When he landed after a twenty-minute sortie he was met by the Station Commander (Gp. Capt. Cockfield), the CO, the press, and a bottle of champagne. Afterwards, a barrel of beer was organised for a squadron celebration, and Jack proceeded to down a half-yard of ale in admirable style! During the Second World War he had flown Spitfires and Vengeances on the Arakan front (where of course 30 Squadron had been prominent) and afterwards had been involved in the evacuation of wounded troops from Korea. Members of the squadron presented an inscribed silver cigarette box to him to mark the occasion.

The recovery phase of Exercise *Ranular* occupied 30 Squadron early in November 1969, after which the CO received a message of congratulation from 38 Group which ended with permission for a short Station stand-down. Later in the month some route-flying took place, but an out-of-the-ordinary task was the airlift of three fourteen-seat helicopters from Milan to Kuwait for the Kuwait Air Force. December saw the final Changi slip sortie, after which the crew returned in a VC-10.

Christmas festivities included a party for twenty-eight children from three homes run by Wiltshire County Council. A film show, a conjurer and a good tea provided by squadron wives added up to an enjoyable afternoon, and then Santa Claus in the form of M.Eng. Davies arrived in a Hercules which was opened for a tour by the children, shepherded by two squadron members.

Most of the squadron's work in January 1970 was connected with exercises. Two ran simultaneously, *Wildwood* to Nairobi and *Woolfram* to Addis Ababa, but without doubt the most interesting for the crews was Exercise *Palm Toddy*, a detachment to Sharjah for support training. One squadron member described the detachment.

"30 Squadron's answer to the ousting from the desert training area in Libya was a home-spun exercise at Sharjah. Lunchtime on 24th January saw three crews in the bar. After a short siesta 30 entertained the officers of RAF Sharjah. Monday saw the commencement of flying, one aircraft u/s and one delayed at Akrotiri, left one for TST and one to go to Bahrain and inspect the strips. Tuesday to Thursday saw a host of three-ship formations around the excellent low-level cross-country routes of Muscat and Oman. Friday was a dropping day to help out everyone's training task. Friday night 30 were entertained by Sharjah and Saturday night a party finished a first class detachment. Sunday saw four Hercules depart for Fairford and return." Not exactly a tedious event, it appears!

Most of the trips flown in February were eastward in direction, as far as Changi, but a few flights were made to Antigua and Anguilla, and to Goose Bay and on to Offutt AFB or Ottawa. Opportunities were taken to hold several parties during the month, one of them by way of congratulations to MAQM Riddle on the award of the Long Service & Good Conduct Medal and to Sgt. Cooper, who received the AOC-in-C's Commendation.

Exercise *Thread* in March 1970 brought about the reactivation of Hal Far airfield on Malta, which had closed three years earlier. At the same time, competition for the Lord Trophy took place. During the exercise, a DZ at Comiso in Sicily was used, the Hercules landing at Sigonella. In addition, one crew took part in a drop on a DZ near Akrotiri in Cyprus. 30 Squadron came fifth in the Lord Trophy contest, but *Thread* proved its value in terms of Transport Support experience for the crews taking part. Another interesting task, arranged in conjunction with Hawker Siddeley Aviation, was a demonstration of role equipment to the Italian Air Force and Army at Practica del Mare. The 30 Squadron crew, headed by Flt. Lt. M. Cannon, laid out a DZ on the airfield and scored a bulls-eye with a one-ton auto drop. On a trip to Marseilles (Marignane) Sqn. Ldr. Henley carried out successful helicopter loading trials in conjunction with Sud Aviation and ATDU personnel from Abingdon and afterwards improved Anglo-French relations in the 'Las Vegas' bar!

At a squadron guest night held at South Cerney on 23rd March the guests were Mr. A. W. 'Bill' Bedford, the former chief test pilot of Hawker Siddeley Aviation at Dunsfold, and Sqn. Ldr. P. L. Whitaker DFC, a CO of the squadron in its Valetta days. Mr. Bedford made a short speech about the Harrier aircraft and ended by saying "I can understand why my son joined Thirty after seeing a notice in the squadron reading 'Silence — aircrew sleeping'!"

The main commitment for 30 Squadron in April 1970 was the deployment phase of Exercise *Bersatu Padu*, a five-nation exercise in the Far East which was due to last until August. Its main aim was to train and exercise the forces of the five nations in advance of British withdrawal from the area. Phase 1 involved the deployment of men and materials from the UK, and in this phase 30 Squadron flew fifteen sorties, after which a message of appreciation was received from the AOC-in-C of Air Support Command. Other tasks in April were limited, but included trips to Lima in Peru for Strike Command backup and one to Eskisehir in Turkey to deliver 250 Red Cross tents to alleviate the suffering caused by an earthquake at Gediz.

According to squadron records, the highlight of activities in May 1970 was Exercise *Cross Check*, in which two crews in one Hercules spent two weeks on an exchange with 436 (Tusker) Squadron of the Canadian Armed Forces. 47 Squadron also provided an aircraft and two crews, and characteristically one aircraft was unserviceable on the day of departure, the delay meaning a night stop at Gander instead of Ottawa. On the second day the two Hercules met at Namao, Alberta, accompanied by two of 436 Squadron's C-130Es, for a week of transport support which culminated in a night drop with 435 (Chinthe) Squadron as part of Exercise *Nemesis North*. A move was then made to CAF Base Uplands at Ottawa for two days of socialising and route preparation for a difficult task. An eight-hour flight took 30 and 436 Squadrons

to Whitehorse in the Yukon, where the crews stopped for a day and a half before flying to Thule over many of the Dewline and Arctic weather stations. One of the Canadian aircraft diverted to Inuvik to evacuate a seriously ill Eskimo child, which caused the captain to remark "This makes the whole job worthwhile." Next day was scheduled for a tour of weather stations at such places as Eureka and Resolute Bay, places probably never before visited by Air Support Command. The flight continued via Frobisher to Uplands, where two days were spent in recuperation after an arduous two weeks, before the transatlantic crossing. Altogether this exercise was deemed a great success, and the crews looked forward to the visit of 436 Squadron to Fairford in September.

Further trouble flared up in Northern Ireland in June 1970, and 30 Squadron was again involved in ferrying troops to the Province, hampering normal squadron activities. However, one unusual task was to airlift a Lightning simulator to Kuwait, which had recently acquired a number of Lightning fighters. July's work included the withdrawal phase of Exercise *Bersatu Padu*, which did not go exactly according to plan but had been completed by the end of the month. One casualty was Flg. Off. Rest, who developed chicken-pox at Changi and had to remain there for some days.

As so much of the squadron silver had been lost in past years, Sqn. Ldr. Henley was kind enough to present a bonbon dish to add to the small collection. To celebrate his posting out, he was in turn presented with a squadron tankard during a guest night on 21st August. Operationally, that was a quiet month, many personnel being on leave.

Members of the squadron were pleased to welcome on 10th September personnel of 28 Squadron South African Air Force, led by Col. Beeton from SAAF Headquarters. They flew as observers on a low-level cross-country route around East Anglia. The crew, captained by Flt. Lt. Humphries, dropped a load within thirty yards of the bullseye on the DZ and within fifteen seconds of the designated time. To celebrate, a barrel of beer was soon dealt with after the return to Fairford!

September 1970 included a return visit by 436 Squadron CAF from Ottawa, which added a great deal to the social calendar and tested everybody's stamina! After arrival on 11th September, the first week was spent in the UK, but characteristic English weather hampered activity, including a visit to the SBAC show at Farnborough. On 18th September a mass departure for Gibraltar took place, and next day the aircraft flew in loose formation to Akrotiri, where five days were spent in carrying out a large number of cross-

*Hercules XV196 and another parked on a coastal airfield, thought to be Heraklion in Crete.*

country exercises and supply drops on Ladies Mile DZ, all in excellent weather. The fleet returned to Fairford on 23rd September via a night stop at Luqa, and next day a mixed all-ranks party was held in the sergeants' mess as a farewell gesture. Only after the Canadians had departed were certain losses discovered, which fact was felt to warrant a mass invasion of Ottawa at a later date!

October 1970 was long remembered as a 'doom month' for postings, as many captains and navigators had received ground postings to such outposts as Gan and Upavon. Wg. Cdr. Ward, who was posted to Sharjah as OC Flying at the end of the month, made a most unusual presentation to the squadron before he left — a gleaming model of a racehorse at full gallop, mounted on a wooden base and accompanied by a framed explanation of the squadron motto. During the month, Air Quartermasters were retitled as Air Loadmasters; there was mixed reaction to this change, which was made to reflect their skill in calculating load weights and dispositions.

The main activity in November 1970 was Exercise *Follicle*, to which 30 Squadron sent two aircraft and four crews, led by Sqn. Ldr. Waddingham, to work with other Hercules, Andovers and Argosies. Personnel were the guests of 46° Aerobrigata, but as accommodation was limited, half of them lived in tents. Luckily the weather was better than normal for the time of year. Between 2nd and 13th November, low-level sorties, paratroop drops and cargo drops were carried out, and the exercise culminated in a series of two stream assaults to Sicily and Sardinia in daylight and two at night. As Italian parachutes were not compatible with the RAF aircraft, Italian troops had to use RAF parachutes, which demonstrated the need for standardisation of equipment in NATO. Due to *Follicle*, route flying was limited, but one trip involved taking relief supplies to Bahrain for onward despatch to the East Pakistan (now Bangladesh) cyclone disaster area.

1970 ended with a memorable two-week 'westabout' in XV219, captained by Flt. Lt. Huntington and Flt. Lt. Rowland. Most of the freight flown from Fairford to Singapore consisted of disposable nappies, but on arrival at McClellan AFB the crew was told that a high-density load of radio equipment had to be taken aboard for Gan. Five hours later XV219 was loaded to perfection, although one needed to be a mountain climber to reach the facilities at the rear end! The other significant event that month was the arrival of a new CO, Wg. Cdr. D. N. Galpin, who came from 10 Squadron, which was flying VC10s at Brize Norton.

January 1971's 'route of the month' award, had there been such a thing, would have gone to Flt. Lt. Cane and his crew, who gallantly volunteered to collect Hercules XV223 from the Lockheed factory at Marietta, Georgia, where it had been under repair following a brake fire at JFK Airport, New York some time previously. This task was completed after a most enlightening stay in nearby Atlantic City and a tour round the vast production lines of C-130 and C-5 aircraft.

## Goodbye to Fairford

Between 10th and 12th February, 30 Squadron moved from Fairford to Lyneham to begin a new lease of life. For several weeks members of the squadron were busy in dismantling acres of chinagraph board, removing coffee bars and collecting assortments of trophies, each of which was testimony to the valour and dedication of a long-forgotten aircrew or mission. But once at Lyneham, the squadron personnel rapidly settled into their new buildings, and with 24, 36 and 47 Squadrons created what was reputed to be not only the largest Hercules force outside the USAF but the best anywhere. To mark the arrival and formally welcome 30 and 47 Squadrons, the Station Commander, Gp. Capt. Yetman, met the COs and representative members of the squadrons. This event was covered by local and national press and television.

Now established at Lyneham, 30 Squadron took part in Exercise *Donkey Trot* in March 1971. The venue was Sharjah in the Persian Gulf, an area familiar to past members of the squadron. Low flying over rugged mountains and featureless desert gave valuable experience to newer crew members. The highlight of the detachment was a resupply mission at Saiq airfield, which was at an altitude of 6500 feet in the Jebal Akhdar. There, 20,000 lbs. of Avtur was dropped in drums by parachute to replenish dwindling

fuel supplies for AAC helicopters, a refreshing change from routine for the Hercules crews. While at Sharjah, the detachment was visited by AVM Crowley-Milling, the AOC 38 Group.

Another out-of-the ordinary task was flown on 20th March, when Flt. Lt. N. Smith and crew dropped 23 soldiers on an unmarked DZ near Liege in Belgium, although subsequently many of them were ambushed and captured by 'opposing forces'.

Exercise *Deep Stream* in April 1971 involved dropping a wide variety of army stores over a DZ at Comiso in Sicily, the four Hercules operating from Hal Far in Malta. Another mission of unusual nature flown that month involved the collection from Sao Paolo in Brazil of members of the Joint Services Expedition who had been on a geological survey on Elephant Island in the Antarctic.

30 Squadron's transport support involvement continued, useful experience being gained in May when many crews took part in low-level stream assault practice on the Froghill DZ in the Stanford Battle Area in Norfolk. Following this came a low-level route and paradrop in Denmark. Training world-wide included the incidental delivery of a helicopter to NASA at Langley Field, Virginia.

Exercise *Donkey Trot* at Sharjah was the third at that location since the squadron reformed. The new CO, Wg. Cdr. Galpin, and two others represented 30 Squadron in competition with the other three Lyneham squadrons. Two overland routes were flown by day and one over the sea by night to deliver a large variety of supplies onto the DZ at Juweiza. Flt. Lt. J. Lambert and his crew excelled themselves by scoring 11 direct hits out of the total of 39 reached by the combined squadrons. From an RAF Station in the Middle East which was being closed down, Muharraq, a large backlog of freight was transported to Lyneham, a task which would be repeated elsewhere as similar Gulf Stations were disbanded.

During the first two weeks of July, 30 Squadron joined the other Lyneham-based squadrons at Machrihanish to compete over a series of selected low-level routes in the highlands and islands. Unusually good weather allowed maximum training value to be extracted from this exercise, and 30 Squadron secured first place in the competition.

On 25th September 1971 there was an Open Day for the families of all 30 Squadron members, the first time such an occasion had been arranged. Everyone over the age of twelve enjoyed a flight in a Hercules captained by either Sqn. Ldr. Pettinger or Sqn. Ldr. Ed Waddingham, who had organised the event. Vast quantities of food and refreshments were consumed and everyone enjoyed the day. Another extra-mural activity was the voyage along the Thames undertaken by four of the squadron's navigators. Embarking in a MS9 dinghy at Lechlade on 22nd October, the crew arrived at Teddington Lock eight days later. What, if anything, this exploit proved is not recorded!

The tragic loss of a 24 Squadron crew in Hercules XV216 in the Mediterranean on 9th November 1971 cast a shadow over all the Lyneham squadrons. Five 30 Squadron crews had been taking part in the exercise at Pisa, named *Coldstream*, between 8th and 19th November, and the squadron was represented at the memorial service held at Pisa on 21st November. That month also saw the departure of the squadron's first sortie to Korea since equipping with the Hercules.

Towards the end of 1971 the conflict between India and Pakistan influenced 30 Squadron's activities, and four crews under the CO were deployed to Masirah for possible action. Another crew, captained by Flt. Lt. Horsley, was obliged to spend Christmas at Masirah during a 'tramp' around Africa, but enjoyed very warm hospitality provided by the Station Commander of that outpost.

## Withdrawal from Malta

International affairs dominated 30 Squadron's activities in January 1972. On 28th December 1971 the Maltese government had decreed that British forces were to leave the island within three days, which was clearly an impossibility. Eventually a revised departure by 31st March was set, and a period of intense planning for the withdrawal under Operation *Mature* began under the control of the Station Commander at RAF Luqa. All non-essential flying by the RAF from Luqa and all training flights from the UK were stopped, and numerous flights from there to the UK carrying equipment and stores were flown by 30 Squadron crews. Air Support Command's Detachment Commander at Luqa was Sqn.

Ldr. Ed Waddingham, 30 Squadron's senior captain, whose efforts contributed greatly to the success of the initial withdrawal.

During the same month, 30 Squadron was heavily involved in Exercise *Cadnam*, under which troops and equipment were positioned in what was then British Honduras and is now Belize. Within about twelve hours from the initial warning, almost all the available crews had assembled for positioning by VC-10 as slip crews at Santa Maria or Nassau. The following week was spent in trying to trace each crew's whereabouts, but eventually most of them were located. Meanwhile, a few other crews had already left on an exercise which involved routing through the United States to Darwin in Australia. These crews were more difficult to find; indeed, the crew captained by Flt. Lt. J. Farley were apparently forgotten for a week before being traced to Guam!

All this added up to a personnel shortage in February, particularly in co-pilots and loadmasters, but enough were available for a westabout training mission which lasted two weeks. It involved landings at Nandi in Fiji, at Perth, and at Christchurch in New Zealand, which one crew member descibed as "....like Chippenham on a Sunday, so who wants to stay?" A destination never previously visited by 30 Squadron was Midway Island in the Pacific, but the crew who went there decided that as it was only a larger version of Wake Island it was hardly worth another trip.

A second phase of Exercise *Cadnam* was mounted in March 1972, but much of 30 Squadron's effort that month went into providing crews for lifting troops to Northern Ireland. It was considered that trouble might flare up over the Easter period, and eight aircraft were despatched on 30th March and two more on 1st and 2nd April, but no general call-out was ordered. At the time, the emphasis on tactical support flying was increasing, and 30 Squadron crews flew three formation sorties per week, two on a squadron basis and one as part of a wave of nine Hercules from the Lyneham Wing as a whole. At the end of March, however, this plan was postponed for a month to allow preparation for two formations each of over thirty aircraft to be flown in the late summer.

Early in April a series of intensive tactical training courses designed to bring Lyneham crews up to a required standard of flying in large formations began. Training for this, under what was known as the Joint Air Transport Force (JATFOR) was in three parts: firstly, individual aircraft flew in sections of three over a period of four days, then two sections joined, and finally twelve aircraft flew together. 30 Squadron allocated ten crews for this task, which was flown over the West Country and Scotland in sorties of up to three hours. Luckily, Exercise *Cadnam* came to an end over the Easter period, releasing crews for other pressing tasks. One special sortie went to Nouadhibou in Mauretania to support a Shackleton which had a damaged oleo. The 30 Squadron crew considered that two hours in that forbidding place was quite enough, but the Shackleton crew had been there for two weeks!

By May 1972, 30 Squadron had four crews allocated to JATFOR, plus a stream commander and two stream leaders. A problem was that constant training for JATFOR had an adverse effect on routine continuation training, which often had to be cancelled at short notice. The climax for the month was a visit from the AOC-in-C, an event noted somewhat cynically in the squadron records. "Despite frantic efforts resulting from an over-large sense of guilt" said the diarist "we failed to prove an untidy squadron and to celebrate we had a squadron party the same evening."

With five squadrons now at Lyneham, 30 Squadron appeared to have the opportunity of good routes once every five months. June was one of the 'bad' months,, and apart from one crew which supported the Red Arrows for five weeks (Ascot 3894), a schedule to Calgary and a VIP return flight (Ascot 3323) from St. Catherine's Airport, Niagara, where the Red Arrows had been performing, the emphasis was on JATFOR training, now referred to as Exercise *Champion Hurdle*.

However, the exercise was amost cancelled at the end of July, when the whole Station was engaged in Exercise *Four Square*, a major reinforcement of troops in Northern Ireland. Within 48 hours of the movement order being issued, 4000 troops and their equipment were flown from Gutersloh to Aldergrove. 30 Squadron acted with its usual aplomb, with up to thirteen crews involved. One crew achieved a fifteen minute turn-round, landing to take-off, at Aldergrove, which was considered something of a record. The

Army 'top brass' were impressed, and NAAFI staff at Gutersloh were pleased with the extra trade!

Meanwhile Sqn. Ldr. Quaife and crew were on a westabout trip from Wake Island to Hong Kong when they had to divert to Manila in the Phillipines with propeller trouble. There they were asked to assist in flood relief operations, as the islands had just suffered great damage form the worst typhoon in living memory. After six days of concentrated flying, the crew was thanked personally by the then President of the Phillipines, Marcos, and his wife and appeared on local television.

At long last Exercise *Champion Hurdle* came to head in August, when over thirty Hercules aircraft from Lyneham took part in a mass assault by dropping elements of 16 Parachute Brigade onto Imber DZ on Salisbury Plain by day and night. The main force was led by Sqn. Ldr. C. J. Horsley of 30 Squadron. This exercise marked the end of the introductory phase of JATFOR, during which assault training techniques for paratroops were altered, and the hope was now for a standardised efficient approach to tactical flying which had not been previously achieved.

In August 1972 the whole country was living under the threat of a prolonged strike by dockers, which particularly affected the Hebrides, Orkneys and Shetlands, where the inhabitants relied on sea transport for almost all their supplies. So during the week of 12th to 18th August, 30 Squadron took part in providing essential supplies by air, flying to Tiree, Kirkwall, and Sumburgh. The strike was then called off, perhaps because its perpetrators saw that alternative methods of transport were available.

September's tasks included troop movements to and from Northern Ireland and Canada and a fighter squadron move from West Raynham to Laarbruch. A crew led by Flt. Lt. Mike Kemp was in Greece for Exercise *Deep Furrow*, in which they dropped military equipment and paratroops, while other crews helped resupply the Army in Sharjah and the Sultan of Oman's Air Force at Salalah. On top of all this, the largest exercise for many years, *Strong Express*, in which all NATO countries took part, was held to test reinforcement of NATO's flanks. 30 Squadron flew 28 missions, mostly carrying supplies and equipment to and from Norway and several airfields on the way.

### The biggest drop since Arnhem

30 Squadron was just as busy in October, joining the largest airborne assault mounted over mainland Europe since the Second World War. Designated *Ruby Signet*, the exercise demonstrated the capability of the UK Joint Airborne Task Force in spectacular style. In two phases, on 16th and 18th October, 34 and 35 Hercules dropped 1400 paratroops and about 450 tons of vehicles, equipment and supplies onto a DZ at Zealand in Denmark. The stream commander was 30 Squadron's CO, Wg. Cdr. D. N. Galpin, and the leading crews were specially selected from 30 Squadron. It was due to their capabilities that the drops were made with great precision. Afterwards, special thanks were received from the CO of 16 Parachute Brigade, who had been the first man to 'hit the silk' and who had found his boots touching the ground right on target. A task not unconnected with tactical operations involved several sorties to a landing strip at Upavon Gallops to test a new type of metal strip surface laid by the Army.

A very unusual task came 30 Squadron's way in November 1972 – Operation *Deep Freeze*, the annual resupply by air of the Antarctic research base at McMurdo Sound. When RAF aircraft were needed urgently to supplement US Navy flights from Christchurch to McMurdo one crew from each of the five Lyneham squadrons, two Hercules and groundcrews were sent to Christchurch. The detachment commander, Sqn. Ldr. Quaife, had already visited the home base of *Deep Freeze* at Quonset Point, Virginia, for briefing. 30 Squadron was represented by Sqn. Ldr. Waddingham and his crew. Six sorties were flown by 30 Squadron onto McMurdo's ice runway and the operation was deemed a great success in several ways. Not only had the purpose of the operation been achieved, but the exercise had provided some good training in working in extreme climatic conditions, with unfamiliar weather and polar navigation.

On Christmas Day 1972 a standby crew was called out to take medical and other equipment to Managua, the capital of Nicaragua,

*A 30 Squadron crew flying their Hercules down a valley in Nepal during Exercise* Khana Cascade *in 1973.*

after an earthquake. Flt. Lt. Allison and his 30 Squadron crew flew the first military aircraft into the area, less than 48 hours after the disaster. After a long stage via Gander, they landed at Bermuda, where they persuaded the airport services to provide fuel and then pressed on to Managua after only a short rest. On their return flight the aircraft became unserviceable at Bermuda, so they became a slip crew, taking over a Managua-bound aircraft from a 24 Squadron crew. After completing a second mercy mission they eventually returned to Lyneham on New Year's Day 1973. Their return was regarded by the whole squadron as a pleasing finale to a year in which 30 Squadron had played a leading part.

Relief operations occupied most of 30 Squadron's time in February 1973, when two aircraft were used to ferry supplies from Khartoum to Juba in the Sudan under the auspices of the United Nations. Many miles away in Nepal, the Government had asked for aid after two years of crop failure, and Operation *Khana Cascade* was organised to provide relief. Hercules crews of 30 Squadron formed part of the detachment, and one of them carried out the first reconnaissance of potential dropping zones and the first drop. *Khana Cascade* continued in March, with airlifts mounted from Bhairawa and Biratnagar, providing a great deal of unusual and demanding flying for the crews. Following the completion of the operation, messages of congratulation were received from the Nepalese Government.

Wg. Cdr. B. P. Earle took command of 30 Squadron on 20th March 1973, and squadron crews took part in Exercise *Pale Jade*, a movement of Phantom fighter squadrons to the Far East. Other tasks included carrying troops to Canada and the Gambia for exercises. In June Exercise *Alexandria Express*, a NATO scheme to deploy forces in Europe's south-east flank, involved the squadron in nine deployment flights and five recovery flights. Far bigger was

Exercise *Deep Furrow*, a Priority 1 exercise involving British, American and Turkish forces held in Turkish Thrace. A 36-aircraft Hercules formation which flew from Incirlik to a DZ north of the Bosphorus included nine flown by 30 Squadron crews, while another seven flew deployment and recovery phases.

Fuel shortages affected the performance of the Hercules fleet at the end of 1973, and in December the task was cut by thirty per cent. On trips of more than 600 miles, captains were told to use long-range cruise techniques in an effort to conserve fuel. To add cheer to the situation, 30 Squadron was proud to retain the Crosscheck Trophy for the best performance on low-level cross-country flying and a harness pack drop. Competition for the Trophy had been held at Trenton in Canada between 10th and 19th October, four crews under Sqn. Ldr. Gillmore, Sqn. Ldr. Waddingham, Flt. Lt. Bailey and Flt. Lt Howard representing 30 Squadron. A further attempt to wrest the Trophy from 30 Squadron was made between 12th and 25th May 1974, when 436 Squadron of the Canadian Armed Forces paid a visit to Lyneham. The competition took place at Machrihanish, and again 30 Squadron was victorious.

On 20th July 1974 an evacuation of British and foreign holiday-makers from Cyprus began, followed by reinforcement of UN forces. All available crews were used, and 35 sorties were made by 30 Squadron. The operation was completed on 28th July, although a few crews were still being called out, particularly in the middle of August. For the rest of that year, low-level Transport Support work was practised intensively, and included a detachment to Machrihanish to take advantage of the many valleys in the Highlands.

Then in January 1975 a problem affecting all flying was discovered — a suspect condition in the Hercules mainplane. The temporary result was a reduction in the amount of fuel carried, which affected the operational range of the aircraft. A refuelling stop at Keflavik in Iceland was therefore introduced for transatlantic flights.

These restrictions did not, however, prevent a three-crew detachment being set up in Cyprus on a seven-week rotational basis with the other Lyneham squadrons. Wg. Cdr. Earle and Sqn. Ldr. Gray planned the operation and led the first detachment, with Sqn. Ldr. R. C. Parsley as Detachment CO, Flg. Off. R. A. Case as operations officer and SAC Shaw providing administrative support. They soon found that there was a local security threat and had to carry out guard duty. By the end of the month flights were being made to Malta, Teheran, the Gulf states, Sudan and Nairobi, although two Hercules had been grounded when cracks in the wing centre section were found. The detachment came to an end early in August, when it was decided that resupply flights to Stations in the Gulf area would be made direct from Lyneham. One crew, however, would spend an extended period at Masirah to operate a shuttle to Seeb and Salalah.

## Would 30 survive?

The Defence Review of March 1975, which specified that two squadrons of Hercules were to be disbanded within twelve months, was received with resignation by 30 Squadron members, although nobody knew whether they would be affected. Morale remained high, and was boosted by a guest night held on 24th March to mark the squadron's 60th anniversary. Among those present were AVM N. E. Hoad, the AOC of 46 Group, and eight former Commanding Officers. On 25th September the MoD announced that aircrew would be reallocated between the four remaining Hercules squadrons, a message which reduced the tension still felt by some squadron members. Between November 1975 and January 1976 30 Squadron received 36 new aircrew members from 36, 48 and 70 Squadrons as well as from the OCU, but a small number of men would be posted.

30 Squadron, always good at creating precedents, established another one in May 1974. In a working day of ten hours five minutes in the air, Flt. Lt. Grange and his crew dropped 420 troops in 53 runs, with ten intermediate landings. After this, a message of appreciation was received from 1 Parachute Training School, the squadron's 'customer'.

On 10th October three crews were called upon at short notice to airlift troops and equipment to Belize in Central America, ostensibly on a jungle survival exercise. A slip pattern was set up by positioning crews at Gander in Newfoundland and Nassau in the Bahamas, and on 5th November the first Hercules to make use of this arrangement landed at Belize. For the next two weeks there was a flight every two hours, delivering troops and their kit and ground support equipment for Harriers and Puma helicopters. During November, 30 Squadron crews flew 390 hours on this task. In November, the MoD decided to reorganise the work load between the squadrons at Lyncham; the changes were to have a lasting impact on 30 Squadron. From that time, 24 and 30 Squadrons were to operate only on long-distance missions, while 47 and 70 Squadrons would devote most of their time to Transport Support duties. Until disbanding on 1st January 1976, 48 Squadron would also fly routes. This meant that 30 Squadron would no longer be involved in parachute delivery and low-level flying tasks.

In view of an increasing number of sectarian incidents in Co. Armagh, it was decided that a Spearhead Battalion would be deployed to Northern Ireland, so on 6th January 1976, 30 Squadron flew three sorties to Belfast at short notice. Resupply flights to Belize continued, but from February these were flown by a single crew. However, in April the Belize operation came to an end, and the slip patterns were reintroduced to facilitate withdrawal.

At the same time, the Belfast squadron at Brize Norton, 99 Squadron, was disbanded. One of the side-effects of the withdrawal of the Short Belfast aircraft from RAF service was that the Hercules fleet took over most of its tasks. For 30 Squadron, the first such task was to fly to Kingston, Jamaica, via Gander in the first week of June 1976, though the purpose is not revealed. Ironically, the Belfast was in great demand six years later, when the RAF had to hire the very same aircraft from its civilian owners to help in the Falklands campaign!

Ever committed to good public relations, 30 Squadron hosted a visit from the Mayors and Mayoresses of Calne, Chippenham and Wootton Bassett on 12th October 1976. Three days later at a special parade the squadron was presented with the Lord Trophy by the AOC 38 Group, AVM P. G. Williamson CBE DFC, an ironic tribute to the squadron which had withdrawn from the transport support role!

Occasional flights to Belize continued, and in January 1977 provided some excitement for Flt. Lt. Clode and his crew. While they were flying at 25,000 feet ninety miles west of Bermuda, the Burndept homer in the Hercules began to pick up distress signals. When this was reported to air traffic control the captain was given permission to reduce height to 1000 feet, and after forty minutes a red light was spotted in the darkness and rain and reported to the US Coast Guard, who found and recovered the vessel *Rampart* adrift with engine trouble.

A sixteen-day trip to Australia with staff of the Royal Aircraft Establishment began in February, routing via the United States, Honolulu and Fiji. Less exotic, there was the threat of a general strike in Northern Ireland in April 1977, which prompted a deployment of security forces to Aldergrove under Operation *Productivity*. In this, seven crews of 30 Squadron flew twelve sorties in addition to their routine *Banner* commitment. During May the squadron was busy with no less than sixteen different exercises. Early in the month five crews took part in supporting the deployment of 54 Squadron Jaguars to Luqa in Malta, 13 Squadron Canberras from Luqa to Villafranca and 5 Squadron Lightnings from Luqa to Binbrook. Another task was to aid the deployment of Canberras to Teheran and to recover a MoD sales team from Shiraz and Isfahan.

This pattern of work continued in June, a month which included another unplanned search and rescue incident. Flying between Gander and Gutersloh, Flt. Lt. Hunter and crew were asked by Shanwick Oceanic Control Centre to loiter off Ireland, where a single-engined Cherokee aircraft inbound to Shannon had reported engine trouble. Using the Burndept homer, the navigator found the Cherokee sixty miles off course and for two and a half hours it was shepherded by Ascot 5908 until relieved by a Nimrod three hundred miles west of Shannon. The Hercules then diverted to Lyneham. Subsequently, the squadron received a letter of appreciation from the rescue centre.

## Trouble in Belize

An increase in political tension between Guatemala and Belize in June 1977 prompted an operation to reinforce the British garrison in Belize. On 5th July all routine flights and exercise for 30 Squadron were cancelled, and army freight and ground equipment for Harriers was loaded onto the Hercules. Seventeen crews of 30 Squadron were involved, and flew 482 hours on the operation, which lasted five days. When they reverted to normal work, the squadron took part in the Royal Jubilee Review of the RAF. In the static display at Finningley on 29th July, 30 Squadron was represented by Flt. Lt. Robinson, while Flt. Lt. Green and Flt. Lt. Butterworth captained aircraft in the flypast. The event was repeated next day for the benefit of the general public.

30 Squadron retained the Lord Trophy in convincing style in September 1977 after carrying out a successful search exercise culminating in dropping Lindholme equipment at sea. The three crews involved gained 798.5 points of a possible 900, and Flt. Lt. Nicholls came first in the individual competition. During October, eighteen different exercises were supported by 30 Squadron, 82% of them within Europe, although a number of more exotic places were visited. Significantly, special VIP flight Ascot 1120, commanded by the CO and captained by Sqn. Ldr. Wright, took a Government team headed by Lord Carver on a tour of southern Africa in a quest for a settlement of the Rhodesian problem. The route was via Luqa and Nairobi to Dar-es-Salaam and then to Salisbury for a four-day stop. After that the party flew to Gabarone and Johannesburg and on to Lusaka and Lagos. In all, the flight took two weeks and presented a number of problems to the crew. Information on scheduled times was often not available until the previous evening, and in areas of poor communications it was sometimes difficult to complete diplomatic clearance and route planning before take-off.

The major event in November 1977 for all member nations of NATO was Exercise *Avon Express*. For this, Fairford airfield was reactivated, and six crews of 30 Squadron took part by flying in US equipment and personnel from Ramstein, including loads not previously carried by RAF Hercules aircraft. After giving support to 13 Squadron on the way to Singapore via Bushire and Colombo, 30 Squadron flew five sorties in December from the UK to Bermuda, where there had been civil disturbance following the execution of the Governor's assassin. At the end of the year, it was found that the squadron had flown more hours in 1977 than in any year since the advent of the Hercules. Route tasks carried out had totalled 634 in a flying time of 8177 hours 35 minutes, and in addition continuation training occupied crews for 307 hours 35 minutes.

Regular support flights to Belize and Northern Ireland continued, and in July 1978 flood-relief supplies were flown to Sudan by Sqn. Ldr. Wright and his crew, who left Lyneham at 03.10 on the morning after the Officers' Mess Summer Ball! 30 Squadron won the Lord Trophy for the third time in succession in September 1978, two of the three crews being placed first and second in the final order. Manning problems in November brought about a period of reduced activity, and although the work was enough to keep crew members occupied they would have appreciated more.

One event which gave a 30 Squadron crew some anxiety occurred in December 1978 during the return flight of a Belize resupply task. On their way from Nassau to Gander, Flt. Lt. Lines and his crew encountered severe clear air turbulence which had not been forecast, and the aircraft dropped from 29,000 feet to 22,000 feet before control was regained. They diverted to Halifax, Nova Scotia, where the Hercules was checked for structural damage. None was found, which did much to restore confidence in the strength of the Hercules.

A delicate political situation developed in Iran in January 1979, and several Hercules were positioned at Bahrain to ferry British and other foreigners out from Ahwaz and Mazid-i-Suleiman. Early in February, when events in Iran reached a climax with the overthrow of the Shah, the withdrawal scheme was activated, and several hundred British citizens were flown to Akrotiri. In this operation, one 30 Squadron crew was involved. Towards the end of January, Sqn. Ldr. Wright was the captain of a VIP-qualified crew of a Hercules which took Admiral Sir Henry Leach GCB and Maj. Gen. Pollard, the Chief Engineer of BAOR, to Diego Garcia via Kuwait and Seeb to take part in a joint services expedition.

In July 1979, 30 Squadron was given 36 hours to nominate two crews to fly supplies from Guatemala to Managua in war-torn Nicaragua, and Flt. Lt. Kemp and Flt. Lt. Busby were selected. The original schedule was amended when the Hercules reached Belize, the new plan specifying Panama as the loading point, as the Red Cross could not guarantee the aircraft's safety in Guatemala. The mission began on 16th July, each sortie carrying 34,000 lbs. of food and medical supplies. Next day, however, Flt. Lt. Busby was arrested by National Guardsmen at Managua and the crew were taken to the airport terminal. As Sandanistas had just taken control of Managua city, the National Guard suspected that his aircraft was full of them! By the time Flt. Lt. Kemp arrived on 18th July the airport was swarming with deposed National Guardsmen, seventy or eighty of whom tried to commandeer the Hercules as soon as he had unloaded, but the attempt was thwarted by quick thinking and talking by the crew. Flt. Lt. Kemp took off as rapidly as possible for Panama, where they remained to continue the shuttle. The mission ended on 28th July after nineteen sorties had moved 562,000 lbs. of supplies.

A sad task carried out by Flt. Lt. Noon and his crew in August was to airlift back to England the bodies of Lord Mountbatten and members of his family who had been assassinated by the IRA. For this mission the Hercules flew to the Irish Air Corps airfield at Baldonnel (Casement). During that month Wg. Cdr. Alan Tolhurst came to the end of his tenure as CO of 30 Squadron, and flew his last crossing of the Atlantic in support of two Buccaneer aircraft from Laarbruch which were on a proving flight to Gander via Lajes. In his place Wg. Cdr. Barry Latter took command.

In 1979 the most significant operation was *Agila*, which took place in December as a result of the Lancaster House talks. It involved deployment of personnel and equipment of the UK Monitoring Force to Salisbury (now Harare) in Zimbabwe, and 30 Squadron provided nine crews from 19th December for a slip pattern. Most of them were, however, back in time for Christmas. After the new year, two Gazelle helicopters of the AAC were flown to Salisbury to reinforce the Monitoring Force. Recovery of personnel and equipment took place in March 1980.

## Stretching the 'Albert'

The most important modification programme carried out on the RAF's Hercules fleet began in 1980 after the successful trials of a prototype, and involved the 'stretching' of thirty aircraft by the insertion of an additional section of fuselage to provide a 37% increase in cargo capacity. This work was carried out by Marshall Aerospace at Cambridge, using components manufactured in the United States. The resulting aircraft were reclassified as the Hercules C.3, and over the years have been flown by all four squadrons of the Lyneham Wing. In December 1980 Flt. Lt. Tew took one to Colombo, the furthest the C.3 had flown.

By the summer of 1980, 30 Squadron crews were much busier and among other tasks took part in Operation *Titan*, positioning elements of 42 Commando in the New Hebrides for peace-keeping purposes. However, by November only minimal flying was taking place.

Offensive action against the Hercules was not a factor much considered by RAF crews, but in February 1981 a 30 Squadron crew flying to Gatow to exercise the British right to use the Berlin air corridor experienced just such a problem. On landing they found that a fuel tank had been punctured by a bullet fired by Warsaw Pact forces, so they left the aircraft at Gatow to be repaired by Marshall Aerospace and flew home by civil airline.

Another change of CO took place on 25th September 1981, when Wg. Cdr. Latter was appointed as Air Adviser to the British High Commission in Nairobi. He was superceded by Wg. Cdr. A. R. Tolcher, who was immediately immersed in Exercise *Amber Express*, which was designed to resupply and support northern Europe in the event of hostility from Warsaw Pact countries and in which the squadron flew 81 sorties. Errands of mercy, a regular feature of 30 Squadron's work over many years, occupied two crews in November. Arriving just in time, a pregnant woman was carried from Gibraltar to the UK on 25th/26th November. The second mission involved Flt. Lt. Lewendon, the captain of Ascot 4079, who was route-checking Flt. Lt. Holman to Akrotiri and back. In the air, he received a signal asking him to divert to Athens to airlift retired Sqn. Ldr. Eric Williams MC, who had been taken seriously ill on his boat in the Mediterranean. Eric Williams was the officer who had led the 'Wooden Horse' escape during the Second World War. In Athens, the British Ambassador had alerted the RAF, and a full aeromedical team had been flown out by civil airline. Ascot 4079 duly collected Sqn. Ldr. Williams and flew him to Brize Norton, from where he was rushed to hospital in Oxford.

Breaking with tradition, 30 Squadron was joined by its first female Air Loadmaster, Flt. Sgt. I. M. Booker, one of three in the Lyneham Transport Wing being evaluated for a year. She had considerable experience of flying in VC10s based at Brize Norton.

An unusual task was carried out by Flt. Lt. Vince and his crew in December 1981 in support of five Wessex helicopters being flown out for service at Akrotiri. After delays, they left on 12th December for Benson and thence to Dinard in northern France. Bad weather then intervened, but although the helicopters could fly under VFR conditions only they managed to reach Montpelier for a night-stop. They then continued via Athens and Rhodes to Akrotiri, where they arrived 48 hours behind schedule. This task gave the 30 Squadron crew an unusual opportunity for low-level flying. They then flew another Hercules back to base via Naples, where an engine for a Buccaneer was collected for delivery to Honington.

1982, of course, turned out to be a highly significant year for Great Britain — the year in which Argentina attempted to annexe the Falkland Islands. Before that, however, Flt. Lt. Lydiate and his crew had ventured into the area to take a Wasp helicopter to HMS *Endurance* after a similar machine had been lost on an ice floe. Flying Ascot 4891 via Dakar and Recife, he delivered the helicopter at Montevideo before returning as Ascot 4906 via Lajes, where a faulty engine was repaired.

## Operation *Corporate*

By April 1982 Argentina had succesfully occupied the Falklands and the massive operation to regain the islands began. For 30 Squadron the action opened on 2nd April, when Sqn. Ldr. Adams, on a Gibraltar schedule as Ascot 4080, was tasked to preposition slip crews. During the subsequent months, an average of two squadron crews left Lyneham every day. Involvement in the operation was enough to bring out the very best in aircrews and ground crews alike. Although no ban was placed on leave periods, some personnel cancelled their leave voluntarily in order to help. In April, 30 Squadron flew 1228 hours 35 minutes on *Corporate*, as the operation had been named, which in some individual cases amounted to almost 100 hours in the air. For the aircraft flying into Ascension Island, a slip pattern had been established at Dakar by early May to avoid the use of Gibraltar as a refuelling point except for the heaviest loads. Permission was obtained for overweight take-offs from Dakar if necessary. One Hercules was diverted to Porto Santo in Madeira with spares for a Sea Harrier, one of the stream of aircraft being ferried south for the task force. In all, 57 sorties were flown by 30 Squadron in May, totalling 1270 hours by day and 460 at night. For navigators especially, the 28-hour return trip to Ascension was both taxing and rewarding.

To give the Hercules sufficient fuel to fly from Ascension on to the Falklands, a rushed engineering programme was introduced to create an in-flight refuelling capability. Four aircraft were also converted into tankers. On 1st June, 30 Squadron sent Flt. Lt. D. Turner and Flt. Lt. A. Morris to Marham for ground-based training in air-to-air refuelling. That completed, they returned to Lyneham and began practice in receiving fuel from Victor tankers and dispensing it to other Hercules. The land battle was soon over, and British forces secured the unconditional surrender of the Argentines on 14th June. On 23rd June Flt. Lt. P. S. Gregory of 30 Squadron arrived at Port Stanley to join the RAF Detachment. He was joined by Flt. Lt. D. Jackson on 27th June, and during the month, 920 hours were flown by 30 Squadron in support of Operation *Corporate*. The first full 30 Squadron crew to land at Port Stanley, that of Flt. Lt. Milton, arrived on 18th July, closely followed by Flt. Lt. W. Akister and his crew. The squadron provided two AAR receiver crews capable of landing at Port Stanley after two refuellings and a twelve-hour trip from Ascension. During July, 30 Squadron flew 652 hours 20 minutes, of which 216 hours 50 minutes were spent between Ascension and Port Stanley. On three of these sorties, the weather was too bad for a landing at Port Stanley, and so they turned round and flew back to Ascension, a flight time often in excess of twenty hours.

The shuttle between Lyneham and Ascension occupied 398 flying hours in August 1982, and the six crews plying between Ascension and Port Stanley flew 339 hours. Flt. Lt. Milton made a proving flight through Porto Alegre in Brazil and on another occasion had to divert to Montevideo after experiencing fuel transfer problems. Tasks other than *Corporate* were very light until September, when the demands of *Corporate* declined slightly and other work increased accordingly. By now, it was abundantly clear that the airbridge would continue for some time, and the squadron was given the job of training two more AAR crews. Each of the AAR crews at Ascension could expect to fly to and from Port Stanley once every five days. Thus in one month each crew would be in the air for 140 hours, close to the permissible 150 hours maximum. Tanker crews, though, were flying shorter but more regular sorties, rising at 02.00 two days out of three, and refuelling the airbridge aircraft. After flying 90 to 100 hours a month they became very tired and were rotated to the UK.

October saw one aircraft leaving Lyneham every day for Ascension, 30 Squadron's contribution being seven flights per month. Three-month detachments to Port Stanley then began and the length of AAR detachments at Ascension was reduced to two or three weeks. From 30 Squadron, the first tanker crew to be detached to the Falklands was that of Flt. Lt. Turner, and they played a significant part in supporting a Flight of Phantom fighters. During the month the first all-Hercules airbridge flight from Ascension to Port Stanley was made, in order to relieve pressure on the Victor tanker fleet, and it was seen that the Hercules C.1K (tanker) was here to stay. The decision to convert two more Hercules to the tanker role and to increase AAR-qualified crews accordingly was taken in November.

One of the tasks not connected with the Falklands was handled in November 1982 by Flt. Lt. Weston, who flew 70 hours from Lyneham to Hong Kong, where Ghurka troops boarded to be delivered to Brunei, after which the flight took the aircraft to New Zealand. There, equipment used in the Fincastle Trophy by a Nimrod detachment was recovered. Operation *Corporate*

continued, and 30 Squadron was heavily tasked over the Christmas period. One crew, headed by Flt. Lt. Curties, managed to position at Dakar over the holiday, and enjoyed several functions given by the staffs of the British and US embassies.

By early January 1983, all crews at Port Stanley were tanker-qualified, and Sqn. Ldr. Drew was CO of the AAR detachment. Their primary task was now refuelling Phantoms in the air, but they also made mail and supply drops to South Georgia and carried out some maritime reconnaissance sorties in the Falkland Islands Protection Zone. Crews lived in QRA tents on the airfield for two days out of three, but when off duty were accommodated in a Floatel, a converted ship moored in Port Stanley harbour. Lack of leisure time precluded much exploration of the islands, but job satisfaction went some way to making up for this shortcoming. One crew, returning from an AAR sortie during a Station defence exercise, even managed to 'beat up' the airfield without warning! Life was not without incident — one Hercules was about to take off from Port Stanley to refuel two Phantoms when the nosewheel oleo sheared. The end of the runway was thus blocked, but another tanker managed to take off from the reduced length and successfully carried out the refuelling before diverting to one of the South American airfields.

Well away from the South Atlantic, Flt. Lt. Myers was the captain of Ascot 4047, the first RAF aircraft to land at the badly-damaged Beirut International Airport for some time. This Hercules delivered twenty-two soldiers, the advance guard of the British contribution to the Multi-National Peacekeeping Force, before returning to Akrotiri. Only one crew of 30 Squadron was detached to Ascension in March, that of Flt. Lt. Akister, and they flew 80 hours in their three-week detachment. Crews were now living in what was called 'Concertina City', named after the collapsible huts hired from the USAF. Proper beds had replaced camp beds and wooden wardrobes had superceded cardboard ones supplied by the Americans. 30 Squadron continued to provide all three tanker crews at Port Stanley until 5th March 1983, when the monopoly was broken. From April no more freight was carried to Ascension by RAF Hercules, as Belfasts hired from Heavy Lift, with a much greater capacity, were now in full use. It is ironic that the Belfasts were former RAF aircraft which had been sold as redundant, but without their contribution Operation *Corporate* would have been much more difficult to maintain.

Before the onset of the Falklands winter, Flt. Lt. Vince took thirty-three dependents to the site of the helicopter crash in which twenty-seven soldiers had died during the campaign. A short memorial service was held in the back of the Hercules by the padre and wreaths were dropped as the aircraft circled. During May five tanker crews and two airbridge crews of 30 Squadron were detached to Ascension, including the CO, who was pleased to be there and to fly with tanker crews at each location. He remarked "The whole 'feel' of Port Stanley is one of front-line operations and it is good to appreciate that the Hercules force is seen as very much a part of the fighting team."

While the Falklands task did not disappear, attention started to focus on other tasks. *Adventure Express*, held in June 1983, was the largest task in months and as far as 30 Squadron was concerned involved establishing a slip pattern to and from Turkey. In September the squadron gave support to Buccaneers being deployed to Akrotiri to guard the British contingent in the Lebanon. For this, three crews were used at what was already a busy time. In September, Wg. Cdr. Tolcher handed over command of the squadron to Wg. Cdr. J. Bell – another navigator in the 'boss' seat! A chance to meet Hercules crews from another force came in November, when 30 Squadron hosted 46° Aerobrigata, 50° Gruppo, of the Italian Air Force, under Maj. Gagliarini. Together, they carried out low-level sorties around the UK and a training mission to the United States, and a genuine sense of comradeship developed.

At Christmas, a crew headed by Flt. Lt. Curties was scrambled, after minimal post-sortie rest, to fly urgent medical supplies from Ascension to Port Stanley for a sick islander. Afterwards, the CO, Wg. Cdr. Bell, remarked "It gives one a sense of pride to be associated with such men." A new unit, 1312 Flight, had been formed on 20th August 1983 to act as the holding unit for Hercules crews detached to Port Stanley, and in the early part of 1984 30 Squadron maintained two crews on the Flight. A rare casevac mission was flown in February by Flt. Lt. Heath and his crew, who

*Wg. Cdr. John Bell, 30 Squadron's CO, displaying in September 1983 the cleverly-designed squadron badge based on a road sign*
*[RAF Lyneham ref. A.8108].*

airlifted a sick sailor from HMS *Endurance* from a small airstrip on King George's Island in the South Shetland group to Port Stanley.

Back in Europe, a good deal of work was carried out in transporting Marines to their winter training area in Norway. No doubt keen on skiing themselves, several members of 30 Squadron went on a skiing expedition to Germany, taking their wives, the trip being arranged by the German exchange officer of the time, Hptmn. Müller.

Although crews in the South Atlantic were working so hard to maintain the air bridge, the powers that be were not allowing any slackening of service discipline. A signal received from on high in February 1984 complained that crews returning from Port Stanley were travelling in their flying suits. Wg. Cdr. Bell wrote at the time "This is not the way to impress them that their interests are being looked after, and I see such messages as a positive step to undermine morale. Fortunately, such is the calibre of the crews that they can shrug off such burrs, and they continue to tackle the South Atlantic task with willing dedication." It was as well that they did, as in March both 47 and 70 Squadrons were involved in the presentation of new standards and an extra burden then fell onto the broad shoulders of 30 Squadron.

The intrepid Flt. Lt. Akister and his crew, flying Ascot 8173 from Port Stanley to Ascension on the night of 3rd/4th March, found heavy rain and very poor visibility at their destination, with insufficent fuel to reach Dakar or Freetown. They made five attempts to land, but had to overshoot every time. As they could see the sea, with HMS *Uganda* not far offshore, the crew decided to ditch next to the ship. Conditions were too bad to allow another tanker to take off, and as fuel was becoming low, the captain had to continue trying to land at Ascension rather than ditching. With fuel almost exhausted, he resolved to make one last attempt to land. On his sixth approach, runway lights were sighted at a mile and a half, and the Hercules touched down on the flooded runway. Severe turbulence had made many of the sixty passengers sick, many of them from 16 Squadron RAF Regiment. Subsequently, Flt. Lt. Akister was awarded the Queen's Commendation for Valiant Service in the Air, and the ALM, Sgt. McDonagh, was commended by the AOC. Co-pilot was Flg. Off. Oborn, navigator was Flg. Off. Shields and engineer was Flt. Sgt. Dodd.

*The winners of the Arthur Barratt Memorial Prize in 1984: Flt. Lt. Bill Akister, Flg. Off. Paul Oborn, Flt. Lt. Ian Shields, Sgt. Sam McDonagh and Flt. Sgt. Dave Dodd.*

*Hercules C.3 XV301 at Addis Ababa.*

The CO put his thoughts on paper again in April 1984, when he wrote "I'm constantly surprised by the fact that on paper the programme appears unachievable, but we always achieve it. The thanks for this go to the aircrew, who are always willing, and I sometimes wonder if we push them too hard." Things appeared to be easing a little, however, and in Europe a large number of short-range 'day-trip' exercises occupied the squadron in the second half of the year. Typical were the nineteen trips made to ferry BAOR troops from Germany to Benbecula in the Hebrides. Two crews and support staff took the opportunity of a detachment to Pisa to carry out exercises with the Italian Air Force, particularly low-level missions. These they found a great success. Not so enjoyable was the football match held between the squadron and the Italians, as 30 Squadron was beaten soundly. On this detachment, eight service wives accompanied the crew members, adding to the social side of the event.

Though the month of July is a popular time for leave, the squadron still managed to fly some significant sorties, one of which involved taking medical supplies to Katmandu and taking a severely wounded soldier from there to Kuala Lumpur. Entitled Exercise *Nelson's Glory*, the route from Lyneham was via Akrotiri, Bahrain and Bombay to Katmandu and from there via Calcutta to Kuala Lumpur. The homeward stage was via Johor Bahru, Colombo, Bahrain and Akrotiri. During the westward trip the Hercules was subjected to a practice interception by a pair of US Navy F-14 Tomcats flying from an aircraft carrier in the Gulf. In addition to this major task, squadron crews provided support facilities to the Red Arrows during their many performances at air shows, and two crews were detached to Ascension in support of the airbridge. This continued in August, a month in which Wg. Cdr. Bell enjoyed his first tanker detachment on Ascension Island.

September 1984 was the month when NATO held the largest exercise in Europe since the end of the Second World War. In Exercises *Lionheart* and *Bold Gannet*, 30 Squadron crews were involved in all aspects from deployment to recovery. Lionheart involved carrying various units for deployment in Denmark, including the ground crew of 233 OCU, the Harrier conversion unit based at Wittering. More significant was *Bold Gannet*, in which 30 Squadron worked day and night to carry RAF personnel and troops, several crews making landings under Taceval conditions. To supplement operations other than those in the South Atlantic, a crew from the Belgian Air Force under Capt. Daniel Delnaye was attached to 30 Squadron that very busy month. In his report, Wg. Cdr. Bell noted "On paper the tasking appeared impossible. In practice we achieved it easily, which speaks highly for the will of those on 30 Squadron."

## Aid to Ethiopia

Operation *Bushell*, which began in November 1984, was a major part of Great Britain's aid in the Ethiopian famine relief campaign. The people of that unfortunate country faced starvation, and many countries pledged money, foodstuffs and transport. On the first day of the operation, Flt. Lt. Lane was captain of Ascot 5965, the second Hercules in a stream of three to fly into Bole airport, Addis Ababa. His cargo included a Land Rover, a power unit, water and rations for the relief workers, as well as RAF personnel, newspaper reporters and a Ministry of Defence press officer. The way in which the RAF handled its part in the relief operation received worldwide recognition and was reported daily on radio and television. Each supply run, routed via Akrotiri to Addis Ababa and returning via Assab and Jeddah, took 27 hours. Apart from this vital task, RAF Lyneham was on Taceval for several days that month and 30 Squadron crews flew to other UK airfields to simulate flying into Northern Europe under battle conditions.

30 Squadron continued to play an important role in the South Atlantic in the early days of 1985, two crews operating from Port Stanley in support of the garrison. Operation *Bushell* continued, and on one occasion the Station Commander, Gp. Capt. J. Cheshire, flew with Sqn. Ldr. Davidson to visit Lyneham personnel on detachment to Addis Ababa. The squadron continued to play its part in RAF Lyneham's scheduled tasking to Germany, Cyprus and Sardinia (Decimomannu), and in addition managed to involve themselves in Exercise *Red Flag* at Nellis AFB, Nevada. To cap it all, time was found for a visit to a Bass Charrington brewery, a most enjoyable venture but not to be described in detail!

## Seventy glorious years

March 1985 was the 70th anniversary of the formation of 30 Squadron from an *ad hoc* unit in Mesopotamia. The squadron tried to bring all crews back to Lyneham between 22nd and 24th March for the reunion, and managed to do so apart from one crew based in the Falklands. However, work continued, and Exercises *Hardfall*, *Cold Winter* and *Clockwork*, all involving flying to Norway, formed a large part of the month's tasking. There were also trips to Belize carrying a Puma helicopter and to Akrotiri in support of a Phantom squadron. On 23rd March members of the recently-formed 30 Squadron Association arrived at Lyneham for the weekend's events. An excellent reunion dinner in the Wessex Restaurant was attended by over 200 past and present members of the squadron who heard speeches by Wg. Cdr. Bell and by AVM David Dick. Next day a service at St. Michael and All Angels church was followed by an informal lunch during which Wg. Cdr. Bell read out a message from HM the Queen: "The Queen sincerely thanks you and all members of the 30 Squadron Association for your kind and loyal message of greetings sent on the occasion of the 70th anniversary of the formation of No. 30 Squadron RAF. Her Majesty greatly appreciates this message and sends her best wishes to all concerned on this notable occasion."

Apart from several flights between Germany and Northern Ireland under the ongoing Operation *Banner* in April 1985, Operation *Corporate* continued in the South Atlantic. At Ascension, the weather was far from good, as in a five-day period seventeen inches (432mm.) of rain fell. Due to these poor conditions, a tanker was on standby to meet each inbound flight. The highlight of May's work was a special trip to Diego Garcia in the Indian Ocean, Mombasa and Nairobi, the scene of some of 30 Squadron's previous activities.

In the South Atlantic revised schedules for the airbridge operation came into force in June 1985. Each Saturday a tanker crew was to leave Lyneham, 30 and 24 Squadrons alternating. The aircraft would fly to Dakar, Ascension and Port Stanley and then back to Ascension to 'slip' the aircraft to the returning tanker crew. As all take-offs were to be mid-morning (local time), this was considered to be much more civilised. A second weekly airbridge was to leave Lyneham on Tuesdays, 47 and 70 Squadrons alternating. On one trip Flt. Lt. Lane and his crew claimed to have covered the sea between Port Stanley and Ascension in nine hours fifteen minutes, an average groundspeed of 366 knots. Operation Bushell in Ethiopia also continued, and a major exercise, *Albatross Exchange*, was held to deploy 6 and 54 Squadrons to Tirstup and Vaerlose in Denmark from Coltishall and to recover them. Exercise *Jumping Mercury* found Sqn. Ldr. Dunn and his crew at Grand Turk in the Bahamas, to where they took 36 troops of the Royal Corps of Signals from Brize Norton. They also visited Providentiales to check available facilities before returning via Goose Bay to collect the ground crew of a Victor. Two crews spent time in carrying Rapier missile crews between Gutersloh and Benbecula. Ever public-spirited, eight of 30 Squadron's officers led by the CO took

part in a race on the Kennet & Avon Canal to raise money for the Canal Trust and the Bath Cancer Unit. Although the team did not live up to early expectations, the sum of £80 was raised.

Live firing of Rapier missiles at Benbecula in July 1985 involved 30 Squadron crews in carrying elements of the RAF Regiment and Royal Artillery from and to Germany and other UK Stations. Many flights to Gibraltar were also made, but members of the squadron found time to take children from The Limes home for a weekend's camping in Devonshire. This well-planned sortie was led by Sgt. Mike Cole, aided by Flt. Sgts. Casey Jones and Pete Colley. Wg. Cdr. Bell "went along for the ride" and saw that the children thoroughly enjoyed themselves.

Although tasking in August was light, the highlight was a training mission to North America. It called at Stephenville, Ottawa, Scott AFB and McGuire AFB and was diverted to Gander before returning to Lyneham. September was also fairly undemanding, with small-scale activity in Ethiopia and the Falklands and a new task, airfield calibration. For this, one crew carried out seven hours of training at Benson to prepare them for a visit to Mount Pleasant, the new airfield on the Falklands, in October. Wg. Cdr. J. V. Bell spent the month in Ethiopia on Operation *Bushell*, an experience which he found eye-opening. "It was interesting to see what is really happening rather than what the television reporters would have us believe" he reported on returning to Lyneham. "The job being done by the RAF crews is first class. The two aircraft move some 120 tonnes of grain a day and we know it is getting to the people in need. But I was struck by the lack of Ethiopian Government support for the relief effort and, in many cases, by its downright obstructiveness, and I left with the distinct feeling that Ethiopia could do more to help itself. I also felt we were not entirely welcome in what is, after all, a Marxist state."

A number of crews visited Turkey in October to take part in Exercise *Archway Express*, and Germany was a frequent destination. Other crews took part in several unit deployments to

*Wg. Cdr. John Bell handing over command of 30 Squadron to Wg. Cdr. David Adams in February 1986*      *[RAF Lyneham ref. O.192].*

Norway, Denmark, Cyprus and Nairobi and to the Falklands, Gibraltar and Northern Ireland. With the introduction of Tristar aircraft to the airbridge, only two flights per week were undertaken by Hercules. There was now only one tanker at Ascension Island, its crew rotating regularly. As the task was shared with 24 Squadron, each had a departure every other week. With three global route training sorties, 30 Squadron crews were to be found literally all over the world that month.

Relief operations in Ethiopia began to diminish in November, and the last 30 Squadron crew to take part in Operation *Bushell* flew to Addis Ababa. It was expected that RAF involvement would end in December after more than a year of making a vital contribution to the international relief effort. This dedication was recognised when RAF Lyneham received the Wilkinson Sword of Peace for 1985 for its contribution. The sword was received on 7th November by the Station Commander, Gp. Capt. John Cheshire, at a parade which included colour parties from the four squadrons of the Lyneham Transport Wing.

With a reduced commitment in Ethiopia and in the South Atlantic, 30 Squadron crews were able to devote more time from January 1986 to such matters as the annual trips to Norway, when under Exercise *Hardfall* personnel of 3 Commando Brigade were flown to their prospective wartime positions. In a warmer climate, Wg. Cdr. Bell was among the crew of a Caribbean training flight which visited Lajes, Bermuda, Jamaica, Grand Turk and Belize. This proved to be his final long route while on 30 Squadron before his posting to SHAPE HQ in February. In his place came Wg. Cdr. D. N. Adams. Further tasks in February included a number of fighter squadron moves, including 5 Squadron to Decimomannu in Sicily and 228 OCU from there back to Coningsby.

In April 1986 the USAF bombed Libya, which led to the reinforcement of Akrotiri and Gibraltar. Six crews flew from Lossiemouth to Akrotiri and five provided AAR support to Phantom fighters flying out of Gibraltar. Down in the Falklands, Flt. Lt. Rogers and his crew flew the first Hercules into Mount Pleasant airfield at the end of April. In May a number of flights were made by 30 Squadron in support of undersea trials of Tigerfish torpedos being carried out by the nuclear submarine HMS *Conqueror*. These involved two crews shuttling between Cape Canaveral and Andros in the Bahamas, which must have been a very pleasant task.

Always ready for any task which might be called for, a 30 Squadron crew headed by Flt. Lt. Dobson was on a Belize schedule when a flood relief operation in Jamaica was instigated. Flying from Belize, the Hercules worked closely with Puma helicopters of 33 Squadron in a joint effort which was not the first time the two units had cooperated. Flt. Lt. Frazer's crew, meanwhile, was providing support to the Red Arrows on a seven-week tour of the Far East which involved landing at twenty-seven airfields in 97 flying hours.

The major winter exercise in 1986 was *Swift Sword*, otherwise known as *Saif Sereea*, a rapid deployment exercise centred on Masirah which began in November. Lyneham in general was heavily tasked to support Tornados, Jaguars and other types, and one of the most complex slip patterns ever seen at Lyneham was brought into use. Operating conditions were more arduous that even the most experienced crews could remember, but 30 Squadron flew 194 hours in this exercise. Recovery from Masirah was carried out by ten crews of 30 Squadron in December.

When the *Herald of Free Enterprise* capsized at Zeebrugge in March 1987, Sqn. Ldr. Davey and his crew carried firemen from Manston to Koksijde to assist in the tragedy. On the very same night, Flt. Lt. Pratt's aircraft carried the coffins of seven of the crew and passengers of a Chinook helicopter which had crashed in the Falklands from Brize Norton to Odiham, where a guard of honour waited.

Due to the advent of a Tristar schedule to Mount Pleasant in May 1987, it became necessary for each Hercules squadron to fly only one airbridge per month. One of 30 Squadron's most stalwart captains, Flt. Lt. Akister, then retired, with 10,000 hours in his logbook, half of them on Hercules and 2,000 on Operation *Corporate*. Over five years after its implementation, this operation continued to demand 150 hours per month from 30 Squadron crews.

Several major exercises in the summer and autumn of 1987 placed something of a strain on 30 Squadron's resources. In June Exercise *Aurora Express* involved eight crews in a week's detachment to Turkey, where they carried out operations from

Erzerun, an airfield at 5,700 feet altitude. This provided a challenge, particularly as much of the flying was done at night. In September came Exercise *Ocean Safari*, a NATO air/sea exercise in the North Atlantic. 30 Squadron's involvement was to carry personnel and equipment of 43, 100 and 208 Squadrons to Montreal or Landivisiau. *Purple Warrior*, held at West Freugh, followed in November and simulated an out-of-area operation involving the establishment, consolidation and resupply of an airhead. 20,000 personnel of all services took part, and 30 Squadron flew several sorties carrying troops between UK and German airfields and West Freugh. Somewhat more sinister was the introduction in December 1987 of a jamming system to provide the Hercules with a defence against SAM.7 missiles.

By January 1988 the Falklands task had reduced to no more than ten percent of 30 Squadron's activity. In March, however, Exercise *Fire Focus* was held, simulating the reinforcement of the Falklands garrison. This involved large numbers of troops and of Phantom fighters, VC10s, Nimrods, Tristars and Hercules. 30 Squadron crews flew 168 hours on a mixture of tanking and airbridge sorties, but one captain, Flt. Lt. Huskie, had to divert to Montevideo when strong winds at Mount Pleasant prevented his return. Only after two days of strong diplomatic pressure were the crew allowed to leave for Ascension!

Operation *Banner*, still being flown by 30 Squadron crews in support of troops going to or returning from Northern Ireland, played an increasing part in the squadron's efforts from May 1987. Apart from the troops, a number of freight sorties were flown, carrying such items as rotor blades for the Wessex helicopters of 72 Squadron. Also now included was the evacuation of casualties of varying severity, including people injured in bomb blasts. In November 30 Squadron flew an initial sortie to the disused airfield at Ballykelly, which had been reactivated for occasional use.

Four flights carrying Land Rovers and artillery pieces were flown between Manston and Dishforth in May 1988 in connection with an exercise taking place at the Otterburn training area in Northumberland. The squadron was becoming more involved in low level flying and strip landing, and in July planned the airland phases of Exercise *Fast Buzzard*, a simulated protected evacuation of British nationals from a hostile area. This exercise involved the use of Upavon airfield and of an advanced airstrip at Deptford Down on Salisbury Plain.

Wg. Cdr. Adams' final flying task with 30 Squadron was in the deployment of Tornados to the Far East for Exercise *Golden Eagle*, scheduled to take place between August and October 1988. The Hercules of 30 Squadron routed through Thailand and Singapore to Australia to participate in the Australian Bicentennial celebrations, and then returned via Hong Kong, where Wg. Cdr. Adams enjoyed a dining-out night. His successor, from 8th September, was Wg. Cdr. D. M. Guest.

A deployment of Nimrod aircraft to Suda Bay in Crete for Exercise *Niris* in November 1988 was supported by 30 Squadron, and an extra day was added to the programme so that the CO and a Flight commander from 33 Squadron could present a plaque to the Cretan Volunteer Veterans Association in commemoration of the two squadrons' involvement in Crete in 1941. Present at this ceremony were AVM David Dick and Mr. Johnny Vellacott of 30 Squadron Association and a Mr. Frame of 33 Squadron.

The final tanker support sortie by 30 Squadron from Ascension was flown by Flt. Lt. Vince on 27th February 1989, in support of the last scheduled airbridge flight. However, the well-practiced arrangements could be, and were, reinstated in special circumstances. A good deal of 30 Squadron's activity that year was in connection with movements to and from Northern Ireland, flying to Aldergrove as Operation *Banner*. By contrast, the squadron participated in many exercises in Europe. In September Wg. Cdr. Guest captained a Hercules which carried twenty-five members of the 30 Squadron Association to Berlin (Gatow) and First Day Covers were flown between there and Lyneham. General carriage of equipment continued as required, and covered such events as the recovery of a Lynx helicopter of 669 Squadron AAC from a site in Arizona. On that occasion, in December 1989, the Hercules captained by Flt. Lt. D. Hamlin had to be tipped with its nose in the air so that the 'chopper' could be loaded. In the Falklands, a Hercules C.3, the first to be employed in the freighter role on the airbridge, delivered Watchman radar to Air Traffic Control at Mount Pleasant in January

*One Hercules C.1 refuelling another (XV185). Slightly different camouflage is apparent in this picture, taken on 27th July 1988.*

1990. Soon afterwards, Flt. Lt. Roberts of 30 Squadron flew there to calibrate the ILS/PAR, which involved four days of preparation at Benson before flying south with 3,400 lbs. of mail for the troops.

In March 1990 the RAF Hercules fleet reached the milestone of one million flying hours, and a composite crew which included as co-pilot Flt. Lt. Murphy of 30 Squadron made a commemorative flight. Several exercises in the United States and Canada were aided

by 30 Squadron in April, but in May the NATO Tanker Standby was implemented, and Flt. Lt. Henderson flew the first sortie, which was from Kinloss. The standby was shared with 24 Squadron on a two-week rotation, the crews being at 24 to 36-hour readiness. New plans were formulated to train tanker crews within their first year on the squadron, whereas in the past crews had qualified at a late stage of their tours and had invariably been posted soon afterwards.

*An example of the extra-mural activities carried out by 30 Squadron personnel was the hosting of disabled young people from the Bristol area in September 1988.*

Royal visits to RAF Lyneham are by no means unusual, but on 17th May 1990 Her Majesty the Queen came to see 30 Squadron. She was hosted by Wg. Cdr. Guest throughout the reception and lunch, and afterwards inspected a static display in a hangar and was introduced to Flt. Lt. Murphy. Two children from the Limes Home, Swindon, the squadron's adopted charity, stood beside a board on which photographs of many of the activities which had been organised for them were displayed.

With the beginning of the Red Arrows' display season, 30 Squadron again provided logistic support. In June of that year, the aerobatic team visited the Soviet Union, and a crew headed by the CO went with them, flying the first Hercules of 30 Squadron to visit that country. Two nights were spent at Leningrad (now St. Petersburg) and three at Kiev, and on the way home a night at Budapest. The crew was allowed to fly for forty-five minutes in an Antonov 12 'Cub' over the Kiev area with an Antonov test crew. The captain, Capt. Sergei Gorbik, permitted Wg. Cdr. Guest to fly the aircraft, which, with manually-operated controls, was found to be more demanding and tiring than the Hercules. Afterwards, the Russians were taken on a short flight in the 30 Squadron aircraft. In general, tasking in June and July was reduced so that mandatory servicing could be brought up to date.

## Trouble in Kuwait

Then came the preparatory phase of the Gulf War, Operation *Granby*, and 30 Squadron and the other squadrons in the Lyneham Wing were soon in great demand to fly equipment to Dhahran, Thuraut, Bahrain, Seeb and Minhad, near Dubai, where most of the RAF men and equipment were deployed. A crew slip pattern was quickly established at Akrotiri and most other commitments were cancelled. All personnel on leave in the UK were recalled, but no complaints were heard, and in fact several people contacted the squadron to volunteer their services. Morale remained high, even though time between sorties could be as little as fourteen hours. High temperatures at the Gulf airfields might have frayed tempers,

but everyone remained good-humoured and worked very hard. Flying hours on *Granby* in August were 1211, and 1226 in September, when constant resupply flights were made. Unusual loads included elements of a field hospital to Bahrain and a boat for the Royal Marines. As a result of the never-ending workload, several crews found themselves dealing with technical problems, often involving the overheating of the cargo compartment. Fatigue began to show at the end of September, and sickness caused by the heat, different eating patterns, and irregular hours became prevalent.

New destinations for the aircraft of 30 Squadron in October were Tabuk and Jubail, both of which are closer to the Iraqi border than the other airfields. The deployment of the 7th Armoured Brigade, 'The Desert Rats', from Germany to the Gulf occupied the squadron considerably, and 1326 hours were flown on *Granby* in October. Most flights operated from Akrotiri and carried light vehicles and priority freight. Flt. Lt. Turnbull, however, carried a BBC TV crew from Akrotiri to Riyadh.

Back in the UK it was still possible to support the Red Arrows on the last display of the season, in the Channel Islands in September. As his government would not allow him to take part in the war against Iraq, Hptmn. Lebert of the Luftwaffe, the exchange officer, flew the mission, a fact which the older inhabitants of the islands, if they were aware of it, must have regarded as ironic.

Some resumption of training had been possible at the end of October, and flying hours on *Granby* in November were halved. This was partly due to the establishment of a detachment at Riyadh, where three aircraft and six crews from Lyneham set up camp. In command was Sqn. Ldr. Joe Bishop, assisted by MALM Bert Desmond, and the first 30 Squadron crew on the detachment was that of Flt. Lt. Royle. A Tristar flew to Riyadh every day with fifteen or more pallets of general freight which was then transshipped to the Hercules and flown to destinations in the Gulf. During December, 30 Squadron carried elements of 55 Squadron from Masirah to Bahrain, where a detachment of Victor tankers was set up to refuel the VC10s of 101 Squadron. Also airlifted were elements of 845 and 848 Squadrons of the Fleet Air Arm to Jubail

*A 30 Squadron crew at Kuwait (left to right): ATLO, Flt. Lt. Hugh Henderson, Flg. Off. Tony Toner, Flt. Lt. Keith Daulby, Flt. Sgt. Mick Bottomley and Sgt. Jules Lang. This crew flew sorties during the early phases of Operation* Granby *in August 1990 and then completed a four-month detachment to the Falklands. Within a few days of returning to Lyneham they were detached to Riyadh and flew during the climax of the Gulf War.*

*Sqn. Ldr. Williams and his crew at Akrotiri on 18th January 1991. This crew was the last to leave the Gulf as war broke out on 16th January, and was the first to return, two days later. Left to right: MALM Broome, Flg. Off. Vaughan, Sgt. McLaren, Sqn. Ldr. Williams and Flt. Lt. Livingston. This crew was 'bounced' by an unidentified fighter on their return from Bahrein on the night of 20th January 1991, but after five minutes the fighter left the scene, unable to achieve a good position for a kill. Subsequently, intelligence sources reported the fighter as of Libyan origin.*

*Offloading a Hercules of 30 Squadron at Jubail in February 1991, during the Gulf War.*

and four Gazelle helicopters to the same place. In preparation for a forthcoming air war, many loads of munitions, Land Rovers, Skyflash missiles and other equipment were carried in December and over the new year period. A deadline of 15th January 1991 was set for Iraqi withdrawal from Kuwait, and to reinforce the ground forces the 4th Armoured Brigade was flown into the north-eastern part of Saudi Arabia. The pace of operations was so intense that Flt. Lt. Hamlin was authorised to fly between Dhahran and Riyadh on three engines, including his take-off and landing.

Soon after taking leaving Jubail on the night of 15th/16th January, Sqn. Ldr. Williams saw a huge number of aircraft taking off and heading north-east towards Iraq. A dramatic report on BBC World Service, to which the crew were listening on HF radio, confirmed that an air offensive had begun. Three nights later, on their way back to Akrotiri, his crew spotted a fast jet ten miles away on their port side and then eight miles. Eventually it was behind them only three miles away, so Sqn. Ldr. Williams took evasive action, and the intruder lost interest and disappeared. Almost every crew experienced air raids while unloading at Gulf airfields; many saw Scud missiles being destroyed and became accustomed to explosions around their aircraft while over Riyadh as Patriot missile batteries intercepted the Scuds. One such crew, headed by Flt. Lt. Moore, was disconcerted when 'Air Raid Warning Red' was received by radio when they were over Riyadh in cloud, but all Flt. Lt. Moore saw was the glow of Scud missiles descending past his aircraft. Sqn. Ldr. Barter and his crew found the situation all too dangerous after being diverted to Dhahran from fog-bound Jubail. With the airfield under attack, they ran to the safety of an air raid shelter, where they donned gas masks and waited for the raid to finish. During this period, many crew members exceeded 115 hours in the air per month, including the CO.

As the date set for the launch of the land offensive drew nearer the airlift became ever more vital. Practice casualty evacuation flights to Riyadh were made from the forward landing strip at Qaisumah, where a field hospital had been established. Operation *Desert Storm*, the land assault against Iraqi forces in Kuwait, began on 24th February 1991 and Flt. Lt. Henderson made regular low-level flights across the desert to forward airstrips to evacuate casualties. But three days later it was all over.

30 Squadron flew 981 hours in March on *Granby*, largely recovering ammunition and missiles and redeploying troops, but Sqn. Ldr. Oldham had the sad task of flying the bodies of eight victims of the war from Akrotiri to Brize Norton, including the crew of a Tornado. There was a major reduction in the *Granby* tasking in April, flights to the Gulf now carrying humanitarian aid such as food and blankets and returning with service personnel and equipment. On 5th April a squadron party was held to mark the official end of Operation *Granby*, and for the first time for almost a year members of the squadron were able to enjoy a convivial evening together with no thought of a trip to the Gulf next day.

When the plight of Kurdish refugees in northern Iraq became known, relief flights were organised as Operation *Haven*, and on 16th April Flt. Lt. Hamlin flew 30 Squadron's first mission into Turkey, landing at Incirlik and Diyabakir. On the same day Flt. Lt. Cooper carried freight and personnel from Gutersloh to Akrotiri for the establishment of a detachment of Chinook helicopters in Turkey. Heavy loads now being carried often necessitated fuel stops at such airfields as Bari, Brindisi and Palermo in Italy, as not enough fuel could be carried to allow the aircraft to return to Akrotiri after unloading in Turkey, where fuel was not available.

Operation *Haven* continued, but as 24 and 47 Squadrons began a fourteen-day stand-down on 4th May, 30 Squadron became as busy as at any stage of *Granby*. Many of the loads now consisted of 105mm field guns, Land Rovers and tents for the Royal Marines, and if the weather was good it was possible to fly direct to Diyabakir. The Riyadh detachment moved to Bahrain on 12th May. Early in June it was decided that an airfield at Sirsenk in Iraq which had been bombed by the Allies could be reopened, although only half of its 4500-foot runway would be usable. On 14th June Sqn. Ldr. Barter and his crew landed there and became the first members of 30 Squadron to visit Iraq since 1939. Subsequently several more crews made resupply flights to Sirsenk, which was at an altitude of 3500 feet and demanded flying to full Military Operating Standard. Return flights to Akrotiri often carried Royal Marines and their equipment.

*Nose-art came back into prominence during the Gulf War, and this example was applied to a Hercules flown by 30 Squadron.*

The final event in June was a Gulf War flypast over London, for which 30 Squadron provided the lead Hercules crew. Unfortunately weather conditions were so bad that the event had to be cancelled, and it was not possible to offer a salute to those who died in the war.

Away from the Middle East, forty members of the 30 Squadron Association were flown in May 1991 to Crete, where they participated in the fiftieth anniversary of the Battle of Crete and unveiled a memorial to the casualties. On behalf of the squadron, Wg. Cdr. Main, who had taken over as CO in April, laid a wreath in the presence of HRH the Duke of Kent.

30 Squadron then reverted to its normal tasks, which in September included Operation *Grouse Trail* in support of two Phantoms being delivered to the Falklands. They were refuelled by VC10s, while the Hercules refuelled the Nimrod which provided search and rescue cover. Under Operation *Warden*, 30 Squadron supported the deployment of Jaguars and Victor tankers to Adana in Turkey for use in deterring Iraqi attacks on Kurds. This operation continued for some considerable time.

In December 1991, 30 Squadron flew Hercules XV292, painted to celebrate the 25th anniversary of the Hercules in RAF service, to Dobbins Air Force Base in Georgia, where the Lockheed factory was located. On board were representatives of all trades concerned with RAF Hercules operations. The captain that day was Sqn. Ldr. Oborn, and navigator and aircraft commander was the CO.

1992 began with intensive trooping to and from Northern Ireland, January's total passengers amounting to 1550. In February came another 'first' for 30 squadron when Flt. Lt. Wendy Smith became the first operational female navigator in the RAF. Winter exercises in Norway predominated, and use of the new airfield at Fagernes emphasised the need for accurate navigation onto the final approach. South America was visited in a more friendly manner in March 1992, when Sqn. Ldr. Williams flew to Chile to support Harriers and Tornados taking part in the national air show, FIDAE '92, at Santiago. On the way, the Hercules landed at Bermuda, Guayaquil and Charleston, among other exotic places. Flt. Lt. Evans and his crew, meanwhile, were being entertained by the Rumanian Air Force at Constanta, where the Rumanian CAS was present at an excellent banquet.

## The Balkans saga

With the first rumblings of trouble in the Balkans, a 30 Squadron crew under Flt. Lt. Hill left Lyneham on 23rd April 1992 carrying half the British contingent of the UN Peace-keeping Force, consisting of army medical personnel, to Belgrade in Yugoslavia. Resupply flights were made from time to time throughout the rest of the year. In July two crews flew in support of the withdrawal of Phantom aircraft from the Falklands and their replacement by Tornados, and in this case were routed to Ascension via Porto Santo and Dakar. Operation *Jural* took place in August and 290 hours

*Hercules XV292, sporting the badges of RAF Lyneham and all seven units which have flown the Hercules, was a great attraction at the Air Fete at Mildenhall in May 1992* *[author].*

were flown by 30 Squadron crews in carrying personnel and equipment to Dhahran via Akrotiri. Across the Atlantic, Hurricane *Andrew* had struck the Bahamas, and Flt. Lt. Pearson was nominated to fly relief supplies from Belize to the islands. Carrying water purification equipment, food and blankets, the Hercules made a landing on a small rough airstrip on North Eleuthera, which is only seven feet above sea level and over which a wall of water had passed not long before! Later, this crew made an oxygen resupply trip to Homestead AFB in Florida, which they left twelve hours before the hurricane completely destroyed the base.

Another unusual destination was Baku in Azerbaijan, to where Flt. Lt. Robertson and his crew flew in September with a team from JACIG (Joint Arms Control & Investigation Group) from Scampton. Yet another worldwide trip took place in October, when Exercise *Suman Warrior* involved a 30 Squadron crew taking elements of the Gloucester Regt. to Christchurch in New Zealand. In twelve days, landings were made at Brindisi, Bahrain, Colombo, Jakarta, Darwin and Sydney on the outbound journey and Whenapui, Nandi (Fiji), Barber's Point (Hawaii), Travis AFB and St. John's (Newfoundland) on the return flight.

Maintaining 30 Squadron's 'can do' attitude to the job in hand, Flt. Lt. Hill took a crew to Mombasa on 10th December 1992 to take part in Operation *Vigour*, organised to help alleviate famine in Somalia. During the 100 hours of flying, the aircraft was struck by birds on numerous occasions, but returned safely on 16th January 1993. This crew was then replaced by that of Flt. Lt. Turnbull. By then the CO was also in Mombasa, to head the detachment, and expressed his feelings by writing "I was most impressed by the performance of the crews and could not have wished for a more dedicated team."

Two trips on Operation *Grapple* to support UN forces in the former Yugoslavia were made in February, and one of the aircraft had to remain overnight at Split because reports had been received that a Transall aircraft of the Luftwaffe had been fired on from the ground, sustaining damage. As part of the effort being made by the UN to restore peace in the area, Lyneham became heavily involved in Operation *Deny Flight*. Between 18th and 23rd April 1993, 30 Squadron crews flew nine sorties between Leeming and Gioia del Colle in support of Tornado aircraft being deployed, and carried eighty tons of material and seventy passengers. Operation *Gràpple*

continued, and in April seven sorties were flown to Split via Zagreb, carrying 180,000lbs. of freight and 330 passengers in all. Likewise, *Deny Flight* was maintained, and in May a 30 Squadron crew had the sad task of flying bereaved families to and from the funerals of the 70 Squadron crew lost in the crash of Hercules XV193 during a low level exercise in Scotland. This was particularly hard, as strong feelings of comradeship were, and are, felt for the members of the other squadrons in the Lyneham Transport Wing.

By July the two operations in the Balkan area were taking up about ten per cent of 30 Squadron's time, which left time for many other tasks. One of the more significant was the tour of the western states of the USA by the Red Arrows in October 1993, supported once again by 30 Squadron. Sixteen locations were visited in three weeks, and the tour was a pleasant if hard-working finale to the flying career of MALM Desmond, who completed forty years in the RAF, thirty-one as aircrew. Another member of the squadron making his final trip, though not leaving the service, was Wg. Cdr. Main, who took part in a flight to the Caribbean in November.

1994 began with the usual round of flights to Norway carrying Marines for exercises in the snow, but in May an operation was organised to airlift British expatriates from the Yemen, where a civil war was developing. In two sorties, a hundred civilians were flown by Sqn. Ldr. Davey's crew to safety in Djibouti, on the other side of the Red Sea. Another civil war was taking place in Rwanda, creating a human tragedy, and it became clear in August 1994 that humanitarian aid would be required. Five crews of 30 Squadron were among those detailed for the operation, and they flew via Akrotiri, Jeddah and Dar-es-Salaam to Kigali with relief supplies and some troops. The operation lasted ten days before being transferred to C-5 Galaxy heavy-lift aircraft of the USAF. On a lighter note, in July the squadron had taken part in the International Air Tattoo at Fairford to celebrate forty years of flying by the C-130 (Hercules).

Worldwide activity was a feature of 30 Squadron's life in 1995, and included ongoing participation in *Grapple* which involved three crews carrying troops to reinforce the ever-increasing UK commitment in the former Yugoslavia, two flights in support of UN forces in Angola, and an operation to South Africa. It was hoped that trips to that country would become more frequent as international acceptability increased. In August Flt. Lt. Baxter and

*Hercules XV292 at Skopje, with M.Eng. Hamil facing the camera and Flt. Lt. Fryar looking for the captain*                    *[30 Squadron].*

his crew made eleven shuttle flights between Antigua and Montserrat in four days, evacuating people affected by the eruption of the volcano there and resupplying the island with food and stores. This operation was suspended, however, when fierce tropical storms intervened. Ottawa in Canada was the destination of two crews in September, but their mission was a sad one — the retrieval of the bodies of the crew of a Nimrod aircraft which had plunged into Lake Ontario during the Canadian National Exhibition air display.

Peacekeeping operations mounted by UN forces in Croatia and Iraq generated most of 30 Squadron's work in October and November, while in December Operation *Resolute*, unofficially known as Operation *Deny Christmas*, was the main task. This had come about when the peace accord reached in Bosnia led to the end of peace-keeping by the UN and the beginning of NATO involvement under the banner of IFOR (Implementation Force). Seventeen sorties were flown by 30 Squadron to Sarajevo, the first of them by Flt. Lt. Brown and his crew on 4th December, fourteen to Split and six to various destinations in Italy or Germany. Rapid turn-rounds were the norm, and very few instances of aircraft unserviceability were found. The task was reduced in January 1996, but to Flt. Lt. Evans proved a little more exciting, as his aircraft was hit by small arms fire while on radar approach to Sarajevo, fortunately without much effect. *Resolute* continued in February, and formed most of the squadron's tasking. One crew joined the NATO Air Transport Unit at Rimini in Italy, the first time that an RAF Hercules crew had been placed under the control of a NATO unit. Five of the sorties in April were made to Banja Luka, an airfield with limited facilities but no obstacle to the intrepid Hercules crews!

After nearly fifteen years, Hercules tankers were withdrawn from use on 31st March 1996 and were superceded by VC10s. Crews from 30 Squadron then began six-week detachments to the Falklands instead of the normal four months away from home. In April the out-going CO of 30 Squadron, Wg. Cdr. R. K. Gault, made his 'swansong' trip, an epic journey to New Zealand in support of the competition for the Fincastle Trophy. Outbound stages of this flight were made with minimal ground time, and on the return trip the stages were flown at only a marginally less hectic pace. In Wg. Cdr. Gault's place came Wg. Cdr. J. A. Lamonte.

May 1996 was dominated by Exercise *Purple Star*, a tri-service exercise held at Cherry Point MCAS, North Carolina which gave 30 Squadron the chance to demonstrate its capability in the transport support role. It was soon pointed out that the last time that British forces carried out operations in the United States on this scale was during the War of Independence! 30 Squadron sent six crews qualified in low-level flying, and total UK forces amounted to 12,500. Also taking part were RAF Nimrods, VC10s, Harriers, Sea Harriers, Tornados and helicopters. Crews slept in a city of tents, which led to problems, as the weather, wildlife and other crews conspired to deprive people of sleep. During the exercise, crews operated into Camp David, a disused airfield with a 5000-foot runway, practising airlanding insertion of troops, artillery and tracked vehicles. Later, about 150 sorties were flown into Holland Landing Zone, a 3500-foot clay airstrip in the Fort Bragg ranges. Overall, the exercise was deemed a great success, with crews from 47 and 70 Squadrons participating in three airdrops, the last of which involved 146 aircraft over a period of four hours! Recovery to the UK began on 20th May, and the last crew arrived at Lyneham in the first week of June.

In the former Yugoslavia, 30 Squadron crews were kept very busy in support of IFOR, while an increasing tempo of activity in Northern Ireland caused members of the Metropolitan Police Anti-Terrorist Branch to be flown to Aldergrove. In August four *Banner* and seven special sorties were flown.

Conscious of the need to help others less fortunate than themselves, 30 Squadron crews had 'adopted' Nyland School in Swindon, which caters for children with a range of problems, including severe learning difficulties, Downs' syndrome and autism. On 28th June 1996 a party of the children and their teachers visited Lyneham, where they first inspected the fire section and a Hercules. Although the weather was poor, 30 Squadron organised a short flight for them over their school and the Swindon area, and after returning to school the excited children wrote letters of appreciation to the 30 Squadron people who had been involved. A typical letter read "Dear Stuart and Jason, Thank you for the ride in the Hercules it was very go[od] When you open the back I thought I was going to fall out of the Hercules it was scary but it was fun I felt sick I was hapy When We landed then I got out of the Hercules then we had are lunch we were full up. but the day was lovely. With best wishes from....."

*Children of Nyland School in Swindon grouped on the ramp of a Hercules on a wet day, 28th June 1996. This school, for children with special needs, has been the recipient of money raised by 30 Squadron.*

## The Hercules shows its age

By now, the Hercules had been in RAF service for almost thirty years and was beginning to suffer problems. In August 1996 an autopilot failure on climb-out from Goose Bay drew attention to this fact. The aircraft pitched 15° up, and the co-pilot did well to bunt it forward, unfortunately causing minor injury to the air loadmaster in the process. However, the faithful Hercules soldiers on and at the time of writing is about to be only partially replaced by the new 'J' model.

Two trips were made in August under Operation *Jural*, the movement of RAF personnel from Dhahran to Al Kharj, prompted by the US withdrawal after a terrorist attack on military accommodation. Al Kharj has a 14,000 foot runway but is 1600 feet above sea level and suffers temperatures of up to 40ºC, so the Hercules is at the upper end of its operational capability when using the airfield.

Continuing trouble in central Africa was the reason that Canberra PR.9 aircraft were sent there in November 1996 to take photographs of the movement of refugees and of their camps. Flt. Lt. Brennan and his crew went to Entebbe in support of this mission but no sooner had they arrived than the refugees began to walk home to Rwanda, and the problem resolved itself. However, the refugee situation became a problem again in March 1997, when Flt. Lt. Laing's crew flew to Brazzaville as part of an effort to resolve the crisis.

After a break of some months, the Far East was visited in February 1997 by five crews who staged through Akrotiri and Muscat to Colombo, where a slip pattern was established to Bombay, Travandrum and Cochin in India, Kuantan in Malaysia, Brunei and Diego Garcia. In April one crew from each Lyneham squadron took three aircraft to Libreville as part of an international

effort known as Operation *Determinant*. Their stay was to have been two months, but it turned out to be for only half that, for most of which the crews were confined to their hotel. Conditions were far from pleasant, and the only sorties flown were a few to Brazzaville. A peaceful handover to a new government in Zaire brought the operation to an end.

A trip to Moscow with no night stop was carried out in April, the aircraft carrying enough fuel for the return journey. Afterwards, the CO remarked "The bizarre process of paying the ground handling fees in Russia leaves one wondering if the country could ever have organised a viable offensive against NATO."

In Northern Ireland, the incredibly long-running Operation *Banner* continued, some flights still making use of Ballykelly airfield. At Aldergrove there were frequent delays when outgoing troops handed over to their reliefs not at the airport but on the streets of Belfast. This system could cause a delay to the aircraft of up to five hours.

Always involved in raising money for charity, 30 Squadron sent a Hercules to the air show at North Weald in May 1997 and there collected the sum of £1500 for RAFA. In the rear of the aircraft a display of current squadron activity was visited by the general public, and a video of Hercules flying was shown.

In August 1997, under a newly-introduced scheme, members of the Royal Auxiliary Air Force joined the squadron. Although all the RAuxAF aircrew were former Hercules crews, questions were raised on whether they could remain current on type in the thirty days per year that they were allowed to fly and whether they would take up positions held by regular officers.

By October, delays in the introduction of the C-130J model which was intended to replace some of the RAF's C-130K fleet caused the high-level decision to extend the service life of the twenty-five aircraft which were due for withdrawal. Some were modified to take a Litton 92 inertial platform and a separate GPS receiver, while others were to be fitted with HINS, an integrated platform and GPS system. About a quarter of the Hercules fleet was now at Marshall Aerospace at Cambridge, which caused severe availability problems.

When in November 1997 Saddam Hussein denied UN inspection teams the access to Iraq which had formed part of the Gulf War settlement, the Hercules force was called upon to take part in Operation *Bolton*. From Gibraltar, HMS *Invincible* was sent to the Gulf with six RAF Harriers on board to boost its capability, and 30 Squadron crews made seven flights to Gibraltar carrying munitions, stores and personnel. Considerable interest was caused among inhabitants of 'the Rock' at seeing so much Hercules and Harrier activity.

Ever eager to raise money, particularly for service charities, 30 Squadron handed over on 4th December 1997 a cheque for no less than £30,000 to Air Marshal Sir John Kemball on behalf of the Royal Air Forces Association. The celebratory lunch also marked the thirtieth anniversary of the Hercules in RAF service. The money had been raised at air displays, by the sale of David Shepherd prints and at a dining-in night.

An instance of exceptional airmanship and skill on the part of Flt. Lt. M. Fowler of 30 Squadron was recognised by AVM P. O. Sturley, the AOC 38 Group after an event which took place on 5th December 1997. Soon after take-off from Al Kharj air base in Saudi Arabia at night, the co-pilot reported an abnormal stiffness in the aileron controls, and Flt. Lt. Fowler quickly agreed. With the aircraft at 10,000 feet and the ailerons very difficult to move, the co-pilot called 'Mayday', but at first air traffic control seemed not to understand. Eventually the seriousness of the situation was impressed on them, and they vectored the Hercules back to Al Kharj. On final approach the controls almost seized up, and Flt. Lt. Fowler believed he would have to crash-land somewhere near the runway, but at the last minute there was a slight improvement in control and a safe landing was made.

February 1998 was dominated by Operation *Bolton*, in which 30 Squadron crews carried equipment for Tornados to Ali al Salem Air Base in Kuwait. This was a major resupply of the base when offensive action appeared to be likely. Heavily bombed during the Gulf War, the Hardened Aircraft Shelters on the airfield had been destroyed (which does not say much for their effectiveness). Initially, the Hercules were routed through Suda Bay in Crete, but as the Greek Air Force there did not prove helpful Akrotiri came into use instead. The flow of Hercules into Ali al Salem was coordinated by five Lyneham-based captains led by Sqn. Ldr. Campbell, who between them soon organised very short turn-round times. Operation *Bolton* continued through March and April, but by May had been reduced to four sorties for 30 Squadron crews.

Kubinka, the base of Russia's 'Open Skies' Squadron and home to a variety of interesting aircraft from MiG29s to Mainstays, was the destination of a 30 Squadron crew for a visit in April 1998. Intended to be a short visit, it was prolonged by the inflexibility of the Russian system for submitting flight plans. A further trip was made to Russia in May, when Sheremetyevo was visited and found to be very disorganised. An inspection team was also flown to Tallinn in Estonia.

*Posed in front of Hercules C.3 XV210 in 1996 are most of the members of 30 Squadron.*

*Flt. Lt. Fowler of 30 Squadron who, with his crew, managed to land a Hercules with aileron malfunction on 5th December 1997 at Al Kharj.*

In May 1998 the CO attended the RAFA Conference at Blackpool on behalf of RAF Lyneham and received the Lord Tedder Trophy and the Sir Charles Wheeler Trophy. The Lord Tedder Trophy is awarded to the RAF Station which raised the most money, while the Sir Charles Wheeler Trophy is awarded to the Station which raised the most per head of population. 30 Squadron personnel again excelled themselves on 18th July 1998, when Sqn. Ldr. Peter Bundock organised a *Classics on the Wing* concert in the open air. Attended by 8,000 people on a sunny evening, the event included flypasts by a variety of aircraft and a paradrop by the Red Falcons, and raised another £35,000 for RAFA. In August came change of CO, when Wg. Cdr. Lamonte was promoted to Gp. Capt. and replaced by Wg. Cdr. John Barrass MA BSc, who had earlier been a Flight commander on 47 Squadron.

Following a worsening situation in Kosovo, very intensive flying was carried out in June. The need for NATO to provide a rapid response to bring pressure onto the Serbian population saw great efforts being made by the Lyneham Transport Wing in support of movements to Gioia del Colle in Italy under Operation *Deliberate Forge*.

An operation in August 1998 gave the Hercules force another opportunity to show its ability to react quickly to a crisis. This time the trouble spot was the Democratic Republic of the Congo. The first crew to become involved was at Windhoek in Namibia, working on Exercise *Zimbabwe Survey*, and was placed on standby for a short time. Two days later the crew was at Ascension when again placed on standby, and they stayed there for ten days. Then 155 troops of 40 RM Commando arrived and the crew went onto two hours standby. Next day they flew forty-eight Marines to Brazzaville and then positioned themselves at Libreville in Gabon to run an RAF detachment. That done, they returned to Lyneham to be relieved by another aircraft and crew.

On the ground, albeit at a high level, seven members of the squadron journeyed to Nepal to take part in Exercise *Johnson Trek*, three weeks devoted to white-water rafting, a jungle safari and trekking through the world's deepest gorge. The expedition had been organised by Sgt. Dex Mann with the object of distributing supplies to village schools along the route. Another change of scenery came in December, when seven members of 30 Squadron spent three weeks on HMS *Ocean* on a voyage from Maryport in

Florida to Devonport. This new helicopter carrier was on sea trials, and a programme arranged for the RAF men by Lt. Cdr. Burgess included flying in Sea Kings.

Operation *Desert Fox* in December 1998 caused 30 Squadron to produce a large number of crews to fly bombs to Kuwait in support of the Allied bombing campaign to force Saddam Hussein to allow United Nations inspections of suspected weapons of mass destruction. At this stage, the planned slip pattern extended through Christmas and the New Year, involving six crews from the squadron, but in the event the bombing was halted and all crews returned home on Christmas Eve. Fg. Off. Clarke produced a Christmas menu similar to those of the past, and some squadron members were disappointed in not spending Christmas in Cyprus, although they would not admit that to their wives!

During 1998, 30 Squadron flew over 7700 hours in support of operations, on exercises and in continuation training. Work in the Middle East now accounted for most of the operational flying, and unusual destinations visited had included Baku in Azerbaijan, Sibiu in Transylvania and Katmandu. Somewhat surprisingly for crews well-known for their interest in the inner man, they displayed considerable aptitude in the sporting field. Flt. Lt. Rich Woods represented the RAF at rowing, Flt. Lt. Gary Moore was a member of the RAF judo team, Sqn. Ldr. Muse managed the RAF cricket team and Flt. Lt. Duncan Wright and Sqn. Ldr. Nigel Painter took part in trials for the RAF motorsports team.

Both 24 and 30 Squadrons lost their limited but significant transport support capability in January 1999, from which date no more low-level training was carried out and no more crews were detached to 1312 Flight at Mount Pleasant.

## More Balkans activity

The attention of the Lyneham squadrons was again drawn to the Balkans in February in response to another potential crisis. In response to the action of Serbian forces in Kosovo, eleven sorties were flown by 30 Squadron crews under Operation *Agricola*, carrying troops to Skopje in Macedonia to await a possible move into Kosovo. Much of the freight and passengers were flown into Thessaloniki, due to Skopje's proximity to the Kosovan border and possible threats from anti-aircraft batteries. Among the loads of freight were vehicles, aircraft ground equipment, personnel of Signals Units, bombs and ammunition for infantry and armoured units, and personal weapons. More than twenty sorties in support of *Agricola* were flown by 30 Squadron in March, the busiest period at Lyneham since the Gulf War. By April, with the air war escalating and preparations for a ground war well under way, many tasks were routed into Tirana in Albania, where US forces had taken over the operation of air traffic control and had started a reconstruction programme. Off-loading with engines running was normal, but delays at Skopje were becoming common, as the airfield had become saturated.

30 Squadron provided four extra crews daily from May 1999, continuing the squadron 'can do' approach to life. The squadron flew 40% of all operational transport sorties into Macedonia and Albania in May 1999 – a tremendous achievement. In June sixty-four sorties were flown under *Agricola*, including many as part of the British army airlift into Macedonia and continuing support of the offensive from airfields in Italy and Corsica. However, the efforts of the last three months began to diminish in July, allowing a slight reduction in pressure on men and machines. The munitions supply task was completed, but the resupply of the peacekeeping force continued on a reduced scale.

To commemorate those who had lost their lives while in 30 Squadron service, a Roll of Honour board was unveiled in squadron headquarters in July 1999 by AVM David Dick, President of the 30 Squadron Association, and AVM Phillip Sturley, AOC 38 Group.

## Eclipse

The much-heralded total eclipse of the sun gave 30 Squadron some public exposure on 11th August 1999, when Flt. Lt. Weedon captained a Hercules which flew BBC and ITV camera teams over Cornwall. As there was almost total cloud cover on that day, this flight gave the British population their only view of the event, but Flt. Lt. Weedon, who was making sure that the aircraft was at the correct altitude and position, was too busy to see it!

*On board HMS* Ocean, *30 Squadron's sister unit, were (left to right): Sgt. Temple, Flt. Lt. 'Spike' Flynn, Flt. Lt. Pete McNichol, Flt. Lt. Al Davidson, Flt. Lt. Ian Shaw, Flt. Lt. Paul Hughes and Flt. Lt. Dave Frey.*

Yet another trouble spot was visited by 30 Squadron crews when in September 1999 East Timor in Indonesia descended into violence after the population had voted for independence on 30th August. On 8th September the UN Security Council gave the Indonesian Government twenty-four hours to control the uprising, and six days later deployment of a peacekeeping force was sanctioned by the UN. This move was approved by President Habibi on 17th September, and an operation was set in motion. 30 Squadron provided one of three crews from Lyneham, and on 12th September, Flt. Lt. Smith and his crew took off for Akrotiri, Muscat and the Cocos Islands before arriving at Darwin in Northern Australia three days later. They then flew twenty-six paratroops and military vehicles to Dili in Timor and subsequently went there twice a day, a ninety minute flight. The loads included freight for the Ghurka troops, and on the return trips to Darwin they returned with captured weapons and Malaysian troops. Seventeen sorties were flown in October to Dili and Baucau on East Timor and to Brunei. Flt. Lt. Smith and his crew returned to Lyneham that month and were replaced by Flt. Lt. Whitworth's crew. Operation *Langar* was also in force, and consisted of a deployment of British troops to support the International Force for East Timor (INTERFET), and this continued until withdrawal in December.

An earthquake in Turkey in November 1999 caused considerable damage to the towns of Duze and Bolu, and Flt. Lt. Davidson and his crew in XV187 from 30 Squadron flew thirty firemen from several brigades from Manston to Turkey so that they could provide their expertise to the local rescue personnel. In addition, they carried two tons of medical and search equipment and five aeromedical evacuation specialists

from Tactical Medical Wing at Lyneham. On the return journey they carried a RN officer who had been badly injured in the earthquake, but sadly, during the flight he died from his injuries.

The Millennium Year, 2000, began quietly, allowing the CO, Wg. Cdr. Barrass, the opportunity of realising a life-long ambition by leading an expedition to the Zululand region of South Africa. One of the objects of this mission was to restore the graves of those who fell in the Zulu wars of a century earlier. Fourteen members of 30 Squadron took part in the mission and enjoyed a two-hour ceremonial audience with the Zulu king. An appreciable sum of money was raised for RAFA by the sale of first-day covers publicising the expedition.

At less than twenty four hours' notice, four crews from 30 Squadron and others from 47 and 70 Squadrons made shuttle flights in February to Sculthorpe in connections with Exercise *Eagles Flight*, an airland deployment of troops. As it was not in regular use, the airfield at Sculthorpe was regarded as a good substitute for an airfield in a trouble spot such as the Balkans.

Most of the squadron personnel, including the CO, went to St. Mawgan in March 2000 for Exercise *Kernow Palm*, eight days of combat survival lectures, lifeboat drill at sea and a short survival exercise on Dartmoor. While they were in Cornwall, a short sponsored run from St. Mawgan to Land's End was arranged, and £1000 was raised for charity. At the annual reunion of the 30 Squadron Association in April a Service of Remembrance was held in honour of AVM David Dick, who had done so much to support the Association and 30 Squadron. A piece of silver was presented by the squadron to the Association in his honour, and a painting depicting the various operations in which the sqaudron had been involved

*The Roll of Honour boards in the foyer of the 30 Squadron offices at Lyneham*  [RAF Lyneham (LYN/208/4/99)].

*HRH Princess Anne, Honorary Air Commodore of RAF Lyneham, taking the salute during a formal inspection in August 1999, with the 'Green Barrows' formation team overhead, led by a 30 Squadron crew*  [RAF Lyneham (LYN/210/8/99)].

*President of the 30 Squadron Association until his death in 2000, AVM David Dick (seated) at the unveiling of the Roll of Honour boards in 1999. The AOC 38 Group, AVM P. Sturley, is talking to David while Flt. Lt. Mike Wareham looks on* [RAF Lyneham (LYN208/2/99)].

during its 85th anniversary year was unveiled by the artist, Mark Postlethwaite, and the project officer, Flt. Lt. Darren Rawlings.

During May 2000 Operation *Palliser* was carried out to move personnel to Freetown in Sierra Leone, commencing early on 7th May, when Flt. Lt. Baddeley set off from Lyneham. Next day he and his crew made two trips between Dakar and Freetown and on 9th May flew two sorties between Accra and Freetown before returning to Lyneham on 15th May. In all, fifteen crews were involved in the operation, for which a slip pattern was set up at Dakar. Some of the aircraft involved picked up fuel at Tenerife, while lighter-laden aircraft flew direct. Freight carried included blades for Chinook helicopters, Land Rovers, rockets, bombs, water, generators, and water purifiers, and bodies carried included Chinook crews, paratroops, Marines and TV filming crews. In the first three weeks of the operation, 30 Squadron crews flew 308 hours, and continued into June with the deployment of UN troops. A change of hotel to the Meridian President in Dakar brought about an improvement in the health of the crews, who flew their final trips into Freetown on 15th June, although three resupply flights were flown by 30 Squadron in July.

In the spring and summer of 2000, RAFA organised a 'Millennium Link', under which a Scroll was carried between Branches by whatever means were dreamed up by the members. 30 Squadron took part in the scheme by flying the Scroll to Filton, where it was handed over to RAFA's Chipping Sodbury & Yate Branch by WO Iain Norris, SWO at Lyneham. Heavily involved in this project were Flt. Lts. Cochrane and Cockram.

The loss of the Russian Oscar II class submarine *Kursk* off Murmansk in August meant a short-notice task to preposition two aircraft at Trondheim in northern Norway to await permission to fly to Murmansk. They carried two ISO containers holding the LR5, the Royal Navy submarine rescue vessel, and the necessary support equipment and team of divers. The plan was to help recover the 116 sailors trapped in the *Kursk*, but after a week of prevarication the Russians announced that there had been no survivors aboard the submarine and the LR5 was not called upon. Subsequently, the Russian government and Navy were severely criticised in the international press for not accepting help.

Apart from the *Kursk* fiasco, 30 Squadron continued its involvement in the Balkans (Operations *Palatine* and *Agricola*) and the Middle East (Operations *Warden*, *Jural* and *Bolton*) in August, and troops were flown to and from Northern Ireland under the long-standing Operation *Banner*. Two special sorties were flown to Edinburgh Field in Australia via Diego Garcia to deliver and retrieve equipment, while Flt. Lt. Myers led his crew "....kicking and screaming" via Las Palmas in the Canaries to Cape Town to rescue an unserviceable Tornado which had taken part in an air show.

Sierra Leone was still proving to be a trouble spot, and on 21st September a 30 Squadron crew in Ascot 4160 moved Gurkhas, Marines and members of the Royal Irish Regt. to Tenerife before continuing next day to Lungi. Operation *Barrass* was an operation designed to free British military hostages in Sierra Leone. Involving crews from all four Lyneham squadrons, the operation included eight sorties by crews of 30 Squadron, who flew a variety of freight and the crews of Chinook helicopters into the country in support of the ground troops. 30 Squadron's then CO, Wg. Cdr. John Barrass, thus became the only CO to have an operation named after him! Many other flights of a more peaceful nature were made during the month, one of them being a special task in support of the Red Arrows, who were performing their display at Luqa in Malta.

The variety of work undertaken by 30 Squadron crews can be illustrated by the three short-notice tasks, totalling 43 hours 50 minutes, which occured in October 2000. One was a call-out to Akrotiri with ten tonnes of freight, another was a trip to Gibraltar to collect the 55-man crew of the submarine *Tireless*, which had developed a reactor problem. Thirdly came an emergency flight from Pristina, Kosovo, with four casualties who had been injured when their Warrior armoured personnel carrier had rolled down an embankment. In addition, squadron crews flew into airstrips in the Jordanian desert to take part in Exercise *Shifting Sands*, one crew receiving a glowing message of thanks from the Engineering Officer of 25 Squadron for "......completing the task against all the odds." The value of ensuring that all crews were qualified for tactical strip landings had been well demonstrated.

In November Operations *Banner*, *Palatine* and *Bolton* continued to occupy the time of 30 Squadron crews. Tasks in support of Exercise *Air Warrior* began on 11th November, the mission being to recover eight Harriers of 3 Squadron from Nellis AFB to Cottesmore. At Nellis, the equipment was loaded and the long journey via Tinker AFB, Oklahoma and Dover AFB, Delaware, began. The crew stayed at Dover for two nights before making the crossing to Lajes in the Azores on 16th November. After another two nights on the ground, the Hercules arrived at Lyneham on 18th November.

On 12th November the first RAF Hercules to be returned to the United States under the 'buy-back' scheme, XV182, left Lyneham in the hands of Sqn. Ldr. Hill's crew. Using call-sign Ascot 4154, it flew to Gander and next day to Bangor, Maine, and finally on 14th November it made its last flight in RAF hands, to Sussex County Airport, Delaware. It was planned that by the summer of 2001 only 25 of the original Hercules flown by the RAF would remain in service, the final new J-model aircraft having been delivered.

An unusual special task was flown as Ascot 635 on 17th November. Celebrity chef Jamie Oliver had offered to cook a meal for a family who were willing to pledge money for the BBC fund-raising programme 'Children In Need', and the RAF had agreed to fly him and the film crew from Northolt to Birmingham, where the selected family lived. The task was completed with the squadron's usual aplomb and the crew returned to base next day. 30 Squadron's charity fund-raising efforts continued in 2000 with a joint 'Draw 2000' which raised £94,000 for the RAF Association.

## Into the future

On 15th December 2000 the last change of command to be covered in this book took place when Wg. Cdr. Barrass handed over to Wg. Cdr. Peter Dixon. The new century finds 30 Squadron crews keenly carrying out all the tasks allocated to them, and no outsider can fail to be struck by their enthusiasm and willingness to deal with any situation presented to them. Their job must be the best in the Royal Air Force!

*The five Standards of Lyneham squadrons and RAF Lyneham on parade, with 30 Squadron second from right*          [*RAF Lyneham (LYN333/12/00)].*

# Appendix 1: 30 Squadron Bases

| Location | Date |
|---|---|
| **Part 1: Headquarters** | |
| Farnborough | 10.14 |
| (Left for Egypt) | 4.11.14 |
| Ismailia | 20.11.14 |
| (30 Sqn. established) | 24.3.15 |
| Basra | 10.15 |
| Ali Gharbi | 7.12.15 |
| Amara | 16.12.15 |
| Musandaq | 1.16 |
| Sheikh Saad | 1.16 |
| Camp Wadi | 1.4.16 |
| Sheikh Saad | 6.5.16 |
| Arab Village | 9.16 |
| Aziziyah | 3.3.17 |
| Zeur | 5.3.17 |
| Bustan | 8.3.17 |
| Baghdad | 11.3.17 |
| Fort Kermea | 7.4.17 |
| Barurah | 20.4.17 |
| Baghdad | 4.5.17 |
| Baquba | 13.9.17 |
| Sharaban | 18.10.17 |
| Baquba | 25.10.17 |
| Qala Mufti | 2.11.17 |
| Baquba | 2.12.17 |
| Uqbah | 1.3.18 |
| Baquba | 5.4.18 |
| Kifri | late 10.18 |
| Baquba | mid 11.18 |
| Baghdad West | early 12.18 |
| (reduced to cadre) | 9.4.19 |
| Baghdad West | 1.2.20 |
| Hinaidi | 3.12.22 |
| Kirkuk | 19.5.24 |
| Hinaidi | @ 1.25 |
| Kirkuk | @ 4.25 |
| Hinaidi | 15.2.26 |
| Kirkuk | 11.4..26 |
| Hinaidi | 27.10.27 |
| Mosul | 25.10.29 |
| Dhibban/Habbaniya | 19.10.36 |
| Ismailia | 25.8.39 |
| (dets. to Amriya and Helwan) | |
| Ikingi Maryut | 8.7.40 |
| Eleusis | 3.11.40 |
| Paramythia ('A'; Flt.) | 2.41 – 3.3.41 |
| Maleme | 17.4.41 |
| Amriya | 16.5.41 |
| Idku | 14.6.41 |
| LG.102 | 25.10.41 |
| LG.05 | 16.1.42 |
| LG.121 | 23.1.42 |
| (embarked in HMS *Indomitable*) | 25.2.42 |
| Ratmalana | 6.3.42 |
| Dambulla | 31.8.42 |
| Colombo | 15.2.43 |
| Dambulla | 3.8.43 |
| Feni | 23.1.44 |
| Fazilpur | 12.2.44 |
| Comilla | 9.4.44 |
| Yelahanka | 25.4.44 |
| Arkonam | 13.9.44 |
| Chittagong | 5.10.44 |
| Jumchar | 10.12.44 |
| Akyab Main | 24.4.45 |
| Chakulia | 18.5.45 |
| Vizagapatam | 3.7.45 |
| Zayatkwin | 24.9.45 |
| Vizagapatam | 29.9.45 |
| Baigachi | 4.12.45 |
| Bhopal | 1.2.46 |
| Agra | 27.5.46 –1.12.46 |
| Abingdon | 1.11.47 |
| Oakington | 24.11.47 |
| Abingdon | 27.11.50 |
| Benson | 2.5.52 |
| Dishforth | 14.3.53 |
| Eastleigh | 15.11.59 |
| Muharraq | 1.9.64 –6.9.67 |
| Fairford | 1.5.68 |
| Lyneham | 24.9.71 |

## Part 2: Flights

### 'A' Flight

| Location | Date |
|---|---|
| Amara | 5.6.15 ** |
| Ali Gharbi | 6.9.15 |
| Sannaiyat | 16.9.15 |
| Nukhailat | 26.9.15 |
| Kut-al-Amara | 30.9.15 |
| Aziziyah | 6.10.15 |
| Kut-al-Amara | 28.11.15 |
| Ali Gharbi | 7.12.15 |
| Mussandaq | |
| Sheikh Saad | |
| Ora | 16.1.16 |
| Basra | |
| Ora | 8.3.16 |
| Camp Wadi | 1.4.16 |
| Sheikh Saad | 6.5.16 |
| Arab Village | 29.10.16 |
| Shumran | 26.1.17 |
| Sheikh Saad | 2.3.17 |
| Aziziya | 3.3.17 |
| Zeur | 5.3.17 |
| Bustan | 8.3.17 |
| Baghdad | 11.3.17 |
| Kermea | 7.4.17 |
| Barurah | 20.4.17 |
| Baghdad | 4.5.17 |
| Baquba | 13.9.17 |
| Shahraban | 18.10.17 |
| Baquba | 25.10.17 |
| Qalat al Mufti | 24.11.17 |
| Baquba | 8.12.17 |
| Ramadi | 23.2.18 |
| Uqbah | 9.3.18 |
| Hit | 11.3.18 |
| Baquba | 5.4.18 |
| Kifri | early 7.18 |
| Zinjan (Persia) | 20.9.18 |
| Kasvin | 13.11.18 |
| (transferred to 63 Sqn.) | 18.2.19 |
| Mosul | @ 8.19 |
| Baghdad | 15.2.21 |
| Kirkuk | ? |
| Hinaidi | 4.1.24 |
| Mosul | 25.10.29 |
| Sulaimaniya | 27.10.30 |
| Mosul | 4.11.30 |
| Kirkuk | 12.11.30 |
| Mosul | 26.11.30 |
| Halebja | 31.1.31 |
| Kingerban | 2.4.31 |
| Sulaimaniya | 9.4.31 |
| Mosul | 14.4.31 |
| Diana | 23.5.32 |

*** also small detachments at Asani 18.7.15
and Basra 4.8.15*

### 'B' Flight

| Location | Date |
|---|---|
| Basra | 9.11.15 |
| Aziziyah | 15.11.15 |
| Kut-al-Amara | 28.11.15 |
| Ali Gharbi | 7.12.15 |
| Mussandaq | |
| Sheikh Saad | |
| Ora | 16.1.16 |
| Basra | 11.3.16 |
| Camp Wadi | 11.4.16 |
| Sheikh Saad | 6.5.16 |
| Arab Village | 9.10.16 |
| Shumran | 26.1.17 |
| Sheikh Saad | 2.3.17 |
| Aziziya | 3.3.17 |
| Zeur | 5.3.17 |
| Bustan | 8.3.17 |
| Baghdad | 11.3.17 |
| Baquba | 28.3.17 |
| Fort Kermea | 5.4.17 |
| Barura | 20.4.17 |
| Baghdad | 4.5.17 |
| Khan Jadida | 28.6.17 |
| Baghdad | 9.8.17 |
| Falliya | 21.9.17 |
| Madhij | 26.9.17 |
| Falluja | 3.10.17 |
| Ramadi | 23.2.18 |
| Uqbah | 9.3.18 |
| Hit | 11.3.18 |
| Ramadi | 14.4.18 |
| Kifri | 18.7.18 |
| Baghdad West | early 12.18 |
| (reduced to cadre) | |
| Kasvin | @ 8.19 |
| Baghdad | 24.4.21 |
| Hinaidi | |
| Kirkuk | 4.1.24 |
| Mosul | 25.10.29 |
| Kirkuk | 1.11.30 |
| Sulaimaniya | 4.11.30 |
| Mosul | 12.11.30 |
| Diana | |
| Mosul | 23.5.32 |

**'C' Flight**

| | |
|---|---|
| Basra | 27.12.15 |
| Amara | |
| Basra | 4.5.16 |
| Sheikh Saad | 17.5.16 (21.7.16 ?) |
| Arab Village | 14.8.16 |
| Sinn Abtar | 27.1.17 |
| Zeur | 7.3.17 |
| Bustan | 8.3.17 |
| Bawi | 9.3.17 |
| Baghdad | 12.3.17 |
| Kasirin | 29.3.17 |
| Sindiya | 7.4.17 |
| Barura | 19.4.17 |
| Sindiya | 4.5.17 |
| Khan Jadida | 23.6.17 |
| Baghdad | 28.6.17 |
| Baquba | 6.8.17 |
| Sharaban | 18.10.17 |
| Baquba | 25.10.17 |
| Qala al Mufti | 24.11.17 |
| Baquba | 2.12.17 |
| Uqbah | 1.3.18 |
| Baquba | 11.3.18 |
| Tuz Khurmatli (half-Flt.) | 2.5.18 |
| Kifri (half-Flt.) | 26.5.18 |
| Kifri (whole Flt.) | late 10.18 |
| Baquba | mid 11.18 –1.1.19 |
| Bushire | 13.1.19 |
| Baghdad West | 9.2.19 |
| (reduced to cadre) | |
| Mosul | 25.10.29 |
| Kirkuk | 4.11.30 |
| Sulaimaniya | 12.11.30 |
| Mosul | 20.11.30 |
| Kirkuk | 17.1.31 |
| Diana | 12.3.32 |

**Part 3: Group and Wing allegiance (Second World War):**

| | |
|---|---|
| 250 Wing | 21.9.39–8.7.40 |
| 252 Wing | 11.7.40–? |
| 264 Wing | |
| Redesignated 269 Wing and 234 Wing | 24.10.41 |
| ? | 16.2.42 |
| 169 Wing / 222 Group | 23.11.43 |
| 166 Wing / 224 Group | 3.2.44–3.6.44 |
| 225 Group | 3.6.44+–20.8.44 |
| 902 Wing / 224 Group | 10.44–? |
| 904 Wing / 224 Group | 24.4.45 |
| 903 Wing / 224 Group | 13.5.45 |
| 905 Wing | 6.45–7.45 |

# Appendix 2: Squadron Commanders

**RFC Detachment, Egypt**

| | |
|---|---|
| Capt. S. D. Massy | 4th November 1914 |
| | to 24th March 1915 |

**30 Squadron**

| | |
|---|---|
| Capt./Maj. H. L. Reilly | 30th April 1915 |
| Maj. R. Gordon RNAS | 20th November 1915 |
| Maj. S. D. Massy DSO | 24th November 1915 |
| Maj. E. M. Murray MC | 30th May 1916 |
| Maj. J. E. Tennant DSO MC | 7th August 1916 |
| Maj. H. de Havilland DSO | 11th January 1917 |
| Maj. D. A. Westendarp | 21st April 1918 |
| Maj. J. Everidge MC | 24th May 1918 |
| | to 2nd May 1919 |
| Sqn. Ldr. W. Sowery AFC | 31st March 1920 |
| Sqn. Ldr. R. Collishaw DSO OBE DSC DFC | 12th November 1920 |
| Sqn. Ldr. H. Johnstone OBE | 13th December 1922 |
| Sqn. Ldr. J. M. Robb DFC | 19th January 1924 |
| Sqn. Ldr. F. H. Coleman DSO | 3rd June 1925 |
| Sqn. Ldr. H. P. Lale DSO DFC | 7th January 1928 |
| Sqn. Ldr. R. V. Goddard | 11th February 1930 |
| Sqn. Ldr. G. S. N. Johnstone | 9th July 1931 |
| Sqn. Ldr. P. R. T. J. M. I. C. Chamberlayne AFC | 14th July 1932 |
| Sqn. Ldr. A. L. Fiddament DFC | 26th March 1935 |
| Sqn. Ldr. A. J. Rankin AFC | 12th November 1936 |
| Sqn. Ldr. G. H. Stainforth AFC | 25th August 1937 |
| Sqn. Ldr. U. Y. Shannon | 3rd November 1938 |
| Sqn. Ldr. R. A. Milward DFC | December 1940 |
| Sqn. Ldr. F. A. Marlow | 28th June 1941 |
| Sqn. Ldr. G. F. Chater DFC | 10th February 1942 |
| Sqn. Ldr. A. W. A. Bayne DFC | 29th May 1942 |
| Sqn. Ldr. S. R. Peacock–Edwards DFC | 15th February 1943 |

| | |
|---|---|
| Sqn. Ldr. T. A. Stevens | 4th May 1944 |
| Flt. Lt. H. F. Whidborne | 31st May 1945 |
| Sqn. Ldr. T. H. Meyer | 29th July 1945 |
| Sqn. Ldr. R. A. Newbery DFC* | 6th August 1946 to |
| | 1st December 1946 |
| Sqn. Ldr. R. C. Wood | 24th November 1947 |
| Sqn. Ldr. A. McC. Johnstone OBE AFC | 18th January 1948 |
| Sqn. Ldr. A. Reece DSO DFC AFC | 4th March 1950 |
| Sqn. Ldr. R. S. Kerby | 15th August 1951 |
| Flt. Lt. S. R. Dixon | August 1952 |
| Sqn. Ldr. D. A. Peacock DFC | 1st September 1952 |
| Sqn. Ldr. P. L. Whitaker DFC | 4th October 1954 |
| Sqn. Ldr. P. G. Coulson AFC MBE | October 1956 |
| Sqn. Ldr. E. J. Churchill AFC | 19th November 1958 |
| Sqn. Ldr. T. C. Waugh DFC | October 1959 |
| Sqn. Ldr. C. R. Evans | 1st November 1961 |
| Sqn. Ldr. R. A. W. Harrison DFC | 20th December 1963 |
| Sqn. Ldr. R. P. J. King | April 1965 to 7th |
| | September 1967 |
| Wg. Cdr. K. J. Parfit | 10th June 1968 |
| Wg. Cdr. D. N. Galpin | January 1971 |
| Wg. Cdr. B. P. Earle | March 1973 |
| Wg. Cdr. J. R. Hardwick | February 1975 |
| Wg. Cdr. A. C. Tolhurst | July 1977 |
| Wg. Cdr. B. Latter | September 1979 |
| Wg. Cdr. A. R. Tolcher | September 1981 |
| Wg. Cdr. J. V. Bell | September 1983 |
| Wg. Cdr. D. N. Adams | February 1986 |
| Wg. Cdr. D. M. Guest | September 1988 |
| Wg. Cdr. A. P. T. Main MIMgt MIPD MRAeS | April 1991 |
| Wg. Cdr. R. K. Gault OBE | November 1993 |
| Wg. Cdr. J. A. Lamonte | May 1996 |
| Wg. Cdr. J. A. Barrass MA BSc | August 1998 |
| Wg. Cdr. P. G. Dixon | 15th December 2000 |

# Appendix 3: Roll of Honour — Fatalities and Prisoners of War

**Part 1: members of the RFC Detachment and of 30 Squadron who lost their lives.**

### First World War

| Name | Date | Circumstances | Cemetery |
|---|---|---|---|
| ADAMS, Capt. Allen Percy, DFC | 6th March 1919 | Killed in crash of Martinsyde 7461 while bombing Khun | |
| ADAMS, AM Francis Luke (44) (Aus) | (by 11.16) | Captured in the fall of Kut-al-Amara; died of malaria | |
| | | | Baghdad (North Gate) |
| ALLISON, Lt. John Oliver, MC* | 15th May 1918 | Shot down in RE.8 B5876 during raid on Altun Kopri airfield | |
| | | | Basra Memorial |
| ALLSTON, Pte. Frank (M4/122199) | 10th July 1918 | ? | Baghdad (North Gate) |
| ATHERTON, Lt. Francis Wright, MC | 15th May 1918 | Shot down in RE.8 B5876 during raid on Altun Kopri airfield | |
| | | | Basra Memorial |
| BEAN, 2nd. Lt. William Stuart | 21st January 1918 | Shot down in DH.4 A7591 by AA during raid on Kifri | |
| | | | Baghdad (North Gate) |
| BLIGHT, 2/AM Reginald Sampson (30241) | 4th September 1917 | ? | Baghdad (North Gate) |
| BRAUND, 2/AM W. | 28th July 1916 | Captured in the fall of Kut-al-Amara | |
| *(Note 1)* | | | |
| BULLEN, 2/AM Harold (240445) | 23rd September 1916 | Captured in the fall of Kut-al-Amara; left in Kut hospital and died there | |
| | | | Basra Memorial |
| BURN, Lt. William Wallace Allison (Aus) | 30th July 1915 | Killed by party of Zobaah after crashing 25 mls west of Abu Salabh | |
| | | | Basra Memorial |
| BUTLER, 2/AM Sidney George (6242) | 10th August 1916 | Captured in the fall of Kut-al-Amara | Baghdad (North Gate) |
| CANDY, Cpl. William Henry Minter (533) | 30th June 1916 | Captured in the fall of Kut-al-Amara | Baghdad (North Gate) |
| CARPENTER, 2/AM Reginald William (240486) | 31st December 1916 | Captured in the fall of Kut-al-Amara | |
| *(Note 2)* | | | |
| CASTOR, Lance-Sgt. Robert Gregory (11439) | 21st January 1918 | Shot down in DH.4 A7591 by AA during raid on Kifri | |
| | | | Baghdad (North Gate) |
| *(Note 6)* | | | |
| CLARIDGE, 2/AM Lionel Victor (1299) | 1st May 1916 | Captured in the fall of Kut-al-Amara | Basra Memorial |
| COCKERELL, 2nd. Lt. Samuel Pepys | 20th March 1915 | Smallpox | Ismailia |
| CORBETT, Capt. Reginald David de la Court | 25th December 1917 | Captured in the fall of Kut-al-Amara; died of heart failure | |
| | | | Baghdad (North Gate) |
| CRAIG, 2nd Lt. Hedley William | 15th April 1917 | Shot down in BE.2c 4149 by enemy aircraft in combat | |
| | | | Baghdad (North Gate) |
| CROCKER, 2/AM Percy (36992) | 11th June 1917 | Died of septicemea | Amara |
| CURRAN, AM David (49) (Aus) | 16th June 1917 | Captured in the fall of Kut-al-Amara | Baghdad (North Gate) |
| DAGGER, 2/AM Victor (3968) | 29th April 1916 | Captured in the fall of Kut-al-Amara | Basra Memorial |
| DEAN, Pte. William Charles (2245) | 22nd October 1916 | Captured in the fall of Kut-al-Amara | Baghdad (North Gate) |
| DICKEN, 2/AM Tom (39041) | 4th June 1917 | ? | Llanddulas, Denbighs |
| DODD, 2/AM Harry (4894) | 7th August 1916 | Captured in the fall of Kut-al-Amara | Basra Memorial |
| DRAPER, 2/AM Victor George (5809) | 8th May 1916 | Captured in the fall of Kut-al-Amara | Basra Memorial |
| EAVES, 1/AM Joseph Richard (806) | 7th May 1916 | Captured in the fall of Kut-al-Amara; died of enteritis | Basra Memorial |
| EDWARDS, Capt. Aubyn Stanley | 13th May 1918 | Died of wounds received while piloting RE.8 | Baghdad (North Gate) |
| *(Note 8)* | | | |
| FAIRHEAD, 1/AM John William (3388) | 15th October 1916 | Captured in the fall of Kut-al-Amara | Baghdad (North Gate) |
| GEORGE, 2/AM Robert Edgar (7578) | 29th April 1916 | Captured in the fall of Kut-al-Amara | Basra Memorial |
| GILL, 2/AM W. T. C. | ? | Captured in the fall of Kut-al-Amara | Baghdad (North Gate) |
| *(Note 3)* | | | |
| GUTHRIE, 1/AM Richard Casper (14489) | 5th December 1917 | ? | Baghdad (North Gate) |
| HARE, 2/AM Alfred James (7801) | 25th August 1916 | Captured in the fall of Kut-al-Amara | Baghdad (North Gate) |
| HAYWOOD, Lt. Sydney | 26th October 1916 | Killed in accidental crash of Voisin 8523 | Amara War Cemetery |
| KEEFE, 2/AM William (5848) | 7th May 1916 | Captured in the fall of Kut-al-Amara; died at Shumran of enteritis | |
| | | | Basra Memorial |
| KING-HARMAN, Capt. Lawrence Hope | 26th October 1916 | Killed in accidental crash of Voisin 8523 | Amara War Cemetery |
| KIRWAN, Lt. Laird | 20th August 1918 | Killed when RE.8 B6611 stalled and spun in at Baquba | |
| | | | Baghdad (North Gate) |
| LEESON, Lt. Alexander Neve, DSO | 22nd October 1917 | Killed in crash of BE.2e A3088 near Sharaban airfield | |
| | | | Baghdad (North Gate) |
| LORD, AM William Henry (23) (Aus) | 13th July 1916 | Captured in the fall of Kut-al-Amara | Baghdad (North Gate) |

| | | | |
|---|---|---|---|
| MAGUIRE, Lt. Matthew Laurence MC | 25th May 1917 | Shot down in Scout 7034; died as PoW | *Basra Memorial* |
| MANNING, 1/AM George William (22339) | 17th October 1917 | Died of smallpox at Felluja | *Baghdad (North Gate)* |
| MERZ, Lt. George Pinnock (Aus) | 30th July 1915 | Killed by party of Zobaah after crashing 25 mls west of Abu Salabh | *Basra Memorial* |
| MUNRO, AM James (47) (Aus) | 13th October 1916 | Captured in the fall of Kut-al-Amara; died of throat abcess | *Baghdad (North Gate)* |
| NICKOLLS, 2/AM Richard George (7373) | 26th May 1918 | Captured in the fall of Kut-al-Amara | *Baghdad (North Gate)* |
| NIXON, 2/AM F. E. | ? | Captured in the fall of Kut-al-Amara | |
| NUNCY, 2/AM F. | ? | Captured in the fall of Kut-al-Amara | |
| PAGE, Capt. Lance St. Allard March | 20th August 1918 | Killed when RE.8 B6611 stalled and spun in at Baquba | *Baghdad (North Gate)* |
| PALGRAVE, Lance Cpl. George Walter (8444) | 3rd May 1916 | Captured in the fall of Kut-al-Amara | *Kut War Cemetery* |
| PALMER, Capt. Walter Gerard | 5th March 1916 | Shot down by machine-gun fire, Es Sinn | *Basra Memorial* |
| PALMER, Sgt. Thomas Newton (4473) | 13th March 1916 | Died as PoW | *Basra Memorial* |
| PASS, 2/AM William Chris (3318) | 26th January 1917 | Captured in the fall of Kut-al-Amara | *Basra Memorial* |
| PECK, 2nd Lt. Roland Henry | 5th March 1916 | Shot down by machine-gun fire, Es Sinn | *Basra Memorial* |
| PICKERING, Capt. Charles Leigh | 15th April 1917 | Shot down in BE.2c 4149 by enemy aircraft in combat | *Baghdad (North Gate)* |
| PONTING, 2/AM Daniel (7350) | 1st June 1917 | Captured in the fall of Kut-al-Amara | *Basra Memorial* |
| RAYMENT, 1/AM William Charles (49) (Aus) | 11th November 1916 | Captured in the fall of Kut-al-Amara; died of nephritis | *Baghdad (North Gate)* |
| REID, Cpl. Alfred (862) | 6th May 1916 | Captured in the fall of Kut-al-Amara; died of enteritis | *Basra Memorial* |
| ROOTES, 2/AM C (Note 4) | 30th June 1916 | Captured in the fall of Kut-al-Amara | *Baghdad (North Gate)* |
| RUFFELL, Sgt. Reginald (2199) | 2nd August 1916 | ? | *Kirkee (India)* |
| SMITH, 1/AM William (3393) | 19th July 1916 | Died of heatstroke | *Amara War Cemetery* |
| SOLEY, Cpl. Thomas M. (10) (Aus) | June/July 1916 | Captured in the fall of Kut-al-Amara | *Basra Memorial* |
| SUTHURST, 1/AM Frederick (12793) | 15th May 1918 | Fatally wounded by enemy aircraft after raid on Altun Kopri airfield | *Baghdad (North Gate)* |
| TAYLOR, Sgt. Alfred (34145) | 22nd July 1916 | Captured in the fall of Kut-al-Amara; died of dysentery | *Baghdad (North Gate)* |
| TREE, 1/AM George Robert (47330) | 15th July 1917 | Died of heatstroke | *Baghdad (North Gate)* |
| VINCENT, 1/AM Thomas William (2853) | 29th April 1916 | Captured in the fall of Kut-al-Amara | *Basra Memorial* |
| WEBB, Flt. Sgt. Arthur (4477) | 11th June 1916 | Captured in the fall of Kut-al-Amara | *Basra Memorial* |
| WELCH, 1/AM Sidney Basil (4136) | 26th January 1917 | Captured in the fall of Kut-al-Amara | *Baghdad (Angora)* |
| WELLS, 2/AM Samuel John (7870) | 20th September 1916 | Captured in the fall of Kut-al-Amara; died of dysentery | *Baghdad (North Gate)* |
| WILLIAMS, AM Leo T. (16) (Aus) | 13th July 1916 | Captured in the fall of Kut-al-Amara | *Basra Memorial* |

**Between the Wars**

| | | | |
|---|---|---|---|
| CARPENTER, AC Reginald Walter (563074) | 10th December 1938 | Killed in crash of Blenheim K7097 60 mls from Ramadi | |
| COOPER, LAC James (155269) | 3rd September 1930 | Killed in mid-air collision in Wapiti J9489 | |
| COOPER, AC Lewis William (566650) | 10th December 1938 | Killed in crash of Blenheim K7097 60 mls from Ramadi | |
| DAVIES, AC1 Harold (528319) | 29th June 1938 | Killed when Blenheim K7102 crashed on take-off | |
| DELLOW, LAC Leonard Alfred (60764) | 18th September 1920 | Killed when RE.8 crashed near Kazvin | *Teheran Cemetery* |
| DUSTIN, Flg. Off. | ? | ? | |
| EDWARDS, Sgt. Walter (340327) | 7th August 1920 | Died of heatstroke | *Baghdad* |
| GAMBLE, AC1 Frederick Oscar (515816) | 10th December 1938 | Killed in crash of Blenheim K7097 60 mls from Ramadi | |
| GARSIDE, Sgt. Vernon Walter (563794) | 10th December 1938 | Killed in crash of Blenheim K7097 60 mls from Ramadi | |
| HALLIDAY, Flt. Lt. C. G. | 27th June 1929 | Killed in crash near Luqait | |
| HANTON, Flg. Off. | 3rd September 1930 | Killed in mid-air collision in Wapiti J9489 | |
| HUDSON, Sgt. Herbert Victor (363135) | 3rd April 1932 | Fatally wounded in action | |
| KENNEDY, Sgt. Edgar (155685) | 26th July 1926 | Killed in crash of 45 Squadron Vernon at Hinaidi | |
| LOCKE-WATERS, Flg. Off. E. A. | 6th October 1922 | Killed when DH.9A H155 crashed 6 mls from Kirkuk | |
| MOORE, Flg. Off. J. A. | 23rd November 1925 | Killed in crash of DH.9A H120 | |
| NUTTALL, Capt. Frank (2863) MC DFC AFC (Note 5) | 18th September 1920 | Killed when RE.8 D4698 crashed near Kazvin | *Teheran Cemetery* |
| PENNY, Flg. Off. Marcus Glanville | 8th July 1925 | Killed in crash on Qara Dagh, near Malula | |
| RICKABY, AC1 Arthur Algernon (354797) | 23rd November 1925 | Killed in crash of DH.9A H120 | |
| SIDEBOTTOM, Flg. Off. William, DFC | 17th December 1920 | Failed to return from raid on Enzeli | *Teheran Memorial* |
| STEPHEN, Plt. Off. C. A. | 29th June 1938 | Killed when Blenheim K7102 crashed on take-off | |

| | | | |
|---|---|---|---|
| WAUGH, LAC William (358180) | 2nd April 1928 | Killed when DH.9A J7854 spun in near Hillan | |
| WOOD, Plt. Off. J. W. | 2nd April 1928 | Killed when DH.9A J7854 spun in near Hillan | |

**Second World War**

| | | | |
|---|---|---|---|
| ABBOTT, AC1 Kenneth George (651897) | 20th May 1941 | Killed in action in Crete | *Alamein War Memorial* |
| ALEXANDER, Cpl. Norman Bert Jones (529742) | 31st May 1941 | Killed in action in Crete | *Alamein War Memorial* |
| AUSTIN, Sgt. W. G. S. (590881) | May 1941 | Killed in action in Crete | |
| BETTS, LAC Henry Frederick (548425) MM | 20th May 1941 | Killed in action in Crete | *Alamein War Memorial* |
| BROWNE, Sgt. Allan John (400516) | 5th April 1942 | Shot down in combat during Japanese attack (probably in Z5447) | |
| | | | *Colombo (Kantte) Gen. Cem.* |
| BURT, Sgt. Christopher Frederick (539698) | 13th July 1940 | Shot down into sea in Blenheim K7181 | *Alamein War Memorial* |
| BYGRAVE, Sgt. Graham Edgar (532192) | 29th December 1940 | Shot down in Blenheim K7104 during raid on Valona | |
| | | | *Alamein War Memorial* |
| CARD, Flt. Lt. Harry Duncan (37934) | 29th December 1940 | Shot down in Blenheim K7104 during raid on Valona | |
| | | | *Alamein War Memorial* |
| CASWELL, Plt. Off. Garth Elliot (404709) | 5th April 1942 | Shot down in combat during Japanese attack in BG795 | |
| | | | *Colombo (Kanatte) Gen. Cem.* |
| CHILDS, Sgt. Eric Borlase (566516) | 15th November 1940 | Shot down in Blenheim L1120 | *Tirana Park Memorial Cem.* |
| CROCKETT, Plt. Off. | September 1941 | ? | |
| CROOKS, Sgt. John (816150) | 11th April 1941 | Shot down in Blenheim K7095 by Ju 88 | *Phaleron War Cemetery* |
| DAVIES, AC1 Alfred George (972979) | 14th June 1941 | ? | *Phaleron War Cemetery* |
| DAY, Cpl. Cecil George (566247) | 31st May 1941 | Killed in action in Crete | *Alamein War Memorial* |
| FENTON, LAC William (527601) | 31st May 1941 | Killed in action in Crete | *Alamain War Memorial* |
| FISHER, Plt. Off. Herbert Paul Greenwood (78443) | 28th July 1940 | Shot down into sea in Blenheim K7181 | *Knightsbridge War Cem., Libya* |
| FRIDD, Flt. Sgt. Kemsley George (361700) | 31st May 1941 | Killed in action in Crete | *Suda Bay Cemetery* |
| GEFFENE, Flg. Off. Donald (64861) | 5th April 1942 | Shot down in combat during Japanese attack in BE352 | |
| | | | *Singapore Memorial* |
| GERRARD, Cpl. Cecil William (535176) | 24th May 1941 | Killed in action in Crete | *Phaleron War Cemetery* |
| GILLAN, Cpl. Andrew Brown (549579) | 23rd May 1941 | Killed in action in Crete | *Suda Bay Cemetery* |
| GOODHAND, LAC Mervyn Sidney (749664) | 1st June 1941 | Killed in action in Crete | *Alamein War Memorial* |
| GOULDING, Sgt. Frederick (537868) | 30th December 1940 | Killed in action | *Phaleron War Cemetery* |
| HARDY, Wt. Off. Ian Griffiths (420880) RAAF | 17th November 1944 | Killed when Thunderbolt HD298 collided with HD294 at Chittagong | |
| HARRIS, Flg. Off. James Herbert Sidney (112309) | 15th June 1943 | Killed when Hurricane BN379 crashed during dummy attack | |
| | | | *Colombo (Liveramentu) Cem.* |
| HARRISON, Cpl. John Sedgewick (523085) | 31st May 1941 | Killed in action in Crete | *Alamein War Memorial* |
| HENDERSON, AC1 James (1291614) | 11th October 1942 | ? | *Colombo (Kanatte) Gen. Cem.* |
| HOYES, Sgt. Maxwell (561167) | 20th May 1941 | Killed in action in Crete | *Alamein War Memorial* |
| HOYLE, LAC Walter (966707) | 31st May 1941 | Killed in action in Crete | *Alamein War Memorial* |
| HUGGINS, AC1 Thomas Oswald (936570) | 31st May 1941 | Killed in action in Crete | *Alamein War Memorial* |
| INNES-SMITH, Flt. Sgt. (564068) | 28th July 1940 | Failed to return from mission over Libya in Blenheim K7178 | |
| JORDAN, LAC Richard William (539923) | 4th April 1940 | ? | *L'Aiguillon-sur-Mer (Vendee) Communal Cemetery* |
| KEMBER, Sgt. Peter Brian (1314908) | 28th July 1942 | Killed when Hurricane struck side of aircraft carrier | |
| | | | *Singapore Memorial* |
| KENT, Flg. Off. Frederick George (181419) | 12th August 1945 | Killed when Thunderbolt KJ222 crashed on take-off from Vizagapatam | |
| | | | *Madras War Cemetery* |
| KETTON-CREMER, Flg. Off. Richard Thomas Wyndham (75788) | 31st May 1941 | Killed in action in Crete | *Alamein War Memorial* |
| KNODLER, Wt. Off. K. J. RAAF | 14th August 1944 | Failed to return from height climb in Thunderbolt | |
| LAWRENCE, Flt. Sgt. George Edward (1251047) | 3rd April 1942 | Dived into sea off Colombo in Hurricane during patrol | |
| | | | *Singapore Memorial* |
| LEA, Plt. Off. Derryk Austin (41432) | 13th July 1940 | ? | *Alamein War Memorial* |
| LEESE, LAC Herbert Fellows (550459) | 31st March 1941 | ? | *Alamein War Memorial* |
| LISLE, Flt. Sgt. John Brown (R/67604) | 20th April 1942 | Crashed into lake while formation flying in Hurricane BG916 | |
| | | | *Colombo (Kanatte) Gen. Cem.* |
| MATTHEWS, Cpl. Frederick (522484) | 31st May 1941 | Killed in action in Crete | *Alamein War Memorial* |
| McBRIDE, AC2 Ian (926515) | 24th September 1941 | ? | *Alexandria (Hadra) War Cem.* |
| MEREIFIELD, Sgt. John (751514) | 6th November 1940 | Killed in action | *Phaleron War Cemetery* |
| MOONEY, LAC John (292367) | 31st May 1941 | Killed in action in Crete | *Alamein War Memorial* |
| MORRIS, Flt. Sgt. James Pullan (1061260) | 21st September 1942 | Killed in crash of Tiger Moth at Dambulla | |
| | | | *Colombo (Kanatte) Gen. Cem.* |
| NANKIEVELL, LAC | May 1941 | Killed in action in Crete | |
| NEWELL, Wt. Off. Geoffrey George (185141) | 14th August 1944 | Failed to return from height climb in Thunderbolt | |

| Name | Date | Notes | Cemetery/Memorial |
|---|---|---|---|
| | | | *Madras War Cemetery* |
| NIELL, Flg. Off. Robert Nason (404255) | 5th April 1942 | ? | *Colombo (Kanatte) Gen. Cem.* |
| OSWALD, AC1 John Tate (935542) | 31st May 1941 | Killed in action in Crete | *Alamein War Memorial* |
| (Note 7) | | | |
| OVENS, Wt. Off. Louis Anthony DFM (590927) | 5th April 1942 | Shot down in combat in Hurricane BM910 during Japanese attack | |
| | | | *Colombo (Kanatte) Gen. Cem.* |
| PAGET, Flg. Off. Steven (41530) | 18th December 1940 | Shot down in Blenheim during raid on Valona | *Alamein War Memorial* |
| PAXTON, Flt. Sgt. Thomas Galbraith (1053584) | 7th April 1942 | Shot down in BM930 during Japanese attack on 5th April; died of burns | |
| | | | *Colombo (Kanatte) Gen. Cem.* |
| PEASE, Sgt. Frederick (564298) | 29th December 1940 | Shot down in Blenheim K7104 during raid on Valona | |
| | | | *Alamein War Memorial* |
| PERKS, LAC Herbert Thomas Bert (1253663) | 11th June 1942 | Died of typhoid | *Colombo (Kanatte) Gen. Cem.* |
| PENNYSTON, Cpl. Charles (293169) | 23rd May 1941 | Killed in action in Crete | *Suda Bay Cemetery* |
| POLLOCK, Wt. Off. John Albert (Can.9780) | 12th October 1943 | Failed to return from firing exercise in Hurricane BN596 | |
| | | | *Colombo (Liveramentu) Cem.* |
| POOLE, LAC Frank Ernest (526974) | 31st May 1941 | Killed in action in Crete | *Alamein War Memorial* |
| QUILLIAM, LAC Charles Frederick (522358) | 11th October 1943 | Captured in Crete; died in prisoner-of-war camp | |
| | | | *Berlin (Brandenburg) War Cem.* |
| RATLIDGE, Plt. Off. George Waddington (47121) DFC | 12th January 1942 | Missing in action in Hurricane | *Alamein War Memorial* |
| RATTENBURY, Sgt. Bernard Arthur Thomas (1804463) | 24th February 1945 | Killed in crash-landing of Thunderbolt KJ128 at Cox's Bazaar | |
| | | | *Chittagong War Cemetery* |
| SCOTT, Plt. Off. Frederick Arthur (J5225) | 4th January 1942 | Missing in action in Hurricane Z4418 | *(Buried at sea by Royal Navy)* |
| SIGSWORTH, Sgt. George (519458) | 18th December 1940 | Shot down in raid on Valona | *Alamein War Memorial* |
| SMITH, Flg. Off. Basil le Breton (NZ412525) | 13th February 1943 | Died of injuries in Beaufort crash at Colombo | |
| | | | *Colombo (Kanatte) Gen. Cem.* |
| SMITH, LAC Robert Arthur (943134) | 14th March 1945 | Died in prisoner-of-war camp | *Berlin (Brandenburg) War Cem.* |
| SMITH, LAC Sydney (648880) | 30th January 1943 | Died of burns after accident with petrol stove | *Kandy War Cemetery* |
| SPENCER, LAC Harold Kenneth (517191) | 12th October 1940 | ? | *Alexandria (Chatby) Mil. Cem.* |
| STEWART, Sgt. John George (566189) | 15th November 1940 | Shot down in Blenheim L1120 | *Tirana Park Memorial Cem.* |
| STEWART, Cpl. | 28th July 1940 | Failed to return in Blenheim K7178 from mission over Libya | |
| STEWART, LAC Albert (521630) | 20th May 1941 | Killed in action in Crete | *Alamein War Memorial* |
| STONE, LAC George Arthur (569410) | 31st May 1941 | Killed in action in Crete | *Alamein War Memorial* |
| STOTT, Cpl. (? LAC) Donald (526089) | 15th November 1940 | Shot down in Blenheim L1120 | *Tirana Park Memorial Cem.* |
| STURMAN, LAC Thomas William Freeman (530069) | 31st May 1941 | Killed in action in Crete | *Alamein War Memorial* |
| SWANN, Flg. Off. Ian Cheesman (39950) | 13th July 1940 | Shot down into sea in Blenheim K7181 | *Knightsbridge War Cem., Libya* |
| THEOBALD, Plt. Off. Edmund Hugh Craft (67716) | 28th December 1941 | ? | *Halfaya Sollum Cemetery* |
| THOMAS, LAC Denziel Jonah (651354) | 20th May 1941 | Killed in action in Crete | *Alamein War Memorial* |
| THOMSON, AC1 David (701682) | 31st May 1941 | Killed in action in Crete | *Alamein War Memorial* |
| TUBBERDY, Sgt. William (538072) | 18th December 1940 | Shot down in raid on Valona | *Tirana Park Memorial Cem.* |
| VUJOVITCH, Flt. Sgt. S. J. (7129) (Yugoslav) | 31st August 1941 | ? | |
| WALSH, Sgt. Maxwell John Shipp (536838) | 24th May 1941 | Killed in action in Crete | *Cairo War Memorial Cem.* |
| WATERS, Sgt. Victor Alexander (1605509) | 31st October 1944 | Killed when Thunderbolt HD264 failed to become airborne | |
| | | | *Chittagong War Cemetery* |
| WHITEHURST, Cpl. | May 1941 | Killed in action in Crete | |
| WILLIAMS, Cpl. Frank Thomas (365037) | 20th May 1941 | Killed in action in Crete | *Alamein War Memorial* |
| WOOD, LAC Max Godden (526264) | 31st May 1941 | Killed in action in Crete | *Alamein War Memorial* |
| WRIGLEY, Cpl. Hedley (525956) | 31st May 1941 | Killed in action in Crete | *Alamein War Memorial* |
| YOUNG, Sgt. John (523927) | 13th July 1940 | Shot down into sea in Blenheim K7181 | *Knightsbridge War Cem., Libya* |

## Post Second World War

| Name | Date | Notes | Cemetery/Memorial |
|---|---|---|---|
| COUTTS, Flt. Lt. John (3045935) | 24th March 1969 | Killed in crash of Hercules XV180 at Fairford | |
| | | | *All Hallows church, S. Cerney* |
| CROSS, Flt. Sgt. Norman (1620761) | 19th August 1952 | Killed in crash of Valetta VX559 at Benson | |
| GARNES, Sgt. William Esplin (1826786) | 19th August 1952 | Killed in crash of Valetta VX559 at Benson | |
| LOUGH, Sig.3 Phillip Arthur (3001781) | 17th November 1948 | Killed in crash of Dakota KP223 in Russian Zone of Germany | |
| LOMAS, Flt. Sgt. T. F. W. (3006063) | 19th August 1952 | Killed in crash of Valetta VX559 at Benson | |
| LONGMAN, Flg. Off. David George Keith (3150285) | 5th November 1959 | Suicide by poisoning | |
| MOIR, Flg. Off. Gavin Ian (4231906) | 24th March 1969 | Killed in crash of Hercules XV180 at Fairford | *(Scotland)* |
| MAYOUX, Flg. Off. Denis Albert Peter (3516266) | 4th December 1958 | Fell from stationary aircraft | |
| MEDHURST, Flg. Off. Peter Henry (4238889) | 24th March 1969 | Killed in crash of Hercules XV180 at Fairford | |
| | | | *All Hallows church, S. Cerney* |
| McGING, Flt. Sgt. Brian Michael (1924164) | 24th March 1969 | Killed in crash of Hercules XV180 at Fairford | |

|  |  | *All Hallows church, S. Cerney* |
|---|---|---|
| PLUMTREE, Flg. Off. Robin Michael (4232721) | 24th March 1969 | Killed in crash of Hercules XV180 at Fairford |
|  |  | *All Hallows church, S. Cerney* |
| ROBINSON, Plt. Off. Albert (533224) | 20th January 1954 | Killed in crash of Valetta VL282 after take-off from Lyneham |
| ROSE, Flt. Sgt. Wiliam Francis Anthony (1596316) | 4th February 1958 | Killed in crash of Beverley XH118 at Beihan |
| TREZONA, Plt.I Francis Ivor (1316810) | 17th November 1948 | Killed in crash of Dakota KP223 in Russian Zone of Germany |
| WILKINS, Flt. Lt. John Graham (55636) | 25th November 1948 | Died from injuries after crash of Dakota KP223 in Russian Zone of Germany |
| WALSINGHAM, Flg. Off. Alan George (4233039) | 24th March 1969 | Killed in crash of Hercules XV180 at Fairford |
|  |  | *All Hallows church, S. Cerney* |

## NOTES

1. Braund is recorded by the CWGC as Pte. in Devonshire Regt. (2900) No mention of RFC

2. Carpenter is recorded by the CWGC as Pte. in East Surrey Regt

3. Gill is recorded by the CWGC as Pte. in Middlesex Regt (2244)

4. Rootes is recorded by the CWGC as Pte. in East Surrey Regt.

5. Recorded elsewhere as a Flt. Lt.

6. Recorded elsewhere as 2/AM

7. Recorded elsewhere as LAC

8. First names recorded elsewhere as Arthur Strother

## Part 2: members of the RFC Detachment and of 30 Squadron who became prisoners of war

### First World War

| *Name* | *Date* | *Circumstance* |
|---|---|---|
| ADAMS, AM Francis Luke (44) (Aus) | 29th April 1916 | Captured in the fall of Kut-al-Amara; died of malaria in enemy hands |
| ATKINS, Capt. Basil Sydney | 16th September 1915 | Shot down |
| BRAUND, 2/AM W. | 29th April 1916 | Captured in the fall of Kut-al-Amara; died in enemy hands |
| BULLEN, 2/AM Harold (240445) | 29th April 1916 | Captured in the fall of Kut-al-Amara; left in Kut hospital and died there |
| BUTLER, 2/AM Sidney George (6242) | 29th April 1916 | Captured in the fall of Kut-al-Amara; died in enemy hands |
| CAMPBELL, Flt. Sgt. H. | 29th April 1916 | Captured in the fall of Kut-al-Amara |
| CANDY, Cpl. William Henry Minter (533) | 29th April 1916 | Captured in the fall of Kut-al-Amara; died in enemy hands |
| CARPENTER, 2/AM Reginald William (240486) | 29th April 1916 | Captured in the fall of Kut-al-Amara; died in enemy hands |
| CLARKE, 2/AM A. | 29th April 1916 | Captured in the fall of Kut-al-Amara |
| CLARIDGE, 2/AM Lionel Victor (1299) | 29th April 1916 | Captured in the fall of Kut-al-Amara; died in enemy hands |
| CORBETT, Capt. Reginald David de la Court | 29th April 1916 | Captured in the fall of Kut-al-Amara; died in enemy hands |
| COURTHOPE-MUNRO, 2nd. Lt. Caryl Henry | 29th April 1916 | Captured in the fall of Kut-al-Amara; survived |
| CURRAN, AM David (30) (Aus) | 29th April 1916 | Captured in the fall of Kut-al-Amara; died in enemy hands |
| DAGGER, 2/AM Victor (3968) | 29th April 1916 | Captured in the fall of Kut-al-Amara; died that day |
| DEAN, Pte. William Charles (2245) | 29th April 1916 | Captured in the fall of Kut-al-Amara; died in enemy hands |
| DODD, 2/AM Harry (4894) | 29th April 1916 | Captured in the fall of Kut-al-Amara; died in enemy hands |
| DRAPER, 2/AM Victor George (5809) | 29th April 1916 | Captured in the fall of Kut-al-Amara; died in enemy hands |
| EAVES, 1/AM Joseph Richard (806) | 29th April 1916 | Captured in the fall of Kut-al-Amara; died in enemy hands |
| EDWARDS, Capt. Aubin Stanley | 2nd May 1918 | Died 13th May 1918 |
| FAIRHEAD, 2/AM John William (3388) | 29th April 1916 | Captured in the fall of Kut-al-Amara; died in enemy hands |
| FULTON, Lt. Edmund James | 22nd November 1915 | Force-landed behind Turkish lines |
| GEORGE, 2/AM Robert Edgar (7578) | 29th April 1916 | Captured in the fall of Kut-al-Amara; died that day |
| GILL, 2/AM W. T. C. | 29th April 1916 | Captured in the fall of Kut-al-Amara |
| HAIGHT, Capt. Walter Lockwood | 4th March 1918 | Shot down by rifle fire near Hit |
| HANCOCK, 2nd. Lt. Harold Lindsey Watkins | 4th March 1918 | Shot down by rifle fire near Hit |
| HARE, 2/AM Alfred James (7801) | 29th April 1916 | Captured in the fall of Kut-al-Amara; died in enemy hands |
| HOGG, 1/AM J. | 29th April 1916 | Captured in the fall of Kut-al-Amara |
| KEEFE, 2/AM William (5848) | 29th April 1916 | Captured in the fall of Kut-al-Amara; died in enemy hands |
| LANDER, Lt. Thomas Eaton, MC | 6th May 1917 | Force-landed behind Turkish lines |
| LORD, AM William Henry (23) (Aus) | 29th April 1916 | Captured in the fall of Kut-al-Amara; died in enemy hands |
| MAGUIRE, Lt. Matthew Laurence MC | 28th April 1917 | Shot down; died in enemy hands 25th May |
| MILLS, Lt. A. S. | 17th January 1918 | Force-landed RE.8 with engine trouble; repatriated 16th December 1918 |
| MORRIS, Cpl. H. L. | 29th April 1916 | Captured in the fall of Kut-al-Amara; interned in Turkey |

| | | |
|---|---|---|
| MUNDEY, Capt. Stanley Cyril Beresford | 29th April 1916 | Captured in the fall of Kut-al-Amara; survived |
| MUNRO, 2nd. Lt. ? ? | 29th April 1916 | Captured in the fall of Kut-al-Amara |
| MUNRO, AM James (47) (Aus) | 29th April 1916 | Captured in the fall of Kut-al-Amara; died in enemy hands |
| NICKOLLS, 2/AM R. G. | 29th April 1916 | Captured in the fall of Kut-al-Amara; died in enemy hands |
| NIXON, 2/AM F. E. | 29th April 1916 | Captured in the fall of Kut-al-Amara |
| NUNCY, 2/AM F. | 29th April 1916 | Captured in the fall of Kut-al-Amara |
| PALGRAVE, Lance Cpl. George Walter (8444) | 29th April 1916 | Captured in the fall of Kut-al-Amara; died in enemy hands |
| PALMER, Sgt. Thomas Newton (4473) | 29th April 1916 | Captured in the fall of Kut-al-Amara; died in enemy hands |
| PASS, 2/AM William Chris (3318) | 29th April 1916 | Captured in the fall of Kut-al-Amara; died in enemy hands |
| PONTING, 2/AM Daniel (7350) | 29th April 1916 | Captured in the fall of Kut-al-Amara; died in enemy hands |
| RAYMENT, AM William Charles (49) (Aus) | 29th April 1916 | Captured in the fall of Kut-al-Amara; died in enemy hands |
| READ, Sgt. F. | 29th April 1916 | Captured in the fall of Kut-al-Amara; thought to have survived |
| REID, Cpl. Alfred (862) | 29th April 1916 | Captured in the fall of Kut-al-Amara; died in enemy hands |
| REILLY, Maj. Hugh Lambert | 20th November 1915 | Shot down behind Turkish lines |
| ROOTES, 2/AM C. | 29th April 1916 | Captured in the fall of Kut-al-Amara; died in enemy hands |
| ST. JOHN, 2/AM S. | 29th April 1916 | Captured in the fall of Kut-al-Amara |
| SNELL, 2/AM F. | 29th April 1916 | Captured in the fall of Kut-al-Amara |
| SOLEY, AM Thomas (10) (Aus) | 29th April 1916 | Captured in the fall of Kut-al-Amara; died in enemy hands |
| TAYLOR, 2nd. Lt. Walter | 17th January 1918 | Force-landed RE.8 with engine trouble; repatriated December 1918 |
| TAYLOR, Sgt. Alfred (34145) | 29th April 1916 | Captured in the fall of Kut-al-Amara; died in enemy hands |
| TRELOAR, Lt. William Harold | 16th September 1915 | Shot down |
| VINCENT, 1/AM Thomas William (2853) | 29th April 1916 | Captured in the fall of Kut-al-Amara; died that day |
| WEBB, Flt. Sgt. Arthur (4477) | 29th April 1916 | Captured in the fall of Kut-al-Amara; died in enemy hands |
| WELCH, 1/AM Sidney Basil (4136) | 29th April 1916 | Captured in the fall of Kut-al-Amara; died in enemy hands |
| WELMAN, 2nd. Lt. John Barthroppe | 24th October 1917 | Shot down at Kifri |
| WELLS, Capt. T. R. MC | 29th April 1916 | Captured in the fall of Kut-al-Amara; survived and repatriated |
| WELLS, 2/AM Samuel John (7870) | 29th April 1916 | Captured in the fall of Kut-al-Amara; died in enemy hands |
| WHITE, Capt. Thomas Walter DFC | 13th November 1915 | Subsequently escaped |
| WILLIAMS, AM Leo T. (16) (Aus) | 29th April 1916 | Captured in the fall of Kut-al-Amara; died in enemy hands |
| WINFIELD-SMITH, Capt. Stephen Christopher | 29th April 1916 | Captured in the fall of Kut-al-Amara; survived |
| YEATS-BROWN, Capt. Francis Charles Claypon DFC | 13th November 1915 | Subsequently escaped |

## Second World War

| | | |
|---|---|---|
| BEATTIE, Sgt. | May 1941 | Captured in the fall of Crete |
| BELL, AC1 A. (945243) | May 1941 | Captured in the fall of Crete |
| BOND, Cpl. A. W. (520468) | May 1941 | Captured in the fall of Crete |
| CARTER-DERBYSHIRE, LAC G. (649533) | May 1941 | Captured in the fall of Crete |
| CHERRY, LAC D. R. (523919) | May 1941 | Captured in the fall of Crete |
| CULLEN, Flg. Off. T. H. | May 1941 | Captured in the fall of Crete |
| COLLETT, AC1 B. W. (973333) | May 1941 | Captured in the fall of Crete |
| DARCH, LAC N. J. (542821) | May 1941 | Captured in the fall of Crete |
| DASTON, Plt. Off. H. N. M. (79109) | May 1941 | Captured in the fall of Crete |
| DEAR, Cpl. E. A. (506974) | May 1941 | Captured in the fall of Crete |
| DONOHOE, Cpl. T. F. (525047) | May 1941 | Captured in the fall of Crete |
| DOW, AC1 G. D. M. (1012777) | May 1941 | Captured in the fall of Crete |
| DULLAGHAN, LAC E. (615465) | May 1941 | Captured in the fall of Crete |
| EDWARDS, Wt. Off. H. C. (413171) RNZAF | 3rd November 1944 | Taken prisoner after Thunderbolt HD245 crashed during an operation; released from captivity May 1945 |
| EDWARDS, LAC J. (535106) | May 1941 | Captured in the fall of Crete |
| ELLIS, Sgt. | May 1941 | Captured in the fall of Crete |
| EVANS, AC1 M. (701639) | May 1941 | Captured in the fall of Crete |
| GRIFFITH, AC2 S. (945246) | May 1941 | Captured in the fall of Crete |
| GULLIVER, Cpl. H. (528823) | May 1941 | Captured in the fall of Crete |
| GREENHALGH, LAC F. D. (522952) | May 1941 | Captured in the fall of Crete |
| HARRISON, LAC J. S. (523085) | May 1941 | Captured in the fall of Crete |
| HILL, Sgt. | May 1941 | Captured in the fall of Crete |
| HOGG, AC1 S. G. (648064) | May 1941 | Captured in the fall of Crete |
| HOLLAND, LAC | May 1941 | Captured in the fall of Crete (not confirmed) |
| HONEYCOMBE, LAC A. K.(651736) | May 1941 | Captured in the fall of Crete |

| | | |
|---|---|---|
| HUGGINS, AC | May 1941 | Captured in the fall of Crete |
| LARTER, LAC | May 1941 | Captured in the fall of Crete (not confirmed) |
| LAWRENCE, Cpl. R. J. (542042) | May 1941 | Captured in the fall of Crete |
| LEESE, LAC H. F. (550459) | May 1941 | Captured in the fall of Crete |
| LEWIS, AC1 B. (945249) | May 1941 | Captured in the fall of Crete |
| LONGBOTTOM, AC1 H. W. (549658) | May 1941 | Captured in the fall of Crete |
| LYE, AC1 H. (1108074) | May 1941 | Captured in the fall of Crete |
| MATHEWS, Cpl. F. (522484) | May 1941 | Captured in the fall of Crete |
| NICHOLS, AC1 C. M. (570475) | May 1941 | Captured in the fall of Crete |
| PENNYSTONE, Cpl. C. (293169) | May 1941 | Captured in the fall of Crete |
| PICKERING, Sgt. E. W. (566492) | May 1941 | Captured in the fall of Crete |
| PRICE, LAC | May 1941 | Captured in the fall of Crete (not confirmed) |
| PRITTY, AC2 A. H. (939551) | May 1941 | Captured in the fall of Crete |
| QUILLIAM, LAC Charles Frederick (522358) | May 1941 | Captured in the fall of Crete; died in enemy hands |
| RALPH, AC1 H. A. (649534) | May 1941 | Captured in the fall of Crete |
| RUSSELL, Cpl. A. C. (523857) | May 1941 | Captured in the fall of Crete |
| SCOTT, AC | May 1941 | Captured in the fall of Crete |
| SMITH, AC1 R. C. (943134) | May 1941 | Captured in the fall of Crete |
| SPALDING, LAC W. L. (525498) | May 1941 | Captured in the fall of Crete |
| STEEDMAN, LAC J. | May 1941 | Captured in the fall of Crete (not confirmed) |
| STONE, Cpl. (? LAC) Kenneth J. (900633) | May 1941 | Captured in the fall of Crete |
| WAKE, Cpl. K. E. (525505) | May 1941 | Captured in the fall of Crete |
| WALKER, LAC E. W. (358468) | May 1941 | Captured in the fall of Crete |
| WHITE, AC W. G. | May 1941 | Captured in the fall of Crete (not confirmed) |
| WILLIAMS, AC1 B. J. (906873) | May 1941 | Captured in the fall of Crete |
| WILLIAMSON, LAC D. M. (966694) | May 1941 | Captured in the fall of Crete |
| WOOD, LAC M. G. (526264) | May 1941 | Captured in the fall of Crete |
| WORTHINGTON, Cpl. F. (525183) | May 1941 | Captured in the fall of Crete |
| WRIGLEY, Cpl. H. (525956) | May 1941 | Captured in the fall of Crete |
| ZELBART, AC1 A. (774518) | May 1941 | Captured in the fall of Crete |

# Appendix 4: Summary of First World War bombing operations

*Note: While this summary contains information on the main raids carried out by 30 Squadron and its ancestor Flights, not all the minor ones are recorded in any detail in the documents of the time, and may therefore be missing from this list.*

| Date | Target | Aircraft | Bomb-load and remarks |
|---|---|---|---|
| 16.4.15 | El Murra | Two MF, one BE.2A | Seven (out of 9) |
| 22.10.15 | Arab settlement 5 mls. SW of Frasers Post | ? Three | 16 x 2lb., 2 x 20lb., 3 x 30lb. |
| 24.10.15 | Boat-bridge across Diyali river etc. | ? | 100lb. |
| ?.4.16 | Gussabs Fort | Two | ? |
| 12.7.16 | 6 mls. S of Sheikh Saad | Two | ? |
| 14/15.8.16 | Shumran airfield | Three BE.2C | 16 x 20lb., 2 x 100lb. |
| 26.8.16 | Sahil encampment | Four | 12 x 20lb. |
| 30.8.16 | Camp SE of Ataba | ? | 4 x 100lb. |
| 7.9.16 | Camp 4 mls S of Bedrah | Three BE.2C | ? |
| 8.9.16 | Shumran airfield | Two BE.2C | 8 x 20lb., 2 x 100lb. |
| 11.9.16 | Shumran airfield | Five | 8 x 20lb., 1 x 100lb. etc. |
| 12.9.16 | Shumran airfield | One | ? |
| 19.9.16 | Shumran airfield | One BE.2C | 8 x 20lb. |
| 23.9.16 | Shumran airfield | Two | 6 x 20lb. |
| 26.9.16 | Shumran airfield | Seven BE.2C | 4 x 112lb., 40 x 20lb. |
| 30.9.16 | Ammunition dump, Kut | One | 8 x 20lb. |
| 3.10.16 | Shumran airfield | Two | 4 x ? |
| 6.10.16 | Camp E of Gussabs Fort | Two | ? |
| 10.10.16 | Camp E of Gussabs Fort | Four BE.2C | 1 x 112lb., 26 x 20lb., 6 incendiary |
| 17.10.16 | Shumran airfield | Two | 1 x 112lb., 12 x 20lb. |
| 23.10.16 | 'enemy airfield' | ? | 5 x ? |
| 25.10.16 | Cavalry at Ataba | Five BE.2C | 2 x 100lb., 9 x 20lb. |
| 31.10.16 | 'enemy airfield' | One | ? |
| 1.11.16 | Shumran airfield | Two BE.2C | 1 x 112lb., 2 x 100lb., 6 x 20lb. |
| 13.11.16 | Shumran airfield | One BE.2C | 12 x 20lb. |
| 16.11.16 | Enemy camps nr. Alain | ? | ? |
| 20.11.16 | Enemy camps nr. Alain | ? | ? |
| 27.11.16 | Enemy camps nr. Alain | ? | ? |

*(in these three raids a total of 12 x 112lb., 3 x 100lb., 2 x 65lb. and 159 x 20lb. bombs were dropped)*

| Date | Target | Aircraft | Bomb-load and remarks |
|---|---|---|---|
| 14.12.16 | Shumran boat bridge *(2 raids)* | ? | ? |
| 21.12.16 | Bughaila | Seven BE.2C, three Martinsyde | 66 |

*(in December the total number of bombs dropped was 2 x 336lb., 8 x 112lb., 5 x 100lb., 5 x 65lbs. and 334 x 20lb.)*

| Date | Target | Aircraft | Bomb-load and remarks |
|---|---|---|---|
| 18.1.17 | Ataba cavalry camp | One Martinsyde | 2 x 100lb. |
| 20.1.17 | Baghdad | Three Martinsyde | 6 x 100lb. |
| 21.1.17 | Baghdad citadel | Two Martinsyde | 4 x 100lb. |
| ?.1.17 | Camp at Iman Mahdi | One | 2 x 100lb. |
| ?.1.17 | Arab camp | One | 2 x 100lb. |
| 1.17 | (total sorties) Seventeen (day), three (night) | | 1 x 336lb., 3 x 112lb., 22 x 100lb., 60 x 20lb. |
| 2.2.17 | Pontoons at Dahra etc. | One | 7 x 20lb. |
| | Ship at Baghdadi | One | 1 x 20lb. |
| | Troops at Husaini Bend | | 2 x 20lb. |
| | 'enemy airfield' | | 3 x 20lb. |
| ?.2.17 | Bridge and shipping, Shumran One | ? | |
| ?.2.17 | 'enemy airfield' | One | 2 x 100lb. |
| ?.2.17 | Cavalry at Iman Mahdi | One | 1 x 336lb. |
| ?.2.17 | Turkish Flying Corps camp | One | 4 x 20lb. |
| 15.2.17 | 'enemy airfield' | One | 1 x 336lb. |
| | Cavalry at Iman Mahdi | One | 12 x 20lb. |
| | 'enemy airfield' | Three | 7 x 20lb. |
| 16.2.17 | Steamer at Bghailah | One | 1 x 20lb. |
| 17.2.17 | Cavalry at Iman Mahdi | One | 3 x 20lb. |
| ?.2.17 | Shipping at Bghailah | One | 4 x 20lb. |
| ?.2.17 | Barges at Iman Mahdi | Two | 1 x 336lb., 8 x 20lb. |
| 20.2.17 | Barges at Iman Mahdi | One | 2 x 20lb. |
| 21.2.17 | Barges at Iman Mahdi | One | 8 x 20lb. |
| 22.2.17 | 'enemy airfield' | One | 8 x 20lb. |
| 24.2.17 | Retreating troops | ? | 60 x 20lb., 2 x 65lb. |
| 25.2.17 | Pontoon bridge | One | ? |
| | Shipping and troops | ? | 2 x 65lb., 92 x 20lb. |
| 9.3.17 | Kazimain station | One | 1 x 65lb., 46 x 20lb. |
| 10.3.17 | Bridge at Baqubah | One | ? |
| 10.4.17 | Rolling stock at Samarra | One | 4 x 20lb. |
| 12.4.17 | Samarra airfield and rly. | Two | 4 x 65lb., 12 x 20lb. |
| 1.5.17 | Turkish troops, Tekrit | Two | 2 x 65lb., 4 x 20lb. |
| 2.5.17 | Troops at Adhaim | Four BE.2C, two Martinsyde | 32 |
| | Troop columns | One | 8 x 20lb. |
| 27.5.17 | ? | ? | ? |
| 22.6.17 | Ship on R. Tigris | Two Martinsyde | 8 x 65lb. |
| 27.6.17 | Camp S of Tekrit | Four BE.2C | 22 x 20lb. |
| 3.7.17 | Camp nr. Imam Askir | One BE.2C, one Martinsyde | 2 x 65lb., 8 x 20lb. |
| 10.7.17 | Troop columns | Two Martinsyde, one BE.2C | ? |
| 11.7.17 | Infantry and vehicles | One 1 x 20lb. | |
| 18.8.17 | Hit | Three Martinsyde, two BE.2C | 5 x 65lb., 28 x ? |
| 22.8.17 | Fort Hamrin | Two Martinsyde | 12 x 20lb., 2 x 100lb. |
| 27.8.17 | Diwaniyeh | One | 4 x 4.5in, shells |

| Date | Target | Aircraft | Bombs/Notes |
|---|---|---|---|
| 12.9.17 | Four arab camps | Five | ? |
| 25.9.17 | Three camps near Baghdad | Three Martinsydes | ? |
| 29.9.17 | Hostile cavalry | ? | ? |
| 5.10.17 | Ammunition dumps, Hit | Three BE.2C | 16 x 20lb. |
| 9.10.17 | Arab camp at Hillah | Two BE.2C | 6 x ? |
| 16.10.17 | Kifri airfield | Three Martinsydes | 6 x 112lb., 12 x 20lb. |
| 20.10.17 | Retreating troops | Three Martinsydes | 22 x 20lb. |
| 24.10.17 | Camp, Jebel Hamrin | One | 5 x 20lb. |
| 31.10.17 | Kifri airfield | Three Martinsyde, three BE.2C | Three aircraft force-landed, one was shot down |
| 8.11.17 | Camps at Qara Tepe and Nahrin Kopri | Five BE.2C, two RE.8, one Martinsyde | 5 x 112lb., 48 x 20lb. |
| 10.11.17 | ditto | Five | 5 x 112lb., 24 x 20lb. |
| 30.11/1.12.17 | Kifri airfield | Two BE.2C | 16 x 20lb. |
| ?.12.17 | Fort, Qalah Shirwan | One | 6 x 20lb. |
| 19.12.17 | Tuz Khurmatli airfield | Three RE.8 | 1 x 112lb., 18 x 20lb. |
| 28.12.17 | Humr airfield | Three RE.8 | In conjuction with 63 Squadron |
| 30.12.17 | Kifri airfield | Four RE.8, one DH.4 | 34 x 20lb. In conjuction with 63 Squadron |
| 3.1.18 | Humr airfield | Three | 11 x 20lb. In conjuction with 63 Squadron |
| 20.1.18 | Kala Shirwan village | Seven | 40 x 20lb. |
| 21.1.18 | Kifri airfield | Six | In conjuction with 63 Squadron. One DH.4 was shot down |
| 22.1.18 | Kellar village | Two RE.8 | 8 x 20lb. |
| 25/26.1.18 | Kifri airfield and town | One DH.4, one RE.8, one BE.2C | 20 x 20lb. The DH.4 force-landed |
| 1.2.18 | Arab encampment, Nehkidir | One | 5 x 20lb. |
| 13.2.18 | Qara Tepe area | Ten | 56 x ? |
| 22.2.18 | Hit airfield | Three RE.8 | 18 x 20lb. |
| 23.2.18 | Hit airfield | Two RE.8 | ? |
|  | Camp at Saliyah | Two RE.8 | 16 x 20lb. |
| 24.2.18 | Camp at Saliyah | Two RE.8 | 14 x 20lb. |
| 26/27.2.18 | Hit airfield | Five | ? |
| 26.2.18 | von Drueffel's HQ | Two RE.8 | 8 x 20lb. In conjuction with 63 Squadron |
| 27.2.18 | Hit airfield | Seven | ? |
| 1.3.18 | Cavalry nr. Sahiliyah | Two RE.8 | 8 x 20lb. |
| 3.3.18 | Hit airfield | Two RE.8 | 16 x 20lb. |
| 8.3.18 | Retreating troops | ? | 33 x 20lb. |
| 9.3.18 | Haditha airfield | Two RE.8 | 15 x 20lb. |
|  | Camps and retreating troops | Seven RE.8 | 56 x 20lb. |
| 10.3.18 | Troops and transport near Baghdad | Two RE.8 | 15 x 25lb., 1 x 20lb. |
|  | Camps nr. Baghdad and Sahiliyah | Two RE.8 | 16 x 20lb. |
|  | Camps and troops, Baghdad | Two RE.8 | 13 x 20lb. |
| 11.3.18 | von Drueffel's HQ | Two | 2 x 112lb., 4 x 20lb. |
| 12.3.18 | Camp, Khan Baghdad | Two | 9 x 25lb. |
| 21.3.18 | Arab camp, Mandali | Three | 24 x 20lb. |
| 26.3.18 | Transport, river vessels, etc. at Baghdadi | Two RE.8, two Martinsydes | 13 x 20lb., 15 x 25lb. |
| 27.3.18 | Hit airfield | Two RE.8 | 12 x 20lb. |
|  | Troops, river vessels, etc. | Three RE.8, one BE.2c, two Martinsyde | 27 x 20lb., 11 x 25lb. |
| ? | Kifri airfield | One RE.8 | 8 x 20lb. |
| 25.4.18 | Villages in Sinjabis | Two | 11 x 25lb. In conjuction with 72 Squadron |
| 26.4.18 | Troops on road to Kifri | Three RE.8 | 20 x 20lb. In conjuction with 63 Squadron |
| 27.4.18 | Retreating troops | Five | 23 x 25lb., 12 x 20lb. |
| 27.4.18 | Kulawand | One | 8 x 25lb. |
| 28.4.18 | Troops and transport NW of Tuz | Eight | 49 x 25lb., 8 x 20lb. |
| 25.4.18 | Troops, transport and camps | Three RE.8 | 20 x 25lb. |
| 29.4.18 | Retreating troops, Tuz | Four RE.8 | 18 x 20lb., 7 x 25lb. |
| 12.5.18 | Camps near Altun Kopri | Five RE.8 | 38 x 25lb. |
|  | Altun Kopri airfield | One Martinsyde | 9 x 25lb. |
| 12.5.18 | Villages near Arbil | Five RE.8, one Martinsyde | 45 x 25lb. |
| 15.5.18 | Altun Kopri airfield | Six RE.8 | 48 x 20lb. |
| 17.5.18 | Altun Kopri airfield | Five RE.8 | 39 x 20lb. Two aircraft shot down |
| 20.5.18 | Altun Kopri airfield | Four RE.8 | 30 x 25lb. |
| 8.7.18 | Hostile Kurds in Kargamil Pass | Two RE.8 | 16 x 20lb. |
| 11.10.18 | Transport in Shibli Pass (Tabriz road) | Three RE.8 | 18 x 20lb. In conjuction with 72 Squadron. One aircraft shot down |
| 19.10.18 | Kirkuk airfield | Two RE.8 | 12 x 20lb. |
| 23.10.18 | Troops near Kirkuk | Three | ? |
| 24.10.18 | Troops near Kirkuk | One | 8 x 20lb. |
|  | Altun Kopri airfield | Two RE.8 | 6 x 20lb. |
| 24.10.18 | Camp near Mianeh | One | 4 x 20lb. |
| 27.10.18 | Altun Kopri airfield | ? | 10 x 20lb. |
| 28.10.18 | Altun Kopri airfield | One RE.8 | 8 x 20lb. |
| 13.11.18 | Arab camps | Two RE.8 | 4 x 20lb. |
| 24.11.18 | Camp at Mianeh | One | 4 x 20lb. |
| 10.1.19 | Villages in Shamijani valley | Two | 12 x 20lb. |
| 27.1.19 | Robatak | Four RE.8 | 29 x 20lb. |
| 28.1.19 | Robatak | Five | 36 x 20lb. |
| 31.1.19 | Arabs in Samarra area |  | Two RE.8   16 x 20lb. |
| 14.2.19 | Arabs at Nasiriya | One RE.8 | 6 x 20lb. In conjuction with 63 Squadron |
| 20.2.19 | Kaki | One Martinsyde, three RE.8 | 31 x 20lb. |
| 6.3.19 | Khun | ? | ? One aircraft shot down |

# Appendix 5: Summary of Second World War offensive operations

| Date | Target or mission | Aircraft | Bomb-load and remarks |
|---|---|---|---|
| 6.11.40 | Offensive recce Savona, Teplene and Argyrokastram | 3 Blenheims | 250lb bombs |
| 10.11.40 | Kronspol and Sarande | 3 Blenheims | 4 x 250lb bombs each |
| 11.11.40 | Valona docks | 3 Blenheims | |
| 13.11.40 | Dhruno river valley | 3 Blenheims | 2 x 100lb + 6 x 40lb bombs each |
| 14.11.40 | MT on road between Pogradie and Koritsa | 3 Blenheims | 2 x 100lb + 2 x 40lb bombs each |
| 15.11.40 | Position north of Koritsa | 3 Blenheims | 1 x 250lb + 9 x 40lb + 8 x 25lb bombs each |
| 17.11.40 | Elbasa | 2 Blenheims | 2 x 100lb + 2 x 40lb + 8 x 25lb bombs each |
| 21.11.40 | Teplene | 1 Blenheim | |
| 22.11.40 | Argyrokastram | 3 Blenheims | 2 x 250lb + 2 x 40lb + 40 incendiary bombs each |
| 27.11.40 | Valona harbour | 3 Blenheims | 4 x 250lb bombs each |
| 3.12.40 | Sarande harbour | 3 Blenheims | |
| 4.12.40 | Sarande | 2 Blenheims | |
| 6.12.40 | Sarande and Valona | 3 Blenheims | |
| 18.12.40 | Seaplane hangars at Valona | 3 Blenheims | |
| 29.12.40 | Troop concentrations | 3 Blenheims | |
| 30.12.40 | Fighter patrol between Preveza and Levkas | 6 Blenheims | |
| 19.1.41 | Anti-submarine patrol | 2 Blenheims | |
| 25.1.41 | Supply depot and camp at Boultsar | 3 Blenheims | |
| 13.2.41 | Bridge north-east of Tepelene | 3 Blenheims | |
| 14.2.41 | Road near Buzi | 3 Blenheims | |
| 15.2.41 | Buzi area | 3 Blenheims | |
| 18.2.41 | MT and troops in Tepelene area | 4 Blenheims | |
| 20.2.41 | MT and troops in Tepelene area | 4 Blenheims | |
| 28.2.41 | Village east of Tepelene | 3 Blenheims | |
| 1.3.41 | Parkbdai village | 3 Blenheims | |
| | Berat | 3 Blenheims | |
| 6.3.41 | Valona airfield and harbour | 5 Blenheims | |
| 25.3.41 | Scarpanto airfield | 2 Blenheims | |
| | Calato airfield, Rhodes | 3 Blenheims | |
| 28.3.41 | | | |
| 10.4.41 | MT at Bitolj | 5 Blenheims | MT strafed |
| 1.1.42 | 3 x convoy patrols | 6 Hurricanes | |
| 4.1.42 | Convoy patrols throughout day | x Hurricanes | |
| 6.1.42 | Convoy patrols throughout day | x Hurricanes | |
| 7.1.42 | Convoy patrols throughout day | x Hurricanes | |
| 8.1.42 | Convoy patrols throughout day | x Hurricanes | |
| 10.1.42 | Convoy patrols throughout day | x Hurricanes | |
| 11.1.42 | Convoy patrols throughout day | x Hurricanes | |
| 12.1.42 | Patrol over Sollum / Halfaya area | 2 Hurricanes | Attacked Ju 52s |
| 13.1.42 | Patrol over Halfaya | 1 Hurricane | |
| 13.1.42 | Convoy patrols throughout day | x Hurricanes | |
| 14.1.42 | 2 x patrols over Halfaya Pass | 4 Hurricanes | Enemy MT strafed |
| 15.1.42 | Convoy patrols throughout day | x Hurricanes | |
| 17.1.42 | Convoy patrols throughout day | x Hurricanes | Ju 88 shot down |
| 19.1.42 | Convoy patrols throughout day | x Hurricanes | |
| 20.1.42 | Convoy patrol | 1 Hurricane | |
| 21.1.42 | Convoy patrols | 2 Hurricanes | |
| 26.1.42 | Convoy patrols | x Hurricanes | |
| 29.1.42 | Convoy patrols throughout day | 2 Hurricanes | |
| 1.2.42 | Convoy patrols throughout day | 8 Hurricanes | |
| 2.2.42 | Convoy patrol | 2 Hurricanes | |
| 3.2.42 | Convoy patrols | x Hurricanes | |
| 5.2.42 | Standing patrol over LG.121 | 2 Hurricanes | |
| 7.2.42 | Standing patrol over Mersa Matruh | 2 Hurricanes | |
| 8.2.42 | Standing patrol over Mersa Matruh | 2 Hurricanes | |
| 9.2.42 | Standing patrol over Mersa Matruh | 2 Hurricanes | |
| 9.2.42 | Convoy patrol | 2 Hurricanes | |
| 10.2.42 | Standing patrol over Mersa Matruh | 2 Hurricanes | |
| 11.2.42 | Standing patrol over Mersa Matruh | 2 Hurricanes | |
| 13.2.42 | Convoy patrols throughout day | x Hurricanes | |
| 15.2.42 | Convoy patrols throughout day | x Hurricanes | Two S.79s shot down during 30 Squadron's final operation in the Middle East |
| 12.3.44 | Zibingyi (stores dump) | 6 Hurricanes | Strafed |
| 15.3.44 | Shipping on Kaladan and Mayu rivers | 6 Hurricanes | Strafed; little success due gun stop |
| 1.4.44 | Night 'rhubarbs' | 4 Hurricanes | Flown from Feni; little success |
| 5.4.44 | Night 'rhubarbs' | 4 Hurricanes | Flown from Feni; little success |
| 8.4.44 | Night 'rhubarbs' | 4 Hurricanes | Flown from Feni; no targets found |
| 11.4.44 | Night 'rhubarbs' | 4 Hurricanes | Flown from Chittagong; uneventful |
| 7.5.44 | Night 'rhubarbs' | 4 Hurricanes | Flown from Chittagong; one aircraft made attacks on river steamer |

| Date | Target / Operation | Aircraft | Results |
|---|---|---|---|
| 9.5.44 | Night 'rhubarbs' | 4 Hurricanes | Flown from Chittagong; attacked launches and sampans on Mayu and Kaladan rivers |
| 13.5.44 | Night 'rhubarbs' | 4 Hurricanes | Flown from Chittagong; uneventful |
| 16.10.44 | 'Rhubarb' | 4 Thunderbolts | Strafed bashas on Mayu Peninsula |
| 17.10.44 | 'Rhubarb' | 4 Thunderbolts | 80 bashas attacked in Tharagon area |
| 20.10.44 | Offensive recce of Pi-Chaung, Kaladan and Lemro rivers | 6 Thunderbolts | Two-masted boat and bashas attacked |
| 21.10.44 | Offensive recce of Mayu river | 2 Thunderbolts | Bashas at Alechaung strafed |
| 21.10.44 | Stores dumps at Dabrugyaung | 2 Thunderbolts | No results obtained |
| 22.10.44 | Offensive recce of Pi-Chaung and Kaladan | 4 Thunderbolts | No targets found |
| 23.10.44 | Offensive recce of Mayu river | 4 Thunderbolts | |
| 24.10.44 | Enemy camp at Yezogyaung | 4 Thunderbolts | Successful strafe |
| 25.10.44 | Search for enemy river craft on Mayu river | 4 Thunderbolts | Target not found |
| 3.11.44 | Sweep over Mingaladon airfield | 12 Thunderbolts | Two aircraft aborted, one crashed; remainder strafed airfield |
| 4.11.44 | Escort to Liberators raiding Insein (Rangoon) | 12 Thunderbolts | Four aircraft reached target; one enemy aircraft shot down |
| 13.11.44 | Sweep over mouth of Sittang river | 12 Thunderbolts | Uneventful |
| 17.11.44 | Sweep over Rangoon area airfields | 12 Thunderbolts | Enemy aircraft encountered |
| 19.11.44 | Escort to Liberators raiding Mokpalin | 12 Thunderbolts | Enemy aircraft encountered |
| 23.11.44 | Escort to B-24s raiding railway bridge | 12 Thunderbolts | Uneventful |
| 4.12.44 | Supply dump at Kindaung | 6 Thunderbolts | 12 x 500lb GP bombs dropped plus strafing |
| 6.12.44 | Supply dump at Htizwe | 8 Thunderbolts | 16 x 500lb GP bombs dropped |
| 6.12.44 | Bridge at Awrama | 4 Thunderbolts | Failed to find target, so bombed another bridge further east; 8 x 500lb GP bombs dropped |
| 13.12.44 | Escort to Liberators bombing railway bridges on Pegu to Moulmein line | 12 Thunderbolts | Almost uneventful |
| 16.12.44 | Enemy HQ east of Buthidaung | 10 Thunderbolts | Successful bombing and strafing |
| 17.12.44 | Supply dumps east of Thaungdara | 12 Thunderbolts | 500lb GP bombs dropped |
| 18.12.44 | Dumps and assembly depot at southern end of Nataguna valley | 12 Thunderbolts | |
| 19.12.44 | Staging post at Ponnagyun | 12 Thunderbolts | Strafed successfully |
| 20.12.44 | Staging post east of Mayu river | 11 Thunderbolts | Strafed successfully |
| 23.12.44 | Camp at Pazin Chaung | 12 Thunderbolts | Bombed and strafed successfully |
| 25.12.44 | Gun positions at Garadaung | 12 Thunderbolts | Bombed and strafed successfully |
| 29.12.44 | Gun positions and troops east of Thayettabin road | 11 Thunderbolts | Bombed and strafed |
| 30.12.44 | ditto | 12 Thunderbolts | Bombed and strafed |
| 31.12.44 | Paukpingwin | 12 Thunderbolts | Bombed and strafed |
| 2.1.45 | Troops at Minzegyaung | 12 Thunderbolts | Bombed and strafed; 80 killed |
| 3.1.45 | Staging post at Ponnagyun | 12 Thunderbolts | |
| 4.1.45 | Myonaung | 12 Thunderbolts | |
| 5.1.45 | Positions 10 miles north of Myohaung | 11 Thunderbolts | |
| 12.1.45 | Positions on Myebon peninsula | 12 Thunderbolts | Flown from Cox's Bazaar |
| 13.1.45 | Positions near Kangaw | 12 Thunderbolts | Flown from Cox's Bazaar |
| 13.1.45 | River craft near Myebon | 4 Thunderbolts | Flown from Cox's Bazaar; no trace of targets |
| 14.1.45 | Positions on Myebon peninsula | 12 Thunderbolts | Bombed and strafed |
| 15.1.45 | Positions on hill north-east of Teinnyo | 12 Thunderbolts | |
| 16.1.45 | Escort to Liberators raiding Zayatkwin airfield, near Rangoon | 12 Thunderbolts | No opposition |
| 17.1.45 | Positions on hill north of Kantha | 12 Thunderbolts | |
| 19.1.45 | ditto | 12 Thunderbolts | 500lb. bombs dropped |
| 21.1.45 | Assault on Ramree Island | x Thunderbolts | 2 x 500lb GP bombs per aircraft |
| 22.1.45 | Positions on hill south of Myohaung | 12 Thunderbolts | |
| 24.1.45 | Positions east of Kangaw | 12 Thunderbolts | Bombed accurately |
| 24.1.45 | ditto | 12 Thunderbolts | |
| 28.1.45 | Road east of Kangaw | 12 Thunderbolts | Bombed accurately |
| 28.1.45 | ditto | x Thunderbolts | |
| 29.1.45 | Positions north of Kangaw | x Thunderbolts | |
| 29.1.45 | ditto | x Thunderbolts | Napalm dropped for first time |
| 30.1.45 | ? | x Thunderbolts | Napalm dropped |
| 31.1.45 | Positions near Kangaw | 12 Thunderbolts | 500lb GP bombs dropped |
| 31.1.45 | ditto | 12 Thunderbolts | Napalm dropped |
| 1.2.45 | Positions near Kangaw | 12 Thunderbolts | Inconclusive |
| 1.2.45 | 'Rhubarb' to Magwe airield, Magwe satellite and Maida Vale | 12 Thunderbolts | Little activity seen |
| 2.2.45 | Enemy HQ at Kolan | 12 Thunderbolts | Damage to bashas |
| 2.2.45 | Defences at Kangaw | 12 Thunderbolts | |
| 4.2.45 | Defences on Ramree Island | 12 Thunderbolts | Napalm dropped; very successful |
| 5.2.45 | Road bridge at Thangyo | 6 Thunderbolts | 500lb. bombs dropped |
| 5.2.45 | ditto | 6 Thunderbolts | 500lb. bombs dropped; bridge still standing |
| 7.2.45 | Bombing at Sinudeik and offensive recce of Dalet Chaung area | 6 Thunderbolts | |
| 7.2.45 | Jetty at Tamandu | 6 Thunderbolts | Inconclusive |

| | | | |
|---|---|---|---|
| 9.2.45 | Road Bridge at Thangyo | 12 Thunderbolts | Napalm dropped; one direct hit |
| 11.2.45 | Escort to B–24s raiding dumps north of Victoria Lake, Rangoon | 12 Thunderbolts | No enemy reaction |
| 12.2.45 | Counter-battery patrols | 5 Thunderbolts | Uneventful |
| 13.2.45 | Hill feature on Ramree Island | 6 Thunderbolts | |
| 15.2.45 | Sakanmaw and Kywegu | 12 Thunderbolts | Napalm dropped; very successful |
| 15.2.45 | River bridge at An | 12 Thunderbolts | Delayed action bombs; direct hits |
| 16.2.45 | Defensive patrols in Ru–Ywa area | 12 Thunderbolts | |
| 16.2.45 | River bridge at An | 6 Thunderbolts | Delayed action bombs |
| 18.2.45 | An and Aukywa villages | 12 Thunderbolts | Bombed and strafed |
| 19.2.45 | Enemy HQ at Tamandu | 12 Thunderbolts | Inconclusive |
| 20.2.45 | Troops at Kolan, Letmauk and An | 12 Thunderbolts | Good results |
| 20.2.45 | An and Aukywa | 12 Thunderbolts | |
| 21.2.45 | Concentration area on bank of Dalet Chaung | 12 Thunderbolts | |
| 22.2.45 | Concentration area along An Chaung | 12 Thunderbolts | Some fires started |
| 23.2.45 | Positions east of Ru–Ywa | 12 Thunderbolts | |
| 24.2.45 | Kokkomaw | 6 Thunderbolts | Napalm dropped; very successful |
| 24.2.45 | Thekanhtaung | 5 Thunderbolts | Napalm dropped; very successful |
| 25.2.45 | Letmauk and Kolan | 12 Thunderbolts | Napalm dropped; very successful |
| 26.2.45 | Positions near Ru–Ywa | 6 Thunderbolts | |
| 26.2.45 | Enemy camp near Buzo | 6 Thunderbolts | |
| 27.2.45 | Positions near Thangyo | 12 Thunderbolts | |
| 28.2.45 | Escort to B–24s raiding Mingaladon | 12 Thunderbolts | No enemy activity |
| 1.3.45 | Positions near Dalet | 11 Thunderbolts | Napalm dropped |
| 2.3.45 | Daing village | 4 Thunderbolts | Napalm dropped |
| 3.3.45 | Offensive patrols from Thangyo to Tamandu and bombing as ordered | 11 Thunderbolts | Napalm dropped; fires started |
| 4.3.45 | Offensive patrols in Tamadu area | 12 Thunderbolts | Napalm dropped |
| 5.3.45 | Positions south-east of Ru–Ywa | 12 Thunderbolts | 500lb. GP bombs dropped very successfully |
| 6.3.45 | Positions south of Me Taung | x Thunderbolts | |
| 7.3.45 | Positions south of Letmauk | 6 Thunderbolts | |
| 9.3.45 | Escort to B–24s raiding Rangoon | 16 Thunderbolts | Squadron's complete establishment |
| 13.3.45 | 'Cabrank' patrols over landing at Letpan | 16 Thunderbolts | Bombs dropped on pre-arranged targets |
| 14.3.45 | Positions east of Dalet Chaung | 12 Thunderbolts | |
| 15.3.45 | Thawatti East railway bridges | 12 Thunderbolts | Delayed-action bombs dropped; direct hits |
| 18.3.45 | Defences near Taungbwe | 12 Thunderbolts | All bombs in target area but no results |
| 20.3.45 | Thawatti East railway bridges | 12 Thunderbolts | Some direct hits |
| 22.3.45 | Road bridge north-east of Pyinmana | 12 Thunderbolts | Inconclusive |
| 23.3.45 | Dumps south of Prome | 12 Thunderbolts | |
| 24.3.45 | Stores and dumps north of Toungoo | 12 Thunderbolts | Large fire started |
| 25.3.45 | Stores and dumps at Yedashe | 12 Thunderbolts | Direct hits and fires started |
| 26.3.45 | Officers' living quarters at Prome | 12 Thunderbolts | Direct hits |
| 27.3.45 | Dumps near Prome | 10 Thunderbolts | Direct hits |
| 28.3.45 | Station at Gyobingauk | 8 Thunderbolts | Very successful |
| 29.3.45 | Troops and dumps at Ngwedaung | 12 Thunderbolts | Very successful |
| 30.3.45 | Living quarters and oil pumping station at Tharrawaddy | 12 Thunderbolts | Only half the bombs exploded |
| 31.3.45 | Enemy HQ and living quarters south of Henzada | 10 Thunderbolts | |
| 1.4.45 | Dumps along Rangoon to Mandalay railway line at Thagaya | 12 Thunderbolts | |
| 2.4.45 | Oil storage depot at Nyidaw Pagoda | 12 Thunderbolts | Disappointing results; no fires started |
| 3.4.45 | Officers' living quarters at Prome | 12 Thunderbolts | Difficulty in finding target in haze |
| 4.4.45 | Positions on Letmauk to An road | x Thunderbolts | Delayed-action bombs dropped from low level |
| 8.4.45 | Prome | 12 Thunderbolts | |
| 9.4.45 | Railway bridges at Letpadam | 12 Thunderbolts | Successful |
| 10.4.45 | Dumps at Kywebwe | 12 Thunderbolts | Four good fires started |
| 11.4.45 | Paletwa road bridge, east of Toungoo | 12 Thunderbolts | Near misses only |
| 12.4.45 | Positions on Letmauk to An road | 10 Thunderbolts | All bombs in target area |
| 29.4.45 | Letpadan west railway bridge and road bridge | 12 Thunderbolts | Successful |
| 1.5.45 | Targets in Rangoon area | 12 Thunderbolts | |
| 2.5.45 | 'Cabrank' patrols and attacks in Rangoon | 6 Thunderbolts | Two aircraft bombed target area |
| 2.5.45 | 'Cabrank' patrols and attacks | 6 Thunderbolts | Attacks directed from HQ ship |
| 8.5.45 | Positions west of Sittang river | 8 Thunderbolts | |
| 11.5.45 | Troop concentrations at Pasawng | 9 Thunderbolts | Successful |
| 12.5.45 | Troops at Payagyi and Yandon | 12 Thunderbolts | |
| 13.5.45 | Troop concentration at Yethogyi | 12 Thunderbolts | Buildings hit but no troops seen; this was 30 Squadron's final offensive operation |

# Appendix 6: Aircraft used by 30 Squadron

| Serial | Code | Fate |
|---|---|---|

**Maurice Farman S.11 Shorthorn**

| Serial | Code | Fate |
|---|---|---|
| 369 | MF1 ? | Crashed into Suez Canal 26.5.15 |
| ? | MF2 | Destroyed near Baghdad 13.11.15 |
| 5901 | | |
| 5907 | | |
| 5908 | | *Fanny*; destroyed in hangar fire 14.10.16 |
| 5909 | | Wrecked in storm, Orah, 2.5.16 |
| 7346 | | Wrecked in storm, Orah, 2.5.16 |
| 7347 | | |
| 7348 | | |
| 7349 | | To Egypt 17.11.16 |
| 7350 | | To Egypt 17.11.16 |
| A365 | | |
| A366 | | |
| A367 | | |
| A368 | | |
| A369 | | |

**Maurice Farman S.7 Longhorn**

| Serial | Code | Fate |
|---|---|---|
| 712 | | |
| 713 | | |
| ? | | Returned to IEF in Mesopotamia 4.15 |
| ? | | ditto |
| ? | MF7 | |

**Henri Farman F.27 Voisin**

*Note:* These aircraft were RNAS property but as they were flown in the joint RFC/ RNAS operations they are included in this listing for the sake of completeness. They were not numbered in the RNAS series, the numbers shown probably being construction numbers.

| Serial | Code | Fate |
|---|---|---|
| 1540 | | SOC 23.1.17 |
| 1541 | | Shot down by machine-gun fire over Es Sinn 5.3.16 |
| 1542 | | SOC 2.16 |
| 1568 | | To Egypt 25.1.17 |
| 1569 | | To Egypt 25.1.17 |
| 1572 | | To Egypt 25.1.17 |
| 1573 | | *The Infant*; To Egypt 25.1.17 |
| A387 | | |
| A388 | | |
| A389 | | |
| A390 | | |

**Caudron**

| Serial | Code | Fate |
|---|---|---|
| ? | C3 | Shot down 16.9.15 during reconnaissance of Es Sinn |
| ? | C4 | Force-landed 25 mls W of Abu Salabh 30.7.15 |

**Royal Aircraft Factory BE.2c**
(names in italics indicate a presentation aircraft, except for 2702)

| Serial | Code | Fate |
|---|---|---|
| 1757 | | To 14 Sqn. 12.15 |
| 2472 | | |
| 2672 | | |
| 2690 | | SOC 25.11.16 |
| 2702 | | (Single-seat conversion) *Oo–er*; SOC 8.11.17 |
| 4135 | | |
| 4141 | | |
| 4149 | | Shot down during reconnaissance 15.4.17 |
| 4182 | | |
| 4183 | | Crashed on landing at Buburah, 1.5.17 |
| 4186 | | |
| 4191 | | Force-landed 12.9.17 and destroyed |
| 4192 | | SOC 18.4.17 |
| 4194 | | SOC 4.4.17 |
| 4302 | | *Maharajah of Rewa-Bandhava Gwalior*; SOC 19.9.16 |
| 4303 | | |
| 4322 | | SOC 19.9.16 |
| 4323 | | SOC 1.5.16 |
| 4324 | | |
| 4327 | | SOC 5.12.16 |
| 4328 | | SOC 1.5.16 |
| 4347 | | SOC 6.8.17 |
| 4348 | | SOC 6.8.17 |
| 4350 | | |
| 4352 | | |
| 4361 | BE.12A | SOC 6.9.17 |
| 4362 | | To 31 Wing Air Park 25.2.18 (last BE.2C in 30 Squadron service) |
| 4363 | BE.14 | |
| 4364 | | SOC 25.11.16 |
| 4373 | | SOC 15.12.16 |
| 4379 | | |
| 4388 | | |
| 4389 | | |
| 4390 | | |
| 4391 | | |
| 4392 | | |
| 4393 | | |
| 4395 | | |
| 4398 | | |
| 4405 | | |
| 4411 | | SOC 1.5.16 |
| 4412 | | SOC 2.18 |
| 4413 | | |
| 4414 | | Burned to prevent capture, 12.9.17 |
| 4421 | | Engine failed, hit tree 16.8.17. SOC |
| 4423 | | To 31 Wing Air Park 11.2.18 |
| 4431 | | *Manipur* |
| 4432 | | |
| 4434 | | |
| 4438 | | To Egypt by 10.16 |
| 4443 | | |
| 4449 | | SOC 18.1.17 |
| 4458 | | SOC 25.11.16 |
| 4459 | | SOC 11.10.16 |
| 4461 | | |
| 4473 | | |
| 4486 | | SOC 10.17 |
| 4487 | | |
| 4491 | | |
| 4500 | | Lost in action near Samarrah 15.4.17 |
| 4510 | | SOC 13.10.16 |
| 4512 | | Wrecked after engine failure 8.7.16 |
| 4537 | | Crashed in down-wind take-off, 19.1.17 |
| 4540 | | |
| 4558 | | *Ginger*; SOC 16.8.17 |
| 4562 | | To 31 Wing Air Park 1.18 |
| 4564 | | |
| 4573 | | SOC 23.1.17 |
| 4584 | | |
| 4585 | | *Maharaja of Rewa-Bandhava*; collided with German aircraft 3.4.17 and SOC 12.4.17 |
| 4594 | | |
| 4711 | | |
| 4712 | | |
| 5427 | | |
| 5877 | | |
| ? | BE.11 | Crash-landed at Lajj 20.11.15 |
| ? | BE.12 | |

### Royal Aircraft Factory BE.2d

| | |
|---|---|
| 6804 | Force-landed and burnt 31.10.17 |
| 6805 | SOC 7.10.17 |
| A1327 | |
| A1377 | |
| A1385 | |

### Royal Aircraft Factory BE.2e

| | |
|---|---|
| A3068 | *Western Province of the Gold Coast*; To 63 Sqn. |
| A3069 | *Shanghai Race Club No.3*; to 6 Sqn. |
| A3078 | *Bharatpur* |
| A3079 | *Rajputana No. 2*; SOC 28.8.19 |
| A3080 | |
| A3086 | *Punjab No.35 Hariana* |
| A3087 | *River Plate*; to 72 Sqn. |
| A3088 | *The Seven Seas*; crashed 22.10.17 |
| A3089 | *QueensTown Cape* |

### Voisin LA

| | |
|---|---|
| 8518 | SOC 25.11.16 |
| 8523 | *The Mule*; spun in and crashed 26.10.16 |

### Short 184 seaplanes

*Note:* These five aircraft, which arrived at Basra in February 1916, were RNAS property but as they were flown in the joint RFC/RNAS operations they are included in this listing for the sake of completeness.

| | |
|---|---|
| 8044 | Shot down while dropping food supplies to Kut-al-Amara, 12.2.16 |
| 8045 | To Port Said by 8.16 |
| 8046 | To Port Said by 8.16 |
| 8047 | To Port Said by 8.16 |
| 8085 | To Port Said by 8.16 |

### Martinsyde S.1 Scout

| | | |
|---|---|---|
| 4243 | MH5 | Crashed on take-off from Ali Gharbi 14.9.15 |
| 4244 | MH6 | Shot down behind Turkish lines 20.11.15 |
| 4250 | MH8 | Force-landed behind Turkish lines 22.11.15 |
| ? | MH9 | Abandoned at Kut-al-Amara 29.4.16 |

### Martinsyde G.100 and G.102 'Elephant'

| | |
|---|---|
| 7459 | To 72 Sqn. |
| 7460 | Destroyed in hangar fire 11.3.17 |
| 7461 | Crashed while raiding Khun 6.3.19 |
| 7466 | Lost in action 6.5.17 but recaptured from Turks 6.11.17 |
| 7467 | To 72 Sqn. |
| 7468 | To 72 Sqn. |
| 7493 | To 72 Sqn. |
| 7494 | Crash-landed in desert during raid on Kifri airfield, 16.10.17; burnt by crew |
| A1584 | |
| A1594 | To 63 Sqn. |
| A1595 | *Australia No.4; New South Wales No.3*; SOC 25.11.17 |
| A1596 | To 72 Sqn. |
| A3940 | Hit by AA fire in raid on Kifri airfield, 31.10.17; burnt to prevent capture |
| A3943 | |
| A3972 | To 72 Sqn. |
| A3973 | To 72 Sqn. |
| A3974 | To 31 Wing Air Park 10.2.18 |
| A3975 | |

### SPAD S.VII

| | |
|---|---|
| A8806 | *Fifi*; to 72 Sqn. |
| A8807 | SOC 28.8.19 |
| A8808 | To 72 Sqn. |
| A8809 | To 63 Sqn. |
| A8810 | To 72 Sqn. |
| A8811 | To 63 Sqn. |
| A8812 | |

### Bristol Scout 'C'

| | |
|---|---|
| 1265 | |

### Bristol Scout 'D'

| | |
|---|---|
| 7031 | |
| 7033 | |
| 7034 | Lost in action 28.4.17 |
| 7047 | |
| A1763 | |
| A1765 | |
| A1768 | To 63 Sqn. |

### DH.4

| | |
|---|---|
| A7591 | Shot down in raid on Kifri airfield 21.1.18 |
| A7621 | Burnt out after engine fire during raid on Kifri airfield 26.1.18; force-landed 3 mls NE of Qarah Tappah |
| A7623 | |

### RE.8

| | |
|---|---|
| A4339 | |
| A4341 | |
| A4349 | |
| A4351 | SOC 24.1.19 |
| A4352 | |
| A4356 | SOC 22.2.19 |
| A4357 | To 63 Sqn. |
| A4416 | |
| A4658 | SOC 24.1.19 |
| A4659 | |
| A4660 | SOC 28.8.19 |
| A4662 | |
| B3445 | Crash-landed at Surmil landing ground 24.9.18 |
| B3447 | SOC 21.3.19 |
| B3448 | |
| B3449 | Lost in forced landing 40 mls behind Turkish lines 11.10.18 |
| B3450 | Failed to return from reconnaissance 4.3.18 |
| B5006 | Engine failed on take-off, crashed, 2.8.20 |
| B5869 | |
| B5871 | To 63 Sqn. |
| B5873 | |
| B5876 | Shot down by AA during raid in vicinity of Altun Kopri, 15.5.18 |
| B5877 | SOC 28.8.19 |
| B5883 | To 63 Sqn. |
| B6470 | |
| B6560 | Crash-landed at Kufa after enemy action, 10.7.20; burnt on evacuation, 15.7.20 |
| B6582 | |
| B6585 | To 72 Sqn. |
| B6588 | |
| B6591 | To 63 Sqn. |
| B6592 | To 63 Sqn. |
| B6601 | |

| | | |
|---|---|---|
| B6611 | | Crashed at Baquba 20.8.18 |
| B6612 | | To 63 Sqn. |
| B6613 | | To 63 Sqn. |
| B6684 | | |
| B6709 | | |
| B6711 | | |
| B7704 | | To 63 Sqn. |
| B7705 | | |
| C2752 | | Engine failed on take-off from Kufa, 14.7.20; burnt on evacuation 15.7.20 |
| C2755 | | |
| D4697 | | To 63 Sqn. |
| D4698 | | Spun in from 300ft on approach to Kazvin, 18.9.20 |
| D4699 | | Engine failed on take-off, force-landed in river bed at Zamzadi–Hatchem, 12.9.20 |
| D4708 | | Destroyed by fire in hangar, 2.8.20 |
| D6709 | | |
| D6711 | | |
| E1213 | | |
| E1214 | | To 63 Sqn. |
| E1241 | | Force-landed, blown over by gale, 15.4.20 |
| F6006 | | |

**DH.9A**

| | | |
|---|---|---|
| E758 | | |
| E773 | | Crashed in forced landing in Iraqi desert, 14.6.21 |
| E775 | | To Air Depot Hinaidi Training Flt. |
| E776 | | |
| E777 | | Returned to UK for reconditioning by DH |
| E778 | | To 8 Sqn. |
| E780 | | Captured by Bolsheviks 8.12.20 |
| E786 | | To 84 Sqn. |
| E800 | | |
| E802 | | |
| E805 | | Returned to UK for reconditioning by DH |
| E811 | | |
| E816 | | |
| E821 | | Crash-landed in deep snow, Kasvin, 9.2.21 |
| E822 | | Shot down on take-off from Diwaniyah, 28.7.20; abandoned on evacuation |
| E828 | | Returned to UK for reconditioning by DH |
| E843 | | To 8 Sqn. |
| E844 | X | |
| E847 | | |
| E848 | X | To 27 Sqn. |
| E849 | | |
| E850 | | To Air Depot Hinaidi |
| E852 | | |
| E873 | | To 84 Sqn. |
| E889 | | Returned to UK for 1 FTS |
| E911 | | |
| E912 | | |
| E914 | | To 8 Sqn. |
| E915 | | |
| E920 | | |
| E930 | | |
| E944 | X | To 8 Sqn. and returned |
| E945 | | |
| E954 | | To 8 Sqn. |
| E958 | | |
| E961 | | |
| E8497 | | To 47 Sqn. |
| E8498 | | |
| E8512 | | |
| E8513 | | |
| E8514 | | To 84 Sqn. |
| E8580 | | |
| E8602 | | |
| E8643 | | To 55 Sqn. |
| E8651 | | Stalled on turn after take-off from Kirkuk, 24.4.28 |

| | |
|---|---|
| E8652 | To 55 Sqn. |
| E8658 | To 84 Sqn. |
| E8668 | |
| E8684 | |
| E8711 | To Air Depot Hinaidi |
| E8713 | |
| E8755 | |
| E8757 | |
| E8758 | Returned to UK for 207 Sqn. |
| E8805 | To Air Depot Hinaidi |
| E9690 | To 55 Sqn. |
| E9691 | Force-landed in river near Baghdad, 20.2.21 |
| E9894 | To 47 Sqn. |
| E9908 | Engine cut on take-off, 1.9.22 |
| E9911 | |
| E9918 | To 84 Sqn. |
| E9922 | Returned to UK |
| E9930 | |
| E9938 | |
| F1614 | To Air Depot Hinaidi |
| F1615 | |
| F2771 | Returned to UK |
| F2783 | |
| F2785 | Crashed in force-landing on rough ground in desert, 14.5.21 |
| F2809 | |
| F2810 | |
| F2817 | |
| F2833 | To 55 Sqn. |
| F2838 | To 84 Sqn. |
| F2840 | |
| F2846 | To Air Depot Hinaidi |
| F2853 | |
| F2855 | |
| H1 | |
| H24 | |
| H26 | |
| H39 | *Rumble Tumble*; crashed Amman 6.1921 |
| H40 | Crash-landed in snow at Hamadan, Persia, 18.2.21 |
| H43 | |
| H44 | To 14 Sqn. |
| H45 | Force-landed with engine fire, 24.3.22 |
| H49 | |
| H53 | To 55 Sqn. |
| H60 | |
| H66 | To 84 Sqn. |
| H68 | Force-landed with rifle-fire damage 14.6.20; salvaged but DBR |
| H71 | Shot down by rifle fire near Kifl, Iraq, 12.10.20; burnt by Arabs |
| H78 | Force-landed in desert and hit sand ridge, 23.4.22 |
| H80 | Crashed 13.1.21 |
| H81 | Force-landed in sandstorm, overturned in irrigation ditch, Khidire, Iraq, 8.4.21 |
| H86 | To 55 Sqn. |
| H90 | Crash-landed in sandstorm 9.6.21 |
| H101 | |
| H104 | Crash-landed at Baghdad West, 20.6.22 |
| H105 | |
| H107 | |
| H108 | To 84 Sqn. |
| H109 | Crashed on landing on soft ground at Shaibah, 19.5.21 |
| H114 | Engine caught fire; crash-landed at Sulaimaniyah, 5.9.22; burnt on evacuation |
| H119 | Heavy landing at LG.4, Iraq, 30.7.21 |
| H120 | Crashed and caught fire, 23.11.25 |
| H121 | |
| H122 | To Air Depot Hinaidi |
| H145 | To 8 Sqn. |
| H150 | |
| H155 | Crashed 6 miles SW of Kirkuk, 6.10.22, after enemy action |

| | | |
|---|---|---|
| H161 | | Crashed on take-off, 29.7.21, when sand temporarily blinded pilot |
| H3424 | | |
| H3433 | | To 6 Sqn. |
| H3441 | | |
| H3451 | | |
| H3481 | | To 55 Sqn. |
| H3482 | | |
| H3483 | | To Training Flt. Shaibah |
| H3500 | | Tyre burst on landing, 20.8.21; DBR |
| H3504 | | Crash-landed in desert, 25.6.21 |
| H3512 | | |
| H3523 | | To 55 Sqn. |
| H3524 | | To 84 Sqn. |
| H3525 | | To 55 Sqn. |
| H3535 | | |
| H3632 | B | Returned to UK |
| H3633 | | To Air Depot Hinaidi |
| H3634 | | To 47 Sqn. |
| J560 | B | Returned to UK |
| J564 | | |
| J6961 | | To 84 Sqn. |
| J7015 | | Stalled, crashed and caught fire, 11.2.25 |
| J7054 | | To 84 Sqn. |
| J7099 | | To 84 Sqn. |
| J7113 | | To 55 Sqn. |
| J7114 | | Collided in air with H3633, 25.4.27 |
| J7115 | | |
| J7124 | | |
| J7302 | | |
| J7307 | | |
| J7309 | | To AHQ Iraq |
| J7346 | | |
| J7352 | | |
| J7607 | | To 55 Sqn. |
| J7612 | | |
| J7854 | | Spun in while attempting to land near stranded aircraft near Hillan, 2.4.28 |
| J7857 | | |
| J7870 | | To 55 Sqn. |
| J7877 | | |
| J7880 | | |
| J7881 | A | Overturned on landing in gale |
| J8102 | | To 55 Sqn. |
| J8113 | | |
| J8151 | | To 55 Sqn. |
| J8152 | | To 55 Sqn. |

**Wapiti Mk.IIa**

| | | |
|---|---|---|
| J9403 | | To Air Depot, Drigh Road 2.32; returned 4.32 |
| J9404 | | |
| J9405 | | To 55 Sqn. |
| J9406 | | |
| J9407 | G | |
| J9408 | A | |
| J9409 | A | |
| J9410 | | |
| J9411 | | To 55 Sqn. |
| J9412 | | Undershot night landing at Mosul and overturned, 22.3.32; repaired |
| J9413 | | To 84 Sqn. |
| J9414 | | |
| J9485 | | To 5 Sqn. |
| J9487 | | |
| J9489 | | Collided at 4000ft with J9623 8 miles SW of Agra, Iraq, 3.9.30; SOC |
| J9490 | | ex 55 Sqn. ? |
| J9492 | | |
| J9495 | | |
| J9514 | | Crashed 7.8.35 |

| | | |
|---|---|---|
| J9592 | | To 55 Sqn. but still in use by 30 Sqn. for drogue towing to 9.36 |
| J9594 | | To Air Depot, Hinaidi |
| J9619 | | Undercarriage collapsed on landing at Tel Sirwal, 17.7.34 |
| J9620 | | |
| J9621 | | Struck ridge on landing at Diana LG 3.3.30 |
| J9622 | | |
| J9623 | | Collided at 4000ft with J9489 8 miles SW of Agra, Iraq, 3.9.30; SOC |
| J9626 | | |
| J9630 | | Hit by K1396 while stationery awaiting take-off from Mosul, 9.2.33 |
| J9636 | A | |
| J9742 | P | |
| J9840 | | SOC 21.5.35 |
| J9853 | | Hit two armoured cars on musketry range, Mosul, 10.5.35; SOC 15.6.35 |
| K1384 | | SOC 2.8.32 |
| K1389 | | |
| K1393 | | SOC 5.4.35 |
| K1394 | | |
| K1396 | | SOC 13.4.35 |
| K1398 | | SOC 5.10.35 |
| K1402 | | SOC 25.4.35 |
| K1404 | | Engine failed on take-off from Mosul, 14.6.34; hit ditch and overturned; SOC 20.8.34 |
| K1406 | | SOC 15.5.35 |

**Hardy Mk.I**

| | | |
|---|---|---|
| K4050 | | To Air Depot Aboukir for 6 Sqn. |
| K4051 | | ditto |
| K4052 | | ditto |
| K4053 | | ditto |
| K4054 | | ditto |
| K4055 | | ditto |
| K4056 | | ditto |
| K4057 | | Ran away when starting up at Sarsian LG 27.7.36 and hit K4050; SOC 7.1.38 as BER |
| K4058 | | Swung on take-off from Dhibban 7.5.37 and tipped up; SOC 27.7.38 as BER |
| K4059 | | To Air Depot Aboukir for 6 Sqn. |
| K4060 | | ditto |
| K4061 | | Undercarrige leg collapsed at Mosul 19.5.36; overturned; SOC 27.7.36 |
| K4062 | | To Air Depot Aboukir for 6 Sqn. |
| K4063 | | ditto |
| K4064 | | ditto |
| K4065 | | ditto |
| K4066 | | ditto |
| K4067 | | ditto |
| K4068 | | ditto |
| K4069 | | Undercarriage collapsed in heavy landing on flarepath at Dhibban, 12.10.37; SOC 27.7.38 as BER |
| K4070 | | To Air Depot Aboukir for 6 Sqn. |
| K4306 | | (30 Sqn. reserve); transferred To 6 Sqn. |
| K4307 | | ditto |
| K4308 | | ditto |
| K4309 | | ditto |
| K4310 | | ditto |
| K4311 | | ditto |
| K4312 | | ditto |
| K4313 | | ditto |
| K4314 | | ditto |
| K4315 | | ditto |
| K4316 | | ditto |
| K4317 | | ditto |
| K4318 | | ditto |
| K4319 | | ditto |

| | | |
|---|---|---|
| K4320 | | ditto |
| K4321 | | ditto |
| K5920 | | ditto |

**Blenheim Mk.I**

| | | |
|---|---|---|
| K7093 | | Belly-landed in error, Ismailia, 11.9.39; SOC 2.1.40 |
| K7094 | | To 70 OTU |
| K7095 | VT:A | Damaged by return fire from Ju 88 and crash-landed NW of Athens, 11.4.41 |
| K7096 | DP:A;<br>VT:O | Presumed lost in Greece 4.41 |
| K7097 | VT:P | Crashed in desert 60 mls. SW of Habbaniya, 10.12.38, presumed due to weather; 6 killed |
| K7098 | | Undercarriage damaged on take-off and jammed; crash-landed Wadi Gazouza, 28.9.41 |
| K7099 | | To 70 OTU |
| K7100 | VT:V | Damaged by flak and crash-landed at Korousades, Corfu, 5.12.40 |
| K7101 | | Swung on take-off from Habbaniya, 15.6.38, and damaged beyond repair; SOC 14.7.38 |
| K7102 | | Engine cut on take-off from Habbaniya, 29.6.38; stalled and dived into ground; 2 killed |
| K7103 | | Engine cut, belly-landed 14 mls N of Khalkis, Greece, 1.12.40 |
| K7104 | VT:L | Damaged by CR.42s and crashed into sea off Valona, 29.12.40 |
| K7105 | VT:F | To 72 OTU |
| K7106 | VT:G | Overshot landing at Haifa and overturned, 5.10.40; damaged beyond repair |
| K7107 | VT:B | SOC 11.4.40 |
| K7177 | VT:T | Damaged by 'friendly' AA from convoy 27.4.41 and abandoned at Maleme |
| K7178 | VT:P | Missing from escorting reconnaissance aircraft over Libyan frontier, 28.7.40 |
| K7179 | VT:B | To 72 OTU |
| K7180 | VT:V/E | Undershot landing at Haifa and hit fence, 18.10.40; destroyed by fire |
| K7181 | VT:X | Lost in action 13.7.40 |
| K7182 | | |
| L1097 | | To 60 Sqn. |
| L1098 | VT:D/M | To 75 OTU |
| L1120 | VT:N | Shot down by Fiat G.50, crashed NE of Koritsa, Greece, 15.11.40 |
| L1166 | VT:K | Ran out of fuel on return from Tepelini, belly-landed on beach at Zagora, Greece, 21.11.40 |
| L1239 | VT:D | To 1 METS |
| L4917 | VT:G | |
| L6672 | VT:Q | |
| L8378 | | |
| L8398 | VT:B | |
| L8443 | | |
| L8446 | | |
| L8462 | VT:X | |
| L8538 | | To 72 OTU |
| L8541 | | To 211 Sqn |
| L8542 | | To 55 Sqn |
| L8543 | | To 39 Sqn |
| L8544 | | To 60 Sqn |

**Hurricane Mk.I**

| | | |
|---|---|---|
| T9531 | | To 238 Sqn. |
| V7486 | | DBR 11.41 |
| W9132 | | Crashed in forced landing in Edku Lake, 15.9.41 |
| W9235 | | |
| W9238 | | To 151 OTU |
| W9264 | | SOC 30.9.43 |
| W9274 | | |
| W9291 | | To 74 OTU |

| | | |
|---|---|---|
| Z4032 | | To 7 Sqn. SAAF |
| Z4086 | | |
| Z4170 | | SOC 9.8.42 |
| Z4186 | | |
| Z4196 | | SOC 1.3.44 |
| Z4230 | C | |
| Z4232 | | |
| Z4234 | | To 73 OTU |
| Z4249 | | To 208 Sqn. |
| Z4355 | | SOC 3.7.42 |
| Z4419 | | SOC 28.8.44 |
| Z4487 | | |
| Z4492 | | To 252 Wg. |
| Z4635 | | SOC 18.12.41 |
| Z4696 | | To 136 Sqn. |
| Z4709 | | Missing (Halfaya) 28.12.41 |
| Z4710 | | Crashed on landing at LG.102, 29.10.41 |
| Z4718 | T | To 1 Sqn. SAAF ? |
| Z4780 | | |
| Z4839 | | To 73 OTU |
| Z6985 | | To Royal Navy Fighter Sqn. |
| Z6988 | | Undershot night anding at Edku, 23.7.41 |
| Z7000 | | Missing 8.7.42 |
| Z7004 | | Hit ground while carrying out unauthorised aerobatics at Edku, 31.8.41 |
| Z7005 | | To 1 METS |
| Z7012 | | To 335 Sqn. |

**Hurricane Mk.IIb**

| | | |
|---|---|---|
| Z4871 | | To 22 AACU ? |
| Z5447 | | Shot down during attack on Colombo 5.4.42 |
| BE352 | | Shot down during attack on Colombo 5.4.42 |
| BG795 | RS:N | Shot down during attack on Colombo 5.4.42 |
| BG916 | | Hit slipstream of another aircraft and dived into lake, 20.4.42 |
| BM910 | | Shot down during attack on Colombo 5.4.42 |
| BM930 | | Shot down during attack on Colombo 5.4.42 |
| BN596 | | Missing on training flight over Ceylon, 12.10.43 |

**Hurricane Mk.IIc**

| | | |
|---|---|---|
| BN379 | RS:G | Dived into ground near Colombo during dummy attack, 15.6.43 |
| BN399 | RS:A | SOC 5.7.45 |
| BN466 | RS:K | SOC 31.8.44 |
| BN478 | | Crash-landed 20 miles S of Hove airstrip, Burma, 14.6.43 |
| BN483 | | To 9 Ferry Unit |
| BN585 | | To 1 Sqn. IAF |
| BN865 | | SOC 14.10.44 |
| BN512 | | To 135 Sqn. |
| BN780 | | SOC 14.10.44 |
| BN869 | | Collided with Liberator FL911 of 160 Sqn. during fighter affilliation and overshot landing at Ratmalana, 17.7.43 |
| BN900 | | To 135 Sqn. |
| BN901 | | SOC 6.7.44 |
| BN970 | | SOC 30.6.44 |
| BP110 | RS:K | To 1 Sqn. SAAF |
| BP229 | | Crashed 3 or 4 miles S of Vairampatte railway station, Ceylon, 31.3.43 |
| BP478 | RS:I | SOC 23.8.45 |
| BP510 | RS:H | To 451 Sqn. |
| BP586 | RS:X | |
| HL507 | RS:H | |
| HV815 | RS:W | SOC 30.5.46 |
| JS447 | RS:Z | SOC 14.3.46 |
| KW827 | RS:T | SOC 31.8.44 |
| KZ934 | RS:W | SOC 10.1.46 |

| | | |
|---|---|---|
| LB718 | RS:W/X | SOC 28.9.44 |
| LB839 | RS:J | To 261 Sqn. |
| LD123 | | To 42 Sqn. |
| LD175 | | To DGA Comms. Flt. |
| LD185 | RS:D | To 11 Sqn. ? |
| LD240 | | To 1 Sqn. IAF |
| LD266 | | SOC 18.10.45 |
| LD295 | RS:C | SOC 31.8.44 |
| LD299 | RS:R | To 14 Ferry Unit |
| LD337 | RS:B | To 28 Sqn. |
| LD573 | RS:X | SOC 14.2.46 |
| LD618 | RS:K | SOC 8.10.46 |
| LD630 | | SOC 8.10.46 |
| LD780 | RS:I | To 3 Sqn. IAF |
| LD961 | RS:H | SOC 14.10.44 |
| LE440 | RS:U | SOC 27.9.45 |
| LF156 | RS:T | To 11 Sqn. |
| ??651 | | Crashed near Puttalam 12.10.43 |

### Thunderbolt Mk.I

| | | |
|---|---|---|
| FL813 | | Hit by HD103 after landing at Yelahanka, 30.8.44 |
| FL834 | | To 135 Sqn. |
| HB986 | | Broke up when recovering from dive near Yelahanka, 14.8.44 |
| HB995 | | Tail came off in dive, 14.8.44 |
| HD103 | | SOC 28.3.46 |
| HD108 | | DBR in gale, Chakulia, 23.5.45 |
| HD114 | | SOC 26.7.45 |
| HD115 | | To 135 Sqn. |
| HD126 | | SOC 13.9.45 |
| HD131 | | |
| HD134 | | To 135 Sqn. |
| HD151 | | To 34 Sqn. |
| HD156 | | To 135 Sqn. |
| HD158 | | To 135 Sqn. |
| HD177 | | To 73 OTU |

### Thunderbolt Mk.II

| | | |
|---|---|---|
| HD191 | | To 1340 Flt. |
| HD192 | | SOC 28.3.46 |
| HD193 | RS:H | SOC 28.3.46 |
| HD204 | | SOC 28.3.46 |
| HD205 | | Overshot landing at Hathazari, 19.11.44 and went into ditch; DBR |
| HD208 | | SOC 28.3.46 |
| HD243 | | To 60 Sqn. |
| HD245 | | Caught fire in air and hit trees in forced landing near Henzada, 3.11.44 |
| HD248 | | SOC 23.8.46 |
| HD258 | | SOC 30.5.46 |
| HD264 | | Hit mound on take-off from Chittagong and crashed, 31.10.44; DBF |
| HD265 | RS:G | To 79 Sqn. |
| HD267 | | Caught fire when starting up at Arkonam, 22.9.44 |
| HD269 | RS:S | SOC 11.4.46 |
| HD272 | | SOC 28.3.46 |
| HD280 | RS:K | SOC 11.4.46 |
| HD289 | RS:S | Damaged in heavy landing at Chittagong, 9.11.44; not repaired |
| HD294 | | Ran into HD298 while landing at Chittagong, 17.11.44 |
| HD298 | RS:U | Hit by HD294 while landing at Chittagong after operational sortie, 17.11.44 |
| HD299 | RS:J | SOC 28.3.46 |
| KJ128 | RS:X | Tyre burst on landing at Cox's Bazaar, 24.2.45; swung and overturned |
| KJ129 | | SOC 28.3.46 |
| KJ131 | RS:Y | SOC 11.4.46 |
| KJ132 | | Engine cut on approach to Jumchar, 30.12.44, and belly-landed in paddy field |

| | | |
|---|---|---|
| KJ140 | RS:B | DBR in gale at Chakulia, 23.5.45 |
| KJ146 | | To 146 Sqn. |
| KJ149 | RS:I | Hit bund on take-off from Vizagapatam, 24.7.45; damaged undercarriage and abandoned |
| KJ150 | | SOC 11.4.46 |
| KJ155 | | To 258 Sqn. |
| KJ157 | | Collided with HD280 while taxying at Jumchar, 22.1.45 |
| KJ187 | | Swung on take-off from Jumchar, 16.12.44, stalled, crashed and destroyed by fire |
| KJ191 | RS:C | DBR in gale at Chakulia, 23.5.45 |
| KJ193 | | Belly-landed near Ganjam, Orissa, 30.6.45, after pilot taken ill |
| KJ213 | | To 258 Sqn. |
| KJ216 | | SOC 28.3.46 |
| KJ220 | | To 34 Sqn. |
| KJ223 | | SOC 25.4.46 |
| KJ228 | | To 135 Sqn. |
| KJ240 | RS:W | To 135 Sqn. |
| KJ243 | | SOC 14.3.46 |
| KJ246 | | DBR in gale at Chakulia, 23.5.45 |
| KJ258 | | To 42 Sqn. |
| KJ264 | | To 134 Sqn. |
| KJ267 | | DBR in gale at Chakulia, 26.5.45 |
| KJ271 | | Abandoned take-off from Vizagapatam 19.8.45 when smoke came from engine; ground-looped and undercarriage collapsed |
| KJ275 | | To 134 Sqn. |
| KJ276 | | To 134 Sqn. |
| KJ281 | RS:R | SOC 28.3.46 |
| KJ287 | | SOC 28.3.46 |
| KJ313 | | SOC 28.3.46 |
| KJ327 | | SOC 11.4.46 |
| KL183 | RS:R | SOC 28.3.46 |
| KL187 | | To 60 Sqn. |
| KL216 | | SOC 11.4.46 |
| KL222 | RS:W | Caught fire on take-off from Vizagapatam, 12.8.45, and crashed |
| KL287 | | Lost power and belly-landed near Bhopal, 23.3.46 |
| KL308 | RS:C | SOC 11.4.46 |
| KL343 | | Crashed in forced landing near Plassey, Bengal, 22.3.46, after hydraulic leak |
| KL838 | | SOC 12.5.46 |

### Harvard Mk.IIb

| | | |
|---|---|---|
| FE373 | | To Pakistan Air Force 9.47 |
| FE884 | | Damaged beyond repair in gale at Chakula, 23.5.45; SOC 21.6.45 |

### Tiger Moth

?

### Tempest Mk.II

| | | |
|---|---|---|
| PR544 | | To 10 Sqn. RIAF |
| PR545 | | To 10 Sqn. RIAF |
| PR551 | | To 10 Sqn. RIAF |
| PR565 | | To 2 Sqn. RIAF |
| PR566 | RS:V | To 10 Sqn. RIAF |
| PR567 | | To 20 Sqn. |
| PR583 | RS:G | Collided with PR672 in formation and force-landed 30 miles SE of Agra, 10.10.46 |
| PR602 | | To 20 Sqn. |
| PR605 | | To 10 Sqn. RIAF |
| PR617 | | To 10 Sqn. RIAF |
| PR648 | | To 20 Sqn. |
| PR651 | | To 10 Sqn. RIAF |

| | | |
|---|---|---|
| PR652 | | To 20 Sqn. |
| PR653 | | To RIAF |
| PR660 | | To 10 Sqn. RIAF |
| PR661 | | To RPAF |
| PR668 | | To 10 Sqn. RIAF |
| PR672 | RS:A | Collided with PR583 in formation and abandoned 30 miles SE of Agra, 10.10.46 |
| PR686 | | Crash-landed at Bhopal 23.4.46 but later to RPAF |
| PR721 | | To 10 Sqn. RIAF |
| PR729 | | To 10 Sqn. RIAF |
| PR734 | | To 20 Sqn. |
| PR740 | | To 20 Sqn. |
| PR751 | | To 10 Sqn. RIAF |
| PR787 | | To 10 Sqn. RIAF |
| PR801 | | To 10 Sqn. RIAF |
| PR804 | | To 10 Sqn. RIAF |
| PR837 | | To RIAF |
| PR840 | | To RIAF |
| PR842 | | To 10 Sqn. RIAF |

**Dakota Mk.IV**

Aircraft marked with * were officially allocated To RAF Oakington rather than to a squadron, but were flown by 30 Squadron. Those marked $ are known to have been flown by 30 Squadron crews in the Berlin Airlift.

| | | |
|---|---|---|
| KJ930 | | Sold 15.6.53; became G–ANAE |
| KJ975 | | To 46 Sqn |
| KJ994 | | To CFS; returned; to SHAPE, Oslo |
| KK127 * $ | | To 1 PTS |
| KK129 * $ | | To 53 Sqn. |
| KK151 * $ | | Sold 25.2.52; became G–AMRA |
| KN214 $ | | (238 Sqn. aircraft) |
| KN231 $ | | (48 Sqn. aircraft) |
| KN238 * | | Swung on landing at Gatow 1.8.48; undercarriage collapsed |
| KN292 * | | To 24 Sqn. |
| KN330 * $ | | To RAF Waterbeach |
| KN335 | | SOC 12.3.48 |
| KN355 * $ | | To 240 OCU |
| KN360 $ | JN:K | To MAAG 26.8.51 |
| KN367 * $ | | To RAF Waterbeach |
| KN369 * $ | | To RAF Waterbeach |
| KN371 $ | | (1 PTS aircraft) |
| KN380 | | To MAAG 25.2.53 |
| KN383 | JN:M | To MAAG 26.7.54 |
| KN388 | | To RAF Oakington |
| KN393 * | | To Transport Support Training Unit |
| KN397 * | | Sold 21.4.52; became G–AMSV |
| KN402 * $ | | To 18 Sqn. |
| KN406 * $ | | To MAAG 8.4.53 |
| KN410 * $ | | To MAAG 21.4.53 |
| KN415 $ | JN:N | Sold 2.5.52; became G–AMSS |
| KN419 | JN:O | Sold 25.2.52; became VP–KJR |
| KN428 * $ | | SOC 17.2.50 |
| KN433 * $ | | To 27 Sqn. |
| KN442 * | | To 46 Sqn. |
| KN452 | | To Transport Command Examining Unit |
| KN487 * | | Scrapped 17.1.50 |
| KN491 * | | Hit trees at Utecht, Russian Zone of Germany, 24.1.49, while on approach to Lubeck |
| KN492 * $ | | To 18 Sqn. |
| KN495 * $ | | To 18 Sqn. |
| KN497 * $ | | Sold 31.3.53; became G–AMYW |
| KN498 | JN:J | To RAF Oakington |
| KN499 * $ | | To 10 Sqn. |
| KN507 * | | SOC 6.8.48 |
| KN509 * | | Sold 31.3.53; became G–AMYX |
| KN512 $ | | To Belgian Air Force 5.1.50 |
| KN514 * $ | | To 10 Sqn. |
| KN518 | | To 46 Sqn |

| | | |
|---|---|---|
| KN520 * $ | | To MAAG 6.7.53 |
| KN527 $ | | (10 Sqn. aircraft) |
| KN541 | JN:S | To MAAG 26.7.54 |
| KN550 | | SOC 29.6.50 |
| KN566 * | | Sold 26.2.52; became G–AMPO |
| KN567 | | To RAF Waterbeach |
| KN570 * $ | | To 27 Sqn. |
| KN573 * | | To RAF Waterbeach |
| KN577 * $ | | To 53 Sqn. |
| KN581 * $ | | To 10 Sqn. |
| KN590 * | | To RAF Waterbeach |
| KN607 * $ | | To RAF Waterbeach |
| KN608 * | | To RAF Waterbeach |
| KN623 * $ | | To 27 Sqn. |
| KN628 | | Retained as Field Marshal Montgomery's aircraft; sold 20.3.56; became G–AOGZ |
| KN631 * $ | | To 240 OCU |
| KN638 | | Sold 22.4.52; became VP–KJU |
| KN640 * | | To RAF Waterbeach |
| KN647 | | To CFS; returned; to Malta Comms. Flt |
| KN652 | JN:H | Sold 27.1.53; became G–AMYB |
| KN656 * $ | | To 27 Sqn. |
| KN657 $ | | To MAAG 15.7.53 |
| KN700 * $ | | To 206 Sqn. |
| KP214 | | SOC 12.6.50 |
| KP217 * $ | | To 46 Sqn. |
| KP223 * | | Crashed on BABS approach to Lübeck 17.11.48 |
| KP265 | | To MAAG 17.9.54 |
| KP273 | | SOC 16.6.50 |

**Valetta C.1**

| | | |
|---|---|---|
| VL277 | JN:H | became GI airframe 7476M 3.58 |
| VL279 | | To 216 Sqn. |
| VL282 | | Dived into ground 2 miles SSW of Lyneham after take-off, 20.1.54 |
| VW142 | | To 242 OCU |
| VW158 | K | |
| VW163 | JN:A | To 216 Sqn. |
| VW189 | | To 242 OCU |
| VW190 | N | To 242 OCU |
| VW201 | M | To 242 OCU |
| VW203 | W | Collided with Venom WE258 and crashed 1.5 miles W of Boscombe Down, 25.11.52 |
| VW204 | J | Flew into ground 0.5 miles W of Dishforth on overshooting, 20.9.55 |
| VW820 | B | To 242 OCU |
| VW827 | | Lost power and crashed into houses at Iffley, Oxon, 2.5.52 |
| VW835 | H | To 48 Sqn. |
| VW838 | A | To Ferry Support Sqn. |
| VW842 | F | To 242 OCU |
| VW848 | | To 242 OCU |
| VW849 | C | To 242 OCU |
| VW855 | Y | To 242 OCU |
| VW858 | | To Station Flt., Benson |
| VW863 | G | To Middle East Comm. Sqn. |
| VX484 | | To TCASF |
| VX493 | JN:Q | To 110 Sqn. |
| VX494 | V | Sold for scrap 17.3.59 |
| VX525 | | To 52 Sqn. |
| VX559 | | Flew into ground 2 miles N of Benson after night take-off, 19.8.52 |

**Valetta C.2**

| | | |
|---|---|---|
| VX574 | | To Malta Comm. Sqn. |
| VX576 | C | To 233 Sqn. |
| VX577 | | To 2nd TAF Comm. Sqn. |
| WJ504 | | To Coastal Command Comm. Flt. |

**Beverley C.1**

| | | |
|---|---|---|
| XB263 | K | To 47/53 Sqns. |
| XB266 | E | To 84 Sqn. |
| XH118 | A | Two engines failed during downwind landing at Beihan 4.2.58; swung and overturned on sand dune |
| XH119 | B | SOC 3.1.68 |
| XH120 | C; H | To 34 Sqn; returned; to 84 Sqn |
| XH121 | E | |
| XH122 | D | To 84 Sqn |
| XH123 | F; C | To 84 Sqn; returned; to 47 Sqn |
| XH124 | G | To 84 Sqn; returned; to 242 OCU |
| XL130 | H; Y | To 242 OCU; returned; to 84 Sqn |
| XL131 | J | To 47 Sqn |
| XL148 | U | SOC 25.3.70 |
| XL149 | X | became GI airframe 7988M 7.11.67 |
| XL152 | A; J | SOC 25.3.70 |
| XM103 | H | To 242 OCU |
| XM104 | | SOC 14.2.68 |
| XM105 | A | SOC 25.9.69 |
| XM108 | T | SOC 25.3.70 |
| XM109 | | SOC 25.3.70 |
| XM111 | D | To 84 Sqn |
| XM112 | | To 48 Sqn |

**Hercules C.1**

| | | |
|---|---|---|
| XV180 | | Dived into ground after take-off from Fairford 24.3.69; six killed |

All other Hercules aircraft are drawn from the Lyneham Transport Wing pool.

---

**Call-signs**

Post-war, 30 Squadron used Transport Command five-letter radio call-signs, as follows. The fifth letter was the same as the individual letter carried by each aircraft.

| | |
|---|---|
| MODF | Dakotas |
| MORG | Valettas |
| MOSC | Valettas |
| MOBE | Beverleys |

# Index of People and Places

## Places

*NB: place names considered to be of minor significance are not included*

# BIBLIOGRAPHY

*In compiling this book, reference was made to many documents, the more significant of which are listed below.*

'Aircraft of the Royal Air Force 1918–1957' by Owen Thetford
    (Putnam, 1957)
'Berlin Airlift' by Robert Rodrigo (Cassell & Co. Ltd., 1960)
'But Not in Anger' by Christopher Cole and Roderick Grant
    (Ian Allen Ltd., 1979)
'Chronicle of the Twentieth Century'
    (Longman Group UK Ltd., 1988)
'Crete – The Battle and the Resistance' by Antony Beevor
    (John Murray [Publishers] Ltd., 1991)
'Encyclopedia of the Second World War' by Bryan Perrett and
    Ian Hogg (Longman Group UK Ltd., 1989)
'Encyclopedia of Aviation'
    (published by Orbis as an 18-volume partwork)
'In the Clouds Above Baghdad' by Lt. Col. J. E. Tennant DSO MC
    (Cecil Palmer, 1920)
'Iraq 1900–1950' by S. H. Longrigg
    (Oxford University Press, 1953)
'Line!' by Air Cdre. H. F. V. Battle OBE DFC
    (Nicholas Battle,1984)
'Other Ranks of Kut' by P. W. Long
    (Williams & Norgate Ltd., 1938)
'Royal Air Force Thunderbolts' by Geoff Thomas
    (Air Research Publications, 1997)
'The Berlin Airlift' by Ann and John Tusa (Spellmount, 1988)
'The Most Dangerous Moment' by Michael Tomlinson
    (Tisara Prakasakayo Ltd.,1976)
'The Price of Surrender' by Ernest Walker (Blandford Press, 1992)
'The Second World War' by John Keegan (Hutchinson, 1989)
'The Squadrons of the Royal Air Force & Commonwealth'
    by J. J. Halley (Air–Britain, 1988)
'The Valetta' by Bill Overton (Loughborough University, 1996)
'War Planes of the First World War: Vol.2' by J. M. Bruce
    (Macdonald & Co. Ltd, 1968)
'Wings of the Phoenix' (HMSO, 1949)
The personal diary of Cpl. Candy
Articles in Cross & Cockade International Journal:
    Main Show to Side Show —
        the life of Lt. A. E. L. Skinner MC, by Peter Wright
    Mesopotamia; RFC/RAF Operations 1915–1918,
        by Raymond Vann

*Documents held at the Public Record Office, Kew:*

**AIR.1**

| | |
|---|---|
| 140/15/40/306 | Movements of Flights, Mesopotamia, 10.10.15–9.11.17 |
| 361/15/229/2 | Printed history, 1915–1919 |
| 504/16/3/23 | Report on operations in Mesopotamia |
| 691/21/20/30 | History of 30 Squadron, 1914–? |
| 815/204/4/1278 | Personnel for 'X' aircraft park: Force 'D' |
| 1168/204/5/2589 | Egypt detachment, 1915 |
| 204/119/1–8 | |
| 204/119/13 | |
| 204/119/22 | |
| 1685/204/119/ | Various papers |
| 2120/207/72/4 | 31 Wing and 30 Squadron, Mesopotamia |
| 2199/209/22/1–5 | War diaries, WW 1 |
| 2200/209/22/6–14 | ditto |
| 2201/209/22/15–21 | ditto |
| 209/24/7–11 | |
| 209/24/25 | |
| 209/25/1–2 | |
| 209/25/8–19 | |
| 209/25/22 | |
| 209/25/28–29 | |
| 209/25/33 | |
| 226/5/1 | |
| 226/5/4–21 | |
| 2383/226/15/1–5 | War diaries, WW 1 |
| 2263/209/61/1–5 | War diary, detached Flight, Mesopotamia |
| 2388/228/11/88 | |

**AIR.5**

| | |
|---|---|
| 1287 | Iraq Command, 1921–1923 |
| 1288 | ditto, 1924 |
| 1289 | ditto, 1925 |
| 1290 | ditto, 1926 |
| 1291 | ditto, 1927–1929 |
| 1292 | ditto, 1930–1932 |
| 1293 | ditto, 1933–1935 |
| 1294 | ditto, 1936–1939 |

**AIR.20**

| | |
|---|---|
| 552 | War diary, 12.15–1.16 |
| 553 | War diary, 2.16 |
| 554 | War diary, 3.16 |
| 555 | War diary, 4.16 |
| 556 | War diary, 5.16 |
| 557 | War diary, 6.16 |
| 558 | War diary, 7.16 |
| 559 | War diary, 8.16 |
| 560 | War diary, 9.16–10.16 |
| 561 | War diary 10.16–11.16 |
| 562 | War diary, 11.16–12.16 |
| 563 | War diary, 12.16–1.17 |
| 6219 | War diary, 1.17 |

**AIR.26**

| | |
|---|---|
| 299 | 264 Wing, 269 Wing and 234 Wing, 10.41–2.42 |
| 346 | 250 Wing, 9.39–7.40 |
| 348 | 252 Wing, 7.40–? |

**AIR.27**

| | |
|---|---|
| 344 | 30 Squadron Operational Record Book, 1926–1943 |
| 345 | ditto, 1944–1945 |
| 2406 | ditto, 1946–1950 |
| 2606 | ditto, 1951–1954 |
| 2744 | ditto, 1955–1960 |
| 2918 | ditto, 1961–1965 |
| 3052 | ditto, 1966–1971 |

**AIR.28**

| | |
|---|---|
| 41 | Station Operational Record Book, Baigachi |
| 62 | ditto, Bhopal |
| 403 | ditto, Ismailia |
| 666 | ditto, Ratmalana |
| 1069 | ditto, Lubeck |
| 1094 | ditto, Oakington |
| 1469 | ditto, Dishforth |
| 1574 | ditto, Eastleigh |
| 1800 | ditto, Fairford |
| 1854 | ditto, Muharraq |

**AIR.38**

| | |
|---|---|
| 324 | Berlin Airlift Advanced Operations Room log book |
| 325 | ditto |

**AIR.55**

| | |
|---|---|
| 115 | History of RAF Lubeck |

# AIR-BRITAIN – THE INTERNATIONAL ASSOCIATION OF AVIATION HISTORIANS
## FOUNDED 1948

Since 1948, Air-Britain has recorded aviation events as they have happened, because today's events are tomorrow's history. In addition, considerable research into the past has been undertaken to provide historians with the background to aviation history. Nearly 18,000 members have contributed to our aims and efforts in that time, and many have become accepted authorities in their own fields.

Every month, *AIR-BRITAIN NEWS* covers the current civil and military scene. Quarterly, each member receives *AIR-BRITAIN DIGEST*, which is a fully-illustrated quality journal containing articles on various subjects, both past and present.

For those interested in military aviation history, there is the quarterly *AEROMILITARIA*, which is designed to delve more deeply into the background of, mainly, British and Commonwealth military aviation than is possible in commercial publications and whose format permits it to be used as components of a filing system which suits the reader's requirements. This publication is responsible for the production of the present volume and other monographs on military subjects. Also published quarterly is *ARCHIVE*, produced in a similar format but covering civil aviation history in depth on a worldwide basis. Both magazines are well-illustrated by photographs and drawings.

In addition to these regular publications, there are monographs covering type histories, both military and civil, airline fleets, Royal Air Force registers, squadron histories and the civil registers of a large number of countries. Although our publications are available to non-members, prices are considerably lower for Air-Britain members, who have priority over non-members when availability is limited. Normally, the accumulated price discounts for which members qualify when buying monographs far exceed the annual subscription rates.

A large team of aviation experts is available to answer members' queries on most aspects of aviation. If you have made a study of any particular subject, you may be able to expand your knowledge by joining those with similar interests. Also available to members are libraries of colour slides and photographs which supply slides and prints at prices considerably lower than those charged by commercial firms.

There are local branches of the Association in Bournemouth, Central Scotland, Exeter, Gwent, Heston, London, Luton, Manchester, Merseyside, North-East England, Rugby, Sheffield, Southampton, South-West Essex, Stansted, West Cornwall and West Midlands. Overseas in France and the Netherlands.

If you would like to receive samples of Air-Britain magazines, please write to the following address enclosing 50p and stating your particular interests. If you would like only a brochure, please sent a stamped self-addressed envelope to the same address (preferably 230mm by 160mm or over) – **Air-Britain Membership Enquiries (Mil), 1 Rose Cottages, 179 Penn Road, Hazlemere, High Wycombe, Bucks. HP15 7NE**.

Our website may be found at **www.air-britain.com**

## MILITARY AVIATION PUBLICATIONS
(prices are for members/non-members and are post-free)

### Royal Air Force Aircraft series

| | | | | | |
|---|---|---|---|---|---|
| J1-J9999 | (£8.00/£10.00) | K1000-K9999 | (See The K-File) | L1000-N9999 | (£12.00/£15.00) |
| P1000-R9999 | (£11.00/£14.00) | T1000-V9999 | (£12.00/£15.00) | W1000-Z9999 | (£13.00/£16.50) |
| BA100-BZ999 | (£6.00/£7.50) | DA100-DZ999 | (£5.00/£6.00) | EA100-EZ999 | (£5.00/£6.00) |
| FA100-FZ999 | (£5.00/£6.00) | HA100-HZ999 | (£6.00/£7.50) | JA100-JZ999 | (£6.00/£7.50) |
| KA100-KZ999 | (£6.00/£7.50) | LA100-LZ999 | (£7.00/£8.50) | MA199-MZ999 | (£8.00/£10.00) |
| NA100-NZ999 | (£8.00/£10.00) | PA100-RZ999 | (£10.00/£12.50) | XA100-XZ999 | (£9.00/£10.00) |

### Type Histories

| | | | | | |
|---|---|---|---|---|---|
| The Battle File | (£20.00/£25.00) | The Beaufort File | (£11.00/£13.50) | The Camel File | (£13.00/£16.00) |
| The Defiant File | (£12.50/£16.00) | The DH4/DH9 File | (£24.00/£30.00) | The Hampden File | (£12.00/£14.50) |
| The Harvard File | (£8.00/£9.50) | The Hoverfly File | (£16.00/£19.50) | The Martinsyde File | (£24.00/£30.00) |
| The Norman Thompson File (£13.50/£17.00) | | **NEW** The Oxford, Consul & Envoy File (£25.00/£32.00) | | The Scimitar File | (£26.00/£32.00) |
| The S.E.5 File | (£16.00/£20.00) | The Sopwith Pup File | (in preparation) | | |

### Individual R.A.F. Squadron Histories

With Courage and Faith – The History of No. 18 Squadron (£5.00/£6.00)
United in Effort – The Story of No. 53 Squadron (£15.00/£19.00)
Always Prepared – The History of No. 207 Squadron (£22.00/£27.50)

Hawks Rising – The History of No. 25 Squadron (£25.00/£32.00)
Scorpions Sting – The Story of No. 84 Squadron (£12.00/£16.50)
The Hornet Strikes – The Story of No. 213 Squadron (£20.00/£25.00)

Rise from the East – The History of No. 247 Squadron (£13.00/£16.50)

### Naval Aviation titles

The Squadrons of the Fleet Air Arm (£24.00/£30.00)
Royal Navy Aircraft Serials and Units 1911-1919 (£12.00)
Fleet Air Arm Aircraft 1939-1945 (new edition in preparation)

Royal Navy Shipboard Aircraft Developments 1912-1931 (£12.00)
Fleet Air Arm Aircraft, Units and Ships 1920-1939 (£26.00/£32.50)
Fleet Air Arm Fixed Wing Aircraft since 1946 (in preparation)

Royal Navy Instructional Airframes (£14.00/£17.50)

### Other titles

The K-File (the RAF of the 1930s) (£23.00/£30.00)
Aviation in Cornwall (£14.00/£17.50)
Aerial Refuelling at Farnborough 1924-1937 (£11.00/£14.00)

The British Aircraft Specifications File (£20.00/£25.00)
British Air Commission and Lend-Lease (£23.00/£29.00)
Broken Wings – Post-War RAF Accidents (£21.00/£26.00)

The above are available from Air-Britain (Historians) Ltd., 41 Penshurst Road, Leigh, Tonbridge, Kent TN11 8HL
or by e-mail to mike@sales.demon.co.uk. Payment in Sterling only.
Visa, Mastercard, Delta/Visa accepted with card number and expiry date, also Switch (with Issue number).